PIROSKA AND THE PANTOKRATOR

CEU MEDIEVALIA 19

Series Editor: József Laszlovszky

Piroska and the Pantokrator

Dynastic Memory, Healing and Salvation
in Komnenian Constantinople

Edited by
Marianne Sághy and Robert Ousterhout

CEU Department of Medieval Studies
&
Central European University Press
Budapest–New York
Budapest, 2019

© Editors and Contributors 2019
1st edition

This volume is a joint publication by
**Central European University
Department of Medieval Studies**
Nádor u. 9, H-1051 Budapest, Hungary
Telephone: (+36-1) 327-3051, Fax: (+36-1) 327-3055
E-mail: medstud@ceu.edu, Website: http://medievalstudies.ceu.edu
and
Central European University Press
Nádor utca 11, H-1051 Budapest, Hungary
224 West 57th Street, New York NY 10019, USA
Tel: +36-1-327-3138 or 327-3000
E-mail: ceupress@press.ceu.edu
Website: www.ceupress.com

Cover design for the series by Péter Tóth
Cover Illustration: Komnenos panel, Hagia Sophia, Istanbul. Courtesy of Robert. S. Nelson.

All rights reserved. No part of this publication may be reproduced,
stored in a retrieval system, or transmitted,
in any form or by any means, without the permission
of the Publisher.

ISSN 1587-6470 CEU MEDIEVALIA
ISBN 978-963-386-295-7

Library of Congress Control Number:
2019941681

Printed in Hungary

TABLE OF CONTENTS

List of Illustrations vii

Preface ix

Introduction 1
Marianne Sághy

Greek Monasteries in Early Árpádian Hungary 11
Marianne Sághy

What did Piroska see at Home? New Trends in Art and Architecture in the Kingdom of Hungary around 1100 39
Béla Zsolt Szakács

Diplomatic Relations between Hungary and Byzantium in the Eleventh–Twelfth Centuries 63
Attila Bárány

Piroska-Eirene and the Komnenian Dynasty 97
Michael Jeffreys

Komnenian Empresses: From Powerful Mothers to Pious Wives 121
Roberta Franchi

Piroska-Eirene, First Western Empress of Byzantium: Power and Perception .. 143
Maximilian Lau

The Many Faces of Piroska-Eirene in Visual and Material Culture 153
Christopher Mielke

Imperial Women and Religious Foundations in Constantinople 175
Elif Demirtiken

To Each According to their Need: Medical and Charitable Institutions in the Pantokrator Monastery 195
Tyler Wolford

Piroska and the Pantokrator: Reassessing the Architectural Evidence 225
Robert Ousterhout

Piroska-Eirene and the Holy Theotokos 261
Etele Kiss

"A New Mixture of Two Powers:" Nicholas Kallikles and Theodore Prodromos on Empress Eirene 291
Roman Shlyakhtin

Ritual and Politics in the Pantokrator: A Lament in Two Acts for Eirene's Son 305
Foteini Spingou

Concluding Remarks 323
Robert Ousterhout

Appendix 1 Synaxarion 327

Appendix 2 Theodoros Prodromos, "Epitaph of Empress Eirene" 332

Appendix 3 Nicholas Kallikles, "On the tomb of the Despina" 333

Index 335

LIST OF ILLUSTRATIONS

Sághy

Figure 1. The Veszprémvölgy Donation Charter, 1109. MNL OL DL 11 © Hungarian National Archives 21

Figure 2. Seal of King Coloman on the Veszprémvölgy Donation Charter, 1109. MNL OL DL 11 © Hungarian National Archives 22

Figure 3. Ruins of the Veszprémvölgy Greek Nunnery 23

Figure 4. Map: Greek Monasteries in Árpádian Hungary 24

Szakács

Figure 1. Pécs, cathedral, interior of the crypt 40

Figure 2. Eger, reconstructed ground plan by Károly Kozák 42

Figure 3. Dömös, the reconstructed crypt 44

Figure 4. Somogyvár, view of the ruins from the north-east 44

Figure 5. Kosztolány, fresco in the nave, Visitation scene with servant 45

Figure 6. Pécsvárad, fresco in the apse, Angel 46

Figure 7. Holy Crown of Hungary, Greek crown, frontal view, Christ Pantokrator 47

Figure 8. Holy Crown of Hungary, Latin crown, top, Christ Pantokrator 48

Figure 9. Dombó, stone fragment from the Benedictine Abbey with palmette decoration, Muzej Vojvodine, Novi Sad 49

Figure 10. Gyulafehérvár, tympanum of the first cathedral 52

Bárány

Table 1. The Dynastic Relations of Piroska 96

Franchi

Figure 1. Seal of Anna Dalassene (obverse/reverse), 11th century. © Dumbarton Oaks Research Centre, Trustees for Harvard University, Washington, D.C. ... 125

Figure 2. Solidus of Empress Irene, 797–802, Constantinople. © Dumbarton Oaks Research Centre, Trustees for Harvard University, Washington, D.C. ... 128

Mielke

Figure 1. Empress Piroska-Eirene on the Komnenos Panel in the South Gallery of the Hagia Sophia (Istanbul) ... 154

Figure 2. Seal of Eirene Doukaina. Inventory Number BZS.1955.1.4349 ... 157

Figure 3. Seal of "Empress Eirene", possibly seal of Piroska-Eirene as junior empress ... 157

Figure 4. Seal of Piroska-Eirene as sole empress ... 159

Figure 5. Folio 19v of the Tetraevangelion, Jesus Christ, flanked by 'Mercy' and 'Justice' crowning John II and Alexios Komnenos ... 161

Figure 6a. "Empress Eirene" from the Pala d'Oro ... 165

Figure 6b. "Empress Eirene" from the Pala d'Oro, detail ... 166

Figure 7. Electron coin, special coronation issue, Constantinople, 1092/3. ... 167

Demirtiken

Figure 1. Urban Monasteries in Constantinople. © Gunder Varinlioglu ... 174

Ousterhout

Figure 1. Monastery of Christ Pantrokrator (Zeyrek Camii), seen from the east, 2005 ... 241

Figure 2. Same, plan showing phases of construction ... 241

Figure 3. Same, south church, interior, looking southeast, 2002 ... 242

Figure 4. Same, south church, reconstructed west façade ... 242

Figure 5. Same, south church, hypothetical reconstruction of the bema windows ... 243

Figure 6. Same, south church, *opus sectile* floor before conservation, late 1950s ... 243

Figure 7. Same, south church, *opus sectile* floor, detail of the wheel of the zodiac, after conservation, late 1950s 244

Figure 8. Same. South church, *opus sectile* floor, detail of the life of Sampson, showing (counterclockwise) Sampson and the gates of Gaza, Sampson smiting the Assyrians, Sampson and the lion, late 1950s 244

Figure 9. Same, central chapel, interior looking west, showing proposed locations of tombs and mosaic imagery 245

Figure 10. Same, central chapel, section, showing relative heights and sizes of domes 246

Figure 11. Same, east façade, showing the connection between the central chapel (left) and the north church (right, with the joint marked by an arrow, 2005 247

Figure 12. Same, domes and roof of the central chapel and north church, looking north, after the replacement of the lead sheeting and windows, 2002 247

Figure 13. Same, exonarthex seen from the northwest, with the indication of the change in elevation marked by an arrow, 2004 248

Figure 14. Same, section through south church, narthex, and exonarthex, showing the position of the gallery dome above the narthex 249

Figure 15. Same, central chapel, bema window, showing remnants of mosaic in the reveal, with traces of gold leaf on the cornice above, 2004 250

Figure 16. Same, exonarthex, north window, showing remnants of fresco in the reveals, 2005 250

Figure 17. Same, view of the complex from the west, ca. 1840, with the so-called sarcophagus of Eirene to the right 251

Figure 18. Distant view of the complex from the east with the domes of the Fatih Camii rising behind it 252

Kiss

Figure 1. The Holy Virgin from the Hungarian Coronation Mantle (author) .. 273

Figure 2. Visegrád: Fragments of frescoes from the "Deanery Church" 274

Figure 3. The Holy Theotokos with Child, Komnenos panel, Hagia Sophia, Istanbul 275

Figure 4. Alexios, Komnenos panel, Hagia Sophia, Istanbul 276

Figure 5. Emperor John II Komnenos and Alexios crowned by Christ. Cod. Urb. Gr.2, 19v © Bibliotheca Apostolica Vaticana 277

Figure 6a and 6b. Gospel of Matthew, Empress Eirene as Eleémosyné. Cod. Urb. Gr.2., 20v 21r © Bibliotheca Apostolica Vaticana 278, 279

Figure 7. Our Lady of Vladimir (Tretiakov Gallery, Moscow) 280

PREFACE

In 2015, Marianne Sághy invited me to Budapest to participate in a symposium on "Piroska and the Pantokrator," which initiated the process that ultimately led to the publication of this volume. My response at the time was to wonder if I had anything new to say, so I told her I'd be happy to speak, but that I hoped she wasn't planning a publication. Well, not only was she able to convince me to push my research further (and to write the chapter included here), she was also able to convince me to join her as co-editor of the volume. Indeed, it was the unique, persuasive powers and diligence of Marianne that brought this volume into being. As the other contributors will attest, none of us was able to say no when confronted by her infectious enthusiasm.

Alas, Marianne did not live to see *Piroska and the Pantokrator* in print, and one of her final requests of her friends was to see the volume through publication when she was no longer able to do so herself. It is thus our hope that this collection of essays will stand as a lasting tribute to our colleague and friend, Marianne Sághy. It was an honor and a pleasure to collaborate with her on this, her final scholarly project.

May her memory endure.

Robert G. Ousterhout
Philadelphia, October 2018

INTRODUCTION

Marianne Sághy

The Christ Pantokrator, an imposing monumental complex serving monastic, dynastic, medical and social purposes in Constantinople, was founded by Emperor John II Komnenos and Empress Piroska-Eirene in 1118. The nine-hundred-year-old building—the second largest Byzantine religious edifice after Hagia Sophia still standing in Istanbul—represents the most remarkable architectural and the most ambitious social project of the Komnenian dynasty. Scholarship on the Pantokrator is vast. This volume—as its title and cover picture show—, approaches the Pantokrator from a special vantage point focusing on its co-founder, Empress Piroska-Eirene of Hungary. This particular perspective enables its authors to explore not only the architecture, the monastic and medical functions of the complex, but also Hungarian-Byzantine relations, the cultural and religious history of early medieval Hungary, imperial representation, personal faith and dynastic holiness.

When I first visited Istanbul in 2014, I was thrilled not only by the artistic brilliance of the Komnenos mosaic panel and its prominent position in Hagia Sophia, but also by the fact that I stood face to face with a compatriot—the only Hungarian woman from the Middle Ages whose features are known from a portrait made during her life. Despite its idealized character, it is a life-like representation of a flesh-and-blood woman, a fertile wife, a loving mother, a faithful devotee of the Holy Mother of God, a charitable and ambitious founder. Standing before the sole Byzantine empress sailing from Hungary, I had the feeling that I could speak to her and she would respond to me.

I sadly noticed, however, that Piroska-Eirene was hardly more in the Hagia Sophia than a museum-shop ad for visitors, unaware of her life and ignorant of her celebrated foundation, the Pantokrator Monastery just a couple of miles away. The situation cried for remedy. Without further ado, I set upon organizing an international colloquy at the Central European University in Budapest in June 2015 with a packed program thanks to the scholars and institutions who responded to the call. At our meeting, we discussed Piroska's life, achievements and memory in early Árpádian Hungary and Komnenian Byzantium in the context of women and power, monastic foundations, architectural innovations, and spiritual models. This volume represents the rich crop of the Budapest conference, complemented with the papers of those scholars who were unable to attend.

The first scholarly work on the Pantokrator Monastery was inspired by motives not entirely unlike mine. Hungarian Byzantinist Gyula Moravcsik's interest in writing his *Saint Ladislas's daughter and the Pantokrator Monastery in Byzantium* in the early 1920's[1] was kindled by the idea to collect source evidence relevant to Hungarian history in Constantinople.[2] Prisoner of war on the Russian front in 1918, Moravcsik could not assume his fellowship at the Hungarian Research Institute in Constantinople, soon to be swept away in the whirlwind of the collapse of empires. Thus, Moravcsik had not yet visited Constantinople and Piroska at the time of his writing the first systematic collection of Byzantine, Latin and Ottoman evidence about the Pantokrator complex. Although the Hungarian Research Institute in Constantinople ceased to exist in 1918, its series continued to be published for a few years in Budapest. The next volume scheduled by the editors after Moravcsik's work was the architectural description of the Pantokrator/Zeyrek Camii by

---

[1] Gyula Moravcsik, *Szent László leánya és a bizánci Pantokrator-monostor. Die Tochter Ladislaus des Heiligen und das Pantokrator-Kloster in Konstantinopel.* Budapest–Konstantinápoly: A konstantinápolyi Magyar Tudományos Intézet Közleményei–Mitteilungen des Ungarischen Wissenschaftlichen Institutes in Konstantinopel 7–8, 1923.

[2] On a state visit in Istanbul after the opening of the Suez Canal, Emperor-King Francis Joseph received in 1868 four codices from King Mathias of Hungary's celebrated Corvina Libraryas a diplomatic gift from Sultan Abdul Hamid. Only two years after the Compromise with the Hungarians in 1967, the emperor offered the codices to the National Széchényi Library of Hungary. In 1877, Sultan Abdul Hamid gave back 35 codices to Hungary, among them 14 Corvinas, taken from Hungary during the Ottoman conquest: see Béla Erődi, *Csok jasa! A török küldöttség látogatásának emlékkönyve/ Çok yaşa. Türk heyetinin ziyaret'inden hatira kitabi.* Budapest: Mehner Vilmos, 1877. bilingual Hungarian–Turkish reprint edition edited by Géza Dávid–Tibor F. Tóth, translated by Yilmaz Gülen, Budapest: Akadémiai Kiadó, 2001. Between 1877–1918, Hungarian historians sought to recover documents and objects of Hungarian provenience—codices from the royal library of Buda, decorative elements, such as the two Renaissance bronze candlesticks from the Assumption of the Holy Virgin parish church of Buda now in the Hagia Sophia, records and of archbishoprics and bishoprics—in the Ottoman Empire, particularly in the archives of Topkapı Sarayı, along with the memory of famous Hungarian immigrants in the Ottoman Empire from Imre Thököly, Ilona Zrínyi and Ferenc II Rákóczi prince of Transylvania to Lajos Kossuth. After WWI, research expanded to the common Turkic heritage of Turks and Hungarians, hallmarked by Béla Bartók's collection of folk music in Anatolia: see János Sipos, *In the Wake of Bartók in Anatolia.* Budapest: European Folklore Institute, 2000. http://rodosto.hu/en/osmaniye.html

Ferenc Luttor, canon of Veszprém, archaeologist, disciple of Giovanni Battista di Rossi, who had already published a book on Saint Agnes's Basilica in Rome.[3] As one of the first fellows of the Hungarian Institute founded in 1916, Luttor spent a year and a half in Constantinople surveying the Pantokrator. Unfortunately, Luttor's work has never seen the light.[4] In 2013, Géza Nagymihályi, Greek-Catholic priest and art historian, published a life of Saint Piroska written for a wide audience, aiming to promote her cult as well as the knowledge of Byzantine spirituality and culture in Hungary.[5]

International scholarly interest in the Pantokrator was triggered by Paul Gautier's critical edition of its *Typikon*,[6] and even more urgently, by the restoration work carried out in the building in Istanbul's Fatih district. Chapters in Nevra Necipoğlu's *Byzantine Constantinople* address the architecture and the restoration of the Pantokrator,[7] while the volume edited by Sofia Kotzabassi on the Pantokrator demonstrates the key role of the complex throughout the Byzantine centuries[8] and publishes, among other important texts, a critical edition of the two versions of the *synaxarion*,[9] along with its English translation by Paul Magdalino,[10] as well as

---

[3] Ferenc Luttor, *A római Via Nomentana-i Szent Ágnes Egyház*. Veszprém, 1916.

[4] The book was advertised as Ferenc Luttor, *A Zeirek Kilisse Dsami (Pantokrator)* [*The Zeyrek Kilisse Djami (Pantokrator)*]. Pastor in Balatonfüred between 1918–1929, where he built a large church in Neo-Romanesque style, Luttor worked as a canon law expert at the Embassy of Hungary to the Holy See between 1929–1944. In 1948, at the time of the Communist takeover in Hungary, he emigrated to Argentina and died in Plátanos in 1953. On the Constantinople Hungarian Institute see Norbert Nagy, *A Konstantinápolyi Magyar Tudományos Intézet története (1916-1918)*. [The History of the Hungarian Research Institute in Constantinople, 1916-1918.] Balkán Füzetek 7. Pécs, 2010.

[5] Géza Nagymihályi, *Az idegen szent. Árpád-házi Szent Piroska élete és kora*. [The Foreign Saint: Life and Times of Saint Piroska of the Árpád Dynasty.] Budapest: Kairosz, 2013.

[6] Paul Gautier, "Le typikon du Christ Sauveur Pantocrator." *Revue des études byzantines* 32 (1974): 1–145. English translation by Robert Jordan, "Typikon of Emperor John II Komnenos for the Monastery of Christ Pantokratorin Constantinople." In: *Byzantine Monastic Foundation Documents: A Complete Translation of the Surviving Founders' Typika and Testaments*. John Thomas and Angela Constantinides Hero (eds.) Washington D. C.: Dumbarton Oaks Research Library, 2000, 725–781.

[7] Metim Ahunbay and Zeynep Ahunbay, "Restoration work at the Zeyrek Camii, 1997–1998." In: Nevra Necipoğlu (ed.). *Byzantine Constantinople: Monuments, Topography and Everyday Life*. Leiden: Brill. 2001, 117–133; Robert Ousterhout, "Architecture, Art and Komnenian Ideology at the Pantokrator Monastery." In: *Byzantine Constantinople* (op. cit.), 133–152.

[8] Sofia Kotzabassi, ed., *The Pantokrator Monastery in Constantinople*. Byzantinisches Archiv 27. Berlin: De Gruyter, 2013.

[9] Sofia Kotzabassi, "Feasts at the Monastery of the Pantokrator." In: op. cit., 153–190.

[10] Paul Magdalino, "The Foundation of the Pantokrator Monastery in Its Urban Setting." In: op. cit., 33–55.

hitherto unpublished verse by Byzantine poets from the twelfth to the fifteenth century.[11] These publications have greatly enlarged our understanding of the symbolic meaning of the Pantokrator's sacred space, the ritual life of the monastery, as well as Eirene's role in its foundation.

Our volume expands the horizon of research on the Pantokrator by including new issues into the discussion, such as Piroska's Hungarian cultural and spiritual inheritance, Hungarian–Byzantine relations, the power of empresses, imperial monastic foundations in Constantinople, the joining of secular and spiritual power, the construction of dynastic holiness. The purpose of the book is not to enhance Empress Piroska-Eirene's Hungarian origins, but rather to contextualize her within the international perspectives of the Árpád dynasty in the eleventh–twelfth century in which the union of the Greek and Latin empires and Greek and Latin churches was regarded as a feasible political option. The very dedication of the Pantokrator Monastery with its allusion to Christ "the Ruler of All," evokes the notion of "universal domination," one of the key terms of the restoration of the Roman Empire (*renovatio imperii*). Through her father and mother, Piroska united in her person the powers of the West—in the words of Theodoros Prodromos, she ruled all nations and was feared by Germans, Dalmatians, Lombards, Genoans, Africans, Huns and Pannonians. "Ruling over the nations" was an idea endorsed by King Stephen of Hungary, who advocated the advantages of multiethnic societies: the Kingdom of Hungary was not for Magyars alone, but operated as a transnational state, adopting an ideology cherished by steppe nomads and empires alike. Piroska's wedding with John Komnenos came to be perceived as a union of East and West, with cosmic connotations: for Prodromos, it was the marriage of the Sun and the Moon.[12] Apart from political traditions in connection with the restoration of the Roman Empire, Piroska also brought with herself a heritage of dynastic holiness through elevations on the altar "within the family," a trademark of the House of Árpád, as well as a spiritual legacy of religious foundations and religious munificence. The cult of the Mother of God was second only to Byzantium in Hungary, where the Virgin Mary guaranteed the political independence of the kingdom between two empires. Piroska is an excellent "trigger" for re-thinking hypotheses not only about early medieval Hungary, where historical documents are notoriously scarce or incomplete, but also about Komnenian Byzantium, with important, but

---

[11] Ioannis Vassis, "Das Pantokratorkloster von Konstantinopel in der Byzantinischen Dichtung." In: op. cit., 203–250.

[12] *Patrologia Graeca* 133, 1340–1342. See, Gyula Moravcsik, *Az Árpád-kori magyar történet bizánci forrásai.* [Byzantine Sources of the History of Hungary under the Árpádian Dynasty.] Budapest: Akadémiai Kiadó, 1984, 169–171.

scattered source material. Thus, for example, it is possible to revise the paradigm that opposes East and West in the twelfth century and argue that Hungary was not a country "in between" East and West, but sought to unite East and West—at least within the confines of the country.

Our volume contextualizes Empress Eirene within Byzantine society as well. How did she fit into the highly competitive Komnenian court? How did she exploit traditions of pious giving, a domain reserved for, and appropriated by, Byzantine empresses? How did her image and perception change in the court over her reign? The authors of our volume present significant paradigm shifts concerning the power of Byzantine empresses in general and the representation of Piroska-Eirene in particular. Equal partner in the design of an innovative structure of spirituality and healing, her great foundation, the Pantokrator Monastery became, after Eirene's canonization in 1166, a shrine of the "sainted ruler," a new concept in political theology.

If Piroska-Eirene's image changed, so did the plan of the Pantokrator Monastery. Our collection presents the transformation of the building, during the lifetime of its founders, from its religious core into a monument of Komnenian piety and victory, from a monastery into a multifunctional medical and social complex. The papers examine the Pantokrator in comparison not only with other imperial monastic foundations, but also with the mausolea of the very founders of Constantinople, Emperors Constantine and Justinian that the *heroon* of the Komnenoi consciously sought to echo not only in its denomination, but also visually on the city skyline. Yet the Christ Pantokrator and the Theotokos Eleousa churches were not meant only to resurrect or resonate the past, their beautiful icons, refulgent treasures, and dazzling decoration started a new phase of artistic brilliance and exercised a huge impact on the art in Byzantium and beyond.

The chapters of the volume are richly illustrated with photographs not only of the Pantokrator Monastery/Zeyrek Camii, but also of the icons, charters, books, seals, gospel books and mosaic portraits relevant to the architecture of early Árpádian Hungary and the representation of Empress Eirene.

The collection starts with three contributions addressing the problem of Byzantine culture in Hungary and Byzantine–Hungarian relations. My paper on *Greek Monasteries in Early Árpádian Hungary* aims to reconstruct the cultural and spiritual background of young Piroska in Hungary. Focusing on what we know of the Greek monasteries in eleventh–twelfth-century Hungary, particularly on the Veszprémvölgy Greek nunnery, I summarize a century of scholarship and debate about Byzantine monastic and ecclesiastical structures in the Árpádian kingdom. I aim to show that the princess grew up in a kingdom that benefited from, and continued to promote the idea of the restoration of the Roman Empire and where an unprecedented spiritual *aggiornamento* and a remarkable cultural boom took place that combined the best of Byzantine and Latin spirituality. No "country bumpkin" from the margins of Byzantium, no foreigner to Greek culture, Piroska carried an impressive cultural baggage upon her arrival in Constantinople—not least with regard to monastic spirituality and dynastic holiness. It was her ward, King Coloman the Learned who promoted the cult of King Stephen by commissioning Bishop Hartvic to write a new *Life of Saint Stephen* that enhanced Stephen's role as apostle of Hungary, as a munificent benefactor and founder of churches and monasteries at home and hospices in the three holy cities of Christendom, Jerusalem, Rome and Constantinople.

Béla Zsolt Szakács's contribution entitled *What did Piroska see at home? New Trends in Art and Architecture in the Kingdom of Hungary around 1100* presents the extraordinary flourish of the arts under the reign of King Coloman at the turn of eleventh–twelfth century. Cathedrals and monastic churches were rebuilt, the new Romanesque style was adapted in architecture, sculpture and the decorative arts, innovative fresco cycles were painted on church walls, and new royal insignia were created—Szakács thus argues for the early twelfth-century creation of the Holy Crown of Hungary. Even if we cannot tell of what Piroska noticed of the artistic boom, it is unlikely that Coloman's vast Christian culture, European perspective, and his running monumental projects did not have an influence on the young princess's mind. Szakács discusses archaic and new Byzantinizing stylistic elements that permeated visual culture, but suggests that they reached Hungary from Italy rather than from Constantinople.

Attila Bárány revisits *Diplomatic relations between Hungary and Byzantium in the Eleventh–Twelfth Century* and takes issue with earlier scholarship that interpreted King Coloman's marriage to Felicia, the daughter of Count Roger of Sicily in 1097 as an anti-Byzantine move. Emphasizing the importance of the Hungarian alliance to Byzantium at the time of the Norman invasion led by Bohemond of Taranto, Bárány substantiates Coloman's continuing support of Byzantium with the Hungarian signatories to the peace of Devol. Bárány remains cautious in accepting at face value chroniclers' references to a Hungarian foray into Apulia, even if it seems certain that Hungarians did participate in an attack on Bohemond with the help of Venetian ships.

Michael Jeffreys's essay surveys the satisfactions and the anxiety of Komnenian dynasty-making from male and female viewpoints. Thanks to three consecutive fecund imperial women who produced families with eight or more children, the Komnenoi bred a new ruling class for the Empire. Fecundity, however, run out in the third generation: a curse placed on Empress Bertha-Eirene's womb by an angry deposed patriarch increased dynastic anxiety for Emperor Manuel who had to wait twenty-three years for a male heir. In the meantime, Manuel found a bridegroom for his daughter from the Árpád dynasty, Béla-Alexios, whom he raised as a prospective heir. Piroska-Eirene was a model dynasty-maker and her marriage a diplomatic success that lasted up to his son's reign. Jeffreys assesses Byzantine expectations about Princess Piroska—her role as an empress; her public persona in the city; the political importance of her marriage to Hungary and Byzantium; her role in the foundation of the Pantokrator—, and highlights the mutual affection that bound the imperial couple.

Roberta Franchi's *Komnenian Empresses: From Powerful to Pious Mothers* presents the transformation of female power during the Komnenian century. In the late eleventh century, ambitious mothers acted as kingmakers, founders of monastic institutions, and literary patronesses. Female influence behind the throne, however, was short-lived. Franchi argues that the coming of foreign brides reflects the conspicuous transformation of the empress's role in Byzantium from powerful mother to pious wife.

In his paper on *Piroska-Eirene, the First Byzantine Empress from the West: Power and Perception* Maximilian Lau follows up Piroska's progress in the perception and ideology of the Komnenian court, her changing image from a marginal entity to the "Lady of all the West." The first Westerner to become a Byzantine empress, the Hungarian princess was welcomed in Constantinople with calculated, cold silence: neither court records, nor Anna Komnene mention her marriage, and the only poem that refers to her suggests that she should fast "forget her kin." In contrast, upon her death, Empress Eirene is extolled for her "blessed forefathers," starting with Julius Caesar. The empress's ancestry meant to bolster the imperial rhetoric of John's regime, showing that John and Eirene unite the Eastern and Western Empires. Far from her ancestry being an embarrassment to be forgotten, subsumed by a superior, Roman, identity, Lau argues that it became a significant contribution to portrayal of the legitimacy and universality of Komnenian rule. The paradigm shift, along with her role strongly emphasized in the foundation of the Pantokrator Monastery makes a convincing case that Eirene cannot be dismissed as simply devoting herself to philanthropy and raising children.

Christopher Mielke's *The Many Faces of Piroska-Eirene in Visual and Material Culture* inquires about the extent to which Empress Eirene was able to control and define her image in Byzantium. He discusses seals, coins, a mosaic, an enamel plaque, and images in illuminated manuscripts connected to Empress Eirene in the past. Mielke assesses which connections can be valid, and which pieces can tell us about the empress's own agency in the construction of her visual program.

Elif Demirtiken's paper on *Imperial Women and Religious Foundations in Constantinople* focuses on imperial women's monumental patronage. Empresses—be they married, unmarried or dowager; Constantinopolitan, provincial or foreign—had an urge to build in the capital to show their power, to construct their representation, and also to build a place for themselves where to retire in times of hardship. Demirtiken shows that over the five hundred years over the five-hundred years of the Middle Byzantine period, the object of imperial philanthropy shifted from churches to monasteries, possibly because of the latter's multifunctional character. Not only was a monastery capable of accommodating a variety of functions—residence, commemoration, burial—but all these revolved around the concept of the family, echoing the Komnenian take on dynasty and kinship networks. Eirene was the only foreign-born empress with an outstanding family record of impressive religious patronage: King Stephen of Hungary, whose munificence embraced Constantinople as well, might also have been a model for her.

The Pantokrator was seen by Byzantine contemporaries not only as a celebration of piety, but also of victory, a cross between manly virtue and feminine piety. Robert Ousterhout analyzes the "stereo effect" of the female and male references in the textual and material sources and in the symbolic conception of the structure. Surveying the architectural evidence from the South to the North Church, from floor to dome, he argues that the real significance of the Pantokrator consisted in its complexity. Over the eighteen years of its construction, the project was transformed from a single monumental block to a sprawling irregular complex, from a monastic *katholikon* to a multi-functional church cluster. Changes in the design parallel with construction work demonstrate that the imperial couple experimented with something new, determined to create an innovative structure formally, functionally, and symbolically. Despite the ongoing changes, the building preserved its stylistic unity. The first monastery to include a separate mausoleum, the Pantokrator's *heroon* consciously harked back to the mausolea of Constantine and Justinian at the nearby Basilica of the Holy Apostles. If Emperor John II intended it as a victory monument, however, over time, the piety of the empress, the concept of the sainted ruler, and the cult of Saint Eirene prevailed in the Pantokrator.

The *Life of Saint Eirene* highlights that "[Piroska-Eirene] erected the beautiful churches that can be seen there now, hostels and old-age homes, all of which in beauty, situation and construction technique take first place among all previous buildings, both old and recent." Analysing the *Medical and Charitable Institutions in the Pantokrator Monastery*, Tyler Wolford enhances the uniqueness of the medical and social care in the complex closely linked to the uniqueness of the source of all knowledge about the hospital, namely the *typikon* of the Pantokrator. As evidence about the actual functioning of the medical institutions is lacking, the scholarly interpretation of the *typikon* oscillates between "never realized ideal" to "the pinnacle of medieval medicine." Piroska-Eirene's hospital was an elite institution, only imaginable in Constantinople. Its functioning is attested for less than sixty-eight years between 1136–1204. Its demise was due to its far too expensive maintenance as well as to the inability of Manuel Komnenos to repair the aqueduct systems of the capital, as healing was closely connected with water in Constantinople.

Etele Kiss's paper on *Piroska-Eirene and the Holy Theotokos* suggests that Piroska-Eirene studiously kept her life private because it was a life lived in imitation of the Virgin Mary. Presenting the intensely emotional Marian devotion in twelfth-century Christianity and the extraordinary political theology centered on the Mother of God in Hungary and Byzantium, the two countries enjoying her special protection, the author argues that Piroska's Marian spirituality shaped her vocation, drive and personality. Kiss links extant, dispersed, or lost artworks to the empress's spirituality, showing that Christian ideals formed not only Piroska's identity, but also Eirene's imperial image in Constantinople, where she associated herself with the Theotokos and had herself represented as re-enacting the virtues of the Mother of God.

Roman Shlyakhtin compares Nicholas Kallikles's and Theodore Prodromos's epitaphs on Empress Eirene. Both emphasize the empress's impressive combination of earthly power with Christian virtue, yet the end result is very different. Drawing on the *Song of Songs*, Kallikles paints an intimate portrait of Eirene, the loving mother, while Prodromos celebrates the empress as the equal partner of her husband and partaker in his victories. For Shlyakhtin, the two epitaphs should not be read as competitive, but as complementary images of Eirene, reflecting the new "aesthetics of plurality" of which the Komnenian Renaissance is justly famous.

Foteini Spingou's *Ritual and Politics in the Pantokrator: A Lament in Two Acts for Eirene's Son* presents two ways of commemorating Eirene's second son, the *sebastokrator* Andronikos during his burial in the Pantokrator Monastery. Theodore Prodromos composed a three hundred-ninety-three-verse monody, that an anonymous author resumed as an epitaph. Spingou discovers the agency of Andronikos's wife, the *sebastokratorissa* Eirene behind these texts. The widow created a personalized ritual lament in a code appropriate for Komnenian culture: a monody recited at the funeral, and an epitaph that reminded forever the reader not only of Andronikos, but also of the *sebastokratorissa*—even if the latter failed to secure a tomb for herself next to her husband in the dynastic *heroon*.

The essays collected in this volume present fresh scholarship on Piroska and the Pantokrator, approaching the founder and her foundation from multidisciplinary viewpoints and methodologies. We hope that this book will boost further research on the illustrious *synktetor* and her great project. Work on the Pantokrator has just started. The next in line is an international workshop in Istanbul organized for the 900th anniversary of the Pantokrator Monastery's foundation.

At the end of a long editorial process, it is our pleasure to express our gratitude to the persons and institutions who made the conference and the publication of its proceedings possible. In the organization of the colloquy, I enjoyed the unfailing support of the late József Kalota, patriarchal vicar of the Greek Orthodox Church in Hungary, who did not live to see the publication of this book now dedicated to his memory. The conference was opened by His Eminence Arsenios Kardamakis, Metropolitan of Austria and Exarch of Hungary, Pál Fodor, director general of the Research Centre for the Humanities of the Hungarian Academy of Sciences, and Attila Fülöp, Vice-Secretary of State for ecclesiastical affairs, ethnic minorities, and NGOs in the Ministry of Human Capacities, in the presence of His Excellency Dimitri Yannakakis, Ambassador of the Republic of Greece to Hungary. Unfortunately, His Excellency the Ambassador of Turkey was unable to attend. I thank Etele Kiss of the Hungarian National Museum whose generously shared knowledge was enormously helpful in the organization of the conference. The presence of Judith Herrin and Niels Gaul at the colloquy was much appreciated. The support of Daniel Ziemann, head of the Medieval Studies Department at CEU was invaluable and PhD student Ágnes Drosztmér's coordination of the event highly professional.

We thank CEU's Academic Cooperation and Research Support Office (ACRO) for its conference grant, CEU's Medieval Studies Department and Center for Eastern Mediterranean Studies (CEMS), the University of Pennsylvania, the Humanities Institute of the Hungarian Academy of Sciences, the "Lendület Research Group" entitled "Hungary in Medieval Europe" at the History Department of Debrecen University, the Hungarian National Museum, the Research Centre for the Humanities of the Hungarian Academy of Sciences and Budapest's Fifth District, the City Council of Belváros-Lipótváros, who offered the conference dinner.

I am grateful to David Hendrix who made me discover Late Antique and medieval Constantinople and proofread the papers, as well as to my colleague Cristian-Nicolae Gaşpar, lecturer in Classical and Medieval Latin at CEU's Medieval Studies Department and Senior Fellow at the Center for Eastern Mediterranean Studies for translating Nicholas Kallikles's poem *On the tomb of the Despina* into English.

The Image Collections and Fieldwork Archives of the Dumbarton Oaks Research Library, the Bibliotheca Apostolica Vaticana, the Hungarian National Archives, Zoltán Kárpáti and Károly Szelényi generously provided the illustrations.

Special thanks to Jonathan Shepard of the University of Cambridge for taking on the charge of "putting some English fog and fudge" into the papers written by international scholars in the last phase of the editorial work.

Robert Ousterhout's work offered inspiration to the conference. For decades, Robert has been my hero before I came to be personally acquainted with him thanks to Piroska. His contribution to this volume, both spiritual and material, is unmeasurable—the end result of our cooperation, I hope, lives up to the high standard of scholarship he set in Byzantine studies.

GREEK MONASTERIES IN EARLY ÁRPÁDIAN HUNGARY[1]

Marianne Sághy

Where was Princess Piroska (1088?–1134) raised and what kind of education did she receive in Hungary? Due to the complete lack of information about King Ladislaus's daughter in the eleventh–twelfth century historical record in Hungary,[2] the question cannot be answered with any certainty. It is not unreasonable to surmise,

---

[1] Special thanks to Etele Kiss and Jonathan Shepard for their helpful comments on this paper.

[2] The name of the daughter of King Ladislaus and Adelaide of Rheinfelden is not known from eleventh–twelfth century sources, as medieval chroniclers tend to omit queens' and princesses' names. The name "Pyrisk" for Ladislaus's daughter first appears in the fourteenth-century *Illuminated Chronicle* (*Chronicum Pictum*, chapter 156), incorporated into Johannes de Thuróczs's *Chronicle of the Hungarians*, chapter LXIII): "Imperatrix Constantinopolitana filia regis Ladizlai nomine Pyrisk." In: Emericus Szentpétery (ed.), *Scriptores rerum Hungaricarum, vol. I*. Budapest: Magyar Tudományos Akadémia, 1937. The first syllable of the name Pyrisk, just like another Old Hungarian name, Pyrit (from the verb *pirít*, "to roast"), may derive from Greek *pyr* (fire.) The modern reconstruction of the name, "Piroska" echoes the Hungarian adjective *piros* (red), usually explained as a reference to the girl's red hair. Hungarian has two words for "red" (*piros, vörös*), of which "piros" is only used for complexion, never for hair: ginger hair is "vörös." Would the royal couple have named their baby daughter after her healthy complexion? Pre-Christian names are not infrequent among the Árpáds, hence names reflecting character or looks cannot be excluded. From the assumption, however, that the baby must have had a Christian name, stems another theory linking Piroska to the Roman child martyr Saint Prisca, or Priscilla/Prisca, who hosted Saint Paul the Apostle in Rome, a name that would well reflect the Roman ambitions of the girl's grandfather, the anti-emperor Rudolph the Swabian. Piroska/Prisca, however, are not attested as female names or names of saints in Hungarian sources before the fifteenth century: Mór Wertner, *Névmagyarázatok II. Régi magyar női nevek*. [Etymology of names. Old Hungarian Women's Names.]. Budapest: A Magyar Nyelvőr Kiadása, 1917, 58; Katalin Fehértói, *Árpád-kori személynévtár 1000–1301*. [Personal Names in the Árpádian Age, 1000–1301.] Budapest: Akadémiai Kiadó, 2004. In the toponymy, Pyros appears in a charter of 1237 as a village's name in Southern Hungary (Hungarian Piros, Serbian Руменка/Rumenka, German Pioss, today in Voyvodina, Serbia). Legend has it that the village was the dowry of Princess Piroska, who stopped at Piros on her way to Constantinople.

however, that the orphaned princess, apart from a courtly upbringing in Esztergom and/or in Székesfehérvár, was also given a religious education in a cloister. Among the monasteries in eleventh-century Hungary, the Greek Nunnery in Veszprémvölgy near Veszprém, the Hungarian queens' residential and burial town, is considered to have functioned as an educational center for royal princesses. This paper explores the key role of this and other Greek monasteries in the study of the religion and culture of early Árpádian Hungary. While Piroska's formation in the Veszprémvölgy community must remain hypothetical, a survey of what is known of Eastern asceticism in the realm under the reigns of King Stephen I (997–1038), King Andrew I (1046–1060), King Ladislaus I (1077–1095) and King Coloman I (1095–1116) offers a possibility to review sophisticated theories and debates that the presence of orthodox cenobitism and eremitism fuels in Hungarian historiography. To summarize the history of Byzantine monasticism in Hungary is to risk telling in one's own words a story that has often been excellently told before by scholars such as Gyula Moravcsik[3] and Endre von Ivánka.[4] Recent research, however, regards the eleventh century as a unique momentum in the history of Christian asceticism that led to *sui generis* forms of cross-pollination of Greek, Slav, and Latin monasticism.[5] The paradigm shift affects the study of Eastern monasticism in Hungary.[6] The remarkable

---

[3] Gyula Moravcsik, "Görögnyelvű monostorok Szent István korában." [Greek-Language Monasteries in the Age of Saint Stephen.] In: *Emlékkönyv Szent István halálának kilencszázadik évfordulóján* [The Commemoration of the 900th Anniversary of the Death of King Saint Stephen.] Jusztinián Serédi (ed.) Budapest: Magyar Tudományos Akadémia, 1938.vol. I, pp. 389–422; idem, "The Role of the Byzantine Church in Medieval Hungary." *American Slavic and East European Review* 6 (1947): 134–151.

[4] Endre von Ivánka, "Griechische Kirche und Griechisches Mönchtum in mittelalterlichen Ungarn." *Orientalia Christiana Periodica* 8 (1942): 183–194; H. Tóth, Imre. (ed.): *Az ortodoxia története Magyarországon a XVIII. századig.* [The History of Orthodoxy in Hungary up to the 18th century.] Szeged: JATE Szláv Filológiai Tanszék, 1995.

[5] Jean-Marie Sansterre, "Saint Nil de Rossano et le monachisme latin." In: A. Acconcia Longo - S. Luca - L. Perria (eds.) *Miscellanea di studi in onore di P. Marco Petto.* Bollettino della badia greca di Grottaferrata, n.s., 45, 1991, II, 339–386; idem, "Le monachisme bénédictin d'Italie et les bénédictins italiens en France face au renouveau de l'érémitisme à la fin du Xe et au XIe siècle." In: A. Vauchez (ed.), *Ermites de France et d'Italie (XIe–XIVe siècle).* Rome: École française de Rome, 2003, 29–46; Barbara Crostini, "Moral Preaching and Animal Moralizations: the Physiologos in the Eleventh Century between Stoudios and Montecassino." *Νέα Ῥώμη / Nea Rhome. Rivista di studi bizantinistici* 7 (2010): 155–190; Sita Steckel—Niels Gaul – Michael Grünbart (eds.) *Networks of Learning: Perspectives on Scholars in Byzantine East and Latin West, c. 1000–1200.* Berlin-Münster: Lit Verlag, 2014.

[6] Marina Miladinov, *Margins of Solitude. Eremitism in Central Europe between East and West.* Zagreb: Leykam International, 2008; Catherine Keene, *Saint Margaret, Queen of the Scots: A Life in Perspective.* New York: Palgrave Macmillan, 2013; Karen Stark, "Cave of Hermits, Cave of Cult: Saints Andrew-Zoerard and Benedict and the Sacralization of the Medieval Hungarian Land-

number of Greek monasteries are not simply seen as witnesses to the strength of the first Byzantine mission in the Magyar kingdom in the tenth century[7] and the survival of the Byzantine metropolitanate in the realm converted to, and aligning with, Latin Christianity in the eleventh century,[8] but as a sign of Christian unity highlighting Hungary's culture carrier position between East and West.[9] In the freshly converted kingdom, the feeling that Christianity was a single unity transcended dogmatic debates and political tensions. It proved to be stronger than linguistic, ritual and cultic differences that slowly started driving a wedge among Greek and Latin Christians.

This places young Piroska against the background of the unprecedented spiritual *aggiornamento* and a remarkable cultural boom taking place in eleventh-to–twelfth century Hungary. The princess sailed from a royal court with imperial ambitions at the height of its expansionist might. Determined to catch up with neighboring Christian empires—a process that involved rapid and spontaneous appropriation of sophisticated political ideas as well as refined spiritual and cultural goods—the Árpádian kings not only benefited from, but also promoted the idea of the reunification of the Roman Empire (*renovatio imperii*), even by vindicating its leadership. No country "bumpkin" from the margins of Byzantium, no foreigner to Greek culture, Princess Piroska carried an impressive cultural baggage upon her arrival in Constantinople—not least with regard to monastic spirituality.

The Veszprémvölgy Charter

The oldest charter preserved in Hungary is King Stephen's Greek foundation roll of the Veszprémvölgy Nunnery. The fact that a Greek-language charter is the very first authentic deed issued by the king of Hungary who converted his people to Roman Catholicism is only one, and not even the most perplexing, of the questions that this oft-debated document raises. Preserved in a bilingual Greek-Latin transcript

---

scape." In: Meg Boulton–Jane Hawkes–Heidi Stoner (eds.) *Place and Space in the Medieval World*. London: Routledge, 2017.

[7] István Baán, "The Metropolitanate of Tourkia. The Organization of the Byzantine Church in Hungary in the Middle Ages." In: Günter Prinzing- Maciej Salomon (eds.) *Byzanz und Ostmitteleuropa 950–1453. Beiträge zu einer table-ronde des XIX International Congress of Byzantine Studies, Copenhagen, 1996*. Wiesbaden: Harrassowitz, 1999, 45–53.

[8] István Baán, "The Foundation of the Archbishopric of Kalocsa: the Byzantine Origin of the Second Archdiocese in Hungary." In: *Early Christianity in Central and East Europe*. Ed. Przemysław Urbańczyk. Warsaw: Semper, 1997, 67–73.

[9] Florin Curta, "East-Central Europe: the Gate to Byzantium."*Byzantinische Zeitschrift*108/2 (2015): 609-652; Éva Révész, "A keleti kereszténység: szerep, hatás, vagy jelenlét?" [Eastern Christianity in Hungary: role, impact or presence?] *Belvedere meridionale* 21 (2009): 52–64.

made by King Coloman the Learned in 1109, the Greek text is an authentic copy of the original deed, translated into Latin and complemented with an explanation of why a new copy was requested by the religious women from the monarch.[10] The nuns were involved in an unspecified legal process that compelled them to open the original scroll and break its seal, by which the document lost its force and had to be renewed. This is what King Coloman did in 1109 by issuing a *renovatio* that carefully copied the original Greek text, provided a Latin translation to it and corroborated its dispositions.

In the original roll, King Stephen declares that he dedicated, fully furnished, and endowed a monastery near Veszprém to the Mother of God for the salvation of his wife, children, himself, and the entire population of Pannonia. Listing the possessions and privileges bestowed upon the religious community dependent from the metropolitan, the king affirms that God will punish those who violate this grant. The Greek text is undated. When did the foundation of the Veszprémvölgy monastery take place, who was its founder, and what necessitated its foundation? Several hypotheses have been put forward to answer these questions. Some suggest that the Greek religious community of women was established by Stephen's father, Prince Géza (also baptized Stephen), and thus the foundation dates before 997.[11] If Christianity made much progress among the Hungarian tribes under Prince Géza's rule,[12] this theory is contradicted by the issuer's title, who calls himself "king"

---

[10] The charter survived in an authentic copy (the original bilingual copy of Coloman the Learned of 1109, charter A) and a fake copy (the thirteenth-century copy of Coloman's charter, charter B) in Veszprémvölgy monastery (taken over by Cistercian nuns in the thirteenth century) until the Ottoman invasion of Hungary in the mid-sixteenth century. After the fall of Székesfehérvár to the Turks in 1543, the Cistercian nuns fled from Veszprémvölgy to Körmend in Western Hungary. In 1627, Cistercian female orders were dissolved and the properties of the nuns, along with their charters, were transmitted to the Jesuits of Győr. Following the dissolution of the Jesuits in 1773, the two charters were kept in the Archives of the Hungarian Chamber until the twentieth century, when both were deposited in the Hungarian National Archives (DL 11/1 and DL 11/2.) The authenticity of charter A was established by Bálint Hóman, "A veszprémvölgyi 1109. évi oklevél hitelessége."[The Authenticity of the Charter of Veszprémvölgy from 1109.] *Turul* 29 (1911): 123–134 and 167–174, and idem, "Szent István görög oklevele." [Saint Stephen's Greek Charter.] *Századok* 51 (1917): 99–136.

[11] Albin Balogh, "A veszprémvölgyi görög monostor alapítása. A legrégibb magyarországi oklevél." [The Foundation of the Veszprémvölgy Greek Monastery. Hungary's Oldest Charter.] *Regnum* 6 (1944—1946): 21–30; Gyula László, "A magyar pénzverés kezdeteiről." [On the Beginnings of Coin Minting in Hungary.] *Századok* 97 (1963): 382–307; Miklós Komjáthy, "A veszprémvölgyi alapítólevél kibocsátójáról." [Who Issued the Veszprémvölgy Charter?] *Levéltári Közlemények* 42 (1973): 33–49.

[12] Marianne Sághy, "Aspects de la christianisation des Hongrois aux IXe–Xe siècles." *Early Christianity in Central and East Europe*. Przemyslav Urbanczyk (ed.) Warszawa: Semper, 1997: 53–65.

rather than "prince." Others surmise that the foundation served the spiritual needs of Sarolt, Géza's wife, daughter of Prince Gyula of Transylvania, baptized in Constantinople, whose family followed the Greek rite;[13] or for King Stephen's sister, the exiled wife of the Bulgar Czar Gavril-Radomir.[14] On this basis, László Holler argues for a foundation date between 975 and 985.[15] It is, however, contradicted by Veszprém's toponymy: named after the Polish prince Bezprym born in 986–987, the city is first mentioned as Veszprém in the year of the foundation of her bishopric in 1009.[16] The foundation of the Greek nunnery must have preceded that of the bishopric and depended on the Greek "metropolitan of Turkia," whose control over the monastery King Stephen's first charter, issued between 997 and 1001 acknowledged.[17] The charter reflects the success and expansion of Byzantine Christian missions in Hungary led by Bishop Hierotheos of Gyulafehérvár (Alba Iulia, Transylvania, today Romania) from 950 onwards.[18]

The Latin translation of King Stephen's roll in King Coloman's *renovatio* of 1109 further complicates the matter by specifying that the charter's being written in Greek is due to "the language of the founder" (*iuxta linguam auctoris monasterii*.) This cannot fit King Stephen—but could it eventually be an allusion to the religion of his mother, Sarolt? A reference to the Byzantine bride of Prince Emeric, King Stephen's son in the thirteenth-century *Legend of Saint Margaret* (daughter of King Béla IV, who lived in Veszprémvölgy's new Dominican cloister near the Greek monastery) led Gyula Moravcsik to suggest that the Byzantine emperor might have been "the Greek-language founder" of the nunnery.[19] The great Hungarian Byzantinist conjectured that King Stephen "was not the founder of the nunnery, merely sanc-

---

[13] János Melich, *A honfoglaláskori Magyarország* [Hungary in the Age of the Magyar Conquest.] Budapest: Akadémiai, 1925, 29, 39.
[14] Gyula Moravcsik, "The Role of the Byzantine Church in Medieval Hungary." *American Slavic and East European Review* 6 (1947): 143.
[15] László Holler, "Géza vagy István idejében alapították-e a veszprémvölgyi monostort?" [Was the Monastery of Veszprémvölgy founded under the reign of Géza or István?] *Magyar Nyelv* 107 (2011): 257–279; idem, "A veszprémi görög rítusú monostor alapító- és adománylevelének datálásáról és további kérdéseiről." [On the Date and Other Issues of the Foundation and Donation Charter of the Greek Rite Monastery in Veszprémvölgy]. *Magyar Nyelv* 109 (2013): 50–67.
[16] Gutheil, Jenő. *Az Árpád-kori Veszprém.* [*Veszprém in the Árpádian Age.*] Veszprém: Veszprém Megyei Levéltár, 1979; Györffy, *King Saint Stephen.*
[17] István Baán, "The Metropolitanate of Tourkia. The Organization of the Byzantine Church in Hungary in the Middle Ages." Art. cit., 45–53
[18] *Sfântul Ierotei, episcop de Alba Iulia (sec. X).* Ioan Aurel Pop—Jan Nicolae—Ovidiu Panaite. Alba Iulia: Edit. Reîntregirea, 2010.
[19] Gyula Moravcsik, "Görögnyelvű monostorok Szent István korában." [Greek-Language Monasteries in the Age of Saint Stephen.] art. cit.

tioned the foundation and endowed the nunnery with the necessary funds in the same manner as John II Komnenos, Emperor of Byzantium, had done in the case of the Pantokrator Monastery founded by his wife, the Empress Eirene, a Hungarian princess, when, following her death, he issued a charter in 1136."[20] Since Emeric's Greek bride is not mentioned by any other source, Moravcsik declared this an open question,[21] and Géza Érszegi refuted it altogether.[22] Comparing the *auctor* of the monastery to the *protectores* or *defensores* in the Latin Church, Rudolf Szentgyörgyi argues that King Stephen commissioned the metropolitan of Turkia to found the monastery before 1001.[23] Greek bishoprics are unthinkable without monasteries, thus the Greek-speaking *auctor monasterii* was no other than the Greek metropolitan of Hungary.

Where did Greeks come from to Hungary? Not necessarily from the East; they could just as well have arrived from the West. In the tenth and eleventh centuries, the sphere of Byzantine spirituality and culture covered a vast horizon that included North-Eastern Italy and Sicily. Scholars have long brought attention to the fact that Greek influences in Hungary appear not only as a direct result of Greek presence and Byzantine missionary activity in the area, but also thanks to Italian and Germano-Byzantine culture carriers. In 1097, King Coloman married a Norman princess from Sicily, whose retinue included Greek speakers. This led Gyula Czebe, the first editor of the Greek text of the Veszprémvölgy charter to suggest that the original text might have been copied and revised by a Sicilian Greek scribe in King Coloman's court.[24] This hypothesis, however, was rejected: comparative reading of the charter shows that it uses a terminology typical to eleventh-century Byzantine diplomacy[25] and thus opens a window onto the vivid Byzantine culture of King Stephen's court, where a Greek priest worked as a scribe and drafted the document.[26]

---

[20] Gyula Moravcsik, "The Role of the Byzantine Church," art. cit. 143.

[21] Ibid.

[22] Géza Érszegi, "Szent István görögnyelvű okleveléről." [On Saint Stephen's Greek Charter.] *Levéltári Szemle* 38 (1988): 239–249.

[23] Rudolf Szentgyörgyi, "The *auctor monasterii* of the Byzantine Monastery of Veszprém Valley 2." In: Egedi-Kovács, Emese (ed.) *Byzance et l'Occident II: Tradition, transmission, traduction*. Budapest: ELTE Eötvös József Collegium, 2015, 191–202.

[24] Gyula Czebe, "A veszprémvölgyi oklevél görög szövege."[The Greek Text of the Veszprémvölgy Charter.] *Értekezések a történelmi tudományok köréből* 24 (1918): 17–18.

[25] Jenő Darkó, "A veszprémi apácamonostor alapítólevelének 1109-i másolatáról." [On the Renewal of the Foundation Charter of the Veszprém Nunnery in 1109.] *Egyetemes Philológiai Közlöny* 41 (1917): 257–272, 336–351.

[26] Gábor Krajnyák, "Szent István veszprémvölgyi donatiójának görög egyházi vonatkozásai." [The Byzantine Ecclesiastical Aspects of Saint Stephen's Donation Charter to Veszprémvölgy.] *Századok* 59–60 (1925–1926): 498–507.

The Greek–Latin bilingual charter of Veszprémvölgy Monastery—just like King Stephen's praise of multilingual realms in his *Admonitions*[27] and the Greek and Latin parts that constitute the Holy Crown of Hungary—offer compelling proof that in the eleventh–twelfth century, the Magyar Kingdom ambitioned to unite, rather than to distinguish Greeks and Latins. King Stephen's foreigner-friendly policy was part of the conception to assure his sovereignty and exclude the superpowers to dominate in Hungary by establishing a "balance of power" between the German and Greek commonwealths. Favoring both Latin and Greek forms of Christianity was more than good politics in the case of Stephen, himself raised in the Greek rite practiced by his mother. For Stephen, Latin and Greek, Slavic or Hungarian were as many idioms and expressions of a single, indivisible Christianity.[28] The king of Hungary regarded Constantinople and Rome "the two eyes of Christendom" and gave lavish donations to build pilgrim houses in both cities, as well as in Jerusalem, the birthplace of Christianity.[29] The Hungarian hospice buttressed Saint Peter's Basilica in Rome,[30] but the exact location of Stephen's foundation in Constantinople is not known. To the Árpádian kings, rulers of a multiethnic country, the terms 'East and West,' 'Roman Catholicism and Greek Orthodoxy,' 'Byzantium and the Holy Roman Empire of the German Nation' used by modern historiography for a compartmentalization of historical reality, would have simply made no sense.

Kings and Greek Nuns, Queens and Slav Hermits

Apart from its rite and language, the location of the Veszprémvölgy Monastery is also remarkable. As its name indicates, the nunnery was established in the "valley of Veszprém," a steep rocky gorge cut by the rapid Séd Creek, whose abundant waters nurture verdant forests below high cliffs. Having defeated his pagan relative and

---

[27] Jenő Szűcs, "Szent István Intelmei: az első magyarországi államelméleti mű." [Saint Stephen's Exhortations: the First Treatise of Political Theory of State in Hungary.] In: Glatz, Ferenc and Kardos, József (eds.) *Szent István és kora*. [Saint Stephen and His Age.] Budapest: MTA Történettudományi Intézet, 1988, 32–53, English summary: idem, "King Stephen's Exhortations and his State." *The New Hungarian Quarterly* 112 (1988): 89–97; Előd Nemerkényi, "The Religious Ruler in the *Admonitions* of King Saint Stephen of Hungary." In: *Monotheistic Kingship: The Medieval Variants*. Aziz Al Azmeh and János M. Bak (eds.) Budapest: CEU Press, 2004 231–247.

[28] No wonder that King Stephen is the only ruler canonized by both the Latin and the Greek Church.

[29] Györffy, *King Saint Stephen*.

[30] László Blazovich-Géza Érszegi-Éva Turbuly (eds.) *Források Magyarország levéltáraiból (1000–1686)*. [Sources from the Archives of Hungary, 1000–1686] Budapest–Szeged: 1998; László Csorba, *Ricordi ungheresi in Italia*. Budapest: Benda Foto, 2003.

contender Koppány in 1009 near Veszprém, King Stephen established Hungary's first episcopal see in the town, which he offered to his Queen Gisela.[31]Veszprém became "the queen's city," and in the royal coronation ceremony, the consorts of Hungary were to be crowned by the bishop of Veszprém.[32] The nunnery of Veszprémvölgy—similarly to other Greek monasteries scattered throughout the realm of which historical information survive—became a prestigious foundation located near a royal center, not unlike a diplomatic residence. Who were the nuns in Veszprémvölgy? The convent functioned as a spiritual and educational center for royal princesses of Hungary whose prospective husbands included the rulers of Kievan Rus, Bulgaria, Serbia, or Byzantium. Apart from the princesses, daughters of the courtly élite following the Greek rite, Queen Gisela's retinue, and members of the "diplomatic corps" in Hungary were likely to patronize the monastery.

Not only did Veszprém boast with a Greek nunnery outside of the town, her patron saints were warrior saints popular in Byzantium: the bishopric of Veszprém was dedicated to Saint Michael, and its first ecclesiastical building, a rotunda, to Saint George.[33] While the choice of Saint Michael, heavenly leader of the New Israel, may owe less to Byzantine spirituality than to the city's standing on a cliff, the Chapel of Saint George did have direct links to Byzantium: it was built to house the relics of the saint, a gift from Emperor Basil II to his ally King Stephen, acquired during the war against the Bulgars between 1016 and 1018 in Ohrid.

Eastern spirituality permeated yet another monastery, the Benedictine Abbey of Saint Maurice of Bél founded by King Stephen in 1018, at only thirty-four kilometers from Veszprém. The Bél (Bakonybél) monastery stemmed from the

---

[31] Jenő Gutheil, *Az Árpád-koriVeszprém*. [*Veszprém under the Árpádian Kings*.] Veszprém: Veszprém Megyei Levéltár, 1979.

[32] Attila Zsoldos, *Az Árpádok és asszonyaik. A királynéi intézmény azÁrpádok korában.* [*The Kings of the Árpádian Dynasty and their Queens. The reginal institution in the Age of the Árpáds.*]Budapest: MTA Történettudományi Intézet, 2005. The queens were buried in Veszprém, among them Queen Adelaide, Piroska's mother, see András Uzsoki, "Szent László hitvese, Adelhaid királyné, Rudolf német ellenkirály leánya"[Queen Adelaide, wife of Saint Ladislaus, daughter of Rudolph of Swabia] In: *Szent László és Somogyvár: Tanulmányok a 900 éves somogyvári bencés apátság emlékezetére.* Kálmán Magyar (ed.), Kaposvár: Somogy Megyei Múzeumok Igazgatósága 1992, 145–152. Antonio Bonfini, *Rerum Ungaricarum decades,* T. II, edd. Iosephus Fógel- Béla Iványi –Ladislaus Juhász. Lipsiae, 1936, 2, IV, 282 quotes the inscription of the tombstone as "Ladislai regis consortum hic ossa quiescunt." The burial slab is now walled into the 17th-century church of Makranc (today Mokronce, Slovakia): *Súpis pamiatok na Slovensku*, 2, Bratislava: Obzor, 1968, 333.

[33] Jenő Gutheil –Katalin H. Gyürky –Ferenc Erdei—Tibor Koppány, "A veszprémi Szent György egyház és konzerválása."[The Saint George Church of Veszprém and its Conservation]. *Műemlékvédelem* 4/3 (1960): 136–143; Monica White, *Military saints in Byzantium and Rus, 900–1200* (Cambridge: Cambridge University Press, 2013).

hermitage that Günther of Niederaltaich—a Thuringian noblemen, warrior, and escort of Queen Gisela to Hungary—frequented in the deep forests of the Bakony mountains. Converted at the age of fifty to the ascetic life—a *cause célèbre* at the time—Günther made a pilgrimage to Rome and entered the Abbey of Niederaltaich in Bavaria in 1006, where Abbot Godehard gave him permission before long to leave the premises of the monastery and establish himself a hermitage. Günther's intense asceticism drew heavily on the inspiration of Eastern masters of spirituality, such as the Desert Fathers—he even learned Greek for their sake—and cherished a special veneration for Saint John the Baptist, the *Prodromos*. His sermons on his patron saint moved audiences to tears. "A mobile hermit with a large radius of movement"[34] who linked Bavaria with Bohemia and Hungary, Günther was an indefatigable founder of Eastern lavra-type eremitic communities. The success of his mission was not only due to his smattering of Slavic languages, but (primarily) to his unrivaled contacts with the rulers of Bohemia and Hungary. He often dropped by at King Stephen's court in Székesfehérvár: "the blessed Günther, who, drawn by the generosity of the charitable prince, used to visit him often from the land of the Czechs. For whenever he illuminated Stephen's court by the brightness of his arrival, the treasury of the king, placed at his disposal, was emptied in a short time of the things that it contained through their distribution to pilgrims, the poor, the needy, widows and orphans, monasteries and churches."[35]

No similar charitable activities are connected to the nunnery of Veszprémvölgy. Nothing is known about the everyday life and work of the nuns. Luxury needlework, however, is often attributed to the monastery. The golden chasuble offered by the royal couple as a gift to the Provostry Church of the Virgin Mary at Székesfehérvár in 1031[36] is thought to have been embroidered by Queen Gisela and the nuns in Veszprémvölgy.[37] Made of the finest Byzantine silk, the rosette-patterned, bell-shaped chasuble is entirely embroidered in gold thread and was decorated with pearls and gemstones. The cape's back shows a Y-shaped Cross with half-length depictions of angels around the raised arms of the Y, while the vertical element features two images of the Savior: Christ conquers death and tramples on a dragon and a lion; Christ on His throne judges the world. Two bands of prophets and apostles

---

[34] Miladinov, op. cit., 84.
[35] Hartvic, "Life of King Stephen of Hungary" 14. Tr. Nora Berend. In: Thomas Head (ed.) *Medieval Hagiography. An Anthology*. New York: Routledge, 2000, 387.
[36] Later used as the coronation mantle of the kings of Hungary: Ernő Marosi, "The Székesfehérvár chasuble of King Stephen and Queen Gisela." In: *The Coronation Mantle of the Hungarian Kings*. István Bardoly, ed. Budapest: Hungarian National Museum, 2005, 110–113.
[37] Krajnyák, art. cit., 505–506.

in tower-shaped niches surround the Cross, while martyrs figure in circular medallions separated by pairs of birds. The Assumption of the Virgin Mary—the feast of the Székesfehérvár Provostry—is shown at the neck of the chasuble. At the foot of Christ's Cross, King Stephen and Queen Gisela are represented in medallions. The king wears a circlet crown with gemstones, a winged lance in his right hand and an orb in his left. Gisela wears the same crown and holds a tower reliquary in her hand. Between them, the half-length portrait of a young man in a circular frame is probably their son, Prince Emeric, who died in a hunting accident in the very year of 1031. The chasuble's inscriptions contain the names of the figures and Latin hexameters. The execution of the chasuble cannot be linked with any certainty to the monastery of Veszprémvölgy. It might just as well have been produced in an Esztergom or Székesfehérvár royal workshop. Another precious textile, the purple purse of Saint Stephen of Hungary decorated with Old Church Slavonic religious inscriptions in gold thread is also attributed to the Veszprémvölgy nunnery, again without hard proof.[38]

The Monastery of the Holy Mother of God in Veszprémvölgy was but one of several Greek monastic communities in eleventh-century Hungary. Greek monasticism and Eastern eremitism seem to have been the dominant forms of spiritual life in the country at the time. As late as 1204, Pope Innocent III wrote to King Emeric I: "In your realm, there exists only one Latin cenobite monastery, but many Greek."[39] Surviving historical record about the Greek monasteries is uneven, due to the withering away of the Greek cloisters in subsequent centuries and to the rise of Roman Catholic forms of monastic life: as against twenty-seven Benedictine abbeys, only eight Greek monasteries are known in the eleventh–thirteenth centuries:[40] the Monastery of Saint George at Oroszlános (today Banatsko Aranđelovo in Serbia) on River Maros in South-Eastern Hungary, Tihany-Óvár cave monastery at Lake Balaton near Veszprém, the Monastery of Saint Andrew in Visegrád with its dependent cave cells in Zebegény in the Danube Bend near Esztergom, the Monastery of Saint Hyppolitus on Mount Zobor in Nyitra (today Nitra in Slovakia), the Monastery of Saint Panteleimon in Pentele on the River Danube, and the Monastery of Saint Demetrius in Szávaszentdemeter (today Sremska Mitrovica in Serbia) on the River Sava in Southern Hungary.

---

[38] Béla Czobor, *Magyarország történelmi emlékei az ezredéves országos kiállításon.* [Hungary's Historical Monuments and relics at the Millenial Exhibition.] Budapest, 1898–99; Krajnyák, art. cit., 505–506.

[39] Georgius Fejér (ed.), *Codex Diplomaticus Hungariae* II: 447: "In regno tuo unum sit Latinorum coenobium, quam tamen ibidem sint multa Graecorum."

[40] Moravcsik, "Görögnyelvű monostorok Szent István korában." art. cit., 421.

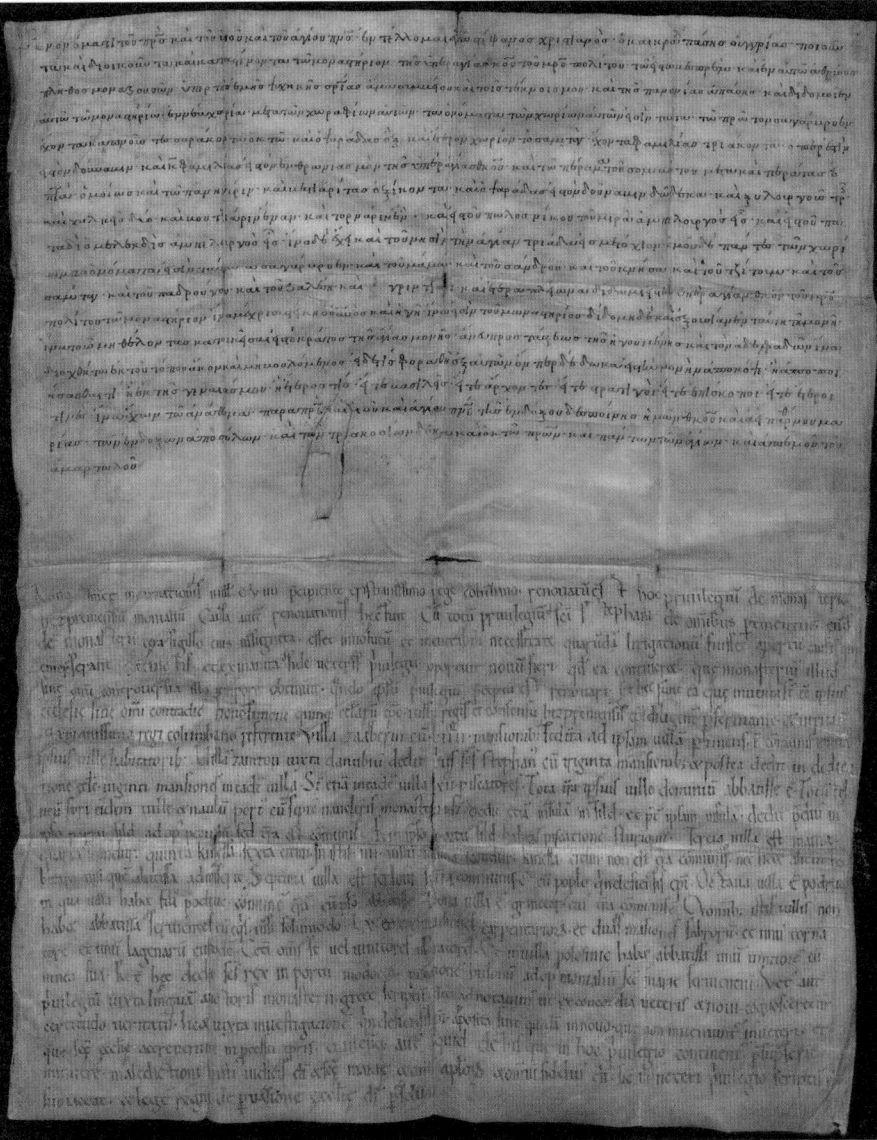

Figure 1. The Veszprémvölgy Donation Charter, 1109. MNL OL DL 11
© Hungarian National Archives

Figure 2. Seal of King Coloman on the Veszprémvölgy Donation Charter, 1109.
MNL OL DL 11 © Hungarian National Archives

Figure 3. Ruins of the Veszprémvölgy Greek Nunnery (© Zoltán Kárpáti)

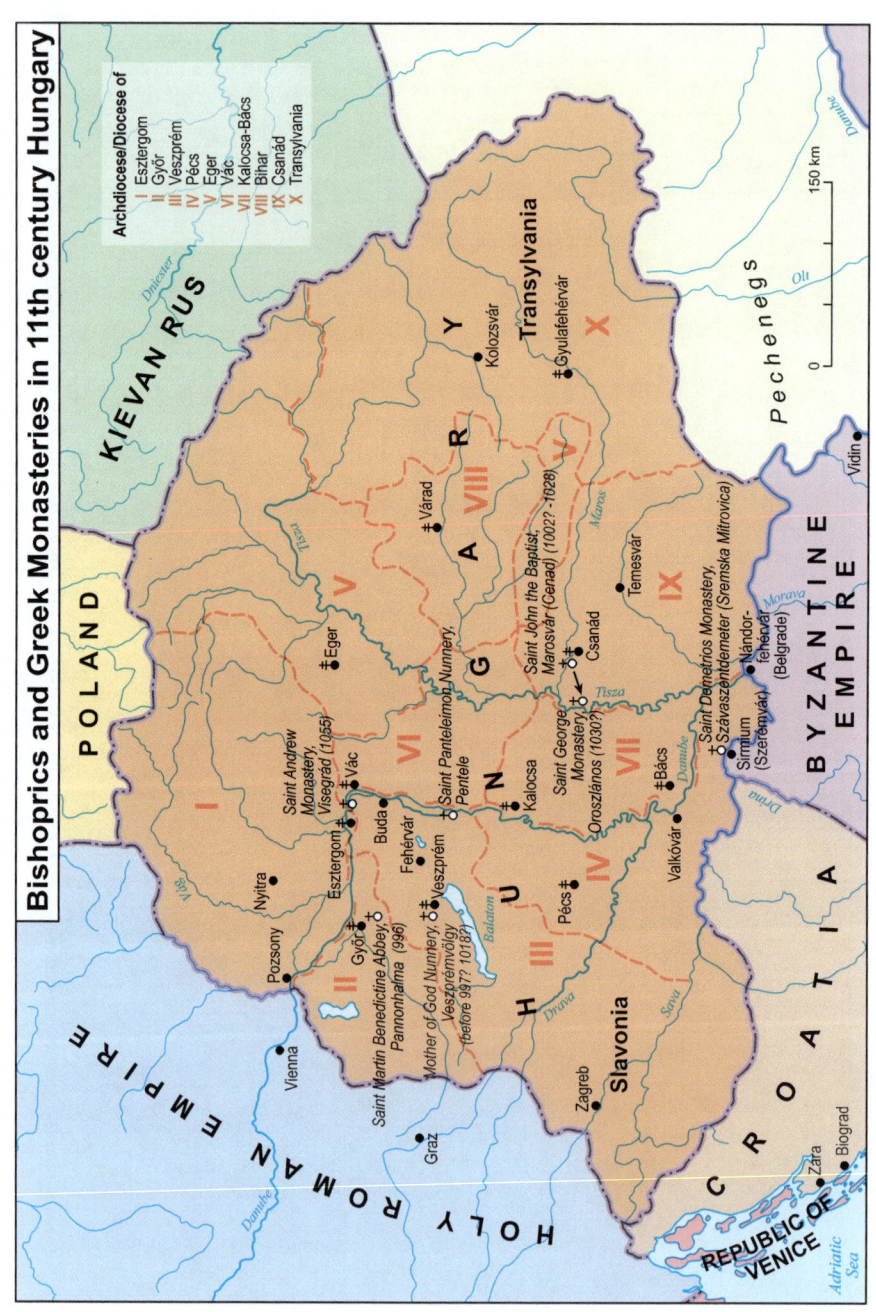

Figure 4. Map: Greek Monasteries in Árpádian Hungary © Attila Sasi

A monastery dedicated to Saint John the Baptist was founded by Prince Ajtony in Marosvár (today Cenad, Romania), the headquarters of his vast territories in Eastern Hungary. In 1028, Ajtony challenged King Stephen and obstructed the transport of salt from Transylvania to Hungary on the River Maros. The king's army led by Csanád defeated Ajtony in the battle at Oroszlános and conquered his lands. Stephen established the bishopric of Csanád in 1030 and appointed Gerard, a Benedictine monk from Venice, as its bishop. Upon his arrival to his see, Gerard transferred the Greek monks of Marosvár to Oroszlános, in a new monastery dedicated to Saint George.[41] In the library of Marosvár Monastery, Gerard found Greek codices that inspired his exegesis of the biblical story of the three youths in the furnace that he possibly composed in the Benedictine Abbey of Saint Maurice in Bakonybél.[42]

In 1055, King Andrew (1046–1060), who had lived as an exile in Kiev and married Anastasia, the daughter of Jaroslav of Kiev, founded a Benedictine abbey dedicated to Saint Anianus of Orléans in Tihany on Lake Balaton[43] and a Greek monastery in Visegrád in honor of his patron saint, Andrew.[44] The Tihany foundation replaced an earlier Greek monastery possibly dedicated to Saint Tychon, whose name survived as the name of the peninsula.[45] Both foundations had clusters of caves nearby for hermits, who lived in individual cells, but constituted an eremitic group (*lavra*).[46] Even Oroszkő—the name of the hermits' caves in Tihany-Óvár—preserves the memory of the Greek monks: even though it means 'Russian Stone', it possibly derives from the Greek *oros* (hill) and thus refers to Tihany as a sacred mount, similarly to Mount Athos (*Hagios Oros*),[47] rather than to the recently arrived

---

[41] "Vita Gerardi Maior" 14, *Scriptores Rerum Hungaricarum* 2, 495; Zoltán J. Kosztolnyik, "The Relations of Four Eleventh-Century Hungarian Kings with Rome in the Light of Papal Letters." *Church History* 46 1977): 33–47.

[42] Gerard of Csanád. *Deliberatio supra hymnum trium puerorum* Gabriel Silagi (ed.) CCCM 49. Turnhout: Brepols, 1978.

[43] *Paradisum plantavit: Bencés monostorok a középkori Magyarországon*. [Paradisum plantavit: Benedictine Monasteries in Medieval Hungary.] Takács, Imre (ed.) Pannonhalma: Bencés Kiadó, 2001; Rudolf Szentgyörgyi, *A tihanyi apátság alapítólevele*. [The Foundation Charter of the Abbey of Tihany.] Budapest: ELTE Eötvös Kiadó, 2014.

[44] Gergely Buzás and Benadett Eszes, "XI. századi görög monostor Visegrádon." [An Eleventh-Century Greek Monastery in Visegrád.] In: *Középkori egyházi építészet Erdélyben /Arhitectura religiosă medievală din Transilvania* IV. Szőcs, Péter Levente and Adrian Andrei Rusu (eds.) Satu Mare, 2007, 49–93.

[45] Rudolf Szentgyörgyi, "A Tihanyi alapítólevél görög helynevei." [Greek Place Names in the Tihany Foundation Charter.]*Magyar Nyelv* 106 (2010): 385–396.

[46] Miladinov, *Margins of Solitude. Eremitism in Central Europe between East and West*, op. cit., 157–167.

[47] Rudolf Szentgyörgyi, "A Tihanyi alapítólevél görög helynevei." [Greek Place Names in the Tihany Foundation Charter.]*Magyar Nyelv* 106 (2010): 295–307.

Kievan monks. The Visegrád Greek monastery had eremitic cells on the opposite bank of the Danube in Zebegény.[48] In 1056, exiles of the Benedictine Monastery of Sázava in Bohemia arrived in Hungary and established themselves near the Monastery of Saint Andrew.[49] In Tihany and Visegrád, Greek and Latin monks and hermits settled in the vicinity of each other. They did not cohabit, but their physical closeness assured that they could draw inspiration from each other. King Andrew's foundation of Benedictine and Orthodox monastic houses and the coexistence of Latin, Greek and Russian monks continue earlier royal models and demonstrate the strength of the conviction of the unity of Christianity in eleventh-century Hungary. The monks regarded Hungary as the "wild East," where, as it was shown by the martyrdom of Gerard of Csanád, it was still possible, as late as in 1046, to die as a martyr, or to live in imitation of the Desert Fathers on sacred mounts, impenetrable forests, and unapproachable cliffs hanging over vast waters.

The appearance of cave heremitism in Hungary is more than a direct echo of the great tradition of monastic *lavra* in Greek and Slav Christianity: it is a sign of the appeal of the Desert Fathers. The attraction of cave eremitism reached as far as Northern Hungary: in the Monastery of Saint Hyppolitus on Mount Zobor in Nyitra (today Nitra in Slovakia), a Polish ascetic, Zoerard-Andrew lived a life modeled on that of the Desert Fathers, especially that of Zosimas, the sixth-century Palestinian monk and confessor of Mary of Egypt. Inspired by his readings, Zoerard used three particular devices of mortification typical of early Christian asceticism: a sleeping stool and a wooden crown with stones hanging on four sides that turned nocturnal repose to torment and affliction, and a metal chain tied around the waist that made everyday existence a constant torture.[50] Zoerard's community also combined Latin Benedictine and Greek Slavonic rites.[51]

The origins of the monasteries in Pentele and Szávaszentdemeter—both localities named after their patron saints, Saint Pantaleimon and Saint Demetrius respectively—are obscure and the presence of Greek monks is only known from

---

[48] János Karácsonyi, "Hogyan jöttek a görög szerzetesek Visegrádra?" [How did Greek Monks Come to Visegrád?] *Katholikus Szemle* 41 (1927). 16–21.

[49] Keene, *Saint Margaret, Queen of the Scots: A Life in Perspective*, op. cit., 20–21.

[50] Miladinov, *Margins of Solitude* 120–123. Eastern asceticism was an inspiration for hermits all over Europe in the eleventh century. Thus, for example, the hermit Godfric in East Anglia designed a specially uncomfortable chair with curving back of shoulder height, so that he could spend all night in prayer, see Andrew Jotischky, "Monastic reform and the geography of Christendom: experience, observation and influence," *Transactions of the Royal Historical Society*, 6th Series 22 (2012), 57–74. I owe this reference to Jonathan Shepard.

[51] Stark, "Cave of. Hermits, Cave of Cult. Saints Andrew-Zoerard and Benedict and the Sacralization of the Medieval Hungarian Landscape." art. cit.

later charters. A charter of Palatine János Drugeth from 1329 refers in an idiosyncratic way—"*begine sine moniales Grecales*"—to the Greek monastery in Pentele. As its patron saint indicates, the monastery of Pentele must have been a Greek male community from the eleventh to the thirteenth century. The charter's wording reflects the blending of the memory of Greek monks and the Saint Catherine begina-community who took over the abandoned cloister after the Mongol invasion of 1241–42.[52]

A letter of Pope Honorius III dated 29 January 1218 mentions the Monastery of Saint Demetrius near the River Száva belonging to the Churches of Saint Theodore of Laberra.[53] In a letter of 1344, Pope Clement VI asks the bishop of Nyitra to settle Benedictine monks in the ancient Monastery of Szávaszentdemeter. The pope explains that Greek, Hungarian and Slav monks had lived here together, yet separately, its abbot depending directly from the patriarch of Constantinople. Since the death of the last Greek abbot some ten years earlier, the monastery stood empty.[54] György Györffy dates the foundation of Szávaszentdemeter Monastery to 1071–1072 and highlights that it was connected to Constantinople, rather than to a Bulgarian bishopric.[55]

Interaction between Latins and Greeks

The heyday of Eastern asceticism in early Árpádian Hungary was a unique moment of the permeability and interaction of Latin and Greek monasticism. The eleventh-century eremitic revival meant the discovery and absorption of Greek and Egyptian monastic models by Latin Christianity: monks flocked to Hungary to re-live the desert experience. The vivacity of Greek and Slav spirituality[56] in the Kingdom of the Árpáds is demonstrated not only by precious Byzantine liturgical

---

[52] Géza Érszegi. "Begine sive moniales grecales." In: *Corde aperto. Tanulmányok Kredics László nyolcvanadik születésnapjára.* [Corde aperto. Essays for László Kredics's Eightieth Birthday.] Veszprém, 2012: 31–45.
[53] György Györffy, *A szávaszentdemeteri görög monostor XII. századi birtokösszeírása* I–II. [The Twelfth-Century List of Land Possessions by the Greek Monastery of Szávaszentdemeter.] MTA II. Oszt. Közleményei 2 (1952) 325–362. és 3 (1953) 69–104.
[54] Péter Tóth, "Egy bizánci szent Magyarországon, egy magyar szent Bizáncban." [A Byzantine Saint in Hungary, a Hungarian Saint in Byzantium.] *Magyar Könyvszemle* 117/1 (2001); Péter Tóth (ed.). *Szent Demeter Magyarország elfeledett védőszentje.* [Saint Demetrius, Hungary's Forgotten Patron Saint.] Budapest: Balassi, 2007.
[55] György Györffy, "Das Güterverzeichnis des griechischen Klosters zu Szávaszentdemeter/ Sremska Mitrovica aus dem 12. Jahrhundert." *Studia Slavica* 5 (1959): 9–74.
[56] Moravcsik, "The Role of the Byzantine Church in Medieval Hungary." art. cit.

vessels,[57] but, above all, by a remarkably versatile architectural language: in Hungary, Greek monasteries tend to follow Latin models, while the Latin churches are built upon Byzantine ones.[58] The momentum of a fused Greek and Latin spirituality lasted well into the twelfth century, when the monk Cerbanus translated Maximus the Confessor and John Damascene from Greek to Latin in the monastery of Pásztó, works that were to be perused all over Western Europe.[59] The Pásztó monk-scholar is identifiable as the Venetian Cerbano Cerbani, an interpreter in the court of John II Komnenos, who left Constantinople in 1124 for Venice, but apparently not stayed there.[60] His presence in North-Eastern Hungary demonstrates the free circulation of monks, texts and scholars around the peripheral regions of the Byzantine world, without necessary reference to, or control by, the imperial capital or the royal court.

The decline of Eastern monasticism in Hungary starts in the twelfth century with the implementation of Gregorian reforms by King Coloman and continues in the thirteenth: a letter of Honorius III written on 20 April 1221 to the archbishop of Esztergom and the abbot of Pilis rules that King Andrew II people the Monastery of Visegrád with Latin monks, because the community, abandoned by the Greeks, decayed in spirit and in resources.[61] The survival of Eastern cenobitism was sealed by the Mongol invasion of Hungary in 1242: during the reign of Béla IV (1235–1270) Benedictines and Cistercians took over the abandoned Greek-rite monasteries, while new mendicant orders settled in towns.

Byzantine Christianity in Hungary was missionary in the tenth century,[62] and monastic in the eleventh. Monasteries—both Latin and Greek—in early

---

[57] Etele Kiss, "Byzantine Silversmiths' Work around AD 1000 between China and the Ottonians: The Beszterec Holy Water Vessel."*Jahrbuch der Österreichischen Byzantinistik* 49 (1999): 301–314.

[58] Miklós Takács, "A magyarországi 11. századi ortodox monostortemplomok térszerkezete." [Raumstruktur der orthodoxen Klosterkirchen im Ungarn des 11.Jh.] In: A *Kárpát-medence, a magyarság és Bizánc*. Ed. Terézia Olajos. Szeged: Acta Universitatis Szegediensis, 2014, 295–323.

[59] István Kapitánffy, "Cerbanus és Maximus-fordítása." In: *Mons Sacer 996–1996. Pannonhalma 1000 éve I*. Pannonhalma: Bencés Kiadó, 1996, 357–368.

[60] Alex Rodriguez Suarez, "From Greek into Latin: Western scholars and translators in Constantinople during the reign of John II." In: Alessandra Bucossi –Alex Rodriguez Suarez (eds.), *John II Komnenos, Emperor of Byzantium. In the Shadow of Father and Son*. London: Publications of the Centre for Hellenic Studies, King's College, 2016, 96–7.

[61] Augustin Theiner (ed.) *Vetera monumenta historica Hungariam sacram illustrantia* I.Romae: Typ. Vaticanis, 1860: 29, nr. 53: "Quae Abbatia de Visegrad Veszpremensis Dioecesis, in qua jus obtinet patronatus, Graecos habet monachos... sibi innotuisse ab Andrea rege Graecos Visegradiensis Monachos disciplinam regularem dissolute observare, proin, si ita compererint, Graecis Latinos substituant."

[62] Jonathan Shepard, "Spreading the word: Byzantine missions," in Cyril Mango, ed., *The Oxford history of Byzantium*. Oxford: Oxford University Press, 2002, 230–247.

Árpádian Hungary were founded by powerful chieftains, princes, kings and hermits. Greek and Slav cenobite and eremitic communities depended from the Greek metropolitan and mushroomed in the vicinity of royal centers, such as Esztergom, Marosvár, Nyitra and Veszprém. Eastern ascetics were contemplative: no mention of their charitable, social or missionary activity survives. However, as the example of Günther of Niederaltaich shows, even the most contemplative of hermits was capable of showing great social sensibility and practical charity. Serving the spiritual needs of kings and queens, high-brow intellectuals, men and women attracted by the spirituality of the Desert Fathers, the fusion of Greek and Latin spirituality was, just like in Italy, promoted by the political and monastic leadership. As Jean-Marie Sansterre observes, "pour l'élite monastique, le sentiment d'unité transcendait les différences."[63] Eastern monasticism was no "hothouse flower" in Hungary.[64] The spiritual, visual and material legacy of the Greek monasteries, even in its fragmented form, suggests that they responded to the needs of wider social circles and took deeper roots in society than hitherto imagined. The laws of King Ladislaus at the Council of Szabolcs in 1092, in the thick of the Gregorian conflict demonstrate the extent to which Byzantine piety permeated religious life in Hungary: priests were allowed to marry, fasting and the sanctification of water followed Greek traditions.[65] The ecclesiastical legislation of Piroska's father evidences the impact of Byzantine monasticism on Christian piety in Hungary.

The legacy of open-minded spiritual interaction between Greeks and Latins was not lost on Princess Piroska. She might have heard edifying stories about King Stephen's Marian piety, his charity towards the poor, and his generous endowments of monasteries, as her ward, King Coloman promoted with brio the cult of the first Christian king in Hungary,[66] commissioning Bishop Hartvic to compose a new *Life*

---

[63] Jean-Marie Sansterre, "Saint Nil de Rossano et le monachisme latin." In: A. Acconcia Longo - S. Luca - L. Perria (eds.) *Miscellanea di studi in onore di P. Marco Petto*. Bollettino della badia greca di Grottaferrata, n.s., 45, 1991, II, 382.

[64] János Karácsonyi, *Szent István király élete*. [Life of King Saint Stephen]. Budapest: Akadémiai, 1904, 75.

[65] János M. Bak, György Bónis - James Ross Sweeney (eds.) *The Laws of the Medieval Kingdom of Hungary, I: 1000–1301*, with a critical essay on previous editions by Andor Csizmadia (The Laws of Hungary, Series I, vol. 1: 1000–1301) (Bakersfield, CA: Charles Schlaks, Jr., Publ., 1989), 55–61, 120–124; Second revised edition in collaboration with Leslie S. Domonkos (Idyllwild, CA: Charles Schlaks, Jr., Publ., 1999), 53–59, 118–122

[66] Coloman was the first to name his son Stephen, and the first king to have himself buried next to the tomb of Saint Stephen in the royal basilica of Székesfehérvár that was to became the royal mausoleum of the House of Árpád.

of King Stephen.[67] This text stated that King Stephen "did not deprive even the royal city, Constantinople, of endowing it with benefactions: he donated a church of wonderful craftsmanship with everything that was necessary."[68] If Empress Eirene's enthusiasm and active participation in the construction of the Pantokrator Monastery was fueled by Byzantine imperial traditions, the empress's Árpádian ancestors provided an inspiring example of lavish giving for religious causes—one wonders if her new foundation was built in relationship to the older establishment of King Stephen.

Appendix

The Veszprémvölgy Charter (1109) [69]

Ἐν ὀνόματι τοῦ πατρὸς καὶ τοῦ υἱοῦ καὶ τοῦ ἁγίου πνεύματος. Ἐντέλλομαι ἐγὼ Στέφανος χριστιανὸς ὁ καὶ κράλης πάσης Οὐγγρίας ποιοῦντα καὶ διοικοῦντα καὶ καταστένοντα τὸ μοναστήριον τῆς ὑπεραγίας Θεοτόκου τοῦ μητροπολίτου τὸ εἰς τὸ Βεσπρὲμ καὶ ἐν αὐτῷ ἀθροίσας πλῆθος μοναζουσῶν ὑπὲρ τῆς ἐμῆς ψυχικῆς σωτηρίας ἄμα συμβίου καὶ τοῖς τέκνοις μου καὶ τῆς Πανονίας ἁπάσης καὶ δίδωμι ἐν αὐτῷ τῷ μοναστηρίῳ ἐννέα χωρία μετὰ τῶν χωραφίων αὐτῶν. Τὰ ὀνόματα τῶν χωρίων αὐτῶν εἰσὶν ταῦτα· τὸ πρῶτον Σαγάρβρυεν ἔχοντα καπνοὺς τεσσαράκοντα ὀκτὼ καὶ ὀψαράδας ἓξ καὶ ἕτερον χωρίον τὸ Σάμταγ ἔχοντα φαμιλίας τριάκοντα, ὅπερ ἐστὶν εἰς τὸ Δούναβιν, καὶ εἴκοσι φαμιλίας εἰς τὸν ἐνθρονιασμὸν τῆς ὑπεραγίας Θεοτόκου καὶ τὸ πέραμα τοῦ Σομβώτου μετὰ καὶ περάτας ἑπτά, ὁμοίως καὶ τὸ πανηγύριν καὶ βεστιαρίτας ἑξήκοντα καὶ ὀψαράδας εἰς τὸ Δούναβιν δώδεκα καὶ ξυλουργοὺς τρεῖς καὶ χαλκεῖς δύο καὶ βουτζιάριν ἕναν καὶ τορνάριν ἕν<αν> καὶ εἰς τοῦ Πωλοσνίκου τοῦ μιρᾶ ἀμπελουργὸς εἷς καὶ εἰς τοῦ Παταδὶ ὁ Μελεκδὶς ἀμπελουργὸς εἷς, ἵνα δὲ ἔχει καὶ τοῦ νησὶν τὴν Ἁγίαν Τριάδα εἰς μετόχιον. Ὁμοῦ δὲ πάντες τῶν χωρίων τὰ ὀνόματα εἰσὶν ταῦτα· α΄ Σαγάρβρυεν καὶ τοῦ Μάμα καὶ τοῦ Σάνδρου καὶ τοῦ Κνῆσα καὶ τοῦ Τζίτουμ καὶ τοῦ Σάμταγ καὶ τοῦ Παδρούγου καὶ τοῦ Ζαλέσι καὶ τοῦ Γριντζάρι. Καὶ ἕτερα πλείονα δίδωμι εἰς τὴν ὑπεραγίαν Θεοτόκον τοῦ μητροπολίτου τὸ μοναστήριον ἵνα μέχρι συστήκει ὁ οὐρανὸς καὶ ἡ γῆ, ἵνα εἰσὶν τοῦ μοναστηρίου. Δίδωμι δὲ καὶ ἐξουσίαν ἐν ταύτῃ τῇ μονῇ ἵνα τοὺς μὴ θέλοντας κατοικῆ-

---

[67] Hartvic's Life of Saint Stephen is undated: Gábor Thoroczkay, "Anmerkungen zur Frage der Entstehungszeit der Hartvik-Legende des Stephan des Heiligen." *Specimina Nova. Pars Prima. Sectio Mediaevalis*(2001), 107– 131 argues for a date between 1097–1099; József Gerics- Erzsébet Ladányi, "A Hartvik legenda keletkezési körülményeiről." [Contextualizing the Hartvic Legend.] *Magyar Könyvszemle* 4 (2004), 317–324, propose a period around 1003.

[68] "Hartvic, "Life of King Stephen of Hungary" 13. op. cit., 386.

[69] Gyula Moravcsik, *Az Árpád-kori Magyar történet bizánci forrásai*. [The Byzantine sources of the history of Árpádian Hungary]. Budapest: Akadémiai Kiadó, 1984, 79–81.

σαι εἰς τὸ κράτος τῆς ἁγίας μονῆς ἄνευ προστάξεως τῆς ἡγουμένης καὶ τῶν ἀδελφάδων ἵνα διωχθήτω ἐκ τοῦ τόπου ἄκων καὶ μὴ βουλόμενος. Εἰ δέ τις φωραθῇ ἐξ αὐτῶν ὧνπερ δέδωκα εἰς τὴν μονήν, ἀποκόψαι ἢ ἀποποιήσασθαί τι, ἢ ἐκ τῆς γενεᾶς μου ἢ ἕτερός τις εἴτε βασιλεῖς εἴτε ἄρχοντες εἴτε στρατηγοὶ εἴτε ἐπίσκοποι εἴτε ἕτεροί τινες ἵνα ἔχων τὸ ἀνάθεμα παρὰ πατρὸς καὶ υἱοῦ καὶ ἁγίου πνεύματος τῆς ἐνδόξου δεσποίνης ἡμῶν Θεοτόκου καὶ ἀειπαρθένου Μαρίας, τῶν ἐνδόξων ἀποστολῶν καὶ τῶν τριακοσίων δέκα καὶ ὀκτὼ πατέρων καὶ πάντων τῶν ἁγίων καὶ ἀπ' ἐμοῦ τοῦ ἁμαρτωλοῦ.

Anno dominice incarnationis millesimo CVIIII precipiente cristianissimo rege Columbano renovatum est hoc privilegium de monasterio Bezpremensium monialium.

Causa autem renovationis hec fuit: cum totum privilegium sancti Stephani de omnibus pertinentiis eiusdem monasterio cera sigillo eius insignita esse involutum et inevitabili necessitate quarundam litigationum fuisset apertum, causis, que emerserant, extinctis et exinanita fide veteris privilegii oportuit novum fieri, quod ea contineret, que monasterium illud sine omni controversia illo tempore obtinuit, quando ipsum privilegium preceptum est renovari.

Et hec sunt ea, que inventa sunt esse ipsius ecclesie sine omni contradictione Simone Quinque Ecclesiarum episcopo iussu regis et consensu Bezpremensis episcopi diligenter perscrutante et veritatem rei christianissimo regi Columbano referente: villa Zaarberin cum LIIII[or] mansionibus, sed terra ad ipsam villam pertinens est communis et silva ipsius ville habitatoribus. Villam Zamtou iuxta Danubium dedit prius sanctus Stephanus cum triginta mansionibus et postea dedit in dedicatione ecclesie viginti mansiones in eadem villa. Sunt etiam in eadem villa XII[cim] piscatores. Tota terra ipsius ville dominium abbatisse est. Totum teloneum fori eiusdem ville et naulum portus cum septem naucleris monasterii sunt. Dedit etiam insulam in Sild et preter ipsam insulam dedit predium in ipso portu Sild ad opus pecudum, sed terra est communis et ipso portu Sild habent piscationem sturionum. Tercia villa est Mama, quarta Scondur, quinta Kinessa, sexta Citim. In istis IIII[or] villis: Mama, Scondur, Kinessa, Citim non est terra communis nec licet alicui habitare, nisi quem abbatissa admiserit. Septima villa est Serlous, sed terra communis est cum populo Quin<que Ec>lesiensis episcopi. Octava villa est Podruc, in qua villa habet filius Podruc communem terram cum populo abbatisse. Nona villa est Grincear, cuius terra communis est. Ex omnibus istis villis non habet abbatissa servientes cum equis, nisi solummodo LX et tres mansiones carpentariorum et duas mansiones fabrorum et unum tornatorem et unum lagenarum custodem. Ceteri omnes sunt vel vinitores et aratores. Et in villa Polosinic habet abbatissa unum vinitorem cum vinea sua. Preter hec dedit sanctus rex in portu Modocea piscationem husonum ad opus monialium sancte Marie servientum. Vetus autem privilegium iuxta linguam auctoris monasterii Grece scriptum ideo adnotavimus, ut ex concordia veteris et novi cognosceretur certitudo veritatis. Licet iuxta investigacionem Quin<que Ec>clesiensis episcopi apposita sint quedam in novo, que non inveniuntur in veteri et que sancte ecclesie accreverunt in processu temporis.

Quincunque autem aliquid de his, que in hoc privilegio continentur, presumpserit minuere, maledictioni iusti iudicis Dei et sancte Marie et omnium apostolorum et omnium fidelium Dei—sicut in veteri privilegio scriptum est—subiaceat et legem regni de pervasione ecclesie Dei persolvat.

Bibliography
Primary Sources

Hartvic, *Life of King Stephen of Hungary*, Tr. Nora Berend. In: *Medieval Hagiography. An Anthology*, ed. Thomas Head (New York/London: Garland, 2000), 379–396.

Vita Maior Sancti Gerardi episcopi, ed. Emericus Madzsar. *Scriptores Rerum Hungaricarum tempore ducum regumque stirpis Arpadianae gestum*, Vol.II, (ed.) Emericus Szentpétery (Budapest: Akadémiai Kiadó, 1938), 480–506.

Czebe, Gyula. "A veszprémvölgyi oklevél görög szövege."[The Greek Text of the Veszprémvölgy Charter.] *Értekezések a történelmi tudományok köréből.* 24 (1918): 17–18.

Fejér, Georgius. *Codex diplomaticus Hungariae ecclesiasticus ac civilis* I–II. Budae, 1829.

Moravcsik, Gyula (ed.) *Az Árpád-kori Magyar történet bizánci forrásai*. [The Byzantine sources of the history of Árpádian Hungary]. Budapest: Akadémiai 1988.

Olajos, Terézia, *Bizánci források az Árpád-kori Magyar történelemhez: kiegészítés Moravcsik Gyula Az Árpád-kori Magyar történet bizánci forrásai című forrásgyűjteményéhez.* [Byzantine Sources for the History of Hungary under the Árpádian Dynasty: Appendices to the work of Gyula Moravcsik.] Szeged: Lectum, 2015.

Silagi, Gabriel, ed. *Gerard of Csanád. Deliberatio supra hymnum trium puerorum*. CCCM 49. Turnhout: Brepols, 1978.

"Vitae S. Gerardi episcopi." Ed. Emericus Madzsar. *Scriptores Rerum Hungaricarum* vol. II, Budapest, 1938, Legenda minor, 461–479; Legenda maior: 480–506.

"Vita s. Güntheri eremitae." Ed. Georg H. Pertz. *Monumenta Germaniae Historica* Scriptores XI, Hannover, 1854, 276–279.

"Vita Stephani Maior." Ed. Emma Bartoniek. *Scriptores Rerum Hungaricarum* vol. II, Budapest, 1938, 377–392.

Bak, János M., Bónis, György, and James Ross Sweeney (eds.) *The Laws of the Medieval Kingdom of Hungary, I: 1000–1301*, with a critical essay on previous editions by Andor Csizmadia (The Laws of Hungary, Series I, vol. 1: 1000–1301) (Bakersfield, CA: Charles

Schlaks, Jr., Publ., 1989), second revised edition in collaboration with Leslie S. Domonkos (Idyllwild, CA: Charles Schlaks, Jr., Publ., 1999).

Theiner, Augustin (ed.) *Vetera monumenta historica Hungariam sacram illustrantia* I–II. Romae: Typ. Vaticanis, 1860.

Thurocz, Johannes de, *Chronica Hungarorum*. Eds. Erzsébet Galántai - Gyula Kristó - Elemér Mályusz, Budapest: Akadémiai Kiadó, 1985–88.

Secondary Sources

Baán, István. "The Metropolitanate of Tourkia. The Organization of the Byzantine Church in Hungary in the Middle Ages." In: Günter Prinzing- Maciej Salomon (eds.) *Byzanz und Ostmitteleuropa 950–1453. Beiträge zu einer table-ronde des XIX International Congress of Byzantine Studies, Copenhagen, 1996.* Wiesbaden: Harrassowitz, 1999, 45–53.

Balogh, Albin. "A veszprémvölgyi görög monostor alapítása. A legrégibb magyarországi oklevél." [The Foundation of the Veszprémvölgy Greek Monastery. The Oldest Hungarian Charter.] *Regnum* 6 (1944—1946): 21–30.

Buzás, Gergely and Eszes, Bernadett. "XI. századi görög monostor Visegrádon." [An Eleventh-Century Greek Monastery in Visegrád.] In: *Középkori egyházi építészet Erdélyben /Arhitectura religioasă medievală din Transilvania* IV. Szőcs, Péter Levente and Adrian Andrei Rusu (eds.) Satu Mare, 2007, 49–93.

Czobor, Béla. *Magyarország történelmi emlékei az ezredéves országos kiállításon.* [Hungary's Historical Monuments and Relics at the Millenial Exhibition.] Budapest, 1898–99.

Crostini, Barbara. "Moral Preaching and Animal Moralizations: the Physiologos in the Eleventh Century between Stoudios and Montecassino." *Νέα Ῥώμη / Nea Rhome. Rivista di studi bizantinistici* 7 (2010): 155–190.

Curta, Florin. "East-Central Europe: the Gate to Byzantium." *Byzantinische Zeitschrift* 108/2 (2015): 609–652.

Darkó, Jenő. "A veszprémi apácamonostor alapítólevelének 1109-i másolatáról." [On the Renewal of the Foundation Charter of the Veszprém Nunnery in 1109.] *Egyetemes Philológiai Közlöny* 41 (1917): 257–272, 336–351.

Érszegi, Géza. "Szent István görögnyelvű okleveléről." [On Saint Stephen's Greek Charter.] *Levéltári Szemle* 38 (1988): 239–249.

———. "Begine sive moniales grecales." In: *Corde aperto. Tanulmányok Kredics László nyolcvanadik születésnapjára.* [Corde aperto. Essays for László Kredics's Eightieth Birthday.] Veszprém, 2012: 31–45.

Fehértói, Katalin. *Árpád-kori személynévtár 1000–1301.* [Personal Names in the Árpádian Age, 1000–1301.] Budapest: Akadémiai Kiadó, 2004.

Font, Márta. *Könyves Kálmán és kora.* [Coloman the Learned and His Age]. Szekszárd: IPF 1999.

Fülöp, Attila–Koppány, Attila. "A crosier from the territory of the Veszprémvölgy convent, *Acta Archaeologica Academiae Scientiarum Hungariae* 55 (2004): 115–135.

———. "A veszprémvölgyi apácakolostor régészeti kutatása (1998–2002). [Archeological Excavations in the Veszprémvölgy Nunnery, 1998–2002.] *Műemlékvédelmi Szemle* 12/1 (2002): 5–40.

Gerics, József and Ladányi, Erzsébet. "A Hartvik legenda keletkezési körülményeiről." [Contextualizing the Hartvic Legend.] *Magyar Könyvszemle* 4 (2004), 317–324.

Gutheil, Jenő. *Az Árpád-kori Veszprém.* [Veszprém in the Árpádian Age.] Veszprém: Veszprém Megyei Levéltár, 1979.

Gutheil, Jenő, H. Gyürky, Katalin, Erdei, Ferenc and Koppány, Tibor. "A veszprémi Szent György egyház és konzerválása."*[The Saint George Church of Veszprém and its Renovation].* *Műemlékvédelem* 4/3 (1960): 136–143.

Györffy, György. *A szávaszentdemeteri görög monostor XII. századi birtokösszeírása* I–II. [The Twelfth-Century List of Land Possessions by the Greek Monastery of Szávaszentdemeter.] MTA II. Oszt. Közleményei 2 (1952) 325–362. és 3 (1953) 69–104.

———. "Das Güterverzeichnis des griechischen Klosters zu Szávaszentdemeter/ Sremska Mitrovica aus dem 12. Jahrhundert." *Studia Slavica* 5 (1959): 9–74.

———. *King Saint Stephen of Hungary.* Tr. Peter Doherty. New York: Columbia University Press, 1994.

H. Tóth, Imre. (ed.): *Az ortodoxia története Magyarországon a XVIII. századig.* [The History of Orthodoxy in Hungary up to the 18th century.] Szeged: JATE Szláv Filológiai Tanszék, 1995.

Holler, László. "Géza vagy István idejében alapították-e a veszprémvölgyi monostort?" [Was the Monastery of Veszprémvölgy founded under the reign of Géza or István?] *Magyar Nyelv* 107 (2011): 257–279.

———. "A veszprémi görög rítusú monostor alapító- és adománylevelének datálásáról és további kérdéseiről." [On the Date and Other Issues of the Foundation and Donation Charter of the Greek Rite Monastery in Veszprémvölgy]. *Magyar Nyelv* 109 (2013): 50–67.

———. "A veszprémi görög rítusú monostoralapító- és adománylevelének datálásáról és további kérdéseiről. Megjegyzések Szentgyörgyi Rudolf tanulmányához." [On the Foundation and Donation Charter of Veszprémvölgy and Further Questions. Observations about the Study of Rudolf Szentgyörgyi].

Hóman, Bálint. "A veszprémvölgyi 1109. évi oklevél hitelessége." [The Authenticity of the Charter of Veszprémvölgy from 1109.] *Turul* 29 (1911): 123–134 and 167–174.

———. "Szent István görög oklevele." [Saint Stephen's Greek Charter.] *Századok* 51 (1917): 99–136.

Ivánka, Endre. "Griechische Kirche und Griechisches Mönchtum in mittelalterlichen Ungarn." *Orientalia Christiana Periodica* 8 (1942): 183–194.

Jotischky, Andrew. "Monastic reform and the geography of Christendom: experience, observation and influence." *Transactions of the Royal Historical Society*, 6th Series 22 (2012), 57–74.

Kapitánffy, István. "Cerbanus és Maximus-fordítása." In: *Mons Sacer 996–1996. Pannonhalma 1000 éve I*. Pannonhalma: Bencés Kiadó, 1996, 357–368.

———. *Hungaro-byzantina. Bizánc és a görögség középkori magyarországi forrásokban.* [Hungaro-byzantina. Byzantium and the Greeks in medieval Hungarian sources.] Budapest: Typotex, 2003.

Karácsonyi, János. "Hogyan jöttek a görög szerzetesek Visegrádra?" [How did Greek Monks Come to Visegrád?] *Katholikus Szemle* 41 (1927). 16–21.

Keene, Catherine. *Saint Margaret, Queen of the Scots: A Life in Perspective*. New York: Palgrave Macmillan, 2013.

Kiss, Etele. "Byzantine Silversmiths' Work around AD 1000 between China and the Ottonians: The Beszterec Holy Water Vessel."*Jahrbuch der Österreichischen Byzantinistik* 49 (1999): 301–314.

Komáromi, László. "A bizánci kultúra egyes elemei és közvetítő tényezői a középkori Magyarországon." [Presence and Carriers of Byzantine Culture in Medieval Hungary.] *Iustum Aequum Salutare* III (2007): 215–228.

Komjáthy, Miklós. "A veszprémvölgyi alapítólevél kibocsátójáról." [Who Issued the Veszprémvölgy Charter?] *Levéltári Közlemények* 42 (1973): 33–49.

Kosztolnyik, Zoltan J. "The Relations of Four Eleventh-Century Hungarian Kings with Rome in the Light of Papal Letters." *Church History* 46 1977): 33–47.

Krajnyák, Gábor. "Szent István veszprémvölgyi donatiójának görög egyházi vonatkozásai." [The Byzantine Ecclesiastical Aspects of Saint Stephen's Donation Charter to Veszprémvölgy.] *Századok* 59–60 (1925–1926): 498–507.

Makk, Ferenc. *The Árpáds and the Comneni: political relations between Hungary and Byzantium in the 12th century*. Budapest: Akadémiai Kiadó, 1989.

László, Gyula. "A magyar pénzverés kezdeteiről." [On the Beginnings of Minting in Hungary.] *Századok* 97 (1963): 382–307.

Marosi, Ernő. "The Székesfehérvár Chasuble of King Stephen and Queen Gisela." In: *The Coronation Mantle of the Hungarian Kings*. English tr. Judit Pokoly. Ed. István Bardoly. Budapest: Hungarian National Museum, 2005: 110–113.

Melich, János. *A honfoglaláskori Magyarország*. [Hungary in the Age of the Magyar Conquest.] Budapest: Akadémiai, 1925.

Miladinov, Marina. *Margins of Solitude. Eremitism in Central Europe between East and West*. Zagreb: Leykam International, 2008.

Moravcsik, Gyula. *Szent László leánya és a bizánci Pantokrator-monostor. Die Tochter Ladislaus des Heiligen und das Pantokrator-Kloster in Konstantinopel*. Budapest-Konstantinápoly: A konstantinápolyi Magyar Tudományos Intézet Közleményei—Mitteilungen des Ungarischen Wissenschaftlichen Institutes in Konstantinopel 7–8, 1923.

———. "Görögnyelvű monostorok Szent István korában." [Greek-Language Monasteries in the Age of Saint Stephen.] In: *Emlékkönyv Szent István halálának kilencszázadik évfordulóján. [Commemoration of the 900th Anniversary of the Death of King Saint Stephen.]* Jusztinián Serédi (ed.) Budapest: Magyar Tudományos Akadémia, 1938.vol. I, pp. 389–422.

———. "The Role of the Byzantine Church in Medieval Hungary." *American Slavic and East European Review* 6 (1947): 134–151.

Nemerkényi, Előd. "The Religious Ruler in the *Admonitions* of King Saint Stephen of Hungary." In: *Monotheistic Kingship: The Medieval Variants.* Al Azmeh, Aziz—János M. Bak (eds.) Budapest: CEU Press, 231–247.

Pop, Ioan Aurel, Nicolae, Jan, and Panaite, Ovidiu (eds.) *Sfântul Ierotei, episcop de Alba Iulia (sec. X)..* Alba Iulia: Edit. Reîntregirea, 2010.

Prinzing, G, Salamon, M., and Stephenson, P. (eds). *Byzantium and East Central Europe.* Cracow: Historia Iagellonica, 2001.

Révész, Éva. "A keleti kereszténység: szerep, hatás, vagy jelenlét?" [Eastern Christianity in Hungary: role, impact or presence?] *Belvedere meridionale* 21 (2009): 52–64.

Rodriguez Suarez, Alex. "From Greek into Latin: Western scholars and translators in Constantinople during the reign of John II." In: Alessandra Bucossi and Alex Rodriguez Suarez (eds.), *John II Komnenos, Emperor of Byzantium. In the Shadow of Father and Son.* London: Publications of the Centre for Hellenic Studies, King's College, 2016), 91–109.

Sághy, Marianne. "La christianisation de la Hongrie." In: *Gerbert l'Européen. Actes du colloque d'Aurillac.* (eds) N. Charbonnel–J.-E. Iung. Aurillac: Société des lettres, sciences et arts La Haute-Auvergne, 1997: 255–262.

———. "Aspects de la christianisation des Hongrois aux IXe–Xe siècles." *Early Christianity in Central and East Europe.* Przemyslav Urbanczyk (ed.) Warszawa: Semper, 1997: 53–65.

Sansterre, Jean-Marie. "Saint Nil de Rossano et le monachisme latin." In: A. Acconcia Longo, S. Luca, L. Perria (eds.) *Miscellanea di studi in onore di P. Marco Petto. Bollettino della badia greca di Grottaferrata,* n.s., 45, 1991, II, 339–386.

Sansterre, Jean-Marie. "Le monachisme bénédictin d'Italie et les bénédictins italiens en France face au renouveau de l'érémitisme à la fin du Xe et au XIe siècle." In: A. Vauchez (ed.), *Ermites de France et d'Italie (XIe-XIVe siècle).* Rome: École française de Rome, 2003, 29–46.

Shepard, Jonathan. *The Expansion of Orthodox Europe: Byzantium, the Balkans and Russia.* Aldershot: Ashgate Variorum, 2007.

——— "Spreading the word: Byzantine missions." In Cyril Mango (ed.) *The Oxford History of Byzantium.* Oxford: Oxford University Press, 2002, 230–247.

Stark, Karen. "Cave of Hermits, Cave of Cult: Saints Andrew-Zoerard and Benedict and the Sacralization of the Medieval Hungarian Landscape." In: Meg Boulton–Jane Hawkes–Heidi Stoner (eds.) *Place and Space in the Medieval World*. London: Routledge, 2017.

Steckel, Sita, Gaul, Niels, Grünbart, Michael. (eds.) *Networks of Learning: Perspectives on Scholars in Byzantine East and Latin West, c. 1000–1200*. Berlin-Münster: Lit Verlag, 2014.

Stojkovski, Boris. "The Greek charter of the Hungarian King Stephen I." Зборник радова Византолошког института /Zbornik radova Vizantološkog instituta LIII, 2016: 127–140 http://www.doiserbia.nb.rs/img/doi/0584-9888/2016/0584-98881653127S.pdf last accessed 10 January 2018.

Szentgyörgyi, Rudolf. "A tihanyi alapítólevél görög helynevei." [Greek Place Names in the Tihany Foundation Charter.]*Magyar Nyelv* 106 (2010): 295–307, 385–396.

———. *A tihanyi apátság alapítólevele*. [The Foundation Charter of the Abbey of Tihany.] Budapest: ELTE Eötvös Kiadó, 2014.

———. "The *auctor monasterii* of the Byzantine Monastery of Veszprém Valley 1." In: Egedi-Kovács, Emese (ed.) *Byzance et l'Occident II: Tradition, transmission, traduction*. Budapest: ELTE Eötvös József Collegium, 2015, 181–190.

———. "The *auctor monasterii* of the Byzantine Monastery of Veszprém Valley 2." In: Egedi-Kovács, Emese (ed.) *Byzance et l'Occident II: Tradition, transmission, traduction*. Budapest: ELTE Eötvös József Collegium, 2015, 191–202.

Szűcs, Jenő. "Szent István *Intelmei*: az első magyarországi államelméleti mű." [Saint Stephen's *Exhortations*: the First Treatise on the Theory of State in Hungary.] In: Glatz, Ferenc—Kardos, József (eds.) *Szent István és kora*. [Saint Stephen and His Age.] Budapest: MTA Történettudományi Intézet, 1988, 32–53.

Szűcs, Jenő. "King Stephen's Exhortations and his State." *The New Hungarian Quarterly* 112 (1988): 89–97.

Takács, Miklós. "A magyarországi 11. századi ortodox monostortemplomok térszerkezete." [Raumstruktur der orthodoxen Klosterkirchen im Ungarn des 11. Jh.] In: *A Kárpát-medence, a magyarság és Bizánc*. (ed.) Terézia Olajos. Szeged: Acta Universitatis Szegediensis, 2014, 295–323.

Thoroczkay, Gábor. "Anmerkungen zur Frage der Entstehungszeit der Hartvik-Legende des Stephan des Heiligen." *Specimina Nova. Pars Prima. Sectio Mediaevalis* (2001), 107–131.

Tóth, Péter. "Egy bizánci szent Magyarországon, egy magyar szent Bizáncban." [A Byzantine Saint in Hungary, a Hungarian Saint in Byzantium.]*Magyar Könyvszemle* 117/1 (2001) http://epa.oszk.hu/00000/00021/00028/0004-213.html (last accessed 1 December, 2017.)

Tóth, Péter (ed.). *Szent Demeter Magyarország elfeledett védőszentje*. [Saint Demetrius, Hungary's Forgotten Patron Saint.] Budapest: Balassi, 2007.

Uzsoki, András. "Gizella királyné sírja Veszprémben van?" [Is Queen Gisela's Tomb to be found in Veszprém?] *Horizont. Veszprém megyei Közművelődési Tájékoztató*, X. (1982) 1. sz. 21.

———. "Szent László hitvese, Adelhaid királyné, Rudolf német ellenkirály leánya"[Queen Adelaide, wife of Saint Ladislas, daughter of Rudolph of Swabia] In: *Szent László és Somogyvár: Tanulmányok a 900 éves somogyvári bencés apátság emlékezetére*. Kálmán Magyar (ed.), Kaposvár: Somogy Megyei Múzeumok Igazgatósága 1992, 145–152.

White, Monica. *Military Saints in Byzantium and Rus, 900–1200* (Cambridge: Cambridge University Press, 2013.

Zsoldos, Attila. *Az Árpádok és asszonyaik. A királynéi intézmény az Árpádok korában.* [*The Kings of the Árpád-Dynasty and their Queens. The Reginal Institution in the Age of the Árpáds.*] Budapest: MTA Történettudományi Intézet, 2005.

WHAT DID PIROSKA SEE AT HOME?
ART AND ARCHITECTURE IN HUNGARY AROUND 1100

Béla Zsolt Szakács

Princess Piroska, daughter of King Saint Ladislaus of Hungary (1077–1095) and Adelhaid of Rheinfeld, was born in the 1080s and until around 1105, when she married the Byzantine crown prince John Komnenos, she lived in Hungary. After her father's untimely death, Piroska became the ward of her cousin, King Coloman the Learned (1095–1116),[1] eldest son of King Ladislaus's brother, King Géza I (1074–1077).[2] Educated to become a priest, Coloman was a consecrated bishop when he was crowned king of Hungary in 1095 due to the unexpected turns in Árpádian dynastic politics. Coloman's vast Christian culture and European perspective contributed significantly to the rise of the arts in Hungary at the turn of the twelfth century. What did Piroska see around her in Hungary? Unfortunately, we cannot tell. By way of a hypothesis, this paper offers a panorama of new artistic trends and novel constructions in the Kingdom of Hungary around 1100.

Cathedrals and Monasteries

A bishop turned king, Coloman completed ecclesiastical organization of Hungary established by his great ancestor, King Stephen (997–1038)[3] with the foundation of

---

[1] Chronica Hungarorum, ed. Emericus Szentpétery, *Scriptores Rerum Hungaricarum tempore ducum regumque stirpis Arpadianae gestarum*. Vol. I, (Budapest: Akadémiai, 1937), 432: "Qui ab Hungaris Cunues Calman apellatur." *Cunues*, in modern Hungarian *könyves*, means "bookish", "book-lover", "learned."
[2] Márta Font, *Koloman the Learned* (Szeged: Szegedi Középkorász Műhely, 2001), 81–82.
[3] Nora Berend, József Laszlovszky and Béla Zsolt Szakács, "The kingdom of Hungary," in *Christianization and the Rise of Christian Monarchy*, ed. Nora Berend (Cambridge: Cambridge University Press, 2007), 319–368.

a new bishopric at Nyitra (Nitra, Slovakia),[4] already home of an important ecclesiastical institution erected above the tomb of two local holy hermits, Andrew Zoerard and Benedict of Szkalka canonized in 1083.[5] The first church of Nyitra was recently excavated by Peter Bednár.[6] It was a single space longitudinal building with an east end that remains unknown; the building was probably reconstructed in the thirteenth century. King Coloman transformed the church of Nyitra into the cathedral of the new bishopric. As Bednar's excavations had limited funds, the architectural consequences of the early twelfth century modifications are unknown; however, a base of a column, found in a secondary position, is closely related to the carvings of the collegiate church of Dömös also from the early twelfth century.[7]

Nyitra was not the only cathedral rebuilt under the reign of King Coloman. The Cathedral of Pécs was destroyed by fire in 1064, an event registered by the *Hungarian Chronicle*.[8] If the cathedral's architecture before the fire remains debated in scholarship, art historians agree that the present structure goes back to around 1100, when the crypt was constructed.[9] The concept of the entire building must have been designed by then. It was an impressive

Figure 1. Pécs, cathedral, interior of the crypt (author)

---

[4] László Koszta, "Die Gründung des Bistums von Nitra," in *Slovakia and Croatia. Historical Parallels and Connections (until 1780)*, ed. Martin Homza, Ján Lukačka and Neven Budak (Bratislava: Department of Slovak History at the Faculty of Philosophy of Comenius University Bratislava – Zagreb: Faculty of Humanities and Social Sciences, University of Zagreb, 2013), 401–407.

[5] Béla Zsolt Szakács, "Three Hungarian Shrines from 1083: Canonization, Reform, and Politics," in *Romanesque: Saints, Shrines and Pilgrimage*, ed. John McNeill (London: British Archaeological Association, in print).

[6] Peter Bednár and Zuzana Poláková, "St. Emmeram's Cathedral," in *The Cradle of Christianity in Slovakia. Nitra Castle and the Cathedral of St. Emmeram*, ed. Viliam Judák, Peter Bednár and Jozef Medvecký (Bratislava: Arte Libris, 2011), 184–205.

[7] Bednár and Poláková, "St Emmeram's Cathedral", 185. For Dömös, see below, notes 22–24.

[8] Szentpétery, *Scriptores*, 362–363.

[9] Gergely Buzás, "A pécsi székesegyházak a román korban" [The cathedrals of Pécs in the Romanesque period], *Archaeologia – Altum Castrum Online*, 2013, http://archeologia.hu/content/archeologia/164/pecs.pdf (last accessed 07/01/2016); Krisztina Havasi, A pécsi középkori székesegyház és a Dómkőtár gyűjteményének rövid története" [Short history of the medieval cathedral of Pécs and the collection of the Cathedral Lapidary], in *A pécsi püspökség évezredes öröksége*, ed. Zsolt Virág (Pécs: Várkastély, 2015), 175–183.

three-aisled Romanesque basilica with wide arcades. The eastern half of the church rose as an elevated chancel above a huge hall crypt. The aisles terminated in semi-circular apses. This type of a large-scale, yet carefully articulated church became widespread around the Mediterranean and in the region of the Alps, in certain cases connected with the ongoing ecclesiastical reforms in the Roman Catholic Church.[10]

The Cathedral of Pécs might not have been the first representative of the new church type in Hungary. According to the *Hungarian Chronicle*, the Cathedral of Vác was constructed by King Géza I and he was buried there.[11] Ongoing excavations of the destroyed building support previous hypotheses on the first cathedral, namely that it was a three-aisled basilica with three semi-circular apses.[12] The preliminary reconstruction of the Cathedral of Vác is partially based on the ground plan of the Benedictine monastery founded by King Géza I at Garamszentbenedek (Hronský Beňadik, Slovakia) before 1075. While the abbey church had a two-tower façade, the Cathedral of Vác was built with a western apse on top of a hall crypt.[13] The tomb of King Géza is supposedly in the middle of the nave of the cathedral.[14] Géza was King Coloman's father: the Cathedral of Vác must have been an important site of family commemoration for the new king. I suggest that the model of the vast cathedral (re)construction project launched in Hungary by King Coloman around 1100 was the Cathedral of Vác.

The reconstruction of the Cathedral of Eger is a case in point. Founded by King Saint Stephen, the early eleventh-century building remains unknown due to its utter destruction in the Ottoman wars of the sixteenth-seventeenth centuries. Its

---

[10] Béla Zsolt Szakács, "Állandó alaprajzok – változó vélemények? Megjegyzések a 'bencés templomtípus' magyarországi pályafutásához" [Constant ground plans – changing ideas? Notes on the Hungarian carrier of the 'Benedictine type' of Romanesque churches], in *Maradandóság és változás*, ed. Szilvia Bodnár et al. (Budapest: MTA Művészettörténeti Kutatóintézet - Képző- és Iparművészeti Lektorátus, 2004), 25–37.

[11] Szentpétery, *Scriptores*, 403.

[12] Ernő Marosi, "Román kor" [Romanesque period] in *A művészet története Magyarországon*, ed. Nóra Aradi (Budapest: Corvina, 1983), 21.; Endre Tóth and Gergely Buzás, *Magyar építészet*, vol. I (Budapest: Kossuth, 2016), 75.; Zoltán Batizi, "Feltárul az ezeréves székesegyház" [The thousand-year cathedral revealed] *Archeologia – Altum Castrum Online*, http://archeologia.hu/feltarul-az-ezereves-szekesegyhaz (last accessed 07/01/2016).

[13] Imre Takács, "Pannonhalma" in *Paradisum plantavit. Bencés monostorok a középkori Magyarországon. Benedictine Monasteries in Medieval Hungary*, ed. Imre Takács, (Pannonhalma: Pannonhalmi Bencés Főapátság, 2001), 317., 671.; Béla Zsolt Szakács, "Dombó és a korai altemplomok Magyarországon" [Dombó and the early crypts in Hungary], in: *Építészet a középkori Dél-Magyarországon*, ed. Tibor Kollár (Budapest: Teleki László Alapítvány, 2010), 682–684.

[14] See in short: *Közkincs-kereső*, 08/19/2015, http://archeologia.hu/vac-rabukkantak-a-kiraly-sirjara-szolnok-felmertek-a-torok-kori-hidat (last accessed 07/01/2016).

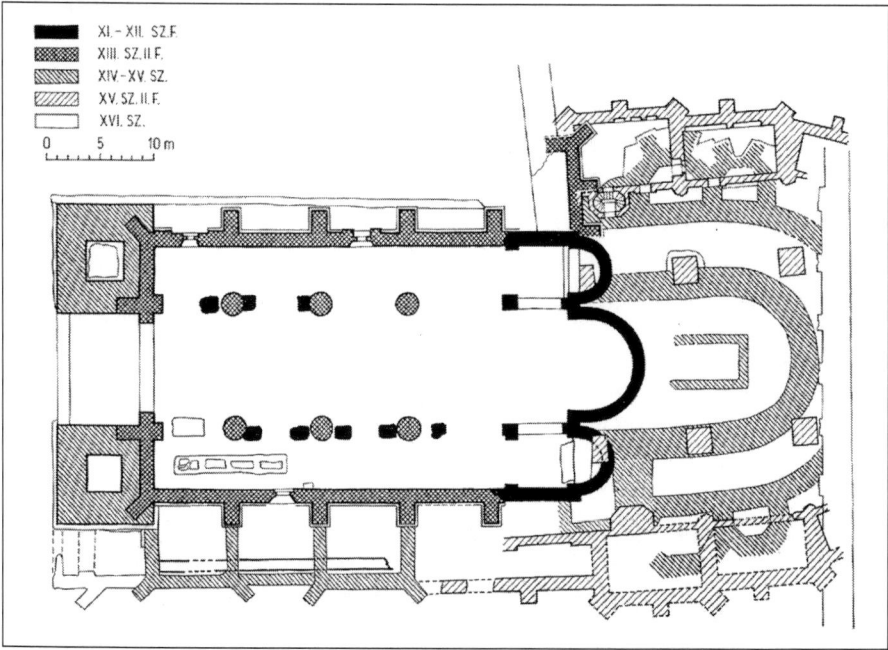

Figure 2. Eger, reconstructed ground plan by Károly Kozák

remains were destroyed subsequently. Started in the nineteenth century, archaeological research has not yet been completed and its results remained largely unpublished. However, there is a consensus in the scholarly literature that the three-apsidal ending of the church dates from the early twelfth century.[15] As to its ground plan, the Cathedral of Győr also belongs to this group. This much transformed building underwent heavy restoration in the early twentieth century when the semi-circular main apse was reconstructed. The side apses are also much restored, however, the north apse still preserves its special disposition. It seems that there was a two-storeyed chapel built at the east end of the northern aisle in the Romanesque peri-

---

[15] Katalin B. Nagy and Melinda Tóth, "Kutaspuszta Árpád-kori templomának díszítése" [Decoration of the Árpád-age church of Kutaspuszta], in *A középkori Dél-Alföld és Szer*, ed. Tibor Kollár (Szeged: Csongrád Megyei Levéltár, 2000), 245 and note 32; Krisztina Havasi, "Egy festett díszű román kori kapuzat és a középkori egri székesegyház kifestésének töredékei" [A painted Romanesque portal and the painted gragments of the medieval cathedral of Eger], *Ars Hungarica* 41 (2015): 223; Gergely Buzás, "Ásatás az egri középkori székesegyházban" [Excavation in the medieval cathedral of Eger], *Archeologia – Altum Castrum Online*, 2016, http://archeologia.hu/asatas-az-egri-kozepkori-szekesegyhazban (last accessed 07/01/2016).

od.¹⁶ Thus, the ground plan of the cathedrals of Pécs, Vác, Eger and Győr are similar, while the upper structures might have been significantly different.

The three-apsidal type was certainly not the only one in use for cathedral rebuilding around 1100. The first phase of the cathedral of Gyulafehérvár (Alba Iulia, Romania) is known from excavations. It had a semi-circular main apse and to aisles with flat east end. The dating of this first phase goes back to a late medieval source which states that it was built by King Ladislaus.¹⁷ Construction might have started back then, but the stone-carvings, including a reused figural tympanum of the south portal, point to a dating after 1100.¹⁸ It is quite possible that the building was begun under King Ladislaus, but its major parts were finished under King Coloman.

The spatial disposition of the medieval cathedral of the Archbishopric of Esztergom is known from a baroque ground plan from around 1763.¹⁹ The cathedral, in decay after the Ottoman wars, was demolished in the early nineteenth century to make space for an imposing Neo-Classical cathedral built on the site. In the Middle Ages, the main apse was rebuilt in Gothic style, but the Romanesque crypt was probably preserved.²⁰ Remarkably, the east end of the aisles terminated in a niche in the interior but had flat façade in the exterior. The apses of the aisles were considerably narrower than the aisles themselves and were positioned asymmetrically. Scholars suggested that the east end preceded the rest of the nave and the aisles which were modernized during the mid-twelfth century.²¹

---

16   Károly Kozák and András Uzsoki, "A győri székesegyház feltárása" [The excavation of the cathedral of Győr], *Arrabona* 12 (1970): 111–159; B. Nagy and Tóth, "Kutaspuszta", note 33.
17   Géza Entz, "A Szent István alapítású erdélyi püspökség első székesegyháza" [The first cathedral of the Bishopric of Transylvania founded by Saint Stephen], in *Doctor et apostol. Szent István-tanulmányok*, ed. József Török (Budapest: Márton Áron, 1994), 101–105; cf. Ernő Marosi,"Magyarországi művészet Szent László korában" [Art in Hungary in the time of Saint Ladislaus], in *Athleta Patriae. Szent László-tanulmányok*, ed. László Mezey (Budapest: Szent István Társulat, 1980), 213.
18   For the tympanum, see Sándor Tóth, "Az aracsi kő rokonsága" [The artistic connections of the stone-caving of Aracs], in *A középkori Dél-Alföld és Szer*, 444. For the stone-carvings, see Krisztina Havasi, "Árpád-kori ornamentális téglák Szakoly lebontott középkori templomából" [Árpád-age decorated bricks from the destroyed medieval church of Szakoly], in: *Középkori egyházi építészet Szatmárban*, ed. Tibor Kollár, (Nyíregyháza: Szabolcs-Szatmár-Bereg Megyei Önkormányzat, 2011), 103.
19   Ernő Marosi, *Die Anfänge der Gotik in Ungarn. Esztergom in der Kunst des 12.–13. Jahrhunderts* (Budapest: Akadémiai, 1984).
20   Gergely Buzás, "Az esztergomi vár románkori és gótikus épületei" [The Romanesque and Gothic buildings of the castle of Esztergom], in *Az Esztergomi Vármúzeum kőtárának katalógusa*, ed. Gergely Buzás and Gergely Tolnai (Esztergom: Vármúzeum, 2004), 11–12.
21   Sándor Tóth, "Esztergom Szent Adalbert-székesegyháza és az Árpád-kori építészet" Saint Adalbert's Cathedral of Esztergom and the Architecture of the Árpádian Age, in *Ezer év Szent Adalbert oltalma alatt,* ed. András Hegedűs and István Bárdos (Esztergom: Prímási Levéltár, 2000), 121–154.

The Esztergom stone carvings datable to around 1100 are related to those found in the collegiate church of Dömös.[22] This is another version of the three-apsidal type. It differs from Pécs and the other twelfth-century cathedrals in the arrangement of the main apse. The three apses do not form a line, but the main apse is connected to the nave by an extra bay elevated over a hall crypt. The crypt has been reconstructed

Figure 3. Dömös, the reconstructed crypt (author)

a few decades ago, however, the general arrangement of this three-aisled church is less known due to the poor preservation of the architectural fragments.

The collegiate church of Dömös is significant because it is relatively well dated with the help of written sources. The ecclesiastical institution was founded by Prince Álmos, the younger brother of King Coloman, after his return from the Holy Land around 1107. The church was consecrated soon after.[23] Despite the rivalry between the two brothers, the architectural elements of Dömös point towards Esztergom, the royal seat of Coloman.[24]

The explosion of cathedral construction under King Coloman's reign is not paralleled by a similar boom in monastic building. The only royal abbey built during this period was the Benedictine monastery at Somogyvár,[25] founded by King Ladislaus around 1091, who invited monks from Saint-Gilles-du-Gard in France to his abbey that became a center of French monastic culture in Hungary for a century. Its architecture,

Figure 4. Somogyvár, view of the ruins from the north-east (author)

---

[22] László Gerevich, "The royal court (curia), the provost's residence and the village at Dömös," *Acta Archaeologica* 35 (1983): 385–409.
[23] Szentpétery, *Scriptores*, 427–428.
[24] Sándor Tóth, *Román kori kőfaragványok a Magyar Nemzeti Galéria Régi Magyar Gyűjteményében* [Romanesque stone-carvings in the Old Hungarian Collection of the Hungarian National Gallery], (Budapest: Magyar Nemzeti Galéria, 2010), 50–56.
[25] Szilárd Papp, "Somogyvár", in *Paradisum plantavit*, 350–353 and 681–683; Kornél Bakay, *Somogyvár. Szent Egyed-monostor* [Somogyvár, Monastery of Saint Giles], (Budapest: Műemlékek Nemzeti Gondnoksága, 2011).

Figure 5. Kosztolány, fresco in the nave, Visitation scene with servant (author)

Figure 6. Pécsvárad, fresco in the apse, Angel (© author)

Figure 7. Holy Crown of Hungary, Greek crown, frontal view, Christ Pantokrator (© Károly Szelényi)

Figure 8. Holy Crown of Hungary, Latin crown, top, Christ Pantokrator
(© Károly Szelényi)

however, followed Hungarian traditions as represented primarily by the monastery of Garamszentbenedek. The abbey church of Somogyvár was equally a three-aisled basilica with three semi-circular apses at the east and flanking towers at the west. The major difference is in the size: as against the 36 m of Garamszentbenedek, the monastery church of Somogyvár was almost 60 m long. The building of Somogyvár, due to the extensive length of the structure and a destructive fire, was finished only in the time of Coloman, attested by coins found during excavations. Following the fire, the new construction phase of the building employed more matured forms of Romanesque architecture, for example pilasters instead of lesenes.[26]

Other monasteries of the same period, such as Sárvármonostor[27] or Ellésmonostor[28] in Eastern Hungary show similar architectural features on a smaller scale. These private foundations followed the architectural models of the royal work-

Figure 9. Dombó, stone fragment from the Benedictine Abbey with palmette decoration, Muzej Vojvodine, Novi Sad (author)

shops. Another important Benedictine monastery built with the same ground plan is Dombó (Rakovac, Serbia).[29] The patron of the abbey is not known, it might have been no other than the archbishop of Kalocsa.[30] While King Coloman generously

---

[26] Melinda Tóth, "A somogyvári bencés apátság és temploma az Árpád-korban" [The Benedictine abbey of Somogyvár and its church in the Árpád-age], in *Szent László és Somogyvár*, ed. Károly Magyar (Kaposvár: Somogy Megyei Múzeumok Igazgatósága, 1992), 221–250.
[27] Sándor Tóth, Sárvármonostor, in *Paradisum plantavit*, 368–370., 690–692.
[28] Lajos Bozóki, "Ellésmonostor faragott kőtöredékeinek stíluskapcsolatai" [Stylistic connections of the stone-carvings of Ellésmonostor], in *A középkori Dél-Alföld és Szer*, 233–240.
[29] Sándor Nagy, *Dombó, középkori monostor és erőd* [Dombó, medieval monastery and fortress], (Újvidék: Forum, 1987); Sándor Tóth, "Dombó," in *Paradisum plantavit*, 359–367 and 686–690.
[30] Levente F. Hervay, "A bencések és apátságaik története a középkori Magyarországon" [The history of the Benedictines and their monasteries in medieval Hungary], in *Paradisum plantavit*, 487.

supported the rebuilding of cathedrals, he shunned monasteries. Coloman is the first king of Hungary to whom no royal monastic foundation can be connected. His royal ancestors were buried in abbeys or cathedrals that they founded, but Coloman, for the first time in his dynasty, chose the vicinity of the holy kings of Hungary, Stephen and Emeric in the royal collegiate church of Székesfehérvár (Alba Regia) as his final resting place.[31] This must have meant a large-scale rebuilding of the collegiate church: the compound piers of this building, even in ruins, still manifest its royal magnificence.[32]

From Palmette Leaves to Romanesque Figural Sculpture

Architectural decoration in Hungary in the second half of the eleventh century is dominated by palmette leave-friezes and spiny acanthus (*acanthus spinosa*) capitals.[33] These motifs speak the architectural language of the Byzantine world and regularly occur from the Caucasus to the Balkan Peninsula. The types popular in Hungary, however, are best paralleled in Italy. The *acanthus spinosa*, a particularly spiny version of the Classical Corinthian capital, originates in Venice and Aquileia, and is widespread along the Adriatic coast from Apulia to Istria and Dalmatia.[34] The palmette friezes were widely used in regions influenced by Byzantium, but the version that consists of two lines of leaves connected by ribbons appears almost exclusively in Hungary. The only comparable example is in the Cathedral of Lund, usually related to North Italian workshops.[35] Thus, the "Byzantine" trends came from Italy to the architectural decoration in Hungary.

---

[31] Pál Engel, "Temetkezések a középkori székesfehérvári bazilikában" [Burials in the medieval basilica of Székesfehérvár], *Századok* 121 (1987): 613–637.

[32] Ernő Marosi, "*A romanika Magyarországon* [Romanesque art in Hungary], (Budapest: Corvina, 2013), 68; Klára Mentényi," Szőlőleveles kőfaragványok. A királyi prépostsági templom új építkezései a 12. század elején"[Stone-carvings with vine-leaves. The rebuilding of the royal collegiate church in the early 12th century], in *Könyves Kálmán és Székesfehérvár*, ed. András Smohay (Székesfehérvár: Székesfehérvári Egyházmegyei Múzeum, in print).

[33] Sándor Tóth, "A 11. századi magyarországi kőornamentika időrendjéhez" [To the chronology of the eleventh-century Hungarian ornamental stone-carvings], in *Pannonia Regia. Művészet a Dunántúlon 1000–1541*, ed. Árpád Mikó and Imre Takács (Budapest: Magyar Nemzeti Galéria, 1994), 54–62; Miklós Takács, "Die sogenannten Palmettenornamentik der christlichen Bauten des 11. Jahrhunderts im mittelalterlichen Ungarn" in *Byzanz – Das Römerreich im Mittelalter*, Teil 3, ed. Falko Daim and Jörg Drauschke (Mainz: Römisch-Germanisches Zenralmuseum, 2010), 411–415.

[34] Miklós Takács, "Ornamentale Beziehungen zwischen der Steinmetzkunst von Ungarn und Dalmatien im XI. Jahrhundert," *Hortus Artium Mediaevalium* 3 (1997): 165–178.

[35] Tóth, *Román kori kőfaragványok*, 11–38.

This style was still popular in Hungary at the end of the eleventh century. A classic representative of the *acanthus spinosa* capital is known from Esztergom. The first workshops applying this style are active in the center of the kingdom (Veszprém, Tihany, Visegrád, Pilis, Szekszárd) in the 1040s-60s. By the end of the eleventh century, a number of buildings attest that this style spread all over the country. Scholars agree that this style appears in Southern Hungary around 1100.[36] Examples include the Benedictine monasteries of Dombó and Bodrogmonostor as well as the collegiate church of Titel, founded by Prince Lampert, younger brother of King Géza and Ladislaus. This trend is not limited to the South but can be detected in the North (Feldebrő)[37] and the East (Sárvármonostor) as well,[38] in monasteries founded by local aristocratic families at the end of the eleventh century.

These sites, however, show not only the dissemination of the architectural traditions and innovations of the "center of the kingdom" (*medium regni*) but also reflect new trends. Dombó and other churches of the South were decorated not only with palmette and acanthus leaves, but figural compositions as well.[39] The signs of a new figural sculpture also appear in monasteries in the Eastern and Northern regions of the kingdom. Moreover, it seems that the coexistence of "Byzantinizing" palmettes and new, figural sculpture are not limited to areas close to the frontiers. A curious capital decorated with spiny leaves in Eger might signal that traditions of the eleventh century lived together with the more innovative forms of Romanesque architecture in major centres of the kingdom.[40]

However, the decoration of the majority of the new buildings constructed around 1100 show dominantly new Romanesque sculpture. Christ enthroned among angels on the inner tympanum of the Cathedral of Gyulafehérvár, is the first

---

[36] Tóth, "Az aracsi kő rokonsága," 435–443.
[37] Edit Szentesi, Ferenc Dávid and Béla Zsolt Szakács, "Feldebrői temlom" [The church of Feldebrő], in *Magyar Művelődéstörténeti Lexikon*, vol. III, ed. Péter Kőszeghy (Budapest: Balassi, 2005), 47–51; Marosi, *A romanika Magyarországon*, 56–61.
[38] Krisztina Havasi, "Sárvármonostor XI. századi kőfaragványainak katalógusa elé" [To the catalogue of the eleventh-century stonecarvings of Sárvármonostor], in: *Középkori egyházi építészet Szatmárban*, 26–59.
[39] See note 29 and Nebojša Stanojev, "A dombói (Rakovac) Szent György-monostor szentélyrekesztői" [The choir-screens of the Saint George's monastery of Dombó (Rakovac)], in *A középkori Dél-Alföld és Szer*, 383–428; idem, "A dombói Szent György-monostortemplom román kori árkádjai" [Romanesque arcades of the Saint George's monastery church of Dombó], in *Építészet a középkori Dél-Magyarországon*, 635–669.
[40] Krisztina Havasi, *A középkori egri székesegyház az 1200-as évek elején* [The medieval cathedral of Eger in the early 1200s], PhD dissertation, Budapest: Eötvös Loránd University, 2011, 75–113, http://doktori.btk.elte.hu/art/havasikrisztina/diss.pdf (last accessed 07/01/2016)

Figure 10. Gyulafehérvár, tympanum of the first cathedral (author)

representative of a novel type of portal decoration in Hungary.[41] Various monsters enliven the corners of the new capitals made for the rebuilding of the collegiate church of Székesfehérvár.[42] Eagles decorate a capital of Esztergom, while another capital is a more classical representative of the Corinthian composition.[43] This mature style is also known near Esztergom, from Dömös,[44] in the reconstructed crypt of the collegiate church where different geometric and ornamental versions of the Early Romanesque decoration abound. Another, much larger capital representing a hunting scene and lions attacking human heads belonged to the nave of the church. This capital is a more mature representative of Romanesque figural sculpture best known from Lombardy. Unfortunately, it is not clear whether it was carved at the time of the foundation of the provostry or somewhat later.[45] Yet another capital, probably originating from Dömös, now in the lapidary of Esztergom, represents sheep on its corner.[46] A similar motif is known from the abbey church of Somogyvár, finished under the reign of King Coloman.[47] These fragments attest that the Romanesque turn in Hungarian architecture was equally characteristic for the arrangement of spaces as well as for sculptural decoration.

---

[41] Tóth, "Az aracsi kő rokonsága," 444.
[42] Tóth, *Román kori kőfaragványok*, 67–72.
[43] Buzás, "Az esztergomi," 12 and 34–35.
[44] Tóth, *Román kori kőfaragványok*, 56–67, 129–130.
[45] *Ibidem*, 131–132 and Tóth, "A 11. századi," 60–61 and note 24.
[46] Hypothesis of Krisztina Havasi, see *Az Esztergomi Vármúzeum kőtárának katalógusa*, 109, no. 2, and 24, note 55.
[47] Tóth, "A somogyvári bencés apátság," 248, Tóth, *Román kori kőfaragványok*, 65 and note 193.

Church Reform and Painted Decoration

The dissemination of mature Romanesque forms is often connected to the reform movement in the Latin Church that started in the second half of the eleventh century.[48] It affected not only the reorganization of the liturgical space or the renewal of the sculpture, but also the fresco decoration of the churches. Unfortunately, very little remains of Romanesque wall paintings in historic Hungary. An early, relatively well-preserved cycle survives in the small village church of Kosztolány (Kostoľany pod Tribečom, Slovakia). The church of Saint George in Kosztolány is variously dated by scholars between the ninth and eleventh century,[49] its frescoes are usually dated to the eleventh century.[50] On iconographical grounds, I argue for the later part of the eleventh century.[51] The best preserved part of the fresco cycle depicts the Infancy of Jesus, including the Annunciation, the Visitation, the Nativity, the Travel and the Adoration of the Magi, and the Flight to Egypt. Most scenes are painted in a strikingly archaic style: the presence of one or two *ancillae* in the Annunciation and the Visitation, the bathing of the infant in the Nativity and the Magi wearing Phrygian hats reflect earlier traditions. The Wandering of the Magi on feet, pointing to the star leading them to Bethlehem, is a rare motif in the Romanesque period. Herbert Kessler convincingly argued that this Infancy cycle was created in Rome during the Gregorian reform in imitation of the decoration of large Early Christian basilicas.[52] The cycle spread from Rome. Even if the frescoes of Kosztolány cannot be directly derived from Rome, we must keep in mind that the church stood in the neighborhood of two outstanding ecclesiastical centres, the

---

[48] Barbara Franzé, ed., *Art et réforme grégorienne en France et dans la péninsule Ibérique* (Paris: Picard, 2015)

[49] Alojz Habovštiak, *Kirche mit Fresken in Kostoľany pod Tribečom* (Nitra: Vydavateľstvo Slovenskej akadémie vied, 1966); Peter Barta, Martin Bóna and Marián Keleši, "Chronometrický výskum murív Kostola sv. Juraja v Kostoľanoch pod Tribečom" [Chronometric Research of Masonry of St. George's Church in Kostoľany pod Tribečom], *Archaeologia historica* 40 (2015): 691–709.

[50] Melinda Tóth, "Falfestészet az Árpád-korban. Kutatási helyzetkép" [Wall-painting in the Árpád-age: the state of research], *Ars Hungarica,* 23 (1995): 140–141; Jana Maříková-Kubková et al., "The Church of St George in Kostoľany pod Tribečom" in *Swords, Crowns, Censers and Books. Francia Media – Cradles of European Culture,* ed. Marina Vicelja-Matijašić (Rijeka: Center for Iconographic Studies, 2015), 213–248; Krisztina Ilkó, "The artistic connections of the Romanesque wall paintings in Kostoľany pod Tribečom (Slovakia)" *Hortus Artium Mediaevalium* 22 (2016): 282–293.

[51] Béla Zsolt Szakács, "Archaism, imitation, provincialism? Notes on the murals of Kosztolány / Kostoľany pod Tribečom", *Convivium* 3/1 (2016): 154–171.

[52] Herbert L. Kessler, *Old St. Peter's and church decoration in medieval Italy* (Spoleto: Centro Italiano di Studi sull'Alto Medioevo, 2002).

royal abbey of Zobor and the Cathedral of Nyitra. The Romanesque frescoes of these churches did not survive and nothing is known of them. Possibly, the cycle in Kosztolány followed the decoration of some important centre with direct connections to leading artistic regions in Europe.[53] King Coloman was not only a learned cleric, a bishop, a promoter of reforms in the Church of Hungary, but also a close ally of the Papacy. Coloman married the daughter of Count Roger I of Sicily in 1097[54] with papal support. Contacts with Rome abounded in Coloman's royal court circle. Moreover, it was Coloman who founded the bishopric of Nyitra and issued two charters in favor of the royal monastery of Zobor,[55] both within a few kilometres from Kosztolány.

Another royal monastery that preserved traces of Romanesque fresco decoration is Pécsvárad in Southern Hungary. The abbey church was destroyed, but the ground floor of a two-storeyed chapel survived.[56] The fresco of the apse is partially restored.[57] So far, an angel came to light, probably flanking the (not yet uncovered) figure of Christ in the middle. The painting style is of high artistic quality. The angel wears the Byzantine imperial dress (*loros*), represented in its traditional form, to be changed under the Komneni. The older fashion is represented on the portrait of King Roger II of Sicily dated to 1143 in the Martorana Church in Palermo. The imperial outfit is frequently used as the dress of archangels in Byzantine art (Nicaea, the Staurothek of Limburg, Cefalù, Monreale, Galliano). Not only the angel's dress, but its face and the painting colors also recall eleventh–twelfth century Byzantine and Italian painting. On the ground of these observations, the fresco can be dated to the late eleventh–early twelfth century.

The Holy Crown

The Pécsvárad angel and the palmette sculpture are not the only artistic features that recall the visual world of Byzantium in the Kingdom of Hungary. There exists a precious object, an imperial gift from Byzantium that Princess Piroska might have

---

[53] Melinda Tóth, "A kosztolányi templom falképei," *Ars Hungarica* 2 (1974): 70.
[54] Font, *Koloman the Learned*, 77–78.
[55] György Györffy, ed., *Diplomata Hungariae Antiquissima I. Ab anno 1000 usque ad annum 1131* (Budapest: Akadémiai, 1992), 382–385, 391–396.
[56] Balázs Bodó, "A pécsváradi bencés monostor építéstörténete az újabb kutatások tükrében" [The building history of the Benedictine monastery of Pécsvárad in the light of new research], in *A középkor és a kora újkor régészete Magyarországon*, ed. Elek Benkő and Gyöngyi Kovács (Budapest: MTA Régészeti Intézete, 2010), 349–386.
[57] Melinda Tóth, *Árpád-kori falfestészet* [Wall-Painting in the Árpádian Age], (Budapest: Akadémiai, 1974), 26–27; Tóth, "Falfestészet az Árpád-korban," 141.

seen with her own eyes. It is the Greek diadem (*corona Graeca*) that forms the lower part of the Holy Crown of Hungary.[58] Originally a separate jewel, the Greek crown is decorated with precious stones and enamels representing Christ, archangels, saints and rulers, among whom Emperor Michael VII Doukas (1071–78) and King Géza I, "faithful king of Hungary." The pointed and arched plaques on the top of the crown show that it was a women's diadem made in Constantinople. As King Géza I married the daughter of Theodulos Synadenos, the crown must have been a gift of Emperor Michael VII to the Byzantine queen of Hungary. What was the destiny of the Greek crown following the dowager queen's return to Constantinople in 1079/80?[59] Similarly to the crown of the first queen of Hungary, Gisella, who offered her royal diadem to the Cathedral of Veszprém where it was preserved until the early thirteenth century,[60] the *Synadene*'s crown also must have been offered as a gift to a prestigious ecclesiastical foundation, possibly the royal basilica in Székesfehérvár. King Coloman was the son of Géza I, the Byzantine princess of the Synadene family was either his mother or his stepmother.[61] Coloman and his niece, Piroska, definitely knew this crown.

Sometime later, the Greek crown was incorporated into a complex structure. A cross of two golden strips decorated with enamel plaques with Latin inscriptions (*corona Latina*) was added to it. The enamel plaques on the Latin crown represent eight apostles and the enthroned Christ flanked by two cypress trees. The same composition decorates the Greek crown. The image on the Latin crown seems to be a direct copy of the Greek one. Since the Greek crown was kept in Hungary, the Latin part must have been made there, too. The inscriptions around the apostle figures on the enamels have a strange lettering, particularly the letters *U* and *T*. This letter font was used in those areas of Western Europe that were under Byzantine rule, for example in Italy up to the middle of the eleventh century. Scholars argued that the Latin plaques were made under King Saint Stephen of Hungary in the early

---

[58] Josef Deér, *Die Heilige Krone Ungarns* (Wien: Böhlaus Nachf., 1966); Éva Kovács and Zsuzsa Lovag, *The Hungarian Crown and Other Regalia* (Budapest: Corvina, 1980); Etele Kiss, "La 'couronne grecque' dans son context," *Acta Historiae Artium* 43 (2002): 39–51; Cecily J. Hilsdale, "The social life of the Byzantine gift: the Royal Crown of Hungary re-invented," *Art History* 31 (2008): 603–631.

[59] Gyula Moravcsik, ed., *Az Árpád-kori magyar történet bizánci forrásai. Fontes Byzantini historiae Hungaricae aevo ducum et regum ex stirpe Árpád descendentium* (Budapest: Akadémiai, 1984) 96.

[60] László Veszprémy, "The Crusade of Andrew II, King of Hungary, 1217–1218," *Iacobus* 13/14 (2002): 87–110.

[61] Attila Zsoldos, *Az Árpádok és asszonyaik* [The Árpádian Dynasty and their Queens], (Budapest: MTA Történettudományi Intézete, 2005), 185; Font, *Koloman the Learned,* 12–13.

eleventh century.⁶² However, similar letters are engraved on King Coloman's ring declaring that this is the royal ring: *annulus Colomanni regis*.⁶³ On the ring's inner side, an apotropaic inscription was still readable in the nineteenth century with the same letters *U* and *T* as on the *corona Latina*. Moreover, the strips of the ring are decorated with golden filigree typical to the eleventh century and rarely used after.⁶⁴ Therefore it is likely that the *corona Latina* was commissioned by King Coloman who integrated it with the Byzantine crown of his (step)mother.⁶⁵ The new royal crown of Hungary was kept in the royal basilica of Székesfehérvár, where it is attested in the middle of the twelfth century.⁶⁶ Székesfehérvár came to be the royal coronation church where all twelfth-century kings of Hungary were crowned—starting with King Coloman.⁶⁷

Conclusion

The turn of the eleventh–twelfth century saw an extraordinary flourishing of the arts in the Kingdom of Hungary. Cathedrals and monastic churches were rebuilt, the new Romanesque style appeared in sculpture, innovative fresco cycles were painted on church walls, and the new royal insignia were created. Artistic prosperity grew from political consolidation. Following the dynastic struggles after the death of Stephen, the first Christian king of Hungary in 1038, the reigns of kings Ladislaus and Coloman brought the long awaited- for stability.⁶⁸ The turn of the century also saw a radical change all over Europe with the spread of mature Romanesque style connected to the reform movement in the Roman Catholic Church. In Hungary, however, Princess Piroska was surrounded with art and architecture much

---

62 Endre Tóth, "A Szent Korona apostollemezeinek keltezéséhez" [On the dating of the Apostle plaques of the Holy Crown], *Communicationes Archaeologicae Hungariae* 16 (1996): 181–209; idem, "The Holy Crown and Coronation Insignia," in *A Thousand Years of Christianity in Hungary*, ed. István Zombori et al. (Budapest: Hungarian Catholic Episcopal Conference, 2001), 37–40.

63 József Hampel, "Kálmán király aranygyűrűje" [The Golden Ring of King Coloman], *Archaeologiai Értesítő* 42 (1908): 11–12.

64 Béla Zsolt Szakács, "Remarks on the filigree of the Holy Crown of Hungary," *Acta Historiae Artium* 43 (2002): 52–61.

65 The dating proposed by György Györffy, *István király és műve* (Budapest: Gondolat, 1977), 356–360, English translation by Peter Doherty *King Saint Stephen of Hungary* (Boulder: Social Science Monographs, 1994). Other scholars date the fusion of the two parts to a later period, see notes 58 and 62.

66 Moravcsik, *Az Árpád-kori magyar történet*, 155.

67 Engel, "Temetkezések," 613–614.

68 Pál Engel, *The Realm of St Stephen. A History of Medieval Hungary*. Translated by Tamás Pálosfalvi. (London and New York: Tauris, 2001), 29–37.

closer to the Byzantine taste. When Piroska arrived in Constantinople around 1105, she encountered a visual language she easily understood. The artistic patronage of the royal court of King Coloman in Hungary might have been an inspiration for Empress Eirene, the great patroness of art and architecture in Byzantium.

Bibliography

Bakay, Kornél. *Somogyvár. Szent Egyed-monostor* [Somogyvár, Monastery of Saint Giles], Budapest: Műemlékek Nemzeti Gondnoksága, 2011.

Barta, Peter, Martin Bóna and Marián Keleši. "Chronometrický výskum murív Kostola sv. Juraja v Kosťanoch pod Tribečom" [Chronometric Research of the Masonry of St. George's Church in Kosťany pod Tribečom], *Archaeologia historica* 40 (2015): 691–709.

Batizi, Zoltán. "Feltárul az ezeréves székesegyház" [The Thousand-Years Old Cathedral Revealed] *Archeologia – Altum Castrum Online*, http://archeologia.hu/feltarul-az-ezer-eves-szekesegyhaz (last accessed 07/01/2016).

Bednár, Peter and Zuzana Poláková. "St. Emmeram's Cathedral," in *The Cradle of Christianity in Slovakia. Nitra Castle and the Cathedral of St. Emmeram*, ed. Viliam Judák, Peter Bednár and Jozef Medvecký. Bratislava: Arte Libris, 2011, 184–205.

Berend, Nora, József Laszlovszky and Béla Zsolt Szakács. "The kingdom of Hungary," in *Christianization and the Rise of Christian Monarchy*. Ed. Nora Berend, Cambridge: Cambridge University Press, 2007, 319–368.

Bodó, Balázs. "A pécsváradi bencés monostor építéstörténete az újabb kutatások tükrében" [The Building History of the Benedictine Monastery at Pécsvárad in the Light of Recent Research], in *A középkor és a kora újkor régészete Magyarországon*. Eds. Elek Benkő and Gyöngyi Kovács. Budapest: MTA Régészeti Intézete, 2010, 349–386.

Bozóki, Lajos. "Ellésmonostor faragott kőtöredékeinek stíluskapcsolatai" [Stylistic Connections of the Stone-Carvings of Ellésmonostor], in *A középkori Dél-Alföld és Szer*, ed. Tibor Kollár. Szeged: Csongrád Megyei Levéltár, 2000, 233–240.

Buzás, Gergely. "A pécsi székesegyházak a román korban" [The Cathedrals of Pécs in the Romanesque period]. *Archaeologia – Altum Castrum Online*, 2013, http://archeologia.hu/content/archeologia/164/pecs.pdf (last accessed 07/01/2016)

———. "Ásatás az egri középkori székesegyházban" [Excavation in the medieval cathedral of Eger], *Archeologia – Altum Castrum Online*, 2016, http://archeologia.hu/asatas-az-egri-kozepkori-szekesegyhazban (last accessed 07/01/2016).

———. "Az esztergomi vár románkori és gótikus épületei" [The Romanesque and Gothic buildings of the Castle of Esztergom], in *Az Esztergomi Vármúzeum kőtárának katalógusa*, ed. Gergely Buzás and Gergely Tolnai, Esztergom: Vármúzeum, 2004, 7–44.

Deér, Josef. *Die Heilige Krone Ungarns*, Wien: Böhlaus Nachf., 1966.

Engel, Pál. "Temetkezések a középkori székesfehérvári bazilikában" [Burials in the Medieval Basilica of Székesfehérvár], *Századok* 121 (1987): 613–637.

———. *The Realm of St Stephen. A History of Medieval Hungary*. Transl. Tamás Pálosfalvi. London and New York: Tauris, 2001.

Entz, Géza. "A Szent István alapítású erdélyi püspökség első székesegyháza" [The First Cathedral of the Bishopric of Transylvania founded by Saint Stephen], in *Doctor et apostol. Szent István-tanulmányok*, ed. József Török (Budapest: Márton Áron, 1994), 101–105.

Font, Márta, *Koloman the Learned*. Szeged: Szegedi Középkorász Műhely, 2001.

Franzé, Barbara (ed.). *Art et réforme grégorienne en France et dans la péninsule Ibérique*. Paris: Picard, 2015.

Gerevich, László. "The royal court (curia), the provost's residence and the village at Dömös." *Acta Archaeologica* 35 (1983): 385–409.

Györffy, György (ed.). *Diplomata Hungariae Antiquissima I. Ab anno 1000 usque ad annum 1131*. Budapest: Akadémiai, 1992.

Györffy, György. *King Saint Stephen of Hungary*. Tr. Peter Doherty. Boulder: Social Science Monographs, 1994.

Habovštiak, Alojz. *Kirche mit Fresken in Kostoľany pod Tribečom*. Nitra: Vydavateľstvo Slovenskej akadémie vied, 1966.

Hampel, József, "Kálmán király aranygyűrűje" [The Golden Ring of King Coloman]. *Archaeologiai Értesítő* 42 (1908): 11–12.

Havasi, Krisztina. "A pécsi középkori székesegyház és a Dómkőtár gyűjteményének rövid története" [Short History of the Medieval Cathedral of Pécs and the Collection in the Cathedral Lapidary], in *A pécsi püspökség évezredes öröksége*, ed. Zsolt Virág, Pécs: Várkastély, 2015, 175–183.

———. "Árpád-kori ornamentális téglák Szakoly lebontott középkori templomából" [Árpádian Decorated Bricks from the Destroyed Medieval Church of Szakoly]. In: *Középkori egyházi építészet Szatmárban*. ed. Tibor Kollár. Nyíregyháza: Szabolcs-Szatmár-Bereg Megyei Önkormányzat, 2011, 92–113.

———. "Egy festett díszű román kori kapuzat és a középkori egri székesegyház kifestésének töredékei" [A Painted Romanesque Portal and the Painted Fragments of the Medieval Cathedral of Eger], *Ars Hungarica* 41 (2015), 222–254.

———. "Sárvármonostor XI. századi kőfaragványainak katalógusa elé" [To the Catalogue of the Eleventh-Century Stonecarvings of Sárvármonostor], in: *Középkori egyházi építészet Szatmárban*. ed. Tibor Kollár. Nyíregyháza: Szabolcs-Szatmár-Bereg Megyei Önkormányzat, 2011, 26–59.

———. *A középkori egri székesegyház az 1200-as évek elején*. [The Medieval Cathedral of Eger in the Early 1200s], PhD dissertation, Budapest: Eötvös Loránd University, 2011, 75–113, http://doktori.btk.elte.hu/art/havasikrisztina/diss.pdf (last accessed 07/01/2016).

Hervay, F. Levente. "A bencések és apátságaik története a középkori Magyarországon" [The History of the Benedictine Order and its Monasteries in Medieval Hungary]. In: *Paradisum plantavit. Bencés monostorok a középkori Magyarországon. Benedictine Monasteries in Medieval Hungary.* ed. Imre Takács, Pannonhalma: Pannonhalmi Bencés Főapátság, 2001, 461–547.

Hilsdale, Cecily J. "The social life of the Byzantine gift: the Royal Crown of Hungary reinvented." *Art History* 31 (2008): 603–631.

Ilkó, Krisztina. "The artistic connections of the Romanesque wall paintings in Kostoľany pod Tribečom (Slovakia)." *Hortus Artium Mediaevalium* 22 (2016): 282–293.

Kessler, Herbert L. *Old St. Peter's and Church Decoration in Medieval Italy.* Spoleto: Centro Italiano di Studi sull'Alto Medioevo, 2002.

Kiss, Etele. "La 'couronne grecque' dans son context." *Acta Historiae Artium* 43 (2002): 39–51.

Koszta, László. "Die Gründung des Bistums von Nitra." in *Slovakia and Croatia. Historical Parallels and Connections (until 1780),* ed. Martin Homza, Ján Lukačka and Neven Budak, Bratislava: Department of Slovak History at the Faculty of Philosophy of Comenius University Bratislava – Zagreb: Faculty of Humanities and Social Sciences, University of Zagreb, 2013, 401–407.

Kovács, Éva and Zsuzsa Lovag. *The Hungarian Crown and Other Regalia.* Budapest: Corvina, 1980.

Kozák, Károly and András Uzsoki. "A győri székesegyház feltárása." [The excavation of the cathedral of Győr] *Arrabona* 12 (1970): 111–159.

Maříková-Kubková, Jana et al. "The Church of St George in Kostoľany pod Tribečom." In: *Swords, Crowns, Censers and Books. Francia Media – Cradles of European Culture,* ed. Marina Vicelja-Matijašić, Rijeka: Center for Iconographic Studies, 2015, 213–248.

Marosi, Ernő. "Román kor" [Romanesque Art]. In: *A művészet története Magyarországon* [The History of Art in Hungary] Ed. Nóra Aradi, Budapest: Corvina, 1983, 21–51.

———. "Magyarországi művészet Szent László korában." [Art in Hungary in the time of Saint Ladislas] In: *Athleta Patriae. Szent László-tanulmányok,* ed. László Mezey. Budapest: Szent István Társulat, 1980.

———. *A romanika Magyarországon.* [Romanesque Art in Hungary] Budapest: Corvina, 2013.

———. *Die Anfänge der Gotik in Ungarn. Esztergom in der Kunst des 12.–13. Jahrhunderts.* Budapest: Akadémiai, 1984.

Mentényi, Klára. "Szőlőleveles kőfaragványok. A királyi prépostsági templom új építkezései a 12. század elején" [Stone-carvings with Vine-Leaves. The Rebuilding of the Royal Collegiate Church in the Early 12th century], in *Könyves Kálmán és Székesfehérvár,* ed. András Smohay, Székesfehérvár: Székesfehérvári Egyházmegyei Múzeum, in print

Moravcsik, Gyula (ed.). *Az Árpád-kori magyar történet bizánci forrásai. Fontes Byzantini historiae Hungaricae aevo ducum et regum ex stirpe Árpád descendentium.* Budapest: Akadémiai, 1984.

Nagy Katalin, B., and Melinda Tóth, "Kutaspuszta Árpád-kori templomának díszítése. [Decoration of the Árpád-age Church of Kutaspuszta] In: *A középkori Dél-Alföld és Szer*, ed. Tibor Kollár, Szeged: Csongrád Megyei Levéltár, 2000, 241–55.

Nagy, Sándor. *Dombó, középkori monostor és erőd* [Dombó, Medieval Monastery and Fortress], Újvidék: Forum, 1987.

Papp, Szilárd. "Somogyvár." In: *Paradisum plantavit. Bencés monostorok a középkori Magyarországon. Benedictine Monasteries in Medieval Hungary.* Ed. Imre Takács, Pannonhalma: Pannonhalmi Bencés Főapátság, 2001, 350–53 and 681–83.

Stanojev, Nebojša. "A dombói (Rakovac) Szent György-monostor szentélyrekesztői" [The Choir-Screens of Saint George's Monastery at Dombó (Rakovac)] In: *A középkori Dél-Alföld és Szer*, ed. Tibor Kollár, Szeged: Csongrád Megyei Levéltár, 2000, 383–428.

Stanojev, Nebojša. "A dombói Szent György-monostortemplom román kori árkádjai." [Romanesque Arcades of Saint George's Monastery Church at Dombó] In: *Építészet a középkori Dél-Magyarországon*, ed. Tibor Kollár, Budapest: Teleki László Alapítvány, 2010, 635–669.

Szakács, Béla Zsolt. "Állandó alaprajzok – változó vélemények? Megjegyzések a 'bencés templomtípus' magyarországi pályafutásához" [Continuity in Ground Plans – Change in Ideas? Notes on the History of the 'Benedictine Type' Romanesque Churches in Hungary] In: *Maradandóság és változás,* ed. Szilvia Bodnár et al., Budapest: MTA Művészettörténeti Kutatóintézet – Képző- és Iparművészeti Lektorátus, 2004, 25–37.

———. "Archaism, Imitation, Provincialism? Notes on the Murals of Kosztolány / Kostoľany pod Tribečom." *Convivium* 3/1 (2016): 154–71.

———. "Dombó és a korai altemplomok Magyarországon" [Dombó and the Early Crypts in Hungary], in: *Építészet a középkori Dél-Magyarországon,* ed. Tibor Kollár, Budapest: Teleki László Alapítvány, 2010, 682–84.

———. "Remarks on the Filigree of the Holy Crown of Hungary." *Acta Historiae Artium* 43 (2002): 52–61.

———. "Three Hungarian Shrines from 1083: Canonization, Reform, and Politics." in *Romanesque: Saints, Shrines and Pilgrimage*, ed. John McNeill. London: British Archaeological Association, forthcoming.

Szentesi, Edit, Ferenc Dávid and Béla Zsolt Szakács. "Feldebrői templom." [The Church of Feldebrő] In: *Magyar Művelődéstörténeti Lexikon*, vol. III, ed. Péter Kőszeghy, Budapest: Balassi, 2005, 47–51.

Szentpétery, Imre (ed.). *Scriptores Rerum Hungaricarum tempore ducum regumque stirpis Arpadianae gestarum.* Vol. I, Budapest: Akadémiai, 1937.

Takács, Imre. "Pannonhalma." In: *Paradisum plantavit. Bencés monostorok a középkori Magyarországon. Benedictine Monasteries in Medieval Hungary.* Ed. Imre Takács, Pannonhalma: Pannonhalmi Bencés Főapátság, 2001, 316–321. and 671–673.

Takács, Miklós. "Die sogenannten Palmettenornamentik der christlichen Bauten des 11, Jahrhunderts im mittelalterlichen Ungarn." In: *Byzanz – Das Römerreich im Mittelalter*, Teil 3, ed. Falko Daim and Jörg Drauschke, Mainz: Römisch-Germanisches Zenralmuseum, 2010, 411–415.

———. "Ornamentale Beziehungen zwischen der Steinmetzkunst von Ungarn und Dalmatien im XI. Jahrhundert." *Hortus Artium Mediaevalium* 3 (1997): 165–178.

Tóth, Endre. "A Szent Korona apostollemezeinek keltezéséhez." [On the Dating of the Apostle Plaques of the Holy Crown] *Communicationes Archaeologicae Hungariae* 16 (1996): 181–209.

———. "The Holy Crown and Coronation Insignia." In: *A Thousand Years of Christianity in Hungary*. Ed. István Zombori et al., Budapest: Hungarian Catholic Episcopal Conference, 2001, 37–40.

Tóth, Endre and Gergely Buzás. *Magyar építészet* [Hungarian architecture], vol. I, Budapest: Kossuth, 2016.

Tóth, Melinda. "A somogyvári bencés apátság és temploma az Árpád-korban." [The Benedictine Abbey of Somogyvár and its Church in the Árpádin Age] In: *Szent László és Somogyvár*, ed. Károly Magyar, Kaposvár: Somogy Megyei Múzeumok Igazgatósága, 1992, 221–250.

———. "Falfestészet az Árpád-korban. Kutatási helyzetkép." [Wall-Painting in the Árpádian Age: the State of Research] *Ars Hungarica* 23 (1995): 140–141.

———. *Árpád-kori falfestészet* [Wall-Painting in the Árpádian Age], Budapest: Akadémiai, 1974.

Tóth, Sándor. "A 11. századi magyarországi kőornamentika időrendjéhez." [To the Chronology of Eleventh-Century Hungarian Ornamental Stone-Carvings] In: *Pannonia Regia. Művészet a Dunántúlon 1000–1541*, ed. Árpád Mikó and Imre Takács (Budapest: Magyar Nemzeti Galéria, 1994), 54–62.

——— "Az aracsi kő rokonsága." [The Artistic Connections of the Stone-Carving of Aracs] In: Kollár (ed.), *A középkori Dél-Alföld és Szer*, ed. Tibor Kollár, Szeged: Csongrád Megyei Levéltár, 2000, 429–448.

———. "Dombó." In: *Paradisum plantavit. Bencés monostorok a középkori Magyarországon. Benedictine Monasteries in Medieval Hungary*, ed. Imre Takács, Pannonhalma: Pannonhalmi Bencés Főapátság, 2001, 359–367 and 686–690.

———. "Esztergom Szent Adalbert-székesegyháza és az Árpád-kori építészet." [Saint Adalbert's Cathedral of Esztergom and the Architecture of the Árpádian Age] In: *Ezer év Szent Adalbert oltalma alatt*, ed. András Hegedűs and István Bárdos, Esztergom: Prímási Levéltár, 2000, 121–154.

———. "Sárvármonostor." In: *Paradisum plantavit. Bencés monostorok a középkori Magyarországon. Benedictine Monasteries in Medieval Hungary*. Ed. Imre Takács, Pannonhalma: Pannonhalmi Bencés Főapátság, 2001, 368–370 and 690–692.

———. *Román kori kőfaragványok a Magyar Nemzeti Galéria Régi Magyar Gyűjteményében* [Romanesque Stone-Carvings in the Old Hungarian Collection of the Hungarian National Gallery], Budapest: Magyar Nemzeti Galéria, 2010.

Veszprémy, László. "The Crusade of Andrew II, King of Hungary, 1217–1218." *Iacobus* 13/14 (2002): 87–110.

Zsoldos, Attila. *Az Árpádok és asszonyaik.* [*The Kings of the Árpád-Dynasty and their Queens. The Reginal Institution in the Age of the Árpáds.*] Budapest: MTA Történettudományi Intézete, 2005.

THE POLITICS OF PIROSKA'S MARRIAGE: BYZANTIUM, HUNGARY AND THE NORMANS IN THE EARLY TWELFTH CENTURY[1]

Attila Bárány

Imperial marriages have always been a form of diplomatic alliance, and never more so than in Byzantium. But to what extent did the union between John II Komnenos and Princess Piroska of Hungary represent a new type of alliance between Hungary and Byzantium? This paper examines the union itself, as well as its political background and the profound consequences it had for the region, and investigates the Byzantino-Hungarian alliance against the Normans of Southern Italy before 1108.

Offering new insights into the date of John and Piroska's marriage, key to understanding diplomatic relations between Byzantium and Hungary and their impact on Central Europe and the Balkans, I argue that this Hungarian alliance was a triumph of diplomacy by a Byzantine court under pressure. I explore the underpinnings of this defensive rapprochement against the Normans of Southern Italy—notably Bohemond of Antioch's aggressive ambitions in the Balkans in 1106–08—and whether Hungary might have participated in the anti-Norman war effort. I also consider how the conquest of Dalmatia in 1105 by King Coloman (1095–1116) and his marriage to an Hauteville princess were received, and how they relate—if at all—to the marriage negotiations between Hungary and Byzantium. The Byzantine Empire, Venice and Hungary had opposing interests in Dalmatia, but for the time being they had to accept Coloman's conquest as a *fait accompli*. Venice did not feel threatened by the marriage tie between a Norman princess and the Hungarian king, but we will show how the conquest of Dalmatia affected Byzantium, and how John and Piroska's marriage formed part of a political *rapprochement*.

---

[1] I would like to express my heartfelt gratitude to Jonathan Shepard for his invaluable help with the English and to Marianne Sághy for her comments and advice.

Hungary was being drawn into the wider conflict, and its occupation of Dalmatia can be seen as a defensive move against the Normans, undertaken in the context of emerging Byzantino-Norman hostility in the Adriatic. A Norman queen did not necessarily lead to the Hungarians' blanket support for Norman ambitions and Coloman's ties with Roger of Sicily encouraged him to move against Bohemond: diversionary activity by the Hungarians in the wake of Bohemond's invading Norman army is not inconceivable. Coloman's Apulian military "adventure" around the time of the Normans' siege of Dyrrachium (Durrës, Albania) has a long modern historiographical tradition, with few doubting its authenticity,[2] not even specialists in Hungary's relations with her neighbors in the eleventh and twelfth centuries.[3] Although an Apulian expeditionary force seems implausible, I will explore whether Hungarian support for the Venetians—obstructing the Normans from landing in Dalmatia—is entirely out of the question.

Finally, the paper investigates Coloman's role in the peace treaty between Bohemond and the Komnenoi signed by Hungarian witnesses in Deabolis (Devol, Albania) in 1108 and the importance of Piroska's Western antecedents. Many Byzantine sources highlight Piroska's German imperial origins, and we will note how important Piroska's "imperial blood" was to the Byzantines throughout the twelfth century: it bolstered not only the interests of Emperor Alexios in the early 1100s, but also the political aspirations of the Komnenian dynasty.

When did Piroska and John's wedding take place?

Anna Komnene does not mention the marriage in her *Alexiad*, but the date can be deduced from her chronology. Alexios moved to Thessalonica in September 1105, and "lingered on in those parts for a year and two months," that is, he stayed in Thessaly until November 1106. When "he was informed that the Norman prince Bohemond of Hauteville was still staying about in Lombardy and as winter was already

---

[2] *Magyarország történeti kronológiája* (Historical chronology of Hungary), vols 1–4, ed. Kálmán Benda. vol. 2, ed. László Solymosi (Budapest: Akadémiai, 1984), vol. 1, (hereafter Kronológia) 100; *Korai Magyar történeti lexikon, 9–14. század* (Encyclopaedia in early Hungarian history, 9th–14th c.), gen. ed. Gyula Kristó (Budapest: Akadémiai, 1994), (hereafter KTML) 315.

[3] Gyula Pauler, *A magyar nemzet történelme az Árpádházi királyok alatt* (The history of the Hungarian nation under the reign of the Árpád dynasty) vols 1-2, (Budapest: MTA, 1893), vol. 1, 271; Ferenc Makk, "Megjegyzések Kálmán külpolitikájához" (Notes for Coloman's diplomacy), *Acta Universitatis Szegediensis. Acta historica* 67 (1980): 21–31. 29; Gyula Kristó, *Az Árpád-kor háborúi* (The wars of the Árpáds) (Budapest: Zrínyi, 1986), 72; István Kapitánffy, *Hungarobyzantina* (Budapest: Typotex, 2003), 167.

setting in, [...] he dismissed all the soldiers" and "returned to Thessalonica."[4] "Whilst he was journeying to Thessalonica, the first son of Prince John was born ... and a little girl was born at the same time. The Emperor attended the services of the commemoration of the Great Martyr Demetrius in Thessalonica."[5] John and Piroska-Eirene's twins were born whilst Alexios was journeying, possibly before the feast of Saint Demetrius. Some scholars mistakenly date the birth of the twins to January 1107, placing the Feast of Saint Demetrius on January 25.[6] This is, however, the Feast of Saint Demetrius the Skeuophylas, but Anna Komnene specifies Demetrius the Great Martyr, celebrated on October 26. The wedding must have taken place nine months before, that is, in mid- or the second half of January 1106. This is not a *terminus ante quem:* the marriage might have taken place several months before, thus in 1105, a date usually accepted by Hungarian historiography.[7] John Zonaras, a reliable twelfth-century chronicler is silent on the wedding, but affirms that before his ascension to the throne, Emperor John Komnenos reached manhood, had married the daughter of the king of the Hungarians, and fathered children.[8] John Kinnamos, a later twelfth-cen-

---

[4] Ἐκεῖνος δὲ ἐγκαρτερήσας ἐπὶ ἐνιαυτὸν ἕνα καὶ μῆνας δύο, ὡς τὸν Βαϊμοῦντον ἔτι <ἐν> τοῖς τῆς Λογγιβαρδίας μέρεσι διατρίβοντα ἐπεπληρο φόρητο, τοῦ χειμῶνος ἐπικαταλαμβάνοντος ἤδη, τοὺς στρατιώτας πρὸς τὰς σφῶν οἰκίας ἐξέπεμψεν, αὐτὸς δὲ τὴν Θεσσαλονίκην καταλαμβάνει. Anna Komnene, ΑΛΕΧΙΑΣ / *Anna Comnenae Porphyrogennitae Alexias*, ed. August Reifferscheid, vols 1-2 (Leipzig: Teubner, 1884); Anna Komnena, *Alexiad*, ed. Diether R. Reinsch and Athanasios Kambylis, vols. 1-2, Corpus Fontium Historiae Byzantinae, 40, (hereafter CFHB) (Berlin–New York, de Gruyter, 2001) (hereafter: AK) XII 4, 4. p. 369.

[5] Ἐν δὲ τῷ τὴν πρὸς Θεσσαλονίκην ἀνύειν ἐτέχθη ὁ πρωτότοκος τῶν υἱῶν τοῦ πορφυρογεννήτου καὶ βασιλέως Ἰωάννου κατὰ τὴν Βαλα βίσταν συνεπαγόμενος ἐν τῷ τίκτεσθαι καὶ ἕτερον θῆλυ. Ἐκεῖσε γοῦν τὴν μνήμην τοῦ μεγαλομάρτυρος Δημητρίου ἐκτελέσας εἰσέρχεται εἰς τὴν μεγαλόπολιν. [Whilst he was journeying to Thessalonica, the first son of Prince John Porphyrogenitus was born at Balabista and a little girl was born at the same time. The Emperor attended the services of the commemoration of the Great Martyr Demetrius in Thessalonica and then returned to the Capital.] AK XII 4, 4. p. 370.

[6] Anna Comnena, *The Alexiad*, transl. E.R.A. Sewter (London: Penguin, 2003) (hereafter Sewter)380. n. 20.; January 1107: Miroslav Marković, "Dva natpisa iz Zadra," (Two inscriptions from Zadar) *Historijski zbornik* 36 (1953): 99–138. 107, 130; Ferdinand Chalandon, *Essai sur le règne d'Alexis Ier Comnène, 1081–1118*, (Paris: Picard, 1900), 239. For Anna's reasons for recording the birth of John's twins see Vlada Stanković, "John II Komnenos before the year 1118", in *John II Komnenos, Emperor of Byzantium: In the Shadow of Father and Son*, ed. Alexandra Bucossi and Alex Rodriguez Suarez (Abingdon: Routledge, 2016), 11–21.

[7] See below, in detail.

[8] [Ioannes Zonaras] Επιτομήιστοριων / *Ioannis Zonarae epitomae historiarum*, ed. Ludwig Dindorf, vols 1-6, (Leipzig: Teubner, 1868–1875) (hereafter Dindorf edn.) vol. 4, Lib. XVIII. 24, 28, p. 246; [Ioannes Zonaras] Χρονικον / *Ioannis Zonarae Annales*, vols 1-2, ed. Moritz Pinder; Επιτομή ιστοριων / *Epitomae historiarum*, vol. 3, ed. Theodor Büttner-Wobst, CSHB, 47–49, (Bonn: Weber, 1841–97) (hereafter Pinder edn.)vol. 3, Lib. XVIII. 24, 18, p. 748; Gyula Moravcsik, *Az Árpád-kori magyar történet bizánci forrásai. Fontes Byzantini historiae Hungaricae aevo ducum et reg-*

tury chronicler notes that John married Irene, "a very chaste woman if ever there was one."[9] Theodore Skoutariotes is the only chronicler who mentions the negotiations preceding the marriage. Although he wrote well after 1282, his narrative is based on accounts dating to the reign of Alexios.[10] Emperor Alexios sent an embassy to Hungary in 1105 to propose the marriage between John and Piroska. Another embassy, led by Eumathios Philokalés, was sent to Coloman somewhat later. This embassy then brought the bride to Constantinople.[11] Skoutariotes hints at the underlying cause of the marriage: "the Western peoples, but no less those of the East, are stirring."[12] The term "Eastern nations" undoubtedly refers to the growing pressure of the Seljuqs, while the term "Western peoples" must allude to the "perturbation" of the ambitious Bohemond, who triggered the Byzantino-Hungarian alliance in the first place. Scholars generally date John's and Piroska's wedding between 1104–1105.[13]

Dalmatia and the Normans

How did Coloman's conquest of the province of Dalmatia on the Adriatic shore affect the wedding negotiations? Two interpretations prevail: one claims that Hungarian foreign policy at the time was pro-Norman, the other that it was pro-Byzan-

---

um ex stirpe Árpád descendentium (Byzantine sources of Hungary under the Árpáds), (Budapest: Akadémiai, 1988), (hereafter ÁMTBF) 101; Írott források az 1050–1116 közötti magyar történelemről (Written sources on Hungarian history 1050–1116), ed. Ferenc Makk, Gábor Thoroczkay (Szeged: Szegedi Középkorász Műhely, 2006), 294.

[9] Ioannes Kinnamos, Ἐπιτομὴτῶν κατορθωμάτων / Ioannis Cinnami Rerum ab Ioannes et Alexio (sic) Comnenis Gestarum, ed. Augustus Meineke, Corpus Scriptorum Historiae Byzantinae, 13, (hereafter CSHB) (Bonn: Weber, 1836), vol. 1, Lib. 4, p. 9–10; John Kinnamos, The Deeds of John and Manuel Comnenus, transl. C. M. Brand (New York, Columbia, 1976),17; Moravcsik, ÁMTBF, 195.

[10] Mátyás Gyóni, "A legkorábbi magyar–bizánci házassági kapcsolatok kérdéséhez" [To the question of the earliest Hungarian–Byzantine matrimonial contacts], Századok 8 (1947): 212–219. 214. On Theodore Skoutariotes see Konstantinos Zafeiris, "The issue of the authorship of the Synopsis Chronike and Theodore Skoutariotes," Revue des études byzantines 69 (2011): 253–263.

[11] Franz Dölger, Regesten der Kaiserurkunden des oströmischen Reiches von 565–1453, vols. 1–3, teil. 2 (München: Oldenbourg, 1924), no. 1220h; Theodoros Skoutariotes, Σύνοψιςχρονική. Synopsis chronice, in Mesaiōnikē vivliothēkē epistasia / Mesaionike Bibliotheke, Bibliotheca Graeca Medii Aevi, ed. Kōnstantinos N. Sathas, vols 1–7, vol. 7 (Paris–Venice: Jean Maissoneuve, 1894) 180–181.; ÁMTBF, 301–302.; The Codex Vaticanus Gr. 1889. version records the marriage only briefly: Theodori Scutariotae Chronica, ed. Raimondo Tocci, CFHB 46, (Berlin–Boston: de Gruyter, 2015)II 338,5, p. 180.; II 341,1, p. 182.

[12] Theodoros Skoutariotes, Σύνοψιςχρονική, 181; ÁMTBF, 301; Also see Dölger, Regesten, no. 1220g.

[13] Nevertheless, recently Jean-François Mourtoux argued for a dating of the marriage to around 10 years before 1104-05: "L'avènement de Jean II: querelles de succession et principes de légitimité (Xᵉ-XIIᵉ siècles)," Diss. Université Paris 4 Sorbonne, 2012. 466–476.

tine. The pro-Norman thesis argues that the marriage must have been concluded before Coloman's conquest in the first half of 1105—not approved, but conceded by the Byzantine court. Alexios was bound to consent because of the military threat presented by Bohemond of Antioch's Normans. The Byzantino-Hungarian *rapprochement* was triggered by Coloman's supposedly strong Norman connections. After all, Coloman's queen was an Hauteville princess, daughter of Count Roger I of Sicily.[14] From the perspective of the Byzantine court, pro-Norman Hungary was a prospective ally of Bohemond's venture against the Empire. Alexios used diplomacy to alienate the Hungarian Árpád dynasty from the Normans. By implicitly accepting Hungarian dominion over Dalmatia, Alexios expected Coloman's neutrality or support against the Normans. The new *entente* was to be sealed by a marriage.[15] Byzantium "handed over" Dalmatia, and, in return, Hungary gave political backing against the Normans, no matter what relations she had maintained with them beforehand. In terms of this agreement, Alexios disapproved of a Venetian campaign against Hungary in 1106.[16]

The pro-Byzantine thesis argues that the Hungarian conquest of Dalmatia in early 1105 or even earlier preceded the marital alliance and was understood as an act of aggression. Byzantium was bound to concede Dalmatia. The Byzantino-Hungarian alliance sealed by the marriage contract months before was, however, so strongly based on mutual interests that it was not disturbed by Coloman's occupation of Byzantine lands.[17] John and Piroska's twins were born on 26 October 1106. From this, it is possible to deduce that their marriage took place *after* Coloman's Dalmatian campaign in the summer of 1105.[18]

---

[14] Gaufredus Malaterra, *De Rebus Gestis Rogerii Calabriae et Siciliae Comitis et Roberti Guiscardi Ducis fratris eius*, ed. Ernesto Pontieri, Rerum ItalicarumScriptores, new edn. vol. 5, pt. 1 (Bologna: Zanichelli, 1927–28); edn. used: *Írott források*, 199–201; József Deér, *A magyar törzsszövetség és patrimoniális királyság külpolitikája* (The foreign policy of the tribal alliance and the patrimonial state), (Kaposvár: Kaposvári Nyomda, 1928), 93; Paul Stephenson, *Byzantium's Balkan frontier. A political study of the northern Balkans, 900–1204*, (Cambridge: Cambridge University Press, 2000), 180; The Norman queen's name is unknown: "Busilla" is wrongly attested, "Felicia" is uncertain: see e.g. Raimund Kerbl, *Byzantinische Prinzessinnen in Ungarn zwischen 1050–1200 und ihr Einfluss auf das Arpaden königreich*, (Wien: Universität, 1979), 61. n. 9; *Írott források*, 200. n. 926.

[15] KTML, 315; Andrew B. Urbansky, *Byzantium and the Danube frontier. A study of the relations between Byzantium, Hungary and the Balkans during the period of the Comneni*, (New York: Twayne, 1968), 30.

[16] Deér, *A magyar törzsszövetség*, 96; Ferenc Makk, *Ungarische Aussenpolitik (896–1196)*, (Herne: Schäfer, 1999), 98.

[17] Makk, "Megjegyzések,"27; Marković, "Dva natpisa,"104–110; Kapitánffy, *Hungarobyzantina*, 78.

[18] Makk, *Aussenpolitik*, 97; Gyula Pauler, "Horvát–Dalmátország elfoglalásáról, 1091–1111. Befejező közlemény" (On the conquest of Croatia and Dalmatia), *Századok* 22 (1888): 197–215, 320–333. 323; Kapitánffy puts the birth between November 1106 and January 1107: *Hungarobyzantina*, 77.

I would suggest that Coloman's conquest of Dalmatia should be regarded through a different lens, not simply as a question of 'aggression' and 'approval.' Byzantine diplomacy was flexible and pragmatic. The Constantinopolitan court was able to accept the *fait accompli*, but long term diplomatic thinking considered the occupation of Dalmatia provisional. Alexios yielded because he was much more concerned with Bohemond of Antioch's aggression.[19] At the beginning of 1105, Bohemond preached the crusade in Italy—against Christians in Byzantium—and I would argue that this must have been the motive behind the diplomatic negotiations preceding John's and Piroska's marriage.

Neither Coloman's Norman marriage in 1097, nor his Dalmatian campaign in 1105, were directed against Byzantium.[20] The Normans of South Italy did not represent a unified front, for the Hauteville family was not a dynasty based around a unified kingdom. Although King Coloman of Hungary had married the daughter of Roger I Count of Sicily in around 1097, a decade later, in 1105–1106, he was not allied to the Normans nor did he support Roger's nephew Bohemond. Furthermore, although Count Roger died in 1101, Bohemond and Roger's 'party' were not on good terms at that time: their conflict went back to the 1070s. Roger had backed Bohemond's brother and rival, Roger Borsa, in the dynastic dispute that followed the death of their father, Robert Guiscard, in 1085.[21] Count Roger had no crusading zeal or anti-Byzantine aspirations and Guiscard's heir, Roger Borsa, lacked ambition to conquer new lands on the Balkans.[22] The brothers had long been entangled in a quarrel. Roger Borsa was supported by his Sicilian uncle, who gave his possessions in Calabria to him.[23] Thus Coloman married into the pro-papal branch of the Haute-

---

[19] Kapitánffy, *Hungarobyzantina*, 167. n. 34.

[20] György Székely, "La Hongrie et Byzance aux Xe–XIIe siècles," *Acta Historica Academiae Scientiarum Hungaricae* 13 (1967): 291–311. 308; Kapitánffy, *Hungarobyzantina*, 75, 166.

[21] Luigi Russo, "Boemondo e la "prima crociata," spunti per un riesame," (Bohemond and the "first Crusade: ideas for a review) in *"Unde boat mundus quanti fuerit Boamundus," Boemondo I di Altavilla, un normanno tra Occidente e Oriente*. Atti del Convegno internazionale di studio per il IX centenario della morte Canosa di Puglia, 5-6-7 maggio 2011, ed. Cosimo Damiano Fonseca, Pasquale Ieva (Bari: Società di Storia Patria per la Puglia, 2015) 122–134. 124, 133; G. A. Loud, *The Age of Robert Guiscard. Southern Italy and the Norman Conquest*, (Harlow: Longman/Pearson, 2000), 255–60.

[22] Robert the Monk's *History of the First Crusade, Historia Iherosolimitana*, transl. Carol Sweetenham (Aldershot: Ashgate, 2005), 91. n. 10; Hubert Houben, *Roger II of Sicily, A Ruler Between East and West*, (Cambridge: Cambridge University Press, 2002), 21; Donald Matthew, *The Norman Kingdom of Sicily* (Cambridge, Cambridge University Press, 2008), 19.

[23] Graham Loud, *Roger II and the creation of the Kingdom of Sicily*, (Manchester: Manchester University Press, 2012), 8–9; Russo, *Boemondo*, 124, 132, 133.

villes of Sicily, who opposed Bohemond,[24] and Bohemond's planned war against Byzantium only drew Coloman closer to Byzantium. The conquest of Byzantine-ruled Dalmatia by Coloman did not turn Hungary against Byzantium. The marriage of Piroska and John created a fresh alliance for Coloman, while Alexios found a new diplomatic partner in the Hungarian king, one able to protect Dalmatia from Bohemond's imminent invasion. Coloman was not looking to Bohemond to conquer Byzantine territory for him. Dalmatia had long been threatened by the Normans,[25] and the Dalmatian cities sought to escape Bohemond's control.[26] Between January and September 1105, Bohemond recruited volunteers and prepared his fleet in the Adriatic ports of Bari and Taranto.[27] In 1107, as Bohemond sailed towards the Balkans, Dalmatia feared a Norman invasion.[28] As the Dalmatian cities knew how hard conditions of Norman rule were, they preferred to live under the protection of a less demanding power. They were content with Hungarian dominion.

Dalmatia and Venice

Hungarian expansion towards the Adriatic in the early 1090s had met with Venetian opposition: although nominally Byzantine, Dalmatia stood in Venice's sphere of interest. Byzantium relied on Venetian military aid, sealed with a chrysobull in 1082. To strengthen her rule and to halt King Ladislaus of Hungary's conquest of Dalmatia in 1091, Byzantium called in Norman mercenaries led by Godfrey of Melfi—thereby setting a dangerous precedent. Defending Byzantine interests, the Normans gained control over Dalmatia—the key to the Balkans—and paved the way for a possible invasion of Byzantium itself. The tensions and conflict of interest between Venice and the Normans were palpable at the start of the First Crusade. Venice supported the crusaders reluctantly, in order not to alienate Byzantium,[29]

---

[24] Houben, *Roger*, 21.
[25] Stephenson, *Byzantium's Balkan Frontier*, 180.
[26] Early in 1073–75 the Normans led expeditions to Dalmatia, and acquired certain territories and cities.
[27] *Chronicon ignoti civis Barensis* / Anonymus Barensis *Chronicon,* Rerum Italicarum Scriptores raccolta degli storici Italiani dal cinquecento al millecinquecento, ordinata da L.A. Muratori (hereafter RIS) (Mediolanum: Sociates Palatina, 1723–51) (hereafter Anonymous of Bari) vol. 5, 145–158. 155; Georgios Theotokis, "Bohemond of Taranto's 1107–8 campaign in Byzantine Illyria—Can it be viewed as a Crusade?," *Rosetta* 11 (2012): 72–81. 73.
[28] "Normanni saepe per mare loca Dalmatiae inquietarent, et per terram aliquando se extendisset ad fines Pannoniae": Laurentius de Monacis, *Chronicon de rebus venetis*, (RIS vol. 8, Apppendix) (Venice: Remondiniana, 1758), 1–320, (hereafter Monacis) 93.
[29] Georgios Theotokis, *The Norman Campaigns in the Balkans, 1081–1108*, (Woodbridge: Boydell, 2014) 203; D.M. Nicol, *Byzantium and Venice*, (Cambridge: Cambridge University Press, 1988), 74.

and in the midst of the Crusade, in 1097, Alexios charged the Doge of Venice with the defence of Dalmatia. The Venetian fleet controlled the Dalmatian cities. As the crusaders travelled along the Danube in Hungary, King Coloman also preferred not to challenge Venetian domination over Dalmatia and in 1098, they signed a treaty (*convention amicitiae*). Respecting Byzantine interests, the treaty implacably opposed Norman expansion.[30] When the Normans conquered Antioch in 1098, armed conflict broke out, triggering war with Byzantium. In 1103, Byzantine rule was formally reinstated over Dalmatia; but since Constantinople was preoccupied with Bohemond from 1104 onwards, it was unable to exert its power over the region and Dalmatia came under Hungarian control. The Doge did not object, because Venice was also engaged in fighting the Normans in the Adriatic. Alexios managed to unite Hungary and Venice in a large coalition against the Normans, and Doge Ordelaffo Falier's magnificent golden retable (*Pala d'Oro*) in the Basilica of Saint Mark, decorated with Alexios's portrait in cloisonné enamel made by Constantinopolitan craftsmen, was made to commemorate Byzantino-Venetian cooperation in 1105.[31]

Prince Álmos, the Germans and the Normans

King Coloman's marriage with the daughter of Roger of Sicily—one of the Papacy's staunchest allies—was directed against the German Emperor Henry IV's Hungarian pretensions,[32] particularly since Roger's other daughter, Maximilla was married to Henry IV's rebellious son, Conrad. Swearing loyalty to the Pope, Conrad became an anti-King.[33] Coloman's brother, Prince Álmos, sought German help in seizing the throne and left for the Salian court at the turn of 1105–06.[34] However, Henry offered only nominal backing and so Álmos sought support in Poland, invading Hungary with his brother-in-law, Prince Bolesław III. Álmos and Bolesław had been married to the two daughters of Sviatopolk II, Grand Duke of Kiev, sometime between 1102 and 1104, and Kiev pursued first a pro-Polish, then a pro-German policy. His marriage did not help Álmos's pretensions, however, and Coloman was

---

[30] Stephenson, *Byzantium's Balkan Frontier*, 197.
[31] Alexios's portrait was replaced by that of Falier in 1115: Nicol, *Byzantium and Venice*, 65.
[32] Ferenc Makk, *The Árpáds and the Comneni*, (Budapest: Akadémiai, 1989), (hereafter Makk, Comneni)13.
[33] I. S. Robinson, *Henry IV of Germany 1056–1106*, (Cambridge: Cambridge University Press, 1999), 279, 286–88, 290–92, 295, 297, 300.
[34] Makk, *Aussenpolitik*, 99; Makk, *Comneni*, 14.

able to conclude an anti-German pact of friendship with Bolesław in 1106.[35] Winning over Bolesław and thus bringing to an end Álmos's pretensions to the throne was Coloman's great achievement—and one in which Byzantino-Hungarian relations played a role: the Byzantine alliance strengthened Hungary's position vis-à-vis Henry IV. Defeated, Prince Álmos went on pilgrimage to Jerusalem in 1107,[36] stopping en route in Constantinople, where he met political figures as well as Piroska-Eirene.[37] Álmos's presence in Constantinople coincided with Bohemond's invasion—perhaps not by accident—and he met one of Bohemond's relatives, Tancred, in Antioch. Travelling through the Balkans in the autumn of 1107—at the same time as Bohemond was laying siege to Dyrrachium—Álmos returned to Hungary for the consecration of a church at Dömös near Esztergom in 1107/8.[38] Given Álmos's lengthy and tenacious search for supporters, it is likely that he sought to exploit Bohemond's attack on Byzantium and Coloman—now Alexios's ally—might have expected Norman aggression against his dominion in the Balkans. On Álmos's journey back to Hungary, perhaps along the Albanian coastline and through Dalmatia, he would have crossed Norman-controlled areas and thus he could have tried to make contact with Bohemond and sought his backing. After a brief stay in Dömös, Álmos fled to the court of Henry V, the new German king, spending the Easter of 1108 in Passau.[39] Álmos's manoeuvers must have triggered Coloman's campaign to Dalmatia in the spring of that year—on 25 May 1108, he issued a charter for Trau (today Trogir in Croatia)[40]—and he had good reason to be present in Dalmatia, given Álmos's recent contact with the Normans and Henry V's threatened attack on Hungary. Bohemond and Henry were willing to coordinate military action against Coloman and the former, who had fallen out of favor with Pope Paschal II after the deviation of the crusade and his siege of the Christian city of Dyrrachium, waged a

---

[35] Makk, "Megjegyzések," 26; *Scriptores Rerum Hungaricarum tempore ducum regumque stirpis Arpadianae gestarum*. ed. Imre Szentpétery et al. vols 1-2, (Budapest: Akadémiai, 1937–1938), new edn. 1999. ed. Kornél Szovák, László Veszprémy, (hereafter SRH) vol. 1, 426–27.

[36] Makk, *Comneni*, 14.

[37] The Legend of Saint Emeric refers to Álmos's stay in Constantinople during the prince's pilgrimage. SRH vol. 2, 456; Makk, *Comneni*, 132. n. 61.

[38] SRH vol. 1, 427; Deér, *A magyar törzsszövetség*, 105–6; György Györffy, "A lovagszent uralkodása (1077–1095)," (The reign of the knightly saint) *Történelmi Szemle* 10 (1977): 533–564.

[39] SRH vol. 1, 429; Makk, *Aussenpolitik*, 100.

[40] *Diplomata Hungariae antiquissima* praefuit Georgius Györffy; adiuverunt Johannes Bapt. Borsa. (Budapest: Akadémiai, 1992), vol. 1, (hereafter DHA) 357; *Regesta regum stirpis Arpadinae critico–diplomatica*, vols. 1-2, ed. Imre Szentpétery, Iván Borsa (Budapest: Akadémiai, 1923–87) (hereafter RA) vol. 1. 41; György Györffy, "A XII. századi dalmáciai város privilégiumok kritikájához (Critical notes on the 12th c. city privileges) *Történelmi Szemle* 10 (1967): 46–56. 49.

war of succession against his brother, Roger Borsa, a papal ally.[41] A German attack would have forced Coloman to withdraw from the Adriatic: and this is exactly what happened. In September 1108, Henry and Álmos launched a major assault on Pozsony (Bratislava, Slovakia) and raided up to the valley of the River Vág (Vah) on the pretext that Hungary had "trespassed" upon imperial possessions in Dalmatia.[42] At the same time, Bohemond attacked Dalmatia. The Germans invaded Hungary in late summer, but preparations had started well before, so Henry could not have foreseen Bohemond's failure. In October, Bolesław III's troops arrived to support Coloman and in early November, the Hungarian army went on the offensive, forcing Henry to sue for peace.[43] During the German threat against Hungary, the Normans were engaged in a long siege of Dyrrachium as well as fighting the Byzantines along the coast of Illyricum and Epirus. The military encounters between Hungary and the Normans in 1108 stemmed from the political situation created by the alliance between the Árpáds and the Komnenoi, an alliance sealed by the marriage of John and Piroska.

Byzantium and the Normans

Byzantino-Norman relations had long been tense. Constantinople saw Antioch as a territory unjustly seized: the Orthodox patriarch of Antioch was forced to resign and was replaced by a Latin cleric.[44] Alexios resorted to military force against Bohemond, dispatching an army to retake the ports of Cilicia and Northern Syria, no doubt with a view to attacking Antioch itself.[45] War was prevented when Bohemond was taken captive in 1100 by the Dānishmand ruler Malik Aḥmad Ghāzī

---

[41] Giancarlo Andenna, "Boemondo e il papato," (Bohemond and the Papacy) in *"Unde boat mundus quanti fuerit Boamundus,"* 85–104.

[42] "Colomannus fines regni nostri, scilicet in locis maritimis invaserit": Ekkehard of Aura (Uraugiensis), *Chronica*, Monumenta Germaniae Historica (hereafter MGH) Scriptores in Folio (hereafter SS) vol. 6, (Chronica et annals aevi Salici) ed. D. G. Waitz, P. Kilon (Hannover: Hahn, 1844), 1–267 (hereafter Ekkehard) 242; Annalista Saxo, *Reichskronik*, ed. D. G. Waitz, P. Kilon. MGH SS vol. 6 (Chronica et annales aevi Salici) (Hannover: Hahn, 1844), 542–777. 539; Kapitánffy, *Hungarobyzantina*, 168.

[43] Makk, *Aussenpolitik*, 159.

[44] Thomas S. Asbridge, *The Creation of the Principality of Antioch, 1098–1130*, (Woodbridge: Boydell, 2000), 94, 195–99; Rudolf Hiestand, "Boemondo I e la prima *Crociata*," (Bohemond and the First Crusade) in *Il mezzogiorno normanno–svevo e le crociate*. Atti delle quattordicesi megiornate normanno–sveve Bari, 17–20 ottobre 2000 a cura di Giosuè Musca (Bari, Centro di studi normanno–svevi Università degli Studi di Bari—Mario Gallina, 2002), 65–94. 85; Jonathan Harris, *Byzantium and the Crusades*, (London: Continuum, 2006), 75–76.

[45] Asbridge, *Principality of Antioch*, 47–53.

and spent three years in prison.⁴⁶ His release was secured by the payment of a huge ransom in May 1103.⁴⁷ Bohemond immediately sought revenge and engaged in a war on two fronts: against the Dānishmands and against the Byzantines, whom he blamed for his captivity. Alexios offered a huge prize for Bohemond's head and asked Malik Ghāzī "to deliver him to his power as he wished him to die so that he could no longer harm" his realm.⁴⁸ Byzantine aggressions against Norman possessions in Syria continued as the Armenians of Cilicia rebelled against their Latin masters,⁴⁹ and Bohemond found his principality hard-pressed by the Byzantines: their navy patrolled Cyprus and the Cilician ports, and south of Antioch, supported Raymond of St. Gilles.⁵⁰ During the Norman campaign against the Seljuqs, the Byzantines gained firm control over Cilicia,⁵¹ and in May 1104 Bohemond suffered a disastrous defeat at the hands of the Seljuqs at Harran (Sultantepe, Turkey);he left Antioch to Tancred and sailed for Italy early that winter.⁵²

---

46 Fulcher of Chartres, *A history of the expedition to Jerusalem, 1095–1127*, transl. Frances Rita Ryan, ed. Harold S. Fink (Knoxville: University of Tennessee Press, 1969) (hereafter Fulcher) Lib. I. XXV. 1–2. pp. 134–35; [Albert of Aachen/Aix] *Historia Ierosolimitana: history of the journey to Jerusalem*, ed. and transl. Susan B. Edgington (Oxford: Clarendon Press, 2007), Lib. II. 27. p. 525 (hereafter Albert of Aachen); Ibn al-Athīr, *Chronicle for the crusading period from al–Kāmil fi'l–ta'rīkh*, transl. D.S. Richards (Aldershot: Ashgate, 2006–7), 32; *Armenia and the Crusades: tenth to twelfth centuries: the Chronicle of Matthew of Edessa*, transl. A. E. Dostourian (London: University Press of America, 1993), (hereafter Matthew of Edessa) Lib. II. 134. pp. 177–78.

47 Guibert de Nogent, *The deeds of God through the Franks*, transl. and ed. Robert Levine (Woodbridge: Boydell, 1997), Lib. VII. p. 159; Fulcher, Lib. II. XXIII. p. 175; Ibn-al Athīr, 60; Matthew of Edessa, Lib. III. 14. p. 191; Asbridge, *Principality of Antioch*, 31.

48 Albert of Aachen, Lib. IX. 34. p. 681; [Ordericus Vitalis] *The ecclesiastical history of Orderic Vitalis*, ed. and transl. Marjorie Chibnall (Oxford: Clarendon Press, 1983) vol. 5, Lib. X. 354–56; Giuseppe Morea, *Marco Boemondo d'Altavilla*, (Canosa: Centro di servizio e programmazione cultura le regionale, 1986), 81; Ralph-Johannes Lilie, *Byzantium and the Crusader States*, trans. J. C. Morris, J. E. Ridings (Oxford: Clarendon, 1994), 71.

49 Radulph of Caen / Radulfo Cadomensi, *Gesta Tancredi in expeditione Hierosolymitana*, in Recueil des historiens des Croisades (hereafter RHC), Historiens occidentaux, par les soins de l'Académie royale des inscriptions et belles-lettres, (Paris: Imprimerie nationale, 1844–95) (hereafter RHC Occ.) vol. 3, 587–716. Lib. CLI. 712; Asbridge, *Principality of Antioch*, 32.

50 Theotokis, "Bohemond," 72; R. B. Yewdale, *Bohemond I, Prince of Antioch*, (Princeton, Princeton University, 1924), 102–105; Harold S. Fink, "The Foundation of the Latin States, 1099–1118," in *History of the Crusades, The first hundred years*, gen. ed. Kenneth Meyer Setton, ed. M. W. Baldwin (Madison: University of Wisconsin Press, 1969), 368–409. 390.

51 Ibn-al Athīr, 79; Asbridge, *Principality of Antioch*, 56; Raoul Manselli, "Normanni d'Italia alla prima crociata, Boemondo d'Altavilla," (The Normans of Italy in the First Crusade. Bohemond) *Japigia* 11 (1940): 45–79; 154–184. 177.

52 Fulcher, Lib. II. XXVI. 1–2. p. 177, lib. II. XXVII. 1. p. 177; Radulph of Caen, Lib. CLIII. 713; Matthew of Edessa, Lib. III. 18. pp. 192–93; Asbridge, *Principality of Antioch*, 32.

Landing in Bari in January1105, Bohemond set out to organize a new crusade[53] and started to build a fleet.[54]

In a letter to Pope Paschal II, Bohemond levelled charges against Byzantium[55] and at the start, Paschal encouraged support for Bohemond's "just" war,[56] giving him "the banner of St. Peter."[57] The pope held the Byzantine emperor responsible for the failure of the Crusade in 1101.[58] Bohemond's call aroused enthusiasm[59] in France: "a countless host of Franks and Germans," almost "the whole of the West," joined his banner[60] and he "gathered enormous forces from every county and city," "going round to all the villages decrying the Emperor."[61] Bohemond allied with the Capetians by marrying Constance, daughter of King Philip I, while his brother Tancred married another of Philip's daughters.[62] Bohemond invented the "recruiting tour" for the Crusades, circulating his pro-Norman propaganda throughout Western courts. Even Ekkehard of Aura bought into this, writing that Alexios had assaulted pilgrims.[63]

---

[53] Yewdale, *Bohemond*, 100–10.

[54] Dieter Girgensohn, "Boemondo I," in *Dizionario Biografico degli Italiani*, vol. 11, (1969) [http://www.treccani.it/enciclopedia/boemondo-i_%28Dizionario-Biografico%29/—10 Aug 2017]

[55] Harris, *Byzantium and the Crusades*, 88; Flori, Jean. "Bohémond, croisé modele." in *"Come l'orco della fiaba,"* studi per Franco Cardini, a cura di Marina Montesano (Firenze: SISMEL—del Galluzzo, 2010), 123–32. 131.

[56] Michael Angold, *The Byzantine Empire, 1025–1204*, (London: Longman, 1997), 144.

[57] "... signiferum Christi exercitus eum constitit, vexillumque sancti Petri ei tradens": Bartolf of Nangis, *Gesta Francorum expugnantium Iherusalem*, in RHC Occ. vol. 3, 487–543 (hereafter Bartolf of Nangis) Lib. LXV. 538.

[58] Theotokis, *Norman Campaigns*, 201.

[59] *Narratio Floriacensis de captis Antiochia et Hierosolyma*, RHC Occ. V. 356–63. 361; Lilie, *Byzantium and the Crusader States*, 72–75; Asbridge, *Principality of Antioch*, 94.

[60] AK XII 1, 2, p. 359.; tr. Sewter, 369; AK XII 9, 2, p. 381–82; tr. Sewter, 392; Fulcher, Lib. II. XXIX. 1. p. 181; "." .innumerabilem tam equitum quam peditum multitudinem ab eiseduxit, et non solum de Galliis, verum et de toto Occidente": *Narratio Floriacensis*, 361; William of Malmesbury, *Gesta regum Anglorum*, ed. and transl. R.A.B. Mynors (Oxford: Clarendon Press, 1998), vol. 1, Lib. IV. 387. p. 693; Anonymous of Bari, 155; Luigi Russo, "Il viaggio di Boemondo d'Altavilla in Francia (1106), un riesame," (Bohemond's journey in France, a review) *Archivio Storico Italiano* 163 (2005): 3–42.

[61] AK XII 1, 2, p. 359.; tr.Sewter, 369.

[62] [Romuald of Salerno] *Romoaldi II archiepiscopi Salernitani annales*, ed. Wilhelm Arndt, MGH SS vol. 19, Annales aevi Suevici, (Hannover–Stuttgart: Hahn, 1866), 387–461. 414; Bernard von Kugler, *Bohemund und Tancred, Fürsten von Antiochien*, (Tübingen: Fues, 1862), 28; Harris, *Byzantium and the Crusades*, 88; Hiestand, *Boemondo*, 68, 85; Jean Flori, *Bohémond d'Antioch: Chevalier d'aventure*, (Paris : Payot, 2007), 7–10.

[63] Ekkehard, 220–221; Gerhard Rösch, "Der «Kreuzzug» Bohemunds gegen Dyrrachion 1107/1108 in der lateinischen Tradition des 12. Jahrhunderts," *Römische Historische Mitteilungen* 26 (1984): 181–

Did Bohemond of Antioch actively seek to make war on Byzantium?[64] Did Pope Paschal II and those who took the cross in France know that the expedition was to be diverted? Did the Normans act in collusion with the papacy, an ally of Hungary? If Bohemond acted without papal sanction, Coloman was entitled to take steps against him. Bohemond sought allies against the Byzantine Emperor[65] and recruited troops for an invasion of Byzantium,[66] although nowhere was it officially stated that they would occupy Constantinople.[67] Was Paschal II aware of these Norman designs to depose Alexios?[68] It is hard to believe that the pope was unaware of Bohemond's plans or that he was powerless to restrain him. The political climate in Rome was ripe for an attack on Byzantium.[69] Alexios had to prepare for the worst,[70] particularly when Bohemond embraced the cause of a pretender to the throne, a supposed son of the deposed Emperor Romanos IV Diogenes (1068–71).[71] The troubles in Antioch and Cilicia gave Bohemond a pretext to go against the "tyrant" and "replace him" on the throne.[72] Thus, he promised "wealthy towns and castles"[73] to all who bore arms against the Emperor, envisioning the establishment of crusader

---

190. 184–89; Brett Edward Whalen, "God's Will or Not? Bohemond's Campaign Against the Byzantine Empire (1105–1108)," in *Crusades. Medieval worlds in conflict*, ed. Thomas F. Madden, James L. Naus, Vincent Ryan (Farnham: Ashgate, 2010), 111–126. 115; Luigi Russo, "*Convergenze e scontri, per une riconsiderazione dei rapporti greco-normanni nei secoli XI–XII*," (Convergences and clashes, for a reconsideration of Greek-Norman relations in the 11th–12th centuries), in *Fedi a confronto, ebrei, cristiani e musulmani fra X e XIII secolo*, atti del convegno di studi, San Vivaldo, Montaione, 22–24 settembre 2004, a cura di Sergio Gensini (Firenze: Montaione, Polistampa, 2006), 263–278. 276.

[64] J. G. Rowe, "Paschal II, Bohemund of Antioch and the Byzantine Empire," *Bulletin of the John Rylands Library* 49 (1966–67): 165–202. 176–80.

[65] "... maxime ab imperatore Constantinopolitano infestatus ... sibi adjutoria quaereret": Bartolf of Nangis, Lib. LXV. 538.

[66] *Historia Belli Sacri*, RHC Occ. vol. 3, 169–229. 228–29; Anonymous of Bari, 155; Albert of Aachen, Lib. IX. 47. p. 702.

[67] Chalandon, *Essai*, 242.

[68] Whalen, "God's Will," 112, 117; Flori, *Bohémond*, 275–77, Yewdale, *Bohemond*, 112–14.

[69] Yewdale found it a "real" crusade with "official" papal sanction. Yewdale, *Bohemond*, 115. See Whalen, "God's Will," esp. 113–17; W. B. McQueen, "Relations between the Normans and Byzantium, 1071–1112," *Byzantion* 56 (1986): 427–69. 462.

[70] Gyula Moravcsik, "Les Relations entre le Hongrie et Byzance à l'époque de croisades," *Revue des Études Hongroises* 8–11 (1933): 301–308. 315; György Székely, "Ungarns Stellung zwischen Kaiser, Papst und Byzanz zur Zeit der Kluniazenserreform," in *Spiritualità cluniacense*. Centro di studi sulla spiritualità medievale, Convegni 2. 12–15 ottobre 1958, (Todi: Accademia Tudertina, 1960), 312–325. 324.

[71] Ordericus Vitalis, vol. 6, Lib. XI. 70; Theotokis, *Norman Campaigns*, 201; Fink, "Foundation," 391.

[72] "contra tyrannum": Ekkehard, 230; Theotokis, *Norman Campaigns*, 200; Whalen, "God's Will," 116.

[73] "... omne armatos secum in imperatorem ascendere commonuit, ac approbatis optionibus urbes et oppida ditissima promisit": Ordericus Vitalis, vol. 6, Lib. XI. 69; Whalen, "God's Will," 118.

kingdoms in Byzantium.[74] The evidence suggests that his army set sail with the intention of overthrowing Alexios and "invading Constantinople."[75]

The sheer scale of Bohemond's enterprise struck terror in Byzantium and forced Alexios to seek allies, including Coloman, since a two-pronged attack was in the air. Allying with his former captor, the Dānishmand ruler now intent on a joint campaign against the Seljuq Sultanate of Rum and Byzantium,[76] Bohemond looked to gain imperial territory: "once we are allied we shall easily ... subdue to our power the lands of the Empire." Alexios was desperate to find allies,[77] and warned Pisa, Genoa and Venice against "being seduced by his [Bohemond's] false words."[78] He was particularly afraid of co-operation between Bohemond and Pisa, remembering that in 1099 the Pisan navy had joined the Normans in devastating Corfu.[79] Such an alliance would also have damaged Coloman's interests, and would have justified an expedition into the Adriatic; and the fact that Bohemond's army included Pisans and Genoese helps explain Venice's counter-action.[80] By 1105, Alexios was isolated and sent an embassy to Fatimid Egypt[81] "to hinder Bohemond from his reputed desire of crossing from Italy." He ordered the commanders of the Western imperial army to gather at Sthlanitza,[82] and considerable forces were recalled from Cilicia and Syria.[83]

---

[74] McQueen, "Relations," 470; Alexēs G. K. Savvidēs, *Byzantino–Normannica. The Norman Capture of Italy and the First Two Norman Invasions in Byzantium*, (Leuven: Uitgeverij Peeters en Departement Oosterse Studies, 2007), 71.

[75] "Boiamundus dux Apuliae contracto unde exercitu, accingitur ad invadendum Constantinopolitanum imperium": [Siegebert of Gembloux] Sigeberti Gemblacensis *Chronica cum continuationibus*, ed. D. L. Bethmann, MGH SS vol. 6, (Chronica et annales aevi Salici) (Hannover: Hahn, 1844), 268–474. 372; George Beech, "A Norman–Italian adventurer in the East, Richard of Salerno 1097–1112," in *Anglo–Norman Studies 15. Proceedings of the Battle Conference 1992 and of the XI Colloquio Medievale of the Officina Di Studi Medievali*, ed. Marjorie Chibnall (Woodbridge: Boydell, 1993), 25–40. 36.

[76] Albert of Aachen, IX. 35. p. 683.

[77] "... foederati uero utrimque ... expugnabimus terram Romanie ... et subiugabimus ... imperatoris regnum et terras": Albert of Aachen, Lib. IX. 35. p. 685; Anton Jenal, "Der Kampf um Durazzo, 1107–1108, mit dem Gedicht des Tortarius," *Historisches Jahrbuch* (der Görres-Gesellschaft) 37 (1916): 285–352. 297; Chalandon, *Essai*, 234–36.

[78] AK XII 1, 2, p. 359; transl. Sewter, 368.

[79] Fink, "Foundation," 374.

[80] Yewdale, *Bohemond*, 116.

[81] Dölger, *Regesten*, no. 1220–1221; AK XII 1, 3, p. 360; transl. Sewter, 369; Ekkehard, 230.

[82] Dölger, *Regesten*, no. 1224; AK XII 3, 1, p. 364; transl. Sewter, 374; Luigi Russo, "L'espansione normanna contro Bisanzio (secoli XI–XII)," (The Norman expansion against Byzantium, 11th-12th centuries) in *Scritti offerti a Mario Troso*, a cura di G. Mastrominico (Ariano Irpino: Centro Europeo di Studi Normanni, 2012), 206–30. 212.

[83] Theotokis, *Norman Campaigns*, 203.

The siege of Dyrrachium: A Hungarian campaign in Apulia?

Bohemond crossed to Avlona/Aulon (Vlorë, Albania) in October 1107 and laid siege to Dyrrachium.[84] The earliest source is the late thirteenth-century Hungarian chronicler Simon of Kéza, who records that Coloman hired Venetian galleys, sailboats, and cargo vessels to ferry an army across to Apulia. Having secured the cities of Monopoli and Brindisi for a faction of their citizens loyal to Venice, they ceded them to the Venetians. The Hungarian army then raided Apulia (Puglia) for three months before crossing back to Dalmatia, leaving behind a Hungarian captain and the banner of the kingdom of Hungary with the Venetians.[85] The story of the Hungarian campaign in Apulia is repeated by mid-fourteenth century Italian chroniclers such as Paolino da Venezia,[86] who knew and drew upon Simon of Kéza's *gesta*. Paolino does not mention that the ships were Venetian, however, or that Monopoli and Brindisi were left under the control of citizens loyal to Venice; he does record the Hungarian captain, but not the banner. The mid-fourteenth century chronicler Andrea Dandolo also borrowed the story, probably through Paolino, with minor modifications. Dandolo emphasizes that Hungary made a pact with the Republic to inflict damage on the Normans, and states that Coloman not only hired ships but set sail himself with his fleet.[87] The story is also incorporated in a fourteenth-century Hungarian chronicle: Coloman hired the ships at a high price and invaded Apulia with a formidable army; but no mention is made of a pact between Venice and Hungary, nor of any banner or Hungarian captain, and the author points

---

[84] Pauler, "Horvát-Dalmátország," 324.

[85] "... galeas, naves et territas cum Venetis solidavit, mittens cum eis exercitum Hungarorum in Apuliam, ubi Monopolim et Brundusium civitates ocuparunt civibus quibusdam fidem Venetis observantibus. Cumque easdem civitates ad tenendum Venetis reliquissent, concitatis ursibus planum Apuliae in quibusdam locis devastantes, tribus mensibus in ea permansere. Tandemque ad naves redeuntes per mare in Dalmatiam revertuntur capitaneo Hungaro et regis Hungariae banerio ibidem cum Venetis derelictis." Simonis de Kéza, *Gesta Hungarorum. The Deeds of the Hungarians*, ed. F. Schaer, L. Veszprémy. (Budapest: CEU Press, 1999), (hereafter Simonis de Kéza)cap. 64.

[86] Paulus Venetus (Paolino da Venezia / Paolino Minorita), *Historia Satyrica* [(Speculum sive) Satyrica rerum gestarum mundi historia] in *Antiquitates Italicae medii aevi*,ed. L. A. Muratori, vols 1-6, (Mediolanum: Societas Palatina, 1738–1742), vol. 4. 951–1034. 969. Also see Tamás Körmendi, *Az Imre, III. László és II. András magyar királyok uralkodására vonatkozó nyugati elbeszélő források kritikája* (A criticism of Western sources for the reigns of Imre, Ladislaus III and Andrew II) PhD–dissertation, (Budapest: ELTE, 2008), 178; László Veszprémy, in Simon of Kéza: *Deeds*, 141. n. 2.

[87] "Colomannus rex misit exercitum in Dalmatiam ... cum Venetorum foedus iniit contra Normannos et pariter exercitum in Apuliam ad eorum dam[p]na mittere statuit. Parata autem classe per Venetos, regius apparatus in Apuliam navigans, Brundusium et Monopolim obtinet, et tribus mensibus Apuliam vastant et redeunt." Andrea Dandolo, *Chronicon Venetum*, RIS (Mediolanum: Sociates Palatina, 1728) vol. 12, 1–525. 259.

out that the cities were only left in usufruct and *not* under the full control of Venice.[88] Drawing on Simon of Kéza, the late fourteenth century Lorenzo de Monacis's *Chronicon de rebus venetis* states that the Hungarians sent a fleet with the Venetians, referring to an alliance, but does not say whether Coloman hired the ships.[89]

A campaign to Apulia appears in Hungarian chroniclers from the fifteenth century onwards and its authenticity has been accepted by most scholars.[90] The first to raise doubts was Jenő Szűcs,[91] although he accepted that the core of the story might have been authentic. He suggests that a campaign in 1108 fed the fiction and that, if not an exceptional naval campaign, the Hungarian expedition was a pro-Byzantine move made in alliance with the Venetians. László Veszprémy argues that "it is not out of the question that such a campaign took place" in Apulia.[92] Indeed, there are reasons to believe that the Hungarian army could have taken part in such an anti-Norman, pro-Byzantine military action. In twelfth-century Hungarian military history, a major campaign to Apulia sounds astonishing. The financial means and the military might of the country did not allow for such a long and exhaustive naval campaign. It was one thing to conquer and control Dalmatia, but quite another to organize expedition hundreds of miles away on foreign territory. However, it is conceivable that a small Hungarian contingent was sent by Coloman to Apulia in the context of cooperation between the Venetians and the Byzantines to defend Dalmatia. To prevent the Normans from taking land bases on the Dalmatian coastline, some troops might have taken part in the naval protection of the cities, most probably transported by Venetian galleys hired by the king. Coloman's preparations for these Dalmatian operations were careful.[93] The

---

[88] "Galeas quoque Venetorum et naves solidans et allocans pecunia maxima exercitum copiosum in Apuliam destinavit. Qui Apulia spoliata per tres menses permanserunt in ea. Ubi etiam Monopolim et Brundusium civitates expugnantes. Venetis ad tenendum pro utilitate regis Colomanni reliquerunt. Ipsi autem in Hungariam ab inde sunt reversi." *Chronici Hungarici compositio saeculi XIV.* in SRH cap. 152. vol. 2, 433.

[89] "Calomanus Rex . . . Venetique contra Normannos confederantur ad invicem. Rex mittit cum Veneta classe exercitum contra eos in Apuliam, capiuntque Monopolim, et Brundusiu, et dum captas civitates Veneti custodirent, Ungari decurrunt hostiliter totam Apuliam, et post damna illata Apulis per tres menses, redicto in dictis terris captis cum venetis Capitaneo Ungaro redeunt in Pannoniam." Monacis, 93.

[90] Pauler, *A magyar nemzet története*, vol. 1, 271; Makk, "Megjegyzések," 29; Kristó, *Árpád-kor*, 72; Kapitánffy, *Hungarobyzantina*, 167; Kronológia, vol. 1, 100; KMTL, 315.

[91] Jenő Szűcs, "Társadalomelmélet, politikai teória és történetszemlélet Kézai Simon Gesta Hungarorumában," (Social and political theory, historical view in Kézai's Gesta) Part 2, *Századok* 107/4 (1973): 823–878. 838, 860.

[92] Veszprémy, in Simon of Kéza, *Deeds*, 141. n. 2.

[93] Ludwig Steindorff, *Die dalmatinischen Städte im 12. Jahrhundert. Studien zu ihrer politischen Stellung und Gesellschaftlichen Entwicklung*, (Köln: Böhlau, 1984), 49–50.

Hungarian military was certainly able to raise a fleet. For example, during the conquest of the Dalmatian islands in 1105, a fleet set sail commanded by Ban Ugra, charged with subduing the peoples of the Gulf of Quarnero (Kvarner).[94] As we have seen, Coloman was in Trau on May 25, 1108, when he issued a charter of privileges for the city.[95] We know nothing of his itinerary earlier that year, apart from the fact that he was present at the consecration of the church in Dömös the very beginning of 1108. He may even have travelled to Dalmatia immediately after the consecration and remained there until the end of May, since the Normans were then threatening to extend their military activities beyond the Albanian coast and into the Southern Dalmatian territories. Venetian galleys, possibly carrying Hungarian troops, may have been patrolling the Dalmatian coastline in the late winter and early spring of 1108, and Coloman may even have decided to supervise the defence in person.

Few contemporary sources mention military activity in Southern Italy connected with Bohemond's Dyrrachium campaign of 1107–1108. There is no hint whatsoever of such activity in Radulphus Tortarius's work describing the siege of Durazzo,[96] and only a solitary mention in the Anonymous of Bari. Indeed, the main twelfth-century chronicler of Sicily, Romuald of Salerno, does not even mention Bohemond's campaign,[97] although he justifies a Venetian blockade during the winter of 1107–1108: following a request in the autumn from Alexios for naval aid,[98] the Venetian navy, led by Ordelaffo Falier, were stationed between the crossing points of Apulia and Illyricum.[99] The *Annales Venetici breves* reports that the doge set sail in December 1107.[100]

In light of the acute military situation in the Adriatic, Alexios made preparations to raise his own fleet "from the coastal cities of Asia and even Europe."[101]

---

[94] Stephenson, *Byzantium's Balkan Frontier*, 199. For the seizure of Arbe/Rab and other islands 13 ships were made ready: "Sint ergo ad praedicta perficienda aptae tredecim naves, quatenus transeuntes per mare in insulam intrare, et civitatem capere valeamus": *Historia s. Christophori Martyris* in *Enchiridion Fontium Historiae Croatiae*, ed. Ferdinand Šišić (Zagreb: Zemaljske Vlade, 1914), 623. It is interesting though that Thomas Archdeacon of Spalato/Split does not mention any detail about maritime warfare.

[95] DHA vol. 1, 357; RA vol. 1, 41; Györffy, "A XII. századi," 49.

[96] Radulphus Tortarius, *Poema de obsidione Dyrrachii*, Cod. Vat. Reg, 1357. in *Rodulfi Tortarii carmina*, ed. Marbury B. Ogle, Dorothy M. Schullian (Rome: American Academy, 1933)

[97] Romuald of Salerno, 414.

[98] Dölger, *Regesten*, no. 1238.

[99] Dölger, *Regesten*, no. 1238.

[100] *Annales Venetici Breves*, ed. Henry Simonsfeld, MGH SS vol. 14, [Supplementatomorum I–XII, pars II. Supplementum tomi XIII] (Hanover: Hahn, 1883), 69–72. 70.

[101] ἅμα δὲ κἀκ τῶν Κυκλάδων νήσων καὶ τῶν παραθαλάσσαν τῆς Ἀσίας πόλεων καὶ αὐτῆς τῆς Εὐρώπης στόλον παρεκελεύσατο ἀπαρτίσαι [At the same time he ordered the Cyclades, and all the maritime towns of Asia and even of Europe, to get a fleet ready]: AK XII 4, 3, p. 369; transl. Sewter, 379.

The Venetians were unable to control the whole of the Adriatic by themselves,[102] and all of Byzantium's forces were needed to cut Bohemond off from his reinforcements. Anna Komnene's reference to "the coastal cities of Europe" may well have included those beyond the borders of Illyricum, stretching up to Dalmatia, and thus raising the possibility of Hungarian participation. Since Illyricum's harbors were now under Greek and Venetian protection, the Norman fleet had to find alternative ports; and since they were also making preparation for warfare inland, Dalmatia could have been regarded as a secondary anchor base. Bohemond's dream was to seize the whole of the Adriatic coast:[103] the *Alexiad* confirms that he intended "to reoccupy Illyricum,"[104] and that the crusader army spread "along the whole Adriatic coastline," which may well have included Dalmatia.[105]

A Byzantine fleet under Isaac Kontostephanos was sent to Dyrrachium "to watch over the straits and to allow nothing whatever to be transported [over]."[106] However, the captain "exceeded his brief" and proceeded to Otranto, where he attacked the city walls; although he was defeated, we might see glimmerings here of an Apulian intervention.[107] The Byzantine forces were certainly prepared for inland warfare, since they included Pechenegs.[108] And Kontostephanos's failure could further help explain Hungaro-Venetian involvement in the Adriatic.

Naval engagements between the Normans and Byzantines lasted until Easter 1108,[109] with our Hungaro-Venetian campaign perhaps taking place that summer. Savvidēs states that the patrols were "regular,"[110] while others note a united Byzantino-Venetian blockade that lasted until September, whereupon the two fleets could resume control of the Adriatic.[111] Bohemond ordered all his ships to be burned, leaving nothing for the Venetians to capture. Venice patrolled the region

---

[102] Angold, *Byzantine Empire*, 251.
[103] Harris, *Byzantium and the Crusades*, 78.
[104] AK XII 1, 1, p. 359; transl. Sewter, 369.
[105] τούτουςγὰρ ἅπαντας συλλεξάμενος‹ἐπὶ› πάσηςτῆςἐντὸς Ἀδρίουὐφήπλωσε γῆςκαὶ τὰἐφεξῆς ἅπαντα λησάμενοςτῇ Ἐπιδάμνῳ προσέβαλεν [Next he dispersed all these troops which he had mustered over the whole country along the Adriatic sea and after ravaging that systematically he attacked Epidamnus]: AK XII 9, 2, p. 382; transl. Sewter, 392.
[106] AK XII 8, 2, p. 378.; transl. Sewter, 388.
[107] Russo, "L'espansione," 212; Yewdale, *Bohemond*, 112–13.
[108] Yewdale, *Bohemond*, 113.
[109] 5 April 1108: *Narratio Floriacensis*, 361. n. f.
[110] Savvidēs, *Byzantino-Normannica*, 77.
[111] Lilie, *Byzantium and the Crusader States*, 75; Russo, "L'espasione," 214; Yewdale, *Bohemond*, 118; Matthew Bennett, "Norman Naval Activity in the Mediterranean c.1060–c.1108." in *Anglo–Norman Studies 15*, 41–58. 56.

for a whole year,[112] while the reorganized Byzantine fleet controlled a wider area than before, leaving Bohemond vulnerable to attack from the sea.[113] Some form of Veneto-Hungarian resistance in the Adriatic might have halted the Normans.[114] The Byzantine fleet came to the assistance of Dyrrachium "with great abundance of food."[115] But since the Byzantines now controlled the sea, Bohemond—unable to "keep open his maritime communications"—was defeated.[116]

Nonetheless, the Byzantines had suffered enormous losses on land and there was an increasing need to recruit fresh forces and to bring new warships to the Adriatic.[117] The situation reached deadlock: it seemed that the Normans would never give up. However, short of food and riddled with disease, their army began to desert.[118] With some success, the Byzantines even tried bribing prominent commanders to switch sides.[119] Lacking supplies and facing epidemics, the Hauteville kinsmen withdrew their support to defend their Italian possessions, and Bohemond finally sued for peace in face of the Byzantine blockade.[120] Seeing Bohemond's failure, Paschal II withdrew support.

Regardless of whether Hungarian forces campaigned in Apulia, they may well have been engaged in defending Dalmatia as part of the Veneto-Byzantine military alliance against Bohemond. In the Otranto campaign, the target was those parts of Apulia under Bohemond's rule. Yet the dispatch of a Hungarian military force to Southern Italy is not unimaginable. Our sources show that Hungarian troops were fighting in Byzantine service in Calabria in the 1050s, where a substantial force (*tagma*) was headed by Hungarian leaders (*domestikos* and *spatharokandidatos*). Such distant military postings were was not unheard of. In the late eleventh century,

---

[112] Yewdale, *Bohemond*, 118; Morea, *Marco Boemondo*, 90; Michael Matzke, "Boemondo e Daiberto di Pisa," in *Boemondo, storia di un principenormanno*, atti del Convegno di Studio su Boemondo, ed. Nunzio Lozito, Benedetto Vetero, Franco Cardini (Lecce: Gelatina, 2003), 95–106. 105; Russo, "L'espansione," 217.

[113] AK XIII 6, 4, p. 401; transl. Sewter, 412; Dölger, *Regesten*, no. 1241; Chalandon, *Essai*, 245.

[114] Stephenson, *Byzantium's Balkan Frontier*, 182.

[115] Albert of Aachen, Lib. X. 45. p. 759.

[116] Ordericus Vitalis, vol. 6, Lib. XI. 104. n. 2; Whalen, "God's Will," 120.

[117] AK XIII 7, 1, p. 403; transl. Sewter, 413.

[118] AK XIII 4, 3–8, p. 395–97.;transl. Sewter, 406–7; Yewdale, *Bohemond*, 120; Harris, *Byzantium and the Crusades*, 78–79.

[119] Albert of Aachen, Lib. X. 445. p. 757; *Narratio Floriacensis*, 362; William of Malmesbury, I. IV. 387. p. 693; Ordericus Vitalis, vol. 6, Lib. XI. 104; Dölger, *Regesten*, no. 1239; Jenal, "Kampf um Durazzo," 307.

[120] AK XIII 8, 6, p. 407; transl. Sewter, 416.

a few Hungarian names are to be found in Calabrian property surveys.¹²¹ "Ungros" appear as a personal name in Byzantine sources, probably as a result of the presence of Hungarian soldiers in South Italy.¹²²

The Treaty of Deabolis (Devol)

Bohemond sued for peace before September 1108.¹²³ Hungary sent envoys to the negotiations that took place in Deabolis: of the 17 signatories "who were present and have signed below, before whom these things were done" two envoys represented the King of Hungary.¹²⁴ Of the twelve witnesses representing the imperial court, two were Hungarians, showing their prominent role in the peace talks. Anna Komnene lists two counts, the "zupanus" (ζουπάνος) Peres and Simon (Περής καὶ Σίμων), "who had come from Dacia from the Kral."¹²⁵ Dacia (Δακῶν) refers to Hungary, and the "Kral" denotes the king (κράλ). The κράλ is further defined as the "co-father-in-law" of the Emperor.¹²⁶ This means the father-in-law of the *basileus* John (the Emperor's son), i.e. a joint kinsman. Although it is commonly argued that this refers to Coloman, the actual ruler of the kingdom, Coloman was not John Komnenos's father-in-law: this was King Ladislaus, now dead.¹²⁷ However, Latin translations of the *Alexiad* use the term "joint" father-in-law (*consocer*).¹²⁸

---

¹²¹ Teréz Olajos, "Egy felhasználatlan forráscsoport a 11. Századi magyar–bizánci kapcsolatok történetéhez," (An uneploited group of sources for the 11ᵗʰ c. Hungarian-Byzantine contacts), *Századok* 132/1 (1998): 215–222. 218–19.

¹²² Teréz Olajos, "Felhasználatlan bizánci forrás a magyarság korai történetéhez," (An unexplored source for the early history of Hungary) *Antik Tanulmányok* 33/1 (1987–88): 24–27.

¹²³ Dölger, *Regesten*, nos. 1242–43.; Negotiations: I. N. Lioubarskij—N. M. Freidenberg, 'Devol'skij dogovor 1108 g. meždu Alekseem Komninomi Boemundom" (The treaty of Devol of 1108 between Alexios and Bohemund), *Vizantijskijvremennik* 21 (1962): 260–274.

¹²⁴ Οἵμέντοι παρουσιάσαντες μάρτυρες καὶ ὑπογεγραφότες, ὧνένανπίον ταῦτα τετέλεστο, εἰσινοῦτοι [But the witnesses who were present and have signed below, before whom these things were done, are as follows]: AK XIII 12, 28, p. 423; transl. Sewter, 434.

¹²⁵ οἱέκτῶν Δακῶνήκοντες ἀποκρισιάριοι παρατοῦκράλη καὶ συμπενθέρου τῆς βασιλείας, ζουπάνος ὁ Περὴς καὶ Σίμων [the envoys who had come from Dacia from the Cral, the Queen's relation, Zupanus Peres and Simon]: AK XIII 12, 28, p. 423; transl. Sewter, 434.

¹²⁶ συμπενθέρος

¹²⁷ ÁMTBF, 107. n. mm; *Írott források*, 334; Dölger, *Regesten*, no. 1243; Gyula Moravcsik, *Szent László leánya és a bizánci Pantokrator–monostor* (St. Ladislaus's daughter and the Pantokrator) (Konstantinápoly (Istanbul): Magyar TudományosIntézet, 1923), 7; Gyóni, "A legkorábbimagyar-bizánci," 216.

¹²⁸ "Inter ceteros legati regis Hungariae (...) qui ex Dacis venerunt apocrisiarii a Crali et consocero regiae maiestatis." Anne Comnène, *Alexiade*, RHC Historiens grecs, publ. par les soins de l'Académie des inscriptions et belles-lettres (Paris: Imprimerie nationale, 1875), vol. 1, 186; Annae Comnenae

The presence of Hungarian witnesses at the Byzantino-Norman peace talks reinforces the possibility that Coloman participated in the military conflict. The list of witnesses contains only a few Greek names, since the Byzantine armed forces included a good number of foreigners.[129] Alexios invited his allies to the peace process, including the Italians, Lombards and Apulians, as well as those Sicilian Normans and Franks who had opposed Bohemond. The Frankish and Norman names represent Byzantium's old allies, Roger Borsa and Roger II, Count of Sicily.[130] Of the twelve imperial witnesses, seven are of Western origin, and even the Byzantines on the list—Basil the Eunuch and the notary Constantine—were commissioners of Bohemond's rival, Richard the Seneschal. Nephew of Robert Guiscard and a close companion to Roger Borsa, he was appointed seneschal of Apulia and Calabria as a move against Bohemond's administrators.[131] Richard of Salerno, Bohemond's cousin, is also attested as a signatory of the peace on the Byzantine side, showing the sharp division within the Hauteville clan against Bohemond.[132] The Norman nobility ranged against Bohemond had also played a part in the conflict, partly because the war had spread into Italy. These pro-Byzantine Normans could have supported the Venetian—and possibly Hungarian—naval war effort in the region.

John Zonaras is silent on both the Byzantino-Hungarian military alliance and on Hungarian participation in the peace with Bohemond, despite being well connected to the imperial court in the 1100s and 1110s and thus, theoretically, being in a position to know. Zonaras describes the circumstances of the Hungarian marriage alliance and goes into detail about Bohemond's marshalling of many of his countrymen, taking up arms against the Romans, crossing the sea, and laying siege to Dyrrachium. He also relates how the siege dragged on, inflicting great losses on the citizens, and how eventually the Emperor proposed peace and sent envoys

---

Alexiadis, vols 1-2, (CSHB 2-3) ed. Ludwig Schopen (Bonn: Weber, 1839–1878), vol. 2, 246; Annae Comnenae *Alexias*, in Patrologia Graeca. ed. J.-P. Migne, (Paris: Imprimerie Catholique, 1864) (hereafter PG) vol. 5, 131. coll. 1026.

[129] Morea, *Marco Boemondo*, 92; Marquis de la Force, "Les conseillers latins du basileus Alexis Comnène," *Byzantion* 11 (1936) 153–65.

[130] In practice it was Adelaide del Vasto, Roger I's consort who ruled as a regent during the minority of Roger II.

[131] Alexander Kazhdan, "Latins and Franks in Byzantium, Perception and Reality from the Eleventh to the Twelfth Century," in *The Crusades from the Perspective of Byzantium and the Muslim World*, ed. Angeliki E. Laiou, Roy P. Mottahedeh (Dumbarton Oaks: Dumbarton Oaks Research Library and Collection, 2001), 83–100. 93–94.

[132] Beech, "Richard of Salerno," 37.

from Thessalonica to Bohemond.[133] The only valuable piece of information he gives is his confirmation that Bohemond also aimed to conquer "other places" and was prepared for inland warfare, which explains why Alexios needed as many allies as possible, perhaps including Hungary.

Latin sources largely ignore the peace of Devol, although they are aware of it. Fulcher of Chartres notes that Bohemond and Alexios signed a peace,[134] and Orderic Vitalis mentions it,[135] while Albert of Aachen glosses over it.[136] The *Historia belli sacri* also notes there was a treaty, without detailing its circumstances;[137] Robert the Monk briefly comments on Bohemond's oath, and discusses the conditions in somewhat greater depth;[138] and the Anonymous of Bari mentions the peace.[139]

William of Tyre states that the peace was established "through the intervention of common friends,"[140] a term which could refer to allies on both sides, with representatives probably being present. Thus, Hungary's involvement, although hypothetical, is not out of the question. The *Narratio Floriacensis* gives some information about the signatories, although it simply mentions the "xii primi" of Emperor Alexios, which agrees with the number given by Anna Komnene.[141] The *Narratio* is the only source to list Alexios's heir, John Komnenos, among those who took an oath on the Devol chrysobull.[142] Anna Komnene confirms that Bohemond agreed to become John's vassal,[143] and the latter is mentioned many times in the treaty's text,[144] possibly shedding light both on John's concerns and on his influence in imperial politics at the time.[145] This, in turn, highlights the significance of his

---

[133] πρὸςτὸν αὐτοκράτορα, συμβάσεις ζητῶν(…) καὶ τὰςσυνθήκας τῶν σπονδῶν ἐποιήσατο[asked for peace from the Emperor (…) and settled the conditions of the treaty]: Zonaras, Ἐπιτομὴ Ἱστοριῶν, vol. 3, Lib. XVIII. 25, 6, p. 750 (Pinderedn.); vol. 4, Lib. XVIII. 22, p. 248 (Dindorf edn.).

[134] Fulcher, Lib. II. XXXIX. 1. p. 93.

[135] Ordericus Vitalis, vol. 6, Lib. XI. 104–5.

[136] Albert of Aachen, Lib. X. 45. pp. 757, 759.

[137] *Historia Belli Sacri*, Lib. CXLII. 229

[138] Robert the Monk, Lib. XVIII. 99.

[139] Anonymus of Bari, 155.

[140] " … ubi communibus intervenientibus amicis … " : William of Tyre, *A History of Deeds Done Beyond the Sea*, tr. and ed. Emily Atwater Babcock, A. C. Krey (New York: Columbia University Press, 1943) (hereafter William of Tyre) Lib. X. VI. 504.

[141] "… impositis manibus ipse et xii primi suae … sacris pignoribus …": *Narratio Floriacensis*, 362.

[142] "… Joanne, filio ejus, juravit omnia …": *Narratio Floriacensis*, 362.

[143] AK XIII 12, 1–24, p. 413–20; transl. Sewter, 429.

[144] Theotokis, *Norman Campaigns*, 213. n. 76.

[145] Asbridge, *Principality of Antioch*, 95.

marriage and the Komnenian scheme of alliances. The treaty always speaks in the plural in terms of Bohemond's allegiance to the "Majesties," Alexios and John.[146]

Bohemond signed a humiliating peace agreement and he returned in "dejection to Apulia."[147] He swore allegiance as a "liege man," obliged to offer military assistance to the Emperor, and also to return Cilicia to him.[148] Antioch duly came under Byzantine overlordship.[149] Why did Bohemond capitulate? It was probably because Byzantium and its allies threatened his possessions in Apulia: an attack on Apulia could not have been left unanswered. Yet if Bohemond's homeland had been attacked by a joint Venetian-Hungarian force, surely he would have used this as propaganda, pressing chroniclers to record such an offensive against Apulia. Nevertheless, this assumption is even more hypothetical since by 1108–09, Bohemond got weaker and was probably not able to control chronicle-writing about him.

I would suggest that there are hints in the poem by Theodore Prodromos, written in 1122, of the role played by the kingdom of Hungary in the making of the treaty of Devol, through its allusion to Piroska-Eirene. It is "You [Empress Eirene] who receive gifts from the Calabrians": it is to Piroska that the recently-defeated Normans of Calabria offer their obeisance and it is no accident that we have mention of the Normans coming to fear Byzantium's power.[150] By implication, Byzantium was grateful to the Hungarians for their help in the war against the Normans and for the support which Piroska-Eirene's marriage provided against the threat from the Norman dukes of Sicily and Calabria.

---

[146] For the importance of John II in the later years of Alexios's reign, and Alexios's trust in him, see Stanković, "John II Komnenos," 14–18.

[147] "... animo deiectus Apuliam rediit ...": William of Malmesbury, vol. 1, Lib. IV. 387. p. 693.

[148] ἄνθρωπος λίζιος, or, ἄνθρωποςπιστὸς : AK XIII 12, 1-2, p. 415;

[149] Angold, *Byzantine Empire*, 156; Harris, *Byzantium and the Crusades*, 79; Lilie, *Byzantium and the Crusader States*, 76–77; Asbridge, *Principality of Antioch*, 94–95.

[150] Λαμβάρδοι καὶ Καλάβροὶ (...) // καὶ πῦρ αἰτναῖον Σικελῶν, φρίσσειτἠνἐσουξσίαν. // καὶ Τυρρηνίον κορυφαί [Lombards and Calabrians (...) Sicilians' fire of the Aetna shudder from your power, and the tops of the Tyrrhenians]: Στίκοι εἰς τὴν στεφηφορίαν Ἀλεξίουτοῦ Κομνηνοῦ : Theodoros Prodromos, *Historische Gedichte*, ed. Wolfram Hörandner. Wiener byzantinistische Studien, 11 (Wien: Verlag der Österreichischen Akademie der Wissenschaften, 1974) I. 177–181. 180.; *Theodori Prodromi versus in coronationem Alexii Comneni*, in Theodorus Prodromus, *Scripta Miscellanea*, PG vol. 133, coll. 1340–42; ÁMTBF, 171. See Nikolaos Zagklas, "Θεόδωρος Πρόδρομος: ἐναλόγιοςποιητήςτου 12ου αἰώνα. Theodóros Prodromos: poeta doctus 12. století," in *Neograeca Bohemica*, Přednášky České společnosti novořeckých studií. Διαλέξεις της Τσεχικής Εταιρείας Νεοελληνικών Σπουδών, 11. (Brno: Akademie věd ČR, 2011) 31–56.

Byzantium and Venice in the 1110s

In the early 1110s, Venice sought to expand its control over Dalmatia with Byzantine support.[151] Although the emperor did not object, neither did he give his backing and the Venetian war against Hungary had to be postponed.[152] Alexios sought to maintain good relations with the Árpáds, partly because he now had ambitions to unite the Roman and Greek Churches and even to become Holy Roman Emperor himself.[153] His ambitions were fed by Pope Paschal II's *rapprochement* with Byzantium, but in the midst of his struggle with Emperor Henry V, Paschal was captured by the German ruler.[154]

Piroska-Eirene: the German Imperial Line

Piroska-Eirene's German imperial descent was a trump card in Alexios's policy in 1111–12.[155] As granddaughter of Rudolf of Rheinfelden, Duke of Swabia and briefly King of Germany, and of Adelaide of Savoy, Piroska-Eirene was the offspring of German emperors, and on her father's side she was related to the Liudolfing (Ottonian) dynasty.

Byzantine diplomacy vigorously highlighted Piroska's noble, even imperial, ancestry.[156] Although writing somewhat later, Theodore Prodromos clearly alludes to Alexios's rivalry with Emperor Henry V, and the *Vita Eirenae* glorifies its subject as "born of blessed parents, Western emperors": the term "blessed" could refer both to King Saint Stephen of Hungary and the Blessed Richeza of Lotharingia.[157] Prodromos praises Eirene as "the lady of all Western nations," to whom she is "related" through both the maternal and the paternal line. "Descended of the King of the Rhine," she is "feared by the Alemanni"—a clear reference to Rudolph of Rhein-

---

[151] Makk, *Comneni*, 16.
[152] Kapitánffy, *Hungarobyzantina*, 79. 88; Makk, "Megjegyzések," 29.
[153] Makk, *Comneni*, 16, 129. n. 99; Whalen, "God's Will," 117.
[154] Angold, *Byzantine Empire*, 145; Harris, *Byzantium and the Crusades*, 91; Chalandon, *Essai*, 260–63.
[155] Kerbl, *Byzantinische Prinzessinen*, Tab. XI.
[156] Barbara Hill, *Imperial women in Byzantium, 1025–1204. Power, patronage, and ideology*, (London: Longman, 1999), 35, 94.
[157] Αὕτη ἡ ἐν βασιλίσσαις ἀοίδιμος γεννητόρωνμέν, προῆλθεν εὐτυχῶν δυσμικῶν μέν βασιλέον [This illustrious empress was born of blessed parents, Western emperors]: *Vita beatae imperatricis Irenes / Vita Irenae*, in ÁMTBF, 115.; Hippolyte Delehaye, *Synaxarium ecclesiae Constantinopolitanaee codice Sirmondiano nunc Berolinensi*, Propylaeum ad Acta Sanctorum Novembris, (Bruxelles: Société des Bollandistes, 1902) 887–890. 887.

felden—and it is within her power to bring to heel the "Lombards and Germans," another reference to Rudolph's rule over Germany in opposition to Henry IV.[158] Prodromos's epitaph on Eirene commemorates an Empress "descended from blessed ancestors, the rulers of the whole western world" and who was "raised by Julius Caesar."[159]

Piroska's marriage was not simply a matrimonial tie in confirmation of a Byzantino-Hungarian alliance, but a major political event with vital diplomatic concerns in the background. The Byzantino-Hungarian alliance strengthened Hungary's position in relation to the Holy Roman Empire. Byzantium, Venice and Hungary had opposing interests in Dalmatia and yet for a short period, cooperation was possible. The fact that Coloman's queen was Norman did not threaten Venice, nor did it entail a pro-Norman policy in Hungary. Coloman's ties with Count Roger of Sicily made him Bohemond's enemy.

This paper has examined the political background of what seems to have been some sort of Hungarian military participation in the war between Bohemond and the Byzantines. Whatever precise form this military action in Apulia may have taken, it must be seen within the framework of the marriage-tie between the Árpáds and the Komnenoi. But even without launching an Apulian campaign, Coloman might have supported Venice in Dalmatia to prevent the Normans from landing, perhaps by creating a diversionary activity in the wake of the invading Normans. Byzantine victory can only have been the result of a joint blockade of the Norman military machine, carried out in liaison with the Venetians.

---

[158] κυρία πάρτον τῶν ἐθνῶν τῶν ἐπὶ τῆςἑσπέρας // ἀπὸ πατρός, ἀπὸ μητρὸς ἐκ τῶν ἀγχιστενμάτον. σὲτρέμουσιν Ἀλαμανοί γένος ῥηγὸς ἐκ Ῥήνου // σοῦ τὰ Γερμανῶν πτήσσουσιν ἔθνη τὴν δυναστείαν (...) [the lady of all Western nations // which are related to you through your father and mother // you are feared by the Germans, who is of the kindred of the King of the Rhine // your rule the German peoples dread]: Στίχοι εἰς τὴν στεφηφορίαν Ἀλεξίουτοῦ Κομνηνοῦ: Theodoros Prodromos, *Historische Gedichte*, I. 179. ÁMTBF, 169–171. 170. Latin translation: "... regina ... populis borealibus ... omnium ad septentrionem gentium domina, patre ac matre legitimis prognata. Te Alamanni ad Rhenum metuunt, tuum imperium Germanorum natio extimescit."*Theodori Prodromi versus in coronationem Alexii*, in *Scripta miscellanea*, PG 133. coll. 1340–42.

[159] Ἐγὼ προῆλθον εὐτυχῶν προπατόρων // ἀρχῆς ἁπάσης δυσμικῆς βασιλέον // Ἰούλιοι Καίσαρες ἐφρέψαντό με [I descended from blessed ancestors, the rulers of the whole western world, I was raised by Julius Caesars]: Ἐπιτάφιοι τῇ μακαρίτιδι βασιλίσσῃ Ῥωμαίων κυρᾷ Εἰρήνῃ ὡς ἀπὸ τῆς κειμένης Ἰούλιοι Καίσαρες ἐφρέψαντό με: Theodoros Prodromos, *Historische Gedichte*, VII. 229–30. 229.; ÁMTBF, 172. Latin transl.: "Orta sum majoribus fortunatis, qui totum Occidentem gubernarunt, a Caesaribus educatam." *Inscriptio sepulcralis ad memoriam imperatricis Romanorum, Irenae, defunctae*, in *Scripta Miscellanea*, PG 133. coll. 1396.; Zagklas, Theodóros Prodromos, 38, 52.

Bibliography
Primary Sources

Albert of Aachen/Aix. *Historia Ierosolimitana: history of the journey to Jerusalem*, ed. and transl. by Susan B. Edgington, Oxford: Clarendon Press, 2007.

Annalista Saxo: [Reichskronik] ed. D. G. Waitz, P. Kilon. MGH SS VI. [Chronica et annales aevi Salici], Hannover: Hahn, 1844. 542–777.

Annales Venetici Breves, ed. Henry Simonsfeld, MGH SS XIV, [Supplementa tomorum I–XII, pars II. Supplementum tomi XIII] Hanover: Hahn, 1883. 69–72.

Armenia and the Crusades: tenth to twelfth centuries: the Chronicle of Matthew of Edessa, transl. by A. E. Dostourian, London: University Press of America, 1993.

Bartolf of Nangis. *Gesta Francorum expugnantium Iherusalem*, In *Recueil des historiens des Croisades, Historiens occidentaux*, par les soins de l'Académie royale des inscriptions et belles–lettres. Paris: Imprimerie Royale, 1844–95. [= RHC Occ.] III. 487–543.

Chronicon ignoti civis Barensis / Anonymus Barensis *Chronicon,* Rerum Italicarum Scriptores raccolta degli storici Italiani dal cinquecento al millecinquecento, ordinata da L.A. Muratori, Mediolanum, Sociates Palatina, 1723–51. [=RIS] V. Mediolanum: Societas Palatina, 1724. 145–158.

Chronici Hungarici compositio saeculi XIV. [= *Chronicon. saec. XIV.*] In *Scriptores Rerum Hungaricarum tempore ducum regumque stirpis Arpadianae gestarum*. ed. by Imre Szentpétery et al. 2 vols., Budapest: Akadémiai, 1937–1938. [New Edn. 1999. ed. by Kornél Szovák, László Veszprémy] [= SRH]

Komnene, Anna. ΑΛΕΧΙΑΣ / *Anna Comnenae Porphyrogennitae Alexias*, ed. August Reifferscheid, 2 vols, Leipzig: Teubner, 1884. [= AK]

Comnenae, Annae *Alexias*, Patrologia Graeca. ed. J–P. Migne. Paris : Imprimerie Catholique, 1864. V. 131. coll. 1026.

Comnenae, Annae *Alexiadis*, I–II. (Corpus Scriptorum Historiae Byzantinae [=CSHB] 2–3). ed. Ludwig Schopen, Bonn: Weber, 1839–1878.

Comnena, Anna: *The Alexiad*, tr. E.R.A. Sewter, Penguin, London, 2003. [= Sewter]

Comnena, Anna: Dandolo, Andrea. *Chronicon Venetum,* RIS, XII. 1728. 1–525

Diplomata Hungariae antiquissima praefuit Georgius Györffy; adiuverunt Johannes Bapt. Borsa. Budapest: Akadémiai, 1992. [= DHA]

Dölger, Franz. *Regesten der Kaiserurkunden des oströmischen Reiches von 565–1453*, 1–3. teil. 2. München: Oldenbourg, 1924.

Ekkehard of Aura [Uraugiensis], *Chronica*, MGH SS. VI. [Chronica et annales aevi Salici] ed. D. G. Waitz, P. Kilon. Hannover: Hahn, 1844. 1–267.

Fulcher of Chartres. *A history of the expedition to Jerusalem, 1095–1127*, transl. by Frances Rita Ryan, edited by Harold S. Fink. Knoxville: University of Tennessee Press, 1969.

Gaufredus Malaterra. *De Rebus Gestis Rogerii Calabriae et Siciliae Comitis et Roberti Guiscardi Ducis fratris eius*, In *Írott források*, 199–201. [ed. Ernesto Pontieri, RIS, V. pt.1. Bologna, Zanichelli, 1927–28.]

Guibert de Nogent. *The deeds of God through the Franks*, transl. and ed. by Robert Levine, Woodbridge: Boydell, 1997.

Írott források az 1050–1116 közötti magyar történelemről. eds. Ferenc Makk, Gábor Thoroczkay. Szeged: Szegedi Középkorász Műhely, 2006.

Historia Belli Sacri, RHC Occ. III. 169–229.

Historia s. Christophori Martyris. In *Enchiridion Fontium Historiae Croatiae*, ed. Ferdinand Šišić. Zagreb: Zemaljske Vlade, 1914.

Ibn al–Athīr. *Chronicle for the crusading period from al–Kāmil fi'l–ta'rīkh*, transl. D.S. Richards, Aldershot: Ashgate, 2006–7.

Kinnamos, Ioannes. Ἐπιτομὴ τῶν κατορθωμάτων / *Ioannis Cinnami Rerum ab Ioannes et Alexio [sic] Comnenis Gestarum*, ed. Augustus Meineke. CSNB, 13. Bonnae, Weber, 1836.

Kinnamos, John. *The Deeds of John and Manuel Comnenus*, transl. C. M. Brand. New York, Columbia, 1976.

Laurentius de Monacis. *Chronicon de rebus venetis*, [RIS Tom. VIII. Apppendix] Venetiis, Remondiniana, 1758. 1–320. [Mediolani 1726]

Moravcsik, Gyula. *Az Árpád-kori magyar történet bizánci forrásai*. Fontes Byzantini historiae Hungaricae aevo ducum et regum ex stirpe Árpád descendentium. Budapest: Akadémiai, 1988. [= ÁMTBF]

Narratio Floriacensis de captis Antiochia et Hierosolyma, RHC Occ. V. 356–63.

Ordericus Vitalis. *The ecclesiastical history of Orderic Vitalis*. Tr. Marjorie Chibnall. Oxford: Clarendon Press, 1983.

Paulus Venetus / Paolino da Venezia / Paolino Minorita. *Historia Satyrica* [(Speculum sive) Satyrica rerum gestarum mundi historia]In *Antiquitates Italicae medii aevi*, ed. L. A. Muratori. 6 vols. Mediolanum: Societas Palatina, 1738–1742. IV. 951–1034.

Petrus Tudebodus / Peter Tudebode. *Historia de Hierosolymitano Itinere*, ed. J. H. Hill, L. L. Hill, Philadelphia: American Philosophical Society, 1974.

Prodromos, Theodore. *Theodoros Prodromos: Historische Gedichte*, edited by Wolfram Hörandner. Vienna: Österreichischen Akademie der Wissenschaften, 1974.

Radulph of Caen / Radulfo Cadomensi. *Gesta Tancredi in expeditione Hierosolymitana*, RHC Occ. III. 587–716.

Robert the Monk. *History of the First Crusade: Historia Iherosolimitana*, tr. Carol Sweetenham. Aldershot: Ashgate, 2005.

Regesta regum stirpis Arpadinae critico–diplomatic, 2 vols., ed. by Imre Szentpétery, Iván Borsa, Budapest: Akadémiai, 1923–87. [=RA]

Romuald of Salerno. *Romoaldi II archiepiscopi Salernitani annales*, ed. Wilhelm Arndt. MGH SS XIX. [Annales aevi Suevici] Hannover–Stuttgart: Hahn, 1866. 387–461.

Siegebert of Gembloux. Sigeberti Gemblacensis *Chronica cum continuationibus*, ed. D. L. Bethmann. MGH SS VI [Chronica et annales aevi Salici] Hannover: Hahn, 1844. 268–474.

Theodore Skoutariotes: Σύνοψις χπρονική. In *Mesaiōnikē vivliothēkē epistasia* / Mesaionike Bibliotheke. Bibliotheca Graeca Medii Aevi. Ed. Kōnstantinos N. Sathas. 7 vols. Vol. VII. Paris—Venise: Jean Maissoneuve, 1894.

Radulphus Tortarius. *Poema de obsidione Dyrrachii*, Cod. Vat. Reg., 1357. In *Rodulfi Tortarii carmina*, edited by Marbury B. Ogle, Dorothy M. Schullian. Rome: American Academy, 1933.

Simonis de Kéza. *Gesta Hungarorum. The Deeds of the Hungarians*, ed. by F. Schaer, L. Veszprémy. Budapest, CEU Press, 1999.

William of Malmesbury. *Gesta regum Anglorum*, edited and translated by R.A.B. Mynors, Oxford: Clarendon Press, 1998.

William of Tyre. *A History of Deeds Done Beyond the Sea*, transl. and ed. by Emily Atwater Babcock, A. C. Krey. New York: Columbia University Press, 1943.

Zonaras, Ioannes. Επιτομή ιστοριων / *Ioannis Zonarae epitomae historiarum*. Ed. Ludwig Dindorf, 6 vols, Leipzig: Teubner, 1868–1875.

Zonaras, Ioannes. Χρονικον / *Ioannis Zonarae Annales*, 2 vols, ed. Moritz Pinder. Επιτομή ιστοριων / *Epitomae historiarum*, Vol. III. ed. Theodor Büttner–Wobst, (CSHB, 47–49.) Bonn: Weber, 1841–97.

Secondary Sources

Andenna, Giancarlo. "Boemondo e il papato." In *"Unde boat mundus quanti fuerit Boamundus." Boemondo I di Altavilla. Un normanno tra Occidente e Oriente* (Canosa di Puglia, 05–09 maggio 2011), edited by Cosimo D. Fonseca, Pasquale Ieva. Bari: Società di Storia Patria per la Puglia, 2015. 85–104.

Angold, Michael. *The Byzantine Empire, 1025–1204*. London: Longman: 1997.

Asbridge, Thomas S. *The Creation of the Principality of Antioch, 1098–1130*. Woodbridge, Boydell, 2000.

Beech, George. "A Norman–Italian adventurer in the East: Richard of Salerno 1097–1112." In *Anglo-Norman Studies 15*. 25–40

Bennett, Matthew. "Amphibious Operations from the Norman Conquest to the Crusades of Saint Louis, c. 1050–c. 1250." In *Amphibious warfare 1000—1700. Commerce, state formation and European expansion*, edited by David J. B. Trim, Mark Charles Fissel. Leiden: Brill, 2006. 51–68.

———. "Norman Naval Activity in the Mediterranean c.1060–c.1108." In *Anglo–Norman Studies 15*. Proceedings of the Battle Conference 1992 and of the XI Colloquio Medievale of the Officina Di Studi Medievali, ed. Marjorie Chibnall. Woodbridge, Boydell, 1993. 41–58.

———. "Amphibious Operations from the Norman Conquest to the Crusades of St. Louis, c. 1050–c. 1250." *Amphibious Warfare 1000–1700*, edited by D. J. B. Trim, M. C. Fissel, Leiden: Brill, 2006. 51–68.

Chalandon, Ferdinand. *Essai sur le règne d'Alexis Ier Comnène, 1081–1118*. Picard: Paris, 1900.

Deér, József. *A magyar törzsszövetség és patrimoniális királyság külpolitikája*. [The Foreign policy of the Magyar Tribal Alliance and of the Patrimonial State] Kaposvár, 1928.

Dölger, Franz. "Ungarn in der byzantinischen Reichspolitik," *Archivum Europae Centro-Orientalis* 8 (1942): 315–412. [Budapest: Sárkány, 1942.]

Fink, Harold S. "The Foundation of the Latin States, 1099–1118." In *History of the Crusades: The first hundred years*, Gen. Ed. Kenneth Meyer Setton, edited by M. W. Baldwin. Madison: University of Wisconsin Press, 1969. 368–409.

Flori, Jean, *Bohémond d'Antioch, Chevalier d'Aventure*. Paris: Payot, 2007.

———. "Bohémond, croisé modele." In *"Come l'orco della fiaba"*: studi per Franco Cardini. A cura di Marina Montesano. Firenze: SISMEL—del Galluzzo, 2010. 123–32.

Girgensohn, Dieter. "Boemondo I," *In Dizionario Biografico degli Italiani*. Vol. 11 (1969). http://www.treccani.it/enciclopedia/boemondo-i_%28Dizionario-Biografico%29/

Gyóni, Mátyás. "A legkorábbi magyar–bizánci házassági kapcsolatok kérdéséhez," [To the Question of the earliest Hungarian–Byzantine Matrimonial Relations] *Századok* 8 (1947): 212–219.

Györffy, György, "A lovagszent uralkodása (1077–1095)," [The Reign of the Chivalric Saint] *Történelmi Szemle* 10 (1977): 533–564.

———, "A XII. századi dalmáciai városprivilégiumok kritikájához [Critical Notes on twelfth-century Urban Privileges] *Történelmi Szemle* 10 (1967): 46–56.

Harris, Jonathan. *Byzantium and the Crusades*. London: Continuum, 2006.

Hiestand, Rudolf. "Boemondo I e la prima Crociata." In *Il mezzogiorno normanno–svevo e le crociate*: Atti delle quattordicesime giornate normanno–sveve Bari, 17–20 ottobre 2000 a cura di Giosuè Musca. Bari: Centro di studi normanno–svevi Università degli Studi di Bari—Mario Gallina, 2002. 65–94.

Hill, Barbara. "Alexios I Komnenos and imperial women," In *Alexius I Komnenos. Papers. Papers of the Second Belfast Byzantine International Colloquium*, edited by Margaret Mullett and Dion Smythe, Belfast: Byzantine Enterprises, 1996. 37–54. 46.

———. *Imperial women in Byzantium, 1025–1204: power, patronage, and ideology*. London: Longman, 1999.

Houben, Hubert. *Roger II of Sicily: A Ruler between East and West*. Cambridge: Cambridge University Press, 2002.

Jenal, Anton. "Der Kampf um Durazzo, 1107–1108, mit dem Gedicht des Tortarius," *Historisches Jahrbuch* [der Görres–Gesellschaft] 37 (1916): 285–352.

Kapitánffy, István. *Hungarobyzantina*. Budapest: Typotex, 2003.

———. "König Ladislaus und Byzanz," *Homonoia* 1 (1979): 73–96.

Kazhdan, Alexander. "Latins and Franks in Byzantium: Perception and Reality from the Eleventh to the Twelfth Century." In *The Crusades from the Perspective of Byzantium and the Muslim World*, edited by Angeliki E. Laiou, Roy P. Mottahedeh, Washington D.C.: Dumbarton Oaks Research Library and Collection, 2001. 83–100.

Kerbl, Raimund. *Byzantinische Prinzessinnen in Ungarn zwischen 1050–1200 und ihr Einfluss auf das Arpadenkönigreich*. Wien: Universität Wien, 1979.

Korai magyar történeti lexikon : 9–14. század. [Encyclopaedia in Early Hungarian History, 9th–14th c.]. Gen. Ed. Gyula Kristó. Budapest: Akadémiai, 1994. [= KTML]

Körmendi, Tamás. *Az Imre, III. László és II. András magyar királyok uralkodására vonatkozó nyugati elbeszélő források kritikája*. [A criticism of Western sources for the reigns of Imre, Ladislaus III and Andrew II] PhD–dissertation, Budapest: ELTE, 2008.

Kristó, Gyula. *Az Árpád-kor háborúi*. [The Wars of the Árpáds] Budapest: Zrínyi, 1986.

———. *Magyarország története 895–1301*. [History of Hungary] Budapest: Tankönyvkiadó, 1984.

Kugler, Bernard von. *Bohemund und Tancred, Fürsten von Antiochien*. Tübingen: Fues, 1862.

Lilie, Ralph-Johannes. *Byzantium and the Crusader States*, trans. J. C. Morris, J. E. Ridings. Oxford: Clarendon, 1994.

Lioubarskij, I. N.—Freidenberg, "N. M. Devol'skij dogovor 1108 g. meždu Alekseem Komninom i Boemundom." *Vizantijskij vremennik* 21 (1962): 260–274.

Loud, G. A. *The Age of Robert Guiscard. Southern Italy and the Norman Conquest*. Harlow: Longman/Pearson, 2000.

———. *The Age of Robert Guiscard: Southern Italy and the Norman Conquest*. London: Routledge, 2000.

———. *Roger II and the creation of the Kingdom of Sicily*, Manchester: Manchester University Press, 2012.

Magyarország történeti kronológiája. 4 vols, ed. by Kálmán Benda. II. ed. by László Solymosi. [=Kronológia] Budapest: Akadémiai, 1984.

Makk, Ferenc. "Megjegyzések Kálmán külpolitikájához," [Notes for Coloman's diplomacy] *Acta Universitatis Szegediensis: Acta historica* 67 (1980): 21–31.

———. *The Árpáds and the Comneni*. Budapest: Akadémiai, 1989.

———. *A turulmadártól a kettőskeresztig*. [From Turul Bird to Double Cross] Szeged: Szegedi Középkorász Műhely, 1998.

———. *Ungarische Aussenpolitik (896–1196)*. Herne: Schäfer, 1999.

Mályusz, Elemér. *Az V. István-kori Gesta.* [A gesta of the age of Stephen V] Budapest: Akadémiai, 1971.

Manselli, Raoul. "Normanni d'Italia alla prima crociata: Boemondo d'Altavilla," *Japigia* 11 (1940): 45-79.; 154-184.

Marković, Miroslav. "Dva natpisa iz Zadra," *Historijski zbornik Srpske akademije nauke* 36 (1953): 99-138.

Marquis de la Force. "Les conseillers latins du basileus Alexis Comnène," *Byzantion* 11 (1936) 153-65.

Matthew, Donald. *The Norman Kingdom of Sicily.* Cambridge: Cambridge University Press, 2008

Matzke, Michael. "Boemondo e Daiberto di Pisa." In *Boemondo: storia di un principe normanno*, atti del Convegno di Studio su Boemondo..., edited by Nunzio Lozito, Benedetto Vetero, Franco Cardini. Lecce: Gelatina, 2003. 95-106.

McQueen, W. B. "Relations between the Normans and Byzantium, 1071-1112," *Byzantion* 56 (1986): 427-69.

Moravcsik, Gyula. "Les Relations entre le Hongrie et Byzance à l'epoque de croisades," *Revue des Études Hongroises* 8-11 (1933): 301-308.

———. *Byzantium and the Magyars.* Amsterdam: Hakkert, 1970.

———. *Szent László leánya és a bizánci Pantokrator-monostor.* [St. Ladislaus's daughter and the Pantokrator] Konstantinápoly [Istanbul]: Magyar Tudományos Intézet, 1923. [= Moravcsik, Pantokrator]

Morea, Giuseppe. *Marco Boemondo d'Altavilla.* Canosa: Centro di servizio e programmazione culturale regionale, 1986

———. *Marco Boemondo d'Altavilla*, Centro di servizio e programmazione culturale regionale: Canosa 1986.

Nicol, D. M. *Byzantium and Venice.* Cambridge: Cambridge University Press, 1988.

Olajos, Teréz. "Egy felhasználatlan forráscsoport : a 11. századi magyar-bizánci kapcsolatok történetéhez," [An unused source group for 11th c. Hungarian-Byzantine contacts], *Századok* 132.1 (1998): 215-222.

———. "Felhasználatlan bizánci forrás a magyarság korai történetéhez," [An unused source for the early history of Hungary] *Antik Tanulmányok* 33.1 (1987-88): 24-27.

Pauler, Gyula. "Horvát-Dalmátország elfoglalásáról, 1091-1111. Befejező közlemény," [On the Conquest of Croatia and Dalmatia] *Századok* 22 (1888): 197-215., 320-333.

———. *A magyar nemzet történelme az Árpádházi királyok alatt.* [The history of the Hungarian nation under the reign of the Árpád kings] 2 vols. Budapest, 1893.

Robinson, I. S. *Henry IV of Germany 1056-1106.* Cambridge: Cambridge University Press, 1999.

Rösch, Gerhard, "Der «Kreuzzug» Bohemunds gegen Dyrrachion 1107/1108 in der lateinischen Tradition des 12. Jahrhunderts," *Römische Historische Mitteilungen* 26 (1984): 181–190.

Rowe, J. G., "Paschal II, Bohemund of Antioch and the Byzantine Empire," *Bulletin of the John Rylands Library* 49 (1966–67): 165–202.

Russo, Luigi. "Boemondo e la "prima crociata": spunti per un riesame." In: *Unde boat mundus quanti fuerit Boamundus, Boemondo I di Altavilla, un normanno tra Occidente e Oriente*, 122–134.

———. "Convergenze e scontri: per une riconsiderazione dei rapporti greco–normanni nei secoli XI–XII." In *Fedi a confronto: ebrei, cristiani e musulmani fra X e XIII secolo*: atti del convegno di studi, San Vivaldo, Montaione, 22–24 settembre 2004, a cura di Sergio Gensini. Firenze; Montaione: Polistampa, 2006. 263–278.

———. "Il viaggio di Boemondo d'Altavilla in Francia (1106): un riesame," *Archivio Storico Italiano* 163 (2005): 3–42.

———. "L'espansione normanna contro Bisanzio (secoli XI–XII)." In *Scritti offerti a Mario Troso*, a cura di G. Mastrominico. Ariano Irpino: Centro Europeo di Studi Normanni, 2012. 206-30.

Savvidēs, Alexēs G. K. *Byzantino–Normannica. The Norman Capture of Italy and the First Two Norman Invasions in Byzantium*, Leuven: Uitgeverij Peeters en Departement Oosterse Studies, 2007.

Steindorff, Ludwig. *Die dalmatinischen Städte im 12. Jahrhundert: Studien zu ihrer politischen Stellung und Gesellschaftlichen Entwicklung*. Köln: Böhlau, 1984.

Stephenson, Paul. *Byzantium's Balkan frontier: a political study of the northern Balkans, 900–1204*, Cambridge: Cambridge University Press, 2000.

Székely, György. "La Hongrie et Byzance aux Xe–XIIe siècles," *Acta Historica Academiae Scientiarum Hungaricae* 13 (1967) 291–311.

———. "Ungarns Stellung zwischen Kaiser, Papst und Byzanz zur Zeit der Kluniazenserreform." In *Spiritualità cluniacense*. Centro di studi sulla spiritualità medievale, Convegni 2. 12–15 ottobre 1958. Todi: Accademia Tudertina, 1960. 312–325.

Szűcs, Jenő. "Társadalomelmélet, politikai teória és történetszemlélet Kézai Simon Gesta Hungarorumában." [Social and Political theory and the Perception of the Past in Simon of Kéza's Gesta] *Századok* 107.4 (1973): 823–878.

Theotokis, Georgios. "Bohemond of Taranto's 1107-8 campaign in Byzantine Illyria—Can it be viewed as a Crusade?" *Rosetta* 11 (2012): 72–81.

———. *The Norman Campaigns in the Balkans, 1081–1108*. Woodbridge: Boydell, 2014.

Urbansky, Andrew B. *Byzantium and the Danube frontier: A study of the relations between Byzantium, Hungary and the Balkans during the period of the Comneni*. New York: Twayne, 1968.

Vattai, Erzsébet P., "Szent László leánya, Piroska–Eiréné bizánci császárné," [St. Ladislaus's Daughter, Piroska-Eirene Empress of Byzantium] *Művészet* 4 (1967): 3–5.

Whalen, Brett Edward. "God's Will or Not? Bohemond's Campaign against the Byzantine Empire (1105–1108)." In *Crusades. Medieval worlds in conflict*, edited by Thomas F. Madden, James L. Naus, Vincent Ryan. Farnham: Ashgate, 2010. 111–126.

Yewdale, R. B. *Bohemond I, Prince of Antioch*, Princeton: Princeton University, 1924.

TABLE I
THE DYNASTIC RELATIONS OF PIROSKA – GERMAN CONTACTS

HOUSE OF ÁRPÁD

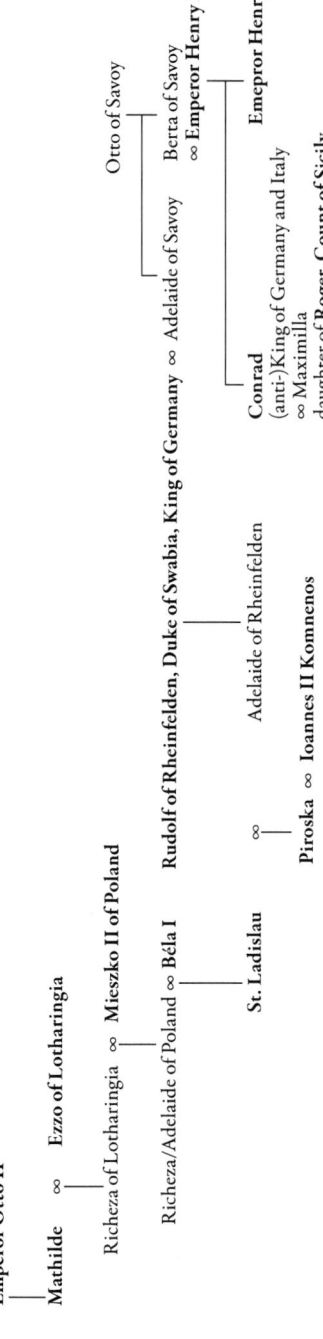

PIROSKA AND THE KOMNENIAN DYNASTY

Michael Jeffreys

I begin with two proposed structures for the Komnenian dynasty, both, I suggest, valid in different ways, one based on males, the other on females. Piroska naturally has a major role in the second. I shall explain both structures in general, with only a simple comment or two on Piroska. I shall then return to discuss her in greater depth, using the limited evidence to suggest what Byzantine society might have expected from her as empress, and what role she might actually have played, especially in the great project she shared with her husband John II, the building of the Pantokrator monastery in the capital.[1]

The Komnenian dynasty[2] seems simple, from the customary masculine perspective. There were three powerful and able emperors who ruled consecutively for a century: Alexios I (1081–1118), John II (1118–1143) and Manuel I (1143–1180).[3] However two decades before Alexios, Isaac I Komnenos (1057–1059) became emperor after a civil war but ruled for just over two years. Isaac fought unsuccess-

---

[1] This plan differs from the presentation made at the conference. There I had an agenda beyond Piroska, an introduction to the material on Hungarian history available in the poems of Manganeios Prodromos, which my wife and I have long been editing. A plan has now been made to present and contextualise this material more fully than is possible here, so concentration is now only on Piroska.

[2] My ideas about the Komnenian dynasty have been stimulated, usually positively but sometimes negatively by the work of Paul Magdalino, and also its partial updating by Vlada Stanković in *Komnini u Carigradu* (Belgrade 2006), which I have consulted through its English summary (pp. 299–314), supplemented by Serbian help at important points.

[3] K. Varzos, *Η γενεαλογία των Κομνηνών* (2 vols.) (Thessaloniki 1984); hereafter Varzos I or II. References to the three major rulers are Alexios I: Varzos I no. 15, p. 87. John II: no. 34, p. 203. Manuel I: no. 81, p. 422. Wives and husbands of Komnenians are discussed (often briefly) in articles devoted to their Komnenian-born spouses: e.g. some information on Piroska may be found under John II (see above).

fully against entrenched interests which were hampering Byzantine progress. In 1159, after a sequence of events which is unclear, Isaac abdicated, his brother John perhaps refused the throne,[4] and for twenty years the Doukai were the dominant dynasty. The reigns of Constantine X Doukas (1059–1067) and Michael VII Doukas (1071–1078) were punctuated by brief periods of rule by Constantine's wife (and Michael's mother) Eudokia (1067, 1071), the military episode of Romanos IV, Eudokia's second husband, climaxing at Mantzikert (1068–1071), and the coup of Nikephoros III (1078–1081).[5] There followed the counter-coup of Alexios I which led to the century of Komnenian emperors. At the end of that century in 1180, the dynasty collapsed conventionally. Alexios II (1180–1183) was left a minor at the death of his father Manuel, and the regency was overturned by Andronikos Komnenos (1183–1185), a son of John II's younger brother Isaac. Andronikos proved a murderous tyrant, particularly against westerners in Byzantium. By 1185, five years after Manuel I's death, Isaac II was emperor, inaugurating a new, short-lived Angelos dynasty.[6]

With a small shift in perspective, a parallel, less obvious structure emerges, basing the dynasty on three prominent females, Anna Dalassene, Eirene Doukaina and Piroska-Eirene. Because it is impossible for the writing of medieval history to overcome its androcentric sources, this pattern will never rival the first structure, though it foreshadows most of it, including useful explications of the beginning and end of the century of rule.

Anna Dalassene was the wife of John Komnenos, who died in 1067. If he did refuse the throne, he must have disappointed her severely, to judge from her later activity as a widow. In the two decades between the abdication of her brother-in-law Isaac I and the successful coup of her son Alexios I, whilst playing a defiant public role unusual for a woman, she forged a union of noble families allied to the Komnenians, using the marriage potential of her eight children and even a grandchild.[7] But she refused to sanction the final alliance to bring her son Alexios I to the

---

[4] Isaac I: Varzos I no. 4, p. 41. His brother John: Varzos I no. 6, p. 49. The refusal of the crown (only in *Nikephoros Bryennios, Historiarum libri quattuor* [ed. Gautier], 81, ll. 7–20) is suspect, as giving the Komnenian family the prominence to justify the coup of 1181.

[5] For a narrative of this complex and decisive period, see Angold, *The Byzantine Empire 1025–1204* (London and New York 1984), 52–8, 92–113 (henceforward Angold, *Byzantine Empire 1025–1204*).

[6] Andronikos I: Varzos I no. 87, p. 493. Alexios II: Varzos II no. 155, p. 454. Isaac II: no. 183, p. 807.

[7] Anna Dalassene: see Varzos no. 6, p. 49. Her children: Manuel married a relative of Romanos IV Diogenes, and their daughter Anna was affianced to the grandson of Nikephoros III Botaneiates (Varzos I, nos. 10 and 19, pp. 61 and 122). Maria married Michael Taronites (no. 11, p. 64). Isaac married the Georgian Eirene of Alania (no. 12, p. 67). Eudokia married Nikephoros Melissenos (no. 13, p. 80). Theodora married Constantine Diogenes, son of Romanos IV (no. 14, p. 85). Alex-

throne, wishing the Komnenians to rule alone. Eirene Doukaina was promoted by the faction of the Doukai, especially her grandfather John (kaisar) and her mother the Bulgarian Maria, to be affianced to Alexios before his coup. Eirene is the second heroine of this female structure. Her marriage joined the Komnenians and Doukai, then the two major imperial families, an alliance which ruled for a century.

Anna Dalassene's role continued after Alexios I's accession. He had to fight hard at once on three fronts, against Normans in the west, steppe nomads in the north and Turks in the east. While he and most male relatives were absent on campaigns, which at first failed more often than they succeeded, Anna remained in charge in the capital with full imperial powers, confirmed by chrysobull. She signed, for example, several documents granting lands to monasteries, and also summarily blinded a rebel claiming to be the son of Romanos IV.[8] As Alexios's position improved around 1096, she retired to the monastery of Pantepoptes which she had founded, dying in 1102.

Anna's importance was matched by other women between 1059 and 1081. When Constantine X fell seriously ill a year before his death in 1067, he set up a regency around his wife Eudokia, to perpetuate the power of the Doukai, through the pair's underage children. He went to extraordinary lengths to stop Eudokia, after his death, from disinheriting them by remarriage or other means.[9] His precautions failed, and at the first military crisis Eudokia married the general Romanos IV Diogenes, making him emperor in a time-honoured way. When Romanos was defeated at Manzikert and again in a civil war, Eudokia was used to validate the new regime, under her son Michael VII. However, she was then exiled by Michael and his advisors, until he abdicated in 1078. Imperial legitimation by marriage to a predecessor's empress was then repeated, with two empresses available for selection by the new ruler Nikephoros III Botaneiates. Eudokia was forestalled by Maria of Alania, empress of Michael VII, a Georgian universally admired for her beauty. Alexios I's coup brought a clash between the two forms of dynasty-building by female agency. The beautiful Maria had adopted and encouraged Alexios, because he supported the claims of her young son. There was great anxiety that Alexios

---

ios, we have seen, married Eirene Doukaina (no. 15, p. 64). Adrianos made another Doukas marriage, with Zoe (no. 16, p. 114). Nikephoros married, but we do not know whom (no. 17, p. 118). More than one of these marriages were uncanonical, but the interests of the dynasty prevailed (see A. Laiou, *Mariage, amour et parenté à Byzance aux XIe–XIII siècles*, Paris 1992, 26).

[8] Chrysobull: Anna Komnene, 101, line 44–103 line 95. The archives of the monastery of Patmos contain many documents showing her and Alexios sharing the bureaucratic responsibility for granting the monastery's first lands. Blinding: Anna Komnene, 292, line 63–293 line 67.

[9] See the text edited by N. Oikonomidès, "Le serment de l'impératrice Eudocie: un episode de l'histoire dynastique de Byzance," *Revue des Études Byzantines* 21 (1963) 73–97.

would marry Maria, not the young Eirene Doukaina, the choice of the Doukai. As we have seen, Eirene won.

After the marriage, Eirene's self-confidence and influence grew. She bore Alexios nine children (though the two youngest died in infancy). She became indispensable when he was struck with arthritis, often following the army in a discreet litter, ready to massage his legs so that he could ride the next day. Alexios famously turned the state into a kind of family enterprise by offering all the Komnenian family, including those married into it, the title of *sebastos* (fem. *sebaste*), the basic, almost exclusive mark of nobility in his new system of dignities.[10]

Piroska was married to John II around 1104, shortly after the death of Anna Dalassene, as Alexios and Eirene Doukaina were completing their family. The marriage bolstered Byzantine defence against the crusader Bohemond of Taranto's attack. It is likely that Piroska soon sensed tension between her new husband and another strong woman, his elder sister Anna Komnene, the historian. Anna, crowned empress as an infant, had reluctantly yielded to the male heir, John II, at his birth. Anna was supported by her mother Eirene Doukaina. Tension between sister and brother climaxed when John inherited the empire on Alexios's death and continued later. The degree of hostility involved is now controversial.[11] Hostility also arose between John and his younger brother Isaac, who would later rebel and depart for the Muslim east.

In contrast to the reigns of Alexios I and Manuel I, that of John II is poorly covered in the sources. John (nicknamed Kaloioannes, Ioannes the Good), is portrayed as a determined soldier and loyal husband. His empress Piroska-Eirene is universally praised for piety and generosity and won broad affection among the people of her new homeland, being eventually canonised there, despite a probable difference in religious practices. She produced eight children, four boys and four girls. Subsequently, her chief achievement was to share the building of the huge monastic complex of the Pantokrator in Constantinople, including the tombs of her clos-

---

[10] P. Magdalino, *The Empire of Manuel I Komnenos* (Cambridge 1993), 180–183 (henceforward Magdalino, *Manuel I*).

[11] L. Neville, *Anna Komnene: the Life and Work of a Medieval Historian* (Oxford 2016), passim (Henceforward "Neville, *Anna Komnene*"). Neville argues convincingly that much of the drama of Anna's history is added in self-defence, to show she is still a woman, though writing in a genre appropriate to men. Her emotions as author are exaggerated: authorial grief approaches a funeral lament, happy memories lead to tears and swooning, and dislike of her brother is transformed into serious hatred. But I think Neville goes too far in saying "She may well have disliked her brother [John II], but there is not much of any reason to think so" (p. 151). Literary enhancement of emotion is one thing, falsification of emotion is another. I think Anna disliked John: only the intensity is in question.

est family. In building a monastery in the capital to house family tombs she followed examples including Anna Dalassene in the Pantepoptes, Eirene Doukaina with the Kecharitomene and her husband Alexios I with Christ Philanthropos.[12] However, textual descriptions of Piroska-Eirene and John suggest conventional stereotypes, raising suspicions that the writers had limited real information.

Three consecutive fecund Komnenian marriages had each produced eight or more children, most with descendants of their own. The family seemed to be breeding a complete new ruling class to fit Alexios's new pattern of nobility. Fecundity is not a fashionable virtue in the twenty-first century, but the dynasty was about to learn its importance in the twelfth. Piroska's sons and sons-in-law died rather early, either in battle or from illness on campaign, including the two eldest sons, as we shall see. Thus, after her death, when John II also died in a hunting accident (1143), it was her fourth son Manuel I who defeated her third son Isaac to claim the throne. Manuel was strongly oriented towards the west, organising his life and court on fashionable western lines. He had an available western fiancée, Bertha von Sulzbach, though he was concerned about her status: their provisional union had been decided for diplomatic reasons when he was the youngest of four princes. Now he was emperor, could he not do better? Another drawback was that despite her western origin her appearance and attitudes did not match his ambitions. It was apparently her refusal to wear cosmetics which offended the court. Manuel had several mistresses and illegitimate children, dimly appearing in the historical record.[13] Still, when Manuel learned that Bertha's powerful kinsman Conrad III of Germany would pass through Constantinople on the Second Crusade (1147), the marriage took place (probably in 1146), and Bertha was renamed Eirene. The key dynastic statistic of Manuel's reign is that his only legitimate son, the future Alexios II, was born to his second wife in 1169, a full twenty-three years after this first marriage. This delay, combined with heavy early mortality in the previous generation, left serious dynastic deficiencies.

Bertha-Eirene had died in 1161. A curse was placed on her womb by an angry deposed patriarch, to prevent the birth of sons and increase dynastic anxiety. She only produced two daughters, Maria and Anna. Maria was crowned empress at birth; Anna did not survive infancy. Beyond cosmetics we know some positive atti-

---

[12] On this sequence of foundations see V. Stanković and A. Berger, "The Komnenoi and Constantinople before the Building of the Pantokrator Complex," in Kotzabassi, *Pantokrator* 3–32; P. Magdalino, "The foundation of the Pantokrator monastery in its urban setting," ibid. 33–56 (henceforward Magdalino, "Urban Setting").

[13] Mistresses: Varzos I, pp. 445–7; Varzos II no. 150, p. 417. Illegitimate children: Varzos II nos. 156, 157 and 157a, pp. 481–504.

tudes of Bertha-Eirene. She sponsored, for example, a simple retelling of the Iliad, to introduce her to Greek culture (though the head of her household would not pay the high price promised). She made a speech (presumably in Greek) to the Senate, expressing pride in Manuel's valor. She also uncovered a conspiracy against him.[14]

Bertha-Eirene's death led to an exhaustive search for a new empress, who should be beautiful and completely above scandal. A war broke out when a potential wife passed the first criterion, but failed the second.[15] Maria of Antioch was selected, and married Manuel in 1161. The mourning period for Bertha-Eirene was kept to a minimum, because of dynastic demands for a male heir. Maria of Antioch dazzled all with her style and beauty, but no heir appeared before the birth of Alexios II (1169).

As well as Manuel's two wives, three other women must be discussed in connection with his reign: his daughter Maria; the widow of his older brother (Piroska's second son, Andronikos) known as Eirene the *sebastokratorissa*; and finally Manuel's chosen fiancée for the young Alexios II, the even younger Agnes of France.

Maria's life was dominated by plans to use her to replace the elusive male heir, by marrying a prince who would succeed her father Manuel. As time passed, speculation over future husbands became frantic: a distinguished list of possible suitors can be drawn up from recorded rumors.[16] The choice finally fell on a Hungarian, the future Béla III, who was brought to Constantinople, renamed Alexios, given a Byzantine education and a high title and affianced to Maria.[17] All this gave her a sense of entitlement which was disappointed when the future Alexios II was born. Béla subsequently married the sister of Maria of Antioch, and succeeded to the Hungarian throne, becoming one of its greatest rulers. If Alexios II had not appeared, Béla might have made an excellent Byzantine emperor.

Eirene the *sebastokratorissa* was probably another non-Byzantine bride imported into the imperial family as the wife of Andronikos, Piroska's second son.[18] She was the most active sponsor of Byzantine literature and manuscript illustration in the mid-twelfth century.[19] After Piroska's first-born Alexios died (from sickness

---

[14] Varzos I, 454–8.
[15] The lady was Mélisende of Tripoli. See Magdalino, *Manuel I*, 72. This is the subject of Constantine Manasses's *Hodoiporikon*; ed. K. Horna, *BZ* 13 (1904), 325–347.
[16] Varzos II, no. 153, p. 439. As well as Béla the suitors include William II of Sicily, John Lackland (son of Henry II of England) and Henry the Lion (son of Frederick Barbarossa); she eventually married Renier, son of the Marquis of Montferrat. See Magdalino, *Manuel I*, 89–93, 100–101.
[17] For Béla in Byzantium, see Magdalino, *Manuel I*, 79–81.
[18] E.M and M.J. Jeffreys, "Who was Eirene the *sebastokratorissa*?," *Byzantion* 64, 1994, 40–68.
[19] She sponsored some manuscripts of the mature work of the Kokkinobaphos master, probably including his masterpieces, the Kokkinobaphos Gospels. His was the best workshop of miniature-

on campaign in Cilicia), Andronikos would have succeeded to the throne at John's death. Unfortunately, Andronikos was asked to transport his brother Alexios's body to the capital, but he also succumbed, probably to the same disease. The ship thus arrived with two princely corpses, the first burials (after Piroska herself) in the Pantokrator monastery. Andronikos's burial there infringed (as we shall see) the monastery's *typikon*.

The *sebastokratorissa* is included here not so much for her political importance, as because the poems of Manganeios Prodromos give many glimpses into her life, as his main patron. Most of the 148 poems offer military news, or the family details sadly missing in the case of Piroska. The *sebastokratorissa* was maliciously accused and persecuted by her brother-in-law Manuel soon after Andronikos's burial. Manganeios repeatedly laments this, without giving a clear reason. We have suggested she was a Norman accused of treachery, for her persecution coincides with wars against the Normans; however, the degree of imperial malice implied is surprising. Manganeios writes about various gaols, including a male prison and the Pantokrator itself, and violence from a drunken gaoler. Manganeios describes events in the lives of all her five children, and family celebrations for weddings and her sons' return from war. He even demands in her name that she be put on trial to test accusations against her. Piroska's two surviving sons, Manuel I and Isaac, were on bad terms, so the *sebastokratorissa*'s first son John became a kind of heir apparent in case Manuel died before longer-term solutions were found. John, as son of Manuel's elder brother, was the next highest-ranking Komnenian male. Relations between emperor, heir apparent and the latter's unhappy imprisoned mother become hard to explain. John was killed by the Turks at the battle of Myriokephalon (1176) under the eyes of his friend the historian William of Tyre;[20] whatever remained of John's expectations passed to his younger brother, another Alexios.

This female-based history of the Komnenian dynasty will end with the arrangements made in Manuel's last years to shore up Alexios II, and their rapid unravelling. Alexios II, probably aged eleven, was married to Agnes, daughter of the King of France, in 1180, just before Manuel's death. She was probably seven. The juvenile rulers were supported by Manuel's widow (and Alexios II's mother),

---

painters in 12th-century Byzantium (see E.M. Jeffreys, "The *sebastokratorissa* Irene as Patron," in L. Theis, M. Mullett and M. Grünbart (eds.), *Female Founders in Byzantium and Beyond*, Wiener Jahrbuch für Kunstgeschichte LX–LXI (2011-2), 177–94, here 184–7). The Kokkinobaphos master was also reponsible for the Gospels of John II, which Etele Kiss in this volume credibly attributes to the sponsorship of Piroska-Eirene, the *sebastokratorissa*'s mother-in-law, who also shared with her a passionate devotion to the Theotokos.

20 William of Tyre (ed. R.B.C. Huygens, H.E. Mayer, G. Rösch, *Guillaume de Tyr, Chronique*. Corpus Christianorum Continuatio Mediaevalis LXIII (Turnhout 1986)), bk. 21, ch. 11 (12), lines 14–15,

Maria of Antioch, as regent; she took the veil as the nun Xene. But the real power was wielded by Alexios, the *sebastokratorissa*'s younger son, just mentioned; he was popularly assumed to be Maria-Xene's lover. This Alexios effectively ruled Byzantium for more than a year, whether acting (with Maria-Xene) as regents for the young ruler or for themselves. Opposition in the streets came from a party centred on Manuel's daughter Maria, now rewarded for her long period as empress-in-waiting by marriage to Renier, son of the Marquis of Montferrat. Though Renier had the title of *kaisar*, this was clearly a consolation prize by which Manuel hoped to keep his daughter loyal to her young half-brother Alexios II. He failed, and the *kaisar* and *kaisarissa* fragmented the remaining support for Manuel's line. Manuel's twenty-three years of marriage without finding a situation of fecundity and producing a male heir left an underage son and daughter-in-law, a frustrated and ambitious daughter and a regency run by Manuel's desperate widow and the young emperor's cousin. These were progressively murdered by the charismatic but elderly and brutal Andronikos I Komnenos, from another branch of the family; only the underage French bride Agnes was spared, for a bizarre marriage to validate the sexagenerian Andronikos as emperor. Andronikos also organised a massacre of Latins in the city. After a Norman attack, he was torn to pieces in the hippodrome.[21]

Piroska in Byzantium

The first part of the above narrative carries the story of Komnenian dynastic women up to Piroska's arrival in Byzantium, while the second continues the tale after her death. Both the first and (with care) the second may be used to predict reactions of the capital's populace to her. Her origin marks an innovation in Komnenian marriages. Most previous spouses at this level of the family were from other Byzantine aristocratic houses, by Anna Dalassene's plan to forge an alliance supporting the Komnenian dynasty. Piroska's was the first Komnenian marriage promoting international support for Byzantium. Numerous prominent Komnenians made similar marriages later, probably including three of Piroska's sons and several grandchildren.

We should now discuss Byzantine expectations about Piroska and how far they may have been met, supporting the scant hard evidence by comparison, analogy and any other methods available. I shall discuss four main subjects, without really disentangling them: the role expected from any Byzantine empress; Piroska's public persona in the city; the political importance of the marriage to Hungary and Byzantium; and the foundation of the Pantokrator, as seen in its *typikon*, with some

---

[21] For a simple narrative of this destructive period, see Angold, *Byzantine Empire 1025–1204*, 263–9.

reference to archaeology. Piroska became popular, but nothing precise may be said over her impact on the wider populace. I shall use the perspective of a well-informed observer close to the palace. Such persons are likely to have influenced wider opinion.

One fact severely distorts the evidence. Most of the imperial women in the above narrative were not weak and subservient. However, they are virtually invisible in the sources until the deaths of their distinguished husbands, when suddenly they spring to life, especially in two areas—supporting the interests of their children and influencing succession to the throne. These areas overlapped. The contrast I am making between working through a live husband and emerging from his shadow as a widow is not new. A recent book on Anna Komnene, the historian,[22] reminds us of the pressure on active Byzantine women to finesse their actions by keeping as far as possible within normal conventions of female behavior. Empresses and other Komnenian women had direct access to great power in their husbands' lifetimes, letting them maintain female reserve by using these channels anonymously. When the husband died, his widow lost his voice and influence, and often had to adopt a more masculine persona, softened by feminine emotion. Eudokia, Maria of Alania, Eirene the *sebastokratorissa* and Maria of Antioch are good examples; the best is Anna Dalassene, whose activities as a widow were so successful that her son Alexios I, when overwhelmed by military duties, made her virtually head of state. Piroska, of course, was not widowed, and could always act through John II. I suggest that she only lived the invisible phase of her life, with no need to leave signs of personal initiative in the historical record. A reserved persona may have attracted her more because of her foreign birth.

Informed Byzantines would know that Piroska's father was Ladislaus I, a fiercely religious king (later canonised), whose reign was devoted to restoring order and unifying and expanding Hungary. His legal system was draconian and implacable. He may have been difficult for a daughter to relate to or follow. The princess lost her mother at age two, and her father at five. Her guardian was her father's nephew and successor, Coloman the Learned (1095–1116), a consecrated bishop with keen cultural interests, who arranged her marriage around the age of sixteen. She was probably aware as his ward that after the first year of his rule saw him managing the armies of the First Crusade through Hungary, the rest of his reign was disturbed by the attacks of his brother Álmos.

As a Hungarian in Constantinople, Piroska at first had to act through John, who directly or indirectly would provide courtly expertise, family support and probably, at first, even the Greek language. She reached Byzantium at an age when her

---

[22] L. Neville, *Anna Komnene: the Life and Work of a Medieval Historian* (Oxford 2016), passim.

non-Greek language skills will have been well developed, making her learn Greek as a foreign language. However both Etele Kiss and Marianne Sághy in this volume remind us that she was raised in Hungary at the Greek nunnery of Veszprémvögly, where there were Greek speakers celebrating orthodox liturgy in Greek, giving her some foundation for her new culture. In any case, it is unknown how many of her duties as a twelfth-century empress were performed verbally in Greek, and how often orthodox Byzantines could see from her reactions if their empress was brought up using the same rites as themselves. Perhaps bilingual attendants and an orthodox chaplain sufficed until her own skills grew.

Piroska-Eirene was presented to the Byzantines by Theodore Prodromos as the empress of all the West. The same fiction was repeated ten years after her death, in a less direct way, with Bertha-Eirene, another foreign bride.[23] This coincidence invites comparisons over the two empresses' reception in the city. While information on Piroska is sparse, for Bertha-Eirene there is a substantial paragraph in Choniates complaining of her obstinacy and tenacity in refusing to wear make-up (face-powder, eye-liner, mascara and blush), which she called feminine nonsense.[24] Choniates implies that Bertha was difficult to live with. The question may be asked (though not easily answered) as to what judgements were made, in similar contexts, about Piroska.

Choniates enjoys making outrageous comments, especially on Komnenians. On the other hand, one wonders whether Piroska's Hungarian upbringing included much familiarity with cosmetics.[25] Perhaps the character of the emperor was crucial in contemporary evaluation of the empress: part of her role was to support her emperor. John II, the bluff, loyal soldier, needed a different empress from Manuel I, with his fashionable tastes, uncertainty over Bertha's status, and willingness to seek solace outside marriage. Contemporary comments probably addressed the conjugal situation, not just the empress's character.

There is little sign of obstinacy and lack of compromise in Piroska's attitude to her husband. Soon after their marriage she fell pregnant. Whether or not she knew she was bearing twins, the pregnancy is unlikely to have been very comfortable. Yet she and John followed the army of Alexios I as he prepared for Bohemond's invasion

---

[23] Piroska: Prodromos (Hörandner) I, lines 85–101, XXV line 95. Bertha: Prodromos XX line 37–40. Max Lau says more on this elsewhere in this volume. Encomia of Piroska may be found in Prodromos, poems I, VII, VIII and 25, and Kallikles (Vassis). They are chiefly concerned with the conflicting symbolisms of Empress, Nun and Death.

[24] Choniates, 53, line 58–54, line 65.

[25] It has been claimed that the mosaic showing Piroska in the south gallery of Hagia Sophia suggests that she is wearing cosmetics: but links between mosaic and actuality are not always simple (discussed in B. Hill, *Imperial women in Byzantium 1025–1204*, (Longman 1999), 90–91).

across the southern Balkans. John had military duties. Piroska, it is suggested, was being kept away from the palace in Constantinople, where Eirene Doukaina was so strongly opposed to her son as to treat his wife and their impending offspring without adequate care.[26] I have always found this threat rather unlikely: Eirene Doukaina plainly supported Anna Komnene against her brother John, but not so fiercely, so early. I would combine the motif of the wicked mother-in-law with a large helping of conventional romance. The newlyweds were closer in age than most aristocratic couples. It seems to me probable that, to enjoy each other's company, they were willing to put up with the discomfort inevitable in a tent, even an imperial tent. Eirene Doukaina had done the same for Alexios, apparently for medical reasons. Piroska's twins were born at Balabista, a village in Macedonia (today Sidirokastro, Greece), not in the *porphyra*, the imperial birthing-chamber in the capital.[27] A quarter-century or more later, Piroska, now in her forties, was again travelling near the main imperial army, shadowing John, who was fighting in central Anatolia. How often did this happen? There was then no reason to keep her from the capital. We know of her journey because she fell sick and died in Bithynia, to John's intense grief.[28] The affection between them will recur in connection with the Pantokrator *typikon*.

The immediate birth of a male heir and a female twin must have caused joy in Byzantium—though the Byzantines were used to fecundity and had not yet tasted its opposite. It will also have confirmed links between the empire and Hungary which the marriage was planned to cement. In the absence of contemporary discussion, or firm dating of the marriage and surrounding events, it is difficult to be sure of precise motivations, as Attila Bárány shows elsewhere in this volume. However, it seems very likely that they again involved the impending attack of Bohemond. When he was defeated, Hungarians were among the signatories of the treaty of Debol.[29] There seems little doubt that Piroska's marriage was regarded as a diplomatic success by both Hungary and Byzantium.

Piroska and the Pantokrator: questions

Piroska's most important action in Byzantium was her share in the foundation of the monastic complex of the Pantokrator. The most revealing document is its *typikon*, with rules for its operation and attendant religious services, written in John II's

---

[26] e.g. V. Stanković, "John II Komnenos before the year 1118" in *John II Komnenos*, 17–18.
[27] Anna Komnene, 370, lines 42–4 describe the birth: the surrounding text can only be explained by the assumption that the couple were following Alexios's army.
[28] Kinnamos, 14 lines 6–8.
[29] Anna Komnene, 423 line 45.

name. The building of the Pantokrator raises questions in many areas. Some relate to the building, the processes leading to the funding and construction in the twelfth century of the largest, best-endowed religious complex in the capital since Justinian. Archeological analysis of the Pantokrator shows one or two major changes of plan. How were these decided, and by whom? Byzantine building practice emphasised continuous adjustments as the building developed, rather than preliminary planning, which was usually sketchy.[30] How far were the sponsors of the project, John and Piroska-Eirene, involved in this micromanagement, and how did the builders learn of their wishes? Analysis of the materials and workmanship proves disappointing, with more spolia than would be expected, often combined hastily and sloppily. Was this the result of time pressures, and if so, when? A "nouveau-riche"[31] aesthetic has been detected—rich materials used with unexpectedly poor taste, particularly towards the end of the project. Whose fault was this?

There was originally only the south church, the *katholikon* of the Pantokrator monastery, a burial site for the emperor and empress, with a body of monks to keep their memory alive with constant prayers for their salvation. That church was finished, and its external surfaces plastered. But later two other churches were added. One, the north church, dedicated to the Theotokos Eleousa, was unfinished when construction began on the other, the burial church of St Michael called the *herōon*. This was built between the other two and involved destruction of several finished northern bays of the south church. All three were almost certainly completed before the *typikon* was written and signed (1136), and probably before the burial of the empress (1134). The last two churches were finished around the same time. St Michael's would become the memorial church of the whole Komnenian dynasty, under John II's successor Manuel I. However, it is clear that the original purpose of John and Piroska-Eirene was more limited. Only their eldest son, Alexios *porphyrogennetos*, was to be buried in the same space as his parents—if he wished it, as the *typikon* says three times.[32] Alexios's twin Maria and their six siblings were to

---

[30] R. Ousterhout, *Master Builders of Byzantium*, (Philadelphia 2008), *passim*. For the Pantokrator used as an example, see pp. 104–8.

[31] R. Ousterhout, "The decoration of the Pantokrator (Zeyrek Camii): Evidence old and new" in A. Ödekan, E. Akyürek and N. Necipoğlu (eds.), *First International Sevgi Gönül Byzantine Studies Symposium* (Istanbul 2010), 439; idem, "Architecture and patronage in the age of John II," in *John II Komnenos*, 146.

[32] *Typikon* (ed. Gautier), p. 79, lines 834–8, p. 83, lines 886–7, p. 89, lines 1009–11. Eng. tr. section 32 (p. 755), section 35 (p. 756), section 44 (p. 759). Does this show John's delicacy, not to pressure his son by pre-empting a decision on his burial place, or does it reflect intense family discussions (even dissensions) on the issue?

be interred elsewhere. The transformation from one church to three during John II's reign is not easy to explain. The increase in scope under Manuel I could easily have been inspired by the neighboring church of the Holy Apostles.

There has been speculation as to who should be called the founder of the monastery, John II or Piroska-Eirene. Most contemporary references cast the empress in this role, suggesting that she had the original idea, turned into reality by money that John provided; however a few sources give the primary role to John.[33] This discussion is not completely arid. It has the potential to make a significant contribution to analysis of aristocratic gender-roles in Byzantium. How did the collaboration work? Did the empress contribute only very general thoughts, leaving John and his builders to work out the details and build them in a masculine way? Doubtless Piroska-Eirene encouraged her husband with smiles and tears, the accepted range of female behavior. Did she also make precise proposals, watch the masterbuilder implement them, and then play a significant role when plans were changed? The choice between these two scenarios will influence views on the relationship between twelfth-century male and female patronage. This case is especially valuable as an example of loving co-operation; gender roles are more commonly studied in more adversarial situations.

Piroska and the Pantokrator: discussion

The first part of the discussion has a simple answer: Piroska was a founder of the Pantokrator. The survival of her name in this role had to compete with so many pressures for its suppression that it must represent a reality. John was a man, an emperor and must have organised the provision of the vast sums required. Unlike his wife, he survived to the end of the project, had the *typikon* written, signed it and took part in any attendant ceremonies. It would have been easy to forget his wife. The best formulation of the answer is that of Paul Magdalino: "The Pantokrator was a work of conjugal devotion, and a monument not so much to the extended imperial kin-group as to the emperor's nuclear family."[34] John wrote an introduction to the *typikon* ensuring that all readers understood it as a joint enterprise. I would like to

---

[33] For example, the Dedication poem implies that Eirene's responsibilities were very wide, while Choniates does not even mention her. See W. Hörandner, "Zur Beschreibung von Kunstwerken in der byzantinischen Dichtung—am Beispiel des Gedichtes auf das Pantokratorklosters in Konstantinopel", in C. Ratkowitsch (ed.), *Sitzungsberichte der Öst. Akad. der Wiss., Phil.-hist Klasse* 735, Vienna 2006: "Der Dichter schreibt also der Kaiserin nicht nur die Initiative, sonder auch die ganze planung der Werkes zu," 214. Cf. Choniates 48, lines 19–28.
[34] Magdalino, "Urban Setting," 41.

add my voice to other experienced readers of twelfth-century documents who claim that this introduction shows unusual emotion, addressing the Almighty:

> ... through thy help I found someone to share its planning, construction and completion, my partner and helper in life, though before the complete establishment of the task she left this world by thy mysterious decision and by her departure cut me apart and left me torn in two.[35]

This is not routine. John formally attributes to his deceased wife much of the credit for this greatest of building projects and refers to her in truly emotional words.

The master mason for the project, known only as Nikephoros, must have made repeated adjustments to the work, because of the techniques of building mentioned above. It is striking that the texts connect him with Piroska rather than John, apart from one passage where John recruits him to help Piroska's project.[36] One reason is obvious. John was a very active general, and in Choniates's version of his deathbed speech, he claims to have spent most of his life in tents.[37] Thus for the campaigning season at least, he was often unavailable to Nikephoros.[38] Piroska-Eirene does not seem a static empress, but she was more accessible than John. Her first and last recorded actions as a Byzantine empress involved following the field army in a tent. When her life's project was nearing completion on a building site in central Constantinople, she cannot have resisted the temptation to leave the palace for discreet visits, especially at crucial moments, when her presence was probably requested.

It is impossible to detail the duties of a Byzantine empress in the twelfth century, since no Komnenian guide to imperial ceremonies survives. Being devout, she must have fulfilled her religious reponsibilities in full. Piroska had to care for her

---

[35] ... διὰ σοῦ συγκοινωνὸν τῆς προθέσεως καὶ τῆς προσαγωγῆς καὶ τῆς πράξεως εὑρὼν τὴν τοῦ βίου κοινωνὸν καὶ συλλήπτορα, κἂν πρὸ τῆς ἐντελοῦς τοῦ ἔργου συστάσεως μετέστη τῶν τῇδε τοῖς ἀρρήτοις σου κρίμασι κἀμὲ συναποτεμοῦσα τῇ μεταστάσει καὶ διχότομον ἀποδείξασα. P. Gautier (ed.), "Le typikon du Christ Saveur Pantocrator," *Revue des études byzantines* 32, 1974. pp. 1–145, here 18–22. The translation is that of Robert Jordan, in J. Thomas and A. Constantinides Hero (eds.), *Byzantine Monastic Foundation Documents*, vol. 2 (Washington DC 2000), 738. V. Stanković gives another perspective: "John II Komnenos behaved more like a family man than any other emperor did during these times, keeping his children close to him and fighting to keep the future of the dynasty within his immediate lineage," "John II Komnenos before the year 1118," in *John II Komnenos*, 21.

[36] Texts collected in Loukaki, "Collaborators."

[37] Choniates, 43, lines 48–9 and 63–64.

[38] We know where he was fighting at the beginning of his reign and again in the 1030s. Information for most of the 1120s is sketchy, with no precision over dates. For a good attempt at a timeline of events, see A. Rodruigez Suarez in *John II Komnenos*, xix–xxi.

children, who covered a range of some fourteen years, demanding varied forms of attention. She had a large household to help, but that added other responsibilities. Family celebrations will have taken up a lot of her time. Probably five of her children married before her death, and she saw several grandchildren. The huge Komnenian clan was constantly celebrating births, marriages and deaths. But, despite all this, with determination she should have been able to respond fairly quickly to Nikephoros's requests. By John's accession in 1118, she would be more or less mistress of her surroundings, even the Greek language, with teenage Byzantine twins to help her. What might she have said to Nikephoros during her visits?

The most significant date in the building of the Pantokrator was when a second church was started next to the monastery's finished *katholikon*. I would suggest that neither the first church nor the other two were likely to have been built in less than five years, suggesting that the crucial moment fell between 1125–1129. The scope of this decision remains obscure. Did it plan the building of both second and third churches? Or was there a second key moment, when it was decided to add a third church, as the second was being built? These questions involve major changes in the purpose of the complex, which we will soon discuss.

But first there are the anomalies Ousterhout indicates in building techniques. Are these due to Piroska-Eirene's influence? Did she demand speedy work, leading to sloppy results? Did John order a rushed job to complete a space for a distinguished, permanent burial for his wife in 1134? Or had her role been to maintain the standard of work, so that it fell sharply when she died? Was the haste caused by the desire to have most of the fabric and personnel in place in 1136, when the *typikon* was signed and published, before John set out for on a long expedition to Syria?[39] He must have wanted to leave the monks praying for his deceased wife as the *typikon* prescribed, and maybe hoped that other parts of the complex would be working too.

Ousterhout speaks of a nouveau-riche aesthetic as a sign that the Komnenians as a dynasty tended to act as parvenus, implying that John was responsible for the lapses in taste. Similar attitudes have been detected in other Komnenians. But we have all learned to say "he or she" rather than using unconsidered masculine pronouns for anonymous achievements. Would it not also be right, when attributing nouveau-riche attitudes, to consider Piroska? She found herself in a world where imperial women had great power and were expected to use it, though not to broadcast it while their husbands were alive. John's absences may have given her effective control over much of the expenditure. We cannot assume that she would react with restraint.

---

[39] The *typikon* of the Pantokrator was signed and dated in October, 1136, while John marched with a large army overland to Cilicia in time for the next year's campaigning season.

We should now examine the change or changes of purpose which occurred when the project's goal increased from one church to three. The purpose of the previous stage was to provide a burial place for John and Piroska and monks to pray for their salvation—in western terms, a chantry chapel on the most lavish scale. Other family members, maybe parents and children, may have been commemorated at a secondary level, but since the *typikon* refers only to the completed complex, we do not know who was included in the original plans. As well as these ceremonies, the monastery claimed primacy within the dynasty for this imperial pair, against rivals including John's siblings Anna and Isaac. The Pantokrator also celebrated the Komnenian dynasty, without blurring the main focus on John and Piroska.

At some time, probably between 1125-9, this format was judged inadequate, and a neighboring but separate north church, the Theotokos Eleousa was begun. I find it hard to understand why, without including the third church as the main focal point. The Theotokos Eleousa was not a monastic church, being open to the public. "Accessible to the outside community and officiated by a lay clergy, the north church opened to a public street through a portico along its north wall, where brackets are preserved."[40] Before it was finished, the third church was begun, and the two were completed together. The most convincing motive for these changes which I have read is the following sentence—where Ousterhout is describing the results of the new architectural format, not exploring its motivation. "... the situation of the imperial tombs was significantly enhanced—the chapel was enveloped by the prayers of two churches, lay and monastic—with which it communicated."[41]

It seems to me likely that a decision was made to build the *herōon*, creating new spaces for the burial of the imperial pair and their eldest son Alexios. But the plans also included elaborate ceremonial for the distribution of alms to the poor and visitations by major Constantinopolitan processions, inserting the new building into the popular religious life of the capital. Family members of those interred there and others would expect to visit. Such events in the monastery would disturb the monks' prayerful duties, and break rules of monastic exclusion. Recent research suggests to my non-archaeological perception the possibility that the Theotokos Eleousa was built as a public entrance to the *herōon*, consecrated ground without the limitations of a monastery.

Let us leave aside this proposal and also the question whether expansion occurred in one step or two. If one views the change through a dynastic prism, what new point was made to those familiar with the *katholikon* when they visited

---

[40] Ousterhout, "Architecture and patronage," 144.
[41] Ibid., 145.

the *herōon*? There was confirmation of previous messages—the importance of the dynasty and the centrality of John II and his family. But the chief emphasis may have been on the other crowned emperor, Alexios, John' eldest son, as heir to the throne, the next link in the chain of Komnenian rulers. The almost complete loss of the mosaics of the *katholikon* makes it impossible to know what they did *not* contain; but I have seen no sign that his role was stressed there. But by being buried in the *herōon*, he is definitively separated from his siblings. Could the message have been largely aimed at them? They, like Alexios, were *porphyrogennetoi*, probably fully so, born in the imperial *porphyra*, rather than at Balabista like Alexios. It is easy to assume that the message of the *herōon* was support for the primacy of Alexios against his siblings.[42] But it is hard to proceed beyond imagination[43] and assumption without identifying an event at the right date to trigger in the builders of the *herōon* the need to send its apparent message.

A Hungarian contribution?

The Pantokrator project promised insights into a good instance of collaboration between an aristocratic Byzantine husband and wife. But information has proved so elusive that the chances of useful results seem small. However, before accepting failure, I wish to examine one dimension of Piroska's situation which may help.

Many aristocratic brides in Constantinople were married at puberty, twelve or thirteen years old. This would make little difference to their future cultural identities if they were Byzantines, continuing development in the same society as before. But if from elsewhere, they would have been barely integrated into the societies from which they came, or aware of the changes occurring at migration. Piroska was a crucial three or four years older. Those with experience of migrants and their children would expect sixteen-year-olds to maintain their previous linguistic skills much better than twelve-year-olds, and to retain a more rounded memory of their origins.[44] Piroska at marriage would have been more a young Hungarian than a juvenile ready to receive the impress of the society (whichever society) where she lived out

---

[42] There is a parallel situation in Hagia Sophia, where the panel including John and Piroska was later supplemented with a mosaic portrait of their son Alexios on a contiguous wall. This is usually dated to Alexios's crowning as co-emperor in 1122; might it perhaps have been later?

[43] For example, I can imagine (without a shred of evidence) an argument in 1125 where Alexios (c. 20 years old) might have been challenged by Andronikos (c. 18) and Isaac (c. 14), with the thought that some of the family were more *porphyrogennetoi* than others.

[44] Most of my professional life was spent teaching Greek migrants in Australia, where this issue arose frequently both at theoretical and practical levels.

her teenage years. She was hardly younger than her husband, not four or five years younger, as was the norm; she would learn of the new society more as his partner than his pupil.

This gives another possible criterion to distinguish her contribution from her husband's in the Pantokrator project. That building shows a history of changes of purpose, detail and aesthetic. Opportunities to make changes (I hope to have shown) were at least as available to Eirene-Piroska as to John. Each change should be examined for Hungarian influence: it is possible that alterations in the plan or the fabric of the Pantokrator may have been caused by early interaction between her Hungarian past and her Byzantine present. Similar reactions would still be possible later, when she would be thinking much more like a Byzantine.

I shall discuss two possible examples. The first is brief and schematic. I suggested that the Theotokos Eleousa might have been built as a non-monastic second entrance to the *herōon*. Were such double entrances to burial sites a Byzantine phenomenon? Or was there any shrine in Piroska's Hungarian heritage which might have suggested it? One thinks of the major royal sites of Esztergom (her birthplace) and Székesfehérvár (St Stephen's basilica). Piroska probably spent most of her Hungarian life in the ancient convent of Veszprémvölgy, must have gone to see her father's tomb (site contested) and probably visited other sacred sites, especially those devoted to the Mother of God. It is difficult to discover how far she was restricted to her convent, especially as royal princesses everywhere often break such rules. If a parallel site may be found in Hungary, it may shed light on her role at the Pantokrator, and maybe confirm a reason for building the Theotokos Eleousa. Unfortunately, I am not qualified linguistically nor in other relevant disciplines to perform this work, and can only recommend it others, chiefly archaeologists who know Hungarian. I have no idea of the answers to any of the questions posed.

The second example is longer and more serious. I have suggested that at a date in the mid to late 1120s, a decision was made to add to the *katholikon* of the Pantokrator other structures to emphasise (among other things) the prominence of John II's nuclear family and to stress the designation of his eldest son, Alexios the co-emperor, as his successor. Why was this decision taken? Like the Komnenians in Byzantium, the Árpáds in Hungary were suffering strife between siblings in the royal family. I will sketch out one of the fiercest of these quarrels.[45] Piroska's father

---

[45] Told in context by F. Makk, *The Árpáds and the Comneni: political relations between Hungary and Byzantium in the twelfth century*, Budapest 1989, 11–17 (henceforward Makk, *Árpáds and Comneni*). See also M. Font, *Koloman the learned: King of Hungary*, Szeged 2001, 1–23 (henceforward Font, *Koloman*).

Ladislaus came to the throne because the two sons of his predecessor, Coloman and Álmos, were underage. He undertook to educate them. Against regular practice, he prepared Coloman, the elder, for a clerical career, while Álmos had a military education suitable for a king. This more or less declared Coloman unsuitable for the royal office, and Ladislaus confirmed this by naming Álmos as his successor just before his own death. Coloman, however, refused to acquiesce, and succeeded in gaining the throne, at the expense of giving his brother other important positions which made him nearly as powerful as himself. The beginning of Coloman's reign was marked by almost yearly attempts by Álmos to replace him. Piroska, however secluded in her convent, must have been aware of these problems before she left for Byzantium. She may have been reminded of them soon after. Álmos passed through Constantinople on his way to the Holy Land in 1107.[46] We do not know if they met. When back in Hungary his attempts to replace Coloman continued. Finally Coloman around 1114 completely lost patience and blinded Álmos, his son Béla and other adherents, a key moment in Hungarian history, for the Hungarian throne soon passed to of the blind Béla and his descendants.

Byzantine-Hungarian relations at the time revolved around the upper Adriatic, where these powers vied with Venice for supremacy. At an uncertain date Byzantium and Hungary found themselves on opposite sides, and Álmos decided to leave Hungary for exile in Constantinople. Ferenc Makk argues that this occurred in 1126, and that Piroska's presence was one reason for choosing exile there.[47] What is certain is that he died there in 1127. Piroska must have met Álmos and probably heard his tale emotionally told in Hungarian, a language she is likely still to have understood but could no longer use well. Major actors in the story were her father and her guardian, the two shadowy men who had governed, mainly from afar, her life in the convent of Veszprémvölgy. How strong was her reaction to Álmos's story? The only evidence we have is the fact that around this time a decision was taken to double approximately the size of the Pantokrator complex and Piroska and John's investment in it, which was already huge. They might at any time have decided that sibling strife demanded major architectural confirmation of John's chosen successor. But the coincidence in dates between Álmos's visit and their decision makes one think that it may have been a trigger. The reception of Álmos later led to hostilities between Byzantium and Hungary.

---

[46] Makk, *Árpáds and Comneni*, 24. Font, *Koloman*, 23–4.
[47] Ibid. Font, *Koloman*, 82–3.

Conclusion

Piroska's life divides neatly into thirds. In the first (1088-c1104), she was an Árpád princess, the religious daughter of the very religious Ladislaus I. She was an orphan, losing both parents by the age of eight, and brought up in a convent. Her father's successor, Coloman, became her guardian. Her childhood will have been comfortable, but perhaps rather unloved. Piroska was then sent to Byzantium, to marry the future John II. She went as a Hungarian teenager, rather older than average Byzantine brides of the time, with considerable understanding of the world she had left.[48]

In the second third (c. 1104–1118) she was the wife of the heir to the Byzantine throne, in a marriage which was probably loving and fulfilling. She performed the expected duty of her position, giving birth to the next generation of the ruling family. She was successfully pregnant seven times in fourteen years, producing four boys and four girls. We know of no unsuccessful pregnancies. During this time she would have been almost invisible, not only from the exhaustion of pregnancy and childbirth, but also because, as a foreigner, she had to rely largely on her husband and his household to relate to a foreign, Greek-speaking environment. As John's beloved wife, her position was privileged, but not as unfettered as she would become later.

The second third ended with two simultaneous changes in 1118, with Piroska around thirty-one. She bore her last child, the future Manuel I, and her husband acceded to the imperial throne. It is not known why she had no more children, but this probably released energy for other activities. Accession to the throne brought John II great responsibilities, but also the power and funds for larger personal projects than before. It seems that the changes of 1118 released pent-up ambitions in both of them. Within a year or two they commenced the reign's largest non-military project, the building of the Pantokrator. Once begun, this lasted for the final third of her life (1118–1134). The sources, as we have seen, suggest that this was a combined conjugal project. Piroska's role was still largely invisible, but she was probably now competent in her own environment, with a large family and increasing numbers of contacts and friends. Behind her feminine reserve she was probably becoming more influential. The monastery and first church of the Pantokrator were completed, celebrating the Komnenian dynasty and the special role of John and Piroska within it.

But my linguistically limited reading of the evidence makes her and her husband seriously worried about fraternal strife and future relations in the Komnenian

---

[48] Contrast Piroska with the three daughters of the *sebastokratorissa* Eirene at the age of 16, having been married at 12 or 13. One was in Vienna, giving imperial legitimation as duke to her husband, the Babenberg Henry II Jasomirgott. The other two were already widows. See Varzos II, no. 129, p. 155; no. 130, p. 161; no. 131, p. 171.

family. She had left Hungary understanding that her ex-guardian and his brother were enemies, and afterwards heard that her father had also been involved. The later news that this enmity led to several blindings will have shocked her. John II's situation in Byzantium was also strained but less violent, with chronic disagreements separating him from his sister Anna (and their mother) and also his brother Isaac, together with wider pressures.[49] The royal pair may have noticed that their own children were already showing signs of the quarrels which would divide them later. Then, probably in 1126, Álmos arrived in the capital, a Hungarian personification of the destructive power of friction between siblings. At around that time, we have suggested that Piroska and John decided to build one, probably two new churches at the Pantokrator. The new buildings set in stone the status of their eldest son as next in the line of Komnenian emperors, excluding his siblings even from being buried with him. Álmos's story may have moved John II, but it is likely to have had a much greater impact on Piroska-Eirene, through his direct linguistic appeal and the important roles played by her father and guardian. I would like to suggest for consideration by experts in Hungarian history that it was she who first proposed the expansion of the site, and then persuaded her husband to find the funds.

Bibliography
Primary Sources

Bryennios, Nicéphore. *Histoire*. Introduction, texte, traduction et notes par Paul Gautier. Bruxelles: Byzantion, 1975.

Choniates, Nicetas. *O City of Byzantium: Annals of Niketas Choniatēs*. Detroit: Wayne State University Press, 1984.

Gautier, Paul. "Le typikon du Christ Saveur Pantocrator." *Revue des études byzantines* 32 (1974), 1–145.

Prodromos, Theodore. *Theodoros Prodromos: Historische Gedichte*, edited by Wolfram Hörandner. Vienna: Österreichischen Akademie der Wissenschaften, 1974.

Manasses, Constantine. *Hodoiporikon*. ed. K. Horna. *Byzantinische Zeitschrift* 13 (1904), 325–347.

---

[49] V. Stanković sums up John's feelings in 1136 as follows: "... John had become a political realist: at forty-nine, having lost his wife and the strongest supporter in his life two years earlier, his lifelong experience of the growing rivalry among his closest relatives had persuaded him that disputes and quarrels over precedence within the Komnenian family would likely never cease," *John II Komnenos*, 15.

Tyr, Guillaume de. *Chronique*. Eds. R.B.C. Huygens, H.E. Mayer, G. Rösch. Corpus Christianorum Continuatio Mediaevalis LXIII Turnhout: Typographi Brepols, 1986.

Secondary Sources

Angold, Michael J., *The Byzantine Empire 1025-1204*. London and New York: Longman, 1984.

Bucossi, Alessandra and Suarez, A. R. *John II Komnenos: Emperor of Byzantium. In the Shadow of Father and Son*. London: Center for Hellenic Studies, 2016.

Font, Márta. *Koloman the Learned, King of Hungary*. Szeged: JATE, 2001.

Hill, Barbara. *Imperial women in Byzantium, 1025–1204: Power, Patronage, and Ideology*. London: Longman, 1999.

Hörandner, Wolfram. "Zur Beschreibung von Kunstwerken in der byzantinischen Dichtung — am Beispiel des Gedichtes auf das Pantokratorklosters in Konstantinopel". In C. Ratkowitsch (ed.), *Die poetische Ekphrasis von Kunstwerken*. Vienna: Österreichischen Akademie der Wissenschaften, 2006, 203–219.

Jeffreys, E. M. and J. M. "Who was Eirene the *sebastokratorissa*?" *Byzantion* 64 (1994), 40–68.

Jeffreys, E.M. "The *sebastokratorissa* Irene as Patron." In: L. Theis, M. Mullett and M. Grünbart (eds.), *Female Founders in Byzantium and Beyond*. Wiener Jahrbuch für Kunstgeschichte LX-LXI (2011–2), 177–94.

Kotzabassi, Sofia ed. *The Pantokrator Monastery in Constantinople*. Byzantinisches Archiv 27. (Berlin: De Gruyter, 2013).

Laiou, Angeliki. *Mariage, amour et parenté à Byzance aux XIe-XIII siècles*. Paris: De Boccard, 1992.

Magdalino, Paul. *The Empire of Manuel I Komnenos*. Cambridge: Cambridge University Press, 1993.

———. "The Foundation of the Pantokrator Monastery in its Urban Setting." In: Kotzabassi, Sofia ed., *The Pantokrator Monastery in Constantinople*. Byzantinisches Archiv 27. Berlin: De Gruyter, 2013, 33–56.

Makk, Ferenc. *The Árpáds and the Comneni: political relations between Hungary and Byzantium in the twelfth century*. Budapest: Akadémiai Kiadó, 1989.

Neville, Leonora A. *Anna Komnene: The Life and Work of a Medieval Historian*. New York: Oxford University Press, 2016.

Oikonomidès, Nicolas. "Le serment de l'impératrice Eudocie: une épisode de l'histoire dynastique de Byzance." *Revue des Études Byzantines* 21 (1963) 73–97.

Ousterhout, Robert G. *Master Builders of Byzantium*. Philadelphia: University of Pennsylvania Museum of Archaeology and Anthropology, 2008.

---. "The Decoration of the Pantokrator (Zeyrek Camii): Evidence Old and New." In: A. Ödekan, E. Akyürek and N. Necipoğlu (eds.), *First International Sevgi Gönül Byzantine Studies Symposium*. Istanbul: Vehbi Koc Vakfı, 2010.

---. "Architecture and Patronage in the Age of John II." In: *John II Komnenos: Emperor of Byzantium. In the Shadow of Father and Son*, eds. Alessandra Bucossi, A. R. Suarez. London: Center for Hellenic Studies, 2016, 135–154.

Stanković, Vlada. "John II Komnenos before the year 1118" In: *John II Komnenos: Emperor of Byzantium. In the Shadow of Father and Son*, ed. Alessandra Bucossi, A. R. Suarez. London: Center for Hellenic Studies, 2016, 11–21.

---. *Komnini u Carigradu*. Belgrade: Vizantoloski in-t SANU, 2006.

Stanković, Vlada, and Berger, Albrecht. "The Komnenoi and Constantinople before the Building of the Pantokrator Complex." In: Kotzabassi, Sofia ed., *The Pantokrator Monastery in Constantinople*. Byzantinisches Archiv 27. Berlin: De Gruyter, 2013, 3–32.

Varzos, Kostantinos. *Η γενεαλογία των Κομνηνών* (2 vols.), Thessaloniki: Kentron Vyzantinon Ereunon, 1984.

KOMNENIAN EMPRESSES:
FROM POWERFUL MOTHERS TO PIOUS WIVES

Roberta Franchi

"In the midst of her court of eunuchs and women, far from the tedium of ceremonies, far from the tumults of the capital, in the quiet peacefulness of flowery gardens, amid the clear sparkle of fountains ... lived ... the Most Pious and Most Happy Augusta, the Christ-loving *basilissa*, the Empress of Byzantium," wrote French historian Charles Diehl in 1906.[1] To deconstruct the Enlightenment prejudices of Montesquieu[2] and Gibbon about Byzantine history, viewed as a period of fall, dominated by weak, subservient, and bad women,[3] Diehl isolated the Byzantine empress, living in magnificent palaces far from the concerns of political affairs, and with a limited access to power. Thus, Diehl declared the empress ultimately powerless. This concept

---

[1] Charles Diehl, *Figures Byzantines* (Paris: Armand Colin, 1906), English tr. Harold Bell - Theresa de Kerpeley, *Byzantine Empresses* (London: Elek, 1964), 5. Diehl's book was a fundamental work on Byzantine empresses.

[2] Montesquieu conceived of the Byzantine Empire as a tragic epilogue to the glory of Rome: Charles Louis de Secondat Montesquieu, *Considérations sur le causes de la grandeur des Romains et de leur décadence* (1734), in R. Caillois (ed.), Montesquieu, *Oeuvres complètes*, 2 vols, (Paris: Gallimard, 1949–1951).

[3] Although fascinated by Byzantium, Edward Gibbon considered the Byzantine period as the triumph of barbarism and Christianity. In particular, he abhorred the promotion of empresses who shared equal positions of authority with the emperors. Praising Eudokia Makrembolitissa and Anna Komnene, he criticized the majority of Byzantine empresses, from Theodora in the sixth century to Irene in the eighth, till Anne of Savoy in the fourteenth century. Theodora's decadence symbolizes the depravity of the Byzantine empire: Edward Gibbon, *The Decline and Fall of the Roman Empire*, revised edition by John B. Bury, 7 vols, (London: Methuen, 1909–1914), chapter 40 (vol. 4, 226–233, on Theodora); chapters 48 and 53 (vol. 5, 200–204, 295–296, Eirene); chapter 53 (vol. 5, 238, and vol. 6, 111, Eudokia and Anna); and chapter 63 (vol. 6, 517, 519–521, 523–527, Anne of Savoy). See also Anne McClanan, *Representations of Early Byzantine Empresses: Image and Empire*, (New York: Palgrave, 2002), 119–120.

remained dominant until recently, when scholars, such as Judith Herrin, Lynda Garland, Barbara Hill, and Liz James revised the connection between women, gender roles, and imperial power in Byzantine society.[4] They reconsidered the notion that Byzantium lacked institutional structure for female rulership and that the empress was able to wield power only in exceptional circumstances as regent.[5] Women's status is difficult to grasp because society is predicted on and around men and male values: men are the positive members, whereas women are the other. Nevertheless, Byzantine imperial women did not sit on the sidelines of their society, uninterested in anything except their domestic affairs: they played an important and often decisive role in social and political history. The lives of the Byzantine empresses must be seen in a broad historical and political context so as to understand the ways their authority and their involvement in politics functioned.[6]

Max Weber defined power as "the probability that one actor within a social relationship will be in a position to carry out his will, despite resistance, regardless of the basis on which this probability rests."[7] Although women's power existed in a framework of male authority and the balance of power in society relied on men, imperial women exerted authority and had goals, which they worked to reach, often in acceptable ways, sometimes by manipulation. The key issue of women and power in Byzantium is not whether women possessed power—they did—, but rather of how and in what sphere they exercised it.[8] The problem can be approached from

---

[4] Lynda Garland, "The Life and Ideology of Byzantine Women: A Further Note on Conventions of Behaviour and Social Reality as Reflected in Eleventh and Twelfth Century Historical Sources," *Byzantion* 58 (1988): 361–393; ead., "'The Eye of the Beholder': Byzantine Imperial Women and their Public Image from Zoe Porphyrogenita to Euphrosyne Kamaterissa Doukaina (1028–1203)," *Byzantion* 64 (1994): 19–39, 261–313; ead., *Byzantine Empresses: Women and Power in Byzantium, AD 527–1204*, (New York: Routledge, 1999); Judith Herrin, "The Imperial Feminine in Byzantium," *Past and Present* 169 (2000): 3–35; ead., *Women in Purple: Rulers of Medieval Byzantium*, (Princeton: Princeton University Press, 2001); ead., *Byzantium: The Surprising Life of a Medieval Empire*, (Princeton: Princeton University Press, 2007); ead., *Unrivalled Influence: Women and Empire in Byzantium*, (Princeton: Princeton University Press, 2013); Barbara Hill, *Imperial Women in Byzantium 1025–1204: Power, Patronage and Ideology*, (London-New York: Longman, 1999); Liz James, *Empresses and Power in Early Byzantium*, (London: Leicester University Press, 2001).

[5] Empresses may have had power as regents for young sons or they may have been consorts, but under these circumstances, they were naturally bound by the wishes and temperaments of their husbands. The common definition of "power" in the ancient world placed legitimate authority solely in the hands of men, while the lives of imperial women remained absent in the political scenario. It is only in the last three decades that Byzantine scholars' interest spread to women's studies.

[6] Women had access to political power through their relationships with the emperor.

[7] Max Weber, *Economy and Society*, (Berkeley: University of California Press, 1978), 53.

[8] Women and power has become a growing research field and produced remarkable results. See, for instance, Mary Erler-Maryanne Kowaleski (eds), *Women and Power in the Middle Ages*, (Athens-Lon-

four angles: the titles by means of people of the imperial court were arranged into a hierarchy; the kinship system; patronage; and ideology. The women of the Komnenian dynasty are a case in point. They dominated the eleventh–twelfth centuries as kingmakers, founders of monastic institutions, and literary patronesses. There was a great contrast, however, between the beginning and the end of this period. The different strategies adopted by women in 1080, 1118 or 1146 signal changes in imperial power: there was the "rise and fall" of female influence "behind the throne."[9] Comparing empresses in the early and in the late Komnenian period, this paper argues that the arrival of foreign brides reveals not only Byzantium's expanding international alliances, but also the conspicuous transformation of the empress's role in Byzantium from powerful mothers to pious wives.

The Komnenian Coup: Motherly Power

The Komnenian dynasty was propelled to power by the motherly concern of powerful women. Alexios Komnenos was not a legitimate heir, but a conspirator whose ascent to the Byzantine throne in 1080 was the result of a coup organized by his "two mothers," Anna Dalassene and Maria of Alania. Nikephoros Botaneiates named a close relative as his heir, rather than his stepson, Constantine Doukas. Maria, however, wanted Constantine to become the next emperor. This is why she adopted Alexios and supported his coup, making Alexios and Constantine adoptive brothers and sealing their alliance. Maria married Nikephoros out of interest and when he ill-served her interests, she organized a conspiracy against her husband. With the help of the Doukas and Dalassene family, Maria created a new power base to oppose the emperor. The conspiracy was successful because her legitimating capacity was high, and the emperor's authority was low.[10] Apart from demonstrating a lack of loyalty to her husband, Maria's ability to create a powerful network of supporters reveals the degree of her influence under the reign of Nikephoros Botaneiates. Her profile points out the existence of a right combination of two worlds: a male world dominated by political matters and a female world with a maternal

---

don: The University of Georgia Press, 1988); Nancy F. Partner (ed.), *Studying Medieval Women: Sex, Gender, Feminism,* (Cambridge, Mass.: Medieval Academy of America, 1993); Marianne Sághy-Nancy F. Partner (eds), *Women and Power in Medieval East Central Europe. Medieval and Modern,* Special Issue of East Central Europe 20–23 (1), 1993–1996.

[9] For women's authority "behind the throne" see the detailed analysis in James, *Empresses and Power,* 83–100.

[10] Lynda Garland-Stephen Rapp, "Mary 'of Alania': Woman and Empress between Two Worlds," in *Byzantine Women: Varieties of Experience, AD 800–1200,* ed. Lynda Garland, (Aldershot: Asgate, 2006), 91–124.

disposition.¹¹ Alexios became emperor and, in order to preserve the political alliances created up before the coup, he named Maria's son, his adopted brother Constantine, as co-emperor. He also married Eirene Doukaina, the granddaughter of John Doukas, and by doing this, he gained the political support of one of the most powerful families in Byzantium.¹²

As Margaret Mullett remarked, motherly care was a trump card in 1080.¹³ Maria justified her disloyalty to her husband by her concern for her son. "If you want to get power, get a mother"—and Alexios had two.¹⁴ Both Maria of Alania and Anna Dalassene were praised by Theophylact of Ohrid for their qualities as a mother.¹⁵ The authority of the mother was a stable feature in Byzantium, where mothers greatly promoted the success of their sons.¹⁶ Alexios came to power thanks to the support of the empress and the activity of his biological mother, Anna Dalassene, who created a strong alliance of families in order to support the success of the Komnenoi. The ambitious Anna preserved the surname of her mother's family since it was a more prestigious family than her father's. In the palace, she was held in high respect and wielded remarkable authority, as Anna Komnene observes in the *Alexiad*:

> Whatever she decrees in writing ... shall have permanent validity ... Whatever decisions or orders are made by her, written or unwritten, reasonable or unreasonable, provided they bear her seal shall be regarded as coming from myself. In years to come they shall have the force of law permanently ... Neither now nor in the future shall my mother be subjected to enquiry or undergo any examination whatsoever at the hands of anybody, whoever he may be.¹⁷

---

11   Thalia Gouma-Peterson, "Gender and Power: Passages to the Maternal in Anna Komnene's Alexiad," in *Anna Komnene and Her Times*, ed. Thalia Gouma-Peterson (New York and London: Garland, 2000), 107–124.

12   Anna Komnene, *Alexiad* 2.2.1–3 (ed. Leib, vol. 1, 66–68). For the critical edition see *Anne Comnène, Alexiade*, edited and translated by Bernard Leib, 3 vols, Paris 1937–1945; English tr. Edgar Robert Ashton Sewter, *The Alexiad of Anna Comnena*, (Harmondsworth: Penguin, 1979), 75–77.

13   Margaret Mullet, "The 'Disgrace' of the Ex-Basilissa Maria," *Byzantinoslavica* 45 (1984): 202–211.

14   Eva Nardi, *Né sole né luna. L'immagine femminile nella Bisanzio dei secoli XI e XII*, (Firenze: Leo Olschki, 2002), 133–139.

15   On Constantine and Anna cf. Theophylact of Ohrid, Or. 4, Λόγος εἰς τὸν πορφυρογέννητον κῦρ Κωνσταντῖνον, ed. Paul Gautier, *Théophylacte d'Achrida, Discours, traités, poésies. Introduction, texte, traduction et notes*, (Thessaloniki: Association de Recherches Byzantines, 1980), 177–211; on Alexios and Anna, cf. Theophylact of Ohrid, Or. 5, Λόγο ςεἰς τὸν αὐτοκράτορα κῦριν Ἀλέξιον τὸν Κομνηνόν, ed. Paul Gautier, *Théophylacte d'Achrida, Discours, traités, poésies*, 214–243.

16   Herrin, "The Imperial Feminine in Byzantium," 28.

17   Anna Komnene, *Alexiad* 3.6.6–8 (ed. Leib, vol. 1, 122).

Fig.1: A seal of Anna Dalassene (obverse/reverse), 11th century. The four-line inscription reads: "Lord, help Anna Dalassene, nun, mother of the emperor." © Dumbarton Oaks Research Center, Trustees for Harvard University, Washington, D.C.

Anna Dalassene possessed the necessary qualities for government and she believed it was correct to exert her power and authority, despite her being a woman. Anna Komnene clearly points out: "the whole executive power was entrusted to his mother alone."[18] She exercised power because she was Alexios's mother: "He (Alexios) was in theory the emperor, but she had the real power."[19] Her position as mother of the emperor appears on her seals as an official title (Fig. 1 FF). Anna Dalassene was a model Komnenian mother, in the right place at the right time to take advantage of the high ideological value of motherhood.

In orchestrating the rise of power of her family, Anna Dalassene played a key role. Alexios gave her a prominent position in the court hierarchy by ensuring that she was addressed by the title of *despoina*.[20] She included herself in the imperial formula of ἡ βασιλεία ἡμῶν when granting property to Christodoulos; moreover, she had her personal formula of δεσποινική for testifying that a document was her own. Anna Dalassene was ambitious, but she used her authority to keep the throne safe for the son. The result is evident: Alexios ruled until he died.[21] Nevertheless, her

---

[18] Anna Komnene, *Alexiad* 3.6.3 (ed. Leib, vol. 1, 120).
[19] Anna Komnene, *Alexiad* 3.7.5 (ed. Leib, vol. 1, 124).
[20] Anna Komnene, *Alexiad* 3.2.7 (ed. Leib, vol. 1, 110). On Anna Dalassene see also Garland, *Byzantine Empresses*, 188–193.
[21] Michael Angold, *The Byzantine Empire: A Political History*, (London-New York: Longman, 1984), 114.

authority was unable to interfere with Alexios's purposes: the status of the *despoina* depended on the emperor.²² In contrast with her powerful authority, the silence about her retirement cannot pass unnoticed: her death is unknown as well as the circumstances of her retirement.²³ According to Zonaras, Anna understood that Alexios was becoming tired of her and she decided to retire before she was removed, to live in imperial state for the rest of her life.²⁴

Alexios was surrounded by women, his mother Anna Dalassene and his wife Eirene Doukaina,²⁵ and he established male authority.²⁶ Alexios elevated the imperial family above the rest of society and the only access to the imperial family was by birth or marriage. The complex system of ranks depended on close relationships to the emperor.²⁷ Within this structure, the effect of the new titles on the women of the family and the gap in privilege between the men and the women cannot pass unnoticed. As a part of the imperial family, Komnenian women shared in its prestige, but inside it, they were subordinated as women. To be a relative of the emperor was a good thing, but it was better to be related on the male side.²⁸ The new titles Alexios gave were destined to his male kin: brothers and sons were eligible for the title of *sebastokratōr*, analogous to *basileus*.²⁹ The highest title granted to brothers-in-law and sons-in-law was *caesar*, they never became *sebastokratores*. The emperor

---

22   See also Anna Komnene, *Alexiad* 3.6.3–8 (ed. Leib, vol. 1, 120–122). For more details see Barbara Hill, "Alexios I Komnenos and the Imperial Women," in *Alexios I Komnenos*, vol. 1: *Papers*, eds. Margaret Mullett and Dion Smythe (Belfast: Belfast Byzantine Enterprises, 1996), 37–54, esp. 39; 50–51.

23   Bernard Leib, "Le silences de Anne Comnène ou ce que n'a pas dit l'Alexiade," *Byzantinoslavica* 19 (1958): 1–11.

24   Zonaras, *Epitome Historiarum* 18.24.9–11 (ed. Büttner-Wobst, vol. 3, 746). For the critical edition see *Ioannis Zonarae Epitome Historiarum*, ed. Moritz Pinder and Theodor Büttner-Wobst, 3 vols, (Bonn: Weber, 1841–1897). It has been supposed that Anna Dalassene was involved in a heretical sect.

25   Paul Lemerle, *Cinq études sur le XIe siècle byzantine*, (Paris: Le monde byzantin, 1977), 298.

26   Angold, *The Byzantine Empire*, 92–135; Hill, "Alexios I and the Imperial Women," 38.

27   See Lucien Stiernon, "Notes de titulature et de prosopographie byzantines: Constantin Angelos (pan) sébastohypertate," *Revue des Études Byzantines* 19 (1961): 273–283; Id., "Notes de titulature et de prosopographie byzantines: Adrien (Jean) et Constantin Comnène, sébastes," *Revue des Études Byzantines* 21 (1963): 179–198; Id., "Notes de titulature et de prosopographie byzantines: a propos de trois membres de la famille Rogerios (XIIe siècle)," *Revue des Études Byzantines* 22 (1964): 184–198; Id., "Notes de titulature et de prosopographie byzantines: sébaste et gambros," *Revue des Études Byzantines* 23 (1965): 222–243; Id., "Notes de titulature et de prosopographie byzantines: Theodora Comnène et Andronic Lapardas, sébastes," *Revue des Études Byzantines* 24 (1966): 89–96.

28   See Hill, *Imperial Women*, 96–119; ead., "Alexios I and the Imperial Women," 40–42.

29   Anna Komnene, *Alexiad* 5.2.4 (ed. Leib, vol. 2, 11).

created a system of male relatives around himself to support him, and he gave them governorships of cities and commands in the army.[30] Alexios placed himself into a male world where high rank and power were the right reward for loyalty. Structurally, women had no place in this system. There were no positions they could fill which brought them remarkable authority. Nevertheless, many women appear in the historiography of the time, reflecting the high profile of "aristocratic" women. Women, as well as men, understood how kinship worked, and they tried to extend their repertoire of kin by creating operating networks.[31] Marriage was the most important tool in creating alliances.[32] Not only were women at this time aware of the strong influence exercised by marriage alliances as a profitable method, but also John Doukas was aware of it. Moreover, Zonaras writes that Alexios arranged the marriages not only of his children, but also those of his brother's children, too.[33] Independent of gender, women and men were equally aware of the importance of marriage.[34] But the effects of power through the manipulation of networks that can be noted prior to the Komnenian coup disappear after it. Eirene Doukaina's influence on the marriage alliances created for the members of her family depends on the fact that many foreign brides took her name upon marriage. However, as wife and mother, Eirene had no powerful and visible role, especially in building marriage alliances.[35] The crisis point of 1118 demonstrates her impotence as a mother in comparison to the women of 1081.[36]

Alexios's daughter, Anna Komnene was raised by influential women. Surrounded by Maria of Alania, her grandmother Anna Dalassene, and her mother Eirene Doukaina, Anna became a capable woman animated by a single purpose:

---

[30] Alexios created a sort of "clan government" in the Komnenian dynasty, using first his mother and brother and then his sons and his sons-in law.

[31] See Angold, *The Byzantine Empire*, 106; Paul Magdalino, *The Empire of Manuel I Komnenos 1143–1180*, (Cambridge: Cambridge University Press, 1993), 180–182; Nicolas Oikonomides, "L'évolution de l'organisation administrative de l'empire byzantin au XIe siècle (1025–1118)," *Travaux et Mémoires* 6 (1976): 125–52.

[32] Maria of Alania may have been the initiator of this idea. See the accounts by Anna Komnene, *Alexiad* 3.2.3 (ed. Leib, vol. 1, 107); Zonaras, *Epitome Historiarum* 18.24.14 (ed. Büttner-Wobst, vol. 3, 747).

[33] Zonaras, *Epitome Historiarum* 18.22.27 (ed. Büttner-Wobst, vol.3, 739–740).

[34] Judit Herrin, "In Search of Byzantine Women: Three Avenues of Approach," in *Images of Women in Antiquity*, eds. Averil Cameron and Amélie Kuhrt (London: Croom Helm 1983), 167–189. As Herrin has demonstrated, marriage contracts and wills are "related legal documents," which provide evidence of women's rights of ownership and control of wealth.

[35] Zonaras, *Epitome Historiarum* 18.28.19–20 (ed. Büttner-Wobst, vol. 3, 761–762).

[36] Hill, *Imperial Women*, 120–152.

Fig 2: Solidus of Eirene, 797–802, Constantinople. © Dumbarton Oaks Research Centre, Trustees for Harvard University, Washington, D.C.

to rule Byzantium with her husband, Nikephoros Bryennios.[37] This aim was not new. The imperial precedents show a variety of models on which Byzantine empresses could draw. During the iconoclastic period, Eirene of Athens and Theodora exerted great authority. Eirene manipulated her son to accomplish her own purpose and seize power. After the death of her husband, the Emperor Leo, when Constantine VI was still young, Eirene assumed power and established her legitimacy.[38] She was the first Byzantine empress to issue coins as a sole ruler, on which the term *basilissa* appeared for the first time (Fig 2 FF).[39]

By asserting her political power, Eirene transformed social life and religious dogma.[40] She played a key role in the restoration of icons. Analogously, Theodora seized power for a short time and ruled as sole empress for a year, after the death of Zoë's husband.[41] Eirene and Theodora highlight the power and prominence of imperial women in Byzantium. When comparing her father's quest for power to her own, however, Anna Komnene acknowledged that she failed where Alexios succeeded.[42]

Alexios designated his son, John, as his heir, but Eirene Doukaina supported their daughter Anna's succession. She sought to convince Alexios to appoint

---

[37] Barbara Hill, "A Vindication of the Rights of Women to Power by Anna Komnene," *Byzantinische Forschungen* 23 (1996): 45–53.

[38] François Halkin, "La vie de l'impératrice Sainte Irène," *Analecta Bollandiana* 106 (1988): 5–27; see also Warren T. Treadgold, "The Unpublished Saint's Life of the Empress Irene," *Byzantinische Forschungen* 7 (1982): 237–251; Garland, *Byzantine Empresses*, 73–94.

[39] Some coins show Irene, labeled *augusta*, on the obverse, and her son, Constantine VI, labeled *basileus*, to the reverse. See Leslie Brubaker-Helen Tobler, "The Gender of Money: Byzantine Empresses on Coins (324–802)," *Gender and History* 12.3 (2000): 572–599, esp. 587–590.

[40] Judith Herrin, "Women and the Faith in Icons in Early Christianity," in *Culture, Ideology and Politics: Essays for Eric Hobsbawn*, eds. Raphael Samuel and Gareth Stedman Jones (London-Boston: Routledge and Kegan Paul 1983), 56–83.

[41] Timothy E. Gregory, *A History of Byzantium*, (Malden: Blackwell Publishing, 2005), 252–253.

[42] Robert Browning, *The Byzantine Empire*, (Washington, D.C.:Catholic University of America, 1992), 204; Dion C. Smythe, "Middle Byzantine Family Values and Anna Komnene's Alexiad," in *Byzantine Women: Varieties of Experience, AD 800–1200*, ed. Lynda Garland, 125–140.

Anna as his heir with her husband Nikephoros Bryennios.[43] Old and ill, the emperor delegated his responsibilities to his wife, who in turn directed all affairs to Nikephoros instead of John.[44] On Alexios's death, however, John was proclaimed emperor.[45] Anna, deeply shaken, gathered the military to depose John. Eirene Doukaina supported her, but her husband withdrewt. Nikephoros did not feel entitled to dispose of the legitimate heir. Anna interpreted Nikephoros's refusal as cowardice: "nature had mistaken the two sexes and had endowed Bryennios with the soul of a woman."[46] Her husband's loyalty to Alexios and John debarred Anna from power. The method of legitimation, used previously by Maria of Alania, would have suited Anna to follow in her mother's, grandmother's and potential mother-in-law's footsteps and become an empress. Eirene's motives for supporting her daughter's claims over those of her son remain unclear, though a desire for authority seems possible. Unfortunately, she was unable to organize Anna's coup and her strategy to ensure the succession of her daughter and son-in-law failed.

Anna's account about her mother is a remarkable source for understanding the role played by Eirene Doukaina. Her physical closeness to Alexios gave her opportunities to share in his decisions, also during his campaign. Anna says that it was because of Eirene's role as ever-vigilant guardian that Alexios brought her with him on campaign, but probably it was better for him to have Eirene under his close supervision rather than on the loose in Constantinople.[47] However, Eirene did not exert authority in the public as Anna Dalassene did. Her concerns were devoted to her family and the care of her husband. She was a good mother, but not a great manipulator. After Nikephoros's death in 1137, Anna withdrew to a monastery in Constantinople founded by her mother, where she spent the rest of her life.[48] Although she did not reach her goal of ruling the empire, she remained an influential woman not only with regard to her status, but also to her culture.[49] Her self-

---

[43] Zonaras, *Epitome Historiarum* 18.28.19–20 (ed. Büttner-Wobst, vol. 3, 761–762). See also Choniates, *Historia* 5–7. For the critical edition see *Nicetae Choniatae Historia*, ed. Jan Louis van Dieten, 2 vols, (Berlin-New York: Walter de Gruyter, 1975); English translation by Harry J. Magoulias, *O City of Byzantium: Annals of Niketas Choniates*, (Detroit: Wayne State University Press, 1984).

[44] Zonaras, *Epitome Historiarum* 18.24.16–17 (ed. Büttner-Wobst, vol. 3, 747).

[45] Zonaras, *Epitome Historiarum* 18.22.29 (ed. Büttner-Wobst, vol. 3, 739).

[46] Susan C. Jarratt-Ellen Quandahl, "To Recall Him … Will Be a Subject of Lamentation: Anna Comnene as a Rhetorical Historiographer," *Rethorica: A Journal of the History of Rhetoric* 26 (2008): 301–335, esp. 305–308.

[47] Anna Komnene, *Alexiad* 12.3.2–8 (ed. Leib, vol. 3, 60–63).

[48] Steven Runciman, "The End of Anna Dalassena," *Annuaire de l'Institut de Philologie et d'Histoire Orientales et Slaves* 9 (1949): 517–524.

[49] Thalia Gouma-Peterson, *Anna Komnene and Her Times*, (New York: Garland Publishing, 2000).

presentation in the *prooimion* to the *Alexiad*, as "daughter of the Emperor Alexios and the Empress Eirene, born and bred in the Purple," as a woman "not without some acquaintance with literature" makes it clear.[50]

Although they exercised power in different ways, Anna Dalassene and Eirene Doukaina are Anna's heroines. Eirene's position next to Alexios as wife and mother was as important in a public sense as Anna Dalassene's control of the civil government.[51] Eirene had no a strong role in the power-building activity of marriage alliances and she was unable to support Anna in getting the throne. At Alexios's ascent, female influence behind the throne was strong enough to seize power; on Alexios's death, in a time of transition the power of the empresses lacked the right influence to ensure female inheritance.

Foreign Princesses: Piety as Power

From the reign of John II, the Komnenian dynasty adapted a new marriage policy by allying with European powers. Piroska of Hungary, the empress of John II, and Bertha of Sulzbach, the empress of Manuel I, were not to become the political manipulators comparable to the women from the great Constantinopolitan families. Far from their homeland, these women were deprived of the reassuring confidence of close networks of family and friends, and lacked a power base in Byzantium.[52] They were unable to interfere in political matters. Foreign-born women were disadvantaged in comparison with other aristocratic women. Not only did they lack the training and appreciation of the way the establishment worked, they were short of family networks supporting them with resources and official support groups.[53]

Piroska-Eirene, the first foreign-born empress of Byzantium, formed an ideal couple with her husband, John II: they loved and respected each other. The emperor paid tribute to Eirene's assistance in the *typikon* of the Pantokrator Monastery that they founded together and he grieved deeply her death.[54] After her mar-

---

[50] Anna Komnene, *Alexiad Prooimion* (ed. Leib, vol. 1, 3).
[51] Anna Komnene, *Alexiad* 7.3.11 (ed. Leib, vol. 2, 101). See also Hill, "A Vindication of the Rights," 52–53.
[52] Garland, *Byzantine Empresses*, 223.
[53] The importance of kinship has been investigated in several articles by Ruth Macrides. See, for instance, Ruth Macrides, "Kinship by Arrangement: The Case of Adoption," *Dumbarton Oaks Papers* 44 (1990): 109–118; ead., "Dynastic Marriages and Political Kinship," in *Byzantine Diplomacy*, eds. Jonathan Shepard and Simon Franklin (Aldershot: Variorum, 1992), 263–280.
[54] Kallikles, *Carmina* 2; 28; 31, on which see also the article by Shlyakhtin in this volume. For the critical edition see *Nicola Callicle: Carmi. Testo critico, introduzione, traduzione, commentario e lessico a cura di Roberto Romano*, (Napoli: Bibliopolis, 1980). See also Ioannis Vassis, "Das Pantokra-

riage, she seems to have devoted herself to her large family and pious works. In his epitaphs of the imperial couple, Theodoros Prodromos highlights the virtues of the empress: Eirene excels by her noble birth, powerful family, noble ancestors (εὐτυχῶν προπατόρων), and fertility. She is presented as the "mistress of the West," educated by the kings of the West (Ἰούλιου Καίσαρες) to be the ideal bride of an emperor. Prodromos praises her as a fertile child-bearer, mother of eight children, four of each sex.[55] She embodies the ideal Byzantine imperial consort, in love with her husband.

A lasting tribute to the imperial dignity vested in the empress consort, Eirene's brilliant mosaic portrait in the Hagia Sophia parallels that of Empress Zoë,[56] even if their character and memory differ greatly. Famous for her multiple marriages, Zoë appears in every eleventh-century chronicle as one of the most important women in Byzantium. Her main function during 1028–1050 was to ensure the peaceful succession of emperors by marrying or adopting the next candidate. She was enabled to do so as she was considered the receptacle of imperial majesty and the heir of the empire.[57] In contrast, Eirene is scarcely mentioned by historians. Choniates's chronicle, even if it begins with the death of Alexios I, does not mention Piroska's marriage to John. Eirene's political power, if she had any, had to be played down. Not only was the political role of women not suitable for an epitaph, and therefore not mentioned, but historians ignored such influence if they could. The ideal wife was not supposed to take any part in politics. A seal which pos-

---

torkloster von Konstantinopel in der byzantinischen Dichtung," in *The Pantokrator Monastery in Constantinople*, ed. Sofia Kotzabassi, (Boston-Berlin: Walter de Gruyter), 203–250; Paul Gautier, "Le Typikon du Christ Sauveur Pantocrator," *Revue des Études Byzantines* 32 (1974): 1–145.

[55] Prodromos, *Carmen* 7 (ed. Hörandner, 299–230). For the critical edition see *Theodoros Prodromos: Historische Gedichte*, ed. by Wolfram Hörandner, (Vienna: Österreichischen Akademie der Wissenschaften, 1974). See especially verses 1–7: Εἴ τις νόμος δίδωσι καὶ νεκροῖς λέγειν, / ἰδοὺ βοὴν πέμψασα κἀγὼ τυμβόθεν / τὰ κατ᾽ἐμαυτὴν ἐκδιδάξω σε, ξένε / ἐγὼ προῆλθον εὐτυχῶν προπατόρων / ἀρχῆς ἁπάσης δυσμικῆς βασιλέων, / Ἰουλίου Καίσαρες ἐθρέψαντό με / καὶ καλλονῆς χάριτες ἐστέψαντό με; and verses 14–17: εἰς φῶς προΐσχω τέτταρας μὲν υἱέας / τῆς πατρογεννοῦς ἐκφυέντας πορφύρας, / ἰδεῖν ἀγαθούς, πῦρ πνέοντας εἰς μάχην, / καὶ τέτταρας δὲ κοσμίας θυγατέρας.

[56] Thomas Whittemore, *The Mosaics of Hagia Sophia at Istanbul: Third Preliminary Report, Work Done in 1935–1938: The Imperial Portraits of the South Gallery* (Oxford: Oxford University Press, 1942), 21–28; Id., "A Portrait of the Empress Zoe and of Constantine IX," *Byzantion* 18 (1946–1948): 223–227; Robin Cormack, "Interpreting the Mosaics of S. Sophia at Istanbul," *Art History* 4 (1981): 131–149, esp. 145; Nicolas Oikonomides, "The Mosaic Panel of Constantine IX and Zoe in St Sophia," *Revue des Études Byzantines* 36 (1978): 219–232.

[57] Garland, *Byzantine Empresses*, 136–157; Hill, *Imperial Women*, 42–55; Barbara Hill-Liz James and Dion Smythe, "Zoe: The Rhythm Method of Imperial Renewal," in *New Constantines: The Rhythm of Imperial Renewal in Byzantium, 4th–13th Centuries*, ed. Paul Magdalino (Aldershot: Variorum, 1994), 215–229.

sibly belonged to Eirene seems to confirm this aspect: the foreign empress preferred to use the title of *augusta* rather than *despoina* or *basilissa* on her seal.[58]

Bertha of Sulzbach arrived at Constantinople in 1142. Celebrating her arrival, Theodore Prodromos praises her noble origins,[59] Choniates highlights her noble family (γένους τῶν ἐπιδόξων καὶ πάνυ λαμπροῦ), and her foreigness.[60] Western empresses were unpopular in Byzantium during the reigns of Manuel and Andronikos I Komnenos. Bertha's ethnic background as a German princess was a disadvantage in Byzantine eyes and she was accused of inflexibility and arrogance.

The wedding of Bertha and Manuel did not take place until 1146. One can only guess her feelings during these four years of waiting. It was her kin who finally pushed Manuel to marry Bertha as Emperor Conrad was already on his way to Byzantium. The physical distance of her kin, however, meant that her family was unable to protect her in a way the Doukas family did Eirene.[61] Close kin networks provided more than protection: they conferred power. A Doukas woman had powerful relatives to implore and the Doukas family was able to interfere on the spot. Commenting on Bertha and Manuel's marriage, Prodromos evokes the Pauline teaching that man is superior to woman so as to proclaim the superiority of New Rome over the old[62]: "If the latter produced the bride, it is the former that gives us the bridegroom, and as we all know that man is superior to woman, it follows that the same relationship should be obtained between the two Empires."[63] This statement reveals that Western empresses were perceived as being culturally inferior.

Bertha had to adapt to new customs, new language, and a different culture. The German princess learned the court's ceremonies and learnt Greek, like many imperial women before her, transferred into the sophisticated Byzantine court culture. Kinnamos remarked that Bertha did not understand the meaning of the dark dress worn by Alexios's wife, as she did not know Byzantine customs and ways of

---

[58] See Hill, *Imperial Women*, 104.
[59] Prodromos, *Carmen* 20 (ed. Hörandner, 321).
[60] Choniates, *Historia* 53–54. See also Alexander Kazhdan, "Latins and Franks in Byzantium: Perception and Reality from the Eleventh to the Twelfth Century," in *The Crusades from the Perspective of Byzantium and the Muslim World*, eds. Angeliki E. Laiou and Roy Parviz Mottahedeh (Washington: Dumbarton Oaks, 2001), 83–100, esp. 86–87; Johannes Irmscher, "Bertha von Sulzbach, Gemahlin Manuels I," *Byzantinische Forschungen* 22 (1996): 279–290. For the importance of having noble origins, see Nardi, *Né sole né luna*, 20–30.
[61] Hill, "Alexios I Komnenos and the Imperial Women," 46–47.
[62] This ideology is central in Byzantine political thought. See Franz J. Dölger, "Rom in der Gedankenwelt der Byzantiner," in did., *Byzanz, und die europäische Staatenwelt. Ausgewählte Vorträge und Aufsätze*, (Ettal: Buch-Kunstverlag, 1953), 83–98.
[63] Prodromos, *Carmen* 20 (ed. Hörandner, 320–321).

life: she interpreted the dress as a sign of mourning instead of celebration.⁶⁴ Bertha commissioned the grammarian John Tzetzes to compose the *Allegories of the Iliad*, an explanation of Homer to the use of the Western-born empress. In his dedication, Tzetzes describes Bertha as "a lady very much in love with Homer" (ὁμηρικωτάτη κυρία).⁶⁵ To demonstrate his zeal, he chose a manuscript with an unusually large format and covered the pages with close script in the hope to be better paid, but he was not recompensed for his efforts: Bertha's treasurer paid just as much as the amount upon which they had agreed. Furious, Tzetzes thought that Bertha was unable to appreciate his work at its full value. He destroyed the first edition of his *Chiliades*, cut short his learned commentary on the *Iliad* at the fifteenth book, and finally left to find another patroness.⁶⁶ Bertha's problems in paying John Tzetzes stemmed from the fact that she did not have access to economic resources in the same way as other aristocratic women. During Manuel's reign, the conspicuous spender was the *sebastokratorissa* Eirene, not the empress. The dowager *sebastokratorissa* had more resources, although her position at court was lower.⁶⁷ Anna Dalassene and Eirene Doukaina displayed more economic power than the other Komnenian empresses. While Anna had been head of the family and had control of its resources (which she largely used to aid her family), Eirene Doukaina was a member of an imperial family and thus she had access to funds.⁶⁸

Tzetzes alludes to cultural differences that express political difference. Exhorted to write a commentary on Hesiod's *Theogony*, Tzetzes had to compose a book for women (γυναικεῖα βίβλος) for his new patroness. Member of the literary circle of the *sebastokratorissa* Eirene, wife of the *sebastokrator* Andronikos, Tzetzes records his pleasure in working for the *sebastokratorissa* "the great friend of human literature" (φιλολογωτάτη).⁶⁹ The contrast with Bertha cannot be greater. Rather

---

⁶⁴ Kinnamos, *Epitome Rerum ab Ioanne et Manuele Comnenis Gestarum*, ed. Meineke, 36.
⁶⁵ Petrus Matranga, *Anecdota Graeca*, 2 vols, (Roma: Bertinelli, 1850; repr. Hildesheim-New York: Olms, 1971), I (2), 1–223, esp. 43; Elizabeth M. Jeffreys, "The Comnenian Background to the 'romans d'antiquité," *Byzantion* 50 (1980): 455–486, esp. 472–473; Michael J. Jeffreys, "The Nature and Origins of the Political Verse," *Dumbarton Oaks Papers* 28 (1974): 141–195, esp. 151.
⁶⁶ Tzetzes, *Epistula* 57 (ed. Leone, 79–84). For the critical edition see *Epistulae*, ed. Petrus Aloisius M. Leone, (Leipzig: Teubner, 1972).
⁶⁷ Elizabeth M. Jeffrey, "The *sebastokratorissa* Eirene as Literary Patroness: The Monk Iakovos," *Jahrbuch der Österreichischen Byzantinistik* 32.3 (1982): 63–71.
⁶⁸ Hill, "Alexios I Komnenos and the Imperial Women," 48–49.
⁶⁹ Manasses, *Breviarum historiae metricum*, ed. Bekker, 3, l. 3. For the critical edition see Constantini Manassis *Breviarum historiae metricum*, ed. Immanuel Bekker, (Bonnae: Weber, 1837). See also Mario Gallina, *Conflitti e coesistenza nel Mediterraneo medievale*, (Spoleto: Fondazione Centro italiano di studi sull'alto medioevo, 2003), 158–162; Elizabeth M. Jeffreys-Michael J. Jeffreys, "Who was Eirene the *sebastokratorissa*?," *Byzantion* 64 (1994): 40–68.

than appreciating her efforts of studying Greek literature, he emphasizes Bertha's foreignness, poor cultural background, and avidity.[70] Had not Emperor Conrad written a letter to Bertha-Eirene, she would be hardly known, due to the silence of the Byzantine chroniclers.[71] Had not Tzetzes written a letter to his friend, the fact that Bertha-Eirene, just like Eirene Doukaina, accompanied her husband on campaign, would have been ignored.[72] Wives did not have a political role, and when a reference to such a role was unavoidable, it is mentioned without adding any other details. Less general visibility for women who came from foreign lands suggests that the lack of relatives residing nearby diminished their visibility as well as their influence. Interestingly, no Byzantine author ever contrasted Piroska or Bertha with Anna Dalassene and Eirene Doukaina. Byzantine court practice allotted various spheres of power to women, but theoretically only mothers were recognized as powerful. The potential of motherhood had been exploited several times in Byzantium by imperial women determined to keep the throne for their sons or, in the case of Irene the Athenian, for herself. Instead, foreign empresses might have played a part on the international political scene, but Byzantine historians only highlight their virtues as ideal wives or their philanthropic activity.[73]

In the south gallery of Hagia Sophia, the imperial mosaic represents Eirene and John in the act of donation, presenting gifts to the Virgin Mary. From the reign of John II, philanthropy opened up new avenues for imperial women. It was an opportunity for involvement in the public sphere as well as for self-expression, even if the venues considered appropriate for women to display their beneficence were limited. Empresses founded churches, monasteries, poorhouses and hospitals. Philanthropy was praiseworthy, even though its real significance in terms of female power was minimized by emphasizing feminine "softheartedness" rather than sponsorship or social concerns.[74] Eirene's involvement in the foundation of the Pantokrator must be placed in this context. In the introduction to the *typikon* of the Pantokrator Monastery, John II mentions his partner and helper in life who was

---

[70] Nardi, *Né sole né luna*, 160–166. The episode clearly demonstrates that in the Byzantine court there were different purposes with different hostilities.

[71] Basil of Ohrid does not mention Bertha's role of mediator between her husband and her relative Conrad of Germany.

[72] Accompanying her husband in times of peace was praiseworthy in an imperial wife, but going with him on campaign was different. Basil of Ohrid does not allude to Bertha accompanying her husband to war in the west.

[73] On the importance of ideology in Byzantine society, see Hill, *Imperial Women*, 181–198.

[74] This type of active public role for women, which evolved in Late Antiquity in the form of euergetism, goes back to the Hellenistic period. See Riet van Bremen, "Women and Wealth," in *Images of Women in Antiquity*, eds. Averil Cameron and Amélie Kuhrt, 223–242.

involved with the planning, construction, and completion of the monastery, but who was torn from him before the completion of the task.[75]

In the twelfth century, traditional ideology required that imperial women appear to be modest, virtuous, pious, and devoted to their families and charitable activity. Such are the portraits of Piroska-Eirene and Bertha-Eirene. Basil of Ohrid's oration for Bertha is very long, but it does not offer the same information about the empress that is contained in the short epitaph for Eirene. There is little about Bertha's noble birth, almost nothing about fertility, because more space is given to descriptions of the grief of the emperor. However, Bertha is praised for her humility, piety, lack of arrogance and vanity, and for her philanthropy. In fact, she took care of widows, orphans, those who had no money to provide dowries for their children although they were well-born, and those who were under the threat of death. She surpassed other women in attending to the needy.[76] Piroska and Bertha incarnate the ideal wife: they were beautiful, well-born, fertile, and pious wives whose public role consisted of dispensing patronage to the needy and behaving in a remarkable manner.

The empresses' role as patronesses also underwent a transformation. Komnenian women were active founders of monasteries: Anna Dalassene founded Pantepoptes, Eirene Doukaina founded Kecharitomene, and Eirene co-founded Pantokrator. Under Manuel, however, the patronage of monasteries by imperial women declined. Evidence of money in the hands of imperial woman has to be inferred from conspicuous spending, since the sources do not specify what money they had or the origin of the money. Anna Dalassene had control over the *sekreton* of the Myrelaion, but, given her position, her patronage took the form of government grants of land and exemptions from tax.[77] Eirene Doukaina endowed Kecharitomene with property, but there is no hint about the source of the property or whether she had the use of the revenues of the monastery, which must have been

---

[75] About the foundation of the Pantokrator monastery, see Sofia Kotzabassi, "The Monastery of Pantokrator between 1204 and 1453," in *The Pantokrator Monastery in Constantinople*, ed. Sofia Kotzabassi, 57–70; Marina Loukaki, "Empress Piroska-Eirene's Collaborators in the Foundation of the Pantokrator Monastery: The Testimony of Nikolaos Kataphloron," in *The Pantokrator Monastery in Constantinople*, ed. Sofia Kotzabassi, 191–202.

[76] See Vasilij Eduardovic Regel-Nikolaj Ivanovic Novosadskij, *Fontes Rerum Byzantinarum: Rhetorum Saeculi XII Orationes Politicae*, 1 (fasc. 1–2), (Leipzig: Zentralantiquariat der Deutsches Demokratischen Republik, 1982), 316–325. Bertha-Eirene took care of the education of her daughters, but she died too soon to have any influence in the marriage.

[77] *Docheiariou*, no. 2, *Actes de Docheiariou, Édition diplomatique*, ed. Nicolas Oikonomides (Paris: P. Lethielleux, 1984), 54–55. As for Christodoulos: Τὸ ἴσον τοῦ δεσποινικοῦ πιττακίου τοῦ καταπεμφθέντος εἰς τὸ σέκρετον τοῦ Μυρελαίου καὶ καταστρωθέντος εἰς μῆνα ἰούνιον ιε´, ἡμέρᾳ τρίτῃ, ἰνδικτιῶνος δεκάτης, ed. Franciscus Miklosich and Joseph Müller, *Acta et diplomata graeca medii aevi sacra et profana*, 6 vols, (Vienna: Gerold, 1860–1890), 6, no. XI, 32–33.

large.[78] Eirene endowed Pantokrator with a small amount of property—monasteries, houses, and rights in villages—in comparison with the endowments of her husband, John Komnenos, who completed the foundation. Kinnamos stresses that the resources given to Eirene by her husband were offered to the foundation of the monastery rather than spent on adornments or her children.[79] Although the dominant ideology did not grant wives economic power, they must have had freedom to spend a certain amount of money, because philanthropy requires money. Within this context, foreign empresses did not seem to have access to the economic resources that the native women did; moreover, they did not have a kin group, and only women with a kin group could operate at a power level when it was required. Piroska was from Hungary, and Bertha from Germany. Transportation into a foreign land must have deprived these women of confidence, money, and a close kin network. Philanthropy and mercy were virtues in common with other imperial women.

Change in Marriage Politics

Transition from Byzantine aristocratic families to international dynasties signaled a change in Komnenian marriage politics. Imperial authority was consolidated by women "on top," but, once restored, male authority soon limited local power networks and allied with foreign—less influential—women.[80] As there is scarce evidence on the ways foreign empresses mobilized their family networks, we can only hypothesize that Piroska-Eirene and Bertha-Eirene continued contacts with their families. In Byzantium, they seem to have largely kept away from politics and government, even from fashionable literary circles. This condition was the result of an active choice, strictly related to their foreign origin.

The changing status of female identity offers us a perspective on the changing nature of female power, encapsulating a different ideology. From the consolidation of the system set up by the male authority, where women were at the fore, we move toward the restoration of male authority in a period of crisis, where women were for-

---

[78] See Kecharitomene *Typikon*, Τυπικὸν τῆς σεβασμίας μονῆς τῆς ὑπεραγίας Θεοτόκου τῆς Κεχαριτωμένης τῆς ἐκ βάθρων νεουργηθείσης καὶ συστάσης παρὰ τῆς εὐσεβεστάτης αὐγούστης κυρᾶς Εἰρήνης τῆς Δουκαίνης κατὰ τὴν αὐτῆς πρόσταξιν καὶ γνώμην ὑφηγηθέν τε καὶ ἐκτεθέν, in *Patrologia Graeca* 127, 991–1128. For a critical edition see Paul Gautier, "Le Typikon de la Théotokos Kécharitômémè," *Revue des Études Byzantines* 43 (1985): 5–166.

[79] Kinnamos, *Epitome Rerum ab Ioanne et Manuele Comnenis Gestarum*, ed. Meineke, 9–10. Critical edition:*Iohannis Cinnami Epitome Rerum ab Ioanne et Manuele Comnenis Gestarum, ad fidem codicis Vaticani recensuit Augustus Meineke*, (Bonn: Weber, 1836); English tr. by Charles M. Brand, *Deeds of John and Manuel Comnenus by John Kinnamos*, (New York: Columbia University Press, 1976), 17.

[80] Barbara Hill, "The Ideal Imperial Komnenian Woman," *Byzantinische Forschungen* 23 (1996): 7–17.

eigners. Transition from mothers who interfered in political affairs and arranged marriage alliances to pious wives cast aside by an emperor who arranged all alliances himself or who remained the main actor reveals a great change over the period.[81]

At the beginning of Alexios's reign, Maria of Alania and Anna Dalassene were powerful mothers, who displayed their efforts in supporting Alexios's success. At the end of Alexios's reign, Eirene Doukaina and Anna Komnene schemed to seize power, but they failed—not because women become less visible and more subordinate within the Komnenian family system, but because the time and the political situation were not propitious.[82] Women were forced to remodel themselves, channeling their energies into philanthropy and family. From the reign of John II, foreign-born empresses redefined the social role of the empress from powerful mothers to pious wives. This is one of the most relevant changes in Byzantine court culture. Imperial women maintained their social role, and invented new avenues to make their status visible in a period of transition.

Piroska-Eirene was undoubtedly the most successful in recasting the role of the empress in Byzantium. The silence of the chronicles about her is compensated by her foundation, the most important religious, charitable and architectural complex that survived of Byzantium: the Pantokrator Monastery. The monastery was presented by its founder as the supreme monument to the imperial victory of the Komnenian family.[83] Although the texts are silent about her, Eirene is commemorated forever in liturgy, in stone and on mosaic. Her piety and charity made her a visible figure in the Byzantine Empire and a canonized saint in the Greek Orthodox Church.[84]

Bibliography

Angold, Michael. *The Byzantine Empire: A Political History*. London and New York: Longman, 1984.

Browning, Robert. *The Byzantine Empire*. Washington, D.C.: Catholic University of America, 1992.

Brubaker, Leslie and Helen Tobler. "The Gender of Money: Byzantine Empresses on Coins (324–802)," *Gender and History* 12.3 (2000): 572–599.

---

[81] Manuel took control over marriage alliances and prohibited his relatives to found monasteries.
[82] Garland, *Byzantine Empresses*, 198.
[83] Paul Magdalino, "The Foundation of the Pantokrator Monastery in Its Urban Setting," in *The Pantokrator Monastery in Constantinople*, ed. Sofia Kotzabassi, 33–55, esp. 44–46.
[84] Garland, *Byzantine Empresses*, 199. See also Vassis, "Das Pantokratorkloster," 226–230.

Cormack, Robin. "Interpreting the Mosaics of S. Sophia at Istanbul," *Art History* 4 (1981): 131–149.

Diehl, Charles. *Figures Byzantines*. Paris: Armand Colin, 1906. English translation: Diehl, Charles, *Byzantine Empresses*, translated by Harold Bell and Theresa de Kerpeley. London: Elek, 1964.

Dölger, Franz J. "Rom in der Gedankenwelt der Byzantiner," in Id. *Byzanz, und die europäische Staatenwelt. Ausgewählte Vorträge und Aufsätze*. Ettal: Buch-Kunstverlag, 1953, 83–98.

Erler, Mary and Maryanne Kowaleski (eds). *Women and Power in the Middle Ages*. Athens-London: The University of Georgia Press, 1988.

Gallina, Mario. *Conflitti e coesistenza nel Mediterraneo medievale*. Spoleto: Fondazione Centro italiano di Studi sull'alto medioevo, 2003.

Garland, Lynda. "The Life and Ideology of Byzantine Women: A Further Note on Conventions of Behaviour and Social Reality as Reflected in Eleventh and Twelfth Century Historical Sources," *Byzantion* 58 (1988): 361–393.

———. "'The Eye of the Beholder': Byzantine Imperial Women and their Public Image from Zoe Porphyrogenita to Euphrosyne Kamaterissa Doukaina (1028–1203)," *Byzantion* 64 (1994): 19–39, 261–313.

———. *Byzantine Empresses: Women and Power in Byzantium, AD 527–1204*. New York: Routledge, 1999.

Garland, Lynda and Stephen Rapp. "Mary 'of Alania': Woman and Empress between Two Worlds," in *Byzantine Women: Varieties of Experience, AD 800–1200*, ed. Lynda Garland. Aldershot: Ashgate, 2006, 91–124.

Gautier, Paul. "Le Typikon du Christ Sauveur Pantocrator," *Revue des Études Byzantines* 32 (1974): 1–145.

———. "Le Typikon de la Théotokos Kécharitôménè," *Revue des Études Byzantines* 43 (1985): 5–166.

Gibbon, Edward. *The Decline and Fall of the Roman Empire*, revised edition by John B. Bury, 7 vols. London: Methuen, 1909–1914.

Gouma-Peterson, Thalia. *Anna Komnene and Her Times*. New York and London: Garland Publishing, 2000.

Gouma-Peterson, Thalia. "Gender and Power: Passages to the Maternal in Anna Komnene's Alexiad," in *Anna Komnene and Her Times*, ed. Thalia Gouma-Peterson. New York and London: Garland Publishing, 2000, 107–124.

Gregory, Timothy E. *A History of Byzantium*. Malden: Blackwell Publishing, 2005.

Halkin, François. "La vie de l'impératrice Sainte Irène," *Analecta Bollandiana* 106 (1988): 5–27.

Herrin, Judith. "In Search of Byzantine Women: Three Avenues of Approach," in *Images of Women in Antiquity*, eds. Averil Cameron and Amélie Kuhrt. London: Croom Helm, 1983, 167–189.

———. "Women and the Faith in Icons in Early Christianity," in *Culture, Ideology and Politics: Essays for Eric Hobsbawn*, eds. Raphael Samuel and Gareth Stedman Jones. London-Boston: Routledge and Kegan Paul 1983, 56–83.

———. "The Imperial Feminine in Byzantium," *Past and Present* 169 (2000): 3–35.

———. *Women in Purple: Rulers of Medieval Byzantium.* Princeton: Princeton University Press, 2001.

———. *Byzantium: The Surprising Life of a Medieval Empire.* Princeton: Princeton University Press, 2007.

———. *Unrivalled Influence: Women and Empire in Byzantium.* Princeton: Princeton University Press, 2013.

Hill, Barbara. "Alexios I Komnenos and the Imperial Women," in *Alexios I Komnenos*, vol. 1: Papers, eds. Margaret Mullett and Dion Smythe. Belfast: Belfast Byzantine Enterprises, 1996, 37–54.

———. "The Ideal Imperial Komnenian Woman," *Byzantinische Forschungen* 23 (1996): 7–17.

———. "A Vindication of the Rights of Women to Power by Anna Komnene," *Byzantinische Forschungen* 23 (1996): 45–53.

———. *Imperial Women in Byzantium, 1025–1204: Power, Patronage and Ideology*, (London and New York: Routledge, 1999).

Hill, Barbara, Liz James and Dion Smythe. "Zoe: The Rhythm Method of Imperial Renewal," in *New Constantines: The Rhythm of Imperial Renewal in Byzantium, 4th–13th Centuries*, ed. Paul Magdalino. Aldershot: Variorum, 1994, 215–229.

Irmscher, Johannes. "Bertha von Sulzbach, Gemahlin Manuels I," *Byzantinische Forschungen* 22 (1996): 279–290.

James, Liz. *Women, Men and Eunuchs: Gender in Byzantium.* London-New York: Routledge, 1997.

———. *Empresses and Power in Early Byzantium.* London: Leicester University Press, 2001.

Jarratt, Susan C. and Ellen Quandahl. "To Recall Him . . . Will Be a Subject of Lamentation: Anna Comnene as a Rhetorical Historiographer," *Rethorica: A Journal of the History of Rhetoric* 26 (2008): 301–335.

Jeffreys, Elizabeth M. "The Comnenian Background to the 'romans d'antiquité,'" *Byzantion* 50 (1980): 455–486.

———. "The *sebastokratorissa* Eirene as Literary Patroness: The Monk Iakovos," *Jahrbuch der Österreichischen Byzantinistik* 32.3 (1982): 63–71.

Jeffreys, Elizabeth M. and Michael J. Jeffreys. "Who was Eirene the *sebastokratorissa*?," *Byzantion* 64 (1994): 40–68.

Jeffreys, Michael J. "The Nature and Origins of the Political Verse," *Dumbarton Oaks Papers* 28 (1974): 141–195.

Kazhdan, Alexander. "Latins and Franks in Byzantium: Perception and Reality from the Eleventh to the Twelfth Century," in *The Crusades from the Perspective of Byzantium and the Muslim World*, eds. Angeliki E. Laiou and Roy Parviz Mottahedeh. Washington: Dumbarton Oaks, 2001, 83–100.

Kotzabassi, Sofia. "The Monastery of Pantokrator between 1204 and 1453," in *The Pantokrator Monastery in Constantinople*, ed. Sofia Kotzabassi. Boston-Berlin: Walter de Gruyter, 2013, 57–70.

Leib, Bernard. "Le silences de Anne Comnène ou ce que n'a pas dit l'Alexiade," *Byzantinoslavica* 19 (1958): 1–11.

Lemerle, Paul. *Cinq études sur le XIe siècle byzantine*. Paris: Le monde byzantin, 1977.

Loukaki, Marina. "Empress Piroska-Eirene's Collaborators in the Foundation of the Pantokrator Monastery: The Testimony of Nikolaos Kataphloron," in *The Pantokrator Monastery in Constantinople*, ed. Sofia Kotzabassi. Boston-Berlin: Walter de Gruyter, 2013, 191–202.

Macrides, Ruth. "Kinship by Arrangement: The Case of Adoption," *Dumbarton Oaks Papers* 44 (1990): 109–118.

———. "Dowry and Inheritance in the Late Period: Some Cases from the Patriarchal Register," in *Eherecht und Familiengut in Antike und Mittelalter*, ed. Dieter Simon. Munich: Oldenbourg, 1992, 89–98.

———. "Dynastic Marriages and Political Kinship," in *Byzantine Diplomacy*, eds. Jonathan Shepard and Simon Franklin. Aldershot: Variorum, 1992, 263–280.

Magdalino, Paul. *The Empire of Manuel I Komnenos 1143–1180*. Cambridge: Cambridge University Press, 1993.

———. "Innovations in Government," in *Alexios I Komnenos*, vol. 1: Papers, eds. Margaret Mullett and Dion Smythe (Belfast: Belfast Byzantine Enterprises, 1996), 146–166.

———. "The Medieval Empire (780–1204)," in *The Oxford History of Byzantium*, ed. Cyril Mango. New York: Oxford University Press, 2002, 169–213.

———. "The Foundation of the Pantokrator Monastery in Its Urban Setting," in *The Pantokrator Monastery in Constantinople*, ed. Sofia Kotzabassi. Boston-Berlin: Walter de Gruyter, 2013, 33–55.

Matranga, Petrus. *Anecdota Graeca*. Roma: Bertinelli, 1850; repr. Hildesheim-New York: Olms, 1971.

McClanan, Anne. *Representations of Early Byzantine Empresses: Image and Empire*. New York: Palgrave, 2002.

Mullet, Margaret. "The 'Disgrace' of the Ex-Basilissa Maria," *Byzantinoslavica* 45 (1984): 202–211.

———. "Alexios I Komnenos and Imperial Revival," in *New Constantines: The Rhythm of Imperial Renewal in Byzantium, 4th–13th Centuries*, ed. Paul Magdalino. Aldershot: Variorum 1994, 259–267.

Nardi, Eva. *Né sole né luna. L'immagine femminile nella Bisanzio dei secoli XI e XII*. Firenze: Leo Olschki, 2002.

Oikonomides, Nicolas "L'évolution de l'organisation administrative de l'empire byzantin au XIe siècle (1025–1118)," *Travaux et Mémoires* 6 (1976): 125–152.

———. "The Mosaic Panel of Constantine IX and Zoe in St Sophia," *Revue des Études Byzantines* 36 (1978): 219–232.

Partner, Nancy F. (ed.). *Studying Medieval Women: Sex, Gender, Feminism*. Cambridge, Mass.: Medieval Academy of America, 1993.

Runciman, Steven. "The End of Anna Dalassena," *Annuaire de l'Institut de Philologie et d'Histoire Orientales et Slaves* 9 (1949): 517–524.

Sághy, Marianne and Nancy F. Partner (eds). *Women and Power in Medieval East Central Europe. Medieval and Modern*, Special Issue of *East Central Europe* 20–23 (1), 1993–1996.

Scott, Joan W. "Gender: a Useful Category of Historical Analysis," *American Historical Review* 91 (1986): 1053–1075.

Smythe, Dion C. "Middle Byzantine Family Values and Anna Komnene's Alexiad," in *Byzantine Women: Varieties of Experience, AD 800–1200*, ed. Lynda Garland. Aldershot: Ashgate, 2006, 125–140.

Stiernon, Lucien. "Notes de titulature et de prosopographie byzantines: Constantin Angelos (pan)sébastohypertate," *Revue des Études Byzantines* 19 (1961): 273–283.

———. "Notes de titulature et de prosopographie byzantines: Adrien (Jean) et Constantin Comnène, sébastes," *Revue des Études Byzantines* 21 (1963): 179–198.

———. "Notes de titulature et de prosopographie byzantines: a propos de trois membres de la famille Rogerios (XIIe siècle)," *Revue des Études Byzantines* 22 (1964): 184–198.

———. "Notes de titulature et de prosopographie byzantines: sébaste et gambros," *Revue des Études Byzantines* 23 (1965): 222–243.

———. "Notes de titulature et de prosopographie byzantines: Theodora Comnène et Andronic Lapardas, sébastes," *Revue des Études Byzantines* 24 (1966): 89–96.

Treadgold, Warren T. "The Unpublished Saint's Life of the Empress Irene," *Byzantinische Forschungen* 7 (1982): 237–251.

Vassis, Ioannis. "Das Pantokratorkloster von Konstantinopel in der byzantinischen Dichtung," in *The Pantokrator Monastery in Constantinople*, ed. Sofia Kotzabassi. Boston-Berlin: Walter de Gruyter, 2013, 203–250.

Whittemore, Thomas. *The Mosaics of Hagia Sophia at Istanbul: Third Preliminary Report, Work Done in 1935–1938: The Imperial Portraits of the South Gallery*. Oxford: Oxford University Press, 1942.

———. "A Portrait of the Empress Zoe and of Constantine IX," *Byzantion* 18 (1946–1948): 223–227.

PIROSKA-EIRENE, FIRST WESTERN EMPRESS OF BYZANTIUM: POWER AND PERCEPTION

Maximilian Lau

The inspiration for this paper lay in noting that all of Piroska-Eirene's successors as Empress until 1204, bar the usurping Emperor Alexios III Angelos's wife Euphrosyne Doukaina Kamatera, were Latins: Western foreigners. With the sole exception of Maria of Alania there had been no foreign empresses of any nationality since Eirene the Khazar had married Constantine V in 732, and these being some of only a few in all of Roman history.

On the one hand, this development may be completely explainable as a direct result of the new political realities that the Komnenoi and Angeloi found themselves confronting: since at least the scholarship produced by Paul Magdalino on the reign of Manuel I Komnenos, there has been the understanding that after the Crusades, dialogue with the Latin west became relevant in the empire in a way that had never been the case before, and its reduced state meant it was more in need of the alliances that marriage with westerners could bring.[1] On the other, however, what did it mean in practical terms that the Empress—the *Augousta*, *Despoina* and *Kyria* of the *Basileon Romaion*—was now no longer a daughter of an imperial noble house, court trained and cognisant of the powers and duties of her position, but a barbarian foreigner? Magdalino may have identified the cause, but the effect, the analysis of the nature and the practice of this new development has yet to be examined in full, and such an analysis must begin with its originator: Piroska-Eirene.

In this paper, I intend to focus my analysis upon the way contemporary court sources in particular reconciled the nature of the empress's ancestry within imperial panegyric to bolster the imperial rhetoric of John's regime, and then to investigate the practical effect of a westerner becoming the Byzantine empress.

---

[1] Magdalino, *The Empire of Manuel I Komnenos*, 99–102; See also: Herrin, *Unrivalled Influence*, 313.

In the *Muses* of Alexios I Komnenos, produced in the early days after the eponymous Emperor's death, Piroska-Eirene goes unmentioned, only the imperial couple's children are referenced as a clear justification as to why John was the rightful heir, fit for the imperial crown as he had already produced suitable heirs of his own.[2] Such a marginalisation of her role was perhaps to be expected in the context of 1118–9, with John's sister Anna Komnene and her noble husband Nikephoros Bryennios still very much a threat, and with the poem having been produced just before, or just after, the plot to kill John in the imperial hunting grounds of the Philopation, as he recuperated from his first campaign in Anatolia.[3]

An insight is however gained as to the perception of foreign princesses in Byzantium in late summer 1119, shortly after the Philopation plot. Though often assumed to take place in 1122 due to its mention by Choniates after John's Serbian expedition, in fact John crowned his eldest son Alexios as his co-Emperor sometime between July 10th and October 7th 1119, as attested by the Neapolitan Chronicles.[4] With John himself not having had a true coronation ceremony amidst the chaos of his elevation, and with the Philopation plot defeated and Laodikeia recaptured over the summer, a demonstration of imperial power and prestige in the capital was overdue, together with festivities to please the citizens of the Queen of Cities. Such festivities are referred to at length by a poem written by the court rhetor Theodore Prodromos for the occasion.[5] In this poem he portrays John rhetorically addressing Alexios's foreign-born bride, likely identified as the Rus princess Dobrodjeja Mstislavna, known as Eupraxia, Eudokia or Eirene in Greek and Latin sources.[6] The iden-

---

[2] *Muses* II, lines 16–7.

[3] Choniates, *Historia*, 10–12.

[4] Ibid., 16–7; "Imperante domino nostro Johannes porfirogenito magno Imperatore anno vicesimo hoctabo: sed et elexium eius filum porfirogenito magno Imperatore anno primo: die prima mensis decembrii indictione tertia decimal neapoli," *Regii neapolitani archive monumenta edita ac illustrate*, ed. A. Spinelli, vol. 5, Naples : ex Regia Typographica, 1858, no. 576, nos. 577 and 579; This dating is reinforced by every subsequent entry in the Chronicle. Further evidence for this dating can be found in the fact that Choniates uses no chronological indicators at this section, "shortly afterwards" used for the Serbian section and "in the summer" used for the Hungarian section, and thus seems to be an aside in the narrative, Choniates, *Historia*, 16–7.

[5] Prodromos, *Gedicte*, Poem I.

[6] She may be identified with the Eudokia in the *PantokratorTypikon*, but equally the Rus sources refer to Dobrodjeja as Eupraxia, though these identifications are not mutually exclusive in the translation to Russian as noted by Gautier. *Pantokrator Typikon*, 43; Gautier, "L'Obituaire du Typikon du Pantocrator," 249, 51; "'Густинская летопись," *PSRL II*, 292; "Ипат'евская летопис," *PSRL II*, 1122; Magdalino, *Empire of Manuel I Komnenos*, 206–7; Chalandon also cites an unknown *Annales de Goustin* who tells us that his wife Dobrodjeja was called Eirene, Chalandon, *Jean II Comnène*, p. 13; Repeated by Hill who sees Dobrodjeja as Alexios's first wife, Hill, *Imperial Women in Byzantium*, 107; The poem by Prodromos does not specifically mention the bride's origin aside

tity of the young Alexios's Empress is sometimes assumed to be Katya, daughter of King David of Georgia, however Varzos and Jeffreys have demonstrated that Alexios Bryennios Doukas, son of Anna Komnene and Nikephoros Bryennios, was almost certainly her husband, and in this very poem of Prodromos he mentions that the bride had been "given from northern lands," further reinforcing their work. [7]

I could discuss further the justifications for both the identity of Alexios's bride and the dating of the coronation ceremony, which provide a number of implications with regards to Byzantine politics, but in reference to Eirene in particular, this poem represents a fairly conflicted portrayal of a foreign empress in the imperial court. On the one hand, Alexios's young empress is called upon by her imperial father-in-law to "forget her kin" (σοῦ γένους ἐπιλάθου), and to merely join together with Alexios in raising Romans.[8] Eirene again goes unmentioned, as though a princess from far Kiev could be told to forget her family and become Roman, the senior *Basilissa* from the neighboring Hungary was another matter, and on which at first Prodromos decides to keep silent, though in the same poem a hint emerges as to how imperial rhetoric came to terms with a foreign empress.

This poem describes that young Alexios as being attended by Dioklians and Dacians, that is Serbians and Hungarians, as his spearcarriers or bodyguards (σοὶ Διοκλέων καὶ Δακῶν ἔθνη δορυφοροῦσι.)[9] This is in the midst of a stanza rhetorically describing Germans quaking in fear of him, a long list of other nations in awe at him, and indeed the far British apparently even praying to him, and so naturally this may not describe a specific part of the ceremony. However, even if it is merely 'rhetorical,' the portrayal of Serbians and Hungarians as the young Alexios's bodyguards, as opposed to any other Christian peoples, is a notable one considering his mother's descent from those very same 'Dacians,' and when brought into contemporary politics opens up a new field of inquiry with regards to Eirene.

Their presence in the first instance conveys the same messages of the legitimacy and the ecumenical rule of the young emperor, just as the Varangian Guard does for John, as discussed in Dion Smythe's article that explored why barbarians stood round about the emperor at diplomatic receptions.[10] The

---

from a reference to her not being the first "to be given from northern lands," and indeed the implication of an embarrassingly 'barbaric' origin of the bride as a Rus princess may represent that would cause Prodromos to call upon her to "forget her kin." Prodromos, *Gedichte*, Poem I, lines 151–61.

[7] Prodromos, *Gedichte*, Poem I, lines 151–61.
[8] *Ibid.*
[9] *Ibid*, line 91.
[10] Smythe, "Why do barbarians stand around the emperor at diplomatic receptions?" 305–12.

presence of Dioklians at court can be readily explained by John and his son's recent campaign in the region in 1117, and the client relationship between the emperor and the Dioklian Prince Grubesa, while that of the Hungarians must derive in the first instance from Piroska-Eirene.[11] Such a presence only grew once John gave hospitality to the fugitive Hungarian Prince Álmos after his flight from his nephew King Stephen II in 1125, though Álmos himself is mentioned as settling on his own estate, allegedly called Constantinia after the prince's Greek name, Constantine.[12] It is this presence that King Stephen seems to have considered as a sword of Damocles above his head, with Álmos just waiting for a moment of weakness before he would attempt to take Hungary with Byzantine support. Whether such was the case or not would depend upon your judgement of Álmos as the sources are not themselves convinced, though the Prince had previously successfully received support from the German emperor in pressing his claim, even though the civil war had eventually been resolved peacefully.[13]

The author of the *Chronicon Pictum* expresses the fear that had Álmos been successful then Hungary would indeed be relegated to the status of an imperial client, just as Serb Dioklea, and personifies this fear by relating an incident with a letter written by Piroska-Eirene to Stephen.[14] Here she expresses her opinion on the relationship between Hungary and the empire, telling Stephen she regarded him as "her [liege]man," a description that apparently led John himself to chastise his beloved wife for speaking out of turn." Stephen's response was to consider it a ter-

---

[11] John is identified as: "Caloioannes Cumano," Priest of Dioklea, Book XLV, 172; Chalandon, *Jean II Comnène*, 69–70; Fine, *The Early Medieval Balkans*, 232.

[12] The exact date of Álmos's flight has been much debated by scholars, with Moravcsik and Chalandon believing that he fled immediately after being blinded around 1116. Makk establishes uncontroversial *terminus post* and *ante quems* however, as he notes that the Hungarian chronicle tells us that Álmos fled "from King Stephen," that both Kinnamos and Choniates place Álmos's flight in the reign of John, and that he died in Constantinople in 1127. He narrows this range of 1118–1127 down however by noting that Álmos's sister Adelheid who was married to the Bohemian Prince Vladislav I was welcomed at court in 1123, something unlikely if Álmos was *persona non grata*, and that Choniates tells us that the war started directly because of Álmos's flight, and that therefore it would not have been many years in advance of the war starting, meaning Álmos arrived in Constantinople around 1125, which Fine also sides with, even if he sees the entire Hungarian wars as happening earlier, discussed in Chapter Five; Choniates, *Historia*, 17; "Chronicon Pictum," 459; Chalandon, *Jean II Comnène*, 57; Moravcsik, *Byzantium and the Magyars*, 77–8; Fine, *The Early Medieval Balkans*, 234–6; Makk, *The Árpáds and the Comneni*, 22–3. On Constantinia and Constantine, "Chronicon Pictum," 442–3, 459; Makk, *The Árpáds and the Comneni*, 22, 131; Tuzson, *Istvan II*, p. 140.

[13] "Chronicon Pictum," 427; Makk, *The Árpáds and the Comneni*, pp. 14–5; Tuzson, *Istvan II*, 77–8; *Catalogus fontium historiae Hungaricae*, 1596.

[14] "Chronicon Pictum," pp. 439–45.

rible slight and thus he mustered an army, which went on to invade Greece and devastate it with "fire and sword."[15] Despite the clarity of the Latin, this incident has been misinterpreted by many scholars, who claim that John made the remarks and Eirene in fact defended the land of her birth as independent, enraging the emperor, and that Stephen went to war to answer the insult to his aunt. Though they could be deriving this from another unreferenced source, it otherwise seems a mistake from early historiography that has been referenced ever since without checking the original source.[16] This incident does however tell us about contemporary Hungarian politics, either at the time of the writing of the *Chronicon Pictum* in the fourteenth century, or earlier whence its sources derived, or indeed whensoever foreign domination was equally feared. The chance that Piroska-Eirene did indeed write such a letter is certainly not impossible. From the imperial side, evidence such as the Holy Crown of Hungary demonstrates that in times of strength the empire did indeed see itself as the regional, if not global, hegemon, and so enforcing such a relationship was not out of the realms of probability as a goal for the revitalised, Komnenian Empire.[17]

Such a context feeds back into Eirene's Western origin. Far from her ancestry being an embarrassment to be forgotten, subsumed by a superior, Roman, identity, it became a significant contribution to portrayal of the legitimacy of imperial rule. As John's reign continued, bar some setbacks such as the Venetian war, he steadily increased imperial authority over Dioklean and Raškan Serbs, Nomadic Cuman and Pecheneg invaders, Turkish lords, both nomadic and settled, including for a few brief years Sultan Mas'ud of Rum himself, and after Eirene's death, Armenian Cilician, Crusader and Arab lords as well.[18] These peoples were in no way

---

[15] "Interea imperatrix Constantinopolitana, filia regis Ladizlai nomine Pyrisk nunciavit regi Stephano dicens regem Hungarie esse hominem suum. Quam etiam contradicentum imperator castigavit. Cum autem hoc audisset rex, pro nimia reputavit iniuria et collecto exercitu in impetus spiritus sui invasit partes Grecie atque alias civitates Grecie igne et gladio devastavit." "Chronicon Pictum," 439–45; Tr. Stephenson, *Byzantium's Balkan frontier*, 208–9.

[16] For this opinion, see Moravcsik, *Byzantium and the Magyars*, 79; Kosztolnyik, *The dynastic policy of the Árpáds*, 104–7.

[17] Stephenson, *Byzantium's Balkan frontier*, 188, 209.

[18] All but Mas'ud from those mentioned are well attested in both primary and secondary literature, Mas'ud's years as an imperial client stems from Michael the Syrian's mention of his deposition by his brother, Arab and subsequent request for aid from John in Constantinople in 1125. The Emperor did indeed provide him with funds to take back his throne. Though no specific mention is made of the details of their arrangement, Mas'ud's subsequent contribution of troops for John's Paphlagonian campaign fits the pattern of John's other client relationships. Michael the Syrian, *Chronicle*, Book 16.2, p. 608.

completely subsumed into the empire, they continued to be governed by their own rulers, and there is no specific evidence that they paid taxes to the imperial fisc, and yet they were subject to the emperor's will. John moves populations seemingly at will, settling Pechenegs in Raška, Raškan Serbs near Nikomedia in Anatolia, and Armenian Cilicians in Cyprus.[19] All of those mentioned above contributed troops at the emperors command for his campaigns, though Sultan Mas'ud was to enact his betrayal with the withdrawal of those troops in the dead of night whilst John laid siege to Gangra, and the Crusader Princes Raymond and Joscelin are famous for gambling in their tent rather than fighting alongside John at the siege of Shayzar.[20] With each campaign John thus secured more troops for the one following, and with such a settlement upon each people the imperial rhetors correspondingly inflated their portrayal of the emperor, and thus found much to gain from celebrating, and not denying, Piroska-Eirene's heritage. Through this celebration, the imperial couple could be portrayed as the ecumenical rulers of all peoples.

In his epitaph for the empress, written after her death in Bithynia in 1133, Prodromos extolls Eirene for her "blessed forefathers," in the tradition of all western Empresses back to no less a figure than Julius Caesar.[21] This may reference Piroska's own descent from the German Emperors of the West through her mother, and indeed she was second cousin to the contemporary emperors Henry V and Conrad, thus John and Eirene unite the Eastern and Western Empires.[22] This is quite a change in tone from the message of "forget your kin" 15 years before, as her status as John's "Lady of all the Western Peoples" (ἐκ γὰρ ἀνάσσης δυσμικοῦ παντὸς γένους) is clearly pushing a new paradigm.[23] The listener is called upon to see the "radiant might" of both John and Piroska-Eirene, as the emperor's victories in the east, west, north and south make them *the* universal rulers, with John's marriage to his "Western Lady" encapsulating the ideology of Byzantium's objective and claim to univer-

---

[19] Pechenegs: Choniates, *Historia*, 16 (with there today being a village called Pečenog in Kraljevo Municipality, Serbia, at 43° 46' 0" N, 20° 46' 0" E); Serbs: Choniates, *Historia*, 16; Charanis, "The Transfer of Population as a Policy in the Byzantine Empire," 142–9; Charanis, "The Slavic Element in Byzantine Asia Minor in the Thirteenth Century," *Byzantion* 18 (Brussels, 1946–8), 69–83; Armenians: Ibn al-Athir, *Chronicle*, 337.

[20] Choniates, *Historia*, 19; Kinnamos, *Epitome*, 14; The possibility that this gambling incident is used by William of Tyre to contrast the idealized crusading behavior of John fighting on the frontline with that of the two Latin Princes and is therefore exaggerated is not to be discounted. William of Tyre, Book 15.1, 675.

[21] "εὐτυχῶν προπατόρων," Prodromos, *Gedichte*, Poem VII, lines 4–6.

[22] With thanks to Attila Bárány for demonstrating the full extent of Piroska's German background at the Conference, c.f. the family tree produced as part of his paper.

[23] Prodromos, *Gedichte*, Poem XXV, line 95.

sal empire.²⁴ Far from her role being minimised, reduced to merely a begetter of heirs and a pious philanthropist, this western lady jointly ruled the land of the Ausones, "συνεξάρξασα τῆς γῆς Αὐσόνων," the latter being Prodromos's poetic ethonym for the Romans.²⁵ This phrase evokes past empresses such as the venerable Eirene Doukaina who, according to Choniates, Alexios I calls his "wife, sharer of his bed and empire." ²⁶ Such a shift is immediately reflected in the poems commemorating the arrival of the German Princess Bertha-Eirene, Manuel's first wife and empress, towards the end of John's reign. With Bertha-Eirene being even more closely connected to the Western empire, the rhetoric surrounding her arrival builds upon the rhetorical tropes established for Piroska-Eirene as a Western empress: her presentation is couched in terms of elder Rome being united with new Rome.²⁷ Though the Emperor Conrad, Bertha-Eirene's brother in law, is referred to as the "ῥὴξ" of elder Rome in a clear diminution of status compared to the Βασιλεύς, "glorious Conrad" is still referred to as a ruler of deepest wisdom and of the noblest of races, "τὸ γένος εὐγενέστατε," which in addition to Bertha-Eiene's beauty and nobility make her the most suitable bride for Manuel.²⁸ As such, the western empress is once again presented as the ideal consort for the eastern emperor, presenting them together as the legitimate universal monarchs, justifying John and Manuel, alongside their respective Eirenes, lordship over other peoples.

The question remains, however, as to how this rhetorical portrayal played out in fact. Evidence is scarce, though when Piroska-Eirene is examined in conjunction with her western successors it can be seen that the western empress of the eastern emperor combined the power of her imperial predecessors with the benefits provided by her upbringing.

Barbara Hill has previously noted that without the surviving letter of the German Emperor Conrad to the princess, which mentions her mediation between the two emperors, "she would be written off as a political non-entity."²⁹ Equally, without the letter of Tzetzes to a friend we would not know that Bertha-Eirene had continued the tradition, set by Alexios I's wife Eirene Doukaina and continued by Piroska-Eirene, of the Empress accompanying her husband on campaign, as Choniates and

---

²⁴ Ibid., Poem VII, lines 15–20.
²⁵ Ibid., Poem VII, line 13.
²⁶ Ὦ γύναι, κοινωνέ μοι λέχους καὶ βασιλείας, Choniates, Historia, 6, Tr. O City of Byzantium, 5; Garland, Byzantine Empresses, 180–198; Hill, Imperial Women in Byzantium, 165–169; Polemis, The Doukai, 70–74.
²⁷ Prodromos, Gedichte, Poem XX, lines 13–4.
²⁸ Ibid. lines 37–9.
²⁹ Hill, Imperial Women, 94.

Kinnamos do not relate anything concerning either of these instances, and yet from the birth of John's eldest twin children in Balabista, Macedonia, while on campaign against the Normans in 1108, and indeed from Eirene's own death in Bithynia while John set out against the Danishmends, we know that Eirene accompanied John on campaign much as her predecessor had done.[30] In court as well, the Western empress was not a passive player, as Choniates relates to us an incident whereby Maria of Antioch overheard the interpreter Aaron Isaakios telling Latin envoys in their own language not to give in immediately to the emperor's demands. She naturally revealed the fact to her husband, which led him to blind Aaron and confiscate his possessions, demonstrating the presence, and indeed active role, of the empress leastwise at one diplomatic reception and negotiation.[31] It was this same empress that briefly dominated the empire after Manuel's death, before Andronikos's coup, and yet somehow some scholars still maintain that such interventions are rare, when in fact we are merely being limited by our later chroniclers, who are focused upon the emperor and so do not have the realism of contemporary court texts.[32] With just one source the portrayal of Bertha and Maria is changed in our historiography, and so we must accept the possibility that Eirene was not only a pious mother and philanthropist, as some studies have judged.[33] These roles were not unimportant in and of themselves, and the impact of Eirene on the *Pantokrator* has itself recently revealed that she collaborated with high ranking officials in the construction of the monastery.[34] One of these collaborators may have been her personal *vestiarios* or treasurer, implying she had a great deal of power over her own household at least.[35] Though these hints remain tantalisingly incomplete, they make a strong case that Eirene cannot be dismissed as simply devoting herself to philanthropy and raising children.[36]

---

[30] Birth of the heirs: Anna Komnene, *Alexias*, Book 12.4, p. 370; On Eirene's death: Choniates, *Historia*, 33; "Vita beatae imperatricis Irenes (Synaxerion 12 August)," Moravcsik, *Az Árpád-kori Magyar Történet bizánci forrásai*, 117 and 120; Prodromos, *Gedichte*, Poem VII, line 24; For a full discussion of imperial women on campaign in the 12th century, see Garland, "Imperial women and entertainment at the middle byzantine court," 181–2. Full information on the role of Lopadion during John's reign can be found in the forthcoming article: Lau, "Ioannoupolis: Lopadion as 'City' and Military Headquarters under Emperor John II Komnenos"

[31] Choniates, *Historia*, 146–7; Garland, *Byzantine Empresses*, 203.

[32] Garland, *Byzantine Empresses*, 199.

[33] *Ibid.*

[34] Loukaki, "Empress Piroska-Eirene's Collaborators in the Foundation of the Pantokrator Monastery: The Testimony of Nikolaos Kataphloron," 191–201.

[35] The exact identity of this figure remains elusive, though his status as a future *Megas Doux* of Hellas attests to his high status.

[36] Garland, Byzantine Empresses, 199.

In this paper I hope to have highlighted one aspect of the study of Piroska-Eirene, and through her the empresses that succeeded her. Much research is still to be done, as my paper must represent preliminary conclusions only as further hints and comparisons will produce a more complete picture of this first Western empress in both perception and power. The change in the portrayal of the empress was part of a broader context of the character of the Komnenian regime, how under John it became a more 'imperial' empire, dealing with client rulers and claiming suzerainty over other nations and peoples in such a way that the rhetoric of imperial rule could benefit significantly from Piroska-Eirene (and her successors) being 'Empress of the West'.

THE MANY FACES OF PIROSKA-EIRENE OF HUNGARY IN VISUAL AND MATERIAL CULTURE

Christopher Mielke

Assessing the power of a medieval consort is hampered by many practical and interpretive issues. The nature of her role means that materials which highlight a queen's or empress's public actions through official documents are given precedence.[1] This problem is easily apparent in the case of Empress Eirene, born Hungarian princess Piroska (d. 1134) and wife of Byzantine Emperor John II Komnenos (d. 1143). While usually her role as an ideal wife and mother who shied away from court intrigues is emphasized, a great deal of scholarship has since accepted her role as co-founder of the Pantokrator Monastery in Constantinople.[2] Since Piroska-Eirene's influence in creating this vast monastic complex was so strong, examining other types of evidence will aid in better understanding her agency in the creation of her own visual program of self-representation. A study done of a reliquary cross commissioned by Piroska-Eirene's mother, Adelaide of Rheinfelden (d. 1090) wife of Hungarian King Ladislas I (r. 1077–1095) has revealed that this object was used not only to signify devotion to God and family, but also to serve as an indicator of wealth, status, prestige, and even

---

[1] Theresa Earenfight, *Queenship in Medieval Europe*. (New York: Palgrave Macmillan, 2013), 26.
[2] Gyula Moravcsik, *Szent László leánya és a bizánci Pantokrator-monostor. Die Tochter Ladislaus des Heiligen und das Pantokrator-Kloster in Konstantinopel*. Budapest–Konstantinápoly: A konstantinápolyi Magyar Tudományos Intézet Közleményei – Mitteilungen des Ungarischen Wissenschaftlichen Institutes in Konstantinopel 7–8, 1923,12–19; Margaret Mullett, "Founders, refounders, second founders, patrons," In *Founders and refounders of Byzantine monasteries*. Ed. Margaret Mullett. Belfast: Belfast Byzantine Texts and Translations, 2007, 19–21; Vassiliki Dmitropolou, "Imperial women founders and refounders in Komnenian Constantinople., In *Founders and refounders of Byzantine monasteries*. Ed. Margaret Mullett, 87–106. Belfast: Belfast Byzantine Texts and Translations, 2007, 89–91.

Queen Adelaide's "Roman-ness."³ While such an approach here will not necessitate using object biography, this study of Piroska-Eirene's mother shows the important of visual and material culture in understanding the agency of medieval royal consorts.

This study will thus discuss several objects and images that have been connected to Piroska-Eirene in the past. These include seals, coins, a mosaic, an enamel plaque, and images in illuminated manuscripts. The main research questions will be first the matter of which connections can be valid, and secondly which pieces can tell us about the empress's own agency in the construction of her visual program. The different types of visual and material culture discussed below will be organized going from those with the strongest connection to the empress and ending with the objects and images with the weakest connection to Piroska-Eirene.

The most famous and oft-cited image of the empress Piroska-Eirene is the mosaic of her on the eastern wall of the southern gallery of the Hagia Sophia (**Fig. 1**). The composition shows four figures total; in the center of the composition is the Virgin Mary holding the infant Christ. To the viewer's left is the emperor John II Komnenos holding a bag of money (ἀποκόμβιον), while to the right of the Virgin is the Empress Piroska-Eirene holding a scroll with the strings tied up in the shape of the Chi-Rho. Around the corner to the right of the Empress is the young co-emperor, Alexios; his inclusion in this panel dates the mosaic to sometime shortly after their coronations. Piroska-Eirene wears a two-tiered pin-

Figure 1. Empress Piroska-Eirene on the Komnenos Panel in the South Gallery of the Hagia Sophia (Istanbul). Photo courtesy of Robert. S. Nelson.

---

³ Christopher Mielke, "Lifestyles of the Rich and (In?)Animate: Object Biography and the Reliquary Cross of Queen Adelaide of Hungary," "Lifestyles of the Rich and (In?)Animate: Object Biography and the Reliquary Cross of Queen Adelaide of Hungary." In *Queenship, Gender, and Reputation in the Medieval and Early Modern West, 1060–1600*. Eds. Zita Eva Rohr and Lisa Benz, 3–27. New York: Palgrave Macmillan, 2016, 6–11, 16–18.

nacled crown with a red veil underneath, a richly embroidered and jeweled red dress with low-hanging sleeves, a blue-green girdle, and the top of a shield-shaped *loros*. The inscription above her head reads "Eirene, the most pious Augusta."[4] This mosaic (only one of three imperial depictions to survive in Hagia Sophia), directly recalls an earlier and nearby panel depicting Constantine IX Monomachos and the Empress Zoe. In the Zoe panel, Christ is enthroned in the center while Constantine is on the left holding the bag of money while Zoe is to the right holding a scroll with Constantine's name on it; this could be due to the fact that the emperor with her was originally Romanos III Argyros and the panel itself has had considerable modification, most likely during the empress's lifetime.[5] The mosaic was erected most likely in reference to an imperial donation to the church of Hagia Sophia. Oikonomides is of the opinion that the patriarch of Constantinople would have commissioned the panels as a gesture of gratitude for imperial donations, as the southern gallery was presumably inaccessible to the public (being used mostly for ecumenical meetings) and the mosaics were meant to be viewed from where the emperor entered the space.[6] The two biggest differences between the Constantine and Zoe panel and the John and Piroska-Eirene panel are namely the dedication to the Virgin Mary and Child in the latter (as opposed to Christ himself in the former) as well as the presence of Alexios as the designated heir, indicating a very clear imperial successor.[7]

If the panel is not an imperial commission, it could explain some of the idiosyncrasies of the mosaic. Several authors have remarked that the face of the empress is at once stiff and like that of a mask, but also representing both the empress as a foreigner and as well as the ideal embodiment of twelfth century Byzantine beauty.[8] Heads and faces in general seem to take on a mostly geometric shape (for example, oval or shield-shaped) but within the space there can be a great deal of individuality; mosaic artists could make use of lines, lighting, variations in flesh tones and color to signify the subject's age or physiognomy. While realistic features may seem stereotyped, they were nonetheless supposed to impart some aspects of physical likeness of

---

[4] "Εἰρήνη ἡ εὐσεβεστάτη αὐγούστα" Thomas Whittemore, *The Mosaics of St. Sophia at Istanbul,* Paris: The Byzantine Institute, 1933–1938, 21–28, 76–82. (henceforth: Whittemore)

[5] Whittemore, 18; Nicolas Oikonomides, "The Mosaic Panel of Constantine IX and Zoe in Saint Sophia," *Revue des études byzantines,* 36 (1978), 221, 228–232 (henceforth: Oikonomides)

[6] Oikonomides, 223–224 suggests that the Zoe panel may have been originally erected to commemorate the capitals of the Hagia Sophia being gilded; Wehli, "II. Komnénosz János és Piroska-Eiréné ábrázolása," 244–245.

[7] Robin Cormack, *Writing in Gold: Byzantine Society and its Icons.*London: George Philip, 1985,197.

[8] Whittemore, 24–26; Barbara Hill, *Imperial Women in Byzantium 1025–1204: Power, Patronage and Ideology/* New York: Longman, 1999, 89–90. (henceforth: Hill)

the person they represent.⁹ Piroska-Eirene's hairstyle here is worthy of comment, as not only is her red-blond hair a marker of her non-Greek origin, but there is no Byzantine equivalent for the bunches of hair framing the side of her face; this has been seen as an identifying marker for her status as a Hungarian princess.¹⁰ Blond hair as well as non-purple clothing (i.e. red and blue) seem to indicate foreign origins of princesses in other twelfth century forms of art.¹¹ That being said, the empress's fair hair, eyes, and skin combined with the darker, drawn eyebrows and flushed cheeks point to strategic use of cosmetics in line with Komnenos-era ideals of beauty.¹² The inclusion of the scroll tied with the Chi-Rho emblem is also worthy of note, as while it obviously recalls the Zoe panel, its exact purpose within the framework of the mosaic is somewhat nebulous. Tünde Wehli is of the opinion that, since Piroska-Eirene founded no monastery of her own, that it is a generic object which is probably meant to represent the ideological and moral privileges granted to the church by the imperial donation.¹³ No doubt, the scroll is meant to refer to an imperial donation to Hagia Sophia, but her assertion that Piroska-Eirene founded no monastery is wrong and outdated and the conclusion that the scroll is simply a generic one needs to be revisited.

Five lead seals from the early twelfth century identify the issuer of the chrysobull as "Empress Eirene."¹⁴ Since titles are frequently used interchangeably, uncovering the identity of the original issuer is a difficult business when other identifying information is not present.¹⁵ For the purposes of this essay, only three of the five seals will be discussed in depth. While the archaeological or documentary con-

---

⁹ Ernst Kitzinger, "Some Reflections on Portraiture in Byzantine Art" in *Art of Byzantium and the Medieval West: Selected Studies*, ed. W. Eugene Kleinbauer, 256–269. Bloomington: Indiana University Press, 1976, 257–258.

¹⁰ Zoltán Kádár, György Németh, Erzsébet Tompos, "A berendezés és a belső díszítés," [Furnishing and Interior Decoration.] In: *A Hagia Szophia,* ed. Zoltán Kádár, et al., Budapest: Képzőművészeti Kiadó, 1987, 65; Géza Nagymihályi. *Árpád-házi Szent Piroska: az idegen szent*. [St. Piroska of the Árpád house: the Foreign Saint]. Budapest: Kairosz Kiadó, 2007, 71.

¹¹ Cecily Hilsdale, "Constructing a Byzantine 'Augusta': A Greek Book for a French Bride." *The Art Bulletin* 87 (2005), 470, 472.

¹² Whittemore, 24–26; Hill, 90–91.

¹³ Tünde Wehli, "II. Komnénosz János és Piroska-Eiréné ábrázolása a konstantinápolyi Hágia Szófia székesegyház mozaikképén" [The Representation of John II Komnenos and Eirene on the mosaics of the Cathedral of Hagia Sophia in Constantinople] in: *Athleta patriae: tanulmányok Szent László történetéhez* [Athleta patriae: historical studies of Saint Ladislas], ed.László Mezey, Budapest: Szent István Társulat, 1980, 244–245.

¹⁴ The numbers in the Dumbarton Oaks seal catalog: BZS. 1951.31.5.43, BZS.1955.1.4348, BZS.1955.1.4349, BZS.1955.1.4561, BZS. 1958.106.490.

¹⁵ For more information on when Komnenian-era empresses are addressed either as *augousta, basilissa* or *despoina*, see Hill, 102–117.

Figure 2. Seal of Eirene Doukaina. Inventory Number BZS.1955.1.4349
© Dumbarton Oaks, Byzantine Collection, Washington, D.C.

Figure 3. Seal of "Empress Eirene", possibly seal of Piroska-Eirene as junior empress. Inventory Number BZS.1958.106.490 © Dumbarton Oaks, Byzantine Collection, Washington, D.C.

text for these seals is unfortunately not known, their presence and the imagery used can be extremely instructive in reconstructing the empress's self-fashioning. One of them shows a half-portrait of the empress holding an orb that reads "The Lord help Eirene Doukaina the *Augousta*" and can easily be attributed to Eirene Doukaina, the wife of Alexios I (**Fig. 2**).[16] The other two seals are a bit more problematic in terms of their identification. Since the inscription only reads "Empress Eirene," it means that the person who employed these two seals could be Eirene Doukaina, Piroska-Eirene of Hungary, or the first wife of Manuel I, Bertha-Eirene of Sulzbach. One of the two unknown seals shows a half portrait of the crowned empress with a scepter in her right hand and an orb in her left (**Fig. 3**). This one seems to be very close in

---

[16] "[Κύριε,]βοήθει Εἰρήνη αὐγούστη τῃ Δουκαίνῃ." George Zacos - Alexander Veglery, *Byzantine Lead Seals* Vol. I. Basel, 1972, no. 103; Hill, 104.

appearance to the lead seal of Eirene Doukaina, and it is tempting to think that this is the seal she used during her widowhood as Byzantine officials changed their seals frequently during their lives when given a new office, though the changes tended to remain conservative.[17] However, the inscription around the border simply refers to the owner as Empress Eirene, with no more room for a further title. While Eirene Doukaina was active as a widow at the monastery she founded at Kecharitomene, her activity there seems to be more towards literary patronage and charitable activities.[18] It thus seems doubtful she would have been issuing documents with a seal during this period where she had been exiled from court, and if she had it seems highly unlikely she would have issued from a seal which did not include her natal name as well.

It seems much more likely that the two lead seals are those of Eirene-Piroska, the one depicting her in a half-portrait issued during her time as junior empress, and the other lead seal showing her standing issued during her time as sole empress from 1118–1134.[19] Junior co-emperors were in the practice of issuing seals, and there is one that survives that has been attributed to Alexios, the son of John II and Piroska-Eirene.[20] Though there are not many analogies for junior empresses issuing documents with lead seals, this explains why the empress's natal family is not mentioned and why the seal appears to be so similar to that of Empress Eirene Doukaina. The third seal depicts the crowned empress standing with a scepter in her left hand, and her right hand on her chest (**Fig. 4**). This has been attributed to Piroska-Eirene for three important reasons: the crown worn by this empress is very similar to the one on the Hagia Sophia mosaic depicting Piroska-Eirene, the inscription on the seal is exactly the same on the mosaic, and the Doukas family name does not appear on this seal either.[21] This seal of Piroska-Eirene is extremely important, not only because it shows her to be the first foreign-born empress to employ the use of a seal, but also because the imagery used on this seal is followed by all the subsequent empresses until Anne of Savoy, the last empress to have a lead seal.[22] Since seals are fairly conservative in their nature, the change from half-portrait to full-length portrait is a rather striking one. If it is indeed showing a transition from her status as junior empress to sole empress, it not only distances herself from her mother-in-law,

---

[17] Nicholas Oikonomides, "The Usual Lead Seal." *Dumbarton Oaks Papers*, 37 (1983), 148, 156.
[18] Hill, 65–169.
[19] Werner Seibt, *Die Byzantinischen Bleisiegel in Österreich*, Vol. I. Vienna: Verlag der Österreichischen Akademie der Wissenschaften, 1978, 105–106 no. 28; Zacos and Veglery, *Byzantine Lead Seals*, Vol. I, 95, no. 106.
[20] Zacos and Veglery, *Byzantine Lead Seals*, Vol. I, 95, #106b.
[21] Zacos and Veglery, *Byzantine Lead Seals*, Vol. I, 94–95, 106.
[22] Zacos and Veglery, *Byzantine Lead Seals*, Vol. I, 101–125 nos. 111, 119, 122, 125, 126, 127.

Figure 4. Seal of Piroska-Eirene as sole empress Inventory Number BZS.1951.31.5.43 Harvard Art Museums/Arthur M. Sackler Museum, Bequest of Thomas Whittemore, Image © Dumbarton Oaks, Byzantine Collection, Washington, D.C.

but also shows a more contemporary image of the empress with the shield-shaped *loros* and not holding an orb. While the loss of the orb may seem like a loss of power in keeping with traditional narratives of Piroska-Eirene's power, the orb was used mostly on seals of empresses regent and regnant in the tenth and eleventh centuries, so as a symbol of worldly authority its inclusion on the seals of Eirene Doukaina and Piroska-Eirene as junior empress had more to do with that tradition. The orb completely falls out of use in the Byzantine regalia under the Palaeologians.[23] While so little has been preserved of her official activity or literary patronage, these seals prove the empress of John II would have been issuing documents well within her right as the Roman *Augousta*.

The question of a portrait of the empress Piroska-Eirene raises its head again in the question of two Byzantine manuscripts held in the Vatican Library: the *Tetraevangelion* (Vat. Urb. gr. 2), and the Barberini Psalter (Barb. gr. 372). The *Tetraevangelion*[24] dates from around 1122–1125, sometime after the coronation of John II and Piroska-Eirene's son Alexios as co-emperor; he appears on folio 19v (the dedication page) with not only a mustache, but also a beard indicating some time has passed between the mosaic and this manuscript.[25] The dedication page makes it

---

[23] Maria G. Parani, *Reconstructing the Reality of Images: Byzantine Material Culture and Religious Iconography (11th–15th Centuries)*. Leiden and Boston: Brill, 2003, 33–34.

[24] "Vat. Urb. gr. 2" accessed online at 27 March 2017, http://digi.vatlib.it/view/MSS_Urb.gr.2.

[25] The date 1128 (6636) is written in a later (probably fourteenth century) hand, though Spatharakis dismisses this, arguing more in favor of a date of 1125. Ioannis Spatharakis, *The Portrait in Byzantine Illuminated manuscripts*. Leiden: Brill, 1976, 82–83; Ioannis Spatharakis, *Corpus of Dated Illuminated Greek Manuscripts to the year 1453*. Leiden: Brill, 1981, vol. I, 41 No. 135 (henceforth: Spatharakis, CDIGM).

clear that the intended audience is imperial, but it is incredibly difficult to tell the relationship between this manuscript and the court. Four manuscripts mention how they were completed during the reign of John II and a copy of the New Testament from 1133 even states it was "Completed on April 30, 6641 (1133) by Theoktistos, during the reign of John (II) Komnenos and his wife Eirene."[26] The imperial family undoubtedly would have had many manuscripts of a religious nature. The great-aunt of John II, Catherine of Bulgaria, wife of Isaac I Komnenos (r. 1057–1059) would have had a lectionary she donated to the monastery of Hagia Trias after she became a nun.[27] Another surviving *Tetraevangelion* from c. 1128 belonged to Ioannes Olontunos, the *domestikos* of Piroska-Eirene.[28] A later Komnenian empress, Maria of Antioch, even seems to have commissioned a manuscript in 1179 meant to welcome Agnes, daughter of Louis VII of France, upon the young princess's arrival in Constantinople to wed Maria's son Alexios.[29]

Two figures in the Vatican *Tetraevangelion* recall the portrait of the empress from Hagia Sophia. The first shows a woman on folio 21r in the initial 'B' at the beginning of Matthew clad in imperial clothing and wearing a tall pinnacled crown and with her hair styled in the similarly distinct way as on the mosaic. There is a strong physical resemblance to the mosaic even though the inscription indicates that the figure here is meant to be 'Mercy'.[30] There is a precedent for imperial portraits formed in such manuscripts, as Michael VII, Maria of Alania and their son Constantine appear in the initial 'M' in the first psalm of folio 1r of the National Library of Russia Cod. gr. 214 (formerly the Leningrad Psalter), though in this case the empress is indicated by her name rather than as an allegorical figure.[31] The other depiction of interest is the dedication page on folio 19v depicting Christ crowning John II and his son, Alexios. Christ is flanked by two allegorical figures; the one to the viewer's left is 'Mercy' wearing a rich purple robe while the figure to right in a blue dress is identified as 'Justice' (**Fig. 5**). The tall crown and hairstyle seem

---

[26] Spatharakis, CDIGM, Vol. I, 42, No. 138. The other three referring just to the reign of John II are Ibid., 38 No. 118, 42 No. 140 and 141.

[27] Spatharakis, CDIGM, Vol. I, 26 No. 77; Charles Diehl, "L'Évangéliaire de l'impératrice Catherine Comnène" *Academie des Inscriptions et Belles-Lettres, Comptes Rendus des Séances de l'Année 1922*, 243–248.

[28] Athos, Vatopedi, Ms. 960 (736).Spatharakis, CDIGM, Vol. I, 78 No. 320.

[29] Hilsdale, "Constructing a Byzantine 'Augusta': A Greek Book for a French Bride": 475–476.

[30] "ἡἐλεημοσύνη." For more on the connection between the empress and this concept, see Etele Kiss's paper in this volume. Ioannis Spatharakis, *Studies in Byzantine Manuscript Illumination and Iconography*. London: Pindar Press, 1996, 79–80; Spatharakis, *The Portrait*, 79–82.

[31] Michael VII has since been erased. Spatharakis, *The Portrait*, 36–37, 80; Spatharakis, CDIGM, Vol. I, 30 No. 93.

to be very similar to Piroska-Eirene's depiction not only on folio 21r of the same volume, but also in the mosaic at Hagia Sophia. Since the *Tetraevangelion* might have been made shortly after the coronation of Alexios (d. 1142) as co-emperor in 1122, her presence in allegorical guise could perhaps be a reference to that as the empress would have been present at the coronation.[32] Since Christ, the source of the emperor's power, is crowning John and Alexios, the figures of Mercy and Justice appealing to Jesus indicate that this is how the emperor wishes to be seen; as a just and merciful ruler.[33] Yet the crowned female figures also recall the role of queens in the medieval West as intercessors.[34] Her purple garb position over John, whispering to Christ are clear indications that this woman was meant to be associated with the court. If 'Mercy' represents Piroska-Eirene, it is possible that her counterpart in blue, 'Justice', could represent the wife of Alexios, either Dobrodeja-Eupraxia of Kiev or Kata-Eudoxia of Georgia.[35] Alexios's first wife clearly predeceased him, so if the *Tetraevangelion* was made sometime after the death of Piroska-Eirene in 1134, it might explain why the two women appear as concepts rather than as people. The consort's role as heavenly intercessor would take on a more literal meaning as well in this interpretation.

Figure 5. Folio 19v of the Tetraevangelion, Jesus Christ, flanked by 'Mercy' and 'Justice' crowning John II and Alexios Komnenos

---

[32] Spatharakis, *The Portrait*, 82.
[33] Cormack, *Writing in Gold*, 196–197.
[34] Earenfight, *Queenship in Medieval Europe*, 11–12.
[35] Rafal T. Prinke, "Kata of Georgia, Daughter of King David IV the Builder, as wife of Sebastokrator Isaakios Komnenos" *Foundations* 3 (2011): 496.

In the case of the *Barberini Psalter*,[36] scholars ascribe the portrait of three figures as a Komnenos-era imperial family. The figure on the left, dressed in blue and gold, is the senior emperor holding a tall staff, with a long dark beard and a covered, pinnacled crown. The junior emperor, in the center (and thus the most important position) is also crowned by an angel, dressed in blue and gold, and holding a book in his left hand. The empress, on the viewer's right, is dressed in red and gold, with a shield-shaped *loros*. Her hair is red and styled in a similar manner to the Hagia Sophia mosaic of Piroska-Eirene, but her crown only has one tire and pinnacles. Ernest De Wald originally identified the three imperial figures on folio 5r as Alexios I Komnenos, his wife Eirene Doukaina, and the young co-emperor as the future John II.[37] Though he is aware of the problems of chronology in relation to the script, Maurizio Bonicatti identified the trio as John II Komnenos, Piroska-Eirene of Hungary, and their son Alexios the co-emperor.[38] The empress's red hair and hairstyle seem to be particularly reminiscent of the mosaic depicting her at the Hagia Sophia. However, Ioannis Spatharakis has noticed several anomalies about the imperial family in the Barberini Psalter. The dedication poem is written in a Palaeologan-era script and the crowns and beards of the two emperors have been altered. The faces of the three figures were re-drawn in black ink, and even the empress's red hair has been added later. The conclusion Spatharakis reached mainly based on the original shape of the crowns was that the three figures originally thus represented Constantine X, Eudokia Makrembolitissa, and the co-emperor Michael and thus dated sometime around the year 1060.[39] On the surface, these alterations tell more about Paleologan ideas about fashion, but the presence of the young co-emperor Michael holding the book indicates that this was likely made for him around the time of his coronation, especially when compared to another psalter dated to 1066.[40] The appearance of the empress (a fourteenth-century rendition) is still very similar to the mosaic of Piroska-Eirene at Hagia Sophia; it makes one wonder when the later illuminator was touching up the imperial family in these images whether or not this mosaic was used as inspiration for creating an image of an idealized empress for the later audience.

The altar retable known as the Pala d'Oro, currently at Saint Mark's Basilica in Venice, is made of Byzantine and Venetian enamels spanning nearly four

---

[36] "The Barberini Psalter" accessed online at 27 March 2017, http://digi.vatlib.it/view/MSS_Barb.gr.372.
[37] De Wald, "The Comnenian Portraits in the Barberini Psalter," 82–84.
[38] Maurizio Bonicatti, "Per l'origine del Salterio Barberiniano greco 372 e la cronologia del Tetravangelo Urbinate greco 2" *Rivista di cultura classica e medioevale* 2 (1960), 44–47, 51, 58–61.
[39] Spatharakis, *Studies in Byzantine Manuscript Illumination and Iconography*, 44–48; Spatharakis, CDIGM Vol. I, 75–76, No. 312. Spatharakis, *Studies in Byzantine Manuscript Illumination and Iconography*, 46–48.
[40] This psalter is in the British Library, Add. 19352.

centuries; beneath the central enamel of the Christ Pantokrator are three enamels depicting (from left to right), Doge Ordaleffo Falier, the Virgin Mary praying with open arms, and (as the Greek inscription states) "Eirene the most pious Empress" (Fig. 6a–b).[41] As it is well known that Falier had commissioned some of the enamels in 1105, it was assumed initially that the empress in question must be Eirene Doukaina, and that the portrait of the doge would originally have been Alexios I Komnenos.[42] However, the enamel depicting Falier (which is slightly smaller than the Eirene enamel) shows that the costume and Latin inscription would have been original and that this enamel was always meant to depict a Venetian doge, while the head had been altered and a halo was added at some later point.[43] This could possibly indicate that this was meant to put the doge on equal footing with the empress when the two enamels were combined, indicating that this Empress Eirene may not have been Falier's immediate contemporary in 1105. The enamels from the upper half of the Pala d'Oro were added by 1345 and the provenience for big enamel plaques like St. Michael and some of the smaller medallions is known. An account of Byzantine clergy visiting Venice in 1438 remarks on an incident where the Byzantine guests corrected the Venetians who had been under the impression that the enamels on the upper part of the Pala d'Oro had come from Hagia Sophia after the Sack of Constantinople in 1204. The visitors recognized the enamels on the upper part as coming from the church of St. Michael at the Pantokrator complex which had been founded by John II and Piroska-Eirene.[44] One of the strongest arguments in favor of this enamel depicting the wife of John II rather than Eirene Doukaina

---

[41] "+EIPINH EYCEBECTATH AVΓOYCTH" Renato Polacco, "The Pala D'Oro." In *St. Mark's: the Art and Architecture of Church and State in Venice*. ed. Ettore Vio. New York: Riverside Book Co., 2003, 227–237, 279; Nagymihályi, *Árpád-házi Szent Piroska*, 73; Holger Klein, "Refashioning Byzantium in Venice, ca. 1200–1400." In *San Marco, Byzatium and the Myths of Venice*. ed. Henry Maguire - Robert S. Nelson, Washington, DC: Dumbarton Oaks Research Library and Collection, 2010, 197–198.

[42] Donald M. Nicol, *Byzantium and Venice: a Study in Diplomatic and Cultural Relations*. Cambridge: Cambridge University Press, 1988, 65–66.

[43] David Buckton -John Osborne. "The Enamel of Doge Ordelaffo Falier on the Pala d'Oro in Venice." *Gesta* 39.1 (2000), 47.

[44] Sylvester Sgyropoulos -Robert Creighton, *Vera historia unionis non verae inter Graecos et Latinos sive consilii Florentini exactissima narratio*. The Hague, 1660, 87; S. Geroulanos - S. Mantzari - M. Papadopoulou, "Canonized Physicians and Healing Saints on the famous Pala d'Oro of San Marco originally from the Pantokrator of Constantinople" 38. *Uluslararası Tıp Tarihi Kongresi bildiri kitabı, 1–6 Eylül 2002= Proceedings of the 38th International Congress on the History of Medicine, 1–6 September 2002*, edited by Nil Sarı, International Society for the History of Medicine, et al, 213–220. Ankara, 2005, 215; Sergio Bettini, "Venice, the Pala d'Oro and Constantinople" In *The Treasury of San Marco, Venice*. ed. David Buckton, 35–64. Milan: Olivetti Press, 1984. 39–42.

or Bertha-Eirene of Sulzbach[45] is how she is addressed in the Greek inscription: "Eirene the most pious Empress" is the exact same formulation found in Piroska-Eirene's seal as well as the mosaic depicting her in the Hagia Sophia.[46] The specific word for empress (*augousta*) is only used to describe a living empress,[47] so it had to have been made before 1134; this means that this enamel stands alone from the medallions on the upper part of the Pala d'Oro, many of which seem to have been made in 1140–1142, possibly as part of a larger plea for better health for the young co-emperor, Alexios Komnenos.[48] There is also the issue of the appearance of the empress on the enamel as well. She is depicted with a richly decorated dress that has the shield-shaped *loros*, holding a long scepter in her right hand, and with a halo, but the head of the empress is different than the one on the mosaic; her hair is dark (though partially visible), and her crown only has one tier, though it has triangular pinnacles and *pendilia* on the side. The fact that the empress's hair is shown is quite significant and could point to an identification of the empress as Piroska-Eirene; the seal of Eirene Doukaina shows only a crown while none of that empress's hair is visible. In any case, the strongest arguments in favor of this enamel from the Pala d'Oro representing the wife of John II are the associations of other enamels on the structure with the Pantokrator monastery, the problematic connections between this enamel and the one showing Ordaleffo Falier, and the title used on the plaque.[49] The small size of the enamel (3.5 x 2.1 cm) makes it difficult to discover the enamel's original context and use.[50] Nonetheless, its presence indicates that the image of the empress (most likely Piroska-Eirene) had high political capital and was important enough to be brought over to Venice and displayed publicly.

Unfortunately, no crown attributed to Piroska-Eirene survives to present, but this is hardly surprising. The only surviving crowns from Byzantine workshops seem to be diplomatic gifts sent abroad, such as the Monomachos crown, the lower part of the Holy Crown of Hungary, enamels from a crown which survive in Preslav, and enamels from the Khakhuli Triptych which appear to have originally been a crown sent to the kingdom of Georgia.[51] Representations of

---

[45] Bettini argues that the enamels would have originally been Manuel I Komnenos and his first wife, Bertha-Eirene. Bettini, "Venice, the Pala d'Oro and Constantinople," 48–54.

[46] Hill, 104.

[47] Hill, 102–108.

[48] Geroulanos, Mantzari and Papadopoulou, "Canonized Physicians and Healing Saints on the famous Pala d'Oro," 220.

[49] Bettini, "Venice, the Pala d'Oro and Constantinople," 48, 50.

[50] Nagymihályi, *Árpád-házi Szent Piroska*, 72.

[51] Magda Bárány-Oberschall, *Konstantinos Monomachos császár koronája* [The Crown of the Emperor Constantine Monomachos.] Budapest: Magyar Történeti Múzeum, 1937. 49–96; Etele Kiss,

Figure 6a. "Empress Eirene" from the Pala d'Oro https://commons.wikimedia.org/wiki/File:Venezia,_pala_d%27oro,_madonna_tra_i_donatori_irene_e_l%27imperatore_Giovanni_II_Comneno,_trasformato_nel_doge_Ordelaffo_Falier.JPG

Figure 6b. "Empress Eirene" from the Pala d'Oro, detail

Figure 7. Electron coin, special coronation issue, Constantinople, 1092/3. The young John II Komnenos is crowned by Christ on the obverse, with the inscription IωΔεCΠOT+KεROHθεI. John's parents Alexios and Eirene are shown on the reverse, with the inscription +AΛεξIωΔε εIPHNAVTU. Inventory Number BZC.1969.8 © Dumbarton Oaks, Byzantine Collection, Washington, D.C.

Piroska-Eirene (such as the mosaic at Hagia Sophia and possibly her seal where she is standing) show her wearing a high, two-tiered pinnacled crown with her unique hairstyle and no pendants, while the seal and coin depicting EireneDoukaina show her wearing a flatter, rounder crown, no visible hair, and multiple pendants. The empress depicted in the *Tetraevangelion* shares the high crown and hairstyle of Piroska-Eirene, which indicates the allegory may have been intentional, demonstrating Piroska-Eirene was the best visual example of mercy incarnate. The Pala d'Oro enamel is much more complicated to interpret, as the black hair of that empress is depicted in a way similar to the mosaic in Hagia Sophia despite the change in hair color, yet the one-tiered crown is more reminiscent of Eirene Doukaina. Yet there is another case where the empress has Piroska's formula, but Eirene Doukaina's visual imagery: the seal of the empress Eirene from the first half of the twelfth century. One possible explanation for the blending could be that the Pala d'Oro enamel and the unknown seal represent Piroska-Eirene as junior empress. Regardless, it is nonetheless significant that images of Piroska-Eirene after 1118 show a clear transition from earlier depictions; in some cases, this method of depicting empresses lasted until Byzantium's twilight years.

It has also been claimed that Piroska-Eirene appeared on bronze coinage of John II. Older works as well as more recent ones give the impression that John II and his wife appeared side by side (Fig. 7).[52] The coin in question is in a rather poor state, but the name of the emperor is clearly visible as that of "Alexios," and the three figures have been identified as Alexios I Komnenos, Eirene Doukaina, and John II as junior co-emperor.[53] This is a case of a clear misidentification, and it seems that there was no coinage issued bearing the portrait or name of Piroska-Eirene. However, the fact that she was ever identified on the coin as the empress is telling of her inconsistent treatment in the secondary literature. As a woman who accompanied her husband on military campaigns, played a leading part in processions, co-founded an impressive monastic institution, and issued documents bearing her lead seal, the wife of John II played a central role in the daily life and administration of the Byzantine court. While she is usually depicted in stark contrast to Eirene Doukaina, the actions of the Hungarian Princess in Constantinople show considerable continuity

---

[52] Lajos Thallóczy, "III. Béla és a Magyar Birodalom" in *III. Béla magyar király emlékezete*. Ed. Gyula Forster, Budapest: V. Hornyánszky, 1900, 64 cites Sabatier who originally thought this coin represented John II and his two sons; Justin Sabatier, *Description générale des monnaies byzantines frappées sous les empereurs d'Orient*, Vol. II. Paris: Rollin et Feuardent, 1862, Vol. II, plate LV, image 1; Kalavrezou, et al. "Appendix: Byzantine Empresses," 310.

[53] The figure is female, not male as had been previously identified. Warwick Wroth, *Imperial Byzantine coins in the British Museum*. Chicago: Argonaut, 1966, 544–545.

in regards to her functions and activity as the Roman Empress Eirene, with her western background portrayed as an advantage in both artistic and rhetorical depictions.

Part of the reason Piroska-Eirene comes across in this study as a standardized yet schizophrenic character is the fact that her image is being used and manipulated by many others around her for many reasons. Her foreignness has been over-emphasized in spite of the fact that she appears crowned and wearing purple; western brides would have been met by women of the Byzantine court who would have not only dressed them in appropriate clothing but who also would have helped these princesses make the transition to court life; Piroska-Eirene would have hardly been an exception in this regard.[54] The objects in which Piroska-Eirene seems to have had the most control over her own, self-fashioned image would have to be the seal(s) she used in her lifetime. This break with tradition is an important one as the empresses who sealed after her all followed in her example. The presence of her issuing lead seals shows an active presence in issuing chrysobulls which is at odds with the oft-repeated image of the empress who shied away from the glitter of the court and the responsibilities of exercising authority. The detailed mosaic of her at Hagia Sophia represents an idealized woman of power; this was most likely a commission from the patriarch of Constantinople as part of a reciprocal arrangement of imperial and ecclesiastic donations. The images of Piroska-Eirene in the *Tetraevangelion* are important as they show her in an allegorical light in contrast to the clear display of power in the imperial portrait of her husband and son. Here the empress is important, but as an idea related to the concept of Mercy, guiding the two emperors behind the scenes. The enamel plaque on the Pala d'Oro, taken from its original context, is a problematic piece, though the argument that it represents Piroska-Eirene is a strong one. Most likely, her image would have been used in this way as some sort of prominent decoration before its removal to Venice.

As an idealized figure, Piroska-Eirene has been very easy to overlook in modern scholarship because much of the primary literature on her is so standardized in her praise. Yet the material and visual culture connected to this empress show how in her lifetime, her image was extremely important and worthy of use in contexts where she might not have had opportunity to fashion her own image. While evidence for Piroska-Eirene explicitly expressing her authority is still minimal, picto-

---

"The State of Research on the Monomachos Crown and Some Further Thoughts." In: *Perceptions of Byzantium and its Neighbors (843–1261)*. Ed. Olenka Z. Pevny, New York: Metropolitan Museum of Art, 2001, 60–76; Timothy Dawson, "The Monomachos Crown: Towards a Resolution," *Byzantina Σymmeikta* 19 (2009): 183–193; Hilsdale, "The Social Life of the Byzantine Gift," 610–617.

[54] Hilsdale, "Constructing a Byzantine 'Augusta': A Greek Book for a French Bride": 468.

rial sources show that the Byzantine court understood her to be in the possession of power, symbolic or otherwise. This is fairly typical for royal consorts of the era and could account for the idealized portrait of this empress given by contemporaries that has thus been the focus of secondary literature thus far. The visual and material sources of Piroska-Eirene show the need for an interdisciplinary examination of all available data in determining the activity and agency of women in the Middle Ages.

Bibliography

Bárány-Oberschall, Magda. *Konstantinos Monomachos császár koronája – The Crown of the Emperor Constantine Monomachos.* Budapest: Magyar Történeti Múzeum, 1937.

Bettini, Sergio. "Venice, the Pala d'Oro and Constantinople" In: *The Treasury of San Marco, Venice,* edited by David Buckton, 35–64. Milan: Olivetti Press, 1984.

Bonicatti, Maurizio. "Per l'origine del Salterio Barberiniano greco 372 e la cronologia del Tetraevangelo Urbinate greco 2." *Rivista di culturaclassica e medioevale* 2 (1960): 41–61.

Buckton, David and John Osborne. "The Enamel of Doge Ordelaffo Falier on the Pala d'Oro in Venice." *Gesta* 39.1 (2000): 43–49.

Cormack, Robin. *Writing in Gold: Byzantine Society and its Icons.* London: George Philip, 1985.

Dawson, Timothy. "The Monomachos Crown: Towards a Resolution." *Byzantina Σymmeikta* 19 (2009): 183–193.

De Wald, Ernest. "The Comnenian Portraits in the Barberini Psalter." *Hesperia* 13.1 (1944): 78–86.

Diehl, Charles. "L'Évangéliaire de l'impératrice Catherine Comnène." *Académie des Inscriptions et des Belles-lettres, comptes-rendus des séances de l'année 1922,* 243–248.

Dmitropolou, Vassiliki. "Imperial women founders and refounders in Komnenian Constantinople." In: *Founders and Refounders of Byzantine monasteries.* Ed. Margaret Mullett, 87–106. Belfast: Belfast Byzantine Texts and Translations, 2007.

Earenfight, Theresa. *Queenship in Medieval Europe.* New York: Palgrave Macmillan, 2013.

Geroulanos, S., S. Mantzari, and M. Papadopoulou. "Canonized Physicians and Healing Saints on the famous Pala d'Oro of San Marco originally from the Pantokrator of Constantinople." *38.Uluslararası Tıp Tarihi Kongresi bildiri kitabı, 1–6 Eylül 2002= Proceedings of the 38th International Congress on the History of Medicine, 1–6 September 2002.* Ed. Nil Sarı, International Society for the History of Medicine, et al, 213–220. Ankara, 2005.

Hill, Barbara. *Imperial Women in Byzantium 1025–1204: Power, Patronage and Ideology.* New York: Longman, 1999.

Hilsdale, Cecily. "Constructing a Byzantine 'Augusta': A Greek Book for a French Bride." *The Art Bulletin* 87 (2005): 458–483.

———. "The Social Life of the Byzantine Gift: The Royal Crown of Hungary re-invented." *Art History* 31.5 (2008): 603–631.

Kádár, Zoltán, György Németh and Erzsébet Tompos. "A berendezés és a belső díszítés," [Furnishing and Interior Decoration.] In: *A Hagia Szophia*. Ed. Zoltán Kádár, et al., 43–50. Budapest: Képzőművészeti Kiadó, 1987.

Kalavrezou, Ioli et al. "Appendix: Byzantine Empresses." In *Byzantine Women and Their World*, edited by Ioli Kalavrezou, et al., 306–312. Cambridge, Harvard University Art Museums, 2003.

Kiss, Etele. "The State of Research on the Monomachos Crown and Some Further Thoughts." In *Perceptions of Byzantium and its Neighbors (843–1261)*. Ed. Olenka Z. Pevny, 60–83. New York: Metropolitan Museum of Art, 2001.

Kitzinger, Ernst. "Some Reflections on Portraiture in Byzantine Art" in *Art of Byzantium and the Medieval West: Selected Studies*. Ed. W. Eugene Kleinbauer, 256–269. Bloomington: Indiana University Press, 1976.

Klein, Holger. "Refashioning Byzantium in Venice, ca. 1200–1400." In *San Marco, Byzatium and the Myths of Venice*. Eds. Henry Maguire and Robert S. Nelson, 193–225. Washington, DC: Dumbarton Oaks Research Library and Collection, 2010.

Mielke, Christopher. "Lifestyles of the Rich and (In?)Animate: Object Biography and the Reliquary Cross of Queen Adelaide of Hungary." In: *Queenship, Gender, and Reputation in the Medieval and Early Modern West, 1060–1600*. Ed. Zita Eva Rohr and Lisa Benz, 3–27. New York: Palgrave Macmillan, 2016.

Moravcsik, Gyula. *Szent László leánya és a bizánci Pantokrator-monostor. Die Tochter Ladislaus des Heiligen und das Pantokrator-Kloster in Konstantinopel*. Budapest-Konstantinápoly: A konstantinápolyi Magyar Tudományos Intézet Közleményei – Mitteilungen des Ungarischen Wissenschaftlichen Institutes in Konstantinopel 7–8, 1923.

Mullet, Margaret. "Founders, refounders, second founders, patrons." In *Founders and refounders of Byzantine monasteries*. Ed. Margaret Mullett, 1–27. Belfast: Belfast Byzantine Texts and Translations, 2007.

Nagymihályi, Géza. *Árpád-házi Szent Piroska: az idegen szent*. [Saint Piroska of the Árpád Dynasty: The Foreign Saint]. Budapest: Kairosz Kiadó, 2007.

Nicol, Donald M. *Byzantium and Venice: a Study in Diplomatic and Cultural Relations*. Cambridge: Cambridge University Press, 1988.

Oikonomides, Nicholas. "The Mosaic Panel of Constantine IX and Zoe in Saint Sophia." *Revue des études byzantines* 36 (1978): 219–232.

———. "The Usual Lead Seal." *Dumbarton Oaks Papers* 37 (1983): 147–157.

Ousterhout, Robert. "Architecture, Art and Komnenian Ideology at the Pantokrator Monastery." In: *Byzantine Constantinople: Monuments, Topography and Everyday Life*. Ed. Nevra Necipoglu, 133–150. Leiden: Brill, 2001.

Parani, Maria G. *Reconstructing the Reality of Images: Byzantine Material Culture and Religious Iconography (11th–15th Centuries)*. Leiden and Boston: Brill, 2003.

Pocoke, Richard. *A Description of the East, and Some Other Countries*, Vol. II. London: W. Bowyer, 1745.

Polacco, Renato. "The Pala D'Oro." In: *St. Mark's: the Art and Architecture of Church and State in Venice*. Ed. Ettore Vio, 227–237. New York: Riverside Book Co., 2003.

Prinke, Rafal T. "Kata of Georgia, Daughter of King David IV the Builder, as wife of Sebastokrator Isaakios Komnenos." *Foundations* 3 (2011): 489–502.

Sabatier, Justin. *Description générale des monnaies byzantines frappées sous les empereurs d'Orient*, Vol. II. Paris: Rollin et Feuardent, 1862.

Seibt, Werner. *Die Byzantinischen Bleisiegel in Österreich*, Vol. I. Vienna: Verlag der ÖsterreichischenAkademie der Wissenschaften, 1978.

Sgyropoulos, Sylvester and Robert Creighton. *Vera historia unionis non verae inter Graecos et Latinos sive consilii Florentini exactissima narratio.*The Hague, 1660.

Spatharakis, Ioannis. *The Portrait in Byzantine Illuminated manuscripts*. Leiden: Brill, 1976.

———. *Corpus of Dated Illuminated Greek Manuscripts to the year 1453*, Vol. I–II. Leiden: Brill, 1981.

———. *Studies in Byzantine Manuscript Illumination and Iconography*. London: Pindar Press, 1996.

Thallóczy, Lajos. "III. Béla és a Magyar Birodalom." [Béla III and the Hungarian Empire] In: *III. Béla magyar király emlékezete* [The Memory of King Béla III]. Ed. Gyula Forster, 57–97. Budapest: V. Hornyánszky, 1900.

Vatican Archives. "Vatican Urb.gr. 2." Accessed 27 March 2017.http://digi.vatlib.it/view/MSS_Urb.gr.2.

———. "The Barberini Psalter." Accessed 27 March 2017.http://digi.vatlib.it/view/MSS_Barb.gr.372.

Wehli, Tünde. "II. Komnénosz János és Piroska-Eiréné ábrázolása a konstantinápolyi Hágia Szófia székesegyház mozaikképén." [Representations of John II Komnenos and Piroska-Eirene on the Mosaics of the Cathedral of Hagia Sophia in Constantinople] In: *Athleta patriae: tanulmányok Szént László történetéhez* [*Athleta patriae*: historical studies of Saint Ladislas]. Ed. László Mezey, 239–246. Budapest, 1980.

Whittemore, Thomas. *The Mosaics of St. Sophia at Istanbul*. Paris: The Byzantine Institute, 1933–1938.

Wroth, Warwick. *Imperial Byzantine coins in the British Museum*. Chicago: Argonaut, 1966.

Zacos, George and Alexander Veglery. *Byzantine Lead Seals* Vol. I. Basel, 1972.

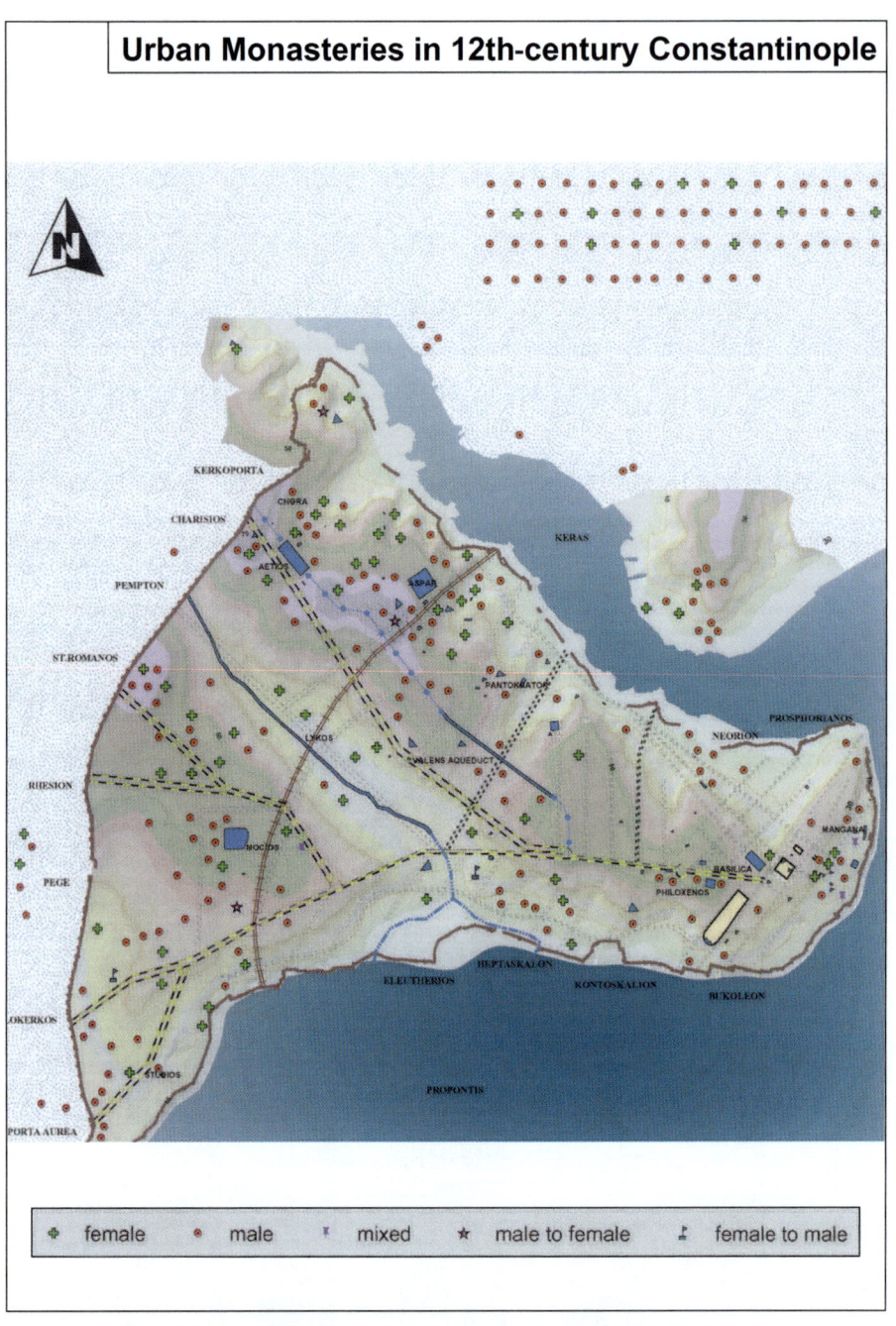

Figure 1. Urban Monasteries in Constantinople. Source: Gunder Varinlioglu, "Urban Monasteries in Constantinople and Thessaloniki: Distribution Patterns in Time and Urban Topography." In *Archaeology in Architecture: Studies in Honor of Cecil L. Striker*, ed. by J. Eremick and D. Deliyannis (Mainz, 2005), 187–98, fig. 1.

IMPERIAL WOMEN AND RELIGIOUS FOUNDATIONS IN CONSTANTINOPLE

Elif Demirtiken

The foundation of churches and monasteries in Byzantium was more often than not a statement of power.[1] Particularly in the capital, the act of foundation encapsulated a variety of symbolic meanings operating on different levels.[2] Churches and monasteries made up the city's sacred geography and at the same time, they created an area where patrons and founders were praised for their piety.[3] The reputation of piety, acquired prestige and visibility, fundamental in a "theatre-state" such as Byzantium, because it led to social acceptance and power. Acquiring prestige through patronage of monumental construction was particularly important for elite women in Byzantium as they had no official roles in state and society: they needed alternative stages for self-representation. The rise of women as sponsors of church and monastery building therefore reflects contemporary social structures that enabled them to initiate foundations.

Between 775 and 1183, thirty-three emperors and thirty-two empresses ruled Byzantium. Two empresses reigned on their own right; two empresses ruled together; and one further powerful woman was invested with authority in state administration, despite not being crowned *augusta*. Fifteen out of thirty-five empresses were recorded as patrons of religious foundations in the capital, in cooperation fourteen women from their close kin. This paper surveys imperial women's

---

[1] Margaret Mullett, ed., *Founders and Refounders of Byzantine Monasteries* (Belfast, 2007); Lioba Theis, Margaret Mullett, and Michael Grünbart, eds., *Female Founders in Byzantium and Beyond* (Vienna, 2013).
[2] Vlada Stanković, "Comnenian Monastic Foundations in Constantinople: Questions of Method and Context," *Belgrade Historical Review* 2 (2011): 47–73.
[3] Robert Ousterhout, "Sacred Geographies and Holy Cities: Constantinople as Jerusalem," in *Hierotopy: The Creation of Sacred Space in Byzantium and Medieval Russia*, ed. Alexei Lidov (Moscow, 2006), 98–116.

religious foundations to answer the question of when and why empresses invested in building in Constantinople. It revisits the backgrounds of the empresses—their marital status, place of origin, and monastic vow—avoiding the usual (over)generalizations in scholarship. At the intersection of research of Byzantine women's history and building programs in Constantinople, this paper explores the patronage of imperial women in the Middle Byzantine period (775–1183) to show what their religious monuments tell us about their power.[4]

The first of the fifteen empresses who founded religious houses in Constantinople in this period is Empress Eirene (regency 780–797, r. 797–802), followed by Maria of Amnia and Theodote, wives of Konstantinos VI (r. 780–797); Theophano, wife of Emperor Staurakios (811); Prokopia, wife of Michael I (r. 811–813); Euphrosyne, wife of Michael II (r. 820–829); Theodora, wife of Theophilos (r. 829–842); Theophano, first wife of Leon VI (r. 886–912); and Elene Lekapene, wife of Konstantinos *porphyrogennetos* (r. 913–959). After Elene, there follows a hiatus in the imperial women's patronage of churches and monasteries in Constantinople from the mid-tenth century until the mid-eleventh century. Then, Zoe *porphyrogenneta* (r. 1028–1054) commissioned the church of Christ *Antiphonetes*, followed by her sister Theodora *porphyrogenneta*, and Eudokia Makrembolitissa, wife of Konstantinos Doukas (r. 1059–1067) and later of Romanos IV Diogenes (r. 1067–1071). Finally, three Komnenian empresses founded monasteries: Eirene Doukaina, wife of emperor Alexios I Komnenos (r. 1081–1118), Empress Piroska-Eirene, wife of John II Komnenos (r. 1118–1143), and Maria of Antioch, second wife of Manuel I Komnenos (r. 1143–1180). It is clear that during this time, just like the earlier period, empresses invested in monumental patronage in Constantinople, the capital of the Byzantine state, continuing a trend of partaking in the imperial virtue of philanthropy. However, the individual names by which the religious houses were known, the holy patrons to whom the foundations were dedicated, and the rise of the imperial couple as (co-)founders under the Komnenoi all suggest that this

---

[4] Lynda Garland, *Byzantine Empresses, Women and Power in Byzantium, AD 527–1204* (London: Routledge, 1999); Barbara Hill, *Imperial Women in Byzantium, 1025–1204: Power, Patronage and Ideology* (London, 1999); Liz James, *Empresses and Power in Early Byzantium. Women, Power, and Politics* (London, 2001); Judith Herrin, "Changing Functions of Monasteries for Women during Byzantine Iconoclasm," in *Byzantine Women Varieties of Experience, 800–1200*, ed. Lynda Garland (Aldershot, 2006), 1-16; Nevra Necipoğlu, ed., *Byzantine Constantinople: Monuments, Topography and Everyday Life* (Leiden, 2001); Paul Magdalino, "Medieval Constantinople," in *Studies on the History and Topography of Byzantine Constantinople* (Aldershot, 2007), I; Cyril Mango, *Studies on Constantinople* (London, 1997); Raymond Janin, *La géographie ecclésiastique de l'empire byzantine 1, Le siège de Constantinople et le patriarcat oecuménique, 3: Les églises et les monastères* (Paris, 1969) and Sofia Kotzabassi, ed. *The Pantokrator Monastery in Constantinople* (Boston, 2013).

period witnessed a change in the motivations of founders and a transformation of the object of monumental religious patronage. The great multifunctional monastic institutions with strong ideological manifestations were to become the pinnacle of a longer development—rooted in more private reasons.

Monumental patronage and religious donation were part of the Classical heritage in Byzantium. Anyone with middling financial means was eager to commission a church or monastery. Emperors, empresses, the members of the imperial family and aristocratic families dominated the scene as benefactors and founders of public religious building in the Empire and in her capital. Building activity in the capital resumed from the second half of the eighth century on, and with the emperor as the prime actor of the re-building of Constantinople. The emperor's interest in religious foundations, especially churches and monasteries, to display his piety, benevolence, and munificence, reached a peak in the eleventh century. According to Paul Magdalino, this process started in the second half of the ninth century under Basil I.[5] In addition to his commission of the *Nea Ekklesia*, Basil I founded the monastery of Diomedes and the convent of St. Euphemia, later incorporated into the monastery of *Petrion/ta Petria*.[6] Before Basil I, in the earlier decades of the Middle Byzantine period, the emperors's reticence in investing in religious foundations may be explained by politics, contested and short reigns, and Iconoclasm.

Imperial women's involvement in religious monumental patronage does not closely follow its male counterpart.[7] Examining areas where Komnenian imperial women exercised power, Barbara Hill concludes her *Imperial Women of Byzantium* by stating that there was a decrease in women's power by the early twelfth century.[8]

---

[5] This is the well-attested patronage of the Komnenoi, which later peaked in the early Palaiologan period; see Hatlie, *Monks and Monasteries*, 257–63; Magdalino, "Medieval Constantinople," I: 27–31.

[6] Magdalino already suggested twenty years ago that this mainly aristocratic building program was perhaps the urban reflexion of Alexios's structural transformation of the Byzantine state; ibid., "Medieval Constantinople," in *Studies on the History and Topography of Byzantine Constantinople* (Aldershot, 2007), I: 78.

[7] For imperial and aristocratic women's patronage of monumental religious buildings, several scholars have focused on specific periods and case studies, however few works are relevant for the current discussion of changing patronage patterns. Leslie Brubaker and Liz James, dealing with the Theodosian and Justinianic imperial women's patronage of churches respectively, tackle how social memory changes previous female foundations. Leslie Brubaker, "Memories of Helena: Patterns in Imperial Female Matronage in the Fourth and the Fifth Centuries," in *Women, Men and Eunuchs, Gender in Byzantium*, ed. Liz James (New York, 1997), 52–75; Liz James, "Making a Name: Reputation and Imperial Founding and Refounding in Constantinople," in *Female Founders*, 63–72.

[8] Hill, *Imperial Women in Byzantium*, 174–80.

Women's visibility and power, diminished as an outcome of the strong re-organization of the state and only rose by the end of the twelfth century, during the crisis of male authority. Social development happened at the expense of women.[9] Is there a similar pattern in the patronage of the women in earlier periods?

Foundations and Power

A pattern of imperial women's patronage of churches and monasteries is evident at a number of religious foundations commissioned during the Middle Byzantine period at moments when the practice coincided with the consolidation of power of the ruling dynasty. Empresses partook in monumental patronage, mostly by founding religious houses, even when the emperors were not necessarily renowned as builders in the capital.[10] This reveals that monumental patronage served the desire of imperial women for visibility, reputation, and social acceptance.[11] A common Byzantine woman was able to take an active part in the daily life of the capital, while elite women were not; they had to rely on others to handle mundane tasks in the city.[12] A woman of high status, therefore, had to seek other means to make an impact in the capital. Religious foundations were ideal to make their names heard and to be remembered without their being physically present.[13]

Empress Eirene, together with her son Constantine VI, restored the churches of St. Anastasios and Theotokos Pege.[14] Eirene was said to have established a women's community on Princes' Islands, built St. Eustathios, restored the relics of St. Euphemia to the monastery dedicated to her at the Hippodrome, and expanded

---

[9] Ibid., 208–17.

[10] For instance, Leo IV, Michael I, and Constantine X did not found religious houses in Constantinople, but their empresses Eirene, Prokopia, Eudokia Makrembolitissa did.

[11] James, "Making a Name," in *Female Founders*, 63–72.

[12] Angeliki Laiou, "Women in the Marketplace of Constantinople," in *Byzantine Constantinople*, 261–273.

[13] This paper focuses on foundation activities; however, it should be noted that imperial women appear as benefactors of monasteries in other ways as well, especially when they have the authority to make decisions independent of the ruling emperor; for example, Theodora, wife of Theophilos, gave Anthemios to her son-in-law Alexios Mousele to convert into a monastery; empresses Zoe and Theodora issued a chrysobull for Nea Mone on Chios and granted privileges to the monasteries of Mangana and St. Michael in Sosthenion; and Anna Dalassene, mother of Alexios I, signed a chrysobull for Patmos. This kind of benefaction points to another way of exercising authority through deeds of piety.

[14] Hesychios Illoustrios, *Patria Konstantinoupoleos*, ed. Theodor Preger, trans. Albrecht Berger, 3.17, 3.142.

a multifunctional complex around St. Loukas.¹⁵ Similar to Eirene's patronage at St. Loukas, although more modest in scale, Elene Lekapene extended the "old" Petrion with a *xenon* and an old-age home (*gerotropheion*) and the complex became to be called *ta Ellenes*.¹⁶ In both cases, the empresses did not establish these foundations for private use. Instead, they displayed the imperial virtue of philanthropy through these complexes, which targeted a wider segment of population and thus, provided a higher degree of visibility and enhanced the reputation of their founders.

In six cases, religious foundations are attributed to empresses, yet evidence for their initial motivations is sporadic. When Constantine VI divorced empress Maria of Amnia to marry Theodote in 795, Maria retreated to her monastery called *ton despoinon*, where she was compelled to take monastic vows.¹⁷ When Michael I abdicated the throne in 813, the usurper Emperor Leo V exiled Empress Prokopia to her monastery, known as *Prokopia/ta Prokopias*.¹⁸ She is noted to have founded palaces in the area as well.¹⁹ Theodora, wife of Theophilos, was known to be a patron of monastic institutions: among others, she founded the monastery of St. Panteleimon *ta Armamentareas* and bestowed properties to it.²⁰ However, unlike Maria and Prokopia, when Theodora lost the favor of her son Michael III, she was not confined to any of the monasteries associated with her; rather, in 858 she was exiled to her mother Theoktiste's monastery called *ta Gastria*.²¹ Another example is Empress Theophano, first wife of Leon VI, who was attributed with building the church of St. Constantine.²² Moreover, Eudokia Makrembolitissa was also exiled to her foun-

---

[15] *Patria*, 3.154, 3.9, 3.85; Theophanes, *Chronographia*, ed. de Boor, trans. Harry Turtledove, AM 6258, 439–440; AM 6295, 480; *Book of Ceremonies*, ed. J. J. Reiske, revised Reinhold Neibuhr (Bonn, 1831), trans. Moffatt, Maxeme Toll (Canberra, 2012), 815.

[16] Theophanes Continuatus, 6.40, ed. Immanuel Bekker, Corpus Scriptorum Historiae Byzantinae (Bonn, 1838), 458–59.

[17] Theodoros Skoutariotes, *Synopsis Chronike*, ed. Constantine Sathas, p. 128.24–26.

[18] Theophanes Continuatus, 1.10, 16–18, ed. Athanasios Kambylis, trans. Michael Featherstone and Juan Signes Codoñer, (Boston/Berlin, 2015), 32–33; Ioannes Skylitzes, *A Synopsis of Byzantine History, 811–1057*, 1.3, trans. John Wortley (Cambridge, 2010), 9; *Patria*,3.153; Ioseph Genesios, *On the Reigns of Emperors*, 1.5, ed. A. Lesmüller and H. Thurn (Berlin, 1978), trans. Anthony Kaldellis (Canberra, 1998).

[19] *Patria* 3.153.

[20] *Patria*3.155; Janin, *Églises*, 52, 386–387.

[21] Theodora's later years are known from numerous sources that do not necessarily agree with one another, yet at least it seems that *ta Gastria* was where she was exiled for some time.

[22] Sermo in Theophano (BHG 1795) cap. 24, pp. 42.28–43.16, ed. Eduard Kurtz (St. Petersburg, 1898); Stephen of Novgorod, *Russian Travelers to Constantinople in the Fourteenth and Fifteenth Centuries*, ed. George Majeska (Washington, 1984), 42; cf. Philip Grierson, "Tombs and Obits of Byzantine Emperors 337–1042," *DOP* 16 (1962): 1–63.

dation dedicated to Theotokos, the monastery of Piperoudion on the Bosporos in 1071.[23] Lastly, Empress Theodora *porphyrogenneta*, whose name appears along her sister Zoe's in distributing privileges to monasteries, was buried in her monastic foundation called *ta Oikoproasteia*.[24] Although little is known about the foundation process of these monasteries, the functions they served are clear: supporting monastic communities, and providing a retirement and/or burial place.

In some cases, there is information about the specific reasons that propelled the empresses to sponsor religious houses. Empress Euphrosyne, daughter of Maria of Amnia and Constantine VI[25] and wife of Michael II, founded the monastery named Euphrosyne *ta Libadia*.[26] When her mother was exiled to the monastery *ton Despoinon*, Euphrosyne was separated from her and spent the early years of her life as a nun in another monastery on the Princes' Islands.[27] Later, she was chosen by Michael II as his second wife even though she renounced the world.[28] She must have founded the monastery of Euphrosyne *ta Libadia* in Constantinople after her marriage in order to house the tombs of her parents and her sister Eirene.[29] Years later, her stepson, Emperor Theophilos forced her to retire in the monastery on the Princes' Islands where she had once taken the veil. Nevertheless, she was buried in the monastery of Euphrosyne.[30] She might have prepared her own tomb along with her family's before Theophilos's rise to power and was able to ensure that her funerary plans were realized.[31] A second example is Empress Zoe *porphyrogenneta*. In addition to sponsoring numerous monastic communities by granting privileges, she founded a church dedicated to Christ *Antiphonetes* to serve as her burial place.[32] Her special devotion to this representation of Christ is recorded by Michael Psellos in a passage entitled "about the *Antiphonetes*," where the historian explains that Zoe commissioned an icon of Christ that revealed prophecies to her.[33] Hence, she

---

[23] Michael Attaleiates, *The History*, 21.3, ed. and trans. Anthony Kaldellis and Dimitris Krallis (DO Medieval Library, 2012), 306–307.
[24] Skoutariotes, *Synopsis Chronike*, p. 163.20–21.
[25] *Prosopographie der mittelbyzantinischen Zeit Online* (hereafter: PMBZ) (Berlin, 2013), no. 1705.
[26] Skoutariotes, *Synopsis Chronike*, cf. Patria 3.77.
[27] Genesios 2.14; Theoph. Cont. 2.24.
[28] Ibid.
[29] Janin, *Églises*, pp. 130–131; Grierson, "Tombs," 1, 3–63.
[30] *Book of Ceremonies*, 2.42.
[31] Theoph.Cont. 3.1. Empress Eirene, too, was exiled to Lesbos but ensured her burial in her foundation on the Princes' Island.
[32] Skoutariotes, *Synopsis Chronike*, p. 163.3–5; Anna Komnene, *Alexias*, 6.3, ed. Diether R. Reinsch, Athanasios Kambylis (Berlin, 2001), 173.
[33] Michael Psellos, *Chronographia*, 6.66, trans. E. R. A. Sewter (London, 1966).

constructed her tomb, lavishly decorated with small columns, silver and other precious metals in a church dedicated to the *Antiphonetes*.³⁴ Euphrosyne seems to have been compelled to establish a mausoleum for her family, whereas Zoe seems to have followed the mid-eleventh century trend of imperial burials in private foundations.

Foundations and Powerlessness

Empresses who founded churches and monasteries during their reign, demonstrated their power through philanthropy and left a permanent mark in the city. There existed, however, yet another category of religious foundations by imperial women. For empresses whose husbands were overthrown or abdicated, proprietary rights at a monastery founded by them become both a refuge and a source of capital. At least two examples show that a monastery could be a welcome solution in moments of crisis.

Empress Theodote, second wife of Constantine VI, presumably lived in the same private palace known as "the house of Isidoros" with her husband, after he was blinded in 797 at the order of his mother Eirene.³⁵ After Constantine's death, Theodote became a nun and, in the first decade of the ninth century, converted the palace into a female monastery named *ta Metanoia*.³⁶ It is possible that Constantine was buried there before his remains were transported to the monastery founded by his daughter Euphrosyne. Theodote must have been buried in this monastery where she spent the last years of her life—her name was not included in the lists of imperial tombs.³⁷ The monastery of Empress Theophano, wife of Staurakios represents a similar case.³⁸ Forced to abdicate in 811 by Michael I Rangabe, Emperor Staurakios took monastic vows.³⁹ Unlike Constantine VI, he was not blinded: his renunciation of the world along with imperial power was a prerequisite for his survival. When he was tonsured, his wife followed suit: Theophano became a nun. Theophanes recounts that Michael I Rangabe granted wealth and privileges to various people upon his coronation, and that Theophano was one of the recipients: she acquired a "fine home known as *ta Hebraika*, for use as a monastery."⁴⁰ The case of Theodote

---

34 The church of Antiphonetes might be close to the church of Virgin Chalkoprateia; see Janin, *Églises*, p. 506.
35 PMBZ no. 7899.
36 Herrin, "Changing Functions of Monasteries," 14–15; b *Patria* II. 65, for the *xenon* of Theophilos.
37 Grierson, "Tombs and Obits," 54–55.
38 PMBZ no. 8163.
39 Theophanes AM 6303, AM 6304, 493–494.
40 Theoph. AM 6304, 494.

and Theophano show that imperial women were successful in using their networks and/or appealing to the new emperor to secure their future.

These examples also reveal a more urgent need of imperial women in distress: they needed a place to live. This concern is best illustrated by empress Catherine of Bulgaria when her husband, Emperor Isaac I Komnenos wanted to abdicate the throne:

> Have you no pity now for us in our desolation? What sort of feeling have you, to take away yourself from the palace, and leave me behind, condemned to a widowhood full of sorrow, and your daughter, a wretched orphan? Nor will that be the end of our sufferings. More dreadful things will follow. Hands, maybe not even friendly hands, will carry us off to faraway places of exile. ... No doubt you will live on after you enter the Church, or perhaps you will die nobly, but what will be left for us? A life worse than death![41]

Trying to change her husband's mind, the empress is aware of what waits for them after they are stripped of their insignia. Embedded in women's collective memories were the fates of previous empresses, such as Eirene, who was promised to be allowed to stay in the palace of Eleutherios in Constantinople, but was nevertheless exiled to the Princes' Islands and then to Lesbos; similarly, imperial women were forced to live at monasteries like the Petrion.

The Komnenian Turn

The Komnenian century was hallmarked by powerful women, starting with Empress Eudokia Makrembolitissa, wife of Constantine X and Romanos IV, and Maria of Alania, wife of Michael VII and later of Nikephoros III. Anna Dalassene, Maria of Bulgaria, Eirene Doukaina, and Maria of Antioch played a prominent and perceptible role in Byzantine society. With the exception of Maria of Bulgaria, who was more reticent to play a public role, and Maria of Alania, who did not found a monastery, these women were renowned for their monastic patronage. As much as it was a part of larger picture of imperial women's foundations in the Middle Byzantine period, the empresses' monastic patronage was shaped by the Komnenian emperors' dynastic strategies to consolidate their power in the Empire. Alexios I estab-

---

[41] Psellos 7.82, trans. Sewter, 248.

lished a new class of *sebastoi* at the top of the state administration, which consisted chiefly of the emperor's relatives and in-laws.⁴² The blood-relatives of the emperor, men and women alike, founded monasteries in the Northwest of the city, on the North-Northeastern slopes of the fifth hill, between the Golden Horn, the northern branch of the Mese and the Constantinian walls. The extant Komnenian monastic structures in Constantinople—the Pammakaristos, Euergetes, and the Pantokrator—constitute impressive structures that reveal a strong focus on dynasty. Women's patronage under the Komneni combined the functions that previous monastic complexes kept separate.⁴³

The first recorded monastic foundation activity of the Komnenian era is the restoration of the Chora monastery by Maria of Bulgaria. The Chora stood close to the Blachernai palace in the North-Western section of Constantinople.⁴⁴ Mother of Empress Eirene Doukaina, Maria of Bulgaria was offered an imperial monastery to restore—it must have been a great honor. Her restoration work around 1081 is likely to have coincided with Anna Dalassene's foundation of the monastery of the All-Seeing Christ (*Pantepoptes*).⁴⁵ In many ways the ideal Komnenian woman, Anna Dalassene was a model mother, admired for her piety and patronage. No empress, she was extremely powerful in the early years of her son Emperor Alexios's reign. As a benefactor, Anna—like Zoe and Theodora—exercised her imperial authority by issuing chrysobulls, granting privileges to monasteries, such as the monastery of St. John the Theologos on Patmos; to the monk John the Faster to establish his monastery in Constantinople; and also for her own foundation of the *Pantepoptes*.⁴⁶ Unfortunately, we have limited evidence about the *Pantepoptes* in Anna's lifetime.⁴⁷ In the 1090s, she retreated to the residences in her monastery, where she was probably buried.⁴⁸ The same monastic pattern recurs once again: once an act of prestige

---

42 Paul Magdalino, *Empire of Manuel I Komnenos 1143–1180* (Cambridge, 1993), 180ff.
43 For the early Komnenian presence in Constantinople, see Vlada Stanković and Albrecht Berger, "The Komnenoi and Constantinople before the Building of the Pantokrator," in *Pantokrator Monastery*, 3–32.
44 Paul Underwood, *The Kariye Djami* (Princeton, 1966), I: 8–13.
45 Janin, *Églises*, 513–15; Vassilios Kidonopoulos, *Bauten in Konstantinopel, 1204–1328: Verfall und Zerstörung, Restaurierung, Umbau and Neubau von Profan- und Sakralbauten* (Wiesbaden, 1994), 28–30; also Cyril Mango, "Where at Constantinople was the Monastery of Christos Pantepoptes?" Δελτίον XAE 20 (1998): 87–8.
46 Hill, *Imperial Women*, 161–65.
47 In 1087, Alexios issued a decree by which he granted some properties of Pantepoptes to Myrelaion and Anna Dalassene approved the transaction. Franz Miklosich, Josef Müller, ed., *Acta et Diplomata Graeca MediiAevi Sacra et Profana, Volume 6: Acta et Diplomata Monasteriorum et Ecclesiarum Orientis Tomus Tertius* (hereafter MM) (Athens, 1890), 25–28, 32–33.
48 Ioannes Zonaras, *Epitome Historion*, 18.24, ed. Theodor Büttner-Wobst (Bonn, 1897), 746.

and piety, monasteries became places of retirement and burial for the founders. It is also noteworthy that *Pantepoptes* was a male monastery. Even though Anna Dalassene took the monastic vow, she did not plan to live the angelic life, not even as an aristocratic nun in her own coenobitic institution.[49]

Early in the twelfth century, Empress Eirene Doukaina founded the monastery of Theotokos *Kecharitomene*.[50] Eirene owned an already extant church in the North-Western part of the city, the narthex of which she restored and also expanded with an exonarthex.[51] The empress built the entire monastery encircling the church, including an outer wall and an inner wall of brick to divide the two courtyards of the convent, and a number of free-standing buildings in it: a dormitory, an adjacent room to the dormitory, other cells for the community, a refectory, a *tropike* behind the refectory's apse for imperial nuns, and various other buildings reserved for the imperial family.[52] As described in the *typikon*, the monastery was a vast foundation (parts of the outer wall measure 224,5 cubits) endowed with several properties.[53] The list of properties includes a small nunnery (*ta Kellaraias*) that the empress received from Patriarch Nicholas III *Grammatikos* (1084–1111) in the same quarter of the city to serve as the cemetery of the nuns.[54] Eirene's imperial residence stood across the street from the convent, to the East.[55] She and Anna Komnene must have spent the last years of their lives in these apartments following their failed coup against John II.[56] It is here that they organized a literary salon; in 1128, for instance, Eirene asked Michael Italikos to improvise an *enkomion* before her *theatron*.[57] While Maria of Alania had to negotiate her living quarters with the

---

[49] As convincingly argued by Vlada Stanković ("Comnenian Monastic Foundations," 53), Anna Dalassene had a special devotion to the All-Seeing Christ, whose icon she carried with her, just as Zoe had a special veneration of Christ Who Responds; see Nikephoros Bryennios, *Materials for History*, ed. Paul Gautier (Brussels, 1974), 131.

[50] *Oxford Dictionary of Byzantium* (Oxford, 1991) s.v. "Irene Doukaina" empress 1081–1118. Paul Gautier, "Le Typikon de la Théotokos Kécharitoménè," *Revue des Études Byzantines* 43 (1985), 5–165; Robert Jordan, trans., "*Kecharitomene*: Typikon of Empress Irene Doukaina Komnene for the Convent of the Mother of God Kecharitomene in Constantinople," in *Byzantine Monastic Foundation Documents: A Complete Translation of the Surviving Founders' "Typika" and Testaments* (hereafter *BMFD*), ed. John Thomas and A. C. Hero (Washington, DC., 2000), 664–717.

[51] Gautier, "Kécharitoménè," 127; Jordan, "*Kecharitomene*," 702–03.

[52] Gautier, "Kécharitoménè," 37–39; Jordan, "*Kecharitomene*," 670–72.

[53] Gautier, "Kécharitoménè," 147–149; Jordan, "*Kecharitomene*," 710–711.

[54] Janin, *Églises,* 188–91; Gautier, "Kécharitoménè," 115; Jordan, "*Kecharitomene*," 699.

[55] Gautier, "Kécharitoménè," 149; Jordan, "*Kecharitomene*," 711.

[56] NiketasChoniates, *O City of Byzantium, Annals of Niketas Choniates*, trans. H. J. Magoulias (Detroit, 1984), 8–11; Zonaras, *Epitome,* 18, pp. 762–66.

[57] Michael Italikos, *Lettres et discours*, 146.1–151.24, ed., Paul Gautier (Paris, 1972).

ruling emperor, and Anna Dalassene had retired to her monastic complex in the heart of the Komnenian quarter of the capital, Eirene Doukaina and Anna Komnene lived close to the palace, but not in the palace; close to the monastery, but, again, not in the monastery.

The *Kecharitomene* was adjacent to the monastery of Christ *Philanthropos*, the foundation associated with Eirene's husband, Emperor Alexios.[58] The founder of the *Philanthropos* is a debated issue: Eirene calls it her husband's foundation, yet Alexios at that time concentrated his attention on his grand foundation of the *Orphanotropheion*. In any case, after Alexios's death, Eirene must have acted as the *ktetor* of both institutions. The joint monasteries of Theotokos *Kecharitomene* and Christ *Philanthropos* represent the first common foundation by an imperial couple in the Middle Byzantine period. Empresses restored or built churches and monasteries with the ruling emperors; more often; however, emperors and empresses commissioned religious houses separately. The twin foundations of Eirene and Alexios reflected for the first time, "in stereo", the philanthropy of the imperial couple, with the male and female communities devoted to Christ and the Theotokos respectively.

This does not mean that the empress lost her individuality, as expressed through her monastic patronage. The *typikon* of the *Kecharitomene* illustrates clearly that, despite being separated only by a wall, the two foundations were independent of each other during the lifetime of the emperor. Three sets of the *typika* of *Philanthropos* and *Kecharitomene* were kept separately in the donor's possession, in the monasteries and in the Hagia Sophia.[59] Although the *typikon* of the Philanthropos did not survive, it is reasonable to assume that the emperor expressed similar concerns in the prologue of the document as the empress: Eirene Doukaina casts herself as a devotee of the Mother of God, emphasizes motherhood as the most valued attribute of a woman, and shows great concern for the female descendants of the family, including in-laws.[60] Not only was the female line of her family given the protectorate of the convent and the right to live in Eirene's imperial residence, but they were also allowed to enter the monastery and to be buried in the exonarthex of the monastic church.[61] Even though Eirene did not include plans for her own burial in the *typikon*, considering her husband's burial in the *Philanthropos* and her expressed

---

[58] Even though the foundational *typikon* of the Philanthropos did not survive, it is reasonable to think that it was similar in size and splendor to the Kecharitomene.
[59] Gautier, "Kécharitoménè," 115, 133; Jordan, "*Kecharitomene*," 698–99, 705.
[60] Gautier, "Kécharitoménè," 19–29; Jordan, "*Kecharitomene*," pp. 664–67.
[61] Gautier, "Kécharitoménè," 131, 133; Jordan, "*Kecharitomene*," 704–05.

wishes for her daughters and grand-daughters, it is likely that she was buried in *Kecharitomene*. In this way, while the monasteries were to remind the viewer of the heavenly family in the urban topography of the city with their domed churches and perimeter walls, they also served the imperial family as their residences outside the palace and at the end, as their resting places.

As for Piroska-Eirene and Maria of Antioch, there is no consensus as to what degree they can be considered "founders." The *typikon* of the monastery of Christ Pantokrator written by Emperor John II Komnenos credits the empress with "its planning, construction, and completion" and records that Eirene donated her wealth to the monastery.[62] Eirene's tomb was placed in the *heroon* of St. Michael that connected the two churches dedicated to Theotokos Eleousa and Christ Pantokrator.[63] The church of Eleousa was completed after Eirene's death, but the monastic complex as a whole parallels the *Kecharitomene–Philanthropos* foundation, where the empress and the emperor both act as founders, the church of Eleousa was accessible to women, while the church of Pantokrator was used by the male monks.[64] The foundation of Pantokrator monastery, thus, developed the model of the adjacent monasteries of *Kecharitomene* and *Philanthropos*. By emphasising the legitimacy of the ruling family, as against the rest of the Komnenoi and their foundations, it highlighted the empress's visibility.

Eirene's son, Emperor Manuel I Komnenos opposed the founding of new monasteries in Constantinople thus posing an obstacle for his second wife, Maria of Antioch. The emperor founded a monastery dedicated to the Archangel Michael *Kataskepe* on the Northern Bosporos outside the capital, but it was fundamentally different in its financial organization from the previous establishments in that it was not endowed with landed property.[65] Representing the third generation of Komnenian emperors, Manuel I had an imperial monastery, the Pantokrator, the greatest of any monastic foundation by the later twelfth century, with a strong emphasis on family and dynasty, including a burial chapel specifically for the ruling emperor and his heirs.[66] Manuel buried there his first wife Bertha-Eirene of Sulzbach in

---

[62] Gautier, "Le typikon du Christ SauveurPantocrator," *Revue des études byzantines* 32 (1974): 29; Robert Jordan, tr., "Pantokrator: Typikon of Emperor John II Komnenos for the Monastery of Christ Pantokrator in Constantinople," in *BMFD*, 738.

[63] Gautier, "Pantocrator," 81; Jordan, "*Pantokrator*," 756.

[64] Gautier, "Pantocrator," 73–77; Jordan, "*Pantokrator*," 753–54.

[65] Choniates, *Annals*, 117–18.

[66] Paul Magdalino, "The Foundation of the Pantokrator Monastery in Its Urban Setting," in *The Pantokrator Monastery in Constantinople*, ed., Sofia Kotzabassi (Boston, 2013), 33–55.

1160.⁶⁷ When Maria of Antioch came to power, despite being a foreigner and having her rule disputed, she also began a foundation work by transforming the house of a certain Michaelitzes into a monastery.⁶⁸ Like many Komnenian founders, she dedicated the monastery to Theotokos the Queen of All (*Pantanassa*). Yet, unlike the other Komnenian foundations, her monastery foundation was located in the Easternmost part of the peninsula, suspiciously distant from the Komnenian core of Constantinople.⁶⁹

The paradigm that empresses strove to convey an ideological message through monumental patronage, however, does not apply to each and every case. Half of the empresses in the Middle Byzantine period were no founders of monasteries. Indeed, even some of the particularly powerful empresses failed to establish religious houses in the city. Maria of Alania is a case in point. Married first to Michael VII between 1072 and 1078, and, after his abdication and retirement to St John of Stoudios as a monk, to Nikephoros III Botaneiates, between 1078 and 1081, thus ensuring the inheritance of her son Constantine.⁷⁰ When Nikephoros III disinherited her son, however, she was powerful enough to support the alliance of the Doukas and Komnenos families that brought Alexios I Komnenos to power.⁷¹ As an empress-consort and a wealthy dowager-empress, Maria was the ideal type of the female Byzantine monastic patron, yet she did not commission a religious house even after she took the veil. At Michael VII's abdication in 1078, Maria retreated to the Blachernai Palace for a brief period. When Alexios I came to power in 1081, Maria lived in the Great Palace until she moved to the palace at Mangana with her son Constantine, then acclaimed co-emperor.⁷² The palace and the monastery of Mangana and the monastery at Hebdomon were already given to Maria of Alania by Nikephoros III and these privileges were confirmed by Alexios I.⁷³ Maria was likely to be content with her possessions thanks to her personal networks, and especially to her relations with the ruling emperor.

---

67 Choniates, *Annals*, 65.
68 Skoutariotes, *Synopsis Chronike*, p. 398.27–30.
69 Ibid.; Janin, *Églises*, 215–16. Maria did not have the time to finish her foundation work, which was finally completed by Isaakios II.
70 Bryennios, pp.143.9–13, 253–255; Zonaras, *Epitome*, 18, p. 714; Anna Komnene, 1.4, p. 18; 3.4, p. 97.
71 Anna Komnene, 2.2 pp. 58–59.
72 Anna Komnene 3.2, p. 91.
73 Zonaras, *Epitome*, 18, p. 733.

Models and Motifs of the Founders

When imperial women appear as founders, what do we know of their motivations? Apart from their close connection to power, what inspired them to establish religious houses? Little can be said for patterns of patronage discernible in the families they came from. Imperial women with strong family connections within Constantinople—Theodote, Prokopia, Euphrosyne, Theophano, Theodora and Zoe, Eudokia Makrembolitissa, and Eirene Doukaina—emerge as monastic founders in the city. Some empresses from the provincial aristocracy Eirene, Maria of Amnia, Theophano, Theodosia—founded monasteries, while others—Thekla, Zoe Zautzina, Eudokia Baina, and Zoe Karbonopsina—did not. Although there is some merit to the idea that foreign-born empresses in the Middle Byzantine period were at a disadvantage in terms of acquiring power, this theory should not be taken too far in relation to their monumental patronage. Byzantines were aware of the significance of family and birth—this is why Nikephoros III was advised to marry Maria of Alania instead of Eudokia Makrembolitissa.[74] It is also true that Catherine of Bulgaria, Maria of Alania, and Bertha of Sulzbach did not found monasteries in Constantinople. However, Catherine was aware of the fate that awaited her upon her husband's abdication; Maria used her networks to secure a residence close to the palace, which happened to be a great monastic complex where she held her own alternative court; and Bertha, who died early, was married to an emperor whose monastic policy did not allow new foundations. How much of their foreign origins played a role in their lack of visibility in the cityscape through pious works is, therefore, open to debate, especially when other foreign-born empresses—Piroska-Eirene and Maria of Antioch—were active as monastic founders.

Secondly, the effect of marital status should be addressed with regard to the empresses' religious and monumental patronage. It has been widely argued that widowhood provided Byzantine women with freedom and the right to manage their wealth.[75] Considering the patronage activities of the Komnenian empresses, Barbara Hill concludes that widowhood was a common trait of those who were actively involved in sponsorship.[76] In the Middle Byzantine period, however, widowhood does not appear to have had a major role in empowering imperial women and propelling them to monumental patronage. Three dowager empresses founded churches and monasteries: Eirene, Theodote, and Maria of Antioch. However, it

---

[74] Anna Komnene 3.2, p. 91.
[75] Angeliki Laiou, *Women, Family and Society in Byzantium* (Aldershot, 2011); eadem, "Women in the Marketplace of Constantinople," 261–73; Hill, *Imperial Women*, 176–79.
[76] Hill, *Imperial Women*, 176–79.

was not widowhood that played the primary role in their sponsoring religious houses. Eirene was a *basilissa;* Theodote converted "the house of Isidoros" into a monastery after Emperor Constantine's death in a difficult period of her life, and it is unclear to what extent her patronage depended on the perks of being a widow. In contrast, Maria of Antioch, was definitely empowered by widowhood: after losing her husband, she acted as a regent and tried to eternalize her name by her piety, by taking the veil and by founding a monastery.[77] Euphrosyne, Theophano, Elene, Zoe, Eudokia Makrembolitissa, Eirene Doukaina, and Piroska-Eirene were all married at the time of their patronage activities. The importance of economic resources in building in the capital is undeniable, yet in the Middle Byzantine period financial means is seldom connected with economic independence acquired by the dowager empress. The Middle Byzantine empress is more often than not a married woman at the time of her monumental patronage.[78]

Lastly, let us consider the issue of taking the veil. Monasteries often functioned as places of (forced) retirement and confinement for their founders, yet the harshness of these varied. For those who lost power, it was sometimes necessary to renounce the world in measures the harshness of these measures varied order to secure a place in it. For example, Theodote and Theophano, wife of Emperor Staurakios, acquired their monasteries upon their husbands' deaths and presumably at the same time they took their vows. For others, if the main motivation for building a church or monastery was to gain a reputation for Christian piety, becoming a nun would further emphasize religious commitment. Four empresses—Theodora *porphyrogenneta*, Zoe *porphyrogenneta*, Eirene-Piroska, and Maria of Antioch—had already taken the monastic vow at the time of their patronage. Theodora was tonsured by her sister Zoe in 1031, more than twenty years before her foundation of *Oikoproasteia*, while for Maria of Antioch, it was a prerequisite to act as a regent after Manuel I's death. Monastic vocation might have gained extra accolade for Zoe, Piroska-Eirene, and Anna Dalassene. However, becoming a nun seems more often to have been a punishment. Three empresses—Maria of Amnia, Prokopia, and Eudokia Makrembolitissa—who commissioned their monasteries as lay patrons were later forced to take the monastic vow in these foundations. Eudokia's case is especially illuminating: she was banished to her foundation at *Piperoudion* in 1071, but only

---

[77] Anna Dalassene and Maria Doukaina were also dowagers at the time of their patronizing monastic foundations.

[78] This picture is in complete contrast to the early Palaiologan pattern of imperial and aristocratic women's monumental patronage; see Alice-Mary Talbot, "Building Activity in Constantinople under Andronikos II: The Role of Women Patrons in the Construction and Restoration of Monasteries," in *Byzantine Constantinople*, 329–43.

after a further decision of the court was she forced to take the veil.[79] Elene Lekapene did not embrace the monastic vocation; not only did she resist confinement in the monastery at the Palace of Antiochos, she also protested when her daughters were coerced to become nuns. Eirene, Theodora, the wife of Theophilos, and Eirene Doukaina were all lay patrons who did not become nuns upon their retirement to monasteries. Eirene even had hopes to stay in a palace in Constantinople after her abdication, yet was sent to exile to first to the Princes' Islands and then to Lesbos, where she died as a lay person. Even though Theodora was forced to retire to the monastery *ta Gastria*, then appeared in the monastery *ta Anthemiou* right before Michael III's assassination in 886, and perhaps travelled to Chrysopolis to bury her son, she did not take the monastic vow. Eirene Doukaina, together with Anna Komnene, was forced into semi-retirement in her imperial apartments described in the *typikon* of the monastery of *Kecharitomene*; neither Eirene nor Anna lived as nuns. All this suggests that a religious house, especially a monastic foundation, might have been planned as a refuge of choice, as opposed to just any place of exile—where the empress was unknown for her largesse, did not have clients, servants or privileges. The backlash of this smart solution, however, was to be compelled to don undesired monastic garments.

Conclusion

The origins of religious houses founded by imperial women were closely connected to dynastic concerns and politics. Foundations occur in two distinct and contrasted periods of time: in times of crisis, and in times of the dynasty's consolidation of power. The monasteries founded by empresses fell in these two groups and served different functions. For the former group, it resulted from an urgent need to secure a retirement home (and sometimes burial place) for the empress, as well as family members, as in the cases of Theodote or Prokopia. By using their networks, empresses were able to choose and to secure where to "retire" and ensure the continuity of their family's memory. However, these monasteries of moderate size did not convey ideological messages. At the time when the family was in power, monastic foundations gained a different meaning as an expression of the empresses' philanthropy. These foundations were meant to represent their immense wealth and social standing, through which they gained more prestige, visibility, and social acceptance in Constantinople. The way in which these empresses—such as Eirene and Elene—declared their power through patronage varied from offering multi-

---

[79] Psellos 7.31, trans. Sewter, 275.

functional complexes with no specific arrangements for their own residence within, to establishing a burial place for themselves. With the Komnenian empresses, all these functions merged to establish stunning and versatile structures in the heart of the city.

The Middle Byzantine empress—married, unmarried, or dowager; Constantinopolitan, provincial, or foreign—had an urge to build in the capital. In the five hundred years between the eighth and the twelfth century, the object of imperial philanthropy shifted from churches to monasteries. Following Zoe *porphyrogenneta*, empresses directed their patronage exclusively to monasteries. It was perhaps because monasteries were so similar to private houses, but with an added dimension of religiosity that protected them from alienation. A monastery was able to accommodate a variety of functions—residence, commemoration, burial— all of which revolved around the concept of the family. It was the Komnenian take on the dynasty and kinship networks that inscribed an unprecedented number of religious foundations onto Constantinople's cityscape. The emphasis of the empresses' foundations shifted from individual piety to familial bonds, and their acts of charity mirrored and complemented the emperors' good deeds—unless they were absorbed by them.

Bibliography
Primary Sources

Attaleiates, Michael. *The History*. Ed. and trans. Anthony Kaldellis and Dimitris Krallis (Washington D. C.: Dumbarton Oaks Medieval Library, 2012).

Bryennios, Nikephoros. *Materials for History*. Ed. Paul Gautier (Brussels, 1974).

Choniates, Niketas. *O City of Byzantium, Annals of Niketas Choniates*. Trans. H. J. Magoulias (Detroit, 1984).

Constantine Porphyrogennetos. *De Cerimoniis Aulae Byzantinae*, CSHB (Bonn 1829). Trans. A. Moffatt and M. Tall. *The Book of Ceremonies*. Canberra, 2012. 2 vols.

Gautier, Paul. "Le Typikon de la Théotokos Kécharitôménè." *Revue des Études Byzantines* 43 (1985), 5–165.

Gautier, Paul. "Le typikon du Christ Sauveur Pantocrator," *Revue des études byzantines* 32 (1974): 1–145.

Genesios, Ioseph. *On the Reigns of Emperors*, 1.5, ed. A. Lesmüller and H. Thurn (Berlin, 1978), trans. Anthony Kaldellis (Canberra, 1998).

Hesychios Illoustrios, *Patria Konstantinoupoleos*, ed. Theodor Preger, *Scriptores originum Constantinopolitanarum*. (Leipzig 1901–1907.)

Italikos, Michael. *Lettres et discours*. Ed. Paul Gautier (Paris, 1972).

Kecharitomene: Typikon of Empress Irene Doukaina Komnene for the Convent of the Mother of God Kecharitomene in Constantinople." Trans. Robert Jordan. In: *Byzantine Monastic Foundation Documents: A Complete Translation of the Surviving Founders' "Typika" and Testaments*. Eds. John Thomas and A. C. Hero (Washington, DC., 2000), 664–717.

Komnene, Anna. *Alexias*. Ed. Diether R. Reinsch, Athanasios Kambylis (Berlin, 2001)

Miklosich, Franz and Josef Müller, ed., A*cta et Diplomata Graeca Medii Aevi Sacra et Profana, Volume 6: Acta et Diplomata Monasteriorum et Ecclesiarum Orientis Tomus Tertius*. (Athens, 1890).

Pantokrator: Typikon of Emperor John II Komnenos for the Monastery of Christ Pantokrator in Constantinople." Trans. Robert Jordan. In: *Byzantine Monastic Foundation Documents: A Complete Translation of the Surviving Founders' "Typika" and Testaments*. Eds. John Thomas and A. C. Hero (Washington, DC., 2000), 737–774.

Psellos, Michael. *Chronographia*. Trans. E. R. A. Sewter (London, 1966).

Skylitzes, Ioannes. *A Synopsis of Byzantine History, 811–1057*, 1.3, trans. John Wortley. (Cambridge, 2010).

Theodoros Skoutariotes, *Synopsis Chronike*, ed. Constantine Sathas.

Theophanes Continuatus, *Chronographiae*. Ed. Athanasios Kambylis, trans. Michael Featherstone and Juan Signes Codoñer, (Boston/Berlin, 2015)

Stephen of Novgorod, *Russian Travelers to Constantinople in the Fourteenth and Fifteenth Centuries*, ed. George Majeska (Washington, 1984)

Zonaras, Ioannes. *Epitome Historion*. Ed. Theodor Büttner-Wobst (Bonn, 1897)

Secondary Sources

Brubaker, Leslie. "Memories of Helena: Patterns in Imperial Female Matronage in the Fourth and the Fifth Centuries," in *Women, Men and Eunuchs, Gender in Byzantium*, ed. Liz James (New York: Routledge, 1997), 52–75.

Garland, Lynda. *Byzantine Empresses, Women and Power in Byzantium, AD 527–1204* (London: Routledge, 1999)

Grierson, Philip. "Tombs and Obits of Byzantine Emperors 337–1042." *Dumbarton Oaks Papers* 16 (1962): 1–63.

Hatlie, Peter. *Monks and Monasteries in Constantinople, 350–850*. (Cambridge: Cambridge University Press, 2007.)

Herrin, Judith. "Changing Functions of Monasteries for Women during Byzantine Iconoclasm," in *Byzantine Women Varieties of Experience, 800–1200*, ed. Lynda Garland (Aldershot: Ashgate, 2006), 1–16.

Hill, Barbara. *Imperial Women in Byzantium, 1025-1204: Power, Patronage and Ideology* (London: Routledge, 1999).

James, Liz. *Empresses and Power in Early Byzantium. Women, Power, and Politics* (London: Continuum, 2001).

———. "Making a Name: Reputation and Imperial Founding and Refounding in Constantinople." In: Theis, Lioba, Margaret Mullett, and Michael Grünbart, eds., *Female Founders in Byzantium and Beyond* (Vienna–Cologne: Böhlau, 2013), 63–72.

Janin, Raymond. *La géographie ecclésiastique de l'empire byzantine 1, Le siège de Constantinople et le patriarcat oecuménique, 3: Les églises et les monastères* (Paris: Institut français des études byzantines, 1969)

Kidonopoulos, Vassilios. *Bauten in Konstantinopel, 1204-1328: Verfall und Zerstörung, Restaurierung, Umbau and Neubau von Profan- und Sakralbauten* (Wiesbaden: Harrassowitz 1994).

Kotzabassi, Sofia. (ed.) *The Pantokrator Monastery in Constantinople*. Byzantinisches Archiv 27. (Berlin: De Gruyter, 2013).

Laiou, Angeliki. "Women in the Marketplace of Constantinople." In: *Byzantine Constantinople: Monuments, Topography and Everyday Life*. Ed. Nevra Necipoğlu (Leiden: Brill, 2001), 261–273.

Laiou, Angeliki. *Women, Family and Society in Byzantium* (Aldershot, 2011)

Magdalino, Paul. "Medieval Constantinople." In: *Studies on the History and Topography of Byzantine Constantinople* (Farnham: Aldershot, 2007)

Magdalino, Paul. "The Pantokrator Monastery in its Urban Setting." in Kotzabassi, ed., *Pantokrator Monastery*, 33–55.

Mango, Cyril. *Studies on Constantinople* (Farnham: Aldershot, 1993).

——— "Where at Constantinople was the Monastery of Christos Pantepoptes?" Δελτίον XAE 20 (1998): 87–88.

Mullett, Margaret ed., *Founders and Refounders of Byzantine Monasteries* (Belfast: Belfast Byzantine Enterprises, 2007)

Necipoğlu, Nevra. ed., *Byzantine Constantinople: Monuments, Topography and Everyday Life* (Leiden: Brill, 2001).

Ousterhout, Robert. "Sacred Geographies and Holy Cities: Constantinople as Jerusalem," in *Hierotopy: The Creation of Sacred Space in Byzantium and Medieval Russia*. Ed. Alexei Lidov (Moscow: Indrik, 2006), 98–116.

Stanković, Vlada. "Comnenian Monastic Foundations in Constantinople: Questions of Method and Context," *Belgrade Historical Review* 2 (2011): 47–73.

Stanković, Vlada and Albrecht Berger, "The Komnenoi and Constantinople before the Building of the Pantokrator." In: *The Pantokrator Monastery in Constantinople*. Ed. S. Kotzabassi. (Berlin: De Gruyter, 2013, 3–32).

Talbot, Alice-Mary. "Building Activity in Constantinople under Andronikos II: The Role of Women Patrons in the Construction and Restoration of Monasteries." In: *Byzantine Constantinople: Monuments, Topography and Everyday Life*. Ed. Nevra Necipoğlu (Leiden: Brill, 2001), 329–343.

Theis, Lioba, Margaret Mullett, and Michael Grünbart, eds., *Female Founders in Byzantium and Beyond* (Vienna–Cologne: Böhlau, 2012).

Underwood, Paul A. *The Kariye Djami* (New York: Pantheon Books, 1966).

"TO EACH ACCORDING TO THEIR NEED": THE VARIOUS MEDICAL AND CHARITABLE INSTITUTIONS OF THE PANTOKRATOR MONASTERY

Tyler Wolford

When Empress Eirene and her husband John II envisioned the completion of the Pantokrator Monastery in Constantinople, they included under its management a sophisticated hospital *(xenon)*. In the study of Byzantine hospitals, the Pantokrator holds a pivotal position. The abundance of detail found within a single document, the *typikon* of the Pantokrator Monastery, dated 1136, easily outpaces any other source on any other Byzantine hospital throughout the long history of the empire.[1] Due to the unique nature of this evidence, the uniqueness of the hospital itself has always been an open question. Building the Pantokrator Hospital alone would have certainly earned them praise enough for their philanthropy, but the imperial couple further envisioned a larger network of medical and charitable institutions operating under the supervision of the Pantokrator Monastery, along with the hospital. The monastery also maintained a leper hospital, an old-age home and a monastic infirmary.

The idea of monasteries supporting various charities and medical institutions was not new to the Byzantine world of the twelfth century. As early as the sixth century, the Monastery of Saint Theodosius in the Judean Desert financed three distinct houses of charity: a traveler's hostel, a poorhouse and a hospital.[2] Like the Pantokrator Monastery, it housed a separate medical institution for its own monks. This is not, of course, to imply that the Monastery of Saint Theodosius was the direct antecedent of the Pantokrator Monastery. This comparison merely prompts us to examine the Pantokrator Hospital in the context of the monastery's other institutions. While the two monasteries supported similar institutions, the list

---

[1] P. Gautier, "Le typikon du Christ Sauveur Pantocrator," *REB* 32 (1974): 26–131, English translation by R. Jordan, in *BMFD*, ed. J. Thomas and A. C. Hero (Washington, D.C., 2000), 28:737–774.
[2] *Der heilige Theodosios: Schriften des Theodoros und Kyrillos,* ed. H. Usener (Leipzig, 1890), 35, 40.

is not exactly the same. Can it be said of the Pantokrator Monastery what Theodore, Bishop of Petra, declared of the Monastery of Saint Theodosius, namely, having "kept fairness in mind in all equality, the ancient tradition of the apostles is fulfilled: 'it was handing over to each according to their need' (Acts 4:35)"?[3]

The Pantokrator Typikon

For answering these questions, scholars are largely dependant upon that one unique document, the *typikon* of the Pantokrator Monastery, composed by Emperor John II Komnenos after the untimely death of Piroska-Eirene. The emperor signed the document in October of 1136, while he was on campaign.[4] It is necessary, therefore, to first address this document on its own terms.

The primary purpose for the creation of any monastic *typikon* was the proper operation of a foundation after the founder's death, but for the *Typikon* of the Pantokrator, another purpose is much more apparent: the personal salvation of John II Komnenos.[5] While the classification of *typika* is often difficult, this feature helps make it the best example of an aristocratic *typikon*.[6] The information contained in this text concerning the operation of the charitable institutions suggests that they existed so that the sick and poor may pray for the soul of the emperor.[7] Other aspects of monastic life, such as the day-to-day activities of the monks, were downplayed or often ignored, especially when compared to other *typika*.[8]

Beyond the purpose of the text, the *Typikon* of the Pantokrator is a document of intent, not one of deeds observed or reported after having occurred. It is always possible that the precepts of the *Typikon* were not enacted as commanded. In fact, there are two specific instances where its instructions may not have been followed. The first is in the establishment of the first abbot of the monastery, Joseph Hagioglykerites. The *Typikon* specifies that the abbot of the monastery should be chosen from the monks of the Pantokrator Monastery or its dependencies. Since the monastery, from which Joseph came, namely the monastery of the Theotokos Pan-

---

[3] *Der heilige Theodosios*, 34.
[4] E. Congdon, "Imperial Commemoration and Ritual in the Typikon of the Monastery of Christ Pantokrator," *REB* 54 (1996): 166.
[5] Congdon, "Commemoration," 162; A. Epstein, "Formulas for Salvation: A Comparison of Two Byzantine Monasteries and their Founders," *ChHist* 50.4 (1981): 399.
[6] C. Galatariotou, "Byzantine Ktetorika Typika: A Comparative Study," *REB* 45 (1987): 92.
[7] P. Horden, "Alms and the Man: Hospital Founders in Byzantium," *The Impact of Hospitals: 300–2000*, edd. J. Henderson, P. Horden and A. Pastore (Bern, 2007), 70–71.
[8] Congdon, "Commemoration," 186; Epstein, "Formulas," 392–393; Galatariotou, "Ktetorika," 107.

tanassa on the island of Hagia Glykeria, was not a dependency of the monastery, he should not have been chosen as the first abbot.[9] While Paul Gautier suggested that either the emperor handpicked Joseph or the island of Hagia Glykeria was added to the monastery's dependencies, it still remains an instance where an assumption made based on the *Typikon* alone would have proven incorrect.[10]

The second instance of possible *typikon* neglect was an abandonment of some aspect of the commemoration ritual for the late emperor.[11] This is known from a letter of the monk Iakonos written to his patron the *sebastokratorissa* Eirene, the daughter-in-law of John II Komnenos. While Iakonos is not specific on exactly how the late emperor failed to achieve his perpetual memory, Michael Jeffreys and Elizabeth Jeffreys have suggested that the commemorations involving the *Hodegetria* icon and the entire monastic community may have been discontinued shortly after the emperor's death in 1143.[12]

While neither of these instances are enough to reject the *Typikon* as evidence, it should promote some caution, particularly in places within the *Typikon* where no other evidence exists for comparison.

The Leper Hospital

The Pantokrator Monastery supported four different institutions: a leper hospital, a monastic infirmary, an old-age home and a medical hospital. The *Typikon* designates that a place be set-aside for those suffering from "the sacred disease" *(hiera nosos)*.[13] This term was understood in classical antiquity as some sort of mental illness, such as epilepsy. By the twelfth century, however, it had come to mean leprosy.

---

[9] *BMFD* 28:751; Gautier, "Pantocrator," 66–67.

[10] Gautier, "Pantocrator," 22; the addition of the island of Hagia Glykeria to the dependencies of the Pantokrator Monastery after the completion of the *typikon* is a likely scenario, considering the monastery owned the village of Bare near Smyrna, according to a 1229 'note of testimony' from the Metropolitan of Smyrna, even though it is not mentioned in the *typikon*, *Acta et diplomata graeca medii aevi*, edd. F. Miklosich and J. Müller (Vienna, 1871), 4:187–189. Also see S. Kotzabassi, "The Monastery of Pantokrator between 1204 and 1453," *The Pantokrator Monastery in Constantinople*, ed. S. Kotzabassi (Boston, 2013), 57–58.

[11] M. Jeffreys and E. Jeffreys, "Immortality in the Pantokrator?" *Byzantion* 64 (1994): 193–201.

[12] Ibid. 200–201; P. Magdalino, however, disagrees with this interpretation, finding it hard to believe that Manuel Komnenos would both neglect his father and honor his mother in the *Life of Saint Eirene*, which was probably composed in his reign, P. Magdalino, "The Foundation of the Pantokrator Monastery in Its Urban Setting" *The Pantokrator Monastery in Constantinople*, ed. S. Kotzabassi (Boston, 2013), 47.

[13] *BMFD* 28:767–768; Gautier, "Pantocrator," 110–113.

Here a leper hospital was established, not a ward dedicated to psychological disorders or a shelter for epileptics.[14]

Of the charitable institutions associated with the Pantokrator Monastery, the leper hospital stands out as markedly different. Unlike the hospital, monastic infirmary or the old-age home, the leper hospital was not physically located in proximity to the monastery itself. Due to the residential and urban nature of the site and thus the difficulty of administrating the leper hospital near the monastery, it was founded near the old-age home (*gerokomeion*) of the Emperor Romanos.[15] The *gerokomeion* in question is probably the ancient leper hospital of Saint Zotikos,[16] refurbished by Romanos III Argyros in the eleventh century after an earthquake.[17] This leper hospital was originally founded in the fourth century north of the Golden Horn, on the so-called Mount of Olives in the region of Pera.[18] The leper hospital, therefore, was an annex to the already established leper hospital.

This explains many of the other ways that the leper hospital stands out. There were chapels at both the hospital and old-age home of the Pantokrator Monastery; even the cemetery at Medikariou, where the dead of the hospital and old-age home were buried, had its own chapel.[19] There are no specific stipulations for the establishment of a chapel at the leper hospital. While the *typikon* does provide the leper hospital with some revenue, it does not specify an amount. It also mentions an allotment that those at the leper hospital already had; this must refer to the finances of the Saint Zotikos Leper Hospital.[20] The omissions concerning the leper hospital may be due to the fact that John II Komnenos could rely upon the well-established institution on the Mount of Olives to provide for the administration and needs of the lepers.

The establishment of the leper hospital annex at the Saint Zotikos Hospital, therefore, attached the newly founded monastery and its charities to a hospital with an ancient tradition. This purposeful association with the past stands in stark contrast to the monastery's other connection to a charitable institution of the past,

---

[14] A. Philipsborn, "'ΙΕΡΑ ΝΟΣΟΣ' und die Spezial-Anstalt des Pantokrator-Krankenhauses," *Byzantion* 33 (1963): 223–230.

[15] *BMFD* 767; Gautier, "Pantocrator," 110–111.

[16] E. Kislinger. "Zur Lage der Leproserie des Pantokrator-Typikon," *JÖB* 42 (1992): 173–175; also see Magalino, "Urban Setting," 38, n. 26.

[17] John Skylitzes, *A Synopsis of Byzantine History, 811–1057*, trans. J. Wortley (Cambridge, 2010), 367–368; M. Aubineau, "Zoticos de Constantinople, nouricier des pauvres et serviteur des lépreux," *AB* 93 (1975): 67–108.

[18] D. Constantelos, *Byzantine Philanthropy and Social Welfare* (New Brunswick, 1968), 166–168.

[19] *BMFD* 28:766; Gautier, "Pantocrator," 106–107.

[20] *BMFD* 28:767–768; Gautier, "Pantocrator," 110–113.

the hospital of the Emperor Theophilos.²¹ While the Pantokrator's leper hospital was added to and augmented the Saint Zotikos Hospital, the Pantokrator Hospital seems to have replaced the hospital of Theophilos.²²

The Monastic Infirmary

The Pantokrator Monastery's medical and charitable institutions were not all public. One institution, the monks' infirmary, was private and used by the monks of the monastery alone. The infirmary was designed to fit six beds and stored two different sets of equipment for dealing with monastic illness. The first consisted of the plasters and oils of a medical cabinet stored in the infirmary. There were, however, no instruments for surgery, which would have been found within the public hospital. The second set included equipment for bathing, such as basins, soap containers and towels. In addition to these, white bread and the best wine were also given to the sick. The staff of the infirmary was comprised of one doctor from the hospital's outpatient clinic and the abbot of the monastery.²³ The doctor, however, did not only treat monks in the infirmary, but also visited those in their cell.²⁴

The infirmary was a feature common to coenobitic monasteries since their invention in the fourth century, but this one has its direct antecedent in the reform monasteries of the eleventh century, especially the Monastery of the Mother of God Evergetis.²⁵ The Evergetis infirmary was equipped with eight beds, a number close to that of the Pantokrator Monastery.²⁶ The major innovation of the Pantokrator Monastery to this system was the integration of the infirmary's doctor within the

---

21   The Pantokrator Hospital's connection to the Theophilos Hospital is made through shared topography, P. Magdalino, "Medieval Constantinople," *Studies on the History and Topography of Byzantine Constantinople* (Aldershot, 2007), 51–52.

22   This contrasts with the remembrance of the Emperor Theophilos in a contemporaneous and irreverent medical satire in which he is the judge of the dead, *Timarion*, trans. B. Baldwin (Detroit, 1984), 64–65.

23   *BMFD* 28:745; Gautier, "Pantocrator," 53.

24   *BMFD* 28:760; Gautier, "Pantocrator," 93.

25   A few monasteries such as Saint Mamas, *BMFD* 32:1017–1018, and Heliou Bomon, *BMFD* 33:1074, explicitly lacked infirmaries, instead entrusting their sick monks to the neighborhood public hospitals.

26   P. Grautier, "Le typikon de la Théotokos Évergétis," *REB* 40 (1982): 87; *BMFD* 22: 497. It is hard to know how this compares to the total number of monks because the *typikon* of the Evergetis declines to set a number of monks. The Nunnery of Theotokos Kecharitomene had twenty-four nuns and thus an infirmary that consisted of a single cell, *BMFD* 27:671, 696. The Monastery of Saint John the Forerunner of Phoberos, however, a monastery of twelve monks, has a four-bed infirmary modeled largely on Evergetis, *BMFD* 30:923, 937.

hospital's medical staff and within the chain of hospital career advancement. Doctors were promoted from this position (possibly also holding, or at least equal to a position within the outpatient clinic) to the hospital's wards.

The term used for infirmary in the Pantokrator is also an innovation, but of a very different sort. The term employed for infirmary in the Evergetis is *nosokomeion*,[27] which seems to be common term for monastic infirmaries in the medieval period.[28] While the *typikon* employs the term *nosokomeion* for its infirmary,[29] it is neither the only nor the main term used. The main term used for the infirmary in the *typikon* is *triklinarion* or *triklinos*.[30] Elsewhere in the text, the *triklinos* of the hospital is mentioned, here clearly meaning a dining hall.[31] This could easily refer to its important role as a place of dining on a more substantial diet, something frequently noted throughout the long history of the monastic infirmaries.[32]

The term *triklinos* for the monastic infirmary, could, however, have a different significance; the term was also used for the various reception halls that are part of Byzantine palaces and mansions, such as the *Chrysotriklinos* or the *Triklinos* of the Nineteen Couches.[33] In the context of the wider use of imperial motifs in a monastery founded by an imperial couple, such as the *opus sectile* floor of the monastic church with parallels in the Great Palace of Constantinople and the fictional palace of Digenis Akritis,[34] it encourages us to consider a palatial model for the Pantokrator Monastery.[35]

This is, however, not the most confusing use of terminology in Byzantine medical and charitable institutions. For instance, the *Typikon* uses the term *gerotropheion*, a variation on the more common term *gerokomeion*. While this institution

---

[27] Grautier, "Théotokos Évergétis," 87.
[28] Miller, *Birth*, 25–26.
[29] I disagree with Jordan, *BMFD* 28:760, and Miller, *Birth*, 25, who both suggested that in line 1065 *nosokomeion* refers to the public hospital, which in its forty other places of mention in the *typikon* is always called some form of *xenon*. I agree with Grautier, "Pantocrator," 92, who translated it as "l'infirmerie" and understood it to be the same as what Jordan has called the Monks' Sanatorium in *BMFD*.
[30] Grautier, "Pantocrator," 53.
[31] *BMFD* 28:762; Gautier, "Pantocrator," 99.
[32] A. Crislip, *From Monastery to Hospital: Christian Monasticism & the Transformation of Health Care in Late Antiquity* (Ann Arbor, 2005), 9–38.
[33] J. Featherstone, "The Great Palace as Reflected in the De Cerimoniis" *Visualisierungen von Herrschaft. Frühmittelalterliche Residenzen—Gestalt und Zeremoniell, Byzas 5*, ed. F. A. Bauer (Istanbul, 2006), 50–53.
[34] R. Ousterhout, "Architecture, Art and Komnenian Ideology at the Pantokrator Monastery," *Byzantine Constantinople: Monuments, Topography and Everyday Life,* ed. N. Necipoğlu (Leidon, 2001), 144.
[35] Magdalino, "Urban Setting," 41–43.

was a public charity, like the medical hospital, for many monasteries the term *gerokomeion* was used to designate the monastery's infirmary, in place of *nosokomeion*, as occurred at the eleventh-century Monastery of the Theotokos Petritzonitissa (Bachkovo, Bulgaria).[36] The aforementioned sixth-century Monastery of Saint Theodosius had a *gerokomeion* that likewise functioned as the monastery's infirmary.[37] Here, however, despite difficult and diverse terms, there is a distinction. The monks were treated in the infirmary, the layman in the public hospital.

The Old-Age Home

The *gerotropheion* of the Pantokrator Monastery was a public hospital, an old-age home, equipped for twenty-four male patients, operated under the direction of a *gerokomos*, chosen among the monks of the monastery.[38] It is almost always associated with the hospital in the *typikon*. The two institutions shared a bathhouse,[39] a bakery,[40] a cemetery[41] and a steward.[42] When those in the *gerotropheion* developed more acute diseases, they were to be transferred to the hospital, not the monastic infirmary.[43] Its orderlies, serving underneath the monastic director of the old-age home, were not monks but paid assistants. The patients, therefore, of the old-age home were not monks, but laymen. An inaugural *ekphrasis* poem for the monastery and the Life of Saint Eirene both note this connection,[44] demonstrating the public nature of the old-age home; it is the only institution, besides the hospital, known from an additional source besides the *typikon*.

When looking for antecedents for the *gerotropheion*, we must not look to monastic infirmaries like the *gerokomeion* of the Monastery of the Theotokos Petritzonitissa, but rather to charitable and public *gerokomeia* such as that called

---

[36] *BMFD* 23:549.
[37] *Der heilige Theodosios*, 40.
[38] *BMFD* 28:767; Gautier, "Pantocrator," 111.
[39] *BMFD* 28:767; Gautier, "Pantocrator," 111.
[40] *BMFD* 28:760, 764; Gautier, "Pantocrator," 91, 103.
[41] *BMFD* 28:766; Gautier, "Pantocrator," 107.
[42] *BMFD* 28:768; Gautier, "Pantocrator," 113.
[43] *BMFD* 28:767; Gautier, "Pantocrator," 111.
[44] Both the inaugural *ekphrasis* and the *Life of Saint Eirene* have recently been reedited. For the ekphrasis, see I. Vassis, "Das Pantokratorkloster von Konstantinopel in der byzantinischen Dictung," *The Pantokrator Monastery in Constantinople*, ed. S. Kotzabassi (Boston, 2013), 203–220. For the Life, see S. Kotzabassi, "Feasts at the Monastery of Pantokrator." *The Pantokrator Monastery in Constantinople*, ed. S. Kotzabassi (Boston, 2013), 160–175. Both have been translated in Magdalino, "Urban Setting," 49–55.

Ta Derma at the tenth-century Monastery of the Theotokos on Mount Tmolos[45] or any of the various *gerokomeia* of Constantinople mentioned in the *Patria*.[46] The successor of this institution seems to be the *gerokomeion* of the Monastery of Kosmosoteira near Bera, founded by Isaac Komnenos in 1152. It was a larger hospital, serving thirty-six patients (compared to the Pantokrator's twenty-four), no doubt due to the fact that Isaac's *gerokomeion* was the only charitable foundation of the monastery, along with a public bath.[47] In many ways, Isaac's *gerokomeion* was a combination of the Pantokrator's *xenon* and *gerotropheion* merged into a single institution. It served as a public hospital and even was found in a separate enclosure outside the main wall of the monastery.[48] This corresponds to the suggested organization of the charitable institutions of the Pantokrator Monastery, as may be gleaned from the inaugural *ekphrasis* poem.[49]

What position did the *gerotropheion* of the Pantokrator Monastery have within the system of charitable institutions? It does not seem to have had its own medical staff, but relied on the medical team of the hospital.[50] It is easy to see it as a simple add-on to the hospital, but this would be untrue. The *gerotropheion*, far from being unnecessary or superfluous, was a vital addition to the monastery. It played a crucial role in allowing the Pantokrator Hospital to develop its advanced medical treatments.

Despite the praise the Pantokrator Hospital received for its medical practice, ancient and medieval medicine was highly ineffective; mortality rates were high.[51] A poem of Theodore Prodromos addresses this contrast in a sophisticated way. Theodore underwent surgery in an unknown twelfth-century Constantinopolitan hospital. When he compares the well-meaning *nosokomos*, his friend, to King Nebuchadnezzar of the Old Testament, it is hard to understand if this is meant to be insulting or simply ironic.[52] The poem suggests the discrepancy between the noble

---

[45] *BMFD* 16:311–312.
[46] Particularly in Book 3: On the Buildings, *Accounts of Medieval Constantinople: The Patria*, ed. and trans. A. Berger (Cambridge, 2013), 142–143; 172–176; 180–181; 184–185; 186–187; 192–193.
[47] *BMFD* 29:825–826.
[48] *BMFD* 29:830, see Miller, *Birth*, 139.
[49] Magdalino, "Urban Setting," 37; 50. An arrangement also alluded to by A. Taylor, "The Pantokrator Monastery in Constantinople: A Comparison of its Remains and its Typikon." *Byzantine Studies Conference Abstract* 3 (1977): 47–48.
[50] *BMFD* 28:767; Gautier, "Pantocrator," 111.
[51] For particularly hospital medicine, see P. Horden, "The Earliest Hospitals in Byzantium, Western Europe, and Islam," *Journal of Interdisciplinary History* 35.3 (2005): 388–389.
[52] Theodore Prodromos, *Historische Gedichte*, ed. W. Hörandner (Vienna, 1974), 431.

ambitions and the reality of Byzantine medicine. John II Komnenos was well aware of this reality; he established a cemetery at the Monastery of Medikariou (north of the Golden Horn) for the hospital and old-age home for this very reason.[53] There could be, however, a long wait between the surgeon's knife and the grave.

What does a hospital do with a patient it cannot cure? Ancient precedent, evident in the medical treatment of Byzantine emperors, was for doctors to abandon patients that they could not cure.[54] Abandonment, however, was not an option for the charitable and philanthropic institutions. Instead they could only transfer patients. For example, Theodore Prodromos did not die in the hospital where he suffered the misery of surgery; instead, he probably passed away in a *gerokomeion*, having been placed there not due to old age, but to his incurable condition.[55]

This transferring of a terminal patient from a hospital to an old-age home or other type of charitable institution was not new to the twelfth century. In the tenth century, a man named Sergios was beaten by thieves and eventually taken to the Euboulos Hospital, a prominent Constantinopolitan hospital located either beside or attached to the Saint Sampson Hospital. After the doctors considered his case hopeless, he was transferred to the "holy house of Nicolas," probably a *gerokomeion*.[56]

Perhaps the best illustration of this process comes from an earlier period, before this became common practice. In the seventh-century miracle collection of Saint Artemios, the *xenodochos* of the Christodotes Hospital in Constantinople is treated unsuccessfully for ten months. Finally, the chief doctor tells him: "You have it [the disease] until the resurrection; for this hernia is untreatable. Nevertheless let us do something to make you comfortable."[57] The Christodotes Hospital seems to have placed a higher value on treatment than on scientific cures. A hospital without an old-age home, to which they might transfer the terminally ill, would have had difficulties in becoming a true medical institution; its beds would have been filled with those incurable, leaving no room for those whose diseases the hospital may have had a chance of curing.

---

[53] *BMFD* 28:766; Gautier, "Pantocrator," 107.
[54] J. Lascaratos, E. Poulakou-Rebelakou and S. Marketos, "Abandonment of Terminally Ill Patients in the Byzantine Era. An Ancient Tradition?" *Journal of Medical Ethics* 25.3 (1999): 254–258.
[55] L. Petit, "Monodie de Nicétas Eugénianos sur Théodore Prodrome," *VV* 9 (1902): 460–463, see T. Miller, "Death in a Xenon?" *Realia Byzantina* 22 (2009): 194.
[56] *Les saints stylites*. Subsidia Hagiographica 14, ed. H. Delehaye (Paris/Brussels, 1923), 218; Miller, "Death," 194.
[57] *Saint Artemios: A Collection of Miracle Stories by an Anonymous Author of Seventh Century Byzantium*, edd. and trans. V. Crisafulli and J. Nesbitt (Leiden, 1997), 133.

The combination of a hospital and old-age home in the same institution could address the medical orientation of institutions with limited information surviving. The list, however, of institutions known to have both a hospital and an old-age home attached to it is not long. It includes the Narses,[58] Myrelaion,[59] Petrion,[60] Mangana[61] and the Pantokrator, all foundations of Constantinople. All of these date to after the tenth century, except for the sixth-century Narses Hospital.[62] Of these, the Myrelaion, Mangana and possibly the Narses are all known to have had doctors present.[63] Still, all but the Narses were imperial investments with various territories and properties in the provinces supplying the mother institution.[64] We are thus dealing with the best-financed hospitals of the capital. Nevertheless, it is difficult to know if the imperial patronage allowed both a *gerokomeion* and hospital to be built together so that the hospital could pursue advanced medical practices, or if the subsequent addition of a *gerokomeion* in turn allowed the hospital to develop a medical focus.

The Medical Hospital

The detailed account of the hospital within the *typikon* has made its contextualization within Byzantine medicine difficult and often controversial. Was everything specified in the *typikon* fully implemented? Peregrine Horden has characterized this as part of a larger debate between "optimists" and "pessimists."[65] For the strict pessimist, the Pantokrator Hospital was an ideal, which almost certainly was never realized in the form described in the *typikon*.[66] For the optimist, it did not contained anything that cannot be found in other Byzantine hospitals and can, therefore, be used to reconstruct those institutions whose evidence is less illuminating.[67] Others consider it a rare example of a pinnacle of medieval medicine, ultimately

---

[58] *The Patria*, 184–185.
[59] Eustathios Rhomaios, *Peira* 15.12; *Jus Graecoromanum* IV, edd. J. Zepos and P. Zepos (Athens, 1931), 53; Miller, *Birth*, 180.
[60] Theophanes Continuates, *HSHB* 45:458.
[61] Skylitzes, *Synopsis,* 444.
[62] For the chronological problems see P. Gautier, "Précisions Historiques sur le Monastère de Ta Narsou," *REB* 34.1 (1976): 101–110.
[63] Miller, *Birth*, 178–185.
[64] Magdalino, *Manuel I Komnenos*, 165.
[65] P. Horden, "How Medicalised were Byzantine Hospitals?" *Medecina e Storia* 10 (2005): 46.
[66] E. Kislinger, "Der Pantokrator-Xenon, ein trügerisches Ideal?" *JÖB* 37 (1987): 173–179.
[67] Miller, *Birth,* xxii; Gautier, "Pantocrator," 9.

unique in the Byzantine Empire.⁶⁸ Scholars, towards the "pessimist" end of this range, often urge caution when trying to use the *Typikon* to understand other Byzantine hospitals.⁶⁹ In the end, the debate is largely about the nature of evidence lacking, which can only be often speculated from the surviving evidence with highly variable interpretation.

It must be admitted that the Pantokrator Hospital did not have a long history. Its lifespan was probably that of a human being, at most sixty-eight years. The birth of this hospital, however, is not clear. Anselm of Havelberg, the agent of the Holy Roman Emperor Lothar, reported seven hundred monks at the Pantokrator Monastery under the Rule of Saint Antony during his visit to Constantinople in the spring of 1136.⁷⁰ It is evident, however, from the observations of Anselm that much of the monastery was built before the emperor signed the *typikon* in October. Since the inaugural *ekphrasis* poem of the monastery, which mentions the hospital, dates between the death of Piroska-Eirene in 1134 and the death of her husband in 1143,⁷¹ the monastery was probably still not complete when Anselm visited. The same conclusion can be found by the internal evidence of the *Typikon*, which may misrepresent the Saint Michael funeral chapel in its architecture, suggesting it may not have been completed by the time of the October 1136 signing.⁷²

Exactly how long the hospital functioned is also not clear. A letter of John Tzetzes, datable to between 1148 and 1160,⁷³ and a poem of the Mangana Poet, datable to 1150,⁷⁴ demonstrate the survival of the hospital at least into the early years

---

68   A. Philipsborn, "Der Fortschritt in der Entwicklung des byzantinischen Krankenhauswesens," *BZ* 54 (1961): 353–354.

69   M. Dols, "The Origins of the Islamic Hospital," *Bulletin of the History of Medicine* 61 (1983): 370; A. Laiou, "Rev. Timothy S. Miller. The Birth of the Hospital in the Byzantine," *AHR* 94 (1989): 426; Horden, "Medicalised," 56–60.

70   Anselm of Havelberg, *Anticimenon: On the Unity of the Faith and the Controversies with the Greeks*, trans. A. Criste, OPraem, and C. Neel (Collegeville, 2010), 73.

71   W. Hörandner, "Zur Beschreibung von Kunstwerken in der byzantinischen Dichtung—am Beispiel des Gedichts auf das Pantokratorkloster in Konstantinopel," *Die Poetische Ekphrasis von Kunstwerken: Eine literarische Tradition der Großdichtung in Antike, Mittelalter und früher Neuzeit*, ed. C. Ratkowitsch (Wien, 2006), 210.

72   Congdon, "Commemoration," 176; but see Ousterhout's essay in this volume.

73   John Tzetzes, *Ioannis Tzetzae Epistulae*, ed. P. Leone (Zeipzig, 1974), 121. This letter (letter 81), however, is one of the few undated letters in Tzetzes's collection. All of the letters from the second set (letters 70–107) all date between 1148 and 1160 (or his death after 1157), after his 1147 move to the Pantokrator Monastery, M. Grünbart, "Prosopographische Beiträge zum Briefcorpus des Ioannes Tzetzes," *JÖB* 46 (1996): 196–223.

74   This poem (poem 59) is currently unedited. M. Jeffreys and E. Jeffreys are currently working on an edition of the works of the Mangana Poet. For a brief description of the poem in question see Magdalino, *Manuel I Komnenos*, 497; M. Jeffreys and E. Jeffreys, "Immortality," 198; Miller, *Birth*, xxi.

of the reign of Manuel Komnenos. If Paul Magdalino is right to associate the *Life of Saint Eirene* with the imperial policies of Manuel Komnenos in the 1170's, evidence for the hospital's existence can be pushed to this date.[75] There is no evidence of the Pantokrator hospital after this time. Hospitals are expensive institutions that require much to upkeep; it is possible the expense was too much.[76] One possible scenario is that the Pantokrator hospital's demise was connected with the inability of Manuel Komnenos to properly repair the aqueduct systems of the capital.[77] Andronikos I Komnenos, during his short reign, would repair the damaged line originally constructed by the Emperor Hadrian.[78] The Pantokrator hospital certainly did not survive the Fourth Crusade, which removed territories and properties making the monastery unable to provide for such an expensive institution.[79]

Turning from the institution's history, the exact layout of the Pantokrator hospital has baffled scholars. John D. Thompson and Grace Goldin mused, "Everything concerning the Pantokrator seems to have come down to us but its floor plan."[80] This has not stopped the projections of the hospital based on the evidence in the *typikon* by Basileios Tsagres[81] and Anastasios Orlandos.[82] While Orlandos's reconstruction in particular helps to demonstrate the size and scope of the hospital, one of its major shortcomings is that it is not bound to the topography of Istanbul or any archaeological evidence.

The *Typikon* itself divides the organization of the hospital into five *ordinoi*. One *ordinos* maintains ten beds for those suffering from wounds or fractures, i.e. a surgical ward, while another has eight beds for acute diseases, including internal

---

[75] Magdalino, "Urban Setting," 47. Two facts are certain about the date of the *Life of Saint Eirene*. First, it is found on twelfth century manuscript, Spyridon, monk of the Laura, and S. Eustratiades, *Catalogue of the Greek Manuscripts in the Library of the Laura on Mount Athos with Notices from Other Libraries* (Cambridge, 1925), 56, No. 415. Secondly, it must date to after the death of John II Komnenos in 1143.

[76] Horden, "Medicalised," 58.

[77] J. Crow, J. Bardill and R. Bayliss. *The Water Supply of Byzantine Constantinople* (London, 2008), 21.

[78] Nicetas Choniates, *O City of Byzantium, Annals of Niketas Choniates*, trans. Harry J. Magoulias (Detroit, 1984), 182.

[79] D. Jacoby, "The Urban Evolution of Latin Constantinople," *Byzantine Constantinople: Monuments, Topography and Everyday Life,* ed. N. Necipoğlu (Leidon, 2001), 290; Kotzabassi, "1204 and 1453," 57.

[80] J. D. Thompson and G. Goldin, *The Hospital: A Social and Architectural History* (New Haven, 1975), 9.

[81] Codellas, "Medical Center," 399.

[82] A. Orlandos, "Ἡ ἀναπαράστασις τοῦ Ξενῶνος τῆς ἐν Κωνσταντινουπόλει μονῆς Παντοκράτορος," *EEBS* 16 (1941): 198–207.

diseases and eye disease. The third *ordinos* is composed of twelve beds set aside for women. The final two *ordinoi* were combined for general patients.[83]

While the *ordinoi* are usually understood as wards divided into individual rooms, the rooms were more likely determined by the presence of a hearth.[84] The *ordinoi*, therefore, would represent the lines of beds that were placed in some relationship to the hearths, which would come closer the sense of the word in other contexts.[85] The hospital contained both a large hearth and two smaller ones in the surgical ward and the women's ward.[86] The hearth was certainly an important feature of the hospital's architecture. At the Kosmosoteria Monastery's *gerokomeion*, Isaac explicitly states that he provides a hearth and firewood because "the physical ailments of those who are sick greatly require warmth."[87]

This idea is supported by an archaeological analogy. Orlandos, in the monasteries of Meteora in Thessaly, located two post-Byzantine infirmaries, one from the Barlaam Monastery and other from the Holy Monastery of the Great Meteora—the two largest monasteries of Meteora.[88] They were small square buildings organized around a central hearth. The surviving cupolas above the hearth contained windows for the smoke of the fire to escape. The beds of the infirmary's patients would have been placed around it in rows. The institutions in question, however, are still monastic infirmaries, not public hospitals, a point well conceded by Orlandos.[89]

However the term *ordinos* is understood, the women's ward was certainly separated in some fashion from the rest of the hospital. Even without considering the long history of gender segregation in Byzantine hospitals, the women's *ordinos* had both its own hearth, chapel and, presumably, latrine.[90] The fact that the hospital had separate accommodations for women was also one of the few details about the hospital mentioned in the inaugural *ekphrasis* poem.[91]

---

[83] *BMFD* 28:757; Gautier, "Pantocrator," 82–83.
[84] Miller, *Birth*, 144–145.
[85] In Maurice's *Strategikon*, a military manual of the late sixth and early seventh century, it refers to either a row of soldiers or of tents in a fortified camp, *Das Strategikon des Maurikios,* ed. G. Dennis (Vienna, 1981), 1.9; 12.B.22. A borrow word from Latin, it usually refers to the rows of seats either in the senate or theatre, Cic. Phil. 2.18.44; Suet. Aug. 44.
[86] *BMFD* 28:762; Gautier, "Pantocrator," 98–99.
[87] *BMFD* 29:831.
[88] N. Vees, "Σύνταγμα ἐπιγραφικῶν μνημείων Μετεώρων καὶ τῆς πέριξ χώρας, μετὰ σχετικῶν ἀρχαιολογημάτων," *Byzantis* 1.4 (1909): 597–598; A. Orlandos, Μοναστηριακὴ ἀρχιτεκτονική, 2nd ed. (Athens, 1958), 76–83.
[89] Orlandos, Μοναστηριακὴ ἀρχιτεκτονική, 84.
[90] *BMFD* 28:761; Gautier, "Pantocrator," 96–97.
[91] Magdalino, "Urban Setting," 50.

Turning from the physical plan to its personnel, the Pantokrator hospital had an impressive staff. The ratio of medical personal to patients is more than one to one, with sixty-five on staff for a capacity of sixty-one beds.[92] Of the doctors, the highest office was that of the *primmikerios*, who oversaw the entire hospital and reviewed the work of the lower ranking doctors.[93] Just below the two *primmikerioi* were the two *protomenitai*, or 'chief doctors,' assigned to the hospital, who held a similar medical supervision role, just underneath the overarching censor of the *primmikerioi*. Two chief surgeons presided over the surgery ward. Two doctors, without special title, were to staff each ward, while four additional doctors, two being surgeons, constitute an outpatient clinic. An extra female doctor was added to the women's ward, whose practice was probably limited to gynecology, in line with the model of women practicing medicine in ancient Greece and Rome,[94] while the outpatient surgeons were also to serve the women in need of surgery. A staff of *hypourgoi*, or nurses, five to each ward, supported the doctors. Two *hyperetai*, or orderlies, in turn, supported them.[95]

The nurses were divided between those who were *embathmoi*, or certified, and those were designated as extra, or *perissoi*. The doctors who served in the outpatient clinic, likewise, bore the status of *perissoi*. A medical metaphor found in the synod decision of Patriarch Stypes Leon, a contemporary of John II Komnenos, helps to shed some light upon these terms.[96] The metaphor describes the teaching and initiation into the medical profession. After proper education and experience, a medical student may be examined by the supreme president of the medical science (ὁ τῆς ἰατρικῆς προεξάρχων) and, if they pass, were awarded their certification.[97] The Pantokrator hospital's requirements for certified medical staff fits well within a larger trend of the reemergence of medical regulation in the twelfth century, with a nearly contemporaneous example is known from Roger II's Sicily, as well as the market regulation manuals of the Islamic world.[98]

Medical examination is also the final step in the process of hospital nurses joining the doctoring ranks. Even though the basic organization of the *hypourgoi*

---

[92] Gautier, "Pantocrator," 9–10.
[93] *BMFD* 28:758; Gautier, "Pantocrator," 86–87.
[94] H. Parker, "Women Doctors in Greece, Rome, and the Byzantine Empire," *Women Healers & Physicians: Climbing a Long Hill,* ed. L. Furst (Lexington, 1997), 136–138.
[95] *BMFD* 28:757–758; Gautier, "Pantocrator," 84–87.
[96] V. Grumel, *Les regestes des actes du patriarcat de Constantinople, I: Les actes des Patriarches, fasc. ii et iii: Les regestes de 715 à 1204,* 2nd ed., ed. J. Darrouzès (Paris, 1989), no. 1007.
[97] V. Grumel, "La profession médicale à Byzance à l'époque des Comnènes," *REB* 7 (1949): 43–46.
[98] D. Stathakopoulos, "On Whose Authority? Regulating Medical Practice in the Twelfth and Early Thirteenth Centuries," *Authority in Byzantium,* ed. P. Armstrong (Farnham, 2013), 232; 237.

is present in the seventh-century *Miracles of Saint Artemios*, there *hypourgoi* were a type of *hyperetai*.[99] An earlier step was a tenth-century epigram written in the Niketas surgical codex of the Hospital of the Forty Martyrs, which included *hypourgoi* among those practicing surgery.[100]

The entire sixty-five-person staff did not all serve at once. Most positions, from the *primmikerios* to the *perissoi* doctors of the outpatient clinic, were staffed with an even number of personnel. This is because the medical personal would alternate each month. The month-by-month service of hospital doctors does not seem to be an innovation of the Pantokrator Hospital, as it is already known from the seventh-century *Miracles of Saint Artemios*.[101]

In addition to the medical staff, the hospital had an administrative staff, which was charged with the overall function of the institution. The highest position was taken by the five *oikonomoi*, or stewards, who oversaw the entire monastery.[102] As for the everyday functioning of the hospital, the top administrator was the *nosokomos*. The majority of his duties revolved about the procurement of material supplies needed in the hospital. In this way, his position overlapped with that of the superintendent. The *nosokomos* was concerned with the hospital in all its aspects, while the superintendent, acting as a cellarer, was largely concerned with the material acquired for the two meals served each day.[103]

While the *Typikon* specifies that the *nosokomos* is an administrative position, the letter written by John Tzetzes to the *nosokomos* of the hospital was clearly addressed to a practitioner of the medical art, for Galen, as Tzetzes writes, was the "originator of [his] craft."[104] Even within the *Typikon* itself there is some confusion with the position of *nosokomos*. When the doctors on staff diagnose a visitor to the outpatient clinic with a serious illness, the *primmikerios* on duty must admit one of the hospital wards.[105] When an inmate at the Pantokrator's *gerotropheion* is diagnosed with a disease more acute than that institution is designed to treat, it is

---

[99] *Saint Artemios*, 130–137.
[100] Miller, *Birth*, 181, n. 90; M. Lauxtermann, *Byzantine Poetry from Pisides to Geometers* (Wien, 2003), 1:206–207.
[101] *Saint Artemios*, 134–135.
[102] *BMFD* 28:768; Gautier, "Pantocrator," 112–115.
[103] *BMFD* 28:760–762; Gautier, "Pantocrator," 92–99.
[104] Tzetzes, *Epistulae*, 121. Tzetzes held a teaching post at the Pantokrator Monastery, see M. Grünbart, "Paideia Connects: The Interaction between Teachers and Pupils in Twelfth-Century Byzantium" *Networks of Learning: Perspectives on Scholars in Byzantine East and Latin West, c. 1000–1200*, edd. S. Steckel, N. Gaul and M. Grünbart (Wien, 2014), 27–28; P. Magdalino, *The Empire of Manuel I Komnenos, 1143–1180* (Cambridge, 1993), 328–329.
[105] *BMFD* 28:758; Gautier, "Pantocrator," 86–87.

the *nosokomos* who must approve his admission into the hospital.[106] Both decisions involve the admission of external patients into the hospital on medical grounds and therefore should be the job of the *primmikerios*.

Timothy Miller has reconciled the administrative and medical roles of the *nosokomos* by suggesting that a former physician would make a logical choice for this position.[107] Tzetzes's letter refers to *Galene*, which was an antidote similar to the *Mithridate* mentioned as a part of the *nosokomos*'s medical kit in the *typikon*.[108] Miller's suggestion that the role of the *nosokomos* is similar to that of the *Aktouarios*—originally a Latin term for an officer who supplied the Roman military—who operated in a similar fashion at the Mangana Hospital seems convincing.[109] Still, there is no reason for Tzetzes to conform to the strict terminology of the *typikon*.

In addition to the personnel already mentioned, the Pantokrator Hospital had on staff an instructor of the doctors, who was hired to "teach the principles of medical knowledge."[110] Venance Grumel has suggested that Michael Italikos, later the metropolitan bishop of Philippopolis, held this post at the Pantokrator hospital.[111] The mother of John II Komnenos, Eirene Doukaina, had appointed him to a post of instructor of the doctors.[112] Chronologically, this would be too early, and Italikos very likely held the same post at another hospital in the capital.[113] Considering his position under the *Aktouarios* Michael Pantechnes, the Mangana Hospital is a better choice for Italikos.[114] Alexandre Philipsborn has considered the position of instructor of doctors at the Pantokrator Hospital to have been inspired by schools attached to Islamic hospitals.[115] While the exact relationship between the Byzantine and Islamic hospital is difficult to establish based on the current state of knowledge,[116] there does not seem to be any proper educational programs in

---

[106] *BMFD* 28:767; Gautier, "Pantocrator," 110–111.

[107] Miller, *Birth*, 17–18, 162–163.

[108] *BMFD* 28:761; Gautier, "Pantocrator," 94–95; Tzetzes, *Epistulae*, 121.

[109] Miller, *Birth*, 149–150.

[110] *BMFD* 28:765; Gautier, "Pantocrator," 106–107.

[111] Grumel, "La profession médicale," 45–46.

[112] Michael Italikos, *Lettres et Discours*, ed. P. Gautier (Paris, 1972), 92–98; 208–210.

[113] Italikos, *Lettres,* 19–21. Although before holding the official title of instructor of the doctors Italikos taught medicine privately, he did seem to have some ambiguous relationship to the Kosmidion, another unspecified hospital, or in fact the hospital at the Kosmidion, Italikos, *Lettres*, 96.

[114] While the post of *aktouarios* is certainly that of a court doctor, because Michael Pantechnes served as the emperor's personal physician, Italikos, *Lettres*, 113–115, the evidence does suggest a connection to the Mangana Hospital between 1081 and 1204, Miller, *Birth*, 149–150.

[115] Philipsborn, "Krankenhauswesens," 355.

[116] One important exception is P. Horden, "Medieval hospital formularies: Byzantium and Islam compared." *Medical Books in the Byzantine World,* ed. B. Zipser (Bologna, 2013), 145–164.

Byzantine hospitals until the twelfth century, which gives credence to Philipsborn's suggestion.

The number of medical personnel at the hospital is impressive, although Horden has retorted that the many provisions in the *Typikon* allow one to "dismiss the hospital as really a heavily-staffed nursing home."[117] What can actually be said then about the specific medicines and therapies dispensed at the hospital? Unfortunately, there are no *xenon* treatment lists written by or ascribed to Pantokrator doctors during its short lifespan.[118]

Instead, it is again the *Typikon* that provides the best clues. The evidence lies in two lists of materials and allotments to be procured by the *nosokomos* and the superintendent. These two lists, however, overlap, especially in terms of materials for medicines. For instance, "the juices, plasters, [and] lozenges" to be provided by the superintendent is a duplication of the more specific "rose-water, oxymel, the liquid of Diospolis, [and] sour grape juice with honey" to be provided by the *nosokomos*; both lists are simply examples of the medications that will be made from the fifty maritime measures of honey provided by each. The ointments and plasters of the *nosokomos*'s list and the hot poultices and enemas of the superintendent both are medicines made from olive oil.[119] In similar fashion, the bread poultice of the *nosokomos* and the dry poultices of the superintendent both deprive from the supplies of barley and wheat. There are, however, a few places where the lists differ. Only the *nosokomos* deals with material for cold cauterizing,[120] while the superintendent is to supply the aromatics, such as "mastic, myrrh, incense [and] gum-ammoniacs." The first abbot of the monastery, Joseph, had authorized a gift of aromatic to be given to John Tzetzes.[121] This probably came from the stores supplied by the superintendent. He was also to supply fruits and eggs, which themselves have medical properties. The combination of these lists demonstrates an important fact about

---

[117] "Medicalised," 54.

[118] For the hospital treatment lists that do exist, mostly recipes from the Mangana Hospital and Myrelaion Hospital, see D. Bennett, "Xenonika: medical texts associated with Xenones in the late Byzantine period" (PhD diss., University of London, 2003).

[119] *BMFD* 28:760–762; Gautier, "Pantocrator," 92–99.

[120] Gautier considered this to be an instrument, "Pantocrator," 95, n. 36. Due to its inclusion with the material acquired by the *nosokomos*, it was possibly instead some agent for cooling a tool for cryotherapy.

[121] Tzetzes, *Epistulae*, 72–73. The inclusion of specifically Arabic aromatics is also important because it demonstrates the influx of *materia medica* from the east in this period. See A. McCabe, "Imported *materia medica*, 4th–12th centuries, and Byzantine pharmacology," *Byzantine Trade, 4th–12th Centuries: The Archaeology of Local, Regional and International Exchange*, ed. M. M. Mango (Farnham, 2004), 291.

the *materia medica* of the ancient and medieval world: there is no clear line to be drawn between nutrition and health, food and medicine.

The meal served in the hospital itself was a well-balanced vegetarian diet. The patients, along with the in-house nursing staff, was given a loaf of bread, beans, vegetables (either peas, legumes or fresh vegetables) and two heads of onion. The hospital's onsite mill and bread oven produced the patients' bread.[122] In addition, they were provided with wine and money to purchase additional food.[123] Edouard Jeansleme and Lysimachos Oeconomos have calculated this meal to be about 3,300 calories a day.[124] The fact that the residents of the old-age home, received 2,500 calories instead, seems to suggest the medical nature of this diet.[125]

While the diet and some medicines are known from the *typikon*, there is a gap concerning medications that were not procured in bulk. While antidotes, such as the *Mithridate* or *Galene*,[126] were probably provided by the hospital, the *typikon* makes it clear this was on a case-by-case basis, probably due to the variety of ingredients required to prepare them.[127] A gardener was one of the jobs a monk may perform in the monastery, thus medicinal plants were probably grown in the monastery garden. Information of this kind, however, should not be expected from the *typikon*; its purpose in this respect was to designate what the *nosokomos* or superintendent must acquire; it did not need to mention what could be produced within the monastery.

The *typikon* also mentions various surgical tools which would be the responsibility of a sharpener, including the following: "lancets, cauterizing irons, a catheter, forceps for drawing teeth, instruments for the stomach and head—simply whatever is necessary for them all."[128] These tools probably represent the continuation of a tradition of surgical tool lists—one survives from the ninth century, another from the eleventh.[129] Both lists contain the tooth puller mentioned in the Pantokrator

---

[122] *BMFD* 28:760, 764; Gautier, "Pantocrator," 92–93, 102–105.

[123] *BMFD* 28:759–760; Gautier, "Pantocrator," 90–91.

[124] E. Jeanselme and L. Oeconomos, "Les oeuvres d'assistance et les hôpitaux byzantins au siècle des Comnènes," *Communication faite au premier congrès de l'histoire de l'art de guérir, Anvers, 7–8 août 1920* (Anvers, 1921) 13.

[125] Gautier, "Pantocrator," 18–19.

[126] While only *Mithridate* is mentioned in the *typikon*, the antidote of *Galene* is the source of the *nosokomos*'s erroneous idea that Galen lived in the time of Christ, Tzetzes, *Epistulae*, 121.

[127] *BMFD* 28:761; Gautier, "Pantocrator," 94–95; G. Watson, *Theriac and Mithridatium: a Study in Therapeutics* (London, 1966), 33–93, esp. 45.

[128] *BMFD* 28:764, Gautier, "Pantocrator," 104–105.

[129] H. Schöne, "Zwei Listen Chirurgischer Instrumente," *Hermes* 38 (1903): 280–284; for the suggestion that these were hospital lists see L. Bliquez, "Two Lists of Greek Surgical Instruments and the

typikon.¹³⁰ It is probably the same tool mentioned in the medical satire of Theodore Prodromos, *Executioner or Doctor*.¹³¹

Bathing was also an important therapy at the Pantokrator Hospital, echoing its importance in the monastic infirmary discussed above. The hospital had its own bathhouse, where each of the patients could bath twice a week, in the presence of nurses and orderlies. If, however, patients required more frequent bathing as a therapeutic treatment, their attending doctor could escort them to the bathhouse "without anyone hindering [them]."¹³²

The material evidence suggests that the location of the monastery, and probably also its hospital, was chosen in order to have constant access to water. Many places of healing throughout the city of Constantinople, not just hospitals, were located near water sources.¹³³ While the numerous cisterns around the Zeyrek Camii demonstrates the importance placed upon the access to water,¹³⁴ these cisterns probably date to the construction of the monastery based on the evidence of the spoliated columns used in their construction.¹³⁵

While the location of the hospital is not known, the Unkapanı Cistern north of the mosque on a lower terrace may have supplied the hospital's water needs.¹³⁶ The Unkapanı Cistern, originally dating to the early seventh century, is much larger than the various smaller cisterns found west of the mosque. The Unkapanı Cistern was fed by the older waterline built originally by the Emperor Hadrian, which seems to have been active at varying points in the monastery's lifetime.¹³⁷ For instance, an anonymous Russian pilgrim of the fourteenth century, who described the monastery as "built of stone with water all around it," could be refer-

---

State of Surgery in Byzantine Times," *DOP* 38 (1984): 191. P. Bouras-Vallianatos takes a more cautious stance on the connection, "Contextualizing the Art of Healing by Byzantine Physicians," *Life is Short, Art Long: The Art of Healing in Byzantium*, ed. B. Pitarakis (Istanbul, 2015), 119–120.

¹³⁰ Schöne, "Zwei Listen," 282.

¹³¹ G. Podestà, "Le satire Lucianesche di Teodoro Prodromo," *Aevum* 21 (1947): 17.

¹³² *BMFD* 28:760; Gautier, "Pantocrator," 90–93.

¹³³ R. Ousterhout, "Water and Healing in Constantinople: Reading Architectural Remains," *Life is Short, Art Long: The Art of Healing in Byzantium*, ed. B. Pitarakis (Istanbul, 2015), 65–77.

¹³⁴ N. Fıratlı and F. Yücel, "Some Unknown Byzantine Cisterns of Istanbul," *Turkiye Turing ve Otomobil Kurumu bellenteni* (1952): 23–26.

¹³⁵ Crow, Bardill and Bayliss, *Water Supply*, 137–139.

¹³⁶ T. Wolford, "Healing on the Fourth Hill: Searching for the Pantokrator Hospital" (An Honors Thesis, Ball State University, 2012), 26. For the Unkapanı Cistern, see P. Forchheimer and J. Strzygowski. *Die Byzantinischen Wasserbehälter von Konstantinpel* (Vienna, 1893), 70.

¹³⁷ Crow, Bardill and Bayliss, *Water Supply*, 134.

ring to the route of this channel.[138] As I have suggested, the disruption of this line and subsequent repair in the reign of Andronikos I Komnenos may be related to the demise of the hospital.[139]

To Each According to Their Need

The Pantokrator Monastery's various charitable and medical institutions operated together to best serve both the monks of the monastery and the greater community of Constantinople. Not only did the inclusion of medical personnel from the monastic infirmary in the hospital's chain of medical advancement and the probable reception of the terminally ill into the *gerotropheion* allow the hospital itself to achieve the medical status for which it is famed, but the combination of charities allowed any possible needy individual to find aid at the monastery. This could range from the niece of an emperor to the anonymous elderly, infirm and poor, or from those temporarily stopping by to use the outpatient clinic to those permanently stricken with the holy disease.

Financing such a range of charities required a great outlay of wealth. Thus the Pantokrator hospital had to be counted among those that were parts of monasteries, or that were former palaces or private residences. One of the major differences, however, between this charitable system and other well-financed monasteries, such as the sixth-century Monastery of Saint Theodosius, is that the Pantokrator Monastery's charities did not segregate by economic status. The rich Monastery of the Mangana, for instance, seems to bear this distinction, having supported three distinct institutions: a *xenon*, *gerokomeion* and *ptochotropheion* or poorhouse.[140] It is clear from the Mangana Poet that the hospital served wealthy members of the Constantinopolitan elite,[141] but the hospital also provided cloaks and shirts for poorer patients, as well as those who must change clothes for medical reasons.[142] In contrast, the evidence suggests that the Pantokrator hospital served both the elite and poor in the same institution.

This is not the only reason it can be asserted that the Pantokrator hospital's medical system was a reaction to the Mangana hospital.[143] The Mangana was not

---

[138] G. Majeska, *Russian Travelers to Constantinople in the Fourteenth and Fifteenth Centuries* (Washington D.C., 1984), 152.
[139] Choniates, *Annals,* 182.
[140] Skylitzes, *Synopsis,* 444.
[141] Miller, *Birth,* xxi.
[142] BMFD 28:757; Gautier, "Pantocrator," 84–85.
[143] Miller, *Birth,* xx.

only the hospital of an active imperial residence and was used by Emperor Alexios Komnenos,[144] but medical manuscripts also cite it just as they might cite Galen or Hippocrates for medical recipes.[145] It may also have had a teaching post, similar to that at the Pantokrator hospital. It is also likely that the separation of the rich from the poor, as evident in the Monastery of Saint Theodosius, is a fuller specialization of individual institutions. The Pantokrator hospital could very well have been a combination of the Mangana's *xenon* and *ptochotrophieon*, just as the Kosmosoteira's *gerokomeion* was a combination of the Pantokrator's *xenon* and *gerotropheion*.

Even though our evidence is lacking for the twelfth century, the Saint Sampson Hospital was also probably at least an equal of the Pantokrator hospital. Its use by the crusaders, which generated the Order of the Knights of Saint Sampson, suggests that it functioned well enough during the previous century.[146] Its antiquity alone bestowed upon it a superiority in the Byzantine mind, similar, no doubt, to the Zotikos Leper hospital, to which the Pantokrator hospital intended to associate.

The Pantokrator hospital's setting, however, was unique. Many factors had to come together to allow hospitals like the Mangana and Pantokrator to flourish. Most importantly this class of elite hospitals had an undeniably Constantinopolitan nature. After Late Antiquity, the greatest hospitals of the Byzantine Empire could only exist in the capital city. The emphasis upon the city of Constantinople at the expense of the other centers of the Greek world, which were rivals of Constantinople in late antiquity, allowed for this concentration not only of capital, money and resources, but also medical knowledge.[147]

Thus, this class of hospitals is a direct result of developments occurring only after late antiquity and the following so-called dark ages of the seventh and eighth centuries. Only then do any references to hospitals begin to appear in medical texts. It also seems that during this period the relationship between the *xenon* and *gerokomeion* was developed, first evident in the tenth-century *Life of Saint Luke the Stylite*.[148] The hospitals' nurses were beginning to join the medical ranks. These

---

[144] John Zonaras, *HSHB* 49:759.

[145] D. Bennett, "Medical Practice and Manuscripts in Byzantium," *Social History of Medicine* 13.2 (2000): 288; Horden, "Medicalised," 63.

[146] T. Miller, "The Sampson Hospital of Constantinople," *BZ* 15 (1990): 127–130; D. Stathakopoulos, "Discovering a Military Order of the Crusades: The Hospital of St. Sampson of Constantinople," *Viator* 37 (2006): 257.

[147] Magdalino, *Manuel I Komnenos*, 109–132. For instance, in late antiquity the center of medical education was Alexandria, which helped to staff a number of hospitals in Egypt, see P. van Minnen, "Medical Care in Late Antiquity," *Ancient Medicine in its Socio-Cultural Context*, edd. P. van der Eijk, H. Horstmanshoff and P. Shcrijvers (Amsterdam, 1995), I:153–169.

[148] *Les saints stylites*, 218.

developments accelerated in the eleventh and twelfth centuries. For example, the medical profession had by the twelfth century become a respected field, which could be a target of satire but not totally rejected.[149] Even when Theodore Prodromos lampooned the medical profession in his satire, *Executioner or Doctor*, he not only assumed Hippocrates and Galen would have been on his side, but he also cited the contemporary doctors who were above his criticism.[150] Teaching also became the purview of the Byzantine hospital for the first time. Both Prodromos's awareness of the medical community and the educational role of the hospital, no doubt, were the result of the popularity and familiarity with medicine, as the doctors themselves we part of the intellectual and political elite of the twelfth century.

When the Pantokrator hospital is compared to the other major hospitals included in the monastic *typika*, the *gerokomeion* of Isaac Komnenos's Kosmosoteira Monastery and the *xenon* of the fourteenth-century Lips Monastery, it shows what happens to the model of the Pantokrator hospital when it is transplanted out of this unique setting. In the case of the Kosmosoteira it is geographically, and for the Lips chronologically.[151]

The Pantokrator Monastery with its network of charities, envisioned by Piroska-Eirene and completed by her husband, due to its unique setting of twelfth-century Constantinople, was able to serve the ill of the city, while also aiding the emperor in his quest for personal salvation. However the Pantokrator hospital is contextualized within the history of medicine, it is hard not to sympathize with the *Life of Saint Eirene*, boasting that, "[Piroska-Eirene] erected the beautiful churches that can be seen there now, hostels and old-age homes, all of which in beauty, situation and construction technique take first place among all previous buildings, both old and recent."[152]

Bibliography

Primary Sources

Acta et Diplomata Graeca Medii Aevi Sacra et Profana: Acta et Diplomata Monasteriorum et Ecclesiarum Orientis. Edd. Franz Miklosich and Joseph Müller. Vienna: Gerold, 1871.

---

[149] A. Kazhdan, "The Image of the Medical Doctor in Byzantine Literature of the Tenth to Twelfth Centuries," *DOP* 38 (1984): 43–51.
[150] Podestà, "Le satire," 14, 21.
[151] Horden, "Medicalised," 55–56.
[152] Magdalino, "Urban Setting," 54.

Anonymous Description of Constantinople. Ed. and Trans. George P. Majeska, *Russian Travelers to Constantinople in the Fourteenth and Fifteenth Centuries*. 114–155. Washington, D.C.: Dumbarton Oaks Research Library and Collection, 1984.

Choniates, Nicetas. *O City of Byzantium: Annals of Niketas Choniatēs*. Detroit: Wayne State University Press, 1984.

Cicero, M. Tullius, *M. Tulli Ciceronis Orationes: Recognovit breviqve adnotatione critica instrvxit Albertus Curtis Clark Collegii Reginae Socius*. Ed. Albert Curtis Clark. Oxford: E Typographeo Clarendoniano, 1918.

Erotikos, Nikephoros. *Typikon of the Monastery of the Mother of God and the old-age Home called Ta Derma*. Trans. John Thomas, *BMFD*, John Philip Thomas and Angela Constantinides Hero, eds. 16:310–312. Washington, D.C.: Dumbarton Oaks, 2000.

Eugenianos, Nicetas. *Monody*. Ed. Louis Petit, "Monodie de Nicétas Eugénianos Sur Théodore Prodrome" *Vizantiiskii vremennik*, no. 9 (1902): 446–63.

Italikos, Michael. *Lettres et discours*. Ed. Paul Gautier. Paris: Institut français d'études byzantines, 1972.

John. *Rule for the Monastery of St. John the Forerunner of Phoberos*. Trans. Robert Jordan, *BMFD*, John Philip Thomas and Angela Constantinides Hero, eds. 30:872–953. Washington, D.C.: Dumbarton Oaks, 2000.

Komnene, Irene Doukaina. *Typikon of the Convent of the Mother of God Kecharitomene*. Trans. Robert Jordan. *BMFD*, John Philip Thomas and Angela Constantinides Hero, eds. 27:649–736. Washington, D.C.: Dumbarton Oaks, 2000.

Komnenos, Isaac. *Typikon of the Monastery of the Mother of God Kosmosoteira*. Trans. Nancy Patterson Ševčenko, *BMFD*, John Philip Thomas and Angela Constantinides Hero, eds. 29:782–858. Washington, D.C.: Dumbarton Oaks, 2000.

Komnenos, John II. *Typikon of the Pantokrator Monastery*. ed. Paul Gautier. "Le typikon du Christ Sauveur Pantocrator." *REB* 32 (1974): 26–131; Trans. Robert Jordan. *BMFD*, John Philip Thomas and Angela Constantinides Hero, eds. 28:737–774. Washington, D.C.: Dumbarton Oaks, 2000.

Havelberg, Anselm of. *Anticimenon: On the Unity of the Faith and the Controversies with the Greeks*. Trans. Ambrose Crite, OPRAEM, and Carol Neel. Collegeville: Liturgical Press, 2010.

Life of Saint Irene. Ed. Kotzabassi, Sofia. "Feasts at the Monastery of Pantokrator." In *The Pantokrator Monastery in Constantinople*, edited by Sofia Kotzabassi, 160–175. Boston: De Gruyter, 2013; trans. Paul Magdalino. "The Foundation of the Pantokrator Monastery in Its Urban Setting." In *The Pantokrator Monastery in Constantinople*, edited by Sofia Kotzabassi, 53–55. Boston: De Gruyter, 2013.

Life of Saint Luke the Stylite. Ed. Hippolyte Delehaye, *Les saints stylites*. Subsidia Hagiographica 14, 195–237. Bruxelles: Société des bollandistes, 1923.

Maurice. *Strategikon*. Edd. George T. Dennis and Ernst Gamillscheg. *Das Strategikon des Maurikios*. Verlag der Österreichischen Akademie der Wissenschaften, 1981.

The Miracles of St. Artemios: A Collection of Miracle Stories by an Anonymous Author of Seventh Century Byzantium. Edd. Virgil S. Crisafulli, John W. Nesbitt, and John F. Haldon, New York: E.J. Brill, 1996.

Mystikos, Nikephoros. *Typikon of the Monastery of the Mother of God Ton Heliou Bomon*. Trans. Anastasius Bandy. *BMFD*, John Philip Thomas and Angela Constantinides Hero, eds. 33:1042–1091. Washington, D.C.: Dumbarton Oaks, 2000.

Pakourianos, Gregory. *Typikon of the Monastery of the Mother of God Petritzonitissa*. Trans. Robert Jordan, *BMFD*, John Philip Thomas and Angela Constantinides Hero, eds. 23:507–63. Washington, D.C.: Dumbarton Oaks, 2000.

Patria of Constantinople. Trans. and ed. Albrecht Berger *Accounts of Medieval Constantinople: The Patria*. Cambridge, Massachusetts: Harvard University Press, 2013.

Petra, Theodore of. *The Life of St. Theodosius*. Ed. Hermann Usener. *Der Heilige Theodosius: Schriften Des Theodoros Und Kyrillos*. Leipzig: B. G. Teubner, 1890.

Philanthropenos, Athanasios. *Typikon of the Monastery of St. Mamas*. Trans. Anastasius Bandy. *BMFD*, John Philip Thomas and Angela Constantinides Hero, eds. 32:973–1041. Washington, D.C.: Dumbarton Oaks, 2000.

Poem for the Encaenia of the Pantokrator Monastery (Inaugural Ekphrasis). Ed. Vassis, Ioannis. "Das Pantokratorkloster von Konstantinopel in Der Byzantinischen Dictung." In *The Pantokrator Monastery in Constantinople*, edited by Sofia Kotzabassi, 203–20. Boston: De Gruyter, 2013; trans. Paul Magdalino. "The Foundation of the Pantokrator Monastery in Its Urban Setting." In *The Pantokrator Monastery in Constantinople*, edited by Sofia Kotzabassi, 49–52. Boston: De Gruyter, 2013.

Prodromos, Theodoros. *Historische Gedichte*. Ed. Wolfram Hörandner. Wien: Verlag der Osterreichischen Akademie der Wissenschaften, 1974.

———. *Executioner or Doctor*. Ed. Giuditta Podestà, "Le satire Lucianesche di Teodoro Prodromo." *Aevum* 21, no. 1/2 (1947): 3–25.

Rhomaios, Eustathios. *Peira*. Edd. Iōnnes D Zepos and Panagiōtēs Zepos. *Jus Graecoromanum*. IV, 5–260. Athens: Phexēs, 1931.

Scylitzes, John. *A Synopsis of Byzantine History, 811–1057*. Trans. J. Wortley. Cambridge: Cambridge University Press, 2010.

Suetonius, C. Tranquillus. *Life of Augustus*. Ed. Maximilian Ihm. Leipzig: Teubner, 1908.

Theophanes Continuates. *Chronographia*. Ed. Immanuel Bekker, *CSHB* 45:3–481, 1838.

Timarion. Trans. Barry Baldwin, Detroit: Wayne State University Press, 1984.

Timothy. *Typikon of the Monastery of the Mother of God Evergetis*. Ed. Paul Gautier, "Le typikon de la Théotokos Évergétis." *REB* 40, no. 1 (1982): 5–101; Trans. Robert Jordan,

BMFD, John Philip Thomas and Angela Constantinides Hero, eds. 22:454–506. Washington, D.C.: Dumbarton Oaks, 2000.

Tzetzes, John. *Letters*. Ed. P. Leone. *Ioannis Tzetzae Epistulae*. Leipzig: B.G. Teubner, 1974.

Zonaras, John. *Annales*. Ed. Moritz Pinder, *CSHB* 49, 1897.

Secondary Sources

Aubineau, Michel. "Zoticos de Constantinople, nouricier des pauvres et serviteur des lépreux." *Analecta Bollandiana* 93 (1975): 67–108.

Bennett, David. "Medical Practice and Manuscripts in Byzantium." *Social History of Medicine* 13, no. 2 (2000): 279–91.

———. "Xenonika: Medical Texts Associated with Xenones in the Late Byzantine Period." Ph.D. Dissertation, University of London, 2003.

Bliquez, L. "Two Lists of Greek Surgical Instruments and the State of Surgery in Byzantine Times." *Dumbarton Oaks Papers* 38 (1984): 187–204.

Bouras-Vallianatos, Petros. "Contextualizing the Art of Healing by Byzantine Physicians." In *Life Is Short Art Long: The Art of Healing in Byzantium*, edited by Brigitte Pitarakis, 104–22. Istanbul: Pera Museum Publication, 2015.

Codellas, Pan S. "The Pantocrator, The Imperial Byzantine Medical Center of XIIth Century A.D. in Constantinople." *Bulletin of the History of Medicine* 12, no. 2 (1942): 392–410.

Congdon, Eleanor A. "Imperial Commemoration and Ritual in the Typikon of the Monastery of Christ Pantokrator." *Revue des études byzantines* 54, no. 1 (1996): 161–99.

Constantelos, Demetrios J. *Byzantine Philanthropy and Social Welfare*. New Brunswick: Rutgers University Press, 1968.

Crislip, Andrew T. *From Monastery to Hospital: Christian Monasticism & the Transformation of Health Care in Late Antiquity*. Ann Arbor: University of Michigan Press, 2005.

Crow, James, Jonathan Bardill and Richard Bayliss. *The Water Supply of Byzantine Constantinople*. London: Society for the Promotion of Roman Studies, 2008.

Dols, M. W. "The Origins of the Islamic Hospital: Myth and Reality." *Bulletin of the History of Medicine* 61, no. 3 (1987): 367–90.

Epstein, Ann Wharton. "Formulas for Salvation: A Comparison of Two Byzantine Monasteries and Their Founders." *Christian History* 50, no. 4 (1981): 385–400.

Featherstone, Jeffrey Michael. "The Great Palace as Reflected in the De Cerimoniis." In *Visualisierungen von Herrschaft: Frühmittelalterliche Residenzen: Gestalt Und Zeremoniell: Internationales Kolloquium 3./4. Juni 2004 in Istanbul*, edited by Franz Alto Bauer. Istanbul: Ege Yayınları, 2006.

Fıratlı, Nezih, and Fikret Yücel. "Some Unknown Byzantine Cisterns of Istanbul." *Turkiye Turing ve Otomobil Kurumu Bellenteni*, 1952, 23–26.

Forchheimer, Philipp, and Josef Strzygowski. *Byzantinischen Wasserbehälter von Konstantinopel*. Vienna: Mechitharisten-Congregation in Wien, 1893.

Galatariotou, Catia. "Byzantine Ktetorika Typika : A Comparative Study." *Revue des études byzantines* 45, no. 1 (1987): 77–138.

Gautier, Paul. "Précisions historiques sur le monastère de Ta Narsou." *Revue des études byzantines* 34, no. 1 (1976): 101–10.

Grumel, Venance. "La profession médicale à Byzance à l'époque des Comnènes." *Revue des études byzantines* 7, no. 1 (1949): 42–46.

———. *Les regestes des actes du patriarcat de Constantinople. 1: Les actes des patriarches, fasc. Ii et iii: Les Regestes de 715 à 1206*. 2nd Ed., ed. J. Darrouzès. Paris, 1989.

Grünbart, Michael. "Paideia Connects: The Interaction between Teachers and Pupils in Twelfth-Century Byzantium." In *Networks of Learning: Perspectives on Scholars in Byzantine East and Latin West, c. 1000-1200*, edited by Michael Grünbart, Niels Gaul, and Sita Steckel, 17–32. Wien: LIT Verlag Münster, 2014.

———. "Prosopographische Beiträge Zum Briefcorpus Des Ioannes Tzetzes." *Jahrbuch der Österreichischen Byzantinistik* 46 (1996): 175–266.

Hörandner, Wolfram. "Zur Beschreibung von Kunstwerken in der byzantinischen Dichtung - Am Beispiel Des Gedichts Auf Das Pantokratorkloster in Konstantinopel." In *Die Poetische Ekphrasis von Kunstwerken. Eine Literarische Tradition*, 203–20, 2006.

Horden, Peregrine. "Alms and the Man: Hospital Founders in Byzantium." In *The Impact of Hostitals, 300-2000*, edited by Peregrine Horden, John Henderson and A. Pastore, 59–76. Peter Lang, 2007.

———. "How Medicalised Were Byzantine Hospitals?" *Medicina e Storia* 10 (2005): 45–74.

———. "Medieval Hospital Formularies: Byzantium and Islam Compared." In *Medical Books in the Byzantine World*, edited by Barbara Zipser, 145–64. Bologna: Eikasmos, 2013.

———. "The Earliest Hospitals in Byzantium, Western Europe, and Islam." *The Journal of Interdisciplinary History* 35, no. 3 (2005): 361–89.

Jacoby, David. "The Urban Evolution of Latin Constantinople (1204–1261)." In *Byzantine Constantinople. Monuments, Topography and Everyday Life*, edited by Nevra Necipoğlu, 277–97, Leiden: Brill, 2001.

Jeanselme, Edouard, and Lysimachos Oeconomos. *Les oeuvres d'assistance et les hôpitaux byzantins au siècle des Comnènes*. Anvers: Imprimerie de Vlijt, 1921.

Jeffreys, Michael, and Elizabeth Jeffreys. "Immortality in the Pantokrator?" *Jahrbuch der Österreichischen Byzantinistik* 44 (1994): 193.

Kazhdan, A. "The Image of the Medical Doctor in Byzantine Literature of the Tenth to Twelfth Centuries." *DOP* 38 (1984): 43–51.

Kislinger, Ewald. "Der Pantokrator-Xenon, ein trügerisches Ideal?" *Jahrbuch der Österreichischen Byzantinistik* (1987): 173–79.

———. "Zur Lage der Leproserie des Pantokrator-Typikon." *Jahrbuch der Österreichischen Byzantinistik* 42 (1992): 171.

Kotzabassi, Sofia. "Feasts at the Monastery of Pantokrator." In *The Pantokrator Monastery in Constantinople*, edited by Sofia Kotzabassi, 153–90. Boston: De Gruyter, 2013.

———. "The Monastery of Pantokrator between 1204 and 1453." In *The Pantokrator Monastery in Constantinople*, edited by Sofia Kotzabassi, 57–70. Boston: De Gruyter, 2013.

Laiou, Angeliki E. "Rev. Timothy S. Miller. The Birth of the Hospital in the Byzantine Empire." *American Historical Review* 94, no. 2 (1989): 426–26.

Lascaratos, J., E. Poulakou-Rebelakou, and S. Marketos. "Abandonment of Terminally Ill Patients in the Byzantine Era. An Ancient Tradition?" *Journal of Medical Ethics* 25, no. 3 (1999): 254–58.

Lauxtermann, Marc Diederik. *Byzantine Poetry from Pisides to Geometres: Texts and Contexts*. Wien: Östereichische Akademie der Wissenschaften, 2003.

Magdalino, Paul. "Medieval Constantinople." In *Studies on the History and Topography of Byzantine Constantinople*, 1–111. Aldershot: Ashgate, 2007.

———. *The Empire of Manuel I Komnenos, 1143–1180*. Cambridge: Cambridge University Press, 1993.

———. "The Foundation of the Pantokrator Monastery in Its Urban Setting." In *The Pantokrator Monastery in Constantinople*, edited by Sofia Kotzabassi, 33–56. Boston: De Gruyter, 2013.

McCabe, Anne. "Imported Materia Medica, 4th-12th Centuries, and Byzantine Pharmacology." In *Byzantine Trade, 4th-12th Centuries The Archaeology of Local, Regional and International Exchange. Papers of the Thirty-Eighth Spring Symposium of Byzantine Studies, St John's College, University of Oxford, March 2004*, edited by Marlia Mundell Mango, 273–92. Farnham: Routledge, 2009.

Miller, Timothy. "The Sampson Hospital of Constantinople." *Byzantinische Forschungen* 15 (1990): 101–35.

———. "Death in a Xenon?" In *Realia Byzantina (Festschrift for Apostolos Karpazolos)*, edited by Sofia Kotzabassi and Giannis Mavromatis, 191–96. Byzantinisches Archiv 22. Berlin: W. de Gruyter, 2009.

———. *The Birth of the Hospital in the Byzantine Empire.* Baltimore: Johns Hopkins University Press, 1985.

Orlandos, Anastasios. "Ἡ Ἀναπαράστασις Τοῦ Ξενῶνος Τῆς Ἐν Κωνσταντινουπόλει Μονῆς Παντοκράτορος." *EEBS* 16 (1941): 198–207.

———. *Μοναστηριακὴ Ἀρχιτεκτονική.* 2nd ed. Athens: The Archaeological Society in Athens, 1958.

Ousterhout, Robert. "Architecture, Art and Komnenian Ideology at the Pantokrator Monastery." In *Byzantine Constantinople: Monuments, Topography and Everyday Life*, edited by Nevra Necipoğlu, 133–52. Leiden: Brill, 2001.

———. "Water and Healing in Constantinople: Reading Architectural Remains." In *Life Is Short, Art Long: The Art of Healing in Byzantium*, edited by Brigitte Pitarakis, 64–77. Istanbul: Pera Museum Publication, 2015.

Parker, Holt. "Woman Physicians in Greece, Rome and the Byzantine Empire." In *Woman Physicians and Healers: Climbing a Long Hill*, edited by Lilian Furst, 131–50. Lexington: University Press of Kentucky, 1997.

Philipsborn, Alexandre. "Der Fortschritt in der Entwicklung des byzantinischen Krankenhauswesens." *Byzantinische Zeitschrift* 54, no. 2 (1961): 338–65.

———. "ΙΕΡΑ ΝΟΣΟΣ und die Spezial-Anstalt des Pantokrator-Krankenhauses." *Byzantion* 33, no. 1 (1963): 223–30.

Schöne, H. "Zwei Listen chirurgischer Instrumente." *Hermes* 38, no. 2 (1903): 280–84.

Spyridon, monk of the Laura, and Sōphronios Eustratiadēs. *Catalogue of the Greek Manuscripts in the Library of the Laura on Mount Athos, with Notices from Other Libraries.* Cambridge: Harvard University Press, 1925.

Stathakopoulos, Dionysios. "Discovering a Military Order of the Crusades: The Hospital of St. Sampson of Constantinople." *Viator* 37 (2006): 255–73.

———. "On Whose Authority?: Regulating Medical Practice in the Twelfth and Early Thirteenth Centuries." In *Authority in Byzantium*, ed. Pamela Armstrong, 227–38. Farnham: Ashgate, 2013.

Taylor, Alice. "The Pantokrator Monastery in Constantinople: A Comparison of Its Remains and Its Typikon." *Third Annual Byzantine Studies Conference* 3 (1977): 47–48.

Thompson, John D. and G. Goldin. *The Hospital: A Social and Architectural History.* New Haven: Yale University Press, 1975.

Van Minnen, Peter. "Medical Care in Late Antiquity." In *Ancient Medicine in Its Socio-Cultural Context, Volume 1: Papers Read at the Congress Held at Leiden University, 13-15 April 1992*, edited by H. F. J. Horstmanshoff, Philip van der Eijk, and P. H. Schrijvers, 1:153–69. Amsterdam: Brill Rodopi, 1995.

Vassis, Ioannis. "Das Pantokratorkloster von Konstantinopel in der byzantinischen Dictung." In *The Pantokrator Monastery in Constantinople*, edited by Sofia Kotzabassi, 203–50. Boston: De Gruyter, 2013.

Vees, Nikos. "Σύνταγμα Ἐπιγραφικῶν Μνημέιων Μετέωρων Καὶ Τῆς Πέριξ Χώρας, Μετὰ Σχετικῶν Ἀρχαιολογημάτων." *Byzantis* 1, no. 4 (1909): 537–626.

Watson, Gilbert. *Theriac and Mithridatium: A Study in Therapeutics*. London: Wellcome Historical Medical Library, 1966.

Wolford, Tyler J. "Healing on the Fourth Hill : Searching for the Pantokrator Hospital." An Honors Undergraduate Thesis, Ball State University, 2012.

PIROSKA AND THE PANTOKRATOR: REASSESSING THE ARCHITECTURAL EVIDENCE

Robert Ousterhout

In this paper I shall discuss the project for which Piroska-Eirene is best remembered: the construction of the Pantokrator Monastery in Constantinople (figs. 1–2). Built between ca. 1118 and 1136 by Piroska-Eirene and her husband, the emperor John II Komnenos, as three large, interconnected churches, the Pantokrator was the most significant Byzantine architectural undertaking of the twelfth century, the core of a unique monastic establishment of singular importance. The chronology is fairly firm, and the documentation for it is unusually good. The enormous project is unlikely to have been begun before 1118, when John assumed the throne; it was completed by 1136, when the monastic *Typikon* was composed.[1] In addition to the surviving church complex, the foundation also included the

---

[1] For a survey of the sources, see R. Janin, *La Géographie ecclésiastique de l'empire byzantin: Les églises et les monastères*, I, iii (Paris, 1969), 515–23; for the building itself, see J. Ebersolt and A. Thiers, *Les églises de Constantinople* (Paris, 1913), 171–207; A. Van Millingen, *Byzantine Churches in Constantinople: Their History and Architecture* (London, 1912), 219–40; both superceded by A.H.S. Megaw, "Notes on the Recent Work of the Byzantine Institute in Istanbul," *Dumbarton Oaks Papers* 17 (1963), 333–64. For the typikon, see P. Gautier, "Le typikon du Christ Sauveur Pantocrator," *Revue des Études Byzantins* 32 (1974), 1–145; and English translation by Robert Jordan in J. Thomas and A. Hero, eds., *Byzantine Monastic Foundation Documents*, Dumbarton Oaks Studies 35, (Washington, D.C., 2000), 725–81, with notes and commentary. For the restoration, see R. Ousterhout, Z. Ahunbay, and M. Ahunbay, "Study and Restoration of the Zeyrek Camii in Istanbul: First Report, 1997–98," *Dumbarton Oaks Papers* 54 (2000), 265–70; and "Study and Restoration of the Zeyrek Camii in Istanbul: Second Report, 2001–05," *Dumbarton Oaks Papers* 63 (2010), 235–56; also M. and Z. Ahunbay, "Restoration work at the Zeyrek Camii, 1997–1998," in N. Necipoğlu, ed., *Byzantine Constantinople: Monuments, Topography and Everyday Life* (Leiden, 2001), 117–32. Most recently, S. Kotzabassi, ed., *The Pantokrator Monastery in Constantinople*, Byzantinisches Archiv 27 (Berlin, 2013), esp. P. Magdalino, "The Pantokrator Monastery in its Urban Setting," 33–55; and a useful bibliography, 251–54.

living quarters for the monks organized within a courtyard, as well as a hospital and an old-age home. The *Typikon* also mentions six dependent monasteries, the monastic cemetery, and a leprosarium, all separate from the main complex.[2] And although the *Typikon* mentions living quarters not yet completed, including those for the founder's use, all of the surviving parts of the complex are described in detail, as if they were already in existence, so we may assume they had been completed by the time of the writing.

Sadly, Piroska-Eirene did not live to see her foundation in its final form. She had passed away in 1134, while accompanying her husband to Bithynia, where he was fighting against the Seljuks. She had assumed the monastic habit, apparently on her deathbed, along with the name Xene, a name appropriate for her status as a monastic, but perhaps also a reference to her foreign origins.[3] As her mortal remains were returned to the capital for burial in the Pantokrator, we might imagine that the final phase of the project was hastened to completion.

The Byzantine sources are equivocal on the matter of patronage. Nikolaos Kataphloron, writing ca. 1136–43—that is, after the foundation of the monastery but before the death of John—credits the conception of the project to Piroska-Eirene, while viewing John as her willing helper: "The queen herself conceived the construction of the house and its perimeter, the enclosure and its palace; but your willingness and labor joined forces with her—for though she conceived the idea, you gave further shape to her thoughts ..."[4] The *Synaxarion* biography, which seems to have taken shape during the reign of Manuel, also credits the project to Piroska-Eirene, while placing John in a secondary role. It includes the charming anecdote of the empress prostrating herself before her husband in the monastery's *katholikon*, "as she washed the sacred floor with her tears," pleading for the funds necessary to expand the project.[5]

John Kinnamos's *History* includes a perfunctory account, written long after Piroska-Eirene's death, which accords with her devout presentation in the *Synaxarion*. It ties the empress directly to the monastery in such a way that the monastery *represents* her and her charity and good works: "... she passed her whole life benefitting persons who were begging for something or other from her. She established a

---

[2] See Magdalino, "Foundation," 36–38.

[3] S. Kotzabassi, "Feasts at the Monastery of Pantokrator," in Kotzabassi, ed., *Pantokrator Monastery*, 159, n. 30.

[4] M. Loukadi, "Empress Piroska-Eirene's Collaborators in the Foundation of the Pantokrator Monastery: The Testimony of Nikolaos Kataphloron," in Kotzabassi, ed., *Pantokrator Monastery*, 191–201, esp. 194–95.

[5] For the text, see Kotzabassi, "Feasts," 173–74; for the translation, Magdalino, "Foundation," 54.

monastery in the name of the Pantokrator, which is among the most outstanding in beauty and size. Such was this empress."[6] The anonymous *Enkainia* epigram, written to celebrate the foundation of the Theotokos Eleousa church at the completion of the vast construction project, seems to credit them both: "The lord seeing the queen impetuously / Rushing to the foundation of a monastery / Gave impetus to her good deliberation."[7] The subsequent lines in the epigram credit the building activity to her. It nevertheless reflects the active presence of John (and the absence of the empress) at the dedication. In contrast, the *Typikon* is written in the voice of John, and Piroska-Eirene's contribution goes unmentioned. Niketas Choniates, writing much later, similarly gives pride of place to John.[8]

Although we may never be able to sort out the specific contributions, John quite literally held the purse strings: in the Hagia Sophia image of the imperial couple (discussed by Christopher Mielke in this volume), John holds the money bag, while Piroska-Eirene offers the deed of donation to the Theotokos.[9] But good deeds, such as the foundation of a monastery enveloped by charitable institutions, fit the pattern of earlier Komnenian philanthropy, although the Pantokrator does so on a grander and more complex scale than any earlier foundation.[10] That said, it seems most likely that Piroska-Eirene initiated the project, and that John supported it and ultimately completed it after her death.

The ambivalence of the texts concerning the patronage of the Pantokrator also reflects the two ways the project would have been understood by its contemporaries: as a celebration of piety (often female) and military valor (usually male). First, following Komnenian precedents, the foundation was a manifestation of piety, for which emphasis given to the role of a saintly empress known for her religious devotion, gentleness, modesty, and compassion.[11] In contrast, the anonymous *Enkainia* epigram presents the Pantokrator as a victory monument, as Magdalino has argued.[12] Indeed, John was at war with the Seljuks at the time, and current events must have played a role in shaping contemporary views of the undertaking. But piety and military valor were the two sides of the Komnenian ideological coin; they were not

---

[6] Ioannes Kinnamos, *Historia*, ed. A. Meineke. *CSHB* (Bonn 1836), 10.6–8, 31.11–13; trans. C. Brand, *Deeds of John and Manuel Comnenus by John Kinnamos* (New York, 1976), 17.

[7] Magdalino, "Foundation," 50.

[8] Niketas Choniates, *Historia*, I.A. van Dieten. *CFHB*, 11/1 (Berlin 1975), 48.20–21.

[9] Thomas Whittemore, *The Mosaics of St. Sophia at Istanbul* (Paris, 1933–1938), esp. 21–28, 76–82.

[10] A point emphasized by Magdalino, "Foundation," passim; for earlier Komnenian foundations, see Vlada Stanković, "The Komnenoi and Constantinople before the Building of the Pantokrator Complex," in Kotzabassi, ed., *Pantokrator Monastery*, 3–31.

[11] For the text, see Kotzabassi, "Feasts," 173–74; for the translation, Magdalino, "Foundation," 54.

[12] Magdalino, "Foundation," 49–52.

mutually exclusive and, in fact, represent the dual concerns of the imperial couple. It is noteworthy that in the military triumph celebrated by John in 1132 following his victory at Kastamon, he opted *not* to enter the city riding in the gilded silver chariot prepared for him. Instead, he placed an icon of the Theotokos in it, while he entered on foot carrying a cross.[13] Thus, in one of John's most public appearances, both religious devotion and military prowess were celebrated simultaneously. In a like manner, Piroska-Eirene was known for her good works but also accompanied her husband to the battlefield in Bithynia. Piety and valor could be manifest in the same person; so too could they be represented by a single monastic foundation.

As determined conclusively by the efforts of A. H. S. Megaw, the south church was the first of the complex to be built, the *katholikon* of the monastery, dedicated to Christ (fig. 3).[14] The church is of the cross-in-square type, with a dome ca. 7.5 m. in diameter, rising ca. 24.5 m. off the floor, making it the largest example of the standard Byzantine church type, and the tallest of the later churches in the capital. In plan, this consisted of a monumental block, measuring 100 Byzantine feet on each side (slightly more than 32 m.)—the dimensions of the dome of Hagia Sophia—with the core of the building enveloped by a broad, two-storied narthex to the west and lateral aisles—that is, assuming there was originally a north aisle symmetrical to the surviving, south aisle.[15] The spacious naos was covered by a 16-sided ribbed dome raised on a windowed drum, with barrel vaults above the crossarms and domical vaults above corner compartments; groin vaults were used in the pastophoria, narthex, gallery, and lateral aisles. Three doors opened from the narthex; an additional three on either side opened into the lateral annexes. The interior was illuminated by windows at several levels: those in the drum of the dome, tripartite windows in the west, north, and south crossarm lunettes; a second, lower level of windows on the north and south; and tall tripartite windows in the apses of the tripartite sanctuary. With its tall proportions and two-storied narthex, from the exterior, the south church would have resembled the Cathedral of Vladimir (fig. 4).[16]

Lavishly decorated, the walls were originally clad in marble, of which the sanctuary revetments survive, with panels of Prokonnesian, verde antico, and rosso

---

[13] Brand, *Deeds*, 20.

[14] Megaw, "Notes," esp. 343–44; reversing the chronology proposed by Van Millingen, *Byzantine Churches*, 233–34.

[15] Partly open, partly closed, the function of the lateral aisles has not been determined; during our investigations of the complex (discussed below), we did not have access to the surviving aisle.

[16] D. Shvidkovsky, *Russian Architecture and the West*. Begun in 1158, perhaps this was an intentional reflection of a Constantinopolitan prototype in early Rus'; although the lateral aisles of the Pantokrator did not include a second story.

antico, with carved doorframes of the same materials. The original columns were of porphyry, as Petrus Gyllius related, but these were replaced in the eighteenth century with the surviving rococo pillars.[17] The marble cornices and capitals were painted or highlighted in gold leaf. The vaults were covered with mosaics, and although none survives, details of their imagery are enumerated in the *Typikon*.[18] The Ottoman mimbar is fashioned from remnants of the templon and ciborium, all reused pieces—as evidenced by the cut-down crosses on the exterior and the monograms on the interior. These might actually belong to a later restoration, although the knotted columns would not have been out of place framing the *proskynetarion* icons flanking the twelfth-century bema.[19] While the elements of the original decoration surviving *in situ* are limited, the sense of its ostentation of the interior is suggested by the Pala d'Oro at San Marco in Venice, which is alleged to have come from the Pantokrator's templon—at least it was recognized as such by the participants in the Council of Florence-Ferrara.[20]

Perhaps the most unusual aspect of the decoration is known only from the archaeological remains. Megaw found hundreds of stained glass fragments in the late 1950s during his limited excavations in the bema of the south church. In addition to a variety of decorative patterns, he also found fragments that represented drapery, inscriptions, and facial features. His proposed reconstruction of the tall apse windows included standing figures surrounded by a decorative background (fig. 5).[21] Megaw also found H-shaped lead cames, indicating that the windows had been set in place in an identical manner to their Western counterparts—that is, demon-

---

[17] Gyllius, *De top. CP*, iv.c.2 ; the style of the rococo embellishments correspond to details at the nearby Laleli Camii, built in 1760–63 by the imperial architect Mehmet Tahir Ağa. It is tempting to credit him with the restoration of the church following the 1766 earthquake, which destroyed the nearby Fatih Camii.

[18] On this, see most recently, Jean-Michel Spieser, "Le monastère du Pantocrator à Constantinople: Le typikon et le monument," in *Many Romes: Studies in Honor of Hans Belting*, eds. I. Foletti and H. Kessler, *Convivium* II/1 (2015), 203–16, with additional bibliography.

[19] Megaw, "Notes," 340–43; R. Ousterhout, "The Architectural Decoration of the Pantokrator Monastery: Evidence Old and New," *Papers of the First Sevgi Gönül Memorial Symposium 2007* (Istanbul, 2010), 432–39; and idem, "The Pantokrator Monastery and Architectural Interchanges in the Thirteenth Century," in *Quarta Crociata: Venezia—Bizanzio—Impero Latino*, eds. G. Ortalli, G Ravegnani, P. Schreiner (Venice, 2006), II: 749–70.

[20] Although it does not specify which of the Pantokrator churches it came from. In his paper in this volume, Christopher Mielke argues that the Empress Eirene represented in the enamels may be Piroska-Eirene; for the text, see Sylvester Syropoulos, IV.25; V. Laurent, *Les 'Mémoires' de Sylvestre Syropoulos sur le concile de Florence (1438–1439)* (Paris: CNRS, 1971), 196 ff.; transl. http://syropoulos.co.uk/translation.htm

[21] Megaw, "Notes," 349–64, esp. 362–64.

strating the early adoption of both a Western European medium and its technology. Megaw believed the glass to have been part of the original decoration of the south church, although his dating of it has not found general acceptance.[22] Chemical analysis of the glass establishes its differences from Western examples, with a composition that would favor Constantinopolitan production.[23]

I would like to think the question of the date is still open. The only other example known from Constantinople was found in the excavations of the Chora (Kariye Camii), apparently coming from the windows of the main apse.[24] The fact that stained glass is known *only* at these two sites encourages us to look at their relative histories, and the only time when that the two were closely related was in the early twelfth century. The Chora was refounded in the 1120s by the *sebastokrator* Isaak and intended to be the setting for his burial. At the time he was a close political ally of his brother John II, although the two soon fell out.[25] After John's death, the sharing of technology and art form seems unlikely: there was no love lost between Manuel and Isaak; and although the Pantokrator may have been maintained during the Latin Occupation, the Chora fell into decrepitude.[26] While a date in the early 1130s may seem precocious when set against surviving examples of stained glass in Western Europe, from a historical perspective this would be the most likely time. Of course the presence of stained glass fits with the Komnenian fascination with the West.

Although invisible beneath the mosque carpets today, most impressive in the south church is its unique *opus sectile* floor, which I like to think is the very floor Piroska-Eirene bathed with her tears (fig. 6). The central space of the naos is divided into nine squares, with large panels and disks of porphyry or *verde antico* framed

---

[22] J. Lafond, "Découverte de vitraux historiés du Moyen Age à Constantinople," *Cahiers Archéologiques* 18 (1968), 231–37, proposed a date ca. 1200 and ascribed the work to a German artisan. F. dell'Acqua, "The Stained-Glass Windows from the Chora and the Pantokrator Monasteries: A Byzantine 'Mystery'?" in *Restoring Byzantium: The Kariye Camii in Istanbul and the Byzantine Institute Restoration*, eds. H. Klein and R. Ousterhout (New York, 2004), 68–77, favors a twelfth-century date, suggesting the period of Manuel Komnenos instead. D. Jacoby, "The Urban Evolution of Constantinople (1204–1261)," in N. Necipoğlu, ed., *Byzantine Constantinople: Monuments, Topography and Everyday Life* (Leiden, 2001), 277–97, suggests they are Venetian additions of the thirteenth century.

[23] Robert H. Brill, *Chemical Analyses of Early Glasses* (Corning Glass Museum, 1999), I, 107, 113; II, 210–12; see also J. Henderson and M. Mundell Mango, "Glass at Medieval Constantinople: Preliminary Scientific Evidence," in C. Mango and G. Dagron, eds., *Constantinople and Its Hinterland* (Aldershot, 1995), 333–56.

[24] Megaw, "Notes," 364–67; reassessed by dell'Acqua, "Stained-Glass Windows," 67–77.

[25] P. Magdalino, *The empire of Manuel I Komnenos. 1143–1180* (Cambridge, 1993), 193.

[26] Magdalino, *Empire*, 193; P.A. Underwood, *The Kariye Djami* (New York, 1966), I, 13.

by interlocking bands of colored marbles. This disks have long since been removed for use elsewhere, but they were arranged in a quincunx pattern, with the spandrels around each disk filled with inhabited rinceaux, with birds, ferocious beasts, mythological creatures, bucolic scenes, and animals of the land and sea. The images would seem to reflect the ideals underlying Byzantine social and political order, as well as general connotations of kingship, power, and order within the well-governed cosmos. Indeed, although there is no direct connection between the two, the themes of the well-ordered cosmos compare favorably to those of the Great Palace floor mosaic of centuries earlier.[27]

Within the Pantokrator floor, two unique panels stand out. At the threshold to the naos, the wheel of the zodiac is represented, with signs of the zodiac and personifications of the seasons, although now much abraded (fig. 7).[28] The unique appearance of the wheel of the zodiac may reflect the Komnenian fascination with astrology. Writers of the period were concerned with the probability of fate, with questions concerning predestination, free will, and the autonomous development of history, and in this context, astrology was revived as a 'scientific' method of determining the future.[29] Exact times of birth were recorded and horoscopes were cast for the purple-born Komnenian children.[30] Similarly, the four scenes from the life of Samson, set immediately before the bema, reflect ideas of Old Testament kingship (fig. 8). Samson was often invoked as a divinely inspired warrior-ruler: his birth and achievements were preordained, his strength the gift of God, his deeds part of the divine plan, Samson was an apposite choice of an antetype for an astrologically inclined emperor.[31]

---

[27] See for example, James Trilling, "The Soul of the Empire: Style and Meaning in the Mosaic Pavement of the Byzantine Imperial Palace in Constantinople," *DOP* 43 (1989), 27–72; also Henry Maguire, *Earth and Ocean: The Terrestrial World in Early Byzantine Art* (University Park, PA, 1987).

[28] See Megaw, "Notes," 335–40; and Ousterhout, "Art, Architecture, and Komnenian Ideology," for a fuller discussion. Note most recently, Xavier Barral i Altet, "Un programme iconographique occidental pour le pavement medieval de l'église du Christ Pantocrator de Constantinople," in *Many Romes: Studies in Honor of Hans Belting*, eds. I. Foletti and H. Kessler, *Convivium* II/1 (2015), 219–32, who, however, emphasizes the Western European parallels for the imagery on the floor, but includes much recent bibliography.

[29] On this subject see Magdalino, *Empire*, 377–82; and idem, *L'Orthodoxie des astrologues: la science entre le dogme et la divination a Byzance (VIIe–XIVe siecle)*, Realités Byzantines 12 (Paris: Lethielleux, 2006).

[30] See A. Kazhdan, "Die Liste der Kinder des Alexios I in einer moskauer Handschrift," *Beiträge zur Alten Geschichte und deren Nachleben,* II (Berlin, 1970), 233–37.

[31] Ousterhout, "Art, Architecture, and Komnenian Ideology," 146–48, for a fuller discussion.

As the odd connections between building units indicate, the south church was completed and finished in all parts before the decision was made to enlarge the complex, and this would seem to accord with the account in the *Synaxarion*. In its original form, the naos was preceded by a broad, five-bayed narthex, and this was likely the original intended burial place for John and Eirene, at least in the initial phase of construction. The central three bays had doorways opening to the exterior and to the naos, but the lateral bays both included arcosolia in their western walls. Megaw suggested that these were originally the intended imperial burial sites.[32] Of course, the narthex had been a common place for interment since Early Christian times, so this would represent a fairly conservative solution for founders' burials, isolated from the liturgy conducted in the naos.[33] At this early point in its history, I suspect the Pantokrator was conceived solely as the burial place of the imperial couple, rather than a family or dynastic mausoleum. Above the narthex was a spacious gallery, extending its full length, with a triple window opening into the naos. It did not extend over the side aisles. Although it is not mentioned in the *Typikon*, this was likely intended to be a space set aside for the founders to worship and oversee the liturgy in relative privacy.[34]

The building was quickly expanded, as Piroska-Eirene had wished. The north church, dedicated to the Theotokos Eleousa, was begun shortly after the completion of the south church; it was also of the cross-in-square type but smaller, less lavishly detailed, less carefully constructed, and it is also less well preserved (see fig. 2). As begun, the two were meant to be distinct elements, both physically and visually, and in fact, the north church is set at a slightly different angle than the south church. They were connected by a single door, where their narthexes joined. At the connection, both the north narthex and the gallery above it were equipped an extra bay, projecting southward to meet the narthex and gallery of the south church. Oddly, the north narthex did not have doors in its western wall opening to the exterior; instead, the north church opened to a public street through a portico along its north wall. Four doorways—one in the narthex and three in the naos—are now blocked, but the north façade preserves a series of marble brackets that once must have supported the portico. Unlike the south church, which was set aside for the

---

[32] Megaw, "Notes," 343; much of this was altered when the complex was enlarged, as discussed below.
[33] See most recently Vasileios Marinis, "Tombs and Burials in the Monastery *tou Libos* in Constantinople," *DOP* 63 (2009), 147–166, esp. 151–52; idem, *Architecture and Ritual in the Churches of Constantinople, Ninth to Fifteenth Centuries* (Cambridge, 2014), 64–76.
[34] Slobodan Ćurčić, 'What was the Real Function of Late Byzantine Katechoumena?' *Byzantine Studies Conference Abstracts* 19, 1993, 8–9.

exclusive use of the monks, the north church was open to the outside community and officiated by a lay clergy.[35]

Of the decoration, little survives. Traces of a mosaic rinceau in red and gold are exposed in one of the north windows. More unusual is the upper cornice, carved with an inhabited vine scroll, framing images of birds, apparently copying a Late Antique prototype.[36] Petrus Gyllius records the columns as Theban granite, but the present piers are probably from an eighteenth- or nineteenth-century restoration.[37] The dome was probably rebuilt at the same time. The rebuilt elements here are simpler in character than the rococo additions in the south church and must represent a separate intervention.

The *Enkainia* poem was composed for the dedication of this church, and this requires some explanation, as the Eleousa church appears second in the construction sequence. As I shall discuss below, the central funeral chapel was begun later but completed at the same time as the north church, and thus the poem celebrated the completion of the vast, sprawling ecclesiastical project. Oddly, the poem begins with an evocation of the Stoa Poikile of ancient Athens, and we may surmise that the extensive portico at the Pantokrator inspired the poet.[38] The portico connected the North Church to Constantinople's street system, and it was by means of this portico that the urban procession came to the church from the Blachernai. And although it has disappeared completely, except for the brackets on the north façade, this must have been an unusual—and particularly visible and impressive—feature of the complex, as well as the point of access for most visitors.[39]

As construction on the north church progressed, it was decided to add a third component, a funeral chapel dedicated to the Incorporeal One, St. Michael.[40] The chapel was sandwiched between the two, and this necessitated the removal of the north aisle of the south church (see fig. 2). Irregular in plan, the central chapel is covered by twin domes. The *typikon* says it is "in the form of a *heroon*"—a term used to designate the nearby mausolea of Constantine and Justinian at the church of the Holy Apostles, and no doubt the Pantokrator was intended to resonate sym-

---

[35] Gautier, "Typikon," 72–81; *BMFD*, 752–56.
[36] Ousterhout, "Decoration," 434.
[37] *De top. CP,* iv.c.2.
[38] Magdalino, "Foundation," 44, 50.
[39] It remains unclear how or where exactly the portico connected into the urban armature; all that remains to indicate its presence are the brackets on the north façade. It nevertheless became part of the network of urban processions honoring the Theotokos; see Magdalino, "Foundation," 44–45; also B. Pentcheva, *Icons and Power: The Mother of God in Byzantium* (University Park, PA, 2006), 165–87.
[40] Gautier, "Typikon," 72–73, 80–83; *BMFD*, 754–57.

bolically with its old and venerable neighbor, as I shall discuss below. The imperial burials were probably clustered at the west end, where there were originally four arcosolia under the west dome. The *Typikon* notes "the dome of the Incorporeal" (Michael) and the "*heroon* of the outside"—most likely to indicate the eastern and western bays of the chapel. It also mentions the tomb of John II (d. 1143), which he requested to share with his son and intended successor Alexios II, who predeceased him (d. 1142), and the tomb of Eirene (d. 1134).[41] Another son, Andronikos, who passed away shortly after Alexios, was also buried there, as well as (somewhat later) Bertha-Eirene, the first wife of Manuel, and finally Manuel himself.[42] We can imagine John and Alexios in the most prominent tomb, with Eirene to one side.[43] Possibly Andronikos was interred in an arcosolium in the lateral wall (fig. 9). The tombs of John and Eirene would have appeared just below the Passion scenes outlined in the Typikon. As I reconstruct them, the Myrrhophores would have appeared immediately above, probably with the Angel gesturing toward their tombs. This is how the same scene was positioned at the tomb of John's brother Isaak at the Kosmosoteira at Ferai.[44] Although the chapel allowed for more prominent burials than the narthex arcosolia, the tombs were still limited in number and may have been intended only for select members of the immediate family.[45] In any event, as the complex grew, it was transformed from the mausoleum of the imperial couple, to a family mausoleum, and ultimately to a dynastic one.

In spite of its significance, the architecture of the chapel is oddly irregular, and with domes of different sizes, set at different heights, and with distinct details (fig. 10). The larger, western dome is ribbed, while the smaller eastern dome is a pumpkin dome. And while the interior walls must have been clad in marble and mosaic, with the exception of the extension of the *opus sectile* floor, added under Manuel to connect to his tomb, nothing of the decoration virtually nothing of the interior decoration survives.[46] Moreover, with the transformation of the building complex into a mosque, large arches were opened between the chapel and the flank-

---

[41] Magdalino, "Foundation," 41.
[42] Ioannis Vassis, "Das Pantokratorkloster von Konstantinopel in der byzantinischen Dichtung," in Kotzabassi, ed., *Pantokrator Monastery*, 203–49, for tomb epitaphs; esp. 230–34.
[43] Géza Nagymihályi, *Árpád-házi Szent Piroska: az idegen szent* (Budapest, 2007), 74, suggests the central arcosolium was that of Piroska-Eirene, but this seems unlikely, as the *Typikon* calls the chapel a *heroon*, as I discuss below.
[44] Robert Ousterhout, "Women at Tombs: Narrative, Theatricality, and the Contemplative Mode," in *Wonderful Things: Byzantium through its Art*, eds. A. Eastmond and L. James (Farnham: Ashgate, 2013), 229–46.
[45] Magdalino, "Foundation," 41.
[46] Megaw, "Notes," 340–43.

ing churches, making the reconstruction of the chapel difficult to imagine. I shall return to this issue below.

An outer narthex and courtyard were added to the south church in this final expansion (see fig. 2 and fig. 13). This expansion destroyed one of the original arcosolia and severely isolated the other, so we suspect the funeral chapel to have been completed before Eirene's death in 1134. With the expansion, the situation of the imperial tombs was significantly enhanced—the chapel was enveloped by the prayers of two churches, lay and monastic—with which it communicated—and it was provided with its own domed bema for the funeral liturgies. The *Typikon* specifies elaborate commemorative services that would hardly have been possible in the limited space of the original narthex.[47] In sum, in the course of 18 years the Pantokrator had been transformed architecturally from a single monumental block to a sprawling irregular complex, and from a monastic *katholikon* to a multi-functioning church cluster.[48]

During the period from 1997 to 2005, I co-directed a program of restoration and documentation at the Pantokrator, which now functions as a mosque known as the Zeyrek Camii.[49] Working together with my Turkish colleagues Profs. Zeynep and Metin Ahunbay of Istanbul Technical University, we were given permission by the Vakıflar Genel Müdürlüğü, which oversees religious foundations. The building had fallen into a dilapidated state, and had been badly restored in the 1960s. The lead sheeting of the roofs had been replaced by reinforced concrete, which has cracked repeatedly and caused leakage throughout the building. Most of our effort was directed toward the roof, where severe cracks became evident with every section of concrete we removed, as well as damage to the fabric of the building caused by the restoration. It was slow, arduous, nerve-wracking work. We were also able to document portions of the building as we worked, although we did not have full access to the interior, nor permission for anything resembling archaeology. With the changing political allegiances in Turkey, unfortunately, our permit was withdrawn in 2004, and we brought our intervention to conclusion in 2005. The

---

[47] Gautier, "Typikon," 80–83; *BMFD*, 756–57; N. P. Ševčenko, "Icons and the Liturgy," *DOP* 45 (1991), 45–57.

[48] Discussed further in Robert Ousterhout, "Contextualizing the Later Churches of Constantinople: Suggested Methodologies and a Few Examples," *Dumbarton Oaks Papers* 54 (2000), 241–50.

[49] For the restoration and for much of what follows, see R. Ousterhout, Z. Ahunbay, and M. Ahunbay, "Study and Restoration of the Zeyrek Camii in Istanbul: First Report, 1997–98," *Dumbarton Oaks Papers* 54 (2000), 265–70; and "Study and Restoration of the Zeyrek Camii in Istanbul: Second Report, 2001–05," *Dumbarton Oaks Papers* 63 (2010), 235–56; also M. and Z. Ahunbay, "Restoration work at the Zeyrek Camii, 1997–1998," in N. Necipoğlu, ed., *Byzantine Constantinople: Monuments, Topography and Everyday Life* (Leiden, 2001), 117–32.

project was turned over to the Istanbul Municipality and given to a contractor who was much more interested in the current function of the building as a mosque than in its history, and the subsequent interventions have been heavy-handed at best. Thus the exterior masonry we had carefully conserved was either covered, painted, or replaced; the interior spaces were plastered and painted, so that there is virtually nothing authentically Byzantine left to see at the site.

Nevertheless, during the period of our project, we were able to observe of the building's fabric close at hand and add some nuances to its construction history. The construction technique shows every indication of haste, to the point of sloppiness and inexactitude—particularly in the later phases, but none was originally exposed. The exterior surfaces were plastered and possibly painted, and the interior encrusted with marble, mosaic, and gilding; it's really *nouveau riche* in flavor. Nevertheless, it is clear that the same workshop was responsible for all parts to the building; the same 'recessed brick' construction technique appears throughout, with wide mortar beds with distinctive etching. In addition, most of the bricks used in construction were reused, with brickstamps dating to the fifth and sixth centuries—probably taken from older buildings on the site.[50] Similarly, the marbles of the interior are spoliated, with the revetments cut from older blocks and columns.[51] In some places, the inexactitude may indicate a mix of newly carved and reused pieces: in the lower cornices of the north church, for example, there is considerable variation in width—between 10 and 18 cm of chamfered surface, often with awkward transitions in the palmette pattern at the corners.[52]

The south church was completed and plastered on the exterior before the second phase was begun. At the gallery level, we exposed several areas where the original plaster was preserved. Later additions abut the pink plaster surface, which were left intact. At the same time, on the upper levels of the building, there are no clear distinctions for phasing between the north church and the funeral chapel. This puzzled us for a long time. When we cleaned the masonry of the east façade, however, we exposed a joint that extends from ground level to just above the prothesis window of the funeral chapel (fig. 11).[53] The window, an afterthought, cuts into the masonry at the southwest corner of the north church, opening into the prothesis of

---

[50] Robert Ousterhout, "The Use and Reuse of Brick in Byzantine Architecture: Lessons from the Zeyrek Camii," *AVISTA Forum Journal* 15/1 (2005), 32–35; idem, "Brickstamps from the Zeyrek Camii," in *Bizans ve Çevre Kültürler: Prof. Dr. S. Yıldız Ötüken Armağan*, eds. S. Doğan and M. Kadiroğlu (Istanbul: Vehbi Koç Vakfı, 2010), 245–53.

[51] Ousterhout, "Architectural Decoration," 432–39.

[52] Ibid, esp. figs. 5–6.

[53] See Ousterhout, Ahunbay, and Ahunbay, "Second Report," esp. 253–54, and fig. 24.

the funeral chapel. The brick courses above it were anchored with the insertion of a reused marble fragment from a window frame. Above this level, the brick courses are continuous and bonded, even though the articulation of the two components remains distinct, with a setback between the two. As the evidence here clearly indicates, the funeral chapel was begun *after* construction the north church was well under way, but two were completed simultaneously.

This relative chronology helps to explain several details in the interior. The cornices are set at the same height in the north church and funeral chapel, even extending between the spaces in the eastern arch, while those in the south church are set at a considerably higher level. The surviving evidence of mosaic and sculptural decoration also corresponds technically and stylistically between the two spaces. In terms of architectural design, the funeral chapel appears as an afterthought, but the evidence of the masonry indicates an uninterrupted process of construction.

Within the funeral chapel there are also indications of changes in the design. It was most likely begun as a single-domed space but was modified during the process of construction. The unique, twin-domed design undoubtedly related to its double function, for it was divided between a liturgical space to the east and the burial area to the west, as the *Typikon* suggests. The large western dome was completed first, and then the smaller eastern dome was built against it, with some unfinished surfaces where the two join (fig. 12).[54] This helps to explain the formal difference between the two, already noted. Because the plan of the eastern bay was already determined, the east dome had to be constructed above an oblong bay, resulting in its unprecedented oval form. The addition of the second dome may have been purely for aesthetic reasons, but it might have also responded to the lighting conditions of the interior: sandwiched between the two churches and framed on the west by the narthex and gallery, the interior would have been quite dark, and the dome's windows provided an additional source of natural light.[55]

Other changes of design were effected when the outer narthex was added, which extended in front the original west façade of the south church. It seems to have been designed as a lower space covered by a sloping wooden roof, the height of which corresponded to the sills of the gallery windows behind it. Clear evidence of the original roofline is provided by the angled line of brick on its exterior north façade, directly above the window arch (fig. 13). During the construction

---

[54] Ibid, 21.
[55] Additional windows were added to the south crossarm vault of the north church for similar reasons; see Ousterhout, Ahunbay, and Ahunbay, "Second Report," esp. 241.

of the outer narthex, however, the masons decided to increase the height and to introduce vaulting. The motivation for this change is unclear; it has resulted in a space that is lofty but dark, with windows positioned only in the lower walls. The original stepped profiles of the pilasters and arches of the original narthex façade were simplified and strengthened, with marble cornices inserted in order to anchor the vaulting. The setbacks of the original arches were cut away to create an angled and slightly concave surface within each, which was probably plastered and painted. The narthex originally opened by three doors, while the outer narthex had a single, axial doorway, with windows in the lunettes of the flanking arcades and large triple windows in the lateral walls. All openings were set below the level of the original roofline, and the vaulting rises in darkness above them.

The addition of the vaulted outer narthex motivated several other alterations. The most important of these was the addition of the dome over the gallery of the south church (that is, above the inner narthex), which blocked the west window of the *katholikon*. The details of the central arcade are considerably different from those of the others, as it was altered to support the dome. Its windows rise above a level of unfinished masonry, indicating that the alteration only occurred *after* the outer narthex was added—that is, when the unfinished area was already covered by the exonarthex roof.

The details of the construction are noteworthy: both the east chapel dome and the narthex gallery dome are twelve-sided pumpkin domes, in contrast to the south church dome and the west chapel dome, which are sixteen-sided ribbed domes. Moreover, the bricks used in the construction of the two pumpkin domes are smaller than the standard bricks used elsewhere. The standard brick size is 38 x 4.5 cm, while those in the east chapel dome measure 24 x 2.5-3.0 cm, and those in the narthex gallery dome measure 30 x 3 cm. Small bricks also appear in remade window arches of the central arcade. It would seem that new sources of brick were employed for the final modifications to the church.

Returning to the narthex gallery dome, the motivation for the addition of yet another dome into an already complex building may seem difficult to explain. But the addition of the vaulted outer narthex eliminated almost all sources of natural light to the inner narthex, and the entrance into the *katholikon* became exceptionally dark. The gallery dome was added in combination with the removal of the vaulting above the central bay of the inner narthex, creating a light well at the entrance (fig. 14). While this seems to be an odd solution, it was imitated elsewhere, at the Kyriotissa in Constantinople and at S. Marco in Venice.[56] The elaborations to

---

[56] As I have discussed elsewhere; see Ousterhout, "Pantokrator Monastery."

the inner and outer narthex areas might also reflect the growing importance of these spaces in monastic ritual.[57]

These changes happened in a gradual, step-by-step process. And although it was completely irregular in its final form, the complex of the Pantokrator is too important for us to dismiss as simply the unfortunate product of an inept designer. The master mason, a certain Nikephoros, was apparently a man of distinction, who was said to have been the *synergates* (co-worker) of Empress Eirene and was lauded as "a new Bezalel." We may puzzle over his design decisions, but he clearly was held in high regard during Byzantine times. Moreover, details of construction, such as the distinctively etched mortarbeds, with boxed X's, indicate that the same workshop of masons was responsible for the entire complex—these details on the south church were covered with plaster before the other churches were added. As I have discussed elsewhere, the *ad hoc* design and construction of the complex actually correspond to Michael Psellos's descriptions of great imperial building projects of the eleventh century—and they might actually represent standard practices.[58] That is, design and construction happened simultaneously, with details determined and modifications introduced as the building rose, the processes inextricably linked. All of this suggests the experimental nature of the imperial couple's project at the Pantokrator: they were intent to create something new—formally, functionally, and symbolically.

One of my thwarted fantasies in the restoration project was to discover areas of the building's original mosaic decoration. While often mentioned in the *Typikon* and in historical texts, the only portion visible was in the window reveal of the north church. We found a similar decorative pattern (figs. 15–16) in the apse window of the *heroon*, and similar patterns in fresco in the exonarthex windows.[59] But we also found thousands of tesserae and fragments of setting plaster in the rubble fill of the roof and windows. And curiously, the nineteenth-century plaster has tesserae mixed into it, all of this indicating that the mosaics must have fallen during earthquakes of the eighteenth and nineteenth centuries or were removed during the subsequent restorations.

Nevertheless, we were able to observe enough of the decorative elements to say something about the stylistic unity of the building project. For example, the palmette pattern of the cornices, with a pinecone marking the corner, matches a group

---

[57] See Marinis, *Architecture and Ritual*, 64–76.
[58] R. Ousterhout, "Contextualizing the Later Churches of Constantinople: Suggested Methodologies and a Few Examples," *Dumbarton Oaks Papers* 54 (2000), 241–50.
[59] Ousterhout, Ahunbay, and Ahunbay, "Second Report," 248–50; Ousterhout, "Decoration," 432–33.

of capitals from the building—one uncovered in situ, another removed to Venice.[60] Another set of capitals were decorated with vine scrolls, either carved or painted, including one now in Berlin. Similar vine scrolls appear on the upper cornice of the north church, which imitates a Late Antique pattern found on a much larger cornice block now in the Istanbul Archaeological Museum. Similar rinceau patterns appear in several different media. And the vine scrolls in paint, *opus sectile*, and marble have distinctive knots joining them where the stems come together. Richly decorated throughout, the *opus sectile*, stained glass, mosaic, and sculpture would have competed visually with each other and probably appeared garish to our eyes. The Byzantines believed in gilding the lily—quite literally: as we uncovered areas of broken cornice and cornice blocks in the fill, we found traces of a red boll (the fixative for gold leaf), as well as areas of gold leaf—which came away with the plaster. Rather than highlighted with gold, the cornices were covered with it.

In its final form, the significance of the Pantokrator was expressed by its complexity; separate functional spaces are clearly distinguished on the exterior, identified by their distinctive apses and domes, which were prominent features on the urban skyline. In the course of less than eighteen years of construction, we witness a dramatic change in architectural style, within a single workshop, and within a single building. And, of course, we also witness the concomitant development of a new kind of expression of political power and familial prestige—something I suspect also developed only gradually—just as the building complex had.[61]

One of the critical clues for understanding the special meanings of the Pantokrator as a mausoleum is the reference in the *Typikon* to the imperial burial chapel as the *heroon*. To my knowledge the only other buildings referred to by this antiquated term of which John would have been aware were the mausolea of Constantine and Justinian at the Holy Apostles.[62] The use of the term must have been intended to draw a comparison between John's new imperial mausoleum and the older and more famous ones nearby. Perhaps its only physical similarity with the Holy Apostles is its five domes, but these were constructed sequentially as the complex grew and not planned from the beginning. Although the two buildings were completely different in their designs, the connection was ideological, associated with their function as imperial mausolea.

I believe there are more specific links between the two complexes. The first depends on how was the term *heroon* understood, as it appears in the Pantokrator

---

[60] For what follows, see Ousterhout, "Decoration," 432–39.
[61] See my comments, Ousterhout, "Contextualizing," 245–46.
[62] I discuss this relationship at greater length in R. Ousterhout, "The Church of the Holy Apostles and Its Place in Later Byzantine Architecture," in press.

Figure 1. Monastery of Christ Pantrokrator (Zeyrek Camii), seen from the east, 2005 (author)

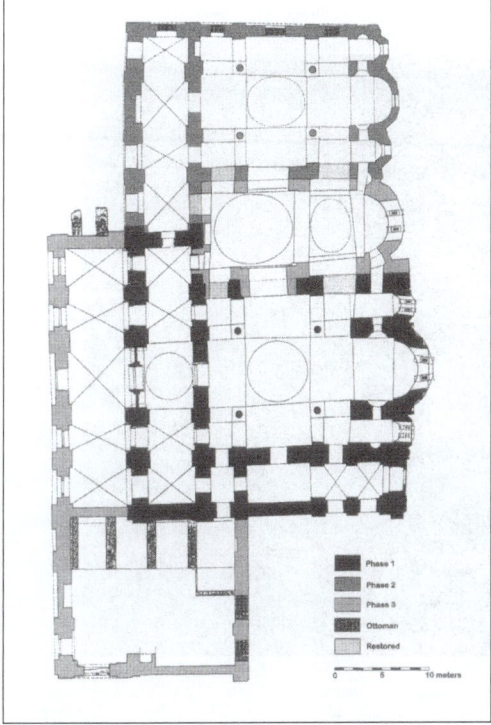

Figure 2. Same, plan showing phases of construction (author, based on Megaw)

Figure 3. Same, south church, interior, looking southeast, 2002 (author)

Figure 4. Same, south church, reconstructed west façade (author, based on Ebersolt and Thiers)

Figure 5. Same, south church, hypothetical reconstruction of the bema windows (Megaw, courtesy of Dumbarton Oaks)

Figure 6. Same, south church, *opus sectile* floor before conservation © The Byzantine Institute and Dumbarton Oaks Fieldwork Records and Papers, late 1950s

Figure 7. Same, south church, *opus sectile* floor, detail of the wheel of the zodiac, after conservation © The Byzantine Institute and Dumbarton Oaks Fieldwork Records and Papers, late 1950s

Figure 8. Same. South church, *opus sectile* floor, detail of the life of Sampson, showing (counterclockwise) Sampson and the gates of Gaza, Sampson smiting the Assyrians, Sampson and the lion © The Byzantine Institute and Dumbarton Oaks Fieldwork Records and Papers, late 1950s

Figure 9. Same, central chapel, interior looking west, showing proposed locations of tombs and mosaic imagery (author, based on a 2014 photograph by A. Vinogradov)

Figure 10. Same, central chapel, section, showing relative heights and sizes of domes (Ebersolt and Thiers)

Figure 11. Same, east façade, showing the connection between the central chapel (left) and the north church (right, with the joint at center), 2005 (author)

Figure 12. Same, domes and roof of the central chapel and north church, looking north, after the replacement of the lead sheeting and windows, 2002 (author)

Figure 13. Same, exonarthex seen from the northwest, with the indication of the change in elevation a diagonal line of brick, 2004 (author)

Figure 14. Same, section through south church, narthex, and exonarthex, showing the position of the gallery dome above the narthex (Ebersolt and Thiers)

Figure 15. Same, central chapel, bema window, showing remnants of mosaic in the reveal, with traces of gold leaf on the cornice above, 2004 (author)

Figure 16. Same, exonarthex, north window, showing wall painting in the reveals, 2005 (author)

Figure 17. Same, view of the complex from the west, ca. 1840, with the so-called sarcophagus of Eirene to the right (Brunet de Presle)

Figure 18. Distant view of the complex from the east with the domes of the Fatih Camii rising behind it—the multi-domed church of the Holy Apostles would have been in the same position as the Fatih Camii in Byzantine times. Thomas F. Mathews, Dumbarton Oaks, Trustees for Harvard University, Washington D. C.

Typikon.⁶³ The term is actually first applied to an imperial mausoleum by Cassius Dio to refer to the Mausoleum of Augustus. Traditionally, the term *heroon* designated the shrine of a hero who has achieved the status of demigod through accomplishments on this earth. Although archaizing, it is used in especial frequency during the Middle Byzantine centuries with respect to the mausolea of Justinian and Constantine: by Constantine Porphyrogennetos, in the *Catalogus Sepulchrorum*, by Cedrenus, by Symeon the Logothete, by Niketas Choniates, in the *vita Ignatii*, as well as in the *ekphrasis* of Nikolaos Mesarites.⁶⁴

In their earthly roles, these emperors were also known as great warriors. Constantine, like Augustus, had brought peace to the empire by putting down the tyranny of his Tetrarchic contemporaries. Justinian, although not a warrior himself, oversaw military campaigns on the European, African, and Asian frontiers, as chronicled by Prokopios and commemorated by the triumphal column and statue in the Augusteion. John, like his father Alexios, went to battle for the security of the empire and was fighting against the Seljuks in Asia when his consort Piroska-Eirene passed away in 1134—that is, immediately before the *Typikon* was written. A *heroon* could be understood as a sort of war memorial, commemorating a victorious military leader. As Magdalino has suggested, the Pantokrator is presented as a monument to imperial victory—at least according to John.⁶⁵

An important distinction of the *heroa* at the Holy Apostles is that they were fully independent funerary structures attached to the church. The church and its annexes had been last used for imperial burial for Constantine VIII, who was inserted into the mausoleum of Constantine a century earlier. Subsequent emperors had not devised a strategy for their own burials, beyond the foundation of grand monastic complexes, where communities of monks could commemorate them *in perpetuum*.⁶⁶ To my knowledge, the Pantokrator represents the first imperial example to include a separate mausoleum, and this marks a significant shift in burial practices. Indeed, the change came about only gradually as the complex grew. Initially the narthex may have been the intended site of the burials, but as the complex was

---

63 Gautier, "Typikon," esp. 72–73
64 Mark J. Johnson, *The Roman Imperial Mausoleum in Late Antiquity* (Cambridge, 2014), esp. 186, with further references, 250, n. 54.
65 Magdalino, "Foundation," 54.
66 See J. P. Thomas, "In Perpetuum. Social and Political Consequences of Byzantine Patrons' Aspirations for Permanence for their Foundations," in *Stiftungen in Christentum, Judentum und Islam vor der Moderne. Auf der Suche nach ihren Gemeinsamkeiten und Unterschieden in religiösen Grundlagen, praktischen Zwecken und historischen Transformationen*, ed. M. Borgolte (Berlin, 2005), 123–35.

enlarged, a separate funerary chapel was added—a substantial structure that competed in scale and prominence with the churches to either side.

A related consideration was the necessity of additional space for the commemorative services at the imperial tombs. At an imperial *heroon* of old, the ceremony of *consecratio* would have honored the *apotheosis* of the emperor, which in Christian terms became the commemoration of the *dies natalis* or the day of death.[67] Constantine the Great was so honored long after his passing by Constantine Porphyrogennetos, as recorded in the *Book of Ceremonies*.[68] Perhaps the *ad hoc* commemorative ceremonies at the Pantokrator, which involved rerouting the procession from the Blachernae, with its *signa* and icons, might be viewed as a reflection of the ceremonies that honored the revered emperors at the Holy Apostles.[69] While other middle and late Byzantine *typika* might specify monastic commemoration of the deceased, there is nothing quite comparable to the ceremonies at the Pantokrator. Moreover, as the *Typikon* indicates again and again, the Pantokrator was an urban monument, provided with its own colonnaded street that linked it to the urban matrix.

Finally, we should consider the concept of the sainted ruler. Constantine was venerated as St. Constantine, and other emperors, even if not sainted, received similar veneration by visitors to the Holy Apostles. Magdalino has suggested that there may be a reflection at the Pantokrator of the Macedonian emperors attempts to co-opt the Holy Apostles as a dynastic *lieu de mémoire* by associating their own familial cult with that of Constantine and royal sainthood.[70] The promotion of the sainted Piroska-Eirene at the Pantokrator seems to mirror attempts to sanctify Theophano, wife of Leo VI, at the Holy Apostles. The promotion of the cult of Piroska-Eirene seems to belong to the period of her son Manuel; it is not mentioned in the *Typikon*.

And what became of Piroska-Eirene's tomb? For centuries a great *verde antico* sarcophagus lay in front of the Pantokrator and was regularly said to be that of St. Eirene (fig. 17). It has since been moved to the narthex of Hagia Sophia.[71] Late Antique in origin, it could not be that of Piroska-Eirene, as it is too large to fit through the door of the church; it must have come from elsewhere. Could it be

---

[67] See the discussion by Johnson, *Roman Imperial Mausoleum*, 88–89.
[68] *de Cer*. 2.6; ed. A. Moffatt and M. Tall, *Constantine Porphyrogennetos, The Book of Ceremonies* (Canberra, 2012), II.532–35
[69] Gauthier, "Typikon," 80–83; N. P. Ševčenko, "Icons and the Liturgy," *DOP* 45 (1991), 45–57; B. V. Pentcheva, *Icons and Power. The Mother of God in Byzantium* (University Park, PA, 2006), 165–87.
[70] Magdalino, "Foundation," 47.
[71] Gyula Moravcsik, *Szent László leánya és a Bizánci Pantokrator Monostor* (Budapest, 1923), 6; also József Deér, *Dynastic Porphyry Tombs of the Norman Period in Sicily* (Cambridge, 1959), 133–34. The first mention of the sarcophagus may be by Richard Pococke, *A description of the East, and some other countries* (London, 1745), II: 130.

from the cemetery that developed around the Holy Apostles, and how close to the Pantokrator did it extend? It is worth noting that the tombs in the *heroon* were set into arcosolia, but the standard practice for privileged burials at this time was for the body to be interred below floor level, with a cenotaph above.[72] To my knowledge, no one has ever looked beneath the floor, so there may still be preserved evidence of imperial burials—although I don't expect excavation any time soon.

The relationship with the Holy Apostles may be particularly important, and although Justinian's church has completely disappeared, there would have been a visual relationship between the two complexes in the Byzantine period. The multi-domed church of the Holy Apostles was part of a large cluster of buildings, which included mausolea to its east, as well as the smaller church of All Saints. Today we can see in the same location the eighteenth-century Fatih Camii and the türbe of Mehmet II. Beneath this rose the cluster of domes of the Pantokrator. Seen from a distance, the two complexes—the Holy Apostles and the Pantokrator—would have merged together (fig. 18).

Even viewed individually, the jumble of domes and disparate building components at the Pantokrator surely meant something to the Byzantine viewer, identifying the site as significant, a place where many things happened. In short, complexity rather than monumentality would have been the dominant visual impression, with the exterior view perhaps more important than the interior. Like the Holy Apostles, the Pantokrator was bound to the urban matrix by porticoes and processions, visible symbols of imperial presence.

In its final form, the complex design of the Pantokrator lay behind the construction of several of the later Byzantine imperial and aristocratic burial churches. Perhaps most important of these was the Monastery *tou Libos*, which consciously followed the church cluster plan developed at the Pantokrator, with the south church added to serve as a grand mausoleum for the immediate family of Michael VIII Palaiologos.[73] However, it is never referred to as a *heroon*—and for good reason: no heroes were involved in its construction. The monastery had been refounded by Theodora, the widow of Michael VIII, himself a usurper to the throne who had died in disgrace as a heretic and was not accorded an Orthodox burial. Their son Andronikos II, who was buried in the church, and was Orthodox, was an

---

[72] On this issue see S. Ćurčić, "Medieval Royal Tombs in the Balkans: An Aspect of the 'East or West' Question," *Greek Orthodox Theological Review* 29 (1984), 175–94.

[73] V. Marinis, "Tombs and Burials in the Monastery *tou Libos* in Constantinople," *DOP* 63 (2009), 147–166; A.-M. Talbot, "Empress Theodora Palaiologina, Wife of Michael VIII," *DOP* 46 (1992) 295–303; Typikon of Theodora Palaiologina for the Convent of Lips in Constantinople, trans. A.-M. Talbot, in *BFMD*, 1254–1286.

unqualified disaster on the battlefield. The Monastery *tou Libos* is diminished both in scale and in imperial stature.

What prevails in the *tou Libos Typikon* is the piety of the empress. Both manly virtue and feminine piety had been asserted in the *Typikon* of the Kecharitomene monastery, written by John's mother Eirene Doukaina, and John's presentation of the Pantokrator emphasizes manly virtue. The inauguration epigram for the Pantokrator included a prayer for imperial victory, and the *heroon* at the Pantokrator stood as a victory monument—at least that is how I read John's intentions. But times and sentiments change. Even within a few decades of his death, the elaborate memorial services specified in the *Typikon* seem to have ceased, and at the same time the cult of St. Eirene was promoted.[74] Later visitors were less interested in bellicose commemorations than they were in saintly relics. As the memory of imperial victory faded, the piety of the empress came to the fore. As I have argued, the Pantokrator was meant to represent both aspects of the Komnenian ideology, and the changed emphasis from manly valor to female piety marks an important shift in later Byzantine thought. In the end, Piroska-Eirene has the last word.

Bibliography
Primary Sources

Constantine Porphyrogennetos. *De Cerimoniis Aulae Byzantinae*, CSHB (Bonn 1829). Trans. A. Moffatt and M. Tall. *The Book of Ceremonies*. Canberra, 2012. 2 vols.

Ioannes Kinnamos. *Historia* Ed. A. Meineke. *CSHB* (Bonn 1836). Trans. C. Brand, *Deeds of John and Manuel Comnenus by John Kinnamos*. New York, 1976.

Gautier, Paul. "Le typikon du Christ Sauveur Pantocrator," *Revue des Études Byzantins* 32 (1974), 1–145.

Niketas Choniates. *Historia*, ed. A. van Dieten. *CFHB*, 11/1 (Berlin 1975).

Byzantine Monastic Foundation Documents. Eds. Thomas, J., P., and A. Hero. Dumbarton Oaks Studies 35. Washington, D.C., 2000, 5 vols.

Secondary Sources

Ahunbay, Metin and Zeynep Ahunbay. "Restoration work at the Zeyrek Camii, 1997–1998," In: *Byzantine Constantinople: Monuments, Topography and Everyday Life*. Ed. Nevra Necipoğlu (Leiden: Brill, 2001), 117–32.

---

[74] Magdalino, "Foundation," 54.

Barral i Altet, Xavier. "Un programme iconographique occidental pour le pavement medieval de l'église du Christ Pantocrator de Constantinople." in *Many Romes: Studies in Honor of Hans Belting*, eds. I. Foletti and H. Kessler, *Convivium* II/1 (2015), 219-32.

Brill, R. H. *Chemical Analyses of Early Glasses*. Corning, 1999. 2 vols.

Ćurčić, Slobodan. "Medieval Royal Tombs in the Balkans: An Aspect of the 'East or West' Question." *Greek Orthodox Theological Review* 29 (1984), 175-94.

———. "What was the Real Function of Late Byzantine Katechoumena?" *Byzantine Studies Conference Abstracts* 19, 1993, 8-9.

Deér, Josef von. *Dynastic Porphyry Tombs of the Norman Period in Sicily*. Cambridge, 1959.

Dell'Acqua, Francesca. "The Stained-Glass Windows from the Chora and the Pantokrator Monasteries: A Byzantine 'Mystery'?" in *Restoring Byzantium: The Kariye Camii in Istanbul and the Byzantine Institute Restoration*, eds. H. Klein and R. Ousterhout. New York, 2004, 68-77.

Ebersolt, Jean, and Adolphe Thiers. *Les églises de Constantinople*. Paris, 1913.

Gilles, Pierre [Petrus Gyllius]. *The Four Books of the Antiquities of Constantinople*. London 1729.

Henderson, Julian, and Marlia Mundell Mango, "Glass at Medieval Constantinople: Preliminary Scientific Evidence." in C. Mango and G. Dagron, eds., *Constantinople and Its Hinterland*. Aldershot, 1995, 333-56.

Jacoby, David. "The Urban Evolution of Constantinople (1204-1261)." in Necipoğlu, ed., *Byzantine Constantinople*. 277-97.

Janin, Raymond. *La Géographie ecclésiastique de l'empire byzantin: Les églises et les monastères*, I, Paris, 1969.

Johnson, M. J. *The Roman Imperial Mausoleum in Late Antiquity*. Cambridge, 2014.

Kazhdan, Alexander. "Die Liste der Kinder des Alexios I in einer moskauer Handschrift." *Beiträge zur Alten Geschichte und deren Nachleben*, II. Berlin, 1970, 233-37.

Kotzabassi, Sofia. "Feasts at the Monastery of Pantokrator." in Kotzabassi, ed., *Pantokrator Monastery*, 153-90.

———, ed. *The Pantokrator Monastery in Constantinople*. Byzantinisches Archiv 27. Berlin, 2013.

Lafond, Jacques. "Découverte de vitraux historiés du Moyen Age à Constantinople." *Cahiers Archéologiques* 18 (1968), 231-37.

Laurent, V. *Les 'Mémoires' de Sylvestre Syropoulos sur le concile de Florence (1438-1439)*. Paris, 1971.

Loukadi, M. "Empress Piroska-Eirene's Collaborators in the Foundation of the Pantokrator Monastery: The Testimony of Nikolaos Kataphloron," in Kotzabassi, ed., *Pantokrator Monastery*, 191-201.

Magdalino, Paul. *L'Orthodoxie des astrologues: la science entre le dogme et la divination a Byzance (VIIe-XIVe siecle)*, Realités Byzantines 12. Paris, 2006.

―――. "The Pantokrator Monastery in its Urban Setting." in Kotzabassi, ed., *Pantokrator Monastery*, 33–55.

―――. *The Empire of Manuel I Komnenos. 1143–1180*. (Cambridge: Cambridge University Press, 1993).

Maguire, Henry. *Earth and Ocean: The Terrestrial World in Early Byzantine Art*. University Park, PA, 1987.

Marinis, Vasileios. "Tombs and Burials in the Monastery *tou Libos* in Constantinople," *Dumbarton Oaks Papers* 63 (2009), 147–166.

―――. *Architecture and Ritual in the Churches of Constantinople, Ninth to Fifteenth Centuries*. (Cambridge: Cambridge University Press, 2014).

Megaw, A.H.S. "Notes on the Recent Work of the Byzantine Institute in Istanbul." *Dumbarton Oaks Papers* 17 (1963), 333–64.

Moravcsik, Gyula. *Szent László leánya és a bizánci Pantokrator-monostor. Die Tochter Ladislaus des Heiligen und das Pantokrator-Kloster in Konstantinopel*. (Budapest-Konstantinápoly: A konstantinápolyi Magyar Tudományos Intézet Közleményei—Mitteilungen des Ungarischen Wissenschaftlichen Institutes in Konstantinopel 7–8, 1923).

Nagymihályi, Géza. *Árpád-házi Szent Piroska: az idegen szent*. [Saint Piroska of the Árpád Dynasty: The Foreign Saint]. (Budapest: Kairosz Kiadó, 2007).

Necipoğlu, Nevra. (ed.) *Byzantine Constantinople: Monuments, Topography and Everyday Life*. (Leiden: Brill, 2001).

Ousterhout, Robert. "Brickstamps from the Zeyrek Camii." in *Bizans ve Çevre Kültürler: Prof. Dr. S. Yıldız Ötüken Armağan*, eds. S. Doğan and M. Kadiroğlu. Istanbul, 2010, 245–53.

―――. "Contextualizing the Later Churches of Constantinople: Suggested Methodologies and a Few Examples." *Dumbarton Oaks Papers* 54 (2000), 241–50.

―――. "The Architectural Decoration of the Pantokrator Monastery: Evidence Old and New." *Papers of the First Sevgi Gönül Memorial Symposium 2007* (Istanbul, 2010), 432–39.

―――. "The Pantokrator Monastery and Architectural Interchanges in the Thirteenth Century," in *Quarta Crociata: Venezia—Bizanzio—Impero Latino*, eds. G. Ortalli, G Ravegnani, P. Schreiner. Venice, 2006, II: 749–70.

―――. "Women at Tombs: Narrative, Theatricality, and the Contemplative Mode." in *Wonderful Things: Byzantium through its Art*, eds. A. Eastmond and L. James (Farnham: Aldershot, 2013), 229–46.

Ousterhout, Robert, Zeynep Ahunbay and Metin Ahunbay. "Study and Restoration of the Zeyrek Camii in Istanbul: First Report, 1997–98." *Dumbarton Oaks Papers* 54 (2000), 265–70.

―――. "Study and Restoration of the Zeyrek Camii in Istanbul: Second Report, 2001–05." *Dumbarton Oaks Papers* 63 (2010), 235–56.

Pentcheva, Bissera. *Icons and Power: The Mother of God in Byzantium*. (University Park, PA: Pennsylvania University Press, 2006.)

Pocoke, Richard. *A Description of the East, and Some Other Countries*. London, 1745.

Ševčenko, Nancy. P. "Icons and the Liturgy," *Dumbarton Oaks Papers* 45 (1991), 45–57.

Shvidkovsky, Dimitry. *Russian Architecture and the West*. New Haven, 2007.

Spieser, Jean-Michel. "Le monastère du Pantocrator à Constantinople: Le typikon et le monument." in *Many Romes: Studies in Honor of Hans Belting*, eds. I. Foletti and H. Kessler, *Convivium* II/1 (2015), 203–16.

Stanković, Vlada. "The Komnenoi and Conastantinople before the Building of the Pantokrator Complex." in Kotzabassi, ed., *Pantokrator Monastery*, 3–31.

Talbot, Alice-Mary. "Empress Theodora Palaiologina, Wife of Michael VIII." *Dumbarton Oaks Papers* 46 (1992) 295–303.

Thomas, J. P. "In Perpetuum. Social and Political Consequences of Byzantine Patrons' Aspirations for Permanence for their Foundations." in *Stiftungen in Christentum, Judentum und Islam vor der Moderne. Auf der Suche nach ihren Gemeinsamkeiten und Unterschieden in religiösen Grundlagen, praktischen Zwecken und historischen Transformationen*, ed. M. Borgolte. (Berlin, 2005), 123–35.

Trilling, James. "The Soul of the Empire: Style and Meaning in the Mosaic Pavement of the Byzantine Imperial Palace in Constantinople." *Dumbarton Oaks Papers* 43 (1989), 27–72.

Underwood, Paul A. *The Kariye Djami*. (New York: Pantheon Books, 1966). 3 vols.

Van Millingen, Alexander. *Byzantine Churches in Constantinople: Their History and Architecture*. London, 1912.

Vassis, Ioannis. "Das Pantokratorkloster von Konstantinopel in der byzantinischen Dichtung," in Kotzabassi, ed., *Pantokrator Monastery*, 203–49.

Whittemore, Thomas. *The Mosaics of St. Sophia at Istanbul*. (Paris: The Byzantine Institute, 1933–38.)

PIROSKA-EIRENE AND THE HOLY THEOTOKOS

Etele Kiss

The portrait of Piroska-Eirene in the south gallery of the Hagia Sophia is one of the most beautiful and most reproduced images of a Byzantine empress since its rediscovery by Thomas Whittemore in 1934.[1] Standing next to her husband, Emperor John II Komnenos and their eldest son Alexios, she is portrayed with a roll in her hand, in an act of donation to the Holy Mother of God with the infant Christ. Her iconic image became the prototype of modern icons and features on the covers of books about Byzantine empresses.[2]

While Piroska-Eirene's image is well-known, her life remains shrouded in obscurity. The only empress canonized by the Orthodox Church in the eleventh and twelfth century, her hagiographical *Life* concentrates on her role in the foundation of the Christ Pantokrator Monastery complex, disclosing little about other traits of her character. Paradoxically, the very exemplarity of Piroska-Eirene's life—her devotion to God and to her husband, the life-long love and mutual fidelity that united them (unusual in Byzantine imperial couples)—conceals, rather than reveals, her personality. John and Piroska-Eirene are among the least known rulers of the Middle Byzantine period: chronicles say little of them, and even less of her. Is it not on

---

[1] The imperial mosaics in Hagia Sophia's south vestibule were discovered by the Fossati brothers in 1848, who recovered them with plaster. Thomas Whittemore and his team rediscovered them in 1934, but cleansing finished only in 1935: Cyril Mango, *Materials for the Study of the Mosaics of Hagia Sophia*, (Washington, D.C.: Dumbarton Oaks,1962, 27–29; Natalia B. Teteriatnikov, *Mosaics of Hagia Sophia, Istanbul: The Fossati Restauration and the Work of the Byzantine Institute*, (Washington, D.C.: Dumbarton Oaks, 1998), fig. 51.

[2] Lynda Garland, *Byzantine Empresses, Women and Power in Byzantium AD 527–1204* (London, New York, Routledge, 1999); Barbara Hill, *Imperial Women in Byzantium 1025–1204* (Harlow: Pearson-Longman, 1999); ironically enough, even Leonora A. Neville's *Anna Komnene, the Life and Work of a Medieval Historian* (Oxford, OUP, 2016), hereafter: Neville, *Anna Komnene* represents Eirene on the cover, while the sister-in-law has hardly a world to say about her in her Alexiad.

purpose that we know so little of the life of the imperial couple? Was it not their own intention to remain private?

This paper suggests that Piroska-Eirene's life remained hidden because it was lived as an imitation of the Holy Virgin. The following of Christ, of the Virgin Mary and of the saints constituted the highest religious ideal of medieval spirituality. The intensity of Marian devotion is the most impressive feature of twelfth-century Christianity. Discussing the extraordinary veneration of the Mother of God in Hungary and Byzantium, the two Christian realms under her special protection, I highlight that the cult of the Holy Virgin deeply impacted spiritual life and sacred art, as well as political theology in Hungary and Byzantium. I wish to argue that the cult of the Theotokos shaped not only national and dynastic spirituality, but also individual vocation, and thus helps understanding Piroska-Eirene's drive and character. The new, emotional devotion to the Mother of God will allow to link dispersed or lost artworks to Piroska's piety and to her great foundation, the Pantokrator Monastery complex. Christian ideals formed not only her soul, but also her imperial image in Constantinople, where she associated herself with the Theotokos and had herself represented as re-enacting the virtues of the Mother of God.

Piroska and the Cult of the Holy Virgin in Hungary

Heavenly helper of kings and simple believers, the Mother of God had been venerated from the beginning of the Christianization of the Hungarian tribes. King Stephen of Hungary had a special veneration for the Holy Virgin, trusted her help in battle and asked for her intercession for the realm.[3] He dedicated several cathedral churches and monasteries in her honor, such as the Greek nunnery of Veszprémvölgy and the Provostry Church of Székesfehérvár, the main royal basilica of the realm.[4] Apart from the legends that attest King Stephen's cult of the Holy Virgin, a rare visual example related to the royal court testifies to the intensity of the king's Marian devotion. An *orans* Virgin Mary in a mandorla surrounded by the four apocalyptic beasts (Fig. 1) is

---

[3] Hartvic, *Life of King Stephen of Hungary*, Tr. Nora Berend. In: *Medieval Hagiography. An Anthology*, ed. Thomas Head (New York-London: Garland, 2000), 379–396.

[4] The Cathedrals of Győr, Csanád, Bihar, Vác were dedicated to the Holy Virgin and she was the co-patroness of the Archbishopric of Esztergom, of the Abbey of Pécsvárad and perhaps also of the Archbishopric of Kalocsa. The Veszprémvölgy Greek nunnery was dedicated to the Most Holy Mother of God. The Royal Provostry of Székesfehérvár, of utmost importance to King Stephen, was dedicated to the Assumption of the Holy Virgin. See Géza Érszegi, "Ég és Föld királynője, Mária." [Mary, Queen of Heaven and Earth], in *Scripta manent, Ünnepi tanulmányok Gerics József professzor tiszteletére* [Festschrift in Honor of Professor József Gerics], ed. Draskóczy, István, (Budapest: Eötvös Lóránd Tudományegyetem, 1994), 37.

represented on the left shoulder of the chasuble donated by King Stephen and Queen Gisela to the Church of the Holy Virgin in Székesfehérvár in 1031.[5] The Leonine inscription around this representation of the *Maiestas Mariae* emphasizes the revelation of her image in the heaven ("*Emicat in celo Sanctae Genitricis imago*"). Depictions of the *Maiestas Mariae* have strong imperial overtones. In the apse of Aquileia, the painting made for the re-dedication of the patriarchal cathedral in July 1031 in the presence of Emperor Conrad II and his son, King Henry III, the Virgin Mary enthroned with her Child is similarly surrounded by a mandorla and the four apocalyptic animals as on the Hungarian chasuble, flanked by rulers and other dignitaries.[6] Henry III arrived to Aquileia from Hungary after having signed a peace treaty with King Stephen. The chasuble's representation of the Virgin Mary in prayer has parallels not only in South German miniatures from the 1030's,[7] but also in eleventh-century Byzantine church apse mosaics, such as Saint Sophia of Kiev or *Nea Moni* in Chios, a probable reflection of the lost apse mosaic of the Blachernai Church.[8]

In Constantinople, the major event in 1030–31 was the discovery of a long lost, pre-iconoclastic icon of the Holy Virgin in the Blachernai shrine. The reappearance of the Blachernai Virgin made a resounding impact on Byzantine cultural and spiritual life. King Stephen might have heard of the reappearance of the Virgin from pilgrims and travellers coming from Constantinople and this might have prompted him to refer to a shining image of the Virgin.[9] Icons of the Virgin kept appearing miraculously in medieval Rome as well.[10]

---

[5] The chasuble later became the coronation mantle, see *The Coronation Mantle of the Hungarian Kings*. István Bardoly, ed. Budapest: Hungarian National Museum, 2005.

[6] For the re-dedication of Aquileia Cathedral under Archbishop Poppo see: Silvia Blason Scarel, (ed.) *Poppone: l'età d'oro del Patriarcato di Aquileia*. Exhibition catalogue. (Aquileia, Museo Civico del Patriarcato), (Rome: "L'Erma" di Bretschneider, 1997), 115–119,148–152.

[7] Augsburg Sacramentary (London BL MS. Harley 2908. f. 123v): the Virgin in prayer is figured in a mandorla, held by angels, but without the four beasts representing her Assumption: Henry Mayr-Harting, *Ottonian Book Illumination*, An Historical Study (London: Harvey Miller, 1991, 1999 (2)) 1, 139–155, fig 89.

[8] Among the different types of icons labeled "Blachernitissa", there is an Orant Virgin *(deomene)* on Constantine IX Monomachos's silver coin, interpreted by Pentcheva as referring to the lost apse mosaic in the Blachernai: B. Pentcheva, Icons and Power, 76., fig. 40, and note 93.

[9] Skylitzes, *Synopsis Historiarum*, (Thurn), 384, 24–28 on the discovery of the Blachernai Virgin in 1030–31. See also John Skylitzes, *A Synopsis of Byzantine History 811–1057* (ed., transl. John Wortley, 2010), 363, and E. Trapp, "Eine wiedergefundene Ikone der Blachernen Kirche," *Jahrbuch der Österreichischen Byzantinistik* 35 (1985): 193–195. Here the icon is clearly referred to as a Virgin holding the Child.

[10] Pietro Zani, *Enciclopedia metodica critico-ragionata delle belle arti: dell' abate D. Piero Zani Fidentino*. (Parma: Tipografia ducale, 1817), pt. 1, vol. 8, p. 161: on one of the best known miraculous images of the Virgin, the icon of Santa Maria in Portico in Campitelli that appeared to a woman named Galla in the sixth century and was highly revered by Gregory the Great.

Almost nothing is known of the medieval decoration of the Provostry Church of the Assumption of the Holy Virgin at Székesfehérvár, except for descriptions in the *Legends of Saint Stephen*[11] and a few mosaic tesserae. The meagre evidence, however, makes it possible to assume that the church had a Byzantine-style apse mosaic representing the Holy Virgin, probably from the original decoration.

The figure of the Holy Virgin on the Székesfehérvár chasuble is a unique source of Marian spirituality from the lifetime of the founder of the Kingdom in Hungary destined to his royal basilica. The chasuble indicates an early devotion to the Holy Virgin in Hungary and discloses unique and innovative aspects of the cult of Mary in the Árpádian dynasty. Its startling emphasis on the supernatural radiance of the image of the Virgin establishes a new, Roman, type of "theology of images," adapted to Western audiences.

The next step in linking the founder of the kingdom to the Holy Virgin was made at the canonization of King Stephen by Piroska's father King Ladislaus in 1083. His wish fulfilled, Stephen died on the day of the Assumption in 1038, and was buried in the Székesfehérvár Basilica of the Holy Virgin, consecrated in haste for the funerals. Since the feast day of Saint Stephen must not have coincided with the feast of the Assumption, Ladislaus chose August 20 for the elevation of his ancestor's relics on the altar. The week of 15–20 August saw not only great religious celebrations in Székesfehérvár, but these were also the "days of justice," when the king, in supreme judge, legislated in court. The "days of justice" started on the Feast of the Assumption—the birth of Mary to divine glory—and ended on the Feast of Saint Stephen, the founder of the kingdom. As the *Vita Maior* of Saint Stephen, composed for his canonisation in 1083, writes:

> This man—King Saint Stephen—was faithful and completely devoted to God in all his acts. He transferred himself together with his kingdom by an oath and offering, with assiduous prayers, to the guardianship of the Mother of God, the ever Virgin Mary. Her glory and honor are so famous among Hungarians, that even the feast of the Assumption of the Virgin is called the Day of the Queen in their language, without the addition of her proper name.[12]

The association of the foundation and the founder with the Holy Virgin, Queen of Heaven must have deeply affected Princess Piroska. Orphaned early—

---

[11] Vita Stephani Maior. In: Emma Bartoniek (ed.) *Scriptores Rerum Hungaricarum* vol. II, Budapest, 1938, 377–392;

[12] Translation by Christian Gaşpar. I thank Gábor Klaniczay for sharing with me the unpublished translation of Saint Stephen's *Legenda Maior*.

she lost her mother at the age of two, her father at the age of seven—, the thought that the Mother of God was the guardian and celestial mother of humankind must have comforted and consoled her. The cult of the Virgin Mary was much more to her than a part of her spiritual education. The letter of Pope Gregory VII written to Piroska's mother Queen Adelaide in 1081 corroborates the suggestion that the Virgin Mary served as a model for queens. Advising Adelaide on reginal demeanor, Gregory focuses on the simplicity and humility of the Virgin:

> Write this in your heart, that the highest Queen of Heaven—who is believed to be exalted over all the choirs of angels, who is the beauty and glory of all women, indeed the salvation and nobility of all the elect, because she alone deserved as virgin and mother to bear naturally God and man, head and life of all good—did not disdain to lead a poor life on earth and to guard herself with all holy humility.[13]

The queen is to follow the example of the Holy Virgin, the "Queen of Heaven" who chose to lead a humble way of life and in following her, she was advised to disdain all earthly and transitory things and glories. The queen was to assist her husband, instil in him the fear of God and persuade him to be merciful towards all. Gregory's letter presenting the Virgin Mary as a model of queens and the scorning of earthly glory as an ultimate virtue was Piroska's most precious heirloom from her mother. She was able to implement its lesson in the Byzantine court, even after becoming an *Augousta*. The papal advice might provide an explanation of why she followed her husband in military campaigns: to exhort her husband to exercise clemency towards captives. It helps understanding of why John and Eirene refrained to punish their relatives who threatened their lives to seize power. The person who profited most from imperial clemency was probably Anna Komnene, who initiated a fatal coup against her brother and did her utmost to pass over John and Eirene's rule in silence in her *Alexiad*.[14] The ill-intentioned historian, paradoxically

---

[13] *Register Gregors VII*, MGH, Epistola Selecta, vol 2. fasc. 2, ed. Erich Gaspar (Berlin: Weidmann, 1923), ep. VIII.22, 564–565 English Translation in Ephraim Emerton, The Correspondence of Pope Gregory VII, Records of Civilization, Columba University Press, 1932, ep. 8, 22. https://epistolae.ccnmtl.columbia.edu/letter/1263.html, last consulted in 01. 01. 2018.

[14] There is, however, a debate raised by Leonora Neville about the lack of evidence of Anna Komnene's plotting against John. See Neville, *Anna Komnene*, 141–151. A different, more traditional approach is outlined by Barbara Hill: "Actions Speak Louder Than Words, Anna Komnene's Attempted Usurpation". in Gouma-Peterson, Thalia (ed.) *Anna Komnene and her times*, Garland, New York, 2000, and Ralph-Johannes Lilie, "Reality and Invention: Reflections on Byzantine Hagiography", in DOP 68 (2014), 178–179.

implemented thereby the imperial couple's spiritual desire to doff all earthly glory. Some other coups came from Isaac, the brother of John in the last years of Piroska's earthly life, but his life was also spared.[15]

Piroska's father, King Ladislaus I (1077–1095) and her cousin, King Coloman the Learned (1095–1116) were outstanding champions of Christianity whose reigns, marked by internal conflict and external expansion, bolstered the process of Christianization in the Kingdom of Hungary.[16] The two kings' far-reaching reform of the Hungarian Church during the Investiture Contest affected the cult of the Virgin Mary: her veneration came to be renewed and reinterpreted by the kings.[17] The Virgin Mary became a constitutional force. Her role in the foundation of the Kingdom was spelled out in the new *Life of Saint Stephen* commissioned by King Coloman. Compiled by Bishop Hartvic, the *Life* claimed that, King Stephen offered his realm on his deathbed to the Virgin Mary.[18] The Holy Virgin thus officially became the Queen of Hungary, patroness of the realm (*Patrona Hungariae*), which, on its turn, became the "Kingdom of Mary" (*Regnum Marianum*).[19] The transformation of King Stephen's and his country's Marian piety into a doctrine of State was singularly reinforced by another claim in the *Life*, namely that the Holy Crown of Hungary was a gift of Pope Sylvester II to King Stephen. The astute combination of these ideas concerned the ultimate source of power in Hungary and conveyed the notion that the Kingdom of the Árpáds was, from its very foundation, sovereign and inde-

---

[15] See Magdalino, P. The Triumph of 1133, in Bucossi, A.–Suarez, A. R. eds. *John II. Komnenos, Emperor of Byzantium*, Routledge Abingdon, 2016. 63–66.

[16] Pál Engel, *The Realm of St Stephen: A History of Medieval Hungary, 895–1526*. London: I.B. Tauris, 2001; Attila Bárány, "The Expansion of the Kingdom of Hungary in the Middle Ages (1000–1490)". In Berend, Nóra (ed.) *The Expansion of Central Europe in the Middle Ages*. Ashgate Variorum. 2012, 333–380.

[17] King Ladislaus's veneration of the Holy Virgin is demonstrated by his dedication of the Bishopric of Várad to the Queen Virgin Mary. For later representations of Ladislaus's Marian devotion, see Terézia Kerny, "Szent László hódolata Szűz Mária előtt (XIV–XIX. század)." [Saint Ladislaus Honoring the Virgin Mary, 14–15th century]. In: *Ghesaurus. Tanulmányok Szentmártoni Szabó Géza hatvanadik születésnapjára*. István Csörsz Rumen (ed.) Budapest: MTA Irodalomtudományi Intézet, 2010. http://plone.iti.mta.hu/rec.iti/Members/szerk/ghesaurus-1/Kerny-Ghesaurus.pdf

[18] Bishop Hartvic, *Life of King Stephen of Hungary*, Tr. Nora Berend, in *Medieval Hagiography. An Anthology*, ed. Thomas Head (New York/London: Garland, 2000), 379–396.

[19] László Németh, "A Regnum Marianum állameszme." [Regnum Marianum as a Theory of State.] *Regnum Egyháztörténeti Évkönyv* (1940–1941): 223–292; Lajos Nagyfalusy, "Le culte de la sainte Vierge en Hongrie". H. Du Manoir de Juaye (ed.) *Maria. Études sur la Sainte Vierge* vol 4. (Paris: Beauchesne, 1956), 645–670; Dezső Dümmerth, "A Mária országa-eszme és Szent István" [The Political Doctrine of the Regnum Marianum and Saint Stephen.], in *Doctor et apostol: Szent István-tanulmányok* [Doctor et apostol. Studies on Saint Stephen], eds. J. Török – P. Erdő (Budapest: Márton Áron Kiadó, 1994), 171–197.

pendent not only from any Roman Empire (Byzantine and German), but also from the papacy.[20] Hartvic's *Life of Saint Stephen* made it manifest that King Coloman put his kingdom on a par with Rome and Constantinople.

The rise of the cult of the Virgin as patroness of Hungary at the end of eleventh century is signalled by a puzzling visual relic, the fragments of a monumental marble icon representing a Virgin *Hodigitria* from the Benedictine Abbey of Pécsvárad founded by King Stephen. The frame of the icon is not typically Byzantine, it resembles to late eleventh-century royal stone carving in Hungary. The original location of the icon is unknown, it might have been brought to Hungary from the Balkans.[21] It might as well have been produced by a royal stone-carving workshop for Pécsvárad. If so, it is a stunning expression of Marian piety in South-Western Hungary, a region with dynamic Byzantine traditions. The icon thus channelled Byzantine cult practices to an important Benedictine Abbey, dedicated to the Holy Virgin that was established by the recently canonized founder of the kingdom.

The Greek nunnery in Veszprémvölgy dedicated to the Most Holy Mother of God (*Yperagia Theotokos*) was founded by Saint Stephen near Veszprém, "the queen's city", where Piroska's mother, Queen Adelaide was buried. Royal princesses, among them Piroska must have been educated in this monastery, taking part in the daily course of Greek liturgy and assisting occasionally at the Latin mass in Veszprém Cathedral. Piroska's alleged sojourn in this monastery immersed her in Greek language as well as Greek liturgy. The queens of Hungary—Anastasia of Kiev, wife of Andrew I, or the Synadene, queen of King Géza I—, who came from the

---

[20] King Coloman appropriated the cult of the Virgin to assert the independence of his kingdom from the papacy the same way as the bishops of Rome used the cult of *Virgo Regina* in Late Antiquity to mark their independence from the emperor. The cult of *Virgo Regina* had a constitutional role in Rome: Ursula Nilgen, "Maria Regina – Ein politischer Kultbildtypus." *Römisches Jahrbuch für Kunstgeschichte*, 19 (1981): 1–33; Gerhard Wolff, "Icons and Sites. Cult images of the Virgin in mediaeval Rome", in Vassilaki, Maria (ed.), *Images of the Mother of God*, ed. M. Vassilaki (Aldershot: Ashgate 2004): 37–39; B. V. Pentcheva, *Icons and Power: the Mother of God in Byzantium*, (Pennsylvania: Penn State University Press, 2006), 21–30, and passim.

[21] Imre Takács – Árpád Mikó (eds.) *Pannonia Regia* Exhibition Catalogue. Budapest: Hungarian National Gallery, 1993, 59 and Cat. Nr. I-28 (Sándor Tóth). A wonder-working icon of the Mother of God is described by Pál Esterházy, *Mennyei Korona az az Az egész Villágon lévő Csudálatos boldogságos Szűz képeinek röviden feltett eredeti képekkel* [Heavenly Crown, or the miruclous images of the Holy Virgin in the world, with original images, 1680] as imported in the late Middle Ages from Sofia to Pécsvárad, and it is tentatively identified with this marble icon by Balázs Bodó, "A pécsváradi bencés monostor építéstörténete az újabb kutatások tükrében" [The architectural History of the Benedictine Abbey of Pécsvárad in the light of recent research], in: Elek Benkő – György Kovács (eds.): *A középkor és a kora újkor régészete Magyarországon*. [Archaeology of the Middle Ages and the Early Modern Period in Hungary.] (Budapest: MTA Régészeti Intézete, 2010): 365. The two Pécsvárad icons, however, might have been different objects.

Byzantine liturgical tradition, equipped the royal monasteries with liturgical books, vessels and icons, thus propagating new trends in Byzantine spirituality and art.

A markedly novel feature in eleventh-century Byzantine spirituality was the increasing interest in the infancy of the Virgin.[22] The Church focused on the human aspects of Mary's earthly life. King Ladislaus decreed the Nativity of the Virgin a feast at the Synod of Szabolcs in 1092; the feast of the Entrance of the Virgin into the Temple is attested a century later.[23] The Virgin's exemplary life became a model in the education of royal princesses. Little is known about Marian devotion in early Árpádian monasteries, be they Greek or Latin. Fresco fragments found in the "Deanery Church" of Visegrád may indicate all the same that painted cycles of the *Life of the Virgin* decorated these monasteries. These fragments have puzzled researchers since their discovery in the 1970's, as their quality, style, and iconography point towards Byzantine workshops.[24] From countless tiny fragments, the head of a servant girl in an interior setting (Fig. 2), and the head of an old man with white beard and white hair were reconstructed; yet other fragments represent young girls. The find can be interpreted as part of a narrative sequence, but not as a Christological cycle. The *Life of the Virgin* would be a good guess for the narrative: if so, the frescoes might have represented the Nativity, the Visitation, or the Entry into the Temple, with servant girls from the house of Joachim and Anne, or with the "daughters of Jerusalem" accompanying the young Virgin. Fragments of intricately patterned textile backgrounds and lavish fake marble suggest a palatial setting for the scenes. As the reconstruction of the fresco scenes is in its initial stages, the interpretation must remain hypothetical, yet there is no doubt about the high quality of the painting that reveals a royal commission and the presence of foreign, probably Byzantine, masters.[25] The dating of the frescoes is debated: art historians Sándor Tóth and Melinda Tóth argue for the late eleventh century, but the stratigraphy is mid-eleventh century.[26] The frescoes might be

---

[22] Jacqueline Lafontaine-Dosogne, *Iconographie de l'enfance de la Vierge dans l'Empire Byzantin et en Occident,* 1, Bruxelles 1964, 1992.

[23] *Rerum Hungaricarum monumenta Arpadiana.* ed. Stephan Endlicher. (St Gallen, Scheitlin-Zollikofer, 1849) 332:39

[24] Gergely Buzás – Orsolya Mészáros, "A középkori Visegrád egyházainak régészeti kutatásai." [Archaeological Research of the Churches of Medieval Visegrád] *Magyar Sion* 44 (2008), 71–72; Bea Mecsy, "Magyarország egyik legrégibb festészeti emléke. A visegrádi esperesi templom falképtöredékei." [One of the earliest paintings of Hungary: Mural fragments from the Visegrád Deanery Church] *Ars Perennis, 2nd Conference of Young Art Historians,* Budapest: Centrart, 2009, 19–21.

[25] The Byzantine origin of the frescoes has been made clear by the many Greek letters found among the fragments.

[26] Melinda Tóth, "Falfestészet az Árpád-korban." [Wall Painting in the Árpádian Age], *Ars Hungarica*: 23 (1995), 139

connected to the arrival of a Greek Orthodox bride from Kiev or Byzantium with her retinue of young ladies-in-waiting.

The Greek monastery dedicated to Saint Andrew founded by King Andrew I in the vicinity of the "Deanery Church" in Visegrád was an important spiritual centre for queens of Russian or Byzantine origin. In the Saint Andrew Monastery, only small monochrome fresco fragments were found. The relation of the workshops active in Visegrád cannot be surely established. Details—such as the servant girls' crossed headband on the frescoes from the "Deanery Church"—suggest a dating between 1050–1080, on the basis of the frescoes in Saint Sofia of Kiev and by Byzantine manuscripts from the second half of the eleventh century, as headbands disappear towards the end of the century.[27] The style of the Visegrád frescoes is slightly different from those preserved in Kiev. Did King Andrew I and Queen Anastasia invite masters from Kiev or from Constantinople? Impossible to know, as so many early Kievan churches were destroyed. The Kievan frescoes, however, were created at that time by Constantinopolitan masters, and evoke thus lost Constantinopolitan models. The existence of such high quality frescoes in auxiliary churches of the Visegrád royal centre lead us to assume that similar ones might have existed about the *Life of the Virgin* in the royal monasteries of Visegrád and Veszprémvölgy, but these fresco cycles are now completely lost.

The Visegrád fresco fragments indicate that Byzantine monumental painters (and perhaps mosaic artists) introduced the latest trends of Constantinopolitan iconography even to the royal court of Hungary. The childhood of the Virgin was a model in the education of royal princesses. Images of the young Virgin "portrayed on the heart" must have impressed Piroska and shaped her inner life as well as her behavior.[28] Exquisite and intimate, these new representations might have sparkled early on her interest in artistic innovation—a marked feature of her commissions in Constantinople. The Kokkinobaphos manuscripts from the second quarter of the twelfth century parade an extensive cycle of the *Life of the Virgin*, decorated with splendid miniatures made by one of the leading masters of the Komnenian court of Piroska-Eirene's time.[29]

---

[27] The Birth of the Virgin scene in Kiev: H. Logwin, *Kiewer Sophienkathedrale*, (Kiev: Mistectvo, 1971), fig. 156–157. The scene is depicted with the Entry of the Virgin in a Constantinopolitan Lectionary (Vat gr. 1156, fol. 246V, or fol. 268v).

[28] Cynthia Hahn, *Portrayed on the Heart. Narrative Effect in Pictorial Lives of Saints from the Tenth through the Thirteenth Century*. Berkeley-Los Angeles: University of California Press, 2001.

[29] Jeffrey C. Anderson, "The Illustrated Sermons of James the Monk, Their Dates, Order, and Place in the History of Byzantine Art." *Viator* 22 (1992): 84–85, hereafter Anderson, *James the Monk*. Anderson, followed by the majority of subsequent scholarship, helds the Paris Manuscript of the Kokkinobaphos sermons for the original, and dated it close to the Gospel Book of Emperor John II Komnenos (Cod. Urb. Gr. 2).

Piroska's childhood in Hungary also taught her to value family bonding. Her understanding of the ideal family life did not stem from experience, but from monastic education. This might explain of why she became an assiduous founder (*ktetor*) and provider of monasteries and charities. Even if no records of Piroska's life survive in Hungary, it is possible to assume that her devotion to the Holy Virgin goes back to her childhood years. The art and spirituality of the Hungarian royal court bear out this hypothesis.

Eirene and the Cult of the Theotokos in Constantinople

Empress Eirene led a private life. By the time she became *Augousta*, she already had given birth to seven children, and was expecting her son, the twice *porphyrogenitus* Manuel. Eirene is represented in Byzantine chronicles and modern scholarship alike as a modest and reserved wife, and as a loving mother devoted to her children. This hardly brings out her character, and even less does it offer a glimpse into her spiritual life. Strikingly, while three counsellors in practical matters are recorded in connection with the founding of the Pantokrator Monastery, Eirene's spiritual advisors go unmentioned.[30] The empress's spiritual autonomy is reflected in her only securely identifiable portrait in the Hagia Sophia, where she pays homage to the Theotokos. (Fig. 3). The portrait is usually dated to 1118, when John II assumed power, while Alexios's portrait is usually considered an addition from around 1122, the year of his alleged crowning as co-emperor. However, there is no sign of alteration on the mosaic composition and Alexios's coronation took place probably earlier. The representation of the Theotokos with the Child is a distant, but clear echo of the late tenth-century mosaic in the lunette above the southwest entrance, where the Mother of God is enthroned with the Divine Logos between the emperors Constantine and Justinian, the founders of the Queen of the Cities and of the Great Church respectively (Fig. 4). The official votive images of the emperors underwent subtle transformations in the Middle Byzantine period. On the Komnenian as well as on the Constantine and Justinian panel, the Theotokos looks into the spectator's eye, the asymmetrical traits of her face add to the vivacity of the representation. The Constantine panel parades a more Classical, more detached Theotokos. The representation of the Child is different. Christ is smaller, does not look directly

---

[30] Nikephoros, the domestikos, Joannes Olyntenos, and an unnamed official, later *megas dux* of Hellas: see Maria Loukaki, "Empress Piroska/Eirene's Collaborators in the Foundation of the Pantokrator Monastery. The Testimony of Nikolaos Kataphloron." In: Sofia Kotzabassi, *The Pantokrator Monastery in Constantinople*. (Boston/Berlin: De Gruyter, 2013), 191–202. Hereafter: Kotzabassi, *Pantokrator*.

at the spectator, and has a more adult look that manifests the unity of His divine and human nature: He is God's Wisdom and Logos. On the Komnenian portrait, the infant Christ is larger and, despite the construction of the face in concentric circles, more baby-like. He looks directly at the spectator. This rendering makes Him stand apart from the childlike Christ in Hagia Sophia's apse mosaic modelled after a Late Antique type. Christ on the Komnenian mosaic recalls the Emmanuel portraits in contemporary or slightly earlier churches, such as the Virgin Eleousa in Veljusa Monastery Church from 1085. This Christ may also allude to the birth of the *porphyrogenitus* Manuel. The childlike representation of the Divine Logos insinuates the increased importance of family life and children in Komnenian imperial ideal and ideology. The name of the imperial couple's youngest son ("God is us") expresses his parents' thanksgiving for their imperial power acquired in the teeth of fierce opposition on the part of John's mother Eirene Doukaina and his crafty sister, Anna Komnene. Above all, however, Manuel's very name was meant to declare the association between the Holy Family and the imperial couple: an association that was not lost on imperial panegyrists under Manuel's reign.

Empress Eirene's portrait in the *Megale Ekklesia* fulfilled a threefold role. The representation of the act of donation showed the way secular rulers were supposed to appear before the Divine Majesty. As a double act of gratitude, John and Eirene "give back to God that is His" according to the words of the liturgical *Anaphora*, while giving thanks to Him and His Mother for bestowing upon them the sole rule of the Empire in 1118. The representation of the holy rulers of the Roman Empire, the imperial portraits are hieratic, iconic images. Iconic portraits, nevertheless, showed individual characteristics as required by the legacy of Classical Antiquity. In Eirene's case, interest in her physiognomy was not entirely innocent, neither did it simply comply with the mandatory display of the beauty of the *Augousta*. The empress's red complexion had a major role in imperial panegyrics as a sign of her descent from the "Western emperors", demonstrating the rarely achieved oecumenical aspect of Komnenian rule.

The imperial couple's almost perfectly symmetrical face and slightly sideward glance towards the Holy Virgin, addressee of their prayers and donations, is a traditional feature of imperial portraiture since Late Antiquity, eloquently brought out by Anna Komnene' portrayal of her parents, Alexios Komnenos and Eirene Doukaina, written about a quarter of century later.[31] Eirene-Piroska is a stunning beauty with moonlike face, auburn hair, and an intelligent gaze. Her sharp, closed

---

[31] Anna Comnena, *Alexias* (rec. Diether R. Reinsch, Athanasios Kambylis) Corpus Fontium Historiae Byzantinae LX/1, (Berlin: de Gruyter, 2001) 3.3.2–3. p. 93,85- 95,58, *The Alexiad of the Princess Anna Comnena*, transl. by Elizabeth A. S. Dawes, (Abingdon: Routledge, 2005), 54–55.

mouth betrays willpower and purpose, features lacking from the expression of her husband and her son. If my reading of Eirene's image is correct and her official portrait indeed aims to express her purpose, it cannot be anything else but the will to achieve her cherished project, the Pantokrator Monastery complex. Before assessing this hypothesis, along with the cult of the Theotokos in the Pantokrator, I propose to discuss a little-known illustration of a celebrated manuscript.

Imperial Portraits in Cod. Urb. Gr. 2

Codex Urb. Grec. 2, now in the Apostolic Library of the Vatican, a small, not too richly illuminated Gospel Book is one of the most precious twelfth-century manuscripts known usually as the Gospels of John II Komnenos. Its prominence rests on two grounds. The first miniature (fol 10v) of the manuscript, just following the Canon tables, features Christ crowning Emperor John II Komnenos and his son and co-emperor Alexios. Christ is flanked by two princesses (or young empresses) personifying the virtues of Mercy (*Eleémosyné*) and Justice (*Dikaiosyné*) (Fig 4.). The two emperors look somewhat older than on the mosaic in the Hagia Sophia: Alexios is shown fully grown up. The traditional dating of the codex to around 1128 is very likely, but not proven.[32] This manuscript is the best early work of the Kokkinobaphos Master, an illuminator who worked on an array of luxury books, such as Isaak Komnenos's *Seraglio Octateuch* and on one (or both) of the Kokkinobaphos manuscripts.[33] The patron of the Gospel Book is not known, but s/he must have been a member of the imperial family. The Gospel Book's small dimensions suggest personal, rather than institutional use. Empress Eirene is absent from the coronation scene, but appears on the next page, a large composition introducing the Gospel of Matthew, read on the Sunday before Christmas, with the Genealogy of Christ through Joseph. The miniature represents the Nativity of Christ and Evangelist Matthew at his writing desk. The initial B hides a personification of *Eleémosyné* (Fig 5.), who is no other than Empress Eirene, recognizable of her awesome auburn hair.[34] Other gospels have no figural initials in this Gospel Book, and to my knowledge no similar initial B exists in Byzantine Gospel illumination. *Eleémosyné* is often represented on the margins of Psalters as an emperor or an empress, with an olive branch

---

[32] Based on a later Greek inscription with this date, corroborated by the style of the manuscript. See the bibliography in W. D. Wixom and H. C. Evans eds. *The Glory of Byzantium*. Exh. cat. (New York: Metropolitan Museum 1997), Cat. Nr. 144. Hereafter *The Glory of Byzantium*

[33] Jeffrey C. Anderson, "The Illustrated Sermons of James the Monk: Their Dates, Order, and Place in the History of Byzantine Art." *Viator* 22 (1991), 69–120.

[34] Ioannis Spatharakis, *The Portrait in Byzantine Illuminated Manuscripts* (Leiden: Brill 1976), 79–80.

Figure 1. The Holy Virgin from the Hungarian Coronation Mantle (author)

Figure 2. Visegrád: Fragments of frescoes from the "Deanery Church" – Magyar Nemzeti Múzeum Mátyás Király Múzeuma Visegrád (author)

Figure 3. The Holy Theotokos with Child, Komnenos panel, Hagia Sophia, Istanbul. Courtesy of Robert S. Nelson.

Figure 4. Alexios, Komnenos panel, Hagia Sophia, Istanbul. Courtesy of Béla Zsolt Szakács

Figure 5. Emperor John II Komnenos and Alexios crowned by Christ. Cod. Urb. Gr.2, 19v
© Bibliotheca Apostolica Vaticana

Figure 6a. Gospel of Matthew, Empress Eirene as Eleémosyné. Cod. Urb. Gr.2., 20v 21r © Bibliotheca ApostolicaVaticana

Figure 6b. Gospel of Matthew, Empress Eirene as Eleémosyné. Cod. Urb. Gr.2., 20v 21r © Bibliotheca ApostolicaVaticana

Figure 7. Our Lady of Vladimir (Tretiakov Gallery, Moscow)

crown.[35] The three-shaped branch in her hand may allude to the olive tree and to the Psalter allegories, yet Eirene's representation as Mercy is utterly unique. This type was conceived for this particular manuscript. Influenced by Byzantine models, the representation of Mercy/ Charity as a ruler was widespread in Western iconographical cycles, as it is shown by the Charity of David (or of an unnamed emperor) on the ivory cover of the Queen Melisenda Psalter,[36] by the Charity as an empress and divine leader of the virtues on a mosaic in the central dome of the Basilica of San Marco in Venice[37] and in the Cloister of Monreale Cathedral[38], or by the Charity of an unnamed princess in the Psalter of Saint Elisabeth of Hungary.[39] These representations, however, are later than the Komnenos Gospel Book, and might have been indirectly inspired by it. The personification of *Eleémosyné* on the previous page of the Komnenos Gospel Book might feature one of Piroska-Eirene's daughters, as their attires and hairstyles are similar. The owner of the manuscript seems to have appreciated these associations.

The special position of Eirene's allegorical portrait in the context of the Nativity and the genealogy of Christ is intriguing. This biblical passage has imperial allusions in Western manuscripts, such as the Gospel Book of Otto III from Trier, where the coins representing the emperor and his ancestors are placed in analogy with the genealogy of the incarnate Divine Logos.[40] The empress's cryptoportrait is shown in the Sankt Gereon Gospel Book of Cologne, fol. 22v, representing Emperor Otto III with his mother, Empress Theophanu and his grandmother, Adelaide on the coins, thus linking them directly to the genealogy of Christ.[41] The association of the Roman emperor with the genealogy of Christ goes back to Eusebius of Caesarea's Christianization of Hellenic political thought. God is the prototype of every ruler: this thought dominates Ottonian political theology and

---

[35] Elias Antonopoulos, Miséricorde-Olivier: agents et attributs. *Byzantion* 51 (1981), 345–385.
[36] British Library, Egerton 1139, from the Holy Land around 1130. *The Glory of Byzantium*, Cat. Nr. 259.
[37] Otto Demus, *The Mosaic Decoration of San Marco Venice* (ed. by Herbert Kessler), (Washington: DO. 1988), Pl. 20A.
[38] Represented on the capital with the Presentation of the Cathedral by William II, together with other virtues. Only Charity has an imperial crown and an inscription: *Deus Caritas Est*. See: http://cenobium.isti.cnr.it/seadragon/index.php?site=monreale&image=W8Sh82E last consulted on 10 Febr. 2018.
[39] Cividale del Friuli, Museo Archeologico Nazionale, Achivi e Biblioteca, cod CXXXVII, Fol 173r, made in Reinhardsbrunn (?) between 1201–1208 for Elizabeth's parents-in-law, Hermann of Thuringia and Sofia of Wittelsbach.
[40] A. Wieczorek and H.-M. Hinz, eds. *Europas Mitte um 1000* Exhibition Catalogue, (Stuttgart: Theiss, 2000), Cat. Nr. 02.04.01. Hereafter *Europa's Mitte*.
[41] *Europa's Mitte*, Cat. Nr. 02.04.02.

art.⁴² The Komnenos Gospel Book, however, only hints at the basic assumption of Christian Hellenism that God is impersonated in the emperor. Neither is Empress Eirene equated with the Virgin Mary: she represents the *Theotokos*'s main virtue: Mercy. *Eleémosyné* reappears in the dedication of the Pantokrator Monastery's north church to the Theotokos Eleousa. By divine grace, Eirene's outstanding mercifulness makes her the embodiment of the Virgin Mary's charity, who cooperates with God in the salvation of humankind by giving birth to Christ.

The reason why Mercy is present at the opening passage of the Gospel of Matthew is explained in biblical commentaries. The Incarnation of Christ is the personification of God's love for humankind (*Philanthropia*), the divine counterpart of Mercy (*Eleémosyné*). Humans receive the divine Child into their heart through charity and humility, exhorts John Chrysostom his flock in his homilies on the Gospel of Matthew.⁴³ It is hard to imagine a more deeply religious compliment for a humble and unpretentious empress than representing her as one of the divine virtues of the Holy Theotokos. This compels us to think that Eirene must have been the owner of the Gospel Book, or that she commissioned it as a gift for her family.

Empress Eirene, the Pantokrator and the Theotokos

The Pantokrator Monastery complex is presented in the sources as Empress Eirene's life achievement. Thanks to this impressive monument, she was able to realize the dream to be remembered as the embodiment of Mercy after her death. Her great foundation, even if she did not see its completion and inauguration, opened her the road of salvation: she died reassured that thanks to the prayers of the monks and the poor, she would inherit the Kingdom. The churches of the monastic complex were in use in Eirene's lifetime, but their official inauguration ceremonies, not yet mentioned in the *Typikon*, took place only after the dedication of the monastery on August 4 and August 11 in 1136.⁴⁴ Thus, the equipment, if not the mosaic decoration of the churches belong to a later period. It is impossible to tell who offered the furnishings mentioned in the *Typikon*, in panegyrics, in epigraphy, found in frag-

---

42 W. C. Schneider, "Imperator Augustus und Christomimetes. Das Selbstbild Ottos III. in der Buchmalerei." In: *Europas Mitte um 1000, Handbuch zur Ausstellung* 2, 798–808, with previous literature.

43 Mercy is a divine virtue: this is what prompts Christ to take on human flesh and save humanity: David Rylaardsdam, *John Chrysostom on Divine Pedagogy: The Coherence of his Theology and Preaching.* (Oxford: OUP 2014), 43. For the idea of mercy linked to Matthew's narrative of the Nativity see Saint John Chrysostom, *Homilies on Matthew*, Hom IV, 19–20 and Hom V, 9. Nicene and Post-Nicene Fathers, Vol. 10, tansl. George Prevost, rev. M. B. Riddle, ed. Philip Schaff (Buffalo New York: Christian Literature Publishing Co., 1888) 98–99.

44 Sofia Kotzabassi, "Feasts at the Monastery of Pantokrator." In Kotzabassi, *Pantokrator*, 157–159.

ments during excavations, or preserved in Venice to the churches: Eirene or John II? Inscriptions on the Theotokos icons—such as the enamel fragment found during the excavations with the inscription *di hés aei proeisin hé sótéria*, or the icon donated probably later by Andreas *Panhypersebastos*—do not mention Empress Eirene.[45] Her name as a donor is absent in connection with the icons listed in the *Typikon,* and her *Vita* is not linked to any icon.[46] This is all the more striking because John II does not fail to emphasize in the *Typikon* and we read also in the *Synaxarion* narratives that the Pantokrator Monastery was not only founded, but also designed with the help of her wife. At the resounding triumphal procession of Constantinople in 1133, the icon of the Virgin *Hodigitria* sat on the place of honor on the richly adorned chariot, preceded by the emperor on foot.[47] All male members of the imperial family participated in the triumph: Eirene's role in it is unmentioned. The processions inside the churches and outside the Pantokrator monastery, the regular Friday procession with the *Hodigitria* icon diverted to the Pantokrator Monastery, the weekly *Presbeia* processions with the icons of the Church of the Theotokos *Eleousa*, the yearly commemoration of the founders with the *Hodigitria* icon make only sense if the churches had already been dedicated and connected with the commemoration of the imperial dynasty—of which the first to be buried here was Piroska-Eirene.[48] The processions of the wonderworking Theotokos icons must have been initiated by John, rather than Eirene in the Pantokrator. It may well be that Eirene did not have a special wish to establish miraculous icons in her foundation.

The lost icon of the Church of the Theotokos Eleousa raises important questions. Is it related to the icon of the Mother of God from Vladimir? The Vladimirskaya reportedly came as a gift given to Russia around 1130 (Fig 6)[49]. Is the Vladimirskaya a later, thirteenth-century copy of the original icon lost during

---

[45] Arthur H. S. Megaw, "Notes on Recent Work of the Byzantine Institute in Istanbul," *Dumbarton Oaks Papers* 17 (1964), 348, fig. 18–19, Kotzabassi, *Pantokrator*, 224–226.

[46] In sharp contrast with her husband's numerous dedications on the Theotokos icons: Nicola Callicle, *Carmi*. ed. Roberto Romano (Neapel: Bibliopolis, 1980), 15 (89–91, 139–140), 20 (95, 142); Ioannis Vassis, "Das Pantokratorkloster von Konstantinopel in der byzantinischen Dichtung," in Kotzabassi, *Pantokrator*, 224–226.

[47] Paul Magdalino, The Triumph of 1133, in *John II Komnenos, Emperor of Byzantium In the shadow of father and son*, ed. A Bucossi and A. Rodriguez Suarez (Abingdon: Routledge, 2016), 53–70.

[48] M. Butyrskij "Vyzantiyskoe bogosluzhenie u ikony soglasnogo tipiku monastyria Pantokratora 1136 goda." [Byzantine service of the icon according to the Typikon of the Pantokrator Monastery of the year 1136] in Alexei M. Lidov, (ed.), *Chudatvornaia ikona v Vizantii i Drevnei Rusi*, [Miracle-working icons in Byzantium and old Russia] (Moscow: Martys, 1996) 145–58, and B. V. Pentcheva, *Icons and Power*, 165–187.

[49] It was reportedly brought to Russia by a Greek Metropolitan called Michael. Later traditions credit Lukas Chrysoberges, a patriarch during the reign of Manuel Komnenos, with this gift.

the Tatar destruction of Vladimir in 1238?⁵⁰ After its cleaning in 1922, this theory was rejected. Much scholarly ink was spelt on the symbolism of the Virgin of Tenderness (*Glykophylousa*), where the embrace of the Virgin and Child is often interpreted as an expression of Mary's intercession for humankind and of her anguish before the Passion of her Son.⁵¹ These emotionally charged images—along with the Pietà (*Threnos*), Mary embracing her dead Son—are seen as the visual expression of a new, sentimental spirituality in the twelfth century. No direct evidence links, however, the Virgin of Tenderness with the Theotokos *Eleousa* Church.⁵² The Blachernai Church's *Glykophylousa* type icon was venerated as Patroness of Constantinople already in the tenth century. A copy of such an icon was given as a gift to the Bulgarians possibly in 927. Emperor John Tzimiskes recovered this copy in 971 as the most precious trophy of his victory over the Bulgarians. John the Deacon mentions an icon representing Christ and His Holy Mother in embrace. The illustration of Tzimiskes's triumphal procession in Skylitzes's Chronicle preserved in Madrid identifies it with a *Glykophylousa* type icon.⁵³ A mirror image of the Vladimir Theotokos is also depicted in the New Church of Toqalı kilise in Cappadocia, dated to 940–960.⁵⁴ The early twelfth-century Georgian-Byzantine Sinai hexaptych represents among the most venerated icons the Virgin Mother embracing her divine Child with the inscription *Blachernitissa*.⁵⁵ Thus, under the Komnenian emperors, the most important example of the embracing Mother and Child icons was among the holy icons of the Blachernai Theotokos, Patroness of Constantinople and of the Empire. *Eleousa* frequently appears as a title on icons under the Komnenians with terms such as "Intercessor", "Advocate of the human race", but usually without the Child. The inventory of the Virgin *Eleousa* monastery near Veljusa, founded by Monk (and later Bishop) Manuel in 1080 and endowed, among others, by John II

---

50   Nikodim Kondakov's hypothesis was rejected by Viktor Lazarev, but followed by Konrad Onasch, Ivan Bentchev and György Ruzsa, "Remarques sur l'icone de la Vierge de Vladimir." *Acta historiae artium Acad. Scient. Hung.*, 37, 1994–95, 105–112. Usually, the faces of the Virgin and the Child, and a few details are held to be from the twelfth century, see. Yurij I. Bobrov, *Istorya restauratsii drevnyerusskoy ikonopissy* [History of the Restoration of Old-Russian Icon Painting], (Moscow: Chudozhnik, 1987), 74.

51   Hans Belting, *Likeness and Presence*. Transl. Edmund Jephcott (Chicago and London: The University of Chicago Press, 1994), 281–282, 287, 583, note 78. Hereafter Belting *Likeness*.

52   Mirjana Tatić-Đurić, "Eleousa, A la recherche du type iconographique," *Jahrbuch der österreichischen Byzantinistik*, 25 (1976): 259–267, Pentcheva, *Icons and Power*, 177–180.

53   Belting, *Likeness*, fig. 107.

54   Belting, *Likeness*, fig. 173.

55   Zaza Skhirtladze, "The Image of the Virgin on the Sinai Hexaptych and the Apse Mosaic of Hagia Sophia, Constantinople." *Dumbarton Oaks Papers* 68 (2014), 373–374, 378, figs. 6–7.

Komnenos, lists an important icon that represents the Virgin and child embracing his mother and speaking to her (*enkardion, eulalaton*). This was not, however, the titular icon, being only the fifth in line.[56] The extant icons of the Veljusa monastery have different inscriptions prior to the thirteenth century.

The existence of icons of the Virgin embracing the child during the twelfth century is evidenced not only in Byzantine art, but also in twelfth-century Western copies made after Byzantine prototypes. Well-known examples include the miniature in the Commentary on Isaiah by Jerome from Cîteaux dated to around 1115–25, with the representation of the Virgin as a flower of the tree of Jesse following the prophecy of Isaias,[57] the seal of Schwarzrheindorf Church and nunnery, dated to 1172 and alluding to a Byzantine icon in their possession,[58] or again a Madonna in the Sacramentary from Messina Cathedral from 1180–90 (Madrid, Bibl. Nac. Cod 52, fol 80r).[59] The Vladimir Theotokos thus might reflect the concerns of the Komnenian court and high clergy in regard of the role of sacred art.

Did the Eleousa Church of the Pantokrator Monastery have an icon of the Virgin of Tenderness? Was it the titular icon of the Church? Was it painted in Piroska-Eirene's lifetime? These questions remain unanswered. Icons of the Virgin embracing the child, however, were in circulation in Constantinople during Eirene's lifetime. Their emotional appeal was surely not lost on the empress, who easily recognised herself in the tender embrace of a Mother and also in her anguish about the fate of her Son as the earthly empress also felt towards her imperial children. Eirene created solid family bonding in the imperial family and this is prominently reflected in James Kokkinobaphos's miniatures, whoever his patron was.

Constantinopolitan life in the twelfth century was marked by an overwhelming presence of icons, mainly those of the Theotokos, and by the processions connected with them. The imperial couple was bound to participate in these processions, such as the Tuesday processions of the *Hodigitria*. John II Komnenos modified this procession and prescribed new ones for the commemorations over the tombs of the imperial couple in the *Typikon* of the Pantokrator. The icons of the Holy Mother of God are often described by art historians as becoming more and more intimate. In this process, the reign of John and Piroska-Eirene constitutes an important phase with the propagation of a *Virgin of Tenderness* icon, reflected on the icon of the Mother of God from Vladimir. Intimacy invades the imperial family as well. Yet, as we have seen, icon painting does not progress in a linear development,

---

[56] Belting *Likeness* 284, n. 93, Text 25 C.
[57] Dijon, Bibl. Mun. Ms 129, Fol 4v-5r, *The Glory of Byzantium*, 446
[58] Belting *Likeness*, fig 200,
[59] *The Glory of Byzantium*, Cat. Nr. 316

at least as far as the icons of the Theotokos are concerned. The embracing Virgin of Tenderness is present much earlier, whereas the cult of the *Hodigitria* reaches its climax only later under the Palaeologan emperors. Did Piroska-Eirene influence this process?

Conclusion

The curious lack of Eirene's icon dedications may lead us to think that the empress concentrated her attention on economic resources and practical matters to bring under roof her great foundation. Or, we may assume that Eirene remained emotionally aloof from icon veneration since she came from Hungary, where Byzantine piety was present, but the cult of the icons was less intense than in Constantinople. Eventually, we may consider that in contrast to the feverish icon worship in the Constantinopolitan Church and in personal devotion, the empress explored alternative avenues—the works of mercy—to implement the teaching of the Gospels in her life. The representation of Charity (*Misericordia*) as an empress and leader of the virtues was a central theme on some slightly later Western examples as we saw earlier. The representation of Empress Eirene as Mercy in the Vatican manuscript, however, is not an echo of Western prototypes, but a genuine and cogent actualization of the empress's ideal role as the embodiment of Charity.

Eirene—and the manuscript's painter—actualized in a highly humane way the main themes of imperial ideology: the imperial dynasty' relation with the family of Christ, and the empress's enacting the main virtue—Mercy/Charity—of the Holy Mother of God. The empress thereby gave a fascinating visual exegesis for the Nativity of the Logos in an imperial context.

Clemency towards captives, defeated enemies and other criminals, ban on capital punishment and mutilation, as many different aspects of mercy are highlighted as distinctive features of John II Komnenos's reign. According to Niketas Choniatis, it was his clemency that turned John's reign into a new Golden Age.[60] The making of the Golden Age, however, resulted from the inseparable cooperation of the imperial couple. Piroska-Eirene's upbringing and faith were instrumental in the transformation of the Komnenian Empire: not only its Western orientation, but also its mercifulness stemmed from her heritage and spirituality.

---

[60] Paul Magdalino, "The triumph of 1133," 53.

Bibliography

Primary Sources

Alexiad [The] of the Princess Anna Comnena. Tr. Elizabeth A. S. Dawes. (Abingdon: Routledge, 2005)

Callicle, Nicola. *Carmi*, ed. Roberto Romano. (Napoli: Bibliopolis, 1980)

Comnena, Anna. *Alexias.* rec. Diether R. Reinsch, Athanasios Kambylis. (Berlin: de Gruyter, 2001)

Esterházy, Pál. *Mennyei Korona az az Az egész Villágon lévő Csudálatos boldogságos Szűz képeinek röviden feltett eredeti képekkel* [The heavenly Crown, or the miraculous images of the Holy Virgin spread over the whole world, with original images, 1680]

Hartvic, *Life of King Stephen of Hungary*, Tr. Nora Berend. In: *Medieval Hagiography. An Anthology*, ed. Thomas Head (New York/London: Garland, 2000), 379–396.

John, Chrysostom Saint. "Homilies on Matthew." *Nicene and Post-Nicene Fathers*, Vol. 10, tr. George Prevost, rev. M. B. Riddle, ed. Philip Schaff (Buffalo New York: Christian Literature Publishing Co., 1888)

Register Gregors VII, Monumenta Germaniae Historica, Epistola Selecta, vol. II. fasc. 2. ed. Erich Gaspar (Berlin: Weidmann, 1923)

Rerum Hungaricarum monumenta Arpadiana ed. Stephan Endlicher, (St Gallen: Scheitlin-Zollikofer, 1849)

Scylitzae Ioannis Synopsis Historiarum. Corpus Fontium Historiae Byzantinae, V, ed. Joannes Thurn (Berlin, de Gruyter, 1973)

Skylitzes, John. *A Synopsis of Byzantine History.* Tr. John Wortley. (Cambridge, New York: Cambridge University Press, 2010)

Vita Maior Sancti Gerardi episcopi. ed. Emericus Madzsar. *Scriptores Rerum Hungaricarum tempore ducum regumque stirpis Arpadianae gestum*, Vol.II, (ed.) Emericus Szentpétery (Budapest: Akadémiai Kiadó, 1938): 480–506.

Secondary Sources

Anderson, Jeffrey C. "The Illustrated Sermons of James the Monk, Their Dates, Order, and Place in the History of Byzantine Art." *Viator* 22 (1992): 69–120.

Antonopoulos, Elias and Miséricorde, Olivier. "Agents et attributs." *Byzantion* 51 (1981): 345–385.

Belting, Hans. *Likeness and Presence.* Tr. Edmund Jephcott (Chicago and London: The University of Chicago Press, 1994)

Bobrov, Yurij Grigorievitch. *Istorya restauratsii drevnyerusskoy ikonopissy.* [History of the Restauration of Old-Russian Icon Painting] (Moscow: Chudozhnik, 1987)

Bodó, Balázs, "A pécsváradi bencés monostor építéstörténete az újabb kutatások tükrében." [Architectural history of the Benedictine Abbey of Pécsvárad in the Light of Recent Research], in: *A középkor és a kora újkor régészete Magyarországon* [Archaeology of the Middle Ages and the Early Modern Period in Hungary], eds. Benkő, Elek – Kovács, Gyöngyi (Budapest: Magyar Tudományos Akadémia Régészeti Intézete, 2010), 349–386.

Blason Scarel, Silvia (ed.) *Poppone: l'età d'oro del Patriarcato di Aquileia.* Exhibition catalogue. (Aquileia, Museo Civico del Patriarcato–Rome: "L'Erma" di Bretschneider, 1997)

Bucossi, Alessandra - Rodriguez Suarez, Alex (eds.) *John II Komnenos, Emperor of Byzantium In the Shadow of Father and Son* (Abingdon: Routledge, 2016)

Butyrskij, M. "Vyzantiyskoe bogosluzhenie u ikony soglasnogo tipiku monastyria Pantokratora 1136 goda." [The Byzantine Rite in Front of an Icon According to the Typicon of the Pantocrator Monastery at Constantinople of the year 1136] in Alexei M. Lidov (ed.), *Chudatvornaia ikona v Vizantii i Drevnei Rusi.* [Miracle-working Icons in Byzantium and Old Russia], (Moscow: Martys, 1996)

Buzás, Gergely and Mészáros, Orsolya. "A középkori Visegrád egyházainak régészeti kutatásai.". [Archaeological Research of the Churches of Medieval Visegrád], *Magyar Sion* 44 (2008): 71–103.

Demus, Otto. *The Mosaic Decoration of San Marco Venice.* (Washington, D. C.: Dumbarton Oaks, 1988)

Dümmerth, Dezső. "A Mária országa-eszme és Szent István" [The Political Doctrine of the Regnum Marianum and Saint Stephen] in *Doctor et apostol: Szent István-tanulmányok* [Doctor et apostol. Studies on Saint Stephen], ed. Török, József (Budapest: Márton Áron Kiadó, 1994)

Garland, Lynda. *Byzantine Empresses, Women and Power in Byzantium AD 527–1204.* (London-New York: Routledge, 1999)

Győrffy, György. *István király és műve.* [King Stephen and his Achievement] (Budapest: Corvina, 1977)

Hahn, Cynthia. *Portrayed on the Heart. Narrative Effect in Pictorial Lives of Saints from the Tenth through the Thirteenth Century.* (Berkeley-Los Angeles: University of California Press, 2001)

Hill, Barbara. *Imperial Women in Byzantium 1025–1204.* (Harlow, Pearson-Longman, 1999)

Horváth, János and Székely, György (eds.), *Középkori kútfőink kritikus kérdései.* [Critical questions of Hungarian Medieval written sources] (Budapest: Akadémiai Kiadó, 1974)

Horváth, János. "Quellenzusammenhänge der beiden Gerhard Legenden." *Acta Antiqua* 1960: 439–454.

Klaniczay, Gábor. *Holy Rulers and Blessed Princesses: Dynastic Cults in Medieval Central Europe* (Cambridge: Cambridge University Press, 2002).

Kotzabassi, Sofia. "Feasts at the Monastery of Pantokrator." In Kotzabassi, *Pantokrator,* 156–158.

———. *The Pantokrator Monastery in Constantinople.* (Boston/Berlin: De Gruyter, 2013)

Lafontaine-Dosogne, Jacqueline. *Iconographie de l'enfance de la Vierge dans l'Empire Byzantin et en Occident* 2 vols, (Brussels: Koninklijke Academie van België, 1964–1965)

Logwin, Hryhory Nikonovic. *Kiewer Sophienkathedrale.* (Kiev: Mistectvo, 1971)

Loukaki, Maria. "Empress Piroska/Eirene's Collaborators in the Foundation of the Pantokrator Monastery. The Testimony of Nikolaos Kataphloron." in Kotzabassi, *Pantokrator*, 191–202.

Németh, László. "A Regnum Marianum állameszme." [Regnum Marianum as a Theory of State.] *Regnum Egyháztörténeti Évkönyv* (1940–1941): 223–292

Mango, Cyril. *Materials for the Study of the Mosaics of Hagia Sophia.* (Washington, D.C.: Dumbarton Oaks, 1962)

———. "Theotokoupolis" in *Mother of God, Representations of the Virgin in Byzantine Art.* ed. Maria Vassilaki, Exhibition catalogue (Athens: Benaki Museum, 2000): 17–25.

Mayr-Harting, Henry. *Ottonian Book Illumination, An Historical Study.* (London: Harvey Miller, 1991, 1999 (2))

Mecsy, Bea. "Magyarország egyik legrégibb festészeti emléke. A visegrádi esperesi templom falképtöredékei." [One of the earliest paintings of Hungary: Mural fragments from the Visegrád "Deanery Church"] *Ars Perennis, 2nd Conference of Young Art Historians.* (Budapest, Centrart, 2009), 19–21.

Megaw, Arthur H. S. "Notes on Recent Work of the Byzantine Institute in Istanbul." *Dumbarton Oaks Papers* 17 (1964), 333–371, Figs. 1–35.

Nagy-Falusy, Louis. "Le culte de la sainte Vierge en Hongrie," in *Maria. Études sur la Sainte Vierge vol. 4,* ed. Du Manoir de Juaye, Hubert (Paris: Beauchesne, 1956): 645–670.

Neville, Leonora Alice. *Anna Komnene, the Life and Work of a Medieval Historian.* (Oxford: Oxford University Press, 2016)

Nilgen, Ursula. "Maria Regina – Ein politischer Kultbildtypus." *Römisches Jahrbuch für Kunstgeschichte,* 19 (1981): 1–33.

Pentcheva, Bissera V., *Icons and Power: the Mother of God in Byzantium,* (Pennsylvania: Penn State University Press, 2006)

Ruzsa, György. "Remarques sur l'icone de la Vierge de Vladimir." *Acta historiae artium Acad. Scient. Hung.,* 37 (1994–95): 105–112.

Rylaardsdam, David. *John Chrysostom on Divine Pedagogy: The Coherence of his Theology and Preaching.* (Oxford: OUP 2014)

Schneider, Wolfgang Christian. "Imperator Augustus und Christomimetes. Das Selbstbild Ottos III. in der Buchmalerei," In: *Europas Mitte um 1000, Handbuch zur Ausstellung* 2 Wieczorek, Alfred and Hinz, Hans-Martin eds. (Stuttgart: Theiss, 2000): 798–808.

Skhirtladze, Zaza. "The Image of the Virgin on the Sinai Hexaptych and the Apse Mosaic of Hagia Sophia, Constantinople." *Dumbarton Oaks Papers* 68 (2014): 369–386.

Spatharakis, Ionnis. *The Portrait in Byzantine Illuminated Manuscripts.* (Leiden: Brill 1976)

Takács, Imre – Mikó, Árpád (eds.) *Pannonia Regia* Exhibition Catalogue. (Budapest: Hungarian National Gallery, 1993)

Tatić-Đurić, Mirjana. "Eleousa, À la recherche du type iconographique," *Jahrbuch der österreichischen Byzantinistik* 25 (1976): 259–267.

Teteriatnikov, Natalia. *Mosaics of Hagia Sophia, Istanbul: The Fossati Restauration and the Work of the Byzantine Institute.* (Washington, D.C.: Dumbarton Oaks, 1998)

Tóth, Melinda. "Falfestészet az Árpád-korban." [Wall Painting in the Árpádian Age.] *Ars Hungarica* 23 (1995):137–153.

Trapp, Erich. Eine wiedergefundene Ikone der Blachernen Kirche, *Jahrbuch der Österreichischen Byzantinistik* 35 (1985): 193–195.

Vassis, Ioannis. "Das Pantokratorkloster von Konstantinopel in der byzantinischen Dichtung." In Kotzabassi, *Pantokrator*,

Wieczorek, Alfred – Hinz, Hans-Martin eds. *Europas Mitte um 1000* Exhibition Catalogue, (Stuttgart: Theiss, 2000)

Wixom, William D. – Evans, Helen C. *The Glory of Byzantium. Art and Culture of the Middle Byzantine Era, A.D. 843 1261.* New York: Metropolitan Museum of Art, 1997.

Wolff, Gerhard. "Icons and Sites. Cult images of the Virgin in mediaeval Rome."In: *Images of the Mother of God*, ed. Maria Vassilaki (Aldershot: Ashgate, 2004): 23–49.

"A NEW MIXTURE OF TWO POWERS:"
NICHOLAS KALLIKLES AND THEODORE PRODROMOS ON EMPRESS EIRENE

Roman Shlyakhtin

The epitaphs of the imperial couple in the Pantokrator Monastery were composed by the court physician and poet Nicholas Kallikles, one of the intellectuals who, along with Theodore Prodromos renewed imperial discourse in the reign of John II Komnenos.[1] Eirene's tomb is a meeting point for two generations of Komnenian poets. This paper compares the different images of Empress Eirene in Kallikles's and Prodromos's epitaphs.[2] While Kallikles focuses on the family, Prodromos extols imperial glory.

Kallikles at Court

Nicolas Kallikles, court physician to Alexios I Komnenos and poet laureate of John II, remains in the shadow of the more famous (and better edited) Theodore Prodromos. His life is little known. Mentioned by three twelfth-century Byzantine authors, Theophylact of Ochrid, Anna Komnene and Theodore Prodromos, his chronology remains approximative. Born at the end of the eleventh century,[3] he studied medicine in Constantinople, perhaps as a disciple of Michael Psellos.[4] By 1115, Kallikles

---

[1] I would like to thank Marianne Sághy and Robert Ousterhout for their unfailing assistance in improving the argument of this paper.

[2] Nicola Kallikles, *Carmi*, ed. Roberto Romano (Naples: Bibliopolis, 1980) (hereafter: Kallikles, *Carmi*). Kallikles's poetry is understudied. P. Magdalino, *The Empire of Manuel I Komnenos*, 361–362, lists him among the physicians. Dionysos Stathakopulos, "John Komnenos: A Historiographical Essay," in *John II Komnenos: Emperor of Byzantium. In the Shadow of Father and Son*, ed. Alessandra Bucossi, A. R. Suarez (London: Center for Hellenic Studies, 2016), 4.

[3] Krumbacher, *Geschichte die Hochsprachische Literatur*, 344.

[4] For other possible students of Psellos see D. Krallis, "Attaleiates as Reader of Psellos," in *Reading Michael Psellos*, ed. C. Barber, D. Jenkins, (Leiden: Brill, 2006) 167–191.

became Emperor Alexios I Komnenos's court physician and thus a member of the Byzantine elite. Despite his prominence in the imperial court, no information exists about his official rank. He owned a rich library containing manuscripts of Galenus and was probably a professor of medicine at the school of the Holy Apostles.[5] Theophylact of Ohrid calls Kallikles "our Asklepios" and praises his medical knowledge.[6] Listing Kallikles among Alexios's doctors, Anna Komnene uses the same epithet and praises the "marvellous Kallikles" who helped relieve her father's suffering in his last days.[7] Together with a doctor called Lizix, Theodore Prodromos calls Kallikles a "true healer" in a period of bad doctors.[8]

The question of the absence of Kallikles's literary activity before 1118, in the "golden age of Byzantine literature" under Alexios I remain open - there is not a single poem that one can safely date to the age before 1118.[9] As a poet, Kallikles flourished under John II Komnenos. He composed the emperor's epitaph in the Pantokrator Monastery that suggests that Kallikles outlived the emperor and died after 1143. In the following centuries, Kallikles was famous as a doctor *and* writer. The title of one of his poems in the fourteenth-century manuscript labels him as "the most educated teacher of the doctors lord Nikolas Kallikles," thus recognizing him both as a medic and a poet.

Kallikles's surviving poetry—thirty-one poems contained in the *Codex Marcianus Graecus* Z 524[10]—is dated between 1118 and 1143.[11] Roberto Romano divides the works in two categories: "funerary orations" and "dedications"—yet, paradoxically, Kallikles's most popular verse was an epigram on a stone statue of Saint George. As a poet, the former court doctor had a definite interest in death. He wrote epitaphs as well as verses on objects decorating the tombs, such as the funerary verse of the *logothete* Gregory Kamateros as well as a verse on the icon of Savior

---

[5] Roberto Romano, "Introduzione," in Kallikles, *Carmi*, 13–17.
[6] Kallikles, *Carmi*, 57–61.
[7] Anna Komnene, *Alexiad*, ed. Kambylis-Reinsch, XV, 499.91–92: ὑπερφυής; reproduced in Kallikles, *Carmi*, 61–62. The episode is absent in the most recent monograph on Anna Komnene. See L. Neville, *Anna Komnene: Life & Work of Medieval Historian* (Oxford: Oxford University Press, 2016).
[8] Romano, "Introduzione," 16.
[9] Margaret Mullett, "Alexios the Enigma," in *Alexios I Komnenos*, ed. M. Mullett, D. Smyth, (Belfast: Belfast Byzantine Enterprises, 1996), 3–4.
[10] Andreas Rhoby, "Zur Identifizierung von bekannten Autoren im Codex Marcianus graecus 524," *Medioevo greco* 10 (2010), 167–204; Foteini Spingou, "The Anonymous Poets of the Anthologia Marciana: Questions of Collection and Authorship," *The author in Middle Byzantine literature: modes, functions, and identities*, Byzantinisches Archiv 28, (Berlin: de Gruyter, 2014), 139–153.
[11] R. Romano, "Tradizione Manoscritta e Edizione" in Nicola Kallikles, *Carmi*, 43–54.

that Kamateros's wife placed above the tomb.[12] In some cases, Kallikles composed the epitaph before the death of the commissioner, such as John II Komnenos's long funerary poem.[13] In another case, the poet turned the funerary matter into a rather lively iambic dialogue between the tomb and the wanderer—an innovative piece that deserves an article on its own.[14]

The function of Kallikles's poem is disputed. His epitaphs written for the members of the imperial dynasty must have been read and inscribed on the defunct person's tomb. The poet's professional interest in death made him one of the important bards of the early Komnenian period. He composed funerary poems not only for imperial officials, but also for the imperial couple.

The Poet and the Empress: Same Court, Different Circles

Princess Piroska of Hungary arrived in Constantinople around 1104–5,[15] completely unnoticed by Byzantine authors. Choniates and Anna Komnene ignore the Hungarian princess altogether in their works, and court poets fail to mention Empress Eirene in their epigrams: her absence from the poetic laments on her defunct son Alexios is particularly conspicuous.

Did Kallikles know Empress Eirene? They lived in the same court, knew the same people, visited the same churches, but they might have never met. The Pantokrator Monastery is a case in point. Eirene was the co-founder of the complex, and Kallikles wrote the dedicatory inscription to the icon of Christ the Savior donated to the imperial foundation highlighting that Christ grants victory against enemies from East and West.[16] Yet there is no sign that Eirene and Kallikles were in personal contact—the poem's last line refers to John, "Lord of the Ausonians," not to Eirene.

Kallikles composed funerary orations for Eirene's family members and close relatives, such as Eudoxia Komnene and the *sebastos* John Roger.[17] The oration for John Roger is a rare example of the Byzantine praise for the foreign prince in imperial service that explicitly mentions his origins and praises his multiple military virtues. The poem summarizes the life of John Roger, compares him with Scipio and

---

[12] Kallikles, *Carmi*, 92–93, 96–97.
[13] Kallikles, *Carmi*, 112, sub "Versus conscripti in sepulchrum Ioannis Comninis adhuc viventis," 2: κατά ἐντολὴν ἐκείνου.
[14] Kallikles, *Carmi*, 83–85
[15] Ferenc Makk, *The Árpáds and the Komneni: Political Relations Between Hungary and Byzantium in the 12th Century*. (Budapest: Akadémiai Kiadó, 1989), 12–14.
[16] Kallikles, *Carmi*, 78–80. Carmi, 78–80, particularly at 80:2: Αὐσόνων ἄναξ
[17] Kallikles, *Carmi*, 91–92; 93–95.

Scaurus,[18] extols his enlistment in Byzantine service and its consequence, a flow of rich gifts.[19] Kallikles's interest in the *sebastos* John Roger might have been sparkled by his connections with his mother-in-law, the dowager empress Eirene Doukaina. Celebrated patroness of Byzantine poets in the 1120s, Doukaina was at the center of the court's intellectual circle to which Kallikles belonged,[20] as Anna Komnene's sympathetic description of him seems to suggest. The doctor-poet gives a vivid testimony to his contacts with Eirene Doukaina, evidenced not only in poetry, but also in other sources, in the poem in which he described the cross that the dowager empress donated—perhaps to the Pantokrator Monastery.[21] In this poem, he calls Eirene "empress" (βασιλίς).

However, nothing hints to Empress Eirene's contacts with the courtly network of poets and scholars.[22] Thus, in 1134, the poet wrote the epitaph of an empress whose patronage he did not enjoy and whom he never called "empress" in his writings.[23] This is why Kallikles's representation of Eirene is particularly intriguing.

Wife and Mother: The Image of Eirene in Kallikles's poems

Kallikles mentions Eirene in two compositions: *On the tomb of the Despina*, a 25-line epitaph (*Carmen* 28 in Romano's edition) and in the epitaph of John II in the Pantokrator Monastery.[24] Eirene's epitaph is unique in Kallikles's œuvre in that this is the only funerary poem dedicated to the memory of a woman—all the rest is written to commemorate men. Even without being Kallikles's patroness, Empress

---

[18] Kallikles, *Carmi*, 94.17: ἦν Σκηπίων ἢ Σκαῦρος ἢ Κάτλος νέος, probably Marcus Aemilius Scaurus, consul of 115 BC.

[19] Kallikles, *Carmi*, 94.17, 32–35.

[20] Nicolas Kallikles, "In Crucem Ab Irena Ducaena Oblatam," in Kallikles, *Carmi*, 81.6, Kallikles explicitly names Eirene Doukaina "empress" (βασιλίς). For Eirene Doukaina's literary patronage see E. Jeffreys, "Literary Trends in the Constantinopolitan Courts of the 1120s and the 1130s," in *John II Komnenos: Emperor of Byzantium. In the Shadow of Father and Son*, op. cit., 111. Positive evidence is lacking on Kallikles's belonging to Doukaina's circle as did Prodromos, Italikos or Basilakes.

[21] Kallikles, *Carmi*, 81–82. Various manuscripts have different variants: "To the beautiful wooden (cross) adorned by the ruling lady."

[22] Empress Eirene's position in the complex power network of the Komnenian family is interesting. John did not leave Eirene with his female relatives and brought her out of the capital in 1106 so that she does not have to meet Anna Komnene and Eirene Doukaina. See Vlada Stanković, "John II Komnenos Before the Year 1018," in *John II Komnenos: Emperor of Byzantium. In the Shadow of Father and Son*, op. cit., 17–18.

[23] No epitaph for Eirene Doukaina survives in Kallikles's corpus.

[24] Stathakopoulos, "John Komnenos: A Historiographical Essay," art. cit., 4 argues that the poem was performed after John's death.

Eirene was important enough that an unnamed patron commission the poet to compose her epitaph.

The epitaph's title, *On the tomb of the Despina*, appears in a thirteenth-century manuscript. One can understand the complex task of addressing the empress in the poem if one realizes that Kallikles does not name Eirene, he calls her "the Lord's bride" (νυμφη θεου). The image derives from the *Song of Songs* that inspires the poem. Kallikles describes the deceased as "black and beautiful and adorned," a literary quote from the Old Testament *epithalamium*. The epitaph also focuses on the family of Eirene and her children. Kallikles addresses John as "King and God and groom" and suggests Eirene to protect her orphaned children.

> Oh open to them your feelings, now as before
> And give them mother's care as usual[25]

It is a remarkable innovation that an epitaph be inspired by an epithalamium. Kallikles's fusion of funerary commemoration and wedding celebration results in an outstanding spiritual homage to the empress. Eirene's death becomes a mystical marriage with Christ.[26] The beauty and virtue of the deceased empress is her asceticism: it is her "imperial outfit" that fastens "the ruby of her outstanding virtue" to the "gold and pearls" of her imperial crown. Eirene joined spiritual and earthly virtue.

Kallikles quotes directly the splendid epithalamic text of the Old Testament when he calls the empress "black and beautiful."[27] Eirene was obviously not "black"—the mosaic of Hagia Sophia depicts her as a ginger-haired, white-cheeked beauty. In the Christian allegorical interpretation of the Solomonic verse "darkness" does not refer to physical quality, but to the soul standing before God and accepting His grace. The bride sees the beauty of the Lord reflected in herself, and rejoices that she is attractive for His sake.

"Dark and comely," she discharges "javelins of lighting" βολίδας ἀστραπηβόλους). These are God's weapons (*Book of Wisdom* 5:21) to defend the righteous on

---

[25] Kallikles, *Carmi*, 106.1–25: ἄνοιγέ σου τὰ σπλάγχνα καὶ νῦν ὡς πάλαι/ καὶ τὴν συνήθη μητρικὴν θάλψιν δίδου. I thank Cristian-Nicolae Gaşpar for his advice on translation.

[26] Richard Alfred Norris, *The Song of Songs: Interpreted by Early Christian and Medieval Commentators*. (Grand Rapids: Eerdmans, 2003); E. Ann Matter, *The Voice of My Beloved: The Song of Songs in Western Medieval Christianity* (Philadelphia: University of Pennsylvania Press, 1990).

[27] For the interpretations of "black and beautiful" see Paul J. Griffiths, *The Song of Songs* (Grand Rapids: Brazos Press, 2011), 17–19. For the uses of the Song of Songs for praise in the twelfth century, see K. Linardou, "The Couch of Solomon, a Monk, a Byzantine Lady and the Song of Songs," *The Church and Mary Studies in Church History*, ed. R. N. Swanson, (Woodbridge: Suffolk and Rochester, NY, 2004), 73–85.

the face of the Earth.[28]. Kallikles changes the agency: it is Eirene, not the Almighty Lord who discharges lighting. This is a new take on Eirene: Kallikles hints not only at the righteousness of the deceased, but possibly also to personal traits of character. Eirene, after all, might not have been as "peaceful" as we would think. This stunning image powerfully equates Eirene's concern for the poor with the work of God.

The poet fuses God's image with Emperor John, the bridegroom who had taken her into the bridal chamber. Finally, Kallikles addresses Eirene and asks her to look at her children who request her mercy. She should take them in her arms and "warm them as mothers do." Kallikles thus asks for the empress's heavenly intercession for her children at the Lord.

Roberto Romano calls this epitaph an "imperial funerary poem."[29] From the formal point of view, he is right. Associating John Komnenos with the *Song of Songs'* bridegroom is in accordance with Kallikles's poetic invention. Following imperial traditions, the poet compares the emperor to King Solomon.[30] Even more significant is, however, the family setting and the familial atmosphere of the poem.

Thanks to Kallikles's daring recycling of the *Song of Songs,* the imperial couple will become the prototype of conjugal union symbolizing the union of the soul and the body. In the *Song of Songs,* bride and bridegroom live a joyful union, while in the epitaph, husband and wife are separated by grim death. What remains of their union are the children in need of motherly care. Eirene is now associated with the Mother of God, able to mediate between her progeniture and God. The cry of the children, at the same time, is the only clue that the poem is about Empress Eirene, as there are no references to the origins, deeds, or role as co-founder of Pantokrator of the deceased. In Kallikles's epitaph, the deceased is wife and mother, who sometimes "discards javelins."

Undoubtedly imperial, the poem is also very personal. Eirene and John are bride and bridegroom, a happy couple blessed with children. Nothing is said about

---

[28] Wisdom 15:21.
[29] Romano, "Introduzione," 18.
[30] King Solomon represents the image of the ideal ruler in Byzantium: Jonathan Bardill, "Anicia Juliana, King Solomon and the Gilded Ceilings of the Church of St. Polyeuktos in Constantinople," *Late Antique Archeology* 3 (2006): 339–370; C. Rapp, "Old Testament Models for Emperors in Early Byzantium," in *The Old Testament in Byzantium*, ed. P. Magdalino, R. Nelson (Washington: Dumbarton Oaks Research Library and Collection, 2010), 175–199, esp. 184–186; for eleventh-century examples see Robert Ousterhout, "New Temples and New Solomons: The Rhetoric of Byzantine Architecture" in *The Old Testament in Byzantium*, op. cit., 248–250. Alexios I Komnenos saw Solomon as the paradigm of the capable ruler: Margaret Mullett, "The Imperial Vocabulary of Alexios I Komnenos," in *Alexios I Komnenos*, ed. M. Mullett, D. Smyth, (Belfast: Belfast Byzantine Enterprises, 1996), 392–393. For other images of Solomon in the reign of Manuel, see Paul Magdalino, *The Empire of Manuel I Komnenos*, 416, 447.

their official status. The absence of the imperial titles is, indeed, striking. Kallikles mentions *basileus* once, and never calls Eirene *empress* or *augusta*. The abandon of official titulature and the personal tone makes the epitaph quite unique. The personalization may parallel on purpose Eirene's personality, who did not bask in her imperial status, and in death deposed all worldly glory.

Kallikles's epitaph hardly provides new information about Eirene, but reinforces the notion of her spiritual virtues, godliness, devotion, and humility. Eirene is one of the rare persons who combined imperial power with spiritual virtue. A loving mother, she is a sorely missed partner, whose name the poet did not bother to mention.[31] A slightly different image is disclosed in another poetical description of Eirene, the epitaph of John II Komnenos.

The funerary poem composed for the emperor in the Pantokrator Monastery is a long, 126-line work. Its title in medieval manuscripts refers to John, the "holy autocrat." Kallikles here focuses on John's deeds.[32] The difference is striking between Eirene's short, personal, family-oriented and yet deeply spiritual epitaph, and the imperial narrative in John's commemoration. The poem glorifies the emperor in Theodore Prodromos's style, listing his noble deeds and victories over foreign enemies. No mention here of personal feelings or children. Comparing John to King David, Kallikles highlights that John conquered Goths and Persians (that is, Cumans and Seljuk Turks), built new cities and resettled barbarian tribes. Eirene is mentioned in passing at John's ascension to heaven:

> You come there together with your wife
> Who took part in your life and your crown.[33]

Remarkably, Eirene is presented as an equal partner to John, sharing his life and his power. Thus, Eirene's image changes from poem to poem, depending on the inspiration of the author, and on the commission of his patron. The epitaph presents the defunct empress as the 'bride of the Lord' with a powerful imagery taken from the *Song of Songs*. John's epitaph presents the empress as wife (σύζυγα), sharing her

---

[31] In Byzantine historical narrative, the absence of the personal name may indicate the author's uneasiness towards the nameless character (see Psellos's notable absence of in Michael Attaleiates's *Historia*). Poetry is different—funerary poems rarely mention the name of the deceased, e.g. it is absent in the poem Kallikles wrote on Andronikos Palaiologus's tomb: Kallikles, *Carmi*, 85–86.

[32] Kallikles, *Carmi*, 112.

[33] Kallikles, *Carmi*, 116.110–112: τούτῳ προσῆλθες ἄρτι σὺν τῇ συζύγῳ, // ἣ συμμετέσχε καὶ βίου σοι καὶ στέφους.

husband's responsibility. This is not without analogies with the other funerary poem written about Eirene by Theodore Prodromos.

The Epitaph for the Princess from Abroad: Eirene in the Works of Prodromos

Theodore Prodromos is a poet from a generation after Kallikles. He appears in the imperial court with Kallikles at the peak of his influence as a doctor. Prodromos's first poem dates from 1120,[34] and while his extant work show him as a talented author of epigrams and funerary orations, he was much more than that. His numerous hymns, bridal songs, poems for the *demos*, panegyrics, epigrams and grammatical treatises shaped intellectual discourse in Komnenian Constantinople. Prodromos's poetic impact surpassed Kallikles's, demonstrated by the great number of his poetic imitators and the manuscripts that conserved his verse. He was often commissioned to compose funerary poems, for example, a lengthy epitaph for Anna Komnene's daughter-in-law, Theodora.[35] His poems show great variety, but death represents a significantly lesser interest for him than for Kallikles.

Prodromos, too, composed a funerary poem for Eirene.[36] Despite the similarity in size, Prodromos's epitaph is different from Kallikles's epitaph. First of all, Prodromos entitles his poem "A funeral verse for the blessed empress of the Romans, *kyra* Eirene" (while the title of Kallikles's poem is much more obscure).[37] In the title, he explicitly labels Eirene as "blessed empress of the Romans" (if Kallikles' title is authentic, she is called a "lady," *despina*).

While Kallikles does not hint at the origins of the empress, Prodromos says that she is a foreigner.[38] Beginning the poem with a short introduction about Eirene's dynasty—"a foreigner born from fortunate forefathers"—, Prodromos generously includes Julius Caesar among the empress's ancestors.[39] This makes Eirene

---

[34] For a recent overview see N. Zagklas, Theodore Prodromos: The Neglected Poems and Epigrams. Edition, Tr. and Comm.)'. PhD diss., (Vienna: University of Vienna, 2014).

[35] This epitaph has 191 lines, similar to the panegyrics: Theodore Prodromos, *Historische Gedichte*, ed. Hörandner, 381–389.

[36] Preserved in three different manuscripts: Vat. 305 s (13th cent), Vat. 1126 a (14th century), Bodleian Rock 18 a (1348) and London Add 10014 b (16th cent). Theodore Prodromos, *Historische Gedichte*, ed. Hörandner, 229.

[37] Theodore Prodromos, *Historische Gedichte*, ed. Hörandner, 229.3

[38] Theodore Prodromos, *Historische Gedichte*, ed. Hörandner, 229.3: τὰ κατ' ἐμαυτὴν ἐκδιδάξω σε, ξένε

[39] It is worth noting that Prodromos avoids the direct labeling of Eirene's homeland. The Hungarians, Paionians of Byzantine rhetoric, were often present in the list of imperial enemies and this mentions would hardly be suitable in the context of imperial funerary poem. Theodore Prodromos, *Historische Gedichte*, ed. Hörandner, 229.6: Ἰούλιοι Καίσαρες ἐθρέψαντό με.

a rather suitable match for her husband, "The son of Alexios, ruler of Rome, the strong Ἰοάννης born in the purple room."[40]

For Prodromos, Empress Eirene is not only a fertile wife, who brought four sons and four daughters to her husband, but also co-ruler with the emperor, who participates in the victories of her husband:
You won over the raise of the Sun, you prevail over sunset
You prevail over the North and over heated South.[41]

Prodromos informs his readers that Eirene having taken the monastic vow, died in Bithynia,[42] and her corpse was shipped back to Constantinople. He ensures the grieving family and subjects that the empress will receive "her portion in Heaven."

Two Epitaphs, One Empress

Kallikles's and Prodromos's epitaphs on Empress Eirene represent an interesting case when two poets use same subjects, images in a different sense and a different way. Both tell the story of the empress who wore "purple clothes" and imperial regalia, but combined them with spiritual virtue. Their construction of the image and the memory of the deceased empress is, nevertheless, different. Kallikles draws on the Bible to create an intimate picture of Eirene, who "hurled lightings," but loved to hug her children. In contrast, Theodore Prodromos highlights Eirene's foreign origin (calling her "foreign lady," ξένη), and using imperial rhetoric to portray the empress as an equal partner of her husband and partaker in his victories. She actively participates in the military deeds of John II, whom Prodromos praises in other poetical works. In some way, the image of Eirene in Prodromos recalls the image of another foreigner, *sebastos* John Roger, praised by Kallikles.[43]

---

[40] Ῥώμης δ' ἄναξ κράτιστος Ἀλεξιάδης//πορφυρογεννὴς εὐτυχὴς Ἰωάννης. Theodore Prodromos, *Historische Gedichte*, ed. Hörandner, 229.8–9: English translation by Gyula Moravcsik, *Byzantium and the Magyars*. (Budapest: Akadémiai Kiadó, 1970), 76. The poet stresses John's descent from Alexios, showing that Alexios's children competed for their share in their father's symbolic heritage: V. Stanković, "John II Komnenos Before the Year 1018," 19–20; K. Linardou, "Imperial Impersonations: Disguised Portraits of the Komnenian Prince and His Father," in *John II Komnenos: Emperor of Byzantium. In the Shadow of Father and Son*, ed. A. Bucossi, A.R. Suarez, (London: Center for Hellenic Studies, 2016), 155–183; See also M. Angold, "Alexios I Komnnenos: An Afterword," in *Alexios I Komnenos*, ed. M. Mullett, D. Smyth, (Belfast: Belfast Byzantine Enterprises, 1996), 406–407.

[41] νίκας πρὸς αὐγὴν ἡλίου καὶ πρὸς δύσιν/ νίκας πρὸς ἄρκτον καὶ νότου θερμὸν κλίμα. Theodore Prodromos, *Historische Gedichte*, ed. Hörandner, 230.19–20.

[42] Theodore Prodromos, *Historische Gedichte*, 230.24: it is not clear which monastery she joined.

[43] Kallikles describes the *sebastos* as the "new Scipio" and military victor, and Prodromos describes Eirene as the descendant of Caesar: is it a common trait in portraying foreigners in Komnenian poetry?

The difference between the two epitaphs may be due to different authorial agendas. Kallikles was the doctor of the imperial family, a person who knew Alexios and his children close enough for Anna Komnene to mention him as late as in the 1150s. He belonged to the Alexian court, yet wrote poetry under the reign of John. He was an intellectual belonging to Eirene Doukaina's circle, and a doctor with a certain interest in death. Theodore Prodromos, on his turn, was the court's discourse-monger, the author of the new kind of imperial poetry that praised and glorified John II's military prowess and his many triumphs in East and West. What was the subject of an internal, "family story" for Kallikles, became, for Prodromos, a topic of external propaganda.

Eirene's tomb, thus, becomes a unique *lieu de mémoire* of the meeting of two authors with different agendas. It is tempting to read the two funerary poems as a rhetorical competition between Prodromos and Kallikles, who rivaled each other to create a fine funerary poem for the deceased empress with the main patroness—dowager empress Eirene Doukaina—still present in the audience.[44] If it is so, then this is the first known case of the alleged "rhetorical contests" in Komnenian literature, John's expedition to Palestine being the second.[45] However, absence of information on the performative aspect of two poems and the lack of data on twelfth-century *theatron* prevents us to make a definite statement. *Theatrons* may have existed in the eleventh century, but nothing is known on rhetorical contests under John II Komnenos, especially whether they included funerary poetry.[46]

I suggest reading the poems of Kallikles and Prodromos not as competitive, but as complementary images of Eirene. Kallikles wrote about the deceased empress in biblical terms and praised her motherly feelings while Prodromos depicted her as a foreign descendant of Julius Caesar, a militant empress, who together with her husband conquered West, East, North and South and then took the monastic habit. These two images, rather than excluding, complement each other like the pieces of a mosaic. The two poems reflect the celebrated plurality in literature and in the visual arts that is recognized as the hallmark of the Komnenian Renaissance starting in John's reign and reaching its peak under Manuel Komnenos's long rule.

---

[44] Elizabeth Jeffreys, "Literary Trends," 111 argues that the *theatron* appeared in the circle of Eirene Doukaina in the twelfth century. For a *theatron* under the reign of Manuel I Komnenos see Magdalino, *The Empire*, 411–412.

[45] John II expedition to Syria and Palestine in 1139 was the subject of panegyrics: Michael Italikos, *Lettres et Discourse*, ed. P. Gautier (Paris: Institut français d'études byzantines. 1962), 239–245; *Nicephori Basilacae Orationes et Epistulae*, ed. A. Garzya. (Leipzig: Teubner, 1984), 48–74.

[46] Floris Bernard, *Writing and Reading Secular Poetry in Byzantium, 1025–1081* (Oxford: Oxford University Press, 2014), 255–257.

How do the two poems contribute to our knowledge of the empress's personality? Neither Prodromos nor Kallikles offer biographical facts about the deceased, none of them praises the empress's patronage of artists and poets. The absence of any hint to Eirene's patronage speaks volumes in the context of late Komnenian aristocratic women's artistic maecenate. Eirene gave birth to eight children, duly mentioned by the poets, but did not participate in the circle of imperial patrons of the arts. In contrast, the *sebastokratorissa* Eirene, wife of *sebastokrator* Andronikos Komnenos—very much like Eirene Doukaina before her—, patronized writers including Prodromos and Constantine Manasses, who composed the *Breviarum Chronicum*, one of the most popular Byzantine rhymed chronicles[47] climaxing in Alexios I Komnenos's ascension to the throne.[48] The Norman-born *sebastokratorissa* Eirene was a generous sponsor in the Constantinopolitan court,[49] while the Hungarian-born Empress Eirene stayed aloof from the artistic circles of socialites of the like of Eirene Doukaina and Anna Komnene. Nevertheless, the empress did contribute to the emergence of the Komnenian spiritual revival and artistic renaissance as the wife of John II, as the co-founder of the Pantokrator Monastery and as the mother of Manuel I Komnenos. In a different way, Kallikles and Prodromos praise her precisely for this achievement.

Bibliography
Primary Sources

Komnene, Anna. *Alexias*. Ed. Diether R. Reinsch, Athanasios Kambylis (Berlin, 2001).

Basilakes, Nikephoros. *Nicephori Basilacae Orationes et Epistulae*. Ed. A. Garzya. (Leipzig: Teubner, 1984).

Italikos, Michael. *Lettres et Discourse*, ed. P. Gautier (Paris: Institut français d'études byzantines. 1962), 239–245.

Kallikles, Nicola. *Carmi*, ed. Roberto Romano (Naples: Bibliopolis, 1980)

Manasses, Constantine. *Breviarium Chronicum*. Ed. O. Lampsidis. (Athens: Institute of Greek and Roman Antiquities, 1996).

---

[47] Constantine Manasses. *Breviarium Chronicum*. Ed. O. Lampsidis. (Athens: Institute of Greek and Roman Antiquities, 1996).
[48] Constantine Manasses, *Breviarum Chronicum*, ed. Lampsidis, 358.6609–6620.
[49] E. Jeffreys, "Sebastokratorissa Irene as a Patron," *Wiener Jahrbuch für Kunstgeschichte* 60 (2012): 177–194; K. Linardou, "The Couch of Solomon, a Monk, a Byzantine Lady and the Song of Songs," *The Church and Mary Studies in Church History*, ed. R. N. Swanson, (Woodbridge: Suffolk and Rochester, NY, 2004), 73–85; Nikolas Kallikles, "On the Tomb of Despina," lines 10–11.

Prodromos, Theodore. *Theodoros Prodromos: Historische Gedichte*, ed. Wolfram Hörandner. Vienna: Österreichischen Akademie der Wissenschaften, 1974.

Secondary Sources

Angold, Michael. "Alexios I Komnenos: An Afterword," in *Alexios I Komnenos*, ed. M. Mullett, D. Smyth, (Belfast: Belfast Byzantine Enterprises, 1996), 398–417.

Bardill, Jonathan. "Anicia Juliana, King Solomon and the Gilded Ceilings of the Church of St. Polyeuktos in Constantinople." *Late Antique Archeology* 3 (2006): 339–370.

Bernard, Floris. *Writing and Reading Secular Poetry in Byzantium, 1025–1081* (Oxford: Oxford University Press, 2014).

Griffiths, Paul J. *The Song of Songs* (Grand Rapids: Brazos Press, 2011).

Jeffreys, Elizabeth. "Sebastokratorissa Irene as a Patron," *Wiener Jahrbuch für Kunstgeschichte* 60 (2012): 177–194.

———. "Literary Trends in the Constantinopolitan Courts of the 1120s and the 1130s," in *John II Komnenos: Emperor of Byzantium. In the Shadow of Father and Son.*

Krumbacher, Karl. Geschichte der byzantinischen Litteratur von Justinian bis zum Ende des oströmischen Reiches (527–1453). (München: Beck, 1891).

Krallis, Dimitris. "Attaleiates as Reader of Psellos." In: *Reading Michael Psellos*. Eds. C. Barber and D. Jenkins, (Leiden: Brill, 2006), 167–191.

Linardou, Kelly. "The Couch of Solomon, a Monk, a Byzantine Lady and the Song of Songs." In: *The Church and Mary Studies in Church History*. ed. R. N. Swanson, (Woodbridge: Suffolk and Rochester, NY, 2004), 73–85.

———. "Imperial Impersonations: Disguised Portraits of the Komnenian Prince and His Father," in *John II Komnenos: Emperor of Byzantium. In the Shadow of Father and Son*, ed. A. Bucossi, A.R. Suarez, (London: Center for Hellenic Studies, 2016), 155–183.

Magdalino, Paul. *The Empire of Manuel I Komnenos. 1143–1180.* (Cambridge: Cambridge University Press, 1993.)

Makk, Ferenc. *The Árpáds and the Komneni: Political Relations Between Hungary and Byzantium in the 12th Century.* (Budapest: Akadémiai Kiadó, 1989).

Matter, Elizabeth Ann. *The Voice of My Beloved: The Song of Songs in Western Medieval Christianity* (Philadelphia: University of Pennsylvania Press, 1990).

Moravcsik, Gyula. *Byzantium and the Magyars*. (Budapest: Akadémiai Kiadó, 1970)

Mullett, Margaret "Alexios the Enigma," in *Alexios I Komnenos*, ed. M. Mullett, D. Smyth. (Belfast: Belfast Byzantine Enterprises, 1996), 1–11.

———. "The Imperial Vocabulary of Alexios I Komnenos." In: *Alexios I Komnenos*, ed. M. Mullett, D. Smyth. (Belfast: Belfast Byzantine Enterprises, 1996), 392–393.

Stathakopulos, Dionysos. "John Komnenos: A Historiographical Essay." In: *John II Komnenos: Emperor of Byzantium. In the Shadow of Father and Son*, ed. Alessandra Bucossi, A.R. Suarez. (London: Center for Hellenic Studies, 2016), 3–11.

Neville, Leonora Alice. *Anna Komnene: The Life and Work of a Medieval Historian* (Oxford: Oxford University Press, 2016).

Norris, Richard Alfred. *The Song of Songs: Interpreted by Early Christian and Medieval Commentators*. (Grand Rapids: Eerdmans, 2003).

Ousterhout, Robert. "New Temples and New Solomons: The Rhetoric of Byzantine Architecture." In: *The Old Testament in Byzantium*. Eds. P. Magdalino, R. Nelson (Washington: Dumbarton Oaks Research Library and Collection, 2010), 223–253.

Rapp, Claudia. "Old Testament Models for Emperors in Early Byzantium." In: *The Old Testament in Byzantium*. Eds. P. Magdalino, R. Nelson (Washington: Dumbarton Oaks Research Library and Collection, 2010), 175–199.

Rhoby, Andreas. "Zur Identifizierung von bekannten Autoren im Codex Marcianus graecus 524," *Medioevo greco* 10 (2010), 167–204.

Spingou, Foteini. "The Anonymous Poets of the Anthologia Marciana: Questions of Collection and Authorship." In: *The author in Middle Byzantine literature: modes, functions, and identities*. Byzantinisches Archiv 28 (Berlin: de Gruyter, 2014), 139–153.

Stanković, Vlada, "John II Komnenos Before the Year 1018." In: *John II Komnenos: Emperor of Byzantium. In the Shadow of Father and Son*, ed. Alessandra Bucossi, A. R. Suarez, (London: Center for Hellenic Studies, 2016), 11–21.

Zagklas, Nikolaos. Theodore Prodromos: The Neglected Poems and Epigrams (Edition, Translation and Commentary. Unpublished PhD diss., University of Vienna, 2014.

RITUAL AND POLITICS IN THE PANTOKRATOR: A LAMENT IN TWO ACTS FOR EIRENE'S SON

Foteini Spingou

At the time when the plans of Empress Eirene and Emperor John II's tombs were designed in the *heroon* of the Pantokrator complex, no one would have predicted the nearly simultaneous passing away of their two sons. Neither would the imperial couple be able to foresee the dynamic activity of their daughter-in-law, the *sebastokratorissa* Eirene, another foreign bride, whose acts of patronage rivalled those of her mother-in-law.[1] This paper highlights an intricate set of texts on the burial of Eirene's second son, the *sebastokrator* Andronikos, in conjunction with his wife's wishful thinking to have herself buried with his husband in the Church of St. Michael at the Pantokrator.

Andronikos died suddenly.[2] In August 1142, as he escorted the mortal remains of his elder brother Alexios, the heir to the throne from Cilicia to the imperial capital, the young prince fell ill and left the earthly kingdom. Andronikos's death

---

[*] I am grateful to Robert Ousterhout for his reading of my paper. Special thanks to Elizabeth and Michael Jeffreys and Marc Lauxtermann, who commented on earlier drafts, one of which was presented at the conference "Literature as Performance," 5–7 July 2013 in Athens, organised by Niki Tsironis.

[1] On the comparison see E. Jeffreys, "The *Sebastokratorissa* Irene as Patron," *Female Founders in Byzantium and Beyond*, eds. L. Theis, M. Mullett, and M. Grünbart, Wiener Jahrbuch für Kunstgeschichte 60/61 (Cologne, Weimar, Vienna: 2014), 192–93. The reconstruction of Eirene's life by Konstantinos Varzos *Ἡ γενεαλογία τῶν Κομνηνῶν*, Βυζαντινά κείμενα καὶ μελέται 20, (Thessaloniki, 1984), 366–78, has to be treated with caution. On Eirene, see also E. Jeffreys and M. Jeffreys, *Iacobi Monachi epistulae* (Turnhout, 2009), XXIV–XXIX. The life of *sebastokratorissa* Eirene remains little known. The forthcoming publication of Manganeios Prodromos's poems and the commentary by Elizabeth and Michael Jeffreys will shed a new light to her life and the political intrigues of her time.

[2] On Andronikos, see Varzos, *Γενεαλογία*, no. 76, I: 357–79. On the death of the brothers see Varzos, *Γενεαλογία*, I: 359–61. Varzos's interpretation of the relevant passage in the *History* by William of Tyre should be treated with caution.

was commemorated in a series of funerary poems, not only because he was—albeit briefly—the heir to the throne, but also because his widow was a major supporter of literature and arts in twelfth-century Constantinople.[3]

Two poems were composed in commemoration of Andronikos's passing and the bitter fate of his widow and children. The first, a verse composition of 393 lines is to be found in Theodore Prodromos's collected works.[4] The second, a summary of Prodromos's verses, is preserved unattributed in the famous *Anthologia Marciana* (hereafter *AM*), the vast anthology of Komnenian poetry collected in the early thirteenth century.[5] A monody in prose was written by Michael Italikos[6] in consolation of Andronikos' father, Emperor John II. In contrast to the monody, the two poems highlight the agony of the *sebastokratorissa* Eirene. I argue that Prodromos's poem was performed at the funeral, while its summary was meant as a verse inscription on Andronikos's tomb in the Pantokrator. The latter's prominent ritual character not only honors the deceased, but also intends to secure the precarious position of his widow.

The Poem of the Anthologia Marciana

The poem can be found in one of the books of the AM with anonymous poetry, *Sylloge B*.[7] It was first published by Ioannis Vassis in 2013. For the reader's convenience, the *appendix* reproduces the text (with minimal changes from Vassis's edi-

---

[3] On this point, see Jeffreys, "The *sebastokratorissa* Irene as patron," 177–94 with further bibliography.

[4] W. Hörandner, ed., *Theodoros Prodromos: historische Gedichte,* (Vienna, 1974), no. 45, 414–26. Hereafter: Prodromos, *Monody*.

[5] Ms. Venice, Marcianus Graecus 524 (XIII ex.). For the text and its translation see the appendix, and the following paragraph for its editions.

[6] P. Gautier, ed., *Michel Italikos: Lettres et discours,* (Paris, 1972) no. 11, pp. 130–34. Hereafter: Italikos, *Monody*.

[7] Ms. Venice, Marcianus Graecus 524 (XIII ex.), ff. 106v–07. On ms. Marc. gr. 524 and the poetic anthology see: Sp. Lambros, "ΟΜαρκιανὸς κῶδιξ 524," *Neos Ellenomnemon* 8 (1911): 3–59, 123–92 (the reference to the poem in question can be found in p. 145, no. 220); E. Mioni, *Bibliothecae Divi Marci Venetiarum Codices Graeci Manuscripti. Thesaurus Antiquus*, vol. 2 (Rome, 1981), 399–407; P. Odorico and Ch. Messis, "L'anthologie Comnène du cod. Marc. gr. 524: Problèmes d'évaluation," in: *L'épistolographie et la poésie épigrammatique: projets actuels et questions de méthodologie. Actes de la 16e table ronde organisée par Wolfram Hörandner et Michael Grünbart dans le cadre du XXe Congrès international des études byzantines. Collège de France-Sorbonne, Paris, 19–25 Août 2001,* W. Hörandner and M. Grünbart, eds., (Paris, 2003), 191–213; and F. Spingou, "Words and Artworks in the Twelfth Century and Beyond: The Thirteenth-century Manuscript Marcianus Gr. 524 and the Twelfth-Century Dedicatory Epigrams on Works of Art," unpublished DPhil thesis, University of Oxford, 2013, where I identified for the first time the division of the anthology in chapters.

tion) and translation as they will appear in my forthcoming edition of the three Syllogae, where it bears the number B57.[8] As the poem is dissociated from its original context, its function is unknown. Its length is appropriate for a tomb epigram or an epitaph. In contrast, Prodromos's poem is clearly entitled a monody—a function confirmed by its inordinate length.

The name of the poem's author in the *AM* is unknown, as is the date of its composition. The title and the text offer information about the deceased and the place of his final rest. The title reads:

> Εἰς τὸν ἐν τῇ μονῇ τοῦ Παντοκράτορος τάφον τοῦ σεβαστοκράτορος
> καὶ πορφυρογεννήτου κυροῦ Ἀνδρονίκου ὡς ἀπὸ τῆς συμβίου αὐτοῦ,
> τῆς σεβαστοκρατορίσσης κυρᾶς Ἄννης.
> On the tomb of the sebastokrator and purple-born Andronikos
> in the Pantokrator monastery, on behalf of his wife, the sebastokratorissa Anna.

As I have argued elsewhere, the titles of the anonymous poems derive from the poets' working books and as such are trustful witnesses of the poems' historical contexts.[9] They often contain details that the main text does not include, and they were available only to someone living at the time of the poems' composition. The few updates that can be found either summarise for or make the text relevant to a late twelfth-century audience.

In the epigram, Andronikos's wife laments the loss of her husband. The poem starts with an *anaphora* to the personified tomb: "Oh tomb, what a bitter name! What a terrible sight! How many lifeless bodies do you hide within a small stone?"[10] In vv. 5–10, Eirene speaks about the one who was laid to rest: noble by

---

[8] I. Vassis, "Das Pantokratorkloster von Konstantinopel in der byzantinischen Dichtung," in ed. S. Kotzabassi, *The Pantokrator Monastery in Constantinople*, (Boston and Berlin, 2013), 230–31. F. Spingou, *Poetry for the Komnenoi. The Anonymous Poetry from the Anthologia Marciana: Sylloge B, and C* (in preparation).

[9] See F. Spingou, "The Anonymous Poets of the Anthologia Marciana" in *Byzantine Authorship: Theories and Practices*, A. Pizzone, ed., (Berlin, 2014), p. 139–53. For a general consideration of the title of the poems see: A. Rhoby, "Labeling Poetry in the Middle and Late Byzantine Period," *Byzantion* 85 (2015), 259–83, esp. 263. On the Anthologia Marciana, see F. Spingou, "Byzantine Collections and Anthologies of Poetry," in *A Companion to Byzantine Poetry*, eds. W. Hörandner, A. Rhoby and N. Zagklas (forthcoming)

[10] On questions at the beginning of a lament see M. Alexiou, *Ὁ τελετουργικὸς θρῆνος στὴν ἑλληνικὴ παράδοση* (Athens, 2002) and also eadem, *The Ritual Lament in Greek Tradition*, second edition, revised by D. Yatromanolakis and P. Roilos (Lanham, MD, 2002)

birth, but also a good general. Then, in vv. 11–22, the previous happy life is contrasted with the new situation.[11] Subsequently (vv. 23–33), she expresses her sorrow and her wish to be buried with him, since only then she will find peace.[12] Finally, she beseeches God for the salvation of her husband and to grant him a place in Paradise (vv. 34–36).

The *purple-born* Andronikos mentioned in the title has been identified with Andronikos the second son of John II Komnenos. He is the only Andronikos of the imperial line of the Komnenoi who was born in purple (v. 7).[13] Andronikos was probably struck by the same illness that caused the death of his brother Alexios the co-emperor, whose body Andronikos escorted to Constantinople.[14] The bodies of the two brothers were brought to Constantinople by their third brother, Isaac. Their funeral took place in Constantinople in the summer of 1142, following John II's return from Cilicia.[15]

The text must have been written at the time of Andronikos's death. The reference to νῦν in v. 12 with the meaning "in this present occasion" speaks of a recent event. Also, the reference to παῖδας ("children") for Andronikos's offspring further corroborates a date close to Andronikos death. The title offers the unique information that the tomb of the *sebastokrator* Andronikos was in the Pantokrator Monastery—without providing any further detail. There can be little doubt that Andronikos's burial place is no other than the monastic complex founded by Empress Eirene-Piroska and her husband John II Komnenos as a family mausoleum and the symbol of their dynasty.[16]

The poem is one of the many ὡς ἀπὸ προσώπου ("on behalf of") verse fashionable in the Byzantine court.[17] Andronikos's wife was the celebrated *sebastokratorissa* Eirene, one of the most prominent patronesses of visual arts and literature in

---

[11] On *Antithesis*, see Alexiou, Θρῆνος, 270–88.
[12] On double and common burials, see Spingou, "Lamenting," as in fn. 28 and p. 284.
[13] The identification of the Andronikos in question with Andronikos, the son of Alexios I, who also bore the title of sebastokrator (Varzos, Γενεαλογία, no. 35; I: 229–237) should be eliminated as he was not born in the purple, and he died in 1130/1, before the construction of the Church St. Michael, and his wife predeceased him.
[14] John Kinnamos, A. Meineke, ed., *Ioannis Cinnami epitome rerum ab Ioanne et Alexio Comnenis gestarum*, CSHB 23 (Bonn, 1836), §10, p. 24, transl. C.M. Brand, *Deeds of John and Manuel Comnenus* (New York, 1976), p. 27. Cf. Michael Italikos, *Monody*, 131, 10–20. For the identification see also Vassis, "Pantokratorkloster," 232. On Alexios see Varzos, Γενεαλογία, no. 74; I: 339–48.
[15] On that point see below ###.
[16] See Ousterhout in this volume.
[17] I. Drpić, *Epigram, art, and devotion in later Byzantium* (Cambridge, 2016), 87–98.

the Komnenian court, particularly in her widowhood.[18] However, it remains unclear why the title names her *sebastokratorissa* Anna, instead of Eirene.

Sebastokratorissa Anna?

One possible suggestion is that the name of the *sebastokratorissa* lacked in the original and a later copier added her name, mistaking her for Agnes of France, wife of Andronikos I Komnenos (r.1183–85), who assumed the name Anna upon her arrival to Byzantium. Such a clumsy mistake and historical inaccuracy, however, is without parallel in the Anthologia Marciana. The redactor of the anthology, who worked around 1200, and the main scribe of the manuscript, who lived in the late thirteenth century, would certainly have known of the humiliating end of Andronikos I.[19]

Konstantinos Varzos suggests that the name is the *sebastokratorissa* Eirene's monastic name.[20] Anna would have been a suitable monastic name for her. She assumed the name Eirene (Peace) as a foreign bride,[21] but Anna, the mother of the Theotokos, would seem particularly appropriate for an Orthodox mother. Unfortunately, Varzos does not support his solution with any evidence other than the title of our poem and I have not been able to corroborate this suggestion further. There is no firm evidence that the *sebastokratorissa* Eirene assumed the monastic habit or resided in a convent. On the contrary, she had been imprisoned numerous times, exiled, and forced to follow Manuel on his expeditions.[22] She resided in the Pantokrator complex for three years, and received medical treatment to cure her fragile health.[23] Living outside the monastic premises was not exceptional in the case of an

---

[18] See Jeffreys in this volume.

[19] Nichetas Choniates, *History*, ed. J. van Dieten, *Nicetae Choniatae historia*, CFHB 11/1, (Berlin, 1975) 349, 10–350, 38, trans. H. Magoulias, *O City of Byzantium: Annals of Niketas Choniates*, Byzantine texts in translation (Detroit, 1984), 192–93. On Andronikos I, see Varzos, Γενεαλογία, no. 87; I: 493–638. On the identification of the scribe to the main compiler of the *Anthologia Maricana* see my "Words and Artworks," 47–49.

[20] Varzos, Γενεαλογία, I: 378.

[21] E. Jeffreys and M. Jeffreys, "Who was Irene the Sevastokratorissa?" *Byzantion* 64 (1994) 40–68; A. Rhoby, "Verschiedene Bemerkungen zur Sevastokratorissa Eirene und zu Autoren in ihrem Umfeld," *Nea Rhome,* 6 (2009), 308–20; and more recently Jeffreys, "The ebastokratorissa Irene as a Patron," 178. The name is indicative of her being "a true outsider," rather than simply coming from the Norman groups settled in Constantinople. Her role upon marrying the emperor's son and second in line to the succession of the throne was to bring peace / *eirene*.

[22] See Varzos, Γενεαλογία, 368–71.

[23] Varzos, Γενεαλογία, 371.

aristocratic widow who took monastic vows following the death of her husband.[24] Now, why Eirene was confined in various places rather than retiring to a monastery remains unclear. Similarly, although it is plausible to surmise that the *sebastokratorissa* became a nun at the end of her life, even perhaps on her deathbed, it is unclear why sources would remain silent about her assuming the name Anna. In that case, the title in the *AM* might have been updated after the initial composition, as it has been done for at least one other poem in the same compilation—perhaps it is the only testimony of *sebastokratorissa*'s short (or long) life as a nun.[25]

Monody or Verse Inscription?

The anonymous compiler of the *AM* did not copy the epigrams from works of art or tomb monuments *in situ*, but from other manuscripts. The only way we can reconstruct the text's original function is from the evidence provided by the title and the text itself.

The voice of the wife, speaking in the second person, coupled with the strong emotional tone, suggest that this text is a monody, the funerary dirge sung during the burial. The poem is the only indication that Andronikos was buried in the Pantokrator monastery, nothing else is known about his burial. The St. Michael funerary chapel (the *heroon*) was built as an integral part of the Pantokrator complex as a burial place for the imperial family. Andronikos and his brother were buried on the same day. No eulogy has survived for Alexios, but the *Typikon* of the Pantokrator hints to him being buried in the tomb prepared John in the *heroon*. Theodore Prodromos verse monody and Michael Italikos's prose monody were offered as λογικαὶ χοαί ("offerings of *logos*") during Andronikos's burial.[26]

Michael Italikos's monody presents Andronikos's personality differently from the poetic version. Italikos portrays Andronikos as a man-at-arms and as a future emperor. He addresses and consoles only the emperor-general, John, for the loss of his sons.

---

[24] See for example, Sophia Komnene, wife of *pansebastos sebastos* Theodore Dokianos, who became nun Sossana shortly after the death of her husband, but she continued raising her children, presumably outside the convent. Varzos, *Γενεαλογία*, no. 29; I: 169–72.

[25] See Spingou, "The Anonymous Poets," 143.

[26] Italikos, *Monody*, title: Μονῳδία εἰς τὸν σεβαστοκράτορα κῦρ Ἀνδρόνικον, τὸν υἱὸν τοῦ βασιλέως κυροῦ Ἰωάννου τοῦ πορφυρογεννήτου θανόντα, ὅτε ἐκόμιζεν ἐξ Ἀττάλιας νεκρὸν τὸν ἀδελφὸν αὐτοῦ κῦρ Ἀλέξιον τὸν πορφυρογέννητον. The term λογικαὶ χοαί is used by Italikos, 134, 10: Ταῦτά σοι καὶ παρ' ἡμῶν χοαὶ προσήχθησαν λογικαί. Prodromos, *Monody*, title: Στίχοι ἴαμβοι μονῳδικοὶ ἐκ προσώπου τῆς σεβαστοκρατορίσης ἐπὶ τῷ αὐτῷ ὁμοζύγι.

Theodore Prodromos's monody, written, like the poem of the *AM*, on behalf of the *sebastokratorissa* Eirene, has a highly emotional tone. Prodromos presents Andronikos the man: Eirene laments for the loss of her dear husband, but also as a soldier-husband, whose return was eagerly awaited in the family home. Now, his wife and children lament over his dead body and wait for Andronikos's answer in vain.[27] Eirene gives mythological examples of laments, suggesting that objects and animals also mourn with her the loss of Andronikos. Eirene says that she pronounces these words in front of the painted portrait of her husband,[28] whose prayers she beseeches for herself and their children.

The similarity between Prodromos's 393-verse monody and the anonymous thirty-seven-verse epitaph is remarkable.[29] The narrator Eirene laments her fate. She conceives of herself as a tree, torn down by the death of her husband[30]; she is a fruit in bloom struck by untimely decay[31]; Andronikos is her light (φωσφόρος), which suddenly darkened.[32] The two poems use the same mythological parallel: the lament for Phaethon, clearly referred to by Prodromos, not named in the *AM*. In both poems, the tears shed for Andronikos are golden, not amber.[33]

Despite these similarities, Theodore Prodromos's authorship of the two poems cannot be established. Apart from parallel passages, there are also many differences between the poems: in Prodromos's monody the Heliades are crying; in the *AM* poem, Eirene assumes the status of a mourning Heliade. The similarities are often twelfth-century literary *topoi*—such as the reference to story of Phaethon, recurring in epitaphs and monodies of Michael Italikos, Euthymios Tornikes, Nike-

---

[27] Prodromos, *Monody*, vv. 112–50.
[28] Cf. Theodore Prodromos, *Monody*, vv. 366–83. This portrait could have been either a portable painting or a fresco/mosaic in an arcosolium. As Robert Ousterhout noted: his uncle Isaak had portraits of his parents displayed at his tomb in the Kosmosoteira monastery, and specifies that his own "made in the vanity of boyhood" be left at the Chora monastery. This suggests that portraits (portable ones) may have been common at upper-class tombs. For a discussion and bibliography on arcosolia see F. Spingou, "Lamenting: Tomb Epigrams and Epitaphs," in in *Texts on Byzantine Art and Aesthetics 3: Visual and Textual Culture in Later Byzantium (1081–ca. 1330)*, ed. eadem, series editor Ch. Barber (Cambridge, forthcoming), II.7.
[29] The similarity is observed by I. Vassis, "Pantokratorkloster," esp. p. 234.
[30] Prodromos, *Monody*, 334–35, cf. *AM B57*, 12.
[31] Prodromos, *Monody*, 30–32, cf. *AM* B57, 1. See also the reference to the common burial (Prodromos, *Monody*, 346–48, cf. *AM* B57, 32–4), the Hyacinth=Blue (Prodromos, *Monody*, 240, cf. *AM* B57, 8).
[32] Prodromos, *Monody*, 221–23, cf. *AM* B57, 16–7.
[33] Prodromos, *Monody*, 197–200.

tas Choniates, and Manganeios Prodromos.[34] The similarity between the two poems is due either to the poet of the *AM*'s immediate access to Prodomos's lament, or to the common cultural background and education of the two poets. It seems most likely that the anonymous poet was present at the funeral and heard Prodromos pronouncing his monody. Access to an oral source would help to explain the differences between the two poems.

It would have been odd if both texts were performed as monodies at the funeral: repetitions would have been tedious. The overlaps between the two texts suggest that that the poem in the *AM* was meant as a tomb epigram. Internal evidence corroborates this view. The voice of the closest kin is typical for tomb epigrams in Byzantium. References in the text point to an actual funerary monument (1. ἀλγεινὴ θέα, 5. νεκρὸς γὰρ ἐντὸς..., and so on). The references to λίθος (vv. 2, 30) and to a πέτρινος λαξευτὸς τάφος (v. 32) point to a sarcophagus, as those placed in the *arcosolia*. The reference to the salvation of the deceased also confirms the inscriptional use of the text.

A text consisting of thirty-six lines is not too long to be inscribed in the Pantokrator, where two other long verse epigrams have been recovered, one of 145 lines,[35] and another of at least forty-four lines.[36] The latter was engraved on the base of the Stone of the Unction placed next to the tomb of Emperor Manuel I in the *heroon*. The inscription resembles the tomb epigram in the *AM* in that it is presented in the voice of the wife, Mary of Antioch, who laments her deceased husband, Manuel. I will return to this parallel later. Now let us turn to the political implication of the tomb epigram in the *AM*.

The Logistics of a Verse Inscription

The anonymous tomb epigram seems to have been composed soon after the death of Andronikos—or perhaps some months after his death. The *typikon* of the Pantokrator monastery is the most accurate source for the *heroon*, composed in 1136,

---

[34] See Italikos, ed. Gautier, *Michel Italikos*, no. 3, p. 88, 1–4; Euthymios Tornikes, ed. J. Darrouzès, "Les discours d'Euthyme Tornikès (1200–1205)," *Revue des études byzantines* 26 (1968): no.. 3, §29, Niketas Choniates, J. van Dieten, *Nicetae Choniatae orationes et epistulae*, Corpus Fontium Historiae Byzantina, 3 (Berlin, 1972), no. 3, p. 19, l. 21–23; cf. Manganeios, E. and M. Jeffreys, eds. (forthcoming), poems no. 50 and 108.

[35] Reported in the 1570s by Theodosios Zygomalas, see Vassis, "Pantokratorkloster," 203–20.

[36] Reported in the late eighteenth century by Meletios of Ioannina, see Vassis, "Pantokratorkloster," 239–42. The text has been previously translated in English by Cyril Mango (C. Mango, "Notes on Byzantine monuments," *Dumbarton Oaks Papers* 23–24 (1970) 372–75, esp. 372–73 = *Studies on Constantinople* (Variorum Reprints, 1993) XVI, for a revised translation based on the new edition see F. Spingou, "Lamenting," appendix.

before the burials of Alexios, Andronikos, and John II. Neither John, nor his ghost-writer who penned the *typikon*, anticipated the premature deaths of the two brothers.[37] Organizing a personalized burial for the deceased, as suggested by the epigram, required time.

John II was in Cilicia when Alexios and Andronikos died, but, according to imperial encomiast John Italikos, he was present at the state funerals of his sons.[38] To make the necessary arrangements for leaving his army and return to Constantinople he required time.[39] John remained in Cilicia until at least 25 September.[40] The journey itself, probably by boat, should not have taken too long. At a rough estimate, a boat trip from near İskenderun (where John is last attested) to Constantinople takes between eleven and sixteen days.[41] This may leave enough time for the preparations for the funerals to have taken place, and the rhetors to write their epitaphs in prose and verse.

The Ritual Function of the Verse Inscription

Scholars suggest that the verses were inscribed on the funerary monument, as it was incorporated into the original plan of the *heroon*, perhaps months after the death of the brothers, but before the passing of John II in 1143.[42] The verses are connected to

---

[37] P. Gautier, "Le typikon du Christ Sauveur Pantocrator," *REB* 32 (1974), 1–145; English translation by Robert Jordan in J. Thomas and A. Hero, eds., *Byzantine Monastic Foundation Documents*, Dumbarton Oaks Studies, (Washington, D.C., 2000), 725–81 (hereafter: *Pantokrator Typikon*)

[38] Italikos, *Monody*, 132, 12–13. The two brothers might have been buried individually but probably on the same day. Evidence is offered by the monody of Michael Italikos for the *sebastokrator* Andronikos. Italikos begins his oration with a reference to the burial of Alexios as a very recent event (Πενθοῦμεν καὶ τοῦτο <τὸ> δεύτερον πένθος, ὥσπερ μὴ ἀρκοῦντος τοῦ πρώτου εἰς κοινὴν συμφοράν πλὴν ὅσον τοῦ πρώτου βαρύτερον...); Italikos, *Monody*, 133.

[39] John's presence at the funeral is not confirmed by Kinnamos and Choniates (see Kinnamos, ed. Meineke, 24; transl. Brand, p. 27; Choniates, van Dieten, 38, 13–19, transl. Magoulias, p. 22). Choniates attests that John did not retreat his army from the Eastern regions. However, it is possible that he returned to Constantinople for the winter, as he did a year earlier (see Choniates, van Dieten, 37, 75–84, transl. Magoulias, *op. cit.*, 21). John died in April 1143 at a camp in Cilicia, after a hunting accident. On John's Syrian campaign see F. Chalandon, *Jean II Comnène (1118–1143) et Manuel I Comnène (1143–1180)* (Paris, 1912), 175–93 and P. Magdalino, *The empire of Manuel I Komnenos, 1143–1180* (Cambridge, 1993), 38–42.

[40] On 25 September 1142 John is attested to be near Bagras, at modern district of İskenderun, Turkey (Chalandon, *Jean II Comnène*, 187).

[41] Distance: 887 NM, according to Imray chart M20. Average speed: between 2.2 and 3.2 kn, cf. estimates offered in R. Gertwagen and E. Jeffreys, *The age of the dromon: the Byzantine navy ca. 500–1204,* The medieval Mediterranean 62, (Leiden, 2006) 351.

[42] On the planning of the *heroon* and its tomb, see Ousterhout in this volume.

the monody that Theodore Prodromos, the Komnenian poet laureate, pronounced during Andronikos's state funeral. Why would the *sebastokratorissa* Eirene wish to inscribe verses on her husband's tomb in the form of a lament months after the death of her beloved? Why would she need to wait for a comparable text to be pronounced at the funeral? I suggest that the text had a ritual function with particular implications for the admittedly precarious political position of the *sebastokratorissa* Eirene and her children following her husband's death.

Inscriptions address different recipients and transmit multilayered messages. Placed in a church, they address God, the Theotokos, the saints, and the Eternal Reader. Eirene (vv. 34–36) addresses God, asking for the salvation of her husband's soul. Should the inscription remain visible, the presence of a tomb epigram links the dedicator and the deceased—a link that would have been otherwise invisible at the funeral? The word νῦν in v. 12 is consistent with the present, being expressive of both the time of the offering and of the reading. Even if viewers were unable to read it (either because of illiteracy or ignorance of the Greek), the existence of the inscription inspired awe and admiration for the deceased (and his relatives).[43]

If the beholder were able to read it, the inscription could become the focal point of ritual.[44] The beholder would begin a private, repetitive commemoration each time he re-enacts the contents of the epitaph. The reader is thus transformed into a mediator addressing supernatural agents, Christ, Mary, or a saint. Readers would be moved to recite by the stipulation that such a commemoration would assist in Andronikos's salvation.[45] One is thus immersed in a prescribed synesthetic and kinesthetic event.

The recipient would *hear* the epigram written in verse. Verse has a ceremonial significance in itself. The meter makes a text appear special as the recipient can easily hear its rhythm, the musical aspect of the poem. Then, because the tombs were

---

[43] On this see e.g., A. Papalexandrou, "Echoes of Orality in the Monumental Inscriptions of Byzantium," in *Art and Text in Byzantine Culture*, ed. L. James (Cambridge, 2007), 161–87.

[44] On the question of accessibility for inscriptions, see, e.g., Drpić, *Epigram, Art and Devotion*, 48–66, with further bibliography. On rituals and their definition see R. Rappaport, *Ritual and Religion in the Making of Humanity*. Cambridge Studies in Social and Cultural Anthropology 110 (Cambridge, 1999), 23–58 (where performance and formality are emphasized); V. W. Turner, *The Forest of Symbols: Aspects of Ndembu Ritual* (Ithaca, NY, 1967), 95 (where the transformative effect is discussed); E. T. Lawson and R. N. McCauley, *Rethinking Religion: Connecting Cognition and Culture* (Cambridge, 1990), 176 (emphasis on the superhuman agent). C. Humphreys and J. Laidlaw, *The Archetypal Actions of Ritual: A Theory of Ritual Illustrated by the Jain Rite of Worship* (Oxford, 1994), 97–98 (on the prescription of acts).

[45] About the necessity of commemorations of the deceased in Byzantine culture, see V. Marinis, *Death and the Afterlife in Byzantium: The Fate of the Soul in Theology, Liturgy, and Art* (Cambridge, 2016), 95–97.

placed in a church the *smell* of the incense would have been predominant and the viewer would automatically *touch* the icons placed at the tomb. The viewer would also *see* the tomb and the epigram. Light entering from the twin dome offered movement to the event. The natural light reflected on the marbles covering the walls. Wall and apse mosaics, and gilded carving would have intensified the play of light. The light's natural movement would have given the impression that the *heroon* was in movement. By 1200, the viewer saw the multicolored "Stone of Unction" and five sarcophagi, many of them decorated with verse inscriptions.[46] Not only did the lights scintillate, but the viewer was encouraged to move while reading the tomb epigrams in the confined space of the *heroon*, whose arches and vaults were decorated with scenes representing the Crucifixion, the Entombment and the Resurrection of Christ. A dynamic relationship was created between tombs, epigrams and mosaics especially since the Anastasis and the Holy Women at the Tomb of Christ were in a prominent relationship to the Komnenian tombs[47]. There was even more movement: according to the *Typikon*, the Friday processions not only passed by the tombs but stopped in front of them with a long prayer (ἐκτενές) being offered to the deceased.[48]

The ritual lament could be read on different levels, it was accessible to the initiated and the uninitiated alike. The simplicity of the language of our poem allows the uninitiated to have a basic interaction with the text. The rhetorical character of the text postulates that the initiated were members of the cultural elite to which the *sebastokratorissa* Eirene belonged.[49] Only the initiated were able to enjoy the *topoi* and the hidden implications of the poem. Not everyone understood the meaning of Phaethon's myth or the Lydian stone (vv. 25–30). But those participating in the literary salons of the twelfth century would have been familiar with it.[50]

The *sebastokratorissa* Eirene was a foreign princess, who for a fleeting moment was positioned to become an empress, with her children in line to be heirs of the

---

[46] The poetic evidence has been collected in Vassis, "Pantokratorkloster," 203–49.

[47] On the depiction of the Holy Women at the Tomb, see R. Ousterhout, "Women at Tombs: Narrative, Theatricality, and the Contemplative Mode," in A. Eastmond and L. James, eds., *Wonderful things: Byzantium through its art* (Farnham/Burlington, 2013), 236–39.

[48] *Pantokrator Typikon*, par. 29, transl. 753–54. See also B. Pentcheva, *Icons and Power: The Mother of God in Byzantium* (University Park, Penn, 2006), 169–73. N. P. Ševčenko, "The service of the Virgin's Lament Revisited," in *The Cult of the Mother of God in Byzantium: Texts and Images*, eds. L. Brubaker and M. B. Cunningham (Burlington, VT, 2011), 253–55.

[49] About this cultural elite, see P. Magdalino, "Cultural change? The context of Byzantine Poetry from Geometres to Prodromos," in *Poetry and its contexts in eleventh-century Byzantium*, eds. F. Bernard and K. Demoen (Farnham/Burlington, 2012), 19–36.

[50] See for example the notes of John Tzetzes about Phaethon in Tzetzes, Chiliades ed. P. L. Leone, *Ioannis Tzetzae Historiae*. Pubblicazioni dell'Istituto di filologia classica. Università degli studi di Napoli, 1 (Naples, 1968), chil. 4, hist. 137, ll. 359–92.

throne.⁵¹ The lament was meant to demonstrate her capacity to participate in social life on that level by commissioning a basic component of a funerary celebration. She was a worthy member of the Constantinopolitan elite, fully acquainted with its cultural products. Eirene's patronage served the same purpose, showing that she belonged to the dominant culture of her time.⁵² The poet does not fail emphasizing Eirene's social role and describe her despair after her loss—a *topos* that reflected reality.

What is particularly interesting is that the poet's focus is Eirene. It is quite remarkable that, after v. 12, the epigram becomes a lament for the *sebastokratorissa*. Motifs used to mourn the deceased are reemployed for Eirene: the blooming yeast harvested early does not refer to Andronikos, as we would expect, but to Eirene.⁵³ Moreover, particularly striking is her promise that she will be buried in the same tomb as Andronikos, in the *heroon*.⁵⁴ The same promise is repeated in Prodromos's monody.⁵⁵ Being buried together might strike the modern reader as odd, but it was a common practice and similar manifestations were frequent in texts from later Byzantium, when family had become a central component of one's social identity.⁵⁶

Yet the symbolism of a double burial is exceptional in this context. A double burial was not foreseen for John II and Piroska-Eirene, the founders of the Pantokrator complex. The only reference to a double burial in the Pantokrator is Alexios's request to his father John that they be buried in the same tomb, as reported in the *Typikon*.⁵⁷ Alexios might have been John's favorite son, or this arrangement reflects on John's high hopes for his co-emperor, heir, and continuator of his dynasty. Eirene's vow also had a strong political undertone, as she would secure that Andronikos's line has a place to the imperial succession. In this respect, Eirene was recognized as a potential troublemaker by Emperor Manuel who expelled her from the court.

It is in this context, installing a tomb inscription with Eirene's voice could be read as a sign of assurance of her stature. Regardless if the inscription was installed before or after Manuel was proclaimed emperor (that is, less than a year after Andronikos's burial), the *sebastokratorissa* publicly demonstrated that she and

---

51 Jeffreys, "The sebastokratorissa Irene as Patron," 178.
52 Ibid., p. 191–93.
53 However, this is not without parallel. Theodore Prodromos, Κατὰ Ῥοδάνθη καὶ Δοσικλέα: 'the lamenting Rodanthe is like rotten apple ("μαραίνεται τὸ μῆλον, ἡ ῥοιὰ φθίνει," 6.299, 258). On the tree motif in mourning see Alexiou, Θρῆνος, 315–17.
54 Vv. 30–34.
55 Cf. Theodore Prodromos, *Monody*, vv. 347–48.
56 See F. Spingou, "Anthologia Marciana, Sylloge B: Epigrams on the Tomb of Two Comnenian Aristocratic Ladies," in *Texts on Byzantine Art and Aesthetics 3: Visual and Textual Culture in Later Byzantium (1081–ca. 1330)*, ed. eadem, series editor Ch. Barber (Cambridge, forthcoming).
57 *Pantokrator Typikon*, par. 32, transl. p. 755, par. 35, transl. 756, par. 44, transl. 759.

her children were members of the Komnenos family with valid claims to the succession. A few decades later, another foreign bride, Maria of Antioch, used the same means to manifest her role in the Palace: an inscription, in which her voice was to be heard, placed next to Manuel's tomb.[58]

Conclusions

The *sebastokratorissa* Eirene's agency behind at least one of the poetic texts created a personalized ritual lament[59] in a code appropriate for Komnenian culture. That lament was staged in two acts. The first act—Theodore Prodromos's monody—began and finished during the funeral. The second act, however, was meant to be perennial: it started each time a viewer stopped and read the text. Space was strictly defined: it was the dynastic mausoleum in the monastery founded by Empress Piroska-Eirene. Even if the *sebastokratorissa*'s remains were not laid to rest there, as her verse alleged, Eirene was always present in the Pantokrator, thanks to her epitaph commemorating Andronikos.[60]

Appendix

Εἰς τὸν ἐν τῇ μονῇ τοῦ Παντοκράτορος τάφον τοῦ σεβαστοκράτορος καὶ πορφυρογεννήτου κυροῦ Ἀνδρονίκου ὡς ἀπὸ τῆς συμβίου αὐτοῦ τῆς σεβαστοκρατορίσσης κυρᾶς Ἄννης

   Ὦ τύμβε, πικρὰ κλῆσις, ἀλγεινὴ θέα,
   πόσους θανόντας ἐν μικρῷ κρύπτεις λίθῳ
   ἑνὸς μὲν ἀνδρὸς συγκαλύπτων ὀστέα,
   ψυχὰς δὲ πολλῶν συντεθαμμένας φέρων;
5 νεκρὸς γὰρ ἐντός, καὶ κόνις καὶ χοῦς μόνον,
   σεβαστοκράτωρ, ὁ γλυκύς μου δεσπότης,
   τὸ πορφυρίζον ἐκ βαφῆς γένους ῥόδον,

---

[58] As in Fn. 36.

[59] For a summary and further bibliography on ritual lament in Byzantium see N. Constas, "Death and dying in Byzantium," in *Byzantine Christianity. A people's history of Christianity* 3, D. Krueger, ed. (Minneapolis, 2010), 128–31.

[60] Indeed, since the tomb epigram does not survive *in situ*, there is a possibility that the inscription never came into existence; this is impossible to know. For this analysis, I relied on the extant evidence (which suggests the existence of that tomb inscription) and examined the intentions of the author and the instigator for the composition of the text.

χρωσθὲν δ᾽ ὑακίνθινον ἐκ τῆς ἀξίας,
ὁ κλεινὸς Ἀνδρόνικος οὐ κλήσει μόνῃ
10 ἔργοις δὲ συντρέχουσιν αὐτὴν δεικνύων,
ᾧ καὶ συνήφθην καὶ συνηυξήθην πόσῳ, | f. 107
καὶ νῦν πεσόντι συγκατερράγην πλέον.
ἤνθισα μικρόν, ἦλθον εὐθὺς εἰς θέρος,
δέδωκα καρπούς, ἦλθεν εὐθὺς ἡ φθίσις,
15 ἤνεγκα παῖδας, ὠρφανίσθησαν τάχει,
ἤκουσα μήτηρ, ἀλλὰ χήρα συντόμως.
ἔκρυψεν, οἴμοι, φωσφόρον μου τὸν μέγαν,
ὁ νυκτοποιὸς τῆς ἐμῆς ψυχῆς τάφος
ἐπ᾽ ἀλλοδαπῆς, ὦ ῥάγηθι καρδία,
20 ὁ καὶ φθονήσας καὶ θέας τοῦ συζύγου.
πολλὴν δ᾽ ἐγὼ μέλαιναν ἠμφιασάμην
ζόφῳ βαφεῖσαν τῆς χυθείσης ἑσπέρας,
καὶ ζῶσα θνήσκω καὶ λαλῶ ψυχῆς δίχα·
ἔχω δὲ καὶ τὰ τέκνα συνθανόντα μοι
25 κἂν ἀέρος πνέωσι λεπτὴν συρμάδα.
ἤγουν γενοίμην δένδρον, οὐ μύθῳ μόνον,
ὡς μικρὰν εὕρω τοῦ μακροῦ λήθην πάθους
ἠλεκτρίνοις δε δακρύοις αὐτὸν βρέχω,
ὃν χρυσίνοις προσῆκε θρηνεῖν δακρύοις,
30 ἤγουν φανείην ταῖς ἀληθείαις λίθος
ὡς εὐτυχήσω ταῖς ἁφαῖς κἂν ἐν κόναις
ὡς πέτρινος δειχθεῖσα λαξευτὸς τάφος
καὶ συλλαβοῦσα τοῦ συνεύνου τὴν κόνιν.
ἀλλ᾽ ὦ πνοῆς τε καὶ χρόνου ζυγοστάτα,
35 τῷ κειμένῳ δὸς οὐρανῶν κληρουχίαν
καὶ σὸν βλέπειν πρόσωπον ἐν τρυφῆς τόποις.

M = Marc. Gr. 524 (XIIIex.), ff. 106–107^v.

Vas =I. Vassis, "Des Pantokratorkloster von Konstantinopel in der byzantinischen Dichtung," in *The Pantokrator monastery in Constantinople*, ed. S. Kotzabassi. (Boston MA—Berlin, 2013), pp. 230–31.

2. μικρᾷ rect.| 8. δὐακίνθινον M | 9. μονῆς M | 10. συντρέχουσανM | 11. πόσον Vas | 20. εἰκαὶM | 21. στολὴν corr. Vas | 24. σκυνθανόνταM | 25. ἀέραM | 26. ἤγοῦνMVas | 27. ἠλεκττρίνοιςM | 30. ἢ γοῦνMVas | 31. τοῖςMκὰ᾽ν M | 32. μόναιςVas | 34 ὦ Vas χρόνων Vas.

On the tomb of the *sebastokrator* and purple-born lord Andronikos in the Pantokrator monastery, as on behalf of by his wife, *sebastokratorissa* lady Anna.

Oh tomb, what a bitter name! What a terrible sight!
How many lifeless bodies do you hide within a small stone,
covering the bones of a single man
and burying with him the souls of many?
5   For the deceased inside, dust and ashes alone,
[is] the sebastokrator, my dear lord,
the rose dyed purple by his family line
and yet coloured blue by his rank,
the famous Andronikos [= victor over men], not only in name
10 but also by performing deeds appropriate to it [his name],
with whom I was joined in wedlock and was lifted high up;
but now that he has died, I have fallen down even deeper.
I blossomed for a short while, but soon the time of harvest was
                                                                         upon me;
I gave fruits, but soon the decay began;
15 I gave birth to children, but quickly they became orphans;
I was called 'mother', but 'widow' soon after.
18 the tomb bringing the darkness in my soul
17 concealed, alas! my great light
19 in foreign lands—oh, break my heart!—
20 the tomb which begrudged me the sight of my husband.
I wear the deepest black plunged
into the dusk of the evening that is spread out.
I am dead while still alive, and I speak without a soul.
My children have died along with me;
25 although they still breathe a light drift of air.
I wish I were a tree, not only in myth [but for real],
that I may find oblivion from my great pain
and that I may rain amber-tears upon him,
who deserves to be to lamented with tears of gold.
30 Or wish I were truly a tomb-stone,
that I may find joy even in touching his dust,
showing myself to be a carved stone tomb
and carrying in myself the ashes of my husband.
But, oh Thou who weighest breath and time,
35 grant that the one who lies here may inherit the heavens
and that he may see Thy face in the pastures of happiness.

Bibliography

Primary Sources

Kinnamos, John. *Epitome*. Ed. A. Meineke. *Ioannis Cinnami epitome rerum ab Ioanne et Alexio Comnenis gestarum*, CSHB 23. Bonn, 1836. Trans.: C.M. Brand, *Deeds of John and Manuel Comnenus*. New York, 1976.

Choniates, Niketas. *History*, Ed. Jan Louis van Dieten, *Nicetae Choniatae historia*, CFHB 11/1. Berlin, 1975). Trans.: Harry Magoulias, *O City of Byzantium: Annals of Niketas Choniates,* Byzantine texts in translation. Detroit, 1984.

Pantokrator Typikon. Ed. Paul Gautier, "Le typikon du Christ Sauveur Pantocrator," *REB* 32 (1974), 1–145; English translation by Robert Jordan in John Jacobs Thomas and Angela Constantindes Hero, eds., *Byzantine Monastic Foundation Documents*, Dumbarton Oaks Studies. Washington, D.C., 2000, 725–81.

Prodromos, Theodore. "Historical Poems." Ed. Wolfram Hörandner, ed., *Theodoros Prodromos: historische Gedichte,* Wiener byzantinistische Studien 11. Vienna, 1974.

Manganeios Prodromos, *Poems*, Ed. Elizabeth and Michael Jeffreys (forthcoming).

Tornikes, Euthymios. *Orations*, Ed. J. Darrouzès, "Les Discours d'Euthyme Tornikès (1200–1205)," *Revue des études byzantines* 26 (1968): 49–121.

Tzetzes, Chiliades ed. Petrus Aloisius Leone, *Ioannis Tzetzae Historiae*. Pubblicazioni dell'Istituto di filologia classica. Università degli studi di Napoli, 1. Naples, 1968.

Secondary Sources

Alexiou, Margaret. Ὁ τελετουργικὸς θρῆνος στὴν ἑλληνικὴ παράδοση. *The Ritual Lament in Greek Tradition*, second edition, revised by Dimitris Yatromanolakis and Panagiotis Roilos. Lanham, MD, 2002.

Chalandon, Ferdinand. *Jean II Comnène (1118–1143) et Manuel I Comnène (1143–1180)*. Paris, 1912.

Constas, Father Maximos. "Death and Dying in Byzantium," in *Byzantine Christianity*. A People's History of Christianity 3, ed. Derek Krueger. Minneapolis, 2010, 128–31.

Drpić, Ivan. *Epigram, Art, and Devotion in Later Byzantium*. Cambridge, 2016.

Gertwagen, Ruthy and Elizabeth Jeffreys. *The Age of the Dromon : the Byzantine Navy ca. 500–1204,* The medieval Mediterranean 62. Leiden, 2006.

Humphreys, Caroline, and Laidlaw, James. *The Archetypal Actions of Ritual: A Theory of Ritual Illustrated by the Jain Rite of Worship*. Oxford, 1994.

Jeffreys, Elizabeth. "The *Sebastokratorissa* Irene as Patron," *Female Founders in Byzantium and Beyond*, eds. Lioba Theis, Margaret Mullett, and Michael Grünbart, Wiener Jahrbuch für Kunstgeschichte 60/61. Cologne–Weimar –Vienna, 2014, 177–9.

Jeffreys, Elizabeth and Michael Jeffreys. "Who was Irene the Sevastokratorissa?" *Byzantion* 64 (1994): 40–68.

———. *Iacobi Monachi epistulae*. Turnhout, 2009.

Lambros, Spyridon. "Ὁ Μαρκιανὸς κώδιξ 524," ["Manuscript 524 of the Biblioteca Nazionale Marciana"] *Neos Ellenomnemon* 8 (1911): 3–59, 123–92

Mango, Cyril, "Notes on Byzantine Monuments," *Dumbarton Oaks Papers* 23–24 (1970): 372–75 = *Studies on Constantinople* (Variorum Reprints, 1993) XVI.

Lawson, E. Thomas and Robert N. McCauley, *Rethinking Religion: Connecting Cognition and Culture*. Cambridge, 1990.

Magdalino, Paul. *The Empire of Manuel I Komnenos, 1143–1180*. Cambridge, 1993.

———. "Cultural Change? The Context of Byzantine Poetry from Geometres to Prodromos," in *Poetry and Its Contexts in Eleventh-century Byzantium*, eds. Floris Bernard and Kristoffel Demoen. Farnham/Burlington, 2012, 19–36.

Marinis, Vasileios. *Death and the Afterlife in Byzantium: The Fate of the Soul in Theology, Liturgy, and Art*. Cambridge, 2016.

Mioni, Elpidio. *Bibliothecae Divi Marci Venetiarum Codices Graeci Manuscripti. Thesaurus Antiquus*, vol. 2. Rome, 1981.

Odorico, Paolo, and Charis Messis. "L'anthologie Comnène du cod. Marc. gr. 524: Problèmes d'évaluation," in: *L'épistolographie et la poésie épigrammatique: projets actuels et questions de méthodologie. Actes de la 16e table ronde organisée par Wolfram Hörandner et Michael Grünbart dans le cadre du XXe Congrès international des études byzantines. Collège de France-Sorbonne, Paris, 19–25 Août 2001*, eds. Wolfram Hörandner and Michael Grünbart. Paris, 2003, 191–213.

Ousterhout, Robert. "Women at Tombs: Narrative, Theatricality, and the Contemplative Mode," in *Wonderful things: Byzantium through its art*, eds. Antony Eastmond and Liz James. Farnham and Burlington, 2013, 229–46.

Pentcheva, Bissera. *Icons and Power: The Mother of God in Byzantium*. University Park, Penn, 2006.

Rappaport, Roy. *Ritual and Religion in the Making of Humanity*. Cambridge Studies in Social and Cultural Anthropology 110. Cambridge, 1999.

Rhoby, Andreas. "Verschiedene Bemerkungen zur Sevastokratorissa Eirene und zu Autoren in ihrem Umfeld," *Nea Rhome*, 6 (2009): 308–20.

———. "Labeling Poetry in the Middle and Late Byzantine Period," *Byzantion* 85 (2015): 259–83.

Ševčenko, Nancy Patterson. "The service of the Virgin's Lament Revisited," in *The Cult of the Mother of God in Byzantium: Texts and Images*, eds. Leslie Brubaker and Mary B. Cunningham. Burlington, VT, 2011.

Spingou, Foteini. "Words and Artworks in the Twelfth Century and Beyond: The Thirteenth-century Manuscript Marcianus Gr. 524 and the Twelfth-Century Dedicatory Epigrams on Works of Art," unpublished DPhil thesis, University of Oxford, 2013.

———. "The Anonymous Poets of the Anthologia Marciana" in *Byzantine Authorship: Theories and Practices*, ed. Aglae Pizzone. Berlin, 2014: 139–53.

———. *Poetry for the Komnenoi. The Anonymous Poetry from the Anthologia Marciana: Syllogae B, and C* (in preparation).

———. "Byzantine Collections and Anthologies of Poetry," in *A Companion to Byzantine Poetry*, eds. W. Hörandner, A. Rhoby and N. Zagklas (forthcoming).

———. "Lamenting: Tomb Epigrams and Epitaphs," in in *Texts on Byzantine Art and Aesthetics 3: Visual and Textual Culture in Later Byzantium (1081–ca. 1330)*, ed. eadem, series editor Ch. Barber (Cambridge, forthcoming), II.7.

Turner, Viktor. *The Forest of Symbols: Aspects of Ndembu Ritual*. Ithaca, NY, 1967.

Varzos, Konstantinos, Ἡ γενεαλογία τῶν Κομνηνῶν [*The Genealogy of the Komnenians*], 2 vols., Βυζαντινά κείμενα καὶ μελέται [Byzantine Texts and Studies] 20. Thessaloniki, 1984.

Vassis, Ioannis. "Das Pantokratorkloster von Konstantinopel in der byzantinischen Dichtung," in ed. S. Kotzabassi, *The Pantokrator Monastery in Constantinople*, Byzantinisches Archiv 27. Boston and Berlin, 2013: 230–31.

CONCLUDING REMARKS

Robert Ousterhout

Outside of Hungary most of us know Princess Piroska as the Empress Eirene. We know her appearance from her portrait in Hagia Sophia and her piety from the foundation of the Pantokrator Monastery. In the portrait, she is depicted with her husband John II Komnenos, flanking the Theotokos with the infant Christ, offering a benefaction to Hagia Sophia. John holds the moneybag, while she holds a scroll that records their donation. Both are regally garbed, in all the trappings of Byzantine rulership. While symmetrical in their poses, John looks proudly straight ahead. Eirene also faces forward, but with her eyes cast demurely to the side—that is, she looks toward the source of imperial power, her husband. She exhibits the appropriate demeanor for a modest, devout, and subservient wife. Aside from her blonde or possibly ginger hair, there is nothing to distinguish her as foreign born, no hint of her Hungarian birth.

There is nothing to marvel at in this thoroughly Byzantine representation. While a foreign-born princess may have been valued for her exotic beauty or the political alliances that came with her, to be the Empress of Byzantium, she had to look, act, and behave as a Byzantine lady of the highest social standing, to provide visible evidence of her assimilation and incorporation into Byzantine culture. We have a near-contemporary document that comprises a sort of primer, or "how-to" guide for a foreign princess, the so-called Epithalamion manuscript, now in the Vatican Library Vat. gr. 1176), which recently has been analyzed by Cecily Hillsdale.[1] It is usually associated with the Princess Agnes, the nine-year-old daughter of Louis VII of France, who was betrothed to the *porphyrogennetos* Alexios, son and succes-

---

[1] Cecily Hilsdale, "Constructing a Byzantine 'Augusta': A Greek Book for a French Bride," *Art Bulletin* 87/3 (2005), 458–83.

sor of Manuel Komnenos, in 1179. The book narrates in a simple vernacular text and parallel images—almost child-like in their simplicity—the *rite de passage* for the young French princess as she is transformed into the Byzantine empress Anna. Piroska must have gone through a similar process. In the case of Agnes, the assimilation seems to have been complete, for in 1203, confronted by the French participants of the Fourth Crusade, the 24-year-old Agnes-Anna claimed, speaking through an interpreter, that she had completely forgotten her mother tongue.

We might expect the same of Piroska-Eirene, who was married to John in 1104 (or shortly thereafter) at the tender age of 16. The question becomes: How Byzantine was she? The answer to this question is a matter of speculation, for the texts are virtually silent on the matter—and many other matters as well. For example, we know virtually nothing about her alleged 'conversion' to Orthodox Christianity. How much did her Catholicism matter in the early twelfth century? There was a tradition of saintly kingship in medieval Hungary, and her father Ladislaus was sainted. But the issue of religious affiliation goes unmentioned with most Western marriages, and I suspect it did not become a critical factor in such situations before the thirteenth century. My colleague Marianne Sághy has speculated that she was educated in a Greek-speaking monastery, and thus arrived in the capital with at least some knowledge of the language—a tempting hypothesis.

The question of language acquisition is important to understand Piroska-Eirene's place in the literary culture of the Byzantine elite. Did she know Greek well enough to participate? Did she, like her mother-in-law and her two foreign-born daughters-in-law, Eirene-Bertha and the *sebastokratorissa* Eirene, maintain her own literary salon, or *theatron*, or stable of poets? She must have associated with poets, for we have two epitaphs recorded for her, one by Theodore Prodromos and the other by Nikolaos Kallikles. Judging from the condescending remarks by poets associated with the *sebastokratorissa* Eirene, wherever she came from, she seems to have been more valued for her pocketbook than her literary acumen.[2] Was Eirene-Piroska similarly a literary parvenue?

Other nagging questions relate to her piety. Did she take the veil while she was married to John, as the *Synaxarion* seems to suggest: it says she had put on the angelic habit as the nun Xene, although it does not say when. Could her piety as expressed in architectural patronage reflect earlier examples, such as the pious Theodosian empresses, who became nuns and constructed churches in the Holy Land?

---

[2] Michael and Elizabeth Jeffreys, "Who was Eirene the Sebastokratorissa?" *Byzantion* 64 (1994), 40–68.

As Eirene came to be promoted as a saint, Theophano, wife of Leo VI seems to have been the role model.³ But there are still a lot of unanswered questions.

While we may never have all the answers, Piroska-Eirene provides a useful historical figure to "think with" about Byzantine culture and cultural relations during the long twelfth century—as the preceding papers amply demonstrate. In a similar way, including Hungary into our picture of East–West relations both broadens and deepens our perspective. We tend to think of Byzantine connections with Western Europe by way of the Mediterranean, but the emerging powers of Central Europe also played a critical role in the politics of the time.

In the final analysis, Piroska-Eirene may remain an enigma, but she nevertheless has left one of the most important religious shrines to survive from Byzantium. It is a *topos* in Byzantine literature that a great building reflects the character of its patron. Cassiodorus expressed it succinctly, centuries earlier: "As is the house, so is the inhabitant."⁴ This is why architectural *ekphraseis* appear frequently in Byzantine biographies. John Kinnamos does so in his almost-telegraphic description of her: "She established a monastery in the name of the Pantokrator, which is among the most outstanding in beauty and size. Such was this empress."⁵ What more did he need to say about her piety, modesty, and magnanimity? In short, we are fortunate that modern Istanbul preserves not one, but two portraits of Piroska-Eirene. One is the famous mosaic in the gallery of Hagia Sophia; the other, I would argue, is the Pantokrator. Let me end with a question: For which of the two would the empress Piroska-Eirene wish to be remembered? If we have understood anything of her character in the preceding essays, the answer should be obvious.

---

3   Paul Magdalino, "The Foundation of the Pantokrator Monastery in Its Urban Setting," in S. Kotzabassi, ed., *The Pantokrator Monastery in Constantinople*, Byzantinisches Archiv 27 (Berlin, 2013), 33–55, esp. 46–47.
4   Cassiodorus, *Variae* VII.5: "talis dominus esse ... quale eius habitaculum."
5   Ioannes Kinnamos, *Historia*, ed. A. Meineke. *CSHB* (Bonn 1836), 10.6–8, 31.11–13; trans. C. Brand, *Deeds of John and Manuel Comnenus by John Kinnamos* (New York, 1976), 17.

APPENDIX 1

Synaxarion

Edited by Sofia Kotzabassi, "Feasts at the Monastery of Pantokrator," in Sofia Kotzabassi (ed.), *The Pantokrator Monastery in Constantinople*. Boston—Berlin: De Gruyter, 2013, 170–175. English translation by Paul Magdalino, "The Foundation of the Pantokrator Monastery in Its Urban Setting." In: Sofia Kotzabassi (ed.), *The Pantokrator Monastery in Constantinople*. Boston – Berlin: De Gruyter, 2013, 50–55.

Τῇ αὐτῇ ἡμέρᾳ μνήμη τῆς ἀοιδίμου καὶ παμμακαρίστου βασιλίσσης καὶ κτητορίσσης τῆς σεβασμίας μονῆς τοῦ Παντοκράτορος σωτῆρος Χριστοῦ Εἰρήνης, τῆς διὰ τοῦ ἁγίου καὶ ἀγγελικοῦ σχήματος μετονομασθείσης Ξένης μοναχῆς

Ἔδει τὴν μεγίστην ταύτην καὶ ὑπερκειμένην τῶν πόλεων, μὴ κάλλει μόνον ἔργων, φθορᾷ χρόνου παραδιδομένων κομᾶν, καὶ διηγήμασι παλαιῶν ἀνδρῶν ἀρετῇ διαβεβοημένων τέρπεσθαι καὶ χαίρειν, ἀλλὰ καὶ τῇ ἀοιδίμῳ βασιλίσσῃ καὶ κτητορίσσῃ τῆς μονῆς τοῦ παντοκράτορος, μᾶλλον ἐγκαυχᾶσθαι καὶ ἐγκαλλωπίζεσθαι· (5) τοῦτο μέν, ὅτι τῶν παλαιῶν ἐκείνων τῷ χρόνῳ ἀμαυρωθέντων, ἀσυντελὴς τοῖς φιλοθεάμοσιν καὶ ἡ ἐκ τούτων τέρψις ἐγεγόνει, τοῦ κάλλους αὐτῶν ἐναποσβεσθέντος (ἀλλ' οὐδὲ εἰ καὶ ἀνακαίνισιν ἐδέξαντο, ἱκανὰ ταῦτα πρὸς τέρψιν ἔδοξαν ἄν· παρὰ τοῦτο γὰρ καὶ ἀτημέλητα προὔκειντο)· τῶν γὰρ ἐξ αὐτῶν κρηπίδων παρ' αὐτῆς τῆς ἀοιδίμου βασιλίσσης ἀνεγερθέντων, νεύσει καὶ γνώμῃ τοῦ κρατίστου βασιλέως, καὶ (10) εἰς δόξαν καὶ εὐχαριστίαν τοῦ δοξάσαντος αὐτοὺς στεφοδότου, τοῦ παντοκράτορος Θεοῦ καὶ σωτῆρος ἡμῶν Ἰησοῦ Χριστοῦ, καλλονῇ καὶ φαιδρότης, οἷς καὶ ἡ μεγαλόπολις αὕτη σεμνύνεται, καὶ τὰ τῷ χρόνῳ γηράσαντα καὶ ἀμαυρωθέντα, ταῖς ἐκ τούτων πεμπομέναις ἀκτῖσι, κατηύγασάν τε καὶ κατελάμπρυναν· τοῦτο δέ, ὅτι καὶ τὰς ἀρετὰς πάσας προσλαβομένη παιδόθεν, καὶ δοχεῖον τῶν ἀγαθῶν γεγενημένη (15) (παρὰ τοῦτο γὰρ καὶ τῷ θεοστέπτῳ καὶ πορφυρογεννήτῳ βασιλεῖ συνήφθη), κόσμος ὡράθη, οὐ μόνον τῶν ἐκ τῆς βασιλικῆς πορφύρας φυέντων καὶ βασιλικῶς ἀνατραφέντων, ὡς τῶν μὲν πρὸ αὐτῆς βασιλισσῶν, σφραγὶς ὥσπερ λογισθεῖσα καὶ γεγονυῖα, τῶν δὲ μετ' αὐτήν, ὡς ῥίζα παντοίων καλῶν καὶ ἀρχέτυπον ἐκμαγεῖον, ἀλλὰ καὶ αὐτῆς τῆς βασιλίδος τῶν πόλεων.

(20) Αὕτη οὖν ἡ ἀοίδιμος βασίλισσα Εἰρήνη, ἐκ γεννητόρων μὲν προῆλθεν εὐτυχῶν καὶ δυσμικῶν βασιλέων· ἐξ ἁπαλῶν δὲ ὡς εἰπεῖν ὀνύχων, ὥσπερ τὰ τῶν φυτῶν εὐγενῆ, ἔδειξεν ὁποίαν ἄρα τὰ κατ' αὐτὴν τὴν ἀπόβασιν δέξηται, τοῖς κρείττοσι μᾶλλον προκόπτουσα, ἢ τῷ χρόνῳ τῆς ἡλικίας κατάδηλος γέγονεν· εἴωθε γὰρ ἡ ἀρετὴ τοὺς ταύτην μετιόντας, κἂν ἐν γωνίᾳ καὶ παραβύστῳ κρύπτωνται, φανεροῦν (25) καὶ ἀνακηρύττειν.

Ἐπεὶ δὲ καὶ ζήτησις γέγονε κόρης εὐόπτου καὶ ἐναρέτου παρὰ τῶν ἀοιδίμων καὶ εὐσεβῶν βασιλέων Ἀλεξίου τοῦ Κομνηνοῦ καὶ Εἰρήνης τῶν ὁμοζύγων, καὶ ταύτην εὗρον πάντα τὰ κάλλιστα ὑπερβλύζουσαν, συνάπτουσι τῷ θεοπαρόχῳ αὐτῶν βλαστῷ καὶ πορφυρογεννήτῳ βασιλεῖ Ἰωάννῃ, καὶ χαρᾶς αὐτίκα καὶ εὐφροσύνης τότε (30) τὰ πάντα ἐπληροῦτο.

Παῖδας οὖν ἐξ αὐτοῦ ἀποτεκοῦσα ἄρρενάς τε καὶ θηλείας ἰσαρίθμους ὀκτώ, ἀνῆξε μὲν τούτους μεγαλπρεπῶς καὶ βασιλικῶς. Τὰ τοῦ βίου δὲ τερπνὰ ὡς οὐδὲν ἡγησαμένη καὶ ταύτην ὡς εἰπεῖν τὴν βασιλείαν, τὸ τοῦ Δαβὶδ ἐν ἑαυτῇ ὑποψιθυρίζουσα, 'τίς ὠφέλεια ἐν τῷ αἵματί μου, ἐν τῷ καταβαίνειν με εἰς διαφθοράν;' νυκτὸς (35) καὶ ἡμέρας οὐκ ἔληγε τὸν θεὸν θεραπεύουσα, ταῖς πρὸς τὴν βασίλειον ἀρχὴν ἀγαθαῖς μεσιτείαις τῶν ἐπιδεομένων ἀντιλαμβανομένη, καὶ παντοίως χειραγωγοῦσα.

Ἀλλὰ καὶ ἐν ἐλεημοσύναις ἔχαιρε διδοῦσα, ἢ λαμβάνουσα· καὶ πρὸ τοῦ στέφους ὅσα ταῖς χερσὶ ταύτης ἐνέτυχον, πένησιν ἐδίδου, καὶ ὀρφανῶν καὶ χηρῶν προστάτις, καὶ μετὰ τὸ στέφος ἐγεγόνει, καὶ τὰ τῶν μοναστῶν καταγώγια, χρήμασι κατελούτισε. (40) τὰ δ' ἄλλα, πῶς διηγήσομαι; τὸ πρᾶον, τὸ ἥσυχον, τὸ ταπεινόν, τὸ πρὸς πάντας συμπαθές, τὸ χάριεν, τὸ εὐόμιλον, τὸ ἀόργητον· οὐδέποτε γὰρ εἰς θυμὸν ἐκινήθη, οὐδὲ πρὸς κάκωσιν τινὸς ἢ λοιδορίαν ἐχώρησεν. Ἀλλ' εἰ καὶ μειδίαμά τι προελθεῖν ἐξ αὐτῆς ἔμελλε, καὶ τοῦτο σωφρονιζόμενον ἦν· ἀεὶ γὰρ καθ' ἑαυτὴν ἐπένθει καὶ ἐσκυθρώπαζεν, ὅτι καὶ ὁ ψαλτὴρ ἐπὶ στόματος ἦν, καὶ τῇ ἐγκρατείᾳ σεμνυνομένη, (45) τῇ τήξει τῶν σαρκῶν ἔχαιρε, τῇ εὐτελεῖ καὶ αὐτοσχεδίῳ τροφῇ χρωμένη, ἀσκητικῶς ζῆν ᾑρεῖτο.

Ταῦτα δὲ πάντα μὴ ἱκανὰ λογισαμένη, πρὸς ὃν εἶχεν ἐν ἑαυτῇ θεοφιλῆ σκοπόν, ὀψέποτε καὶ βραδέως τὸ στέφος τῆς βασιλείας λαβοῦσα, καὶ εἰς τὴν βασίλειον ἀναβιβασθεῖσα ταύτην ἀρχήν, πάντων καταφρονήσασα, καὶ πάντα τὰ ἀναγκαῖα καὶ (50) κατεπείγοντα πρὸς οὐδὲν θεμένη, τὴν βασιλικὴν μονὴν τὴν ἐπονομαζομένην τοῦ παντοκράτορος σωτῆρος Χριστοῦ τοῦ θεοῦ ἡμῶν συνεστήσατο ἐξ αὐτῶν βάθρων, τοὺς νῦν ὁρωμένους περικαλλεῖς ναοὺς ἀνεγείρασα, ξενῶνας τὲ καὶ γηροκομεῖα, κάλλει καὶ θέσει καὶ τῇ τούτων κατασκευῇ, τῶν προγεγονότων παλαιῶν τὲ καὶ νέων τὸ πρωτεῖον ἀράμενα, μεγάλως ἐπὶ τούτοις ἅπασι συναραμένου, καὶ τοῦ τὰς συμμετρίας (55) τῶν τοιούτων οἰκοδομημάτων διαταξαμένου εὐρύθμως καὶ καταλλήλως καὶ προσφυῶς νέου Βεσελεήλ, τοῦ πανεντίμου Νικηφόρου καὶ οἰκειοτάτου ἀνθρώπου αὐτῆς, κατὰ σπουδὴν ὅτι πολλὴν τὰ πρὸς τὴν τούτων ἀπάρτισιν κατεπείγοντος, ὡς μηδὲ κατὰ τὸ ἀρκοῦν τοῖς ὀφθαλμοῖς ὕπνου παραχωρῆσαι, μηδὲ τοῖς κροτάφοις ἀναπαύσεως. Καὶ οὕτω δὴ ταῦτα πάντα τῇ αὐτοῦ συνεργίᾳ ἀπαρτίσασά τε καὶ (60) ἀποκαταστήσασα, τῇ βασιλίδι ταύτῃ τῶν πόλεων, ὡράισμά τι τερπνὸν ἐνεστήσατο, χαίρουσα τῇ τούτων ἐπιτυχίᾳ καὶ καλλονῇ, καὶ τῷ θεῷ εὐχαριστοῦσα. Ἐπεὶ δὲ καὶ μείζονος ἔτι τοῦ βοηθήσοντος ἐδεῖτο, μείζονας καὶ τυγχάνει. τῆς γὰρ τοῦ βασιλέως χειρὸς καὶ ὁμοζύγου αὐτῆς κατὰ καιρόν ποτε δραξαμένη, καὶ ἐν τῷ παρ' αὐτῆς ἀνεγερθέντι περικαλλεῖ ναῷ τοῦ παντοκράτορος θεοῦ καὶ κυρίου (65) ἡμῶν Ἰησοῦ Χριστοῦ εἰσελθοῦσα, καὶ ἑαυτὴν αἰφνηδὸν χαμαὶ προσκαταβαλοῦσα, καὶ τὴν κεφαλὴν τῷ ἱερῷ ἐδάφει προσκολλήσασα, «δέξαι, ὦ δέσποτα, τὸν ἐκ θεοῦ σοι κατασκευασθέντα ναόν» μετὰ δακρύων ἀνεβόησε, τοῖς δάκρυσι δάκρυα προστεθεῖσα καὶ διαβεβαιοῦσα μὴ ἀναστῆναι, εἰ μὴ τὴν τοῦ ποθουμένου πληροφορίαν πράγματος δέξηται. Ὡς δὲ τὸ ἱερὸν ἔδαφος τοῖς δάκρυσι καταπλύνασα, ἠκηκόει (70) τοῦ βασιλέως τὰ καταθύμια ἐπαγγελλομένου ταύτης, ἅπαν τὲ βουλητὸν αὐτῇ περατῶσαι, καὶ τὰ ὑπὲρ δύναμιν ἀγωνίσασθαι παντοίως ἐπί τε ἱερῶν κειμηλίων ἀφιερώσει, ἀκινήτων διαφόρων προσκυρώσει, ἐφ' ᾧ καὶ διὰ κινητῶν καὶ ἀκινήτων καὶ εἰσόδων ἐτησίων τῶν ἁπάντων κατασκευάσαι, τὴν σεβασμίαν ταύτην μονὴν κράτος σχεῖν, καὶ Παντοκράτορα τὸν ἐν αὐτῇ τιμώμενον καὶ σεβόμενον κύριον καὶ (75) θεὸν ἡμῶν Ἰησοῦν Χριστόν, μόνον εἶναί τε καὶ ὀνομάζεσθαι, καὶ λόγοις καὶ ἔργοις τὰ πρωτεῖα κατὰ πάντων φέρειν, ἀνέστη χαρᾶς ἀφάτου καὶ εὐφροσύνης ἔμπλεως.

Καὶ ἡ μὲν ἀοίδιμος βασίλισσα καὶ κτήτορισσα ὥσπερ ὁ ἐπεφέρετο βάρος ἀποθεμένη, ἔχαιρεν ἔκτοτε καὶ ἠγαλλιᾶτο· οὐ πολὺ δὲ τὸ ἐν μέσῳ, καὶ ἐπ' αὐτῆς τῆς Βιθυνῶν ἐπαρχίας γενομένη, πρὸς ὃν ἐπόθει παντοκράτορα Χριστὸν ἐξεδήμησεν, (80) ἐν ταύτῃ τῇ μονῇ κατατεθεῖσα, ἣν ἐκ βάθρων ἀνήγειρε, τῆς δὲ πρὸς αὐτὴν ἐπαγγελίας παρὰ τοῦ εὐσεβοῦς βασιλέως τὸ πέρας λαβούσης καὶ τῆς βασιλικῆς καὶ παντοκρατορικῆς μονῆς τὰ πρῶτα φερούσης κατὰ πάντων καὶ ἐν πᾶσι καὶ πλατυνθείσης, καὶ αὐτὸς ὁ εὐσεβέστατος καὶ ἀοίδιμος βασιλεὺς Ἰωάννης μετ' οὐ πολὺ τὴν ἐπίγειον βασιλείαν ἀποθέμενος, πρὸς τὸν ἐν οὐρανοῖς μεταβαίνει δεσπότην καὶ (85) βασιλέα, τὸ σῶμα τούτου κατατεθὲν ἐν τῇ παρ' αὐτοῦ λαμπρυνθείσῃ βασιλικῇ καὶ παντοκρατορικῇ μονῇ εἰς δόξαν τοῦ παντοκράτορος Χριστοῦ τοῦ ἀληθινοῦ θεοῦ ἡμῶν· ὅτι αὐτῷ πρέπει δόξα, εἰς τοὺς αἰῶνας τῶν αἰώνων ἀμήν.

On the same day, commemoration of Eirene,
the celebrated and most blessed empress
and founder of the venerable monastery of the Pantokrator Savior Christ,
who was renamed as the nun Xene on taking the holy and angelic habit

It was necessary that this most great and supreme city should not just take pride in the beauty of things given over to corruption, and take delight and rejoice in tales of men of old who are renowned for their virtue. Rather, it was right for [Constantinople] to boast of and be embellished by the celebrated empress and founder of the Pantokrator monastery. On the one hand, since the things of old had faded with time, and their beauty was extinguished, they no longer served as sources of delight to their beholders. Not even if they had undergone restoration would they have been sufficient to delight the eye; they still looked neglected. For such were the beauty and brightness of the buildings raised from their very foundations by the celebrated empress, with the consent and approval of the mighty emperor, in glorification and thanks to the Pantokrator our God and Savior Jesus Christ who glorified them with coronation, that the city was dignified by them, and by the rays that they emitted, they illuminated and brightened the buildings that grown old and faded with time. On the other hand, the empress, who had acquired all the virtues from childhood and was a receptacle of all good things—this is why she was joined in marriage to the God-crowned and Purple-born emperor—showed herself to be a veritable ornament, not only to the offspring of the imperial Porphyra raised as emperors, in that she was reckoned to be, as indeed she was, the one who set the seal on all the empresses before her, as well as a root of all good qualities and archetypal mould for those who came after her; she was also an adornment to the Queen of Cities.

This celebrated empress, then, came from parents who were fortunate western kings; from the cradle, so to speak, like the noblest of plants, she showed the way that things would turn out, so that her progress in excellence belied her tender age. For virtue tends to reveal and proclaim those who pursue it, even if they are hidden away in a corner.

When a search for a good-looking and virtuous girl was conducted by the celebrated and pious imperial couple Alexios Komnenos and Eirene, and they found this one brimming with excellent qualities, they joined her to their God-given offspring, the Purple-born emperor; then everything was filled with joy and gladness.

Having borne him male children and as many females to a total eight, she raised them in a royal and splendid manner, but reckoned the pleasures of life and even the royalty itself at nought, whispering to herself the words of David, 'What profit is there in my blood, when I go down to the pit.' (Ps.29,10 [30,9]) She did not desist from ministering to God, by her good intercessions with the imperial power, representing the causes of petitioners, and guiding them in every way. But she also rejoiced in almsgiving, more than in receiving money. Before her coronation, she gave everything that came into her hands to the poor, and after it she became just as much a protector of orphans and widows, and she enriched monastic dwellings with money. How shall I tell of the rest? Her gentleness, her quietness, her humility, her compassion, her cheerfulness, her approachability, her placid nature, for she was never moved to anger, and neither did she malign or insult anyone. And if ever she ventured a smile, this too was done with modesty, for she was ever grieving and sorrowful in private, because the psalter was ever on her lips. She was distinguished by continence, she delighted in the wasting of the flesh, and partaking of a lowly and simple diet, she lived an ascetic life.

Yet considering all this inadequate to the God-loving purpose that she nurtured, slowly and latterly, after receiving the imperial crown and being elevated to imperial power, she disregarded everything else, and setting at nought all necessary and urgent matters, she established from its very foundations the imperial monastery that is named after the Pantokrator Savior Christ our God. She erected the beautiful churches that can be seen there now, hostels and old-age homes, all of which in beauty, situation and construction technique take first place among all previous building, both old and recent. In everything she was greatly assisted by the most worthy Nikephoros, her most trusted household man, truly a new Beseleel. He fittingly ordered the harmonious design of the buildings, driving the construction work with great energy, so that he neither allowed his eyes sufficient sleep, nor rest to his head.

And thus constructing and establishing the whole complex with his collaboration, she set it up as a delightful embellishment for the imperial city, rejoicing in the beauty of the successful result and giving thanks to God.

Now that she needed a greater helping hand, she found it. For on one occasion, taking her husband the emperor by the hand, and entering the lovely church of God the Pantokrator our Lord Jesus Christ, she suddenly threw herself down, pressing her head to the sacred floor. "Receive, O Lord, the church that God has built for you", she exclaimed in tears, adding tears to tears and affirming that she would not get up if the thing that she desired did not receive fulfilment.

As she washed the sacred floor with her tears, she heard the emperor promise what she wanted, to fulfil every one of her wishes, and to do all that was in his power and more, in every way, in the dedication of sacred vessels and in the donation of landed property, in order to contrive that this venerable monastery should prevail over all others in moveable and immoveable property and in annual revenues, just as Our Lord and God the Pantokrator Jesus Christ, who is honored and revered therein, takes precedence over all things. Hearing this, she rose to her feet full of inexpressible joy and cheerfulness.

And so the celebrated empress, as if casting off a weight that had been oppressing her, was glad from that moment and rejoiced. Not long afterwards, when she was in province of Bithynia, she departed to Christ Pantokrator for whom she longed. She was laid to rest in this monastery, which she had raised from its foundations. The promise that she had received from the pious emperor had been fulfilled and the imperial Pantokrator monastery had been extended to take first place over all and among all others. And it was not long before the most pious and celebrated emperor John himself, laying aside the earthly empire, migrated to the Lord and King who is in heaven. His body was laid to rest in the imperial Pantokrator monastery that had been made splendid by him, to the glory of the Pantokrator Christ our true God, for to Him is due glory unto the ages of ages, Amen.

APPENDIX 2

Theodoros Prodromos: "Epitaph of Empress Eirene"

Εἴ τις νόμος δίδωσι καὶ νεκροῖς λέγειν,
Ἰδοὺ βοὴν πέμψασα κἀγὼ τυμβόθεν
Τὰ κατ'ἐμαυτὴν ἐκδιδάξω σε, ξένε.
Ἐγὼ προῆλθον εὐτυχῶν προπατόρων
Ἀρχῆς ἁπάσης δυσμικῆς βασιλέων·
Ἰούλιοι Καίσαρες ἐθρέψαντό με
καὶ καλλονῆς Χάριτες ἐστέψαντό με.
Ῥώμης δ' ἄναξ κράτιστος Ἀλεξιάδης
πορφυρογεννὴς εὐτυχὴς Ἰωάννης,
Ὄρπηξ Κομνηνῶν, εὐθαλὴς Δουκῶν κλάδος,
πάσης διώκτης ἐθνικῆς φυλαρχίας,
Εἰς ἔννομον σύζευξιν ἡρμόσατό με·
ᾧ καὶ συνεξάρξασα τῆς γῆς Αὐσόνων

Εἰς φῶς προΐσχω τέτταρες μὲν υἱέας
τῆς πατρογεννοῦς ἐκφυέντας πορφύρας,
Ἰδεῖν ἀγαθούς, πῦρ πνέοντας εἰς μάχην
καὶ τέτταρες δὲ κοσμίας θυγατέρας.
Ὁρῶ δὲ λαμπρὰ τὰ κράτη τοῦ συζύγου,
νίκας πρὸς αὐγὴν ἡλίου καὶ πρὸς δύσιν,
νίκας πρὸς ἄρκτον καὶ νότου θερμὸν κλίμα.
Τέλος λιποῦσα τὸ στέφος, τὴν πορφύραν,
τὸ βύσσινον πόρπημα, τὴν ἁλουργίδα, τὸ
τῶν μοναστῶν ἐνδιδύσκομαι ῥάκος·
θνήσκω δ' ἐπ' αὐτῆς Βιθυνῶν ἐπαρχίας
Ἄποικος ἐκ τῆς Αὐσόνων βασιλίδος·
κομίζομαι δὲ ναυστολουμένη πάλιν
καὶ τὴν ἐμὴν ἐνταῦθα πιστεύω κόνιν.
Ἀλλ' ὢ πλάσας με καὶ μεταπλάσας πάλιν
ὁ τὴν κάτω δοὺς κοσμικὴν ἐξουσίαν,
καὶ τὴν ἄνω δὸς οὐρανῶν κληρουχίαν.

If the dead are permitted to speak after death,
here is my word from the tomb, traveller,
who are passing here;
I tell you the story of my life, I had been a
descendant of happy and great ancestors who
 bore rule over the whole West.
I was nurtured by the brood of Julius Caesar's,
and crowned by the Graces.
The son of Alexius, ruler of Rome, thestrong
Ióannes born in the purple room,
a flourishing shoot of the Comnenus-Ducas house,
the noble warrior who fought all pagan races, made me his lawful wife according to ancient rites.
With him I ruled the Ausonian land
and bore four noble sons to him
who saw the light of day in the ancient purple room, all great heroes, full of fighting spirit; and I also brought four virtuous girls into the world.
I had been witness to my husband's great deeds, his victories in all parts of the world where the sun rises and sets,
in the North as much as in South.
Yet having left the imperial purple and rooms, having taken off splendid garments and a shining crown, I put on the nun's veil and their rags.
Death reached me in distant Bithynia, far from the walls of Byzantium.
My mortal remains were brought by imperial galley
back to this place where I wished to rest.
God Almighty who hast created me
and gavest me power on the earth below,
give me my heavenly portion in the world above.

Wolfram Hörandner, *Theodoros Prodromos Historische Gedichte*. (Wien: Verlag der Österreichischen Akademie der Wissenschaften, 1974, 229–230.) English translation by Gyula Moravcsik, *Byzantium and the Magyars*. (Budapest: Akadémiai Kiadó, 1970), 76.

APPENDIX 3

Nicholas Kallikles: "On the tomb of the Despina"

Τιμῶμεν ὡς νυμφῶνα σεπτὸν τὸν τάφον·	We honor this holy tomb, as if a bridal chamber,
νύμφη Θεοῦ γὰρ ὧδε κεῖται γνησία,	for a true bride of Christ lies here.
ἔχει δὲ κόσμον οἷον, πηλίκον, πόσον;	How much and great adornment does she have?
τὸν πορφυροῦν χιτῶνα τῆς ἀλουργίδος	A ruler's purple garment drenched in crimson
ἀσκητικοῖς ἱδρῶσιν ἐμβεβαμμένον,	with the sweat of her ascetic toils;
τῷ χρυσομαργάρῳ δὲ τοῦ κράτους στέφει	a crown of power all of gold and pearls,
ἐξ ἀρετῶν πήγνυσι λαμπρὸν λυχνίτην·	made more resplendent by the shining ruby of her virtues.
τὸ μίγμα καινόν, τὰς δύο σκηπτουχίας	The mix is novel: she joined the two sceptres in one!
εἰς ἓν συνῆψεν· ὢ καλῆς ἀπληστίας!	Oh, what excellent avidity!!
ὡς δυνατόν, μετέσχεν, ἰδού, τῶν δύο.	Behold, of both did she partake as much as this could be!
Μὴ σὲ προεῖπεν ἡ Σολομῶντος λύρα,	Is this not what the lyre of Salomon foretold?
'μέλαιναν εἶναι καὶ καλὴν' καὶ κοσμίαν,	That she is black and beautiful and adorned?
ἐξ ἀμφίων μέλαιναν, ἐκ δὲ τοῦ τρόπου	Black on account of her [monastic] garment,
'βολίδας' ἀφιεῖσαν ἀστραπηβόλους;	yet dazzling with the shafts of lightning
Ταῦτ' ἄρα καὶ κατεῖδεν, ἐδράξατό σου	of her good features!
'ὁ βασιλεύς' σου καὶ Θεὸς καὶ νυμφίος	Your King and God and Groom looked upon all these
καὶ τῶν ταμείων ἔνδον 'εἰσήνεγκέ' σε.	and took you by the hand, and brought you into his chamber.
Βαβαί, ταμεῖα ποῖα; βαβαί, πηλίκα;	Oh, what a chamber! Oh, just how great!
ζωῆς ἐκεῖθεν, ἀλλὰ πηγαίας χύσις,	A pouring stream of life comes forth from there,
τρυφῆς ἐκεῖθεν, πλὴν ἀειρρόου βρύσις.	and straight from the source;
Πότιζέ σου τὰ τέκνα, σοῦ πένθους χάριν	A spring of delight gushes forth from there, one that will never dry up.
αὐχμῶντα καὶ διψῶντα καὶ ζητοῦντά σε,	[Of this], pray, make your children drink,
κούφιζε τὰ τρύχοντα, χαύνου τὸ θλίβον,	for parched they are with sorrow, they thirst for you,
ἄνοιγέ σου τὰ σπλάγχνα καὶ νῦν ὡς πάλαι	they seek you.
καὶ τὴν συνήθη μητρικὴν θάλψιν δίδου.	Relieve their pain, relieve their suffering,
	Show your compassion now just as before,
	and with a mother's care comfort them as you always did.

English translation by Cristian-Nicolae Gaşpar

INDEX

A

Adelaide del Vasto, consort of Roger I, Count of Sicily, 83n130
Adelaide of Rheinfelden, 11, 96, 153–54
Adelaide of Savoy, 86, 96,
Adriatic Sea, 80
Agnes of France, 102, 309
aisle, 41–44, 49, 228, 232–33
Ajtony, 25
Albert of Aachen, 84
Alexios I Komnenos, Emperor of Byzantium (1081–1118), 123, 164, 215, 271
Almighty, 110, 296, 332. *See also* God
Álmos, Prince of Hungary, 44, 70–72, 105, 115, 117, 146
Anastasia of Kiev, consort of King Andrew I of Hungary, 25, 267, 269
Anatolia, 144, 148
  central, 107
Andreas *panchypersebastos*, 283
Andrew I, King of Hungary (1046–1060), 12, 25, 26, 267
Andrew II, King of Hungary (1205–1235), 28, 269
Andrew, Saint, 25, 269
Andronikos I Komnenos, Emperor of Byzantium (1183–1185), 98, 104, 132, 206, 214, 309,
Andronikos II, son of Emperor Michael VIII Palailogos, 255
Angelos dynasty (Angeloi), 98, 143

Anianus, Saint, of Orléans, 26
Anna Dalassene, consort of John Komnenos, 98–101, 104–105, 123–27, 129–30, 133–35, 137, 178n13, 182–85, 189
Anne of Savoy, 121n3, 158,
Anonymous of Bari, 79, 84
Anselm of Havelberg, 205
Antioch, 70–73, 75, 85
Antony, Saint, Rule of, 205
Apulia (Puglia, Italy), 6, 50, 77–81, 83, 85, 87
Apulians, 83
Aquileia, 50, 263
Armenians, 73, 148
Árpád dynasty (Árpáds), 11n2, 27, 67, 72, 86–87, 114, 203, 266
Artemios, Saint, 203
asceticism, 12, 19, 26–27, 295
  Eastern, 12, 26n50, 27
Asia, 79, 253
Athens
  ancient, 233
  Stoa Poikile, 233
augusta, 121, 128n39, 132, 155, 156n15, 175, 297
Augusteion, 253
Ausones, 149
Avlona/Aulon (Vlorë, Albania), 77

B

Bachkovo, Bulgaria, 201
Bakony mountains, Hungary, 19
Bakonybél, Hungary. *See* Bél

Balabista, Macedonia, 65n5, 107, 113, 150
Balaton, Lake, Hungary, 20, 25
Balkans, 63, 68–69, 71, 267
Barberini Psalter, 159, 162
Bari, Italy, 69, 74
Basil I, Emperor of Byzantium (867–886), 177
Basil II, Emperor of Byzantium (976–1025), 18
Basil of Ohrid, 134n71, 135
Basil the Eunuch, 83
Basileon Romaion, 143
basileus, 82, 126, 128n39, 297
basilissa, 121, 128, 132, 145, 156n15, 189
bathhouses, 201, 213
bathing, 53, 199, 213
Bavaria, 19
Begina-community, 27
Bél, Hungary, 18, 25
Béla II the Blind, King of Hungary (1131–1141), 115
Béla III, King of Hungary (1172–1196), 102
Béla IV, King of Hungary (1235–1270), 15, 28
Benedictine abbey, 20, 25, 49, 267
Benedictines, 28
Bera, Thrace, 202
Bertha-Eirene of Sulzbach, consort of emperor Manuel I, 101–102, 106, 130, 132–36, 149–50, 157, 164, 186, 188, 234, 324
Bezprym, Duke of Poland (1031–1032), 15
Bible, 299
Bithynia, 107, 148, 150, 226, 228, 299, 331–32
Bohemia, 19, 26
Bohemond I, Prince of Taranto and Antioch (1089–1111), 6, 63–64, 66–77, 79–85, 87, 100, 106–107
Bolesław III (Wrymouth) Duke of Lesser Poland (1108–1138), 70–72
Bosporos, 180, 186
Breviarum Chronicum, 301
Brindisi, 77
Bulgaria, 18, 201
Bulgarians, 284
burial churches, 108, 255,
burial places, 108, 112, 180, 190–91, 232, 308, 310
Byzantine Empire, 63, 121–23, 137, 205, 215. *See also* Byzantium
Byzantine empresses, 104, 110, 121–22, 128, 143, 189, 191, 261, 324

Byzantine liturgical tradition, 268
Byzantine metropolitanate, 13
Byzantine mission, 13
Byzantine poets, 294
Byzantine spirituality, 16, 18, 268
Byzantines, 64, 72–73, 78, 80–81, 83, 87, 105–107, 113, 188, 240. *See also*
Byzantino–Norman relations, 64, 72
Byzantium, 13, 16–18, 50, 54, 57, 63, 67–72, 74–76, 80, 83, 85–87, 98, 104–107, 109, 114–17, 121–24, 128, 130–32, 133, 136–37, 143–44, 148, 168, 175, 177, 262, 269, 296n30, 309, 312, 316, 317n59, 323, 325, 332. *See also* Byzantine Empire

C

caesar, 126
Calabria, 68, 81, 83, 85
Calabrians, 85
Campitelli, church of Santa Maria in Portico, 263n10
Capetians, 74
Cappadocia, New Church of Toqalı kilise, 284
Cassiodorus, 325
Cassius Dio, Lucius, 253
Catherine of Alexandria, Saint, 27
Catherine of Bulgaria, consort of emperor Isaac I Komnenos, 160, 182, 188,
cauterizing, 211–12
Cedrenus, 253
cenobitism, 12, 28
Cerbani, Cerbano (Cerbanus), 28
Chalandon, Ferdinand, 146n12
charity, 29, 137, 191, 195, 201, 226, 281–82, 286
Charity (*Misericordia*). *See* charity
chasuble, 19–20, 263–64
Chios, church of Nea Moni, 263
Chi-Rho, 154, 156
Choniates, Niketas, 106, 109n33, 110, 131–32, 144, 146n12, 149–50, 227, 253, 293, 312, 313n39
Christ, 4, 19, 51, 54–55, 154–55, 160–61, 167, 180, 261–62, 270–72, 277, 281–82, 284, 286, 293, 295, 314–15, 323, 329–31, 333. *See also* Savior
Crucifixion of, 315
Entombment of, 315

Incarnation of, 282
Nativity of, 53, 268, 272, 281, 282n43
Resurrection of, 315
Antiphonetes, 176, 180,
All-Seeing (*Pantepoptes*), 183
Pantepoptes. See All-Seeing
Pantokrator, 163
Philantropos, 101, 185
Christ's Cross, 20
Christodoulos, 125
Chronicon Pictum, 146–47
chrysobull, 69, 84, 99, 156, 169, 178, 183
Chrysopolis, 190
Chrysotriklinos. See Great Palace, palaces: Constantinople
Cilicia, 72–73, 75–76, 85, 103, 111n39, 147
Cilicians, 147–48
Cistercians, 28
Clement VI, Pope (1342–1352), 27
clinics, 199–200, 208–209, 214
Cologne, 281
Coloman I, King of Hungary (1095–1116), 6, 12, 14–16, 22, 28–29, 39–41, 43–44, 50, 52, 54–57, 63–64, 66–72, 75–79, 82–83, 87, 105, 115–16, 266–67
commemoration, 41, 65, 191, 197, 254, 256, 283, 285, 295, 297, 306, 314, 329
Conrad II, Holy Roman Emperor (1027–1039), 70, 96, 101, 132, 134, 148–49, 263
consorts, 18, 83n130, 122n5, 131, 149, 153–54, 161, 170, 187, 253
Constance, daughter of Philip I, King of France, 74
Constantine (Konstantinos) IX Monomachos, Emperor of Byzantium (1042–1055), 155, 164, 263n8
Constantine (Konstantinos) V, Emperor of Byzantium (741–775), 143
Constantine (Konstantinos) VI, Emperor of Byzantium (780–797), 128, 176, 178–81
Constantine (Konstantinos) VII Porphyrogennetos, Emperor of Byzantium (913–959), 176, 253–54
Constantine (Konstantinos) VIII, Emperor of Byzantium (1025–1028), 253
Constantine (Konstantinos) X, Doukas, Emperor of Byzantium (1059–1067), 98–99, 162, 178n10, 182

Constantine I the Great, Roman Emperor, Saint (306–337), 254
Constantine, the notary, 83
Constantinia, 146
Constantinople, 13, 15, 17, 27–28, 30, 55, 57, 66, 70–72, 75–76, 100–102, 105, 107, 110, 113, 115, 128–29, 132, 144, 146n12, 147n18, 153, 160, 167, 169, 175–177, 178n10, 180, 183, 186–91, 202, 204–205, 213–16, 225, 230, 233, 262–63, 267, 269–70, 283–86, 291, 293, 298–99, 306, 308, 309n21, 313, 329, 330
 Blachernai palace, 183, 187
 Blachernai quarter, 233
 churches: Blachernai, 263–64; *Nea Ekklesia*, 177; Christ Antiphonetes, 176, 180–81; *Hagia Sophia*, 106n25, 113n42, 131, 134, 154–56, 158, 160–64, 168–69, 185, 227–28, 254, 261, 270–72, 275–76, 295, 323, 325; Holy Apostles, 8, 109, 233, 240, 252–55, 292; St. Anastasios, 178; St. Constantine, 179; St. Eustathios, 178; Theotokos Chalkoprateia, 181; Theotokos Eleousa, 5, 108, 112, 114, 186, 227, 232, 282–84; Theotokos Kyriotissa (Kalenderhane Mosque), 238; Theotokos Pege, 178
 Constantinian walls, 183
 Convent of Saint Euphemia, 177–78
 Golden Horn, 183, 198, 203
 Hebdomon quarter, 187
 Hippodrome, 178
 hospitals: Christodotes, 203; Euboulos, 203; of the Forty Martyrs, 209; Mangana, 204, 209, 210, 211n118, 214–15; Myrelaion, 135, 183n47, 204, 211n118; Narses, 204; Saint Sampson, 203, 215; Saint Zotikos Leper Hospital, 198–99, 215; Mangana quarter, 178n13; Mangana palace, 187
 Medikariou cemetery, 198, 203
 Mese quarter, 183
 monasteries: All-Seeing Christ (*Pantepoptes*), 99, 101, 135, 183–84; Archangel St. Michael *Kataskepe*, 186; at the Palace of Antiochos, 190; Chora (Kariye Camii), 183, 230, 311; Christ *Philanthropos*, 101, 185; Euergetes, 183; Lips, 216; Mangana, 214; Medikariou, 203; Mother of God Evergetis, 199–200; Myrelaion, 135, 183, 204; Pammakaristos,

183; Pantokrator Monastery, 1–5, 7–9, 16, 30, 97, 100, 103–104, 107–109, 111–17, 130, 134–37, 150, 153, 163–64, 183, 186, 195–202, 204–206, 208–216, 225–27, 228n16, 229–33, 235, 239–41, 253–56, 261, 270, 272. 282–83, 285, 291–94, 296–97, 301, 305, 307–10, 312, 316–17, 323, 325; Petrion/ta Petria, 177, 179, 182, 204; Piperoudion, 180, 189; Prokopia/ta Prokopias, 179; St. Diomedes, 177; St. John of Stoudios, 187; St. Panteleimon *ta Armamentareas*, 179; St. Loukas, 179; ta Anthemiou, 190; ta Ellenes, 177, 179, 182; ta Gastria, 179, 190; ta Hebraika, 181; ta Kellaraias, 184; ta Libadia, 180; ta Metanoia, 181; ta Oikoproasteia, 189; Theotokos *Kecharitomene*, 101, 135, 158, 184–86, 190, 199n26, 256; Theotokos the Queen of All (*Pantanassa*), 187; *tou Libos*, 255–56
mosques: Laleli Camii, 229n17; Zeyrek Camii, 2, 5, 213, 235, 241. *See also* monasteries: Pantokrator monastery.
Mount of Olives, 198
palaces: Great Palace, 187, 200, 231; of Eleutherios, 182
Pera region, 198
Unkapanı Cistern, 213
Council of Florence-Ferrara, 229
Council of Szabolcs. *See* Synod of Szabolcs
court physician, 291–92
court poet, 293
crowns, 20, 26, 55–56, 98, 144, 155, 158, 160, 162, 164, 168, 281, 295, 297, 330, 332–33. *See also* Holy Crown of Hungary
crusades, 68, 71, 74, 75n69, 143
    First (1095–1099), 69–70, 105
    Second (1147), 101
    Fourth (1202–1204), 206, 324
Cumans, 297
Cyprus, 73, 148
Csanád, Hungary. *See* Marosvár bishopric of, 25

D

Dacia, 82
Dacians, 145
Dalassene family, 123

Dalmatia, 50, 63–64, 66–72, 77–81, 86–87
Dalmatians, 4
Dandolo, Andrea, 77
Dānishmands, 73
Danube,
    bend, 20
    River, 20, 70
David, 281, 297, 330
David IV the Builder, King of Georgia (1089–1125), 145
Deabolis (Devol, Albania), 64, 82
Demetrius, Saint (the Great Martyr), 26, 65
Desert Fathers, 19, 26, 29
despoina, 125–26, 132, 143, 156n15
devotion, 109, 153, 180, 184, 227–28, 261, 286–87
    Marian, 9, 103, 262, 264, 266, 268, 270
Digenis Akritis, epic hero, 200
Dioklians, 145–46. *See also* Serbians
Dobrodjeja Mstislavna of Kiev, Rus princess, 144
doctors, 199–200, 203–204, 208–11, 213, 216, 292, 294, 300
    female, 208
Doukas family (Doukai), 98–100, 132, 158
Dömös, Hungary, 40, 44, 52, 71, 79
Drugeth, János, palatine, 27
Durazzo (Durrës, Albania), 77. *See also* Dyrrachium
dynastic strategies, 182
Dyrrachium (Durrës, Albania), 64, 71–72, 79–81, 83

E

ecclesiastical legislation, 29
ecumenical rule, 145
education, 11–12, 102, 115, 135n76, 208, 215n147, 265, 268–70, 312
Egypt, Fatimid, 76
Eirene Doukaina, consort of emperor Alexios I Komnenos, 98–101, 107, 124, 126–30, 133–35, 137, 149, 157–59, 162–64, 168–69, 176, 182–85, 188–90, 201, 256, 271, 294, 300–301
Eirene of Alania, 98
Eirene *sebastokratorissa,* consort of Andronikos, 9, 116, 133, 197, 301, 305–306, 308–309, 311, 314–15, 317, 324

Eirene the Khazar, consort of emperor
    Constantine (Konstantinos) V, 143
Eirene of Athens, Empress (797–802), 176
Ekkehard of Aura, 74
Elene Lekapene, consort of emperor
    Constantine VII, Porphyrogennetos, 176,
    179, 190
Elisabeth of Hungary, Saint, 281
Emeric I, King of Hungary (1196–1204), 20
Emeric, Prince of Hungary (1000/1007–1031),
    Saint, 15–16, 20, 50
Empress of the West. *See* Piroska-Eirene, Empress
empresses
    dowager, 187–89, 294, 300
    foreign, 132, 134, 136, 143, 145
    junior, 157–59, 168
enamel, 7, 55, 70, 154, 162–64, 168–69,
    229n20, 283
epilepsy, 197
epitaphs, 9, 87, 135, 148, 234n42, 291–300,
    307, 311, 314, 317, 324, 332
epithalamium, 295
eremitic revival, 27
eremitism, 12, 20, 26. *See also* hermits
Esztergom, Hungary, 12, 20, 28–29, 43–44,
    51–52, 71, 114
    Archbishopric of, 262
Eudokia Makrembolitissa, consort of emperor
    Constantine X, Doukas, 121, 162, 176,
    178–79, 182, 188–89
Eudoxia (Eudokia) Komnene, consort of
    William VIII of Montpellier, 293
Euphemia, Saint, relics of, 178
Euphrosyne Doukaina Kamatera, consort of
    Emperor Alexios III Angelos, 143
Euphrosyne, consort of emperor Michael II,
    176, 180–81, 188–89
Europe, 26n50, 54, 56, 79–80
    Central, 63, 325
    Western, 28, 55, 230, 325

F

façades, 41, 43, 232–33, 236–38, 242, 247
Falier, Ordelaffo, doge, 70, 79, 165
Ferai (Vira), Church of the Virgin
    Kosmosoteria, 207, 234
princesses, foreign, 130, 144, 315, 323

Fossati brothers, 261n1
foundations, 13–18, 25–27, 30, 50, 52, 55, 101,
    104, 106–107, 110, 118, 134–37, 175–91,
    196, 202, 204, 225–28, 235, 253, 261–62,
    264, 266, 270, 282–83, 286, 293, 323,
    329–31
France, 44, 74, 75
Franks, 74, 83
Frederick I Barbarossa, Holy Roman Emperor
    (1155–1190), 102n16
Fulcher of Chartres, 84
funeral chapel, 205, 233, 235–37
funeral liturgies, 235
funerary dirge, 310
funerary orations, 292–93, 298

G

Galen (Galenus), 209, n112, 215–16, 292
Gangra (Çankırı. Turkey), 148
Gavril-Radomir of Bulgaria, 15
geography, sacred, 175
George, Saint, 18, 20, 25, 53, 292
Gerard of Csanád, Bishop, 25–26
Germans, 70, 72, 74, 87, 145
gerokomeion. *See* old-age home
gerotropheion. *See* old-age home
Géza, Grand Duke of Hungary (early 970s–
    997), 14–15
Ghāzī, Malik Aḥmad, 73
Gisela, Queen (c. 984–1065), Blessed, 18–20,
    263
glass, stained, 229–30, 240
Glykophylousa. *See* Virgin Mary: Virgin of
    Tenderness
God, 14, 153, 231, 261, 264–65, 271, 281–82,
    295–96, 308, 314, 329, 331–33. *See also*
    Almighty
God's love for humankind (*Philanthropia*), 282
Godehard, Abbot, 19
Godfrey of Melfi, 69
Godfric, the hermit, 26n50
Gospel Book, 269n29, 272, 281–82. *See also*
    John II Komnenos, Gospel Book of
Goths, 298
Great Meteora, Holy Monastery, 207
Greece, 147
    ancient, 208

Greek metropolitan, 16, 29, 283
Greek monastery, 15, 25–27, 269
Greek rite, 15, 17–18, 28
Gregorian reforms, 28
Gregory the Great, 263n10
Gregory VII, Pope (1073–1085), 265
Grubeša Branislavjević, Prince of Dioclia (1118–1125), 146
Guiscard, Robert, 68, 83
Günther of Niederaltaich, 19, 29
gynecology, 208
Győr, Hungary, 14, 42–43, 262
Gyula, Duke of Transylvania (980–1003 or 1004), 15
Gyulafehérvár (Alba Iulia, Romania), 15, 43, 51–52

H

Hadrian, Roman Emperor (117–138), 206, 213
Hagia Glykeria, Island, 197
Hagioglykerites, Joseph, abbot, 196
Harran (Sultantepe, Turkey), 73
Hartvic, Bishop, 6, 29–30, 266–67
Hauteville family, 68
healer, 292
Heaven, 263, 297, 299, 319, 331–32
Heliade, -s, 311
Henry II Jasomirgott, Duke of Austria (1141–1156), 116n48
Henry III, Holy Roman Emperor (1046–1057), 263
Henry IV, Holy Roman Emperor (1084–1105), 70–71, 87, 96
Henry V, Holy Roman Emperor (1111–1125), 71, 86, 96, 148
Henry the Lion, 102n16
heritage, 2, 4, 114, 148, 177, 286, 299n40
hermits, 17, 25–26, 29, 40. *See also* eremitism
hermitage, 18–19
hernia, 203
herōon, 5, 8–9, 108, 112–14, 186, 233–34, 239–40, 253–56, 310, 312–13, 315–16
Hesiod, 133
hiera nosos (sacred disease). *See* leprosy
Hierotheos, Bishop, 15

Hippocrates, 215–16
Hodigitria, 267, 283, 285–86. *See also* Virgin Mary
Holy Apostles, school of the, 292
Holy Crown of Hungary, 6, 17, 47–48, 54–55, 147, 164, 266
Holy Land, 44, 115, 281n36, 324
Holy Mother of God. *See* Mother of God (*Theotokos*)
Holy Virgin, 262. *See also* Virgin Mary
  cult of, 262
  church of the Assumption of, 263–64
  Entrance of, into the Temple, 268
  image of, 263, 264, 267n21
  imitation of, 262
  infancy of, 268
Homer, 133
Honorius III, Pope (1216–1227), 27–28
hospitals, 8, 134, 179, 181n36, 195, 199–210, 211, 214–16, 226. *See also* infirmary
  elite, 215
  Islamic, 210
  leper, 195, 197–99
  medical, 197, 201, 204
  public, 199, 200n29, 201–202, 207
House of Árpád, 29n66, 96. *See also* Árpád Dynasty
humility, 135, 265, 282, 297, 300
Hungarian expansion, 69
Hungarian–Byzantine relations, 1, 4
Hungary, 1–7, 10–20, 25–29, 39, 41, 44, 50–53, 55–57, 63–64, 66–67, 69–72, 75, 77, 82, 84, 86–87, 104–107, 114–15, 117, 136, 145–46, 262–64, 266–67, 269–70, 286, 324–25
  Church of, 54
  early Árpádian, 2, 5, 12, 27, 28–29
  Eastern Hungary, 24, 29
  Kingdom of, 4, 54, 56, 85, 264, 266
  Northern, 26
  North-Eastern, 28
  South-Eastern Hungary, 20
  Southern Hungary, 20, 51, 54
  South-Western, 267
  Western, 14n10
Hyppolite, Saint, 20, 26

I

icons, 6, 128, 229, 254, 261, 263, 268, 283–85, 315
  of Christ, 180, 184, 284, 293
  of the Hodigitria, 283, 285. See also *Hodigitria*
  of the Theotokos, 197, 283
  of the Virgin Mary, 263, 267, 284
  of the Blachernai Thetokos, 263, 284. See also Theotokos
iconoclasm, 177
Iliad, 102, 133
Illyricum, 72, 79–80
imperial
  clothing, 160. See also *loros*
  family, 102, 126, 133, 160, 162, 177, 184, 186, 272, 283, 300, 310
  foundation, 293
  ideology, 286
  regalia, 299. See also *pendilia*
  residence, 184–185, 215
  women, 6, 7, 105, 111, 122, 128, 132, 134–37, 150n30, 175–78, 181–82, 188, 190
infirmary, 195, 197–201, 207, 213–14. See also hospital
Innocent III, Pope (1198–1216), 20
intimacy, 285
Investiture Contest, 266
Isaac I Komnenos, Emperor of Byzantium (1057–1059), 97–98, 160, 162
Isaac II Komnenos, *sebastokrator*, 187n69, 230
Isaakios, Aaron, 150
Isaias, 285
Istanbul, 206, 235–36, 240, 277–78, 325
Italikos, John, imperial encomiast, 313
Italikos, Michael, 184, 210, 294n20, 306, 310–11
Italy, 6, 29, 50, 55, 63, 68, 73, 76, 83
  North-Eastern, 16
  Southern, 63, 68, 79, 81–82

J

Jaroslav of Kiev, 25
Jerome from Cîteaux, 285
Jerusalem, 6, 17, 71, 268
Jesse, tree of, 285
Jesuits, 14n10
Joachim, 268
John Damascene, 268
John I Tzimiskes, Emperor of Byzantium (969–976), 284
John II Komnenos, Emperor of Byzantium (1087–1143), 1, 16, 28, 63, 110, 153–54, 162, 167, 176, 186, 196–98, 203, 208, 210, 225, 261, 277, 285–86, 292–93, 297, 300, 308, 323
John II Komnenos, Gospel Book of, 269n29, 272
John Roger, *sebastos*, 293–94, 299
John the Baptist, Saint (*Prodromos*), 19, 25
John the Deacon, 284
John the Faster, monk, 183
Joscelin of Courtenay, Count of Edessa (1119–1131), 183
Judean Desert, 195
Julius Caesar, 7, 87, 148, 298, 300, 332
Justice (*Dikaiosynē*), 160–61, 272
Justinian I, Eastern Roman Emperor (527–565), 5, 8, 108, 233, 240, 253, 255, 270

K

kaisar, 99, 104
kaisarissa, 104
Kamateros, Gregory, *logothete*, 292–93
Kastamon (Kastamonu, Turkey), 228
Kataphloron, Nikolaos, 226
Catherine of Bulgaria, consort of Isaac I Komnenos (1057–1059) 160, 182, 188
katholikon, 8, 108, 111–14, 226, 228, 235, 238
Kata-Eudoxia, daughter of King David IV of Georgia, 145, 161
Khakhuli Triptych, 164
Kiev, 25, 70, 145, 161, 269
  church of St Sophia, 263, 269
Kievan Rus, 18
kingship, saintly, 324
Kinnamos, John, 65, 132, 136, 145, 150, 226, 313, 325
kinship networks, 8, 191
Kokkinobaphos, James, 285
Kokkinobaphos master, 102–103n19, 272
Kokkinobaphos manuscript, 269, 272
Komnene, Anna, 7, 64–65, 80, 82, 84, 100, 105, 107, 121, 124–25, 127–28, 137, 144–45,

184–85, 190, 265, 271, 291–94, 298, 300–301
Komnenian
   dynasty, 64, 72, 87, 97, 103–104, 108, 112, 116, 123–24, 127, 130, 143, 176–77, 186, 308.
   Empire, 147, 286
   period, 123, 293
   poetry, 299n43, 306
   renaissance, 9, 300
Kontostephanos, Isaac, 80, 102
Koppány, Duke of Somogy (962 or 964?–997 or 998), 18
Körmend, Hungary, 14n10
ktetor, 185, 270
kyria, 143

L

Lackland, John, son of Henry II, King of England, 102n16
Ladislaus, King of Hungary (1077–1095), Saint, 11–12, 29, 39, 43, 44, 51, 56, 69, 77, 82, 105, 115–16, 264, 266, 268, 324
Lady of all the Western Peoples. *See* Piroska-Eirene, Empress
laments, 100, 103, 293, 307, 311–12, 314–17
Laodikeia, 144
Late Antiquity, 134n74, 215, 267, 271
Latins, 17, 27, 29, 104, 143
lavra (λάυρα), 19, 25–26
lay patrons, 189–90
Leon Stypes, Patriarch of Constantinople, 208
Leon VI, Emperor of Byzantium (886–912), 176, 179, 254, 325
Leningrad Psalter, former, 160
leprosy, 197–98
Lesbos, 182, 190
lieu de mémoire, 254, 300
liturgy, 106, 137, 232, 267
Liudolfing (Ottonian) dynasty, 86
Lizix, physician, 292
Lombards, 4, 83, n85, 87
Lombardy, 52, 64
Lorenzo de Monacis, 78
loros, 54, 155, 159, 162, 164. *See also* imperial clothing

Lothar III, Holy Roman Emperor (1133–1337), 205
Louis VII the Younger, King of France (1137–1180), 160, 323
Luttor, Ferenc, 3

M

Macedonian emperors, 254
Madrid, 284–85
Magyar Kingdom, 13, 17. *See also* Hungary, Kingdom of
Maiestas Mariae, 263. *See also* Virgin Mary
Manasses, Constantine, 301
Mangana Poet, 205, 214
Manuel I Komnenos, Emperor of Byzantium (1143–1180), 91, 98, 100–103, 106, 108–109, 116, 130, 143, 157, 164n45, 176, 186, 189, 254, 284, 300–301, 312
Manzikert Battle (1068–1071), 99
Margaret of Hungary, Saint (1242–1270), 15
Maria of Alania, consort of emperor Michael VII Doukas and emperor Nikephoros III Boteneaites, 15, 105, 123–24, 127, 129, 137, 143, 160, 182, 184, 187–88
Maria of Amnia, consort of emperor Constantine VI, 176, 179–80, 188–89
Maria of Antioch, consort of emperor Manuel I Komnenos, 102, 104–105, 150, 176, 182, 186–89, 312, 317
Maria of Bulgaria, consort of Andronikus Doukas, 182–83
Maria, daughter of emperor Manuel I, 102
Marian devotion, 262, 266n17, 268. *See also* Virgin Mary
Marian piety, 29, 266–67. *See also* Virgin Mary
Mary of Antioch. *See* Maria of Antioch
Mary of Egypt, 26
Maros, River, 20, 25
Marosvár (Cenad, Romania), 25, 29
Mas'ud I, Sultan of the Seldjuks of Rum (1116–1156), 147–48
Matthew, Evangelist, 160, 272, 278–79, 282
Maurice, Saint, 18, 25
mausoleum/a, 29n66, 181, 232, 234, 240, 253, 255, 308, 317. *See also* Constantinople: mausolea of Constantine and Justinian

Maximilla, daughter of Count Roger I of Sicily, 70, 96
Maximus the Confessor, 28
medical
  institutions, 195, 203, 214
  manuscripts, 215
  personnel, 211, 214
  recipes, 211n118, 215
medicine (science or practice), 202, 208, 210n113, 211–12, 216, 291–92
  ancient, 202
  Byzantine, 203–204
  medieval, 8, 202, 204
  history of, 202
medicines (drugs), 211–12
Megale Ekklesia. See Hagia Sophia
Mehmet Tahir Ağa, 229n17
Mélisende of Tripoli, daughter of Raymond II, Count of Tripoli, 102n15
Melissenos, Nikephoros, 98n7
mental illness, 197
mercy, 136, 168, 286, 296
Mercy (*Eleémosyné*), 160–61, 169, 172, 272, 281–82
Mesarites, Nikolaos, 253
Messina, 285
Messina, Cathedral, 285
Meteora, Barlaam Monastery, 207
Meteora, Thessaly, 207
Michael I Rangabe, Emperor of Byzantium (811–813), 176, 178n10, 179, 181
Michael II, Emperor of Byzantium (820–829), 176, 180
Michael III, Emperor of Byzantium, (842–867), 179, 190
Michael the Syrian, Patriarch of the Syriac Orthodox Church (1166–1199), 147n18
Michael VIII Palaiologos, Emperor of Byzantium (1261–1282), 255
Michael, Saint, 163, 233
Michael, Saint, church of, 108, 163, 178, 186, 305, 308n13
Michael, Saint, of funerary chapel, 310
Middle Ages, 43, 170
  late, 267
Middle Byzantine period, 176–78, 182, 185, 187–89, 261, 270
military virtues, 293

Monastery of Hagia Trias (Holy Trinity), 160
Monastery of the Mother of God *ton Heliou Bomon*, 199n25
Monastery of Kosmosoteira near Bera, 202, 215–16,
Monastery of Kosmosoteira in Ferai, 234, 311n28
Monastery of Saint Theodosius in the Judean Desert, 195
Monastery of Saint Mamas, 199n25
Monastery of the Theotokos on Mount Tmolos, 202
Monastery of the Theotokos Pantanassa (The Queen of All), 187
Monastery of the Theotokos Petritzonitissa in Bachkovo, 201
monastic
  complex, 100, 107, 153, 183, 185–86, 188, 253, 282, 308
  habit, 226, 300, 309
  infirmary, 195, 197–201, 213–14. *See also* infirmary; hospitals
  patronage, 20, 103, 261–62, 267, 270, 272, 275, 282–83, 285–86, 309, 314, 323
Mongol invasion of Hungary, 1241–1242, 27–28
Monk (Bishop) Manuel, 284
monks, 25–29, 44, 108, 111–12, 186, 195–96, 199, 201, 205, 212, 214, 226, 233, 253, 282
  Greek, 25–27
  Latin, 26
  Benedictine, 25, 27. *See also* Benedictines
Monomachos crown, 164
Monopoli, Italy, 77
Monreale Cathedral, Cloister of, 281
Montesquieu, Charles-Louis de Secondat, Baron de La Brède et de Montesquieu, 121
Moravcsik, Gyula, 12, 15–16, 146n12
mosaics, 106n25, 113, 131, 134, 137, 154–56, 158–62, 164, 168–69, 229, 231, 233–34, 236–37, 239–40, 245, 250, 261, 263–64, 269–72, 281–82, 295, 300, 311, 315, 325
mosques, 213, 230, 234–36. *See also* Constantinople: mosques
Most Holy Mother of God (*Yperagia Theotokos*), 267. *See also* Virgin Mary

Mother of God (*Theotokos*), 114, 261–62, 264–65, 267, 270, 285–86, 296. *See also* Virgin Mary of Vladimir, 280, 283–85. *See also* Vladimirskaya
motherhood, 125, 134, 185
Mount Athos (*Hagion Oros*), 25
Mount Tmolos (Bozdağ, Turkey), 202
Mount Zobor (Nitra, Slovakia). *See* Zobor

N

naos, 228, 230–32
narthex, 184, 228, 232, 234–35, 237–39, 249, 253–54
  exonarthex, 184–85, 238–39, 248–50
Neapolitan Chronicles, 144
Nebuchadnezzar, King of Babylon, 202
New Testament, 160
Nicholas III *Grammatikos,* Patriarch of Constantinople (1084–1111), 184
Niederaltaich, Bavaria, 19
Nikephoros Bryennios, 128–29, 144–45
Nikephoros III Boteneiates, Emperor of Byzantium (1078–1081), 98–99, 182, 187–88
Nikephoros, master mason, 110, 239
Normans, 63–64, 66–72, 75–81, 83, 85, 87, 99, 103, 150
nosokomeion. See infirmary
Nyitra (Nitra, Slovakia), 20, 26–27, 29, 40, 54

O

Ohrid (Ochrid Macedonia), 18
old-age home, 179, 195, 197–98, 201, 203–204, 212, 216, 226, 330
Old Testament, 202, 231, 292
Olontunos, Ioannes, the *domestikos* of empress Piroska-Eirene, 160
opus sectile, 200, 230, 234, 240, 243–44
Orant Virgin (*deomene*), 263n8. *See also* Virgin Mary
orb, 20, 157, 159
Orderic Vitalis, 84
Orlandos, Anastasios, 206–207
Oroszkő, Hungary, 25

Oroszlános (Banatsko Aranđelovo, Serbia), 20, 25
Orthodox Christianity, 324
Otranto, Italy, 80–81
Otto III, Holy Roman Emperor (996–1002), 281
Ottoman invasion of Hungary, 14n10
Ottonian political theology, 281

P

Paionians, 298n39
Palaeologians, 159
Palestine, 300
Pannonia, 14
pansebastos, 310n2
Pantechnes, Michael, *aktouarios*, 210
Panteleimon, Saint, monastery of, 20, 179
Paolino da Venezia, 77
papacy, 54, 70, 75, 267
Paschal II, Pope (1099–1118), 71, 74–75, 81, 86
Passau, Bavaria, Germany, 71
Pásztó, Hungary, 28
Patmos, 178n13
Patmos, monastery of St. John the Theologos, 99n8, 183
patronage, monumental, 7, 176–78, 187–89
Patrona Hungariae, 266. *See also* Virgin Mary
Paul, Apostle, Saint, 11n2
peace treaty, 64, 263
Pečenog, Serbia, 148n19
Pechenegs, 80, 148
Pécsvárad, Hungary, 46, 54, 267
  Benedictine abbey, 262n4, 267
pendilia, 164. *See also* imperial regalia
Pentele (Dunaújváros), Hungary, 20, 26–27
Peres, Dacian count, 82
Persians, 297
Peter, Saint, the banner of, 74
Phaethon, 311, 315
philanthropy, 134–37, 150, 176, 179, 181, 185, 190–91, 195, 227
Philip I, King of France (1059–1108), 74
Philippopolis (Thrace, Plovdiv, Bulgaria), 201
Philokalés, Eumathios, 66
Philopation, 144
Pietà (*Threnos*), 284

piety, 5, 8, 29, 100, 130, 135, 137, 175, 177, 178n13, 183–84, 189, 191, 227–28, 256, 262, 266–67, 286, 323, 324–25
  Christian, 29, 189
pilgrimage, 19, 71
Pilis, Hungary, 28, 51
Piros (Rumenka, Serbia), 11n2
Piroska, Hungarian Princess, 11, 13, 29, 39, 54, 56, 63, 153, 264, 293, 323. *See also* Piroska-Eirene
Piroska-Eirene, Empress (1088–1134), 65, 71, 85–86, 98, 100–101, 103, 106, 108–11, 117, 130, 135–37, 143–44, 146–51, 153–64, 168–70, 176, 186, 188–89, 196, 205, 216, 225–30, 232, 234n43, 253–54, 256, 261–62, 269, 281, 283, 285–86, 316–17, 324–25
Pisa, Italy, 76
poets, 233, 291–99, 301, 307, 312, 314, 316, 324
Poland, 70
political theology, 262, 281
poorhouses, 134, 195, 214
porphyra, 107, 113, 330. *See also* purple
porphyrogennetos/-a, -oi (porphyrogenitus). *See* purple-born
poultices, 211
power base, 123, 130
Pozsony (Bratislava, Slovakia), 72
Preslav, Bulgaria, 164
Princes' Islands, 178, 180, 182, 190
Prisca / Priscilla, Saint, 11n2
processions, 112, 168, 233, 254–55, 283–85, 315
Prodromos, Manganeios, 97n1, 103, 305n1, 312
Prodromos, Theodore (Theodoros), 85–87, 106, 131–32, 144–45, 148–49, 202–203, 213, 216, 291–92, 294n20, 297–301, 306–307, 310–12, 314, 316–17, 324, 332
Prokopia, consort of Emperor Michael I, 176, 179, 188–90
Prokopios, 253
prose monody, 310
psalter, 162, 272, 281, 330
Psellos, Michael, 180, 239, 291, 297n31
ptochotropheion, 214. *See also* poorhouse

purple, 130, 156, 160–61, 299, 319, 332–33. See also *porphyria*
purple-born, 231, 307, 308, 318, 330

Q

Quarnero (Kvarner, Croatia), Gulf of, 79
Queen of Cities. *See* Constantinople
Queen of Heaven, 281. *See also* Virgin Mary

R

Raymond of Poitiers, Prince of Antioch (1136–1149), 148
Raymond of St. Gilles, 73
Regnum Marianum, 266
religious donation, 177
reliquaries,
  cross, 153
  tower, 20
Renier, son of the Marquis of Montferrat, 102n16, 104
renovatio imperii, 4, 13
Rhine, River, 86–87
Richard of Hauteville, Seneschal of Apulia and Calabria, 83
Richard of Salerno, 83
Richeza of Lotharingia, Blessed, 86, 96
Robert the Monk, 84
Roger Borsa, Duke of Apulia and Calabria (1085–1111), 68, 72, 83
Roger II, King of Sicily (1130–1154), 54, 83, 208
Roger I, Count of Sicily, 54, 67–68, 83n130
Roman Catholic Church, 41, 56
Roman Empire, 13, 267, 271
Holy Roman Empire, 17, 87
Romanos III Argyros, Emperor of Byzantium (1028–1034), 155, 198
Romanos IV Diogenes, Emperor of Byzantium (1067–1071), 75, 98–99, 176, 182
Rome, 11n2, 17, 19, 53–54, 75, 132, 149, 267, 299, 332
  ancient, 208
  medieval, 263
  Mausoleum of Augustus, 253
  Saint Peter's Basilica, 17
  Saint Agnes' Basilica, 3

Romuald of Salerno, 79
Rudolf of Rheinfelden, Duke of Swabia, antiking of Germany, 11n2, 86, 96
Rudolph the Swabian. *See* Rudolf of Rheinfelden
rulers, sainted, 8, 254

S

Sack of Constantinople (1204), 163
sainthood, royal, 254
Salian court, 70
salvation, 14, 108, 112, 116, 216, 265, 282, 308, 312, 314
Samson (Sampson), 26, 231, 244
Sarolt, Grand Duke Géza's wife (c. 950–c. 1008), 15
Savior, 19, 292–93, 329–30. *See also* Christ
Scaurus, Marcus Aemilius, 294
Schwarzrheindorf, church and nunnery, 285
Scipio, Publius Cornelius, Africanus, 293, 299n43
seals, 14, 22, 124–25, 131–32, 154, 156–59, 164, 168–69, 285, 330
sebaste, 100
sebastoi, 283
sebastokratōr, -es, 9, 126, 133, 230, 301, 305, 307–308, 319
sebastokratorissa, 102–105, 116n48, 133, 137, 301, 305–11, 314–18, 324
sebastos, 100, 293–94, 299. *See also* Theodore Dokianos.
Séd, Creek, 17
Seljuks (Seljuqs, Seljuq Turks), 66, 73, 226–27, 253, 297
Seljuq Sultanate of Rum, 76
Serb Dioklea, 146
Serbia, 11n2, 18, 20, 49, 148n19
Serbians, 144
Serbs, Raškan, 14, 147
Shepard, Jonathan, 26n50
Shayzar, siege of, 148
Sicily, 16, 85
Simon of Kéza, 77–78
Simon, Dacian count, 82
Skoutariotes, Theodore (Theodoros), 66
Sofia, Bulgaria, 267
Sofia of Wittelsbach, 281n39

Hermann I, Landgrave of Thuringia, 281n39
Solomon, 296
Song of Songs, 9, 295–97
Sophia Komnene, consort of Theodore Dokianos, 310n24
Staurakios, Emperor of Byzantium (26 July–2 October 811), 176, 181, 189
Stephen I, King of Hungary (997–1038), Saint, 12–20, 25, 29–30, 41, 50, 55–56, 86, 146, 262–64, 266–67
Stephen II, King of Hungary (1116–1131), 146–47
Sthlanitza (Sthlaniza, Dobrudja), 76
surgeons, 203, 208
surgery, 199, 202–203, 208–209
surgical tools, 212
Sviatopolk II, Grand Duke of Kiev (1083–1113), 71
Sylvester II, Pope (999–1003), 266
Symeon the Logothete, 253
Synadene, consort of King Géza I of Hungary, 55, 267
Synod of Szabolcs (1092), 29, 268
Syria, 73, 76, 111, 300n45
Syria, Northern, 72
Szabolcs, Hungary, 29, 268. *See also* Synod of Szabolcs
Száva (Sava), River, 20, 27
Szávaszentdemeter (Sremska Mitrovica, Serbia), 20, 26–27
Székesfehérvár (Alba Regia), Hungary, 12, 14n10, 19, 20, 29, 50, 52, 55–56, 114, 262–64
  Provostry Church of the Assumption of the Holy Virgin, 19–20, 50, 52, 55–56, 262–64

T

Tancred of Hauteville, Regent of Antioch (1100–1108), 71, 73–74
Taranto, Italy, 69
Taronites, Michael, 98n7
Tetraevangelion, 159–61, 168–69
theatron, 184, 300, 324
Thekla, consort of Emperor Michael II, 188
Theodora *porphyrogenneta*, Empress of Byzantium, (1055–1056), 176, 180, 189

Theodora, consort of emperor Michael VIII Palailogos, 255
Theodora, consort of Emperor Theophilos, 176, 178n13, 179, 190
Theodore Dokianos, *pansebastos sebastos*, 310n24
Theodore of Laberra, Saint, 27
Theodore, Bishop of Petra, 196
Theodote, consort of Emperor Constantine VI, 176, 179, 181, 188–90
Theoktistos, 160
Theophanes the Confessor, 181
Theophano, consort of Emperor Staurakios (811), 176, 181–82, 188–89
Theophano, first consort of Emperor Leo VI, 176, 179, 254, 325,
Theophanu, Empress, mother of Holy Roman Emperor Otto III, 281
Theophilos, Emperor of Byzantium (829–842), 176, 178n13, 179–80, 190, 199
Theophylact of Ochrid, 124, 291–92
Theotokos, 103, 114, 180, 185, 227–28, 262, 270, 272, 282–86, 309, 314, 323. *See also* Mother of God
Thessalonica. Greece, 64–65, 84
Tihany-Óvár, Hungary, 20, 25
Tornikes, Euthymios, 311
Tortarius, Radulphus, 79
Transylvania, 15, 25
Trau (Trogir, Croatia), 71, 79
Trier, 281
triklinarion. See infirmary
triklinos. See infirmary
Tsagres, Basileios, 206
Tzetzes, John, 133–34, 149, 205, 209–11, 315n50
Tychon, Saint, 25
typikon,-a, 103–104, 107–109, 111–12, 130, 134, 184–86, 190, 195–98, 200–201, 204–206, 209–13, 225–27, 229, 232–35, 237, 239–40, 253–54, 256, 282–82, 285, 301, 312–13, 315, 316

U

Ugra, Ban of Slavonia, 79

V

Vág (Vah), River, 72
Varangian Guard, 145
Varzos, Konstantinos, 145, 305n1, 309
Vatican Library, 159, 323
Veljusa, Macedonia, 271, 284–85
    Virgin *Eleousa* monastery, 271, 284–85
Venice, Italy, 25, 28, 50, 63, 69–70, 76–78, 86–87, 115, 162–64, 169, 229, 238, 240, 281, 283
    Pala d'Oro, 70, 162–66, 168–69, 229
    San Marco, 70, 229, 281
vestiarios, 150
Veszprémvölgy, Hungary, 264–65
Vienna, 116n48
Virgin Mary, 4, 9, 134, 154–55, 163, 262–66, 282. *See also Hodigitria; Holy Virgin;* icons, of the Hodigitria, of the Theotokos, of the Virgin Mary, of the Blachernai Theotokos; *Maiestas Mariae;* Marian devotion; Marian piety; Most Holy Mother of God (*Yperagia Theotokos*); Mother of God (*Theotokos*); Orant Virgin *(deomene); Patrona Hungariae*
    Assumption of, 20, 262n4, 263n7, 264
    Nativity of, 268
    Visitation, 270
    Virgin of Tenderness, 284
Visegrád, Hungary, 51, 269
    Deanery Church, 268–69, 274
    St Andrew Monastery, 20, 25–26, 28
Vladimir, Russia, 228, 283–85
Vladimir, Cathedral, 228
Vladimirskaya 283. *See also* Mother of God (*Theotokos*) of Vladimir
Vladislav I, Bohemian Prince, 146n12
votive images, 270

W

Weber, Max, 122
William II the Good, King of Sicily (1166–1189), 102n16, 281n38
William of Tyre, 84, 103, 148n20, 305n2
women as sponsors, 175

X

Xene, 104, 226, 324, 329. *See also* Piroska-Eirene
xenon. See hospital

Z

Zebegény, Hungary, 20, 26

Zobor, Slovakia, 20, 26, 54
Zoe Karbonopsina, consort of Emperor Leo VI, 188
Zoe Zautzina, Empress of Byzantium, (870–c. 899), 188
Zoe, Empress of Byzantium, *porphyrogenneta* (1028–1054), 176, 180, 189, 191
Zonaras, John (Ioannes), 65, 83, 127–27
Zosimas of Palestine, Saint, 26